CW01475579

Artificial Intelligence for Science

A Deep Learning Revolution

editors

Alok Choudhary

Northwestern University, USA

Geoffrey Fox

University of Virginia, USA

Tony Hey

Rutherford Appleton Laboratory, UK

World Scientific

NEW JERSEY · LONDON · SINGAPORE · BEIJING · SHANGHAI · HONG KONG · TAIPEI · CHENNAI · TOKYO

Published by

World Scientific Publishing Co. Pte. Ltd.

5 Toh Tuck Link, Singapore 596224

USA office: 27 Warren Street, Suite 401-402, Hackensack, NJ 07601

UK office: 57 Shelton Street, Covent Garden, London WC2H 9HE

Library of Congress Cataloging-in-Publication Data

Names: Choudhary, Alok N. (Alok Nidhi), 1961– editor. | Fox, Geoffrey C., editor. |
   Hey, Anthony J. G., editor.
Title: Artificial intelligence for science : a deep learning revolution / editors,
   Alok Choudhary, Northwestern University, USA, Geoffrey Fox, University of Virginia, USA,
   Tony Hey, Rutherford Appleton Laboratory, UK.
Description: New Jersey : World Scientific, [2023] | Includes bibliographical references and index.
Identifiers: LCCN 2022039066 | ISBN 9789811265662 (hardcover) |
   ISBN 9789811265679 (ebook for institutions) | ISBN 9789811265686 (ebook for individuals)
Subjects: LCSH: Artificial intelligence--History. | Discoveries in science.
Classification: LCC Q335 .A787143 2023 | DDC 006.309--dc23/eng20221107
LC record available at https://lccn.loc.gov/2022039066

British Library Cataloguing-in-Publication Data
A catalogue record for this book is available from the British Library.

Copyright © 2023 by World Scientific Publishing Co. Pte. Ltd.

All rights reserved. This book, or parts thereof, may not be reproduced in any form or by any means, electronic or mechanical, including photocopying, recording or any information storage and retrieval system now known or to be invented, without written permission from the publisher.

For photocopying of material in this volume, please pay a copying fee through the Copyright Clearance Center, Inc., 222 Rosewood Drive, Danvers, MA 01923, USA. In this case permission to photocopy is not required from the publisher.

For any available supplementary material, please visit
https://www.worldscientific.com/worldscibooks/10.1142/13123#t=suppl

Desk Editors: Soundararajan Raghuraman/Steven Patt

Typeset by Stallion Press
Email: enquiries@stallionpress.com

© 2023 World Scientific Publishing Company.
https://doi.org/10.1142/9789811265679_fmatter

About the Editors

Alok Choudhary is a Chaired Professor in the ECE Department at Northwestern University. He was a faculty member at Syracuse University from 1989 to 1996. He was the founder and chairman of 4C insights, a data science software company. He received his PhD from the University of Illinois, Urbana-Champaign, in the field of Supercomputing and Big Data Science. He served on the Secretary of Energy's Advisory Board on Artificial Intelligence. He served as the chair of EECS Department from 2007 to 2011 at Northwestern University.

He is a recipient of the NSF Young Investigator Award, the IEEE Engineering Foundation award, and an IBM Faculty award. He is a Fellow of IEEE, ACM, and AAAS. He received the distinguished Alumni award from BITS, Pilani, India. He has published more than 450 papers and has graduated 40+ PhD students, including 10+ women PhDs.

Geoffrey Fox received a PhD in Theoretical Physics from Cambridge University, where he was Senior Wrangler as an undergraduate Mathematics degree. He is now a Professor in the Biocomplexity Institute and Initiative and Computer Science Department at the University of Virginia. He previously held positions at Caltech, Syracuse University, Florida State University, and Indiana University after being a post-doc at the Institute for Advanced Study at Princeton, Lawrence Berkeley Laboratory, and Peterhouse College Cambridge. He has supervised the PhD of 76 students. He received the High-Performance Parallel and Distributed

Computing (HPDC) Achievement Award and the ACM/IEEE CS Ken Kennedy Award for Foundational contributions to parallel computing in 2019. He is a Fellow of APS (Physics) and ACM (Computing) and works on the interdisciplinary interface between computing and applications. His current focus is on algorithms and software systems needed for the AI for Science revolution.

Tony Hey received D.Phil. in Theoretical Particle Physics from the University of Oxford in 1970. After post-doctoral research positions at Caltech and CERN, he accepted a tenured position in the Physics Department at the University of Southampton. In the 1980s, he moved to the Electronics and Computer Science Department and started a parallel computing research group. The group designed and built one of the first distributed memory message-passing computing systems and participated in the development of the MPI message-passing standard. In 2001, Tony Hey left Southampton to lead the UK's ground-breaking "eScience" initiative and received a CBE for "services to science" in 2005. He joined Microsoft Research as a Vice President in 2005 and returned to the UK in 2015. He is now Chief Data Scientist at STFC's Rutherford Appleton Laboratory and is a Fellow of the AAAS and ACM in the US, and of UK's Royal Academy of Engineering.

© 2023 World Scientific Publishing Company.
https://doi.org/10.1142/9789811265679_fmatter

Contents

Part A. Introduction to AI for Science

YOUNG, THIN ICE DOMINATES TODAY'S ICE PACK

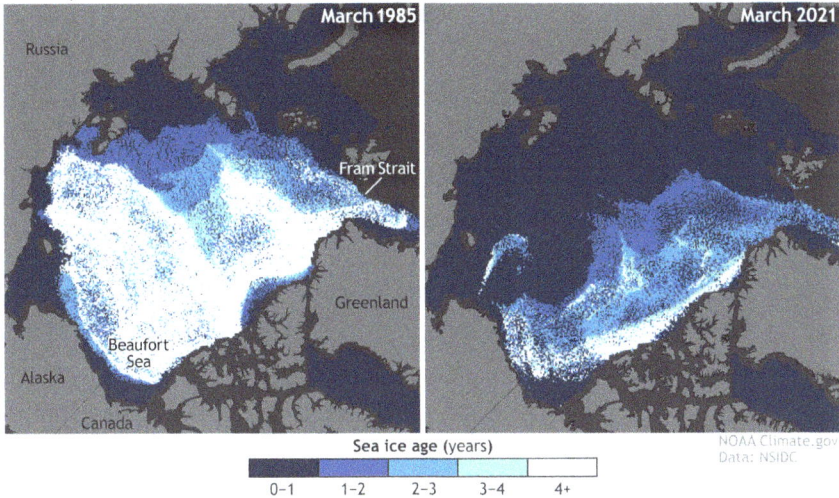

Report from the US National Oceanic and Atmospheric Administration on changes in Arctic ice coverage. Credit: NOAA Climate.gov.

© 2023 World Scientific Publishing Company
https://doi.org/10.1142/9789811265679_0001

Chapter 1

AI for Science

Alok Choudhary[*,§], Geoffrey Fox[†,¶], and Tony Hey[‡,||]

*Electrical and Computer Engineering and Computer Science
Departments, Northwestern University, Evanston, IL, USA*
†*Biocomplexity Institute and Computer Science Department, University of
Virginia, Charlottesville, VA USA*
‡*Chief Data Scientist, Rutherford Appleton Laboratory, Science and
Technology Facilities Council/UKRI, Didcot, UK*
§*a-choudhary@northwestern.edu*
¶*vxj6mb@virginia.edu*
||*tony.hey@stfc.ac.uk*

1. A Brief History of Scientific Discovery

It was Turing Award winner Jim Gray who first used the term "Fourth Paradigm" to describe the next phase of data-intensive scientific discovery [1]. For over a thousand years, the basis of science was purely empirical, based solely on observation. Then in 1687, after the discoveries of Kepler and Galileo, Isaac Newton published his book on the *Mathematical Principles of Natural Philosophy* [2]. This established his three laws of motion that both defined classical mechanics and provided the foundation for his theory of gravity. These mathematical laws of Nature provided the basis for theoretical explorations of scientific phenomena as a second paradigm for scientific discovery. Newton's laws of mechanics were followed nearly 200 years later, by Maxwell's equations for his unified theory of electromagnetism [3], and then, in the early 20th century, by Schrödinger's equation describing quantum mechanics [4]. The use of these two paradigms — experimental observation and theoretical calculation — has been the basis for scientific understanding and discovery for the last few hundred years.

Jim Gray was a member of the "Computer Science and Telecommunications Board" of the US National Academies that had released a study on computing futures. He and the Board then came to the realization that computational science was a third paradigm for scientific exploration. Gray goes on to say:

> *"Then, for many problems, the theoretical models grew too complicated to solve analytically, and people had to start simulating. These simulations have carried us through much of the last half of the last millennium. At this point, these simulations are generating a whole lot of data, along with a huge increase in data from the experimental sciences. People now do not actually look through telescopes. Instead, they are 'looking' through large-scale, complex instruments which relay data to data centers, and only then do they look at the information on their computers."*

Gray concluded that the world of science has changed [1]:

> *"The new model is for the data to be captured by instruments or generated by simulations before being processed by software and for the resulting information or knowledge to be stored in computers. Scientists only get to look at their data fairly late in this pipeline. The techniques and technologies for such data-intensive science are so different that it is worth distinguishing data-intensive science from computational science as a new, fourth paradigm for scientific exploration."*

2. Artificial Intelligence, Machine Learning, and Deep Neural Networks

Soon after the advent of computers, one of the early pioneers, Alan Turing, wrote about his ideas on "machine intelligence". In 1950, in a paper titled "Computing Machinery and Intelligence" he famously considered the question "Can machines think" [5]. However, it was another computer pioneer, John McCarthy, who first used the term "Artificial Intelligence" at a workshop in 1956. McCarthy founded AI research Labs first at MIT and then at Stanford. He later defined Artificial Intelligence (AI) as

> *"The science and engineering of making intelligent machines, especially intelligent computer programs."*

In their recent textbook on AI [6], Russell and Norvig introduce the terms "weak AI" and "strong AI" as follows:

> *"The assertion that machines could act as if they were intelligent is called the weak AI hypothesis by philosophers, and the*

assertion that machines that do so are actually thinking (not just simulating thinking) is called the strong AI hypothesis."

In our applications of AI to science, we will not be concerned with such a distinction and take the weak AI hypothesis for granted. Machine Learning (ML) can be regarded as a sub-domain of AI. In their recent review article [7], Jordan and Mitchell define ML as

"Machine learning addresses the question of how to build computers that improve automatically through experience. It is one of today's most rapidly growing technical fields, lying at the intersection of computer science and statistics, and at the core of artificial intelligence and data science. Recent progress in machine learning has been driven both by the development of new learning algorithms and theory, and by the ongoing explosion in the availability of online data and low-cost computation."

As a final subdivision of the field of AI, Deep Learning (DL) neural networks, illustrated in Figure 1), are a subset of machine learning methods that are based on artificial neural networks (ANNs) [8]:

"An ANN is based on a collection of connected units or nodes called artificial neurons, which loosely model the neurons in a biological brain. Each connection, like the synapses in a biological brain, can transmit a signal to other neurons. An artificial neuron that receives a signal then processes it and can signal neurons connected to it. The 'signal' at a connection is a real number, and the output of each neuron is computed by some non-linear function of the sum of its inputs. The connections are called edges. Neurons and edges typically have a weight that adjusts as learning proceeds."

The input layer consumes data instances from large datasets. The hidden layers collectively learn functions and models, which in turn try to predict the output variable (or variables) of interest. The output variable can be a categorical variable (yes/no, content of an image, or a numerical variable such as stock value). This is just one type of neural network. Some Deep Neural Networks can have over a hundred hidden layers.

The artificial neurons in these networks are arranged in layers going from an input layer to an output layer with connections between the neurons in the different layers. Deep learning neural networks are merely a subset of such ANNs with large numbers of hidden intermediate layers between the input and output layers. DL networks came to prominence when a team led by Geoffrey Hinton, a long-term advocate for the ANN approach to AI, won the ImageNet Image Recognition Challenge in 2012 [9]. Their entry in the competition, AlexNet, was a DL network consisting of 8 hidden layers with the learning phase computed on GPUs. By 2015, progress was such that a Microsoft Research team used a DL neural network with over 150 layers trained using GPU clusters to achieve object recognition error rates comparable to human error rates [10].

Deep learning networks are now a key technology for the IT industry and are used for a wide variety of commercially important applications — such as image classification, facial recognition, handwriting transcription, machine translation, speech recognition, text-to-speech conversion, autonomous driving, and targeted advertising. More recently, Google's UK subsidiary DeepMind has used DL neural networks to develop the world's best Go playing systems with their AlphaGo variants. However, of particular interest for our "AI for Science" agenda is DeepMind's AlphaFold protein-folding prediction system [11]. Their latest version of AlphaFold convincingly won the most recent CASP protein-folding [12]. Nobel Prize winner, Venki Ramakrishnan, has said that [13]

> *"This computational work represents a stunning advance on the protein folding problem, a 50-year-old grand challenge in biology. It has occurred decades before many people in the field would have predicted. It will be exciting to see the many ways in which it will fundamentally change biological research."*

3. AI and Modern Scientific Discovery

As described earlier, it is possible to distinguish four scientific discovery methodologies: (1) experiments, (2) mathematical modeling, (3) computer simulation, and (4) data analytics. Figure 2 illustrates these four paradigms.

Each paradigm has limitations. Experiments can be very slow and difficult to do at scale or even at all. Moreover, large-scale instruments, such as the Large Hadron Collider or the Square Kilometre Array radio telescope, are very expensive to build and maintain. In addition, the output of each experiment is usually analyzed separately, within its own silo so the potential for gaining new knowledge is limited to the analysis of the output and input parameters of individual experiments. However, AI technologies can be applied not just to a single instance of an experiment but also to the analysis of the combined total of information from many such experiments and can help generate new scientific discoveries and insights.

Mathematical models can also have their limitations including the need to simplify assumptions in order to create the models in the first place, and then by our inability to solve the resulting complex set of equations to produce analytical solutions that can be easily explored. In practice, computer simulations can be used to address both of these limitations to a certain

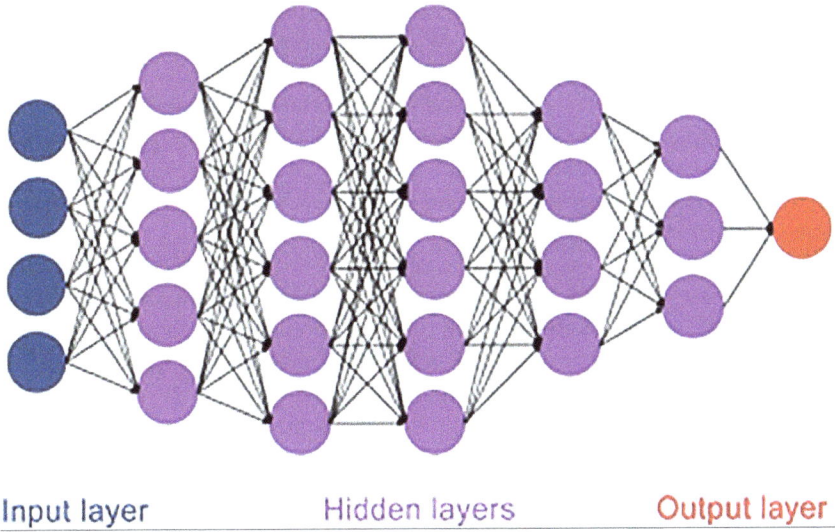

Fig. 1.   An illustration of a neural network.

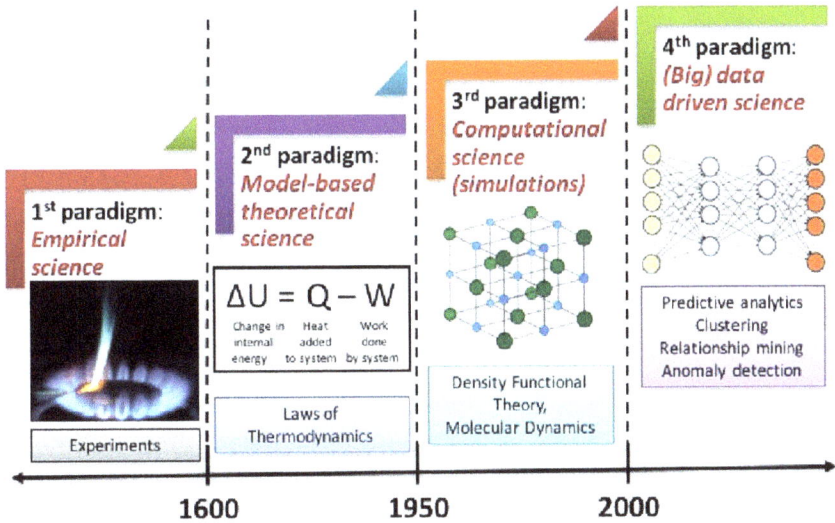

Fig. 2.   Four existing paradigms for scientific discovery.

extent. Simulating the relevant mathematical models for a wide range of different research areas — such as climate science, molecular dynamics, materials science, and astrophysics — has proved very successful. In order to scale discoveries derived from small-scale models, supercomputers are now used routinely for such simulations. Supercomputer performance is now approaching exascale levels in computing power (corresponding to 10^{18} floating point calculations per second). However, even such supercomputer simulations can be limited in several ways. Supercomputers are expensive, and therefore only a small number of such systems exist across the world. Simulations themselves are limited by the mathematical models and data representations being simulated. In addition, one simulation represents only one instance of the problem with a particular set of initial conditions and constraints. Finally, some simulations can take many days or weeks to complete thus limiting the number of simulations that can feasibly be performed, which therefore limits the exploration of large parameter spaces.

An example of these limitations of supercomputer simulations is simulation of climate models which are an urgent problem for humanity. The National Center for Atmospheric Research (NCAR) is a collaborator in a new NSF Center for Learning the Earth with Artificial Intelligence and Physics (LEAP). NCAR scientist David Lawrence says [14]

> *"LEAP is a tremendous opportunity for a multidisciplinary team to explore the potential of using machine learning to improve our complex Earth system models, all for the long-term benefit of society."*

LEAP will focus on using ML technologies to improve NCAR's Community Earth Systems Model (CESM). The CESM model comprises a complex collection of component models that can simulate the interaction of atmosphere, ocean, land, sea ice, and ice sheet processes. However, CESM is limited in its ability to incorporate some important physical processes that are difficult to simulate — such as the formation and evolution of clouds that happen at such a fine scale the model cannot resolve them, and processes to represent land ecology that are too complicated to capture in a simulation. To include an approximation of these important physical processes into CESM, climate scientists have created parameterizations. A major goal of LEAP is to improve these approximations by using machine learning technologies to incorporate learnings from the large amounts of Earth system observational data and high-resolution model simulation data now available.

4. AI for Science Book

This "AI for Science" book is about the application of AI, ML, and DL technologies to the huge scientific datasets generated both by supercomputer simulations and by modern experimental facilities. Huge quantities of experimental data now come from many sources — from satellites, gene sequencers, powerful telescopes, X-ray synchrotrons, neutron sources, and electron microscopes, as well as major international facilities such as the Large Hadron Collider (LHC) at CERN in Geneva and the European X-ray Free-Electron Laser (XFEL) facility at DESY in Hamburg. These sources already generate many Petabytes of data per year and planned upgrades of these facilities will create at least an order of magnitude more data. Extracting meaningful scientific insights from these ever-increasing mountains of data will be a major challenge for scientists. The premise of AI for Science is that such "Big Scientific Data" represents an exciting opportunity for the application of new AI technologies in ways that could be truly transformative for many areas of science.

There are now many international initiatives around the globe that are applying AI technologies to manage and analyze the ever larger and more complex datasets. In the US, the National Science Foundation (NSF) has established 18 National AI Research Institutes with partnerships covering a total of 40 States [15]. In addition, the US Department of Energy (DOE) funds the large-scale facilities and supercomputers at the National Laboratories. In 2019, the DOE Laboratories organized a series of Town Hall meetings, attended by hundreds of scientists, computer scientists, participants from industry, academia, and government, to examine the opportunities for AI to accelerate and potentially transform the scientific research fields under the domain of the DOE's Office of Science [16]. The goal of this endeavor was

> "To examine scientific opportunities in the areas of artificial intelligence (AI), Big Data, and high-performance computing (HPC) in the next decade, and to capture the big ideas, grand challenges, and next steps to realizing these opportunities."

The Town Hall meetings used the term "AI for Science" to broadly represent the next generation of methods and scientific opportunities in computing and data analysis. This included the development and application of AI methods — e.g., machine learning, deep learning, statistical methods, data analytics, and automated control — to build models from data and to use these models alone or in conjunction with simulation data to advance scientific research. The meetings concluded that the use of AI methods in science has the potential to result in major transformations of many areas of scientific research over the next decade. In conclusion, the report concluded that AI technologies can:

- Accelerate the design, discovery, and evaluation of new materials
- Advance the development of new hardware and software systems, instruments, and simulation data streams
- Identify new science and theories revealed enabled by high-bandwidth instrument data streams
- Improve experiments by inserting inference capabilities in control and analysis loops
- Enable the design, evaluation, autonomous operation, and optimization of complex systems from light sources and accelerators to instrumented detectors and HPC data centers
- Advance the development of self-driving laboratories and scientific workflows
- Dramatically increase the capabilities of exascale and future supercomputers by capitalizing on AI surrogate models
- Automate the large-scale creation of FAIR data — Findable, Accessible, Interoperable, and Reusable data

In the UK, the Alan Turing Institute in London is the National Institute for Data Science and Artificial Intelligence [17]. Their "AI for Science and Government" initiative includes a major research effort on AI for Science in collaboration with the UK's National Laboratory at Harwell, near Oxford [18].

5. Summary

This book on "AI for Science" attempts to cover the potential for AI technologies to enable transformational advances in many scientific domains. The book includes chapters written by leading scientists who authoritatively address the challenges and potential of AI technologies for their domain of expertise.

References

[1] J. Gray (2009). Jim Gray on eScience: A transformed scientific method. In T. Hey, S. Tansley, and K. Tolle (eds.), *The Fourth Paradigm: Data-Intensive Scientific Discovery*. Redmond: Microsoft Research.
[2] I. Newton (1687). Mathematical principles of natural philosophy. https://en.wikipedia.org/wiki/Philosophi%C3%A6_Naturalis_Principia_Mathematica (accessed June 2022).

[3] J. C. Maxwell (1865). A dynamical theory of the electromagnetic field. *Philosophical Transactions of the Royal Society of London*, *155*, 459–512.

[4] E. Schrödinger (1926). An undulatory theory of the mechanics of atoms and molecules. *Physical Review*, *28*(6), 1049–1070.

[5] A. Turing (1950). Computing machinery and intelligence. *Mind*, *49*, 433–460.

[6] S. Russell and P. Norvig (2020). *Artificial Intelligence: A Modern Approach*, 4th edn. Pearson Education Limited, New York.

[7] M. I. Jordan and T. M. Mitchell (2015). Machine learning: Trends, perspectives and prospects. *Science*, *349*, 255–260.

[8] Artificial Neural Network. https://en.wikipedia.org/wiki/Artificial_neural _network (accessed June 2022).

[9] A. Krizhevsky, I. Sutskever, and G. E. Hinton (2012). Imagenet classification with deep convolutional neural networks. *Advances in Neural Information Processing Systems*, *25*, 1097–1105.

[10] K. He, X. Zhang, S. Ren *et al.* (2016). Deep residual learning for image recognition. In *Proceedings of the IEEE Conference on Computer Vision and Pattern Recognition*, 27–30 June 2016, Las Vegas, NV, USA, pp. 770–778.

[11] A. W. Senior, R. Evans, J. Jumper, *et al.* (2020). Improved protein structure prediction using potentials from deep learning. *Nature*, *577*, 706–710.

[12] J. Jumper, R. Evans, A. Pritzel *et al.* (2021). Highly accurate protein structure prediction with AlphaFold. *Nature*, *596*, 583–589.

[13] D. Rice (2020). Stunning advance on 'protein folding': A 50-year-old science problem solved and that could mean big things. Protein folding discovery a major breakthrough from DeepMind (usatoday.com) (accessed June 2022). 3 December 2020, https://www.usatoday.com/story/news/nation/2020/12/ 03/protein-folding-discovery-major-breakthrough-deepmind/3809693001/ .

[14] L. Snyder (2021). NCAR will collaborate on new initiative to integrate AI with climate modeling | NCAR & UCAR News (news.ucar.edu) (accessed June 2022). 10 September 2021, https://news.ucar.edu/132809/ncar-will-collaborate-new-initiative-integrate-ai-climate-modeling.

[15] NSF AI Map (accessed June 2022).

[16] AI for science report | Argonne National Laboratory (anl.gov) (accessed June 2022).

[17] Home | The Alan Turing Institute (accessed June 2022).

[18] SCD Scientific Machine Learning (stfc.ac.uk) (accessed June 2022).

© 2023 World Scientific Publishing Company
https://doi.org/10.1142/9789811265679_0002

Chapter 2

The AI for Science Book in a Nutshell

Alok Choudhary[*,§], Geoffrey Fox[†,¶], and Tony Hey[‡,∥]

*Electrical and Computer Engineering and Computer Science
Departments, Northwestern University, Evanston, IL, USA*
†*Biocomplexity Institute and Computer Science Department, University of
Virginia, Charlottesville, VA USA*
‡*Chief Data Scientist, Rutherford Appleton Laboratory, Science and
Technology Facilities Council/UKRI, Didcot, UK*
§*a-choudhary@northwestern.edu*
¶*vxj6mb@virginia.edu*
∥*tony.hey@stfc.ac.uk*

1. Overview

This book is divided into six sections. The first introductory section has two chapters covering AI for Science and describing how this book presents the case for and status of this meme. Then in the second section, "**Setting the Scene**", eight chapters follow, giving examples and establishing the background for our discussion. These cover the driving impact of big data and data science and the striking AI success of AlphaFold in predicting protein structure. Then follow three chapters on observational science with astronomy, gravitational wave detection, and accelerators. The next chapter describes many groundbreaking studies of AI for Science on the first exascale (10^{18} operations per second) supercomputer. The final chapter of this second section describes the role of benchmarking in advancing cross-disciplinary scientific discovery with AI.

The third section, "**Exploring Application Domains**", is the heart of the book with eight subsections each with two chapters discussing AI in a research area in science and engineering. The fields are arranged alphabetically and are Astronomy and Cosmology; Climate Science and Climate Change; Energy covering Fusion and the Electric Power Grid;

Environmental Science with Remote Sensing and Agriculture; Health with Pathology and Epidemiology; Life Sciences with Drugs studied using virtual humans, and the role of AI standards; Materials Science and Engineering including the role of simulation surrogates; and the final subsection is on particle physics describing AI in both experimental analysis and theoretical understanding.

The fourth section, **"The Ecosystem of AI for Science"**, with seven chapters, describes the crosscutting environment that enables AI for Science. We start with the development of ontologies and schema needed to describe all aspects of big data and its analysis. The section ends by showing how Findable, Accessible, Interoperable, and Reusable (FAIR) data are important and can be realized. The section covers the cyberinfrastructure and middleware allowing the complex workflows that typify modern AI for Science. We show how AI enhances our ability to visualize science and the impact of AI. Many chapters stress the need for Uncertainty Quantification for results from AI that can be quite opaque; a chapter describes current approaches to this. Much scientific progress involves sharing of data and people internationally and here can help control the electronic network that links things together. Science is built on experiments and Chapter 32 presents AI approaches for designing optimal experiments and facilities.

The fifth section, **"Perspectives on AI for Science"**, with five chapters, describes ideas that are futuristic and broadly impactful. The chapter on Large Language Models describes how advances in Natural Language Processing (NLP) could lead to a revolution in scientific reasoning. The chapter on autonomous vehicles highlights work in industry that links to both the many science fields built around image processing and the push to robotic experimental laboratories. The latter is described in the following chapter. The last two chapters point to a future with a growing artificial general intelligence and the deep issues stemming from Science's need for causal arguments in contrast to AI's typical discovery of the related but different correlations.

The final section, **"Endpiece: AI Methods and the Concepts Used in the Book"**, has two chapters. The first is a brief handbook of AI methods, and the second reviews the variety of applications, concepts, and methods discussed in the separate chapters of the book.

We now follow with more details about Chapters 3–38.

2. Setting the Scene: Chapters 3–10

Chapters 3 and 4 describe the Big Data environment that is essential for AI to be effective. In **Chapter 3, "Science in the Era of AI: from Patterns to Practice"**, Szalay describes how large scientific datasets are created and curated and the type of skills and collaboration that are needed. He uses examples from databases of simulation results (turbulence, cosmology, and ocean simulation) as well as observational science illustrated by the Sloan Digital Sky Survey SDSS astronomy data with SkyServer access. Cloud and Kubernetes infrastructure are used. In **Chapter 4, "AI in the Broader Context of Data Science"**, Bourne and Alvarado stress that AI demands data to learn from. This implies that AI must be thought of in the broader context of data science with a consideration of the ethical implications of what is being learned, how it can be understood and explained, and how best to present the outcomes for human consumption. Their history of data science suggests a 4+1 model with the 4 Data Science pillars being systems, design, analytics, and ethics, with the +1 being the domain under consideration.

In **Chapter 5, "AlphaFold — The End of the Protein Folding Problem or the Start of Something Bigger?"**, Jones and Thornton describe a recent spectacular success for AI: AlphaFold2 was the star of the 2020 CASP competition predicting the atomic coordinates of protein structures from amino acid sequences. The chapter describes the structure problem and outlines the deep learning solution in AlphaFold2, which predicted a million new protein structures. This is inspiring although it is just the beginning with extensions such as ligands and carbohydrates to be explored. AlphaFold2 builds on earlier Google innovations such as AlphaGo and Transformers. It is instructive that a commercial organization won this competition by exploiting its human capital, AI expertise, and huge computing resources. We expect AI for science broadly to benefit from collaboration between academia, government, and industry. The new methods are pervasive, and multi-disciplinary and multi-organization activities are needed.

In **Chapter 6, "Applications of AI in Astronomy"**, Djorgovski and collaborators describe the use of AI in astronomy, astrophysics, and cosmology. This includes multi-messenger astronomy with an integrated study of multiple wavelengths. Synoptic sky surveys and time-domain astronomy lead to petascale data streams and the need for real-time processing for the classification and identification of interesting events. A typical problem is the separation and classification of stars and galaxies, from data with billions of feature vectors in hundreds of dimensions. Over the past decade, we have seen an exponential growth of the astronomical literature involving a variety of AI applications of ever-increasing complexity and sophistication.

In **Chapter 7, "Machine Learning for Complex Instrument Design and Optimization"**, Barish and collaborators use their experience in large physics experiments such as those that observed gravitational waves using the Laser Interferometer Gravitational-Wave Observatory (LIGO) and that discovered the Higgs boson with the Large Hadron Collider (LHC). Other chapters focus on the use of AI to analyze the data from such instruments, but here Barish looks at AI to address the operational stability and sensitivity of the instrument itself. This is aided by big data produced by operational monitors on existing instruments. AI can be used to minimize noise and produce surrogates to replace simulations. Explainable AI allows the identification of precursors to instrumental anomalies. The chapter concludes by showing how this paves the way for end-to-end AI-driven instrument design.

In **Chapter 8, "Artificial Intelligence (AI) and Machine Learning (ML) at Experimental Facilities"**, Sethian and collaborators discuss both the operation of instruments and analysis of data emphasizing light, neutron, and electron sources. These study fundamental physics, material science, and biological processes with sophisticated new AI techniques for analysis where the price of being wrong is high. The optimization of "self-driving" experiments and AI to guide and choose scientific experiments are presented as are multi-scale methods aimed at cases with limited training data. Theory can be advanced by surrogates.

In **Chapter 9, "The First Exascale Supercomputer: Accelerating AI for Science and Beyond"**, Matsuoka and collaborators present the remarkable Fugaku supercomputer designed around a novel A64FX Fujitsu processor. The design principle across compute, bandwidth, and latency issues are discussed. Benchmarks from Top500, MLCommons, and Green500 demonstrate the prowess of the machine. The machine focuses on accelerating Science with AI and many early projects are summarized. These include flood damage from remote sensing, clustering ensemble of simulations, tsunami flooding, configurational sampling of multicomponent solids, density functional theory, nonlinear modes of the three-dimensional flow field around a cylinder, aerospace design, supernova simulation, quantum spin systems, compression, explainable AI and causality for gene networks and cancer drug resistance, and data representation in a quantum computer.

In **Chapter 10, "Benchmarking for AI for Science"**, Thiyagalingam and collaborators stress the value of benchmarks aimed at the performance on scientific discovery metrics as well as the well-established role in computer performance. This includes studying algorithms and their software instantiations across different scientific fields; understanding both their common features and domain-specific optimizations. A broad discussion of AI for Science is given with examples from weather, climate, and the electron microscopy fields. A taxonomy is needed across fields. The software infrastructure for benchmarking is explained.

3. Exploring Application Domains: Chapters 11–26

3.1. *Astronomy and cosmology*

In **Chapter 11, "Radio Astronomy and the Square Kilometre Array"**, Scaife presents the Square Kilometre Array (SKA), which will be the world's largest radio observatory, consisting of two telescopes in Australia and South Africa gathering about 300 petabytes of data per year each. Instead of the AI starting with custom signal processing hardware at and near the instrument, all processing will be done in software. Deep learning will be used for object detection and morphological classification across a range of astrophysical system types, data augmentation, exploiting rotation, reflection, and preserving symmetries will address the paucity of labeled data. Issues addressed include denoising radio images, Fanaroff–Riley classification of radio galaxies, generation of synthetic populations, the removal of RFI radio frequency interference, and pulsar classification.

In **Chapter 12, "The Rise of the Machines"**, Connolly describes the next generation of survey astronomy with the commissioning of the Rubin Observatory and its Legacy Survey of Space and Time LSST. AI will identify new classes of explosive or transient events, detect potentially hazardous asteroids before they approach the Earth, and map the stellar remnants of galaxies that have merged with the Milky Way. Delivering on this promise requires an ecosystem that provides easy access to data, a software infrastructure that can work for datasets in the 10s of billions of sources, and an educational program that creates a research workforce that can implement robust and scalable AI.

3.2. *Climate change*

In **Chapter 13, "AI for Net-Zero"**, Arribas and collaborators summarize the context for net-zero and explain why AI is a critical technology to accelerate progress in carbon accounting and the decarbonization of the economy. The use of AI for Climate has been an active area of research during the last few years, but there are factors — related to data availability, practical experience deploying AI, and incentives for the use of AI — currently limiting its impact. This chapter discusses how to address those limitations and identifies two critical knowledge gaps (direct measuring of carbon emissions and materials engineering) where AI could make a significant impact to achieve net-zero. Finally, this chapter explains the need to ensure AI itself is environmentally sustainable and discusses how AI must be integrated within people, processes, and policy systems to accelerate the progress toward net-zero.

In **Chapter 14, "AI for Climate Science"**, Stier stresses the need to advance climate science to constrain remaining uncertainties in climate predictions on scales relevant for decision-making. Stier describes how AI will make transformational contributions to climate science with physically constrained, trustworthy, and explainable results realized as Digital Twin Earths. Climate simulations can use AI to parameterize unresolved processes to speedup and down-scale to finer resolutions. AI-based emulation of key climate parameters obtained from the output of large ensembles of complex climate models is promising. There is a growing amount of Earth Observation data, such as cloud patterns, where features can be extracted by AI and provide important constraints on climate models.

3.3. *Energy*

In **Chapter 15, "Accelerating Fusion Energy with AI"**, Cowley and collaborators describe fusion energy, which offers the promise of a clean, carbon-free energy source to power the future. AI can help address a number of challenges in designing, building, and operating next-generation fusion devices due to the highly nonlinear dynamics of fusion plasmas that spans a vast range of temporal and spatial scales. AI is being applied to real-time control of fusion machines, featuring multiple sensors, and recently leveraging reinforcement learning for flexible control. AI is also used to create surrogates that accelerate the fusion simulations at various levels, from complete black-box replacement to the targeted kernel and solver acceleration. These surrogates are fast enough to use in real-time control decisions.

In **Chapter 16, "Artificial Intelligence for a Resilient and Flexible Power Grid"**, Kuruganti and collaborators describe the challenges, needs, and solutions with AI techniques for modern and envisioned sustainable and flexible power grids. The electric grid is an essential, vast, and complex infrastructure that is critical to any nation's basic living, economic growth, security, and practically all aspects of modern society. The electric grids across the globe, particularly in developed countries, are based on very old technologies and are complex and fragile. Modern electric grid infrastructure is also driven by newer sources of power generation (such as solar and wind), that are decentralized, distributed, and dynamic. Reinforcement learning is used for control and trading with distributed solutions attractive to reduce the size of the action space in each instance.

3.4. *Environmental science*

In **Chapter 17, "AI and Machine Learning in Observing Earth from Space"**, Dozier's future-looking chapter has a focus on "Earth

System Science" to understand the complex interplays of atmosphere, land, and oceans that affect climate and climate change. This highlights the importance of observing Earth from space for monitoring trends and providing data for modeling. In this context, AI can integrate water, energy, and carbon fluxes, perform novel unsupervised classification of imagery, and fuse information from multiple sensors to estimate snow water equivalent. Especially ripe for future opportunities are spaceborne missions with imaging spectrometers to launch during this decade.

In **Chapter 18, "Artificial Intelligence in Plant and Agricultural Research"**, Leonelli and Williamson present many AI use cases to address the challenges of climate change and food production and delivery of "precision" farming. Biodiversity, as affected by the changing environment, is a key challenge. The many stakeholders imply the need for transdisciplinary collaborations and attention to data governance. Privacy issues suggest distributed computing solutions, while FAIR and related good data practices must be observed. Computer vision and time series are important data classes.

3.5. *Health*

In **Chapter 19, "AI and Pathology: Steering Treatment and Predicting Outcomes"**, Saltz and collaborators discuss digital histopathology, which is aimed at quantitative characterization of disease state, patient outcome, and treatment response. Gigantic 3D whole slide images can be analyzed by AI using high-performance computing to obtain better results than traditional methods. The analyses encompass multi-resolution detection, segmentation, and classification of objects and complex multi-object structures in gigapixel images at multiple scales. The new personalized deep learning approaches produce assessments of predictive value and reproducibility of traditional morphological patterns employed in anatomic pathology and the discovery of novel diagnostic biomarkers. The ideas in this chapter can be generalized across many biomedical disciplines.

In **Chapter 20, "The Role of Artificial Intelligence in Epidemiological Modeling"**, Marathe and collaborators describe an AI-driven approach for supporting real-time epidemic science based on their experiences with COVID-19 and six other epidemics in the 21st century. This work is characterized by the delivery of real-time assessments to aid government policy decisions at the state and higher levels, Agent-based simulations of the complex socio-technical systems are used with the AI. Marathe describes three large-scale efforts: (i) supporting state and local public health departments on a weekly basis; (ii) weekly forecasting to support the CDC and European CDC Forecasting Hub; and (iii) supporting the CDC Scenario modeling hub.

3.6. *Life sciences*

In **Chapter 21, "Big AI: Blending Big Data with Big Theory to Build Virtual Humans"**, Coveney and Highfield propose to blend AI and physics-based (PB) mechanistic understanding to give what they call "Big AI". An iterative cycle is used in Big AI, where AI hypotheses are tested in physics-based simulations, and the results of PB modeling are used to train AI. The synergy of ML and PB makes Big AI more powerful than traditional "narrow" AI and also marks a step toward general AI. The authors discuss several examples, including epilepsy surgery planning from a virtual brain model; a hybrid example of AI for docking and simulation for scoring binding free energies to evaluate drug candidates; AlphaFold2 with comments on its limitations; GAN for drug discovery; ensemble methods to cope with chaos and extreme sensitivity to input data; enhanced sampling of simulation phase space; and finally surrogates for the fine-grain compute-intensive components of simulations.

In **Chapter 22, "A Roadmap for Defining Machine Learning Standards in Life Sciences"**, Psomopoulos and collaborators describe the DOME life science recommendations from the ELIXIR European Union project supporting reproducibility; benchmarking; fairness; and standardization. This community activity defines approaches, compatible with FAIR principles, for reporting AI and data in biology. They support openness in all aspects of AI in the Life Sciences. DOME links to Bioschemas (Chapter 27) and a best practices toolkit for machine learning Ops (MLOps) in the life sciences.

3.7. *Materials science and engineering*

In **Chapter 23, "Artificial Intelligence for Materials"**, Warren and collaborators explain that the increased use of AI in materials research and development is poised to radically reshape how materials are discovered, designed, and deployed into manufactured products. Materials underpin modern life, and advances in this space have the potential to markedly increase the quality of human life, address pressing environmental issues, and provide new, enabling, technologies that can help people realize their potential. This chapter delves into the many ways that AI is currently being applied to accelerate MR&D, the implications of this revolution, and the new frontiers that are now being opened for exploration. The paucity of data inspires scientific machine learning which incorporates physics into the AI. Applications covered include density functional theory, phase mapping, force-field surrogates, automated materials discovery, design, and control of high-throughput experiments, and recommendations for research.

In **Chapter 24, "Artificial Intelligence for Accelerating Materials Discovery"**, Agrawal and Choudhary continue the discussion of materials science and engineering looking at forward and inverse models leading to a knowledge discovery workflow. Important features of this workflow include data availability (small and big) and the materials design space (big and huge). The forward model is the processing-structure-property-performance science pipeline and the inverse engineering problem is to find possible materials with a desired set of properties. The growing adoption of open data principles in materials science, along with pioneering advances in AI will accelerate the discovery and deployment of advanced materials, realizing the vision of the Materials Genome Initiative.

3.8. *Particle physics*

In **Chapter 25, "Experimental Particle Physics and Artificial Intelligence"**, Rousseau describes AI playing a growing role in experimental particle physics during the last decade including XGBoost winning the HiggsML Kaggle competition in 2014. The focus is on the Large Hadron Collider LHC at CERN. Using inference at the particle level, AI helps identify particles from the signal formed when they scatter in the detector. With inference at the event level, AI helps find the signature of the unstable particles (like the Higgs boson) that are created in the proton collision before decaying almost immediately. Finally, with inference at the experiment level, AI helps refine the measurement of fundamental physics parameters. In addition, AI can speed up event simulation dramatically using AI surrogate models emulating traditional sophisticated but computationally expensive simulators.

In **Chapter 26, "AI and Theoretical Particle Physics"**, Gupta and collaborators describe AI will lead to major advances in theoretical particle physics by reducing the computational cost of simulations with surrogates. Gupta covers lattice Quantum Chromodynamics with the use of normalizing flows for efficient importance sampling in Monte Carlo integration. AI is also used to advance string theories — perhaps the most advanced theoretical idea today — by efficiently searching for the vacuum corresponding to our universe. They note that AI is no more of a black box than computational QCD and the key is to understand errors and biases within each approach. Gauge invariant networks are described as an example of physics-aware AI. They present a data compression algorithm using representation learning with binary variables on quantum annealers.

4. The Ecosystem of AI for Science: Chapters 27–33

In **Chapter 27, "Schema.org for Scientific Data"**, Gray and collaborators describe Schema.org, which was originally introduced by industry to support search over web pages. Machine-readable metadata can be exploited by AI and supports FAIR principles. To go beyond generic concepts, and to address the needs of specific scientific communities, targeted extensions to the Schema.org vocabulary are needed. The Bioschemas community has developed extensions for life sciences types such as genes, proteins, and chemicals. These extensions can be used in markups that can then be exploited by the life sciences community to populate specialist community registries and generate focused Knowledge Graphs across multiple sources. Validation tools and courses and training including the TeSS Training Portal have been developed.

In **Chapter 28, "AI-Enabled HPC Workflows"**, Jha and collaborators discuss the middleware needed by complex workflow applications mixing AI, Big Data, and simulations on HPC systems. The changing requirements with adaptive heterogeneous tasks are illustrated by several examples. Classes of workflows include hybrid HPC-HTC (high throughput computing) workflows; AI-coupled workflows; and edge-to-center workflows, containing distributed AI with HPC workflows (e.g., with all or part of the AI on the edge); workflows of multiscale ensembles with AI improving path through phase space. Surrogates can be used for all or part of an application with three categories: ML-in-HPC, using a full or partial surrogate; ML-out-HPC, ML controls simulation; ML-about-HPC. ML coupled to simulation. The effective performance of these systems is discussed.

In **Chapter 29, "AI for Scientific Visualization"**, Shen and Johnson define scientific visualization as the discipline that utilizes computer graphics and data analysis techniques to extract knowledge from scientific datasets; typically those from an ensemble of science simulations. In this chapter, we review recent works that employ AI techniques to optimize various stages of the visualization pipeline, including prediction, extraction, reduction, rendering, super-resolution, interaction, and comparisons of data. We also present two use cases of deep neural networks for constructing visualization surrogates that allow scientists to explore the space of simulation parameters rapidly with real-time feedback.

In **Chapter 30, "Uncertainty Quantification in AI for Science"**, Bhattacharya and collaborators discuss Uncertainty Quantification (UQ), whose importance is stressed in many other chapters, and focus on a simple important case of deep learning for a multi-layer dense network. (MLP). UQ for deep learning is difficult since the function-space modeled is implicitly specified only by the regularization criteria and is often inscrutable. Furthermore, data-driven methods ultimately capable of representing any data-dependence blur the traditional distinction between aleatoric (statistical) and epistemic (systematic, bias) uncertainty, due to the tight interaction between network architectures, data-representation choices, training methods, and regularization procedures. This chapter presents some strategies to provide uncertainty estimates in DL, from heteroscedastic and quantile aleatoric models, to deep ensembles and Bayesian methods. Principled approaches to ascertain uncertainty, coupled with tools for explainability of predictions, are key to trustworthiness in AI for real-world applications.

In **Chapter 31, "AI for Next Generation Global Network-Integrated Systems and Testbeds"**, Kiran and Newman stress the role of networking to enable worldwide big science in many fields and how the bursty high bandwidth challenges network management systems. The paper initially reviews current network hardware and routing software and its monitoring and standards. Routing, anomaly detection, and classification must be addressed while the routing problem is compared to other areas such as intelligent road traffic. Software-defined networks (SDN) must be considered. Deep learning techniques successfully used include Markov decision processes, autoencoders, encoder–decoder architectures, diffusion convolutional and graph neural networks, LSTM, and reinforcement learning.

In **Chapter 32, "AI for Optimal Experimental Design and Decision-Making"**, Alexander and collaborators stress that the traditional experimental processes are no longer adequate in today's big data frantic fields. Large teams reduce productivity. They propose a Bayesian approach that encodes uncertainty quantification and is joined with advances in AI and natural language processing to confront this crisis head-on. Expert Elicitation constructs prior distribution through well-designed interviews. Optimal Experimental Design OED will reduce model uncertainty with the example of an experiment improving a gene regulatory network.

In **Chapter 33, "FAIR: Making Data AI-Ready"**, Sansone and collaborators look at the FAIR (Findable, Accessible, Interoperable, and Reusable) journey, status, and key next steps. Machine-readable and actionable FAIR data natively understand the semantic context and provide provenance of the information. FAIR data are essential to the future of human–machine collaboration and autonomous machine-to-machine communication. The pharmaceutical sector is used as an example. FAIR is a goal and not an implementation. FAIR describes generalized data, including software, interfaces, and APIs. The role of Schema.org (Chapter 27) is described. Catalogs, metrics, and the packaging together of data and metadata are covered.

5. Perspectives on AI for Science: Chapters 34–38

In **Chapter 34, "Large Language Models for Science"**, Stevens and collaborators observe that the vast majority of scientific literature and the methodology of scientific research is not described by clean, structured data. As scientific research output grows, it is challenging to fully integrate scientific literature into computational practices, develop data-driven hypotheses, probe reasoning, and update old assumptions. However, large language models (LLMs) have significantly advanced natural language processing on colloquial text showing promising capabilities for knowledge-retrieval, question-answering, parsing structured data, and logical reasoning. In this regard, the concept of Foundation models is introduced. Thus, the chapter investigates the assertion that LLMs can advance AI for Science by directly integrating with scientific literature, explainability, and concept-formation, thus advancing the interoperability of AI and HPC with human scientific practice. The chapter provides a broad overview of progress in NLP with LLMs, highlights a set of unique challenges of scientific language modeling, and establishes an LLM road map for scientific hypothesis generation, data parsing, and reasoning.

In **Chapter 35, "Autonomous Vehicles"**, St. John and Janapa Reddi give an overview of the current state of the field for autonomous vehicles and future directions, noting that 94% of vehicle accidents are due to human error. The perception, prediction, and planning steps for data from lidar, radar, and cameras are considered with examples from Waymo, NVIDIA, and Velodyne (lidar) analyzed by deep learning. Autonomous technologies which would reduce or eliminate traffic fatalities due to human error have become a research area of utmost importance. While deep learning methods to perform tasks such as object detection are already commonplace in many applications, the unique safety requirements of autonomous vehicles require strict guarantees with regard to both accuracy and latency, necessitating its own class of machine learning models, using a variety of sensor technologies to provide input data. 3D object detection is particularly important.

In **Chapter 36, "The Automated AI-Driven Future of Scientific Discovery"**, Zenil and King assert that the growing convergence of AI, laboratory robotics, and science affords a once-in-a-generation opportunity to greatly accelerate scientific discovery and create synergies across scientific fields. AI technology for science is generic, and so immediately benefits a wide range of scientific domains. AI-driven experiments will dramatically speed up and improve experimentation. As with cars (SAE0-5), facilities can be classified by their degree of automation. Examples of automated experimental facilities are given in the biomedical arena: Adam and Eve in the Turing Lab, Genesis at Vanderbilt, and of course AlphaFold2.

AI has the potential to actually drive science, accelerating it to super-human rates, thereby benefiting science and providing society with the wherewithal to tackle some of its greatest challenges.

In **Chapter 37, "Toward Reflection Competencies in Intelligent Systems for Science"**, Gil reviews AI for science and envisions a much more expanded role of AI systems that goes beyond simply learning from given data using a given metric. Scientists will need to partner with AI systems that are capable of independent inquiry, proactive learning, and deliberative reasoning, in a collaborative, resourceful, and responsible fashion. The chapter introduces six core competencies (reflection, observation, modeling, probing, extraction, and creation) for AI scientists and expands on one of them — the reflection competency, which involves formulating scientific questions, devising general strategies to answer them, executing methods that implement those strategies, and placing new findings in the context of the original questions. Examples are given from cancer, omics, neuroscience, and flood prediction. Global team science needs to view AI as a collaborator and not just as an assistant.

In **Chapter 38, "The Interface of Machine Learning and Causal Inference"**, Bahadori and Heckerman note that AI has had great successes in exploiting correlations, but this is not necessarily causality. Observation naturally gives correlation, but intervention leads to the study of causality, which lies at the heart of scientific understanding. This chapter reviews the fundamentals of causal inference, using an example where a technique from causal inference is used to advance AI and an example where an AI technique is used to advance causal inference. In the first example with a bird dataset, the chapter shows how the double-regression trick in causal inference can be used to improve the explanations offered by black-box AI algorithms. In the second health example, optimization techniques from AI are used to infer causal relationships.

6. Endpiece: AI Methods and the Concepts Used in the Book — Chapters 39 and 40

In **Chapter 39, "Overview of Deep Learning and Machine Learning"**, the book editors collect descriptions of many major machine and deep learning ideas used in the chapters of this book. The cookbook starts with some overall concepts and then goes over classic machine learning methods: Decision Trees, LightBGM, XGBoost, and Random Forests; Support Vector Machine (SVM); Clustering; and Genetic Algorithms (GA). Then follow some building block concepts for deep learning: Neurons. Weights and Links; Activation: (ReLU, Sigmoid, Tanh, SELU, Softmax); Layers; Loss Function, Optimizer; Stochastic Gradient Descent (SGD) and Batch size; Backpropagation; One-hot Vector; Vanishing Gradient; Hyperparameters and Neural Architecture Search; and dropout. The final section describes useful deep learning architectures: Multi-layer Perceptron, Feed-Forward Network, Fully Connected Network; Convolutional Neural Network; Encoder–Decoder Network; Autoencoder, Variational Autoencoder; Recurrent Neural Network RNN; Long Short-Term Memory Network (LSTM); Gated Recurrent Unit (GRU); Transformer; Generative Adversarial Network (GAN); Reinforcement Learning; Transfer Learning and Pretraining; Foundation Models; and finally What are PyTorch, TensorFlow, JAX, and MXNET?

In **Chapter 40, "Topics, Concepts and AI Methods Discussed in Chapters"**, the book editors present a structured index by scanning Chapters 3–38 for key ideas and recording them in tables. These tables list Nuggets of information, Goals, Concepts, Topics, and targets for AI applications. The chapter identifies Education discussions and Electronic Resources such as datasets and Physical Resources (R) such as instruments. Very important is the list of Methods and Tools (called solutions) in the AI and computing area. The chapter also lists Qualities such as explainability and FAIR principles.

Part B. Setting the Scene

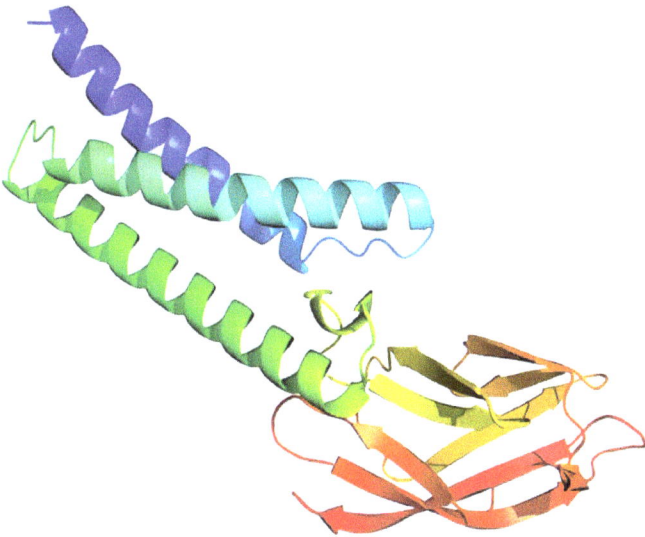

DeepMind's AlphaFold prediction for a Covid protein structure. Credit: DeepMind.

© 2023 World Scientific Publishing Company
https://doi.org/10.1142/9789811265679_0003

Chapter 3

Data-Driven Science in the Era of AI: From Patterns to Practice

Alexander Sandor Szalay

Department of Physics and Astronomy, Department of Computer Science, The Johns Hopkins University, Baltimore, USA
szalay@jhu.edu

1. Introduction

There is a revolution under way in science. Artificial Intelligence tools are not only driving our cars, but they are starting to run our experiments, and recognize new patterns in our data. However, it is increasingly realized that the ultimate quality of the results strongly depends on the quality of the underlying datasets [1,2]. Even the recent breakthroughs in AI are due to large, high-quality datasets, like ImageNet and the AlexNet Deep Neural Network. In this world, it becomes increasingly important to understand the patterns of how today's largest scientific datasets have been created and turn them into best practices. In this chapter, we discuss many of the lessons learned over the last few decades, while working on large-scale data-driven discoveries, and hope that it helps others in the design and execution of future experiments.

Today's science lives in the era of the Fourth Paradigm [3]. Scientific discoveries rely on datasets of unprecedented size. Computers and algorithms are responsible for most of the stages of experiments, from automated data acquisition to the workflows transforming the raw data, to their structured organization and performing the final analyses. While this phenomenon is relatively recent, we have seen a gradual transformation of science since the early 20th century toward ever larger scales. The growth of nuclear and particle physics experimental facilities illustrates this trend toward Big

Science very well: from the first Van Der Graaf generators, we transitioned to Cyclotrons, to Synchrotrons, and to National Accelerator Laboratories by the end of the 20th century. It became also clear that the next generation experiment following these was too large even for the USA (with the canceled SSC project) and the whole world contributed to building the Large Hadron Collider (LHC). This trend was followed (with a few decades' delay) by other sciences, like genomics with the Human Genome Project, or astronomy with the current batch of telescopes under construction with a cost over $1B each such as the Extremely Large Telescope (ELT) or the Square Kilometer Array (SKA).

At the beginning of the 20th century, small-scale experiments rapidly followed one another, quickly superseding each other's results. Consequently, scientific datasets had a relatively short lifetime. With Big Science, where the experiments cost billions, take decades to construct, and even longer to execute, this is all changing. It is unlikely that these experiments will be repeated in an incrementally improved form, thus their data remains here to stay, for decades. The scale and the long lifetime of the data represent new challenges that the community has not been ready to tackle.

By the end of the 20th century, much of the world's science became bimodal: at one end with single researchers and small groups funded by small research grants, and at the other extreme, the Big Science projects, National and International Laboratories, with little in between. The large experiments, due to their extreme scale, became also extremely risk averse, and had to freeze their technologies relatively early, like space missions, and therefore lacked technological and sociological agility.

The rapid evolution of semiconductor technology enables not only faster and cheaper computers but also better detectors and sensors which seem to follow Moore's Law in their increasing capabilities. This rapid annual growth in capabilities is leading to an interesting new trend: the emergence of mid-scale science. Such projects, with budgets of $10M–$100M can retain much more agility, using bleeding edge automation around a unique scientific instrument (a microscope, or a telescope), and can create quite large datasets and analyze them with the latest software technologies (machine learning, AI tools). Examples of these mid-scale projects are the early Sloan Digital Sky Survey [4], or the 1000 Genomes Project [5]. Other forms of mid-scale projects are those with large numbers of inexpensive commodity sensors, which can collect extremely large, crowd-sourced datasets, and their aggregated data can be another way to arrive at major scientific breakthroughs. These materialize not only in science but around data from remote sensing facilities, like Planet Labs (https://www.planet.com/). All these new types of science experiments represent new modalities and require different approaches to data management (and analyses). These mid-scale projects represent the "sweet spot" for science today; this is where the most innovative research is found, liberating enormous amounts of fresh intellectual energy for discoveries.

Data analysis is also undergoing major changes. These trends are remarkably similar to what is happening in the music industry. In the 1960s, everybody purchased vinyl albums, took them home, and listened to them on their own devices. New media, like CDs and DVDs, still largely retained this model — we had to purchase and own the media and play them on our own. With iTunes and MP3, something changed. We were able to access music with a different granularity — we could select and download content one song at a time. We still owned the digital copy and played them on our own MP3 player, but we did not have to purchase and download the rest of the album. The latest evolutionary step came with streaming services, like Pandora and Spotify. Everything is happening somewhere in a cloud, we provide loose preferences, the playlist is assembled for us by AI tools, and the music is streamed to us in a format hidden from us, auto-negotiated between the provider and the end-user device.

There are remarkable similarities in how we analyze scientific data. We used to follow the LP model by carrying the data files from large experiments on magnetic tapes to our home institution, where we analyzed them on our own computers. Later this was followed by sending the data over a different medium (hard disk drives, HDD, then internet download), but the data still followed the granularity of the original organization of the files, and the analysis was done locally. Then we started to place the data into online, indexed databases. Today we can run an SQL query or specify a selection in a web form, and then we get a small, individualized subset of the data, containing exactly what we specified. We then download this extract and analyze it on our local computer — essentially following the iTune pattern of "one song at a time". The third, streaming model is slowly emerging through the likes of Google's Colaboratory or the JHU SciServer, where the data are co-located with the computing, all data selections and transformations are happening server side, and AI tools are performing many of the pattern recognition aspects of the analyses.

There is yet another trend first recognized as part of the Fourth Paradigm [3] — there is an increased convergence and synthesis among the different scientific disciplines. While traditional computational methods in physics, chemistry, and biology were widely different, the data-intensive discoveries and AI techniques equally apply in all domains of science. In the rest of this chapter, we will discuss what our group at JHU has learned over the last few decades working at this frontier, talk about the patterns that we have seen and how these can be translated into best practices, and formal design processes. The discussion is rooted in our personal experience and will reflect on our journey over the last 20 years.

2. Discovering Convergent Patterns

Through former engagements, we learned how widely different areas of science lead to very similar data-intensive activities. This opens the door for synthesizing a common set of practices and tools as part of a data-intensive ecosystem, instead of "reinventing the wheel" in isolation. We started in astronomy, when we built the interactive SkyServer as the platform for the Sloan Digital Sky Survey (SDSS) almost 20 years ago. Over the years, most recently with the help of a large NSF grant, we have transformed this into the general use SciServer, where under the hood we have re-architected the whole platform to be more modular, generically usable, and adaptable from biology to social science [6,7]. The SciServer contains most of the tools that scientists need today under one umbrella — to acquire, store, share, analyze, and publish their data from interactive collaborative explorations of petabytes to running massive workflows.

An efficient convergence strategy requires important interdisciplinary roles that we have identified, from many trial-and-error lessons learned over the last few years. One of the most important aspects of our approach today is how we solidify and fill these roles in a systematic fashion and use these to increase the efficiency of the convergence process at JHU and beyond. In brief, these roles are as follows:

> ***Architects***: mid-career, mature scientists with gravitas, good people skills, who are equally at home in a broad science domain and data science. They are the ones who can most effectively build bridges between the new domain problems and the solution platforms. They are absolutely crucial, but very hard to find and quite difficult to fund.
>
> ***Implementers***: a pool of interdisciplinary postdocs, application programmers, and experienced software engineers who design, prototype, and deliver implementations. Here the key is the diversity of skills and scientific interests combined with cohesive team building. They are also part of rapid deployment teams with the disruptors.
>
> ***Disruptors***: highly innovative faculty, typically early to mid-career, who provide examples and demonstrations of truly disruptive, game-changing solutions at the cutting edge, that turn into templates for future approaches. They work together with the postdocs and programmers who can quickly translate an idea to end-to-end applications.

The convergence is also present in the natural progression and lifecycle of projects and datasets. The creation of a new data resource has several distinct phases:

(a) prototyping and design,
(b) data acquisition, and transformation into a form applicable to analysis,
(c) steady-state hosting operation.

If the data are from an open resource, there are additional steps:

(d) building the trust of the community and creating a wide user base,
(e) establishing sustainable, long-term support once the direct project leading to the dataset comes to an end.

There is a big gap between (c) and (d): it takes an unexpectedly long time to "build trust" with a broad community. This is similar to crossing the infamous "Valley of Death" for startups — it takes substantial additional investment to take a working prototype and make it a polished product. We outline the patterns we have seen over the years as follows:

- The first step is gathering data necessary for the analysis. Everyone needs to collect data, either from experiments and instruments, or through large computer simulations, and/or aggregating data from a diverse set of locations. Our SciServer is especially geared toward efficient data aggregation, as this became probably the most important activity, yet the hardest to support.
- Data need to be organized, cleaned, and calibrated, requiring specific data science and domain expertise and a mixed hardware/software infrastructure that enables fast data transfers, as the data needs to be moved from the instruments to where the processing will take place. We are members of the Open Storage Network collaboration (OSN) that is trying to solve this problem on a national scale [8]. The data organization at this stage reflects the coherence of the data acquisition.
- The data then need to be transformed and organized to a structure that is well aligned with the anticipated science use. This includes building specially sorted data structures or indexed databases. This stage must include a strong interplay between the intended science users and the system architects to optimize storage layout and performance. We have developed a detailed methodology to engage with new groups and help them through this stage. Our two-phase data ingest protocol (introduced by Jim Gray) has worked very well in all our usage scenarios.
- Most data today are accessed through intelligent services, which hide the complexities of the underlying parallel access to massive amounts of data. To design, architect, and implement these services requires a mix of many skills, from database programmers to HPC specialists, web service programmers, and interface specialists. Few research groups have people with even one of these skills. Using economies of scale one can build a critical mass of architects, shared programmers, and interdisciplinary

postdocs with the required mix of expertise to resolve this enduring challenge at every university.

- Creating, maintaining, and serving such open datasets for the whole community requires a cost-effective shared infrastructure that can provide massive economies of scale. We have currently more than 4PB of active-use data available as an open resource and another 20PB spinning for temporary data access and redundant storage. The SciServer has already been successfully ported to both AWS and Azure and is in active use in those platforms, so we can already see a flexible migration path into clouds as their business model will become more affordable for large-scale data.
- The rapid pace of changes in computing technology created constant tensions for science over the last two decades. In scientific publishing, we have relied on commercial publishers as the "trusted intermediaries" between authors and end users of papers. Due to technological advances, this model is crumbling, journals are gradually replaced by open source, electronic alternatives, but for data we do not have a viable model for sustainable data publishing yet. Trust is built over a long time, thus we need to urgently start inventing how to create the "trusted intermediaries" for today's scientific data.
- Datasets at some point of their life become dormant, as the underlying instrument goes out of commission. Some experiments ran for 20 years, at a cost of more than $100M, and the final product is their open and shared dataset. Such high-value data will not be superseded in the near future, and there is an urgent need to come up with a preservation path that is sustainable on the timescale of decades. However, their curation requires different skills than when the data was live and was often recalibrated. We will need to collaborate with University Libraries to create joint convergence teams and prototype models for long-term data preservation, with expertise both in Big Data and curation.

The datasets we are currently hosting are at different stages of their lifecycles in these terms. The SDSS data have an enormous reach: 10M distinct (casual) users, more than 10,000 power users, resulting in more than 10,000 refereed publications. It has achieved the end of (d) and will shortly enter stage (e). Our turbulence database [9,10] is close, it has just entered stage (d), gaining acceptance in the broader turbulence community, having served 183 trillion data points from its 650TB collection to the community. The dataset on magnetohydrodynamic (MHD) turbulence was used already in 2013 [11] to discover that flux freezing breaks down rapidly even in high-conductivity fluids, helping to explain rapid reconnection events in solar flare and coronal mass ejection observations. This discovery was made possible only because the Johns Hopkins Turbulence Databases (JHTDB) contain the entire time-history of the flow that enabled the backtracking (running time backwards) needed to find precursors of reconnection events. Our collaboration in ocean circulation will soon have 2.5PB [11,12], and it is at the end of phase (a). Its progress was substantially accelerated by sharing many low-level tools and methodologies from turbulence (immersive sensors as web services). We have just released Indra, a 1.1PB suite of cosmological simulations, for open use [13]. Indra has just finished stage (c), guided by the Millennium Run DB. Our bioinformatics efforts are at a similar stage, a large archive has been created. Material science is at the beginning of (b), the PARADIM platform [14] involved in building the data resources has been fully using the existing shared SciServer infrastructure for the data acquisition and prototype analyses. They are now ready to go to the next step. There are several projects with a large breakthrough potential at various points within phase (a).

3. Turning Patterns into Formal Processes

Over the years we have developed a more formal methodology to accelerate the process of building science engagements. This is where we take the patterns discussed above and turned them into more formal processes. Our guiding principle is *"Disruptive Assistance"*, where we will help the different groups change their data-intensive approach, through a variety of steps, throughout the lifecycle of their projects. The methodology consists of the following key components:

3.1. *Architecting, rapid prototyping, crossing the first trust gap*

This is a step carried out by the senior people identified as **architects**. At the first deep engagement with a new science project, we ask them to assemble their most important "20 queries" *àla* Jim Gray, as a simple, but prioritized list of plain text questions [15]. The prioritization immediately conveys the information that not every question asked is equally important, or equally frequent, which provides guidance for the overall systems design. This is followed by a data organization plan, rapid prototyping, and developing scalable data ingest plugins. Generally, our philosophy is "disruptive assistance": we teach our collaborators how to help themselves, establishing trust on a local scale. This phase of the projects, to get the first reasonable size of data into a properly designed data system, typically takes 3–4 months.

3.2. Deployment, building global trust

Building global trust involves going beyond the initial group. It also has a longer time scale which is very hard to bridge, due to the previously mentioned "Valley of Death" problem. In today's world of data science, building a resource does not necessary guarantee that the users will automatically appear. Thus, in the beginning we usually focus on a set of key individuals in the particular field. We engage with them and give them additional **implementer** support to bring one of their datasets or tools to our system.

3.3. Creating disruptive applications

These are typically early engagements coming from radically different, sometimes unexpected directions. One example is how astrophysicist Tamas Budavari worked with the Housing Commissioner of Baltimore City to develop a machine learning approach for decision-making when dealing with collapsing vacant houses in Baltimore City [16]. The group of "**disruptors**" play a crucial role for this purpose. Their unusual approaches are then followed by others.

3.4. Developing sustainability

Eventual sustainability will come from a good business proposition: "*With our help you can manage and analyze your data much better, cheaper and faster than alone!*" Various examples already exist of user communities with ongoing research grants budgeting fractional support toward SciServer resources, for both hardware and programmers. For example, the medical field is getting increasingly ready to embrace Big Data, even beyond genomics, and we have been building trust for the last 5 years. Other good examples are turbulence, oceanography, and materials science. Given our increasingly diversified engagements, we expect that these collaborative contributions will be steadily growing and in 5 years, combined with the medical projects, will allow us to be sustainable. Hopefully, this may serve as a model for others.

3.5. Long-term legacy

The costs of long-term stewardship of data are a tiny fraction of the "price" of acquiring the data but represent a challenge in the long term. Our belief is that a possible solution could be found at university research libraries. By mixing scientists who are in charge of datasets with curation experts from the libraries, a credible and sustainable solution can be developed. Securing long-term funding will not be easy, however.

4. Design Principles for Scalability and Computability of Large Datasets

There are many additional lessons from our past projects, learned the hard way, which we present as a set of bullets with the corresponding design principles to be used in our future efforts. The methodology we developed adheres to these principles, and has been successfully used in many different projects to date:

- Not all data and not all queries are equal. Projects have to learn to understand and enumerate the underlying priorities, short-circuiting the communication between Architects and the Projects, leading to substantial speedups in the design process.
- Scalability is hard. Maximal automation and parallelism should be built in from the very beginning. Data should flow seamlessly from instrument to database/data store, with minimal human intervention. This requires a well-defined and strict protocol on file formats, naming conventions, directory structure, to be laid out in a short reference document.
- For a large enough dataset, disks will always fail. Data must be stored in a redundant fashion, ensuring data resiliency, enabling fast recovery at multiple granularities.
- Use a two-phase load, where data are ingested in self-contained blocks, which are then cleaned, validated meticulously, before ingesting into the final data warehouse.
- The whole ingest pipeline should be designed with extreme hardware parallelism in mind, so that future incoming data can be processed on separate servers, up to the final data(base) load.
- Having the final data in a well-designed relational database makes data consistency and reproducibility much easier downstream. Self-documenting, consistent metadata must be fully part of the data system from the beginning. We must capture all geometric and spatial information, positions, and shapes.
- With large enough datasets, statistical errors become small and systematic errors dominate. These can only be discovered with a conscious systematic effort, using redundant observations. Reproducibility requires a well-thought-out quality assurance and calibration process.

- Reproducibility is a central concern, and preserving older versions of the datasets is extremely important. Queries running today on older versions of the data must return the same results as years ago.
- There must be easy access to the underlying raw data to eliminate previously undetected data artifacts detected in subsequent analyses.
- We need a flexible visual browser tied to the database, capable of displaying all the information hierarchically, without having to type an SQL query.
- All value-added code and data should be shareable among collaborating groups.
- Power users should have access to interactive and batch computations with precise control over data locality and easy integration of different frameworks (Jupyter, TensorFlow, PyTorch).
- Use agile development methodologies, built on DevOps principles (http://radar.oreilly.com/2012/06/what-is-devops.html).
- Data must be organized and accessible through parallel I/O operations (e.g., FileDB [17]).
- Scale-out computations (especially Deep Learning) must be extensible to parallel (HPC, cloud) architectures, and be able to use GPUs and other special coprocessors (TPU), and Kubernetes orchestration.
- Computations must be elastically extensible into most major cloud computing platforms. This requires building a system that is "future ready" by making full use of the evolving visions of data-intensive architectures.

5. Economies of Scale — From SkyServer to SciServer

The SDSS science archive [18] pioneered the concept of *server-side analytics* — the backbone of the current science platform concept — in astronomy almost 20 years ago [19] with the release of SkyServer in 2001. SkyServer was the first instance of a publicly accessible astronomical archive available online that embodied the *"bring the analysis to the data"* paradigm [20] and allowed users to run queries against very large datasets and manipulate the data server-side in interactive and batch mode. Recognizing the foundational role of SkyServer in the astronomical community, the National Science Foundation (via the Data Infrastructure Building Blocks program) provided funding to the Institute for Data Intensive Engineering (IDIES) at JHU in 2013 to extend the server-side analysis functionality to all science domains. SkyServer thus became SciServer [15], a fully featured science platform that took building blocks that had served astronomy for more than a decade and built a state-of-the-art collaborative and cross-domain framework around them. SciServer is free to use and anyone can start using it as soon as they register. Data providers and users with larger resource requirements (GPUs, memory nodes) can either add their own to the system, or deploy an instance of SciServer in their own environment. Besides astronomy, SciServer currently supports many additional science domains such as turbulence/fluid dynamics, oceanography, genomics, earth science, materials science, and social sciences.

Data aggregation is hard. A particular challenge is to have rich enough, self-explanatory metadata, formal data models, and appropriate ontologies to describe the meaning of the data. Very often this is the first stumbling block in data aggregation. Many groups have built good data archives from a single coherent data collection. Once we add a second, related but distinct dataset, it is tempting to deeply integrate the two — merge the two data models and ontologies, and create formal links between the appropriate data items. This is a point that many projects cannot get past. One of the reasons is that often the links and relations between the two projects are not unique and they depend on what questions we want to ask. Many to many relationships over large data are very difficult to build and validate. Furthermore, modifying the data models for collections which are close but not identical is also problematic — as they say *"eskimos have 17 words for snow"* while other countries have never seen snow. If the data models in the different entities contain such aliases, it can be very difficult to resolve them in a fashion that will satisfy everybody. The difficulties arise further with the arrival of the third and fourth datasets that need to be integrated pairwise into the previous ones. The number of links to build will rise combinatorically, especially if they are non-unique.

One of the lessons learned in the Virtual Observatory project is that as long as we can access the different collections simultaneously, we may leave it to the users/projects to identify the optimal links that are specific to their own research. We just have to enable them to build the link tables necessary for their well-defined focus and make it easy for them to keep it in a shareable and manageable form. In order to support this, we give our SciServer users their own databases sitting in the same computer room as the core datasets (on the same high-speed backbone), where in order to store such customized links they do not even have to copy the raw data from any of the other collections in order to create new, value-added datasets, they just need to store the links (foreign keys). If the individual deep collections were well documented, motivated and smart users with the right domain expertise have been very quick in finding the right joins.

The result is that in this model we can aggregate new collections easily, *in a linear fashion*, since we only have to deal with each collection in isolation. We just need to load each new dataset into the SciServer and represent its metadata using the same principles and access methods. We

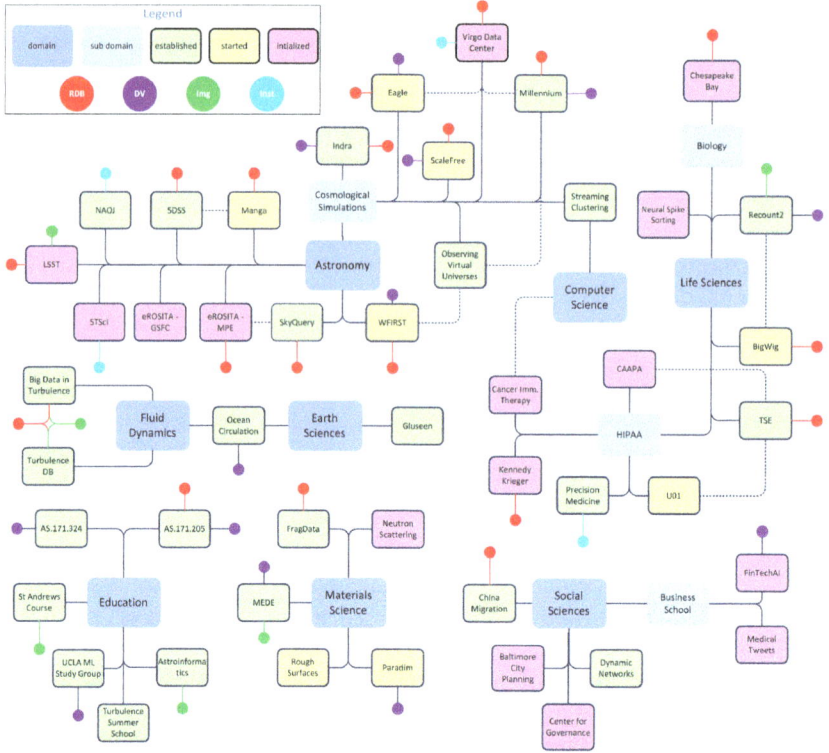

Fig. 1.   A depiction of the current projects on the SciServer, organized by science domains. The chart illustrates the convergence in data-intensive science, how wildly different disciplines can successfully co-exist on the same platform.

call these basic, high-value data collections "*data contexts*". Today we have more than 70 data contexts on the SciServer, most of them public.

Often scientists want to upload their private collection to be co-hosted with the data, as the joins can be performed much more efficiently. This turned out to be an extremely useful feature, and essentially all datasets, at different granularities (single files, data volumes, full databases, single database tables) can all be shared within individuals, groups, or made entirely public (Figure 1).

5.1. *Operating sustainable data services*

We need to help projects to help themselves to create and use their datasets. Our solution is using shared infrastructure, consisting of tens of petabytes of fast storage, a complex data analytics and management platform, the SciServer, and a substantial human capital with two decades of experience. In order to work toward a more shareable data ecosystem, we provide a variety of data services to our collaborating projects. We help them to construct and implement their system, and provide storage and computational infrastructure.

For smaller projects (typically with data below 100TB) we provide free storage for a steady-state operation. For datasets exceeding this threshold, we expect the projects to make a serious effort to secure their own funding for the storage infrastructure, where we would be included as funded partners with a cost recovery for the hardware components. For the first few years, we would operate the data services as part of our infrastructure. This would enable the projects to cross the phase of building public trust. This time scale is long enough for reasonable planning for the long term. We also expect that the data storage landscape will undergo a substantial change during the next 5 years, so this plan needs to be regularly updated.

All datasets are stored in at least three copies: (a) a "hot" version, sitting on very high performance (usually SSD) disks, (b) a "warm" version, mostly on fast HDDs, identical to (a), and (c) a "cold" backup. In case of a failure, the service switches automatically to the warm copy, while the "hot" version is recovered. Our larger databases are all shared, so in case of a failure we only have a single shard to be recovered, typically within 10–15 min. For our most important data, there is also a cold backup onto tape, stored offline in two locations. The most used datasets (like the latest release of SDSS) are served on multiple load-balanced servers. The latest data release of SDSS is typically served from 6 separate instances. These copies serve another purpose as well — we separate the short interactive queries from a medium and long batch queue, as the short ones require random access, while the long scans of the data consist typically of sequential reads.

While providing a lot of shared storage is necessary, the importance of shared, centralized help is primarily in the human capital it represents; how the existing projects emerged from and contributed to the cumulative know-how at this central core; and the way they led to a deeper understanding on how to shorten the transition from prototype to a trusted open dataset and act as force multiplier for the whole organization.

6. Open Science and Large Open Data Collections

Many activities in science today focus on interacting with large datasets. These include efforts leading to the creation of new open data collections and serving them to the science community and far beyond as a shared resource; exploring and analyzing existing collections in innovative ways; and creating a set of shareable tools and building blocks that can be interconnected in many different usage scenarios. These datasets and tools form the basis of new discoveries, and their quality and ease of use are major factors in their ultimate impact, on which future analyses and AI applications can be built. Here we discuss the different activities leading to the creation of large datasets and new, innovative ways of analyzing these, and how we can leverage existing resources and remain agile to respond to new challenges as they emerge.

As more and more scientific datasets are created under the FAIR principles and expectations, there is an urgent need to find the right ways for making the data not only open, but *truly usable* as well. Traditionally, scientists were moving the data to their computers to perform the analyses. With increasingly large amounts of data, this is becoming difficult; as a result, scientists are learning how to "move the analysis to the data", i.e., executing the analysis code on computers co-located with the data repositories, often provided as intelligent data services. In a digital world, we have to rethink not only the "data lifecycle" as most datasets are accessible via services, but we also need to consider the "service lifecycle".

As scientists are becoming increasingly excited about augmenting their analyses with advanced machine learning (ML) and artificial intelligence (AI) techniques, it is important to emphasize the need for well-calibrated reference and benchmarking data [2]. The creation of the ImageNet data challenge was a turning point for Deep Learning, but not many equivalents exist for the different science domains. We have seen an enormous growth in the usage of the SDSS and turbulence data as training sets for ML projects. Large, well-calibrated "AI-ready" reference datasets will enable new breakthroughs in creating new AI applications in science. Reproducibility of scientific results requires open access to the underlying (even raw) data.

There are different patterns on how a large dataset may emerge. The data may originate from a single large experiment or come from aggregating data from a large number of edge devices (sensors, gene sequencers, furnaces, microscopes); they can come from aggregating related but distinct data from all over the world (Virtual Observatory, sociological data, climate observations); they can come from real-time streams (analyses of tweets, Multi-Messenger Astronomy). Large supercomputer simulations also become novel instruments in their own right, and their outputs can now be in petabytes (fluid dynamics, climate modeling, cosmological N-body).

6.1. *Analysis services*

On the SciServer we have currently enough computing resources to support the services and analyses (about 8,000 cores) directly on top of the storage, partly from the conversion of the NSF-funded 100-node Data-Scope cluster (after upgrades) to a virtualized, Kubernetes orchestrated shared environment, where people can run their customized containers with preinstalled tools for the analyses.

Jim Gray used to say: *"You have nothing to fear but success or failure!"* Indeed, one of our fears is that with more and more people looking at heavy Deep Learning tasks, any free computing environment will soon run out of capacity. One way out of this is to put a reasonable limit on free computing for the analyses on the local system, while ensuring that there is an elastic overflow to the commercial clouds, where the most ambitious analyses can be scaled out at the expense of the user.

We are working with AWS and Microsoft to create a fully transparent environment, where some of the computations (and even some of the data) can reside in one of the clouds, and the cost of computation that exceeds what we can provide for free can be executed there, e.g., using an NSF-guaranteed cloud allocation, or they can move some of the data to XSEDE using the Open Storage Network. We already have working versions of the SciServer in both clouds, and we also have direct private fiber into both clouds, potentially enabling us to avoid the ingest and egress fees. This effectively provides a new business model for cloud-based academic computing: the data is permanently stored with us, but we stream just in time into the cloud and pull back the results immediately. Currently, we are working on how to make the whole elastic overflow as seamless as possible. This will also require an investment into novel, streaming algorithms.

The emergence of more and more mid-scale projects will change the nature of scientific computations — they will become increasingly more opportunistic. The computing environments will need to accommodate this. When parts of large datasets sit in different commercial clouds, we will need to think about scenarios when data are streamed "just-in-time" to a place where they can be cross-correlated with other collections. Federated learning is emerging [22], where data aggregations are built locally and then shared across federation boundaries, and the learning is performed on these large aggregations (or sketches), avoiding the need to move the raw data.

7. Long-Term High-Value Datasets

Large datasets are fundamentally changing science. We have many major research efforts, often spanning decades, collecting unheard amounts of data, typically as part of a large collaboration. Much of the analysis of these large, open datasets is carried out by a much broader community, who access the open data archive, typically through intelligent data services. There is an emerging trend in creating Science Portals, intelligent, collaborative data analytics environments, where much of the data analysis can take place. This whole effort started a few decades ago, first in High Energy Physics, now followed by many other disciplines. Today we have such projects on almost every scale of the physical world (LSST, ALMA, SDSS, EOSDIS, EarthCube, OOI, NEON, Materials Genome Initiative, Human Genome Project, Fermilab, CERN LHC). The resulting data are so unique that they will have a useful lifetime extending to several decades, possibly as much as 50–70 years.

The overall cost of these projects is often in the hundreds of millions if not billions. Their data collections represent an enormous national investment, and the data will remain uniquely useful for several decades. There is a lot of effort underway to figure out how one could benefit more from economies of scale, and build a common data ecosystem, shared by all the projects participating in the data collection effort. However, sharing much of the infrastructure has been made difficult by the realization that a lot of the projects require very domain-specific tools and expertise through much of the vertical software stack. Oceanographer's tools have little in common with genomics, particle physics, or astronomy. As a result, much of the development of the data processing and analysis stack has been done in isolation, often "reinventing the wheel", even for components that could be otherwise shared.

However, it gets worse. As the first generation of these large-scale projects is getting close to the end of their lives as far as data collection is concerned, as the original instruments are slowly becoming obsolete, a new challenge is emerging: *what happens to the data after the instruments are shut down?* This is a much harder problem than it may first appear. In order even to address this problem, we need to establish a common "currency" on which one can make easier comparisons and try to formulate a rational decision-making process. Let us try to define and quantify the three different aspects: the price, value, and cost of the data.

The Price of Data is what the cost was to create the data collection from a Big Science project. It includes the capital investment in the facility, the data infrastructure, the cost of operating the instrument, reducing the data, and building and operating an open and accessible data archive with a steady stream of incoming, active data. This is the price of data, how much the funding agencies have invested to create this unique resource. Generally, this process is well understood, and all of the aspects of the project are well under control while the experiment is running.

The Value of Data is reflected in how much science it generates. While it is difficult to put a monetary value on the results of scientific research in an algorithmic fashion, we can use another approximate metric. Each scientific paper published in a refereed journal represents a research effort that costs approximately $100K (more than $10K, less than $1M). This is the amount of research funds spent on paying for students, postdocs, research tools, computer time, to be able to write a credible scientific publication. The number of papers analyzing a dataset gives an indication of how much the members of the research community are willing to spend from their own research funds to work on this particular dataset. Effectively they vote on the value of the data with their own research dollars.

The Cost of Data measures how much it costs annually to curate, preserve, and keep serving the data to the community in an open and accessible way, in a steady state, possibly after the original instrument has been turned off and there is no new data being added to the archive any longer. This task is more than archiving, as the data is in use, through intelligent interfaces, often based on a large database, combined with collaborative data analysis platforms. This requires a lot more than just copying data on disks. Operating systems change, database systems change, web browsers change, computing hardware changes, and the users' expectations are increasing.

7.1. *Comparison of price, value, and cost*

As an example, we can take the Sloan Digital Sky Survey (SDSS). The price of the data to date has been about $200M. The project's data have generated about 9,000 refereed publications, i.e., attracting about $900M of research over this period. One can see from these numbers that it was a very worthy investment from the community's perspective.

After operating the archive for 20 years, we estimate the cost of sustaining the necessary technological advances into the future is approximately $500K/year. Expressing the annual cost in terms of the price: $500K/$200M = 0.25%/year. We can see that a 5% addition to the project's budget would secure the archive for 20 more years. If the continued operation of the archive results in just 5 refereed papers in a year(!), it is still a reasonable investment to keep the archive running.

The numbers for the Rubin Observatory, the current national flagship project for astronomy, are likely to be similar. The price is expected to be around $1.2B by the end of the project, and the cost to be about $6M/year, i.e., $6M/1.2B = 0.5%, similar to SDSS.

The costs are quite small when compared to the price of the data, yet we have no coherent plans or long-term funding mechanisms in place to address this problem, especially if we consider not just the benefits but the risks as well. A potential loss or corruption of just one of these datasets would create an enormous (potentially $B scale) amount of damage to science. It would also surely endanger the national willingness to continue to fund future experiments, if we cannot demonstrate that past investments are adequately protected, preserved, and cared for [23].

7.2. *A sustainable data infrastructure*

We have talked about the cost of long-term data preservation, but not about who are the people maintaining the services. Generally, we have invested a fair amount of funds into cyberinfrastructure, developing data services and software tools. The underlying (often implicit) expectation is that these services will at some point become self-sustaining. Let us analyze the different aspects of this problem.

On the one hand, the expectation is to provide open and free data services for everyone, in line with open science, and the increasing democratization of science. On the other hand, open data is only useful if it is accessible in a practical fashion, implying smart services, operating at no cost to the user. We could place open data into the Amazon cloud, but if every user had to pay with their credit card for both the data access and computations, there would be a lot of unhappy users. Furthermore, in this model somebody still has to pay for the ongoing improvements and evolution of the environment and the user interfaces. Some projects may be able to solicit crowdfunding, but even the arXiv has not been able to survive on voluntary donations only.

In many ways these three facets of long-term data preservation, open/free data, usable/accessible data, and self-sustaining, are similar to the three legs of project management: Fast/Good/Cheap: you can pick any two but not all three. If we want free and accessible data, somebody will have to pay for maintaining the services. If we want free and sustainable, then we can drop the data on disks, leave it there, and hope that nothing bad will happen, but cannot offer high-level, intelligent services. Finally, if we want accessible and sustainable, but have no external funding, we will have to charge user fees, the traditional publishing model. This needs to be recognized and resolved.

7.3. *Who can preserve the data for the long term?*

The biggest lesson to learn from the evolution of scientific publishing is that the community will always need a trusted intermediary to handle the aggregated knowledge, be it in the form of literature or data files. We should look through the required criteria for providing long-term data preservation, who will be this trusted intermediary. We need to find one or more organizations with the following qualities:

i. a long track record with a predictable, stable future,
ii. trusted by the science community,
iii. understands knowledge preservation,
iv. technically capable,
v. can run under a sustainable model,
vi. no single points of failure.

Let us elaborate on these criteria. For the sake of this discussion let us assume that a predictable future means 50 years. Over the last 2 years, some of the federal agencies have not been successful in maintaining a safe haven for their data. Without the science communities' help, we would have seen a major disruption turning into a major disaster for legacy data. It is not clear that even National Laboratories or Federal Research Facilities established around a large instrument will have a stable mission and existence over 50-year timescales.

Probably the longest existing stable organization on Earth is the Catholic Church, followed by universities and their libraries. While the Church is not particularly trusted by the science community, university libraries are, and have been in the service of scientists for hundreds of years. Probably none of us has any doubt that our major research universities will still be around in 50 years, and they will have a library. These libraries may be quite different from today's organizations or holdings, but their mission of preserving scientific knowledge for future generations remains the same.

While today the digital skills of libraries may not be on par with those of some of the more advanced technological centers, they are already disrupted by the digital revolution, and have started aggressively implementing rapid changes required by today's technologies. An association of research libraries, combined with clusters of domain scientists and digital archivists, may provide an almost inevitable solution to the challenges. Having several libraries participating as part of a large federation can avoid having a single point of failure and can provide good access to a wide spectrum of local domain knowledge.

7.4. *Long-term career paths*

Most of today's data archives are overseen by a high-level management group consisting of the personally identifiable information (PII)'s of the instrument, typically of the internationally recognized domain scientists. While they are tenured either at a national laboratory or at a research university, the people who run the data facilities are typically on soft money. Their careers depend on continued grant support for the experiment. The senior data scientists (or better the "data architects") are uniquely indispensable, they make the "trains run on time". Their expertise in the domain science, combined with deep understanding of the underlying data systems, how they have been built, and what functions should they provide to the community, makes the projects successful. They form the bridge between the senior management, the user community, and the lower-level programmers who perform the daily maintenance tasks. Yet, they have no stable career paths.

This contradiction becomes even more pronounced when the datasets move from being "live" to "legacy". These senior data architects, who have spent several decades of their lives, most of their scientific career, living with the same data collection, are the ones who can best oversee the transition of the data toward a long-term hosting. Wherever the data go, they have to go with them.

7.5. *Sustainable funding — A data trust?*

Needless to say, any new organization does not automatically become sustainable. However, libraries are used to raising funds, and endowments if they require funds to acquire and curate a rare specimen, like an old codex. One possible avenue is to seek endowments to build a Data Trust, where the endowment's interest income would cover the cost of data curation. For the future, one can imagine public–private partnerships, where federal agencies would provide a one-time contribution toward a rare data collection, or, e.g., make it possible for a project running for 30 years to start making annual contributions into a fund that would keep accumulating with compound interest, like a retirement account.

7.6. *Privacy concerns*

Jim Gray used to say: "*I love working with astronomers, because their data are worthless!*" The fact that much scientific data do not have any direct monetary value does indeed make life easier. However, this is not true of every dataset. In social sciences and the life sciences, there is a lot of PII, and even in the physical sciences some research has serious commercial and/or confidentiality concerns. It is clear that we need to think carefully about open data and how to ensure privacy and data security.

8. The Path Ahead

Collecting and managing large open datasets is hard. We are still very far away from having a generic, off-the-shelf solution that fits all. Over the last 20 years, we have largely created solutions to challenges as they arose. While we have learned a lot along the way, we are still responding to new challenges as they emerge (long-term data, opportunistic computing, large-scale data mobility). Support from funding agencies is still at best reactive rather than pre-emptive. As a result, much of the funding is used toward solving yesterday's problems.

It is time to think about where the whole science enterprise is heading over a 10-year timescale, and how we can future-proof our computational model. It is clear that individual universities, or even national funding agencies cannot compete with the commercial cloud providers on economies of scale. We can take for granted that given time, a large fraction of scientific data will find a long-term home in commercial clouds. There will be a gradual transition to this world over the years.

Today the cloud environment is too expensive for large-scale scientific data, the costs of storing the data locally are still 5–7 times cheaper than moving to the cloud. Given the steady state of science budgets, it will require a dramatic shift in commercial storage costs to make a commercial cloud model viable. In general, scientists seem to accept weaker robustness guarantees than current cloud offerings in exchange for lower prices. Egress fees also stand in the way of wider acceptance of cloud computing. However, once academic networks establish fast enough private fiber links to the clouds, it should be possible to negotiate a wide waiver of the egress fees for scientific data. This would also advance inter-cloud science analyses. Computing on spot instances is already competitive with the cost of local computing. Once we have fast and cheap ways to move data in and out of the clouds, this becomes a viable way to do opportunistic computing, as has been recently demonstrated [24].

However, as our example of mid-scale instruments shows, we will always need petascale storage locally — this is analogous to the *"first meter problem"*. The need to capture the ultra-fast data bursts coming off high-tech instruments (e.g., cryo-electron microscopes), to buffer them next to the instrument, and then transmit the data for processing and long-term storage to another location, will always be present.

The rapid evolution of GPUs represents another major challenge for scientific computing. Neuromorphic hardware today has a 1-year lifecycle. Everybody wants to use the latest GPU or TPU cards, and new chip architectures follow each other much faster than the traditional CPU release cycles. This provides an increasing incentive to rent as needed, and only purchase a base-level of core facility locally. This means a constant need for elastic overflow and transition of science codes between the local resources and the commercial clouds.

The different clouds provide quite different scale-out environments. While all rely on Kubernetes, and the standard AI packages that are available everywhere, the management scale-out is done quite differently. This means that most science software will need to be re-engineered in the next few years to make both our data and codes ARCO compliant (Analysis Ready and Cloud Optimized), and transportable everywhere [24]. This will require a lot of software engineering efforts — e.g., we need to start using data abstractions that are agnostic as to whether the data comes from POSIX filesystems or cloud Object Stores.

Much of today's science software was written by graduate students. In the future, we will see much more "software carpentry" [25]: reuse from open-source repositories. We will see more involvement of and respect for serious software engineering in science, reflected in new career paths at universities, like the Architects and Implementers mentioned in the previous sections. This transition will take probably a decade, but it is inevitable.

Another aspect of the future will be a revolution in how we collect data. Today we are enamored with the ease with which we can build many inexpensive digital sensors, which collect and save petabytes of data. However, we are getting close to a critical point when we are faced with a difficult decision. The question is *"do we have enough scientific data or do we want more?"* No scientist would ever say NO to this question. But it is the wrong answer to an ill-posed question. Every scientist wants more data that is *relevant* to their research, that contains new information. No scientist wants just more dirty, noisy data that occupies more storage space and takes longer to separate the noise from the relevant items. On one extreme, we can collect everything we can think of and spend the whole budget of our experiment on storage, and then have no resources left to analyze it. On the other extreme, we spend all the money on the instrument, but collect too little data, and do not have a statistically meaningful dataset.

The right trade-off is in the middle, through a judicious use of Pareto's 80–20 rule, which translated to science says that you can do 80% of the science on the (right) 20% of the data that you could potentially collect. The goal is to identify this relevant fraction even before we start gathering data. The best example of this is the Large Hadron Collider, where through the use of sensitive triggers, only a single event is kept out of about 10M. Each experiment needs to decide where to place their own threshold, at 80–20, or 99–1, or 9999–1, but we will each be facing this challenge in the next few years. In the era when we are trusting AI algorithms to drive our cars, it is easy to imagine a world when similar algorithms will soon be running our microscopes and telescopes.

In summary, in spite of tremendous progress over the last few years in how we manage large, high-value scientific datasets, there are plenty of challenges remaining, which will keep us busy ourselves for the foreseeable future.

Acknowledgments

Our work was mentored by the late Jim Gray, and we would like to acknowledge his immense contributions not only to the whole field of data science and databases but to our own effort as well. We would also like to acknowledge a generous support from the Alfred P. Sloan Foundation, the Gordon and Betty Moore Foundation, from Schmidt Futures and the Mark Foundation. Our research has also been supported by various research grants from Microsoft, NVIDIA, and Intel. Several of our projects have been supported by the grants from the National Science Foundation: SciServer has been supported by NSF-1261715, the turbulence database by NSF-1633124 and NSF-2103874, cosmological N-body simulations by NSF-1517007, the ocean circulation modeling by NSF-1835640, the Open Storage network by NSF-1747493.

References

[1] Cory Doctorow blog on Data Cascades. https://pluralistic.net/2021/08/19/failure-cascades/#dirty-data.

[2] N. Sambasivan, S. Kapania, H. Highfill *et al.* (2021). Everyone wants to do the model work, not the data work: Data Cascades in High-Stakes AI. *SIGCHI*, ACM. https://research.google/pubs/pub49953/.

[3] T. Hey, S. Tansley, and K. Tolle (eds.) (2009). *The Fourth Paradigm: Data-Intensive Scientific Discovery.* Redmond: Microsoft Research.

[4] D. G. York, J. Adelman, J. E. Anderson Jr. *et al.* (2000). The Sloan Digital Sky Survey: Technical Summary. *The Astronomical Journal, 120,* 1579.

[5] The 1000 Genomes Project website. https://www.internationalgenome.org/.

[6] The SciServer platform. https://www.sciserver.org.

[7] M. Taghizadeh-Popp, J. W. Kim, G. Lemson *et al.* (2020). SciServer: A science platform for astronomy and beyond. *Astronomy and Computing, 33,* 100412.

[8] The Open Storage Network website. https://www.openstoragenetwork.org/.

[9] The JHU Turbulence database. http://turbulence.pha.jhu.edu.

[10] Y. Li, E. Perlman, M. Wan, *et al.* (2008). A public turbulence database cluster and applications to study Lagrangian evolution of velocity increments in turbulence. *Journal of Turbulence, 9,* N31.

[11] G. E. Eyink, E. Vishniac, C. Lalescu *et al.* (2013). Flux-freezing breakdown observed in high-conductivity magnetohydrodynamic turbulence. *Nature, 497,* 466–469. https://doi.org/10.1038/nature12128.

[12] The Poseidon Project website. https://poseidon.idies.jhu.edu/.

[13] OceanSpy website. https://oceanspy.readthedocs.io/en/latest/datasets.html.

[14] B. Falck, J. Wang, A. Jenkins *et al.* (2021). Indra: A public computationally-accessible suite of cosmological N-body simulations. *Monthly Notices of the Royal Astronomical Society, 506,* 2659. Also *arXiv:2101.03631.*

[15] W. A. Phelan, J. Zahn, Z. Kennedy *et al.* (2019). Pushing boundaries: High pressure, supercritical optical floating zone materials discovery. *Journal of Solid State Chemistry*, *270*, 705.

[16] A. S. Szalay (2017). From SkyServer to SciServer. *The ANNALS of the American Academy of Political and Social Science*, *675*, 202.

[17] P. M. E. Garboden, L. Fan, T. Budavari *et al.* (2019). Combinatorial optimization for urban planning: Strategic demolition of abandoned houses in Baltimore. Working Papers, 2019-5, University of Hawaii Economic Research Organization, University of Hawaii at Manoa. https://ideas.repec.org/s/hae/wpaper.html.

[18] G. Lemson (2018). FileDB, a pattern for querying cosmological simulations. In *Proceedings of the ADASS Conference*, P10.7. https://adass2018.astro.umd.edu/abstracts/P10.7.html.

[19] A. S. Szalay (1999). The Sloan Digital Sky Survey. *Computing in Science & Engineering*, *1*(2), 54.

[20] A. S. Szalay, P. Kunszt, A. R. Thakar *et al.* (2000). Designing and mining multi-terabyte astronomy archives: The Sloan Digital Sky Survey. In *Proceedings of the SIGMOD 2000 Conference*, Dallas, Texas USA May 15–18, 2000, 451–462.

[21] A. S. Szalay (2008). Jim Gray, astronomer. *Communications of the ACM*, *51*(11), 58–65.

[22] V. Wei, N. Ivkin, V. Braverman *et al.* (2020). Sketch and scale: Geo-distributed tSNE and UMAP. In *Proceedings of IEEE Big Data Conference*, *arXiv preprint arXiv:2011.06103*.

[23] A. S. Szalay and B. C. Barish (2019). The emergence of long-lived, high-value data collections. In Astro2020: Decadal Survey on Astronomy and Astrophysics, APC white papers, no. 16; *Bulletin of the American Astronomical Society*, *51*(7), id. 16.

[24] R. Abernathey, T. Augspurger, A. Banihirwe *et al.* (2021). Cloud-Native repositories for Big Scientific Data. *Computing in Science & Engineering*, *23*, 1.

[25] G. Wilson (2016). Software Carpentry: Lessons learned [version 2; peer review: 3 approved]. *F1000Research*, *3*, 62. https://doi.org/10.12688/f1000research.3-62.v2.

© 2023 World Scientific Publishing Company
https://doi.org/10.1142/9789811265679_0004

Chapter 4

AI in the Broader Context of Data Science

Rafael C. Alvarado[*,‡] and Philip E. Bourne[†,§]

School of Data Science, University of Virginia, Charlottesville VA, USA
†*School of Data Science & Department of Biomedical Engineering,*
University of Virginia, Charlottesville VA, USA
‡*rca2t@virginia.edu*
§*peb6a@virginia.edu*

1. Introduction

Here we take a more holistic view of Artificial Intelligence (AI), namely, within the context of data science. Much of the current and future success of AI depends on learning from data and there is an emergent science surrounding data in the most generic sense. Better data means better AI outcomes. Better data can imply more data, more complete, more usable, more comprehensive, or some combination. Characteristics are embodied in the notion of FAIR data [1]. Better outcomes for AI can depend on better hardware and software architectures for managing and manipulating these data. Better outcomes for AI can depend on the human ability to interpret inputs and outputs and last, but by no means least, the success of AI as it impacts humans depends on our ability to manage what is transforming society and our place in it. In short, AI is analytical and should be studied in the broader context of data science which is more comprehensive and driven by practical application. Just as computational sciences emerged from computer science applied to different disciplines; data science has emerged from AI research which has an insatiable need for data and all that implies and is applied across every imaginable discipline. At least this is the view we have taken as we embark on establishing a School of Data Science at the University of Virginia: "*A School Without Walls*".

This is not an article about our school, beyond stating the following as context for how we view AI. Higher education needs a makeover [2].

The siloed nature of learning which separates the humanities and the social sciences from the science, technology, engineering, and medicine (STEM) fields and the lack of emphasis on quantitative skills in many disciplines is leading to a divided society at a time when comprehensive thinking is needed. Furthermore, that many of the innovations in AI have come from outside the halls of academia is no coincidence. It is reflective of an embedded academic culture that needs to embrace innovation from outside its walls and build it into the education and research programs going on within. Starting a school from scratch, which has no predefined culture, is an opportunity to reflect a future in which AI plays an important yet appropriate part, a part that can be researched and taught to future generations of practitioners.

To explore the interplay between data science and AI, we begin with a brief history of data science. This is somewhat subjective as is the definition of data science itself. Ask 10 people what data science is and you get 10 answers — the same as if you asked those same people to define the Internet, yet both are used by those 10 people and millions of others, every day. We follow the brief history with our definition of data science as embodied in the $4 + 1$ model for which AI is a distinct part but by no means the whole definition. We then move to explore AI within this $4 + 1$ framework where the emphasis moves beyond algorithms into the realm of systems, human–computer interaction, ethics, policy, law, justice, psychology, and more. In short, something different than what is typically studied in an engineering school, but we feel is apropos for a school of data science.

2. A Brief History of Data Science — A US Perspective

The origin of data science, in both name and practice, can be traced to the early 1960s. During this period, at least two data science companies, Data Science Corporation and Mohawk Data Sciences, formed by IBM and UNIVAC engineers, respectively, and a major research center, the Data Sciences Lab (DSL) of the Airforce Cambridge Research Labs (AFCRL), were established. These organizations were created to solve a new kind of problem that faced post-war America as it shouldered the burden of becoming the free world's military and industrial superpower: the need to manage and process the vast amounts of electronic data that were being produced by a host of new data-generating technologies. These technologies included wide-area radar arrays, satellites, particle accelerators, high-speed wind tunnels, geophysical sensors, and other advanced instruments used in the physical and military sciences, as well as improved machinery for capturing manually entered data.

The output of these instruments and tools was frequently described as a "data deluge" — data too fast, voluminous, and complex to be processed by traditional statistical methods and existing machines. Today, we call this deluge "big data", a broader and more positively framed concept that emphasizes potential value instead of imminent disaster. One reason for the change in sentiment is the successful development of methods and tools by data scientists and others to manage the deluge.

The problem of managing the data deluge may be described as data impedance: the persistent bottleneck between surplus data production and scarce computational capacity that scientists and engineers face in making sense of raw research data. At the time, in the late 1950s and early 1960s, computers were essentially sophisticated numerical calculators and had not yet incorporated advanced features such as integrated circuits and specialized software required to process and analyze the firehose of data they were tasked to receive, especially in real time. Data processing engineers and scientists had to shape the technology to suit their needs. The close relationship between data science and computer science at the time may account for Peter Naur's proposal in the 1970s to rename computer science to data science [3,4].

To overcome data impedance, researchers turned to the emerging field of artificial intelligence. Pattern recognition, classification, feature engineering, machine learning, and other methods we associate today with data science were all embraced and developed by the DSL and what were then called "data processing scientists" elsewhere to handle this problem. These methods, along with the material conditions that brought them about, pushed the envelopes of both computational machinery and computational thinking. By the 1990s, the fruits of these developments were evident in the successes of machine learning and of the emerging fields of data mining and knowledge discovery in databases that have become the foundation for contemporary data science.

From the 1960s to the present day, the field of data science has prospered quietly within science, industry, and government as the science and art of processing, managing, and extracting value from data. Throughout this period, the role of "data scientist" appears frequently in job ads, news stories, and policy reports relating to the data-driven sciences, from physics to geography.

Although the original formation of data science occurs in the US, the history of the field is international. In the first place, the developments of the DSL and the preceding activity of the Lincoln Laboratory were based explicitly on the achievements of operations research, which was invented in the UK during the Battle of Britain [5]. Over time, as data-intensive science developed throughout the world, the role of the data scientist become recognized in the UK, Europe, and Japan as an essential element of scientific research.

In the 1990s and early 2000s, the term was appropriated by a handful of academic statisticians, first in Japan and then the United States, seeking to expand and rebrand their field in response to the rapid growth and overshadowing effects of computational statistics and data mining [6–9]. However, this usage never caught on. As a group, statisticians did not embrace the call to rename and expand their field [10]. For its part, the established field of data science continued to be recognized by organizations like the NSF, JISC, and CODATA.

In 2008, the primary meaning of the term "data science" shifted. It became associated with the work of data-driven corporations like Google, Facebook, and LinkedIn, firms based on the mass extraction and strategic use of behavioral data. This was the year Facebook's Jeff Hammerbacher appropriated the term and applied it to the work being done at the social media giant to manage the vast amounts of data it was generating and starting to monetize, following the machine learning-based business model invented by Google [11,12]. Partly through the efforts of bloggers like Nathan Yau of FlowingData and industry thought leaders like O'Reilly, the term became viral [13–16]. By 2012, Harvard Business Review [17] had dubbed the field the "sexiest job of the 21st century", based on a quip made in 2008 by Hal Varian, Google's chief economist, in an interview with McKinsey [18].

Following these events, the term went viral and the demand for data scientists in industry increased dramatically. Data science developed into an advanced form of business intelligence, broadly defined, combining elements of statistics, data mining, artificial intelligence, computer science, and a host of recently developed data processing technologies designed to store and process big data — data generated by social media, transactional machinery, embedded sensors, and a variety of other sources in addition to the sources of the data deluge decades earlier. It also became associated with a number of soft skills deriving from its new business context, such as the need to visualize and communicate results and to understand the business value of data, considered to be the new oil [19,20].

The academic response to industry demand was immediate and equally dramatic. Hundreds of master's degree programs in data science and closely related fields were established in the United States and elsewhere, stimulating a preferential attachment process within the academy: as a hot new field attracting students, gifts, and internal resources, many adjacent disciplines — from systems engineering and computer science to statistics and a variety of quantitative and computational sciences — associated themselves with the field. Since data science had no history as a discipline in the academy, these contiguous fields provided the courses and faculty out of which the majority of data science programs were built, resulting in a transformation of data science into an umbrella field, both rich and internally competitive, and often divergent from industry expectation.

In spite of these developments, the core of data science has remained constant throughout its history. Data science is focused on the management and leveraging of data impedance, whether in the context of modeling military airspace, global climate, the human genome, or consumer behavior. In each area of application, a fundamental structure has remained in place: the combination of big data and artificial intelligence to generate value. To be sure, the tools employed by data scientists to extract value from data are not limited to artificial intelligence. Methods from statistics and data analysis play essential roles today, as they have since the beginning, along with those of operations research and statistical physics. But these do not distinguish the field of data science and account for its history and its success. Data science exists and thrives as a separate field because of its deep connection to the technologies of data that stretch back to the days of automated data processing and radar to the current era of social media, big data, cloud computing, data mining, and deep learning.

3. The 4 + 1 Model of Data Science

Given this historical perspective, how to structure a school of data science and identify the role of artificial intelligence within that broader field and institution? This is a question we have pondered at length and arrived at a model that works for us in the context of three deliverables: unique research contributions; education of a workforce suited to a wide variety of verticals; and responsible service to our various stakeholders, locally, nationally, and internationally. We refer to it as the 4 + 1 model.

A common theme throughout the history of data science is that the primary job of the data scientist is to shepherd data as it passes through a sequence of stages. This sequence is often imagined as a pipeline. From its prototypical form in the 1950s as "data processing science" to the CRISP-DM model for data mining in the 1990s [21] to the taxonomy of data science proposed by Mary Mason and Chris Wiggins in 2010 [22], this pipeline has had a remarkably stable form: data are ingested, stored, cleaned, transformed, analyzed, and modeled and then visualized and reported or deployed, depending on the context. Although the image of a pipeline may connote a passive relationship to the data and the technology used to process it, this is deceptive: the work of the data scientist often involves creating or modifying the components — including hardware, software, and models — of the pipeline.

CONTEXT   CONTACT   CONDUIT   CORE

Motivation, e.g. by   Acquisition, e.g.   Processing, e.g. clean,
scientific questions,   discover, represent,   wrangle, explore,
value propositions,   collect, curate   prepare
social needs

A N I M A T I N G   P O L A R I T I E S

Analytics, e.g.
model, evaluate,
tune, test

Assessment, e.g. of   Communication, e.g.   Production, e.g. scale
social, ethical, business,   visualize, narrate,   up, optimize monitor,
and scientific impact   disseminate   secure

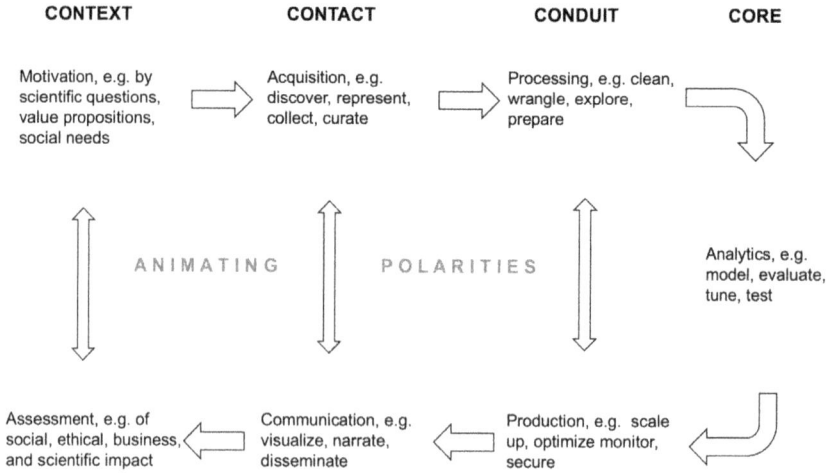

Fig. 1.   The data science parabola.

The components of the data pipeline imply a division of labor, whether carried out by a single person or a team. When viewed as an arc or parabola (Figure 1), where the starting and end points of the pipeline are aligned, we may discern at least four areas of knowledge and expertise involved: the "4" of the 4 + 1 model. Let us consider each of these 4 components.

1. *Data hardware and software systems (the conduit).* Expertise in hardware architectures and software development to support data storage and exploration and to produce performant data products at scale, or other computational tools to support the processing of data. Arises, along with data design, primarily in the two arms of the arc, as data moves in and out of the pipeline. Related to computer science, information technology engineering, cloud computing, DevOps, programming languages, cybersecurity, and other concrete knowledge required to build actual systems.

2. *Data design (the contact).* Expertise in the representation of phenomena by data models so that they may be machine processed and mathematically analyzed, as well as the representation of analytical results to non-experts in decision support and scientific research. Arises in the two arms of the arc, where raw data are incoming and analytical results are outgoing. Related to human–computer interaction, visualization, informatics, knowledge representation, database design, and other fields focused on human and machine communication.

3. *Data analysis and modeling (the core).* Expertise in data analysis and modeling by means of mathematical methods. Arises at the inflection

point of the arc, after data have been prepared for modeling but before the results of modeling have been finalized. Related to statistics, operations research, simulations, machine learning, and other methods. In short, the nexus of AI as most think of it.

4. *Data ethics and value (the context).* Expertise in framing the strategic or scientific value of data and a critical understanding of the social impacts of data products. Arises at the end points of the arc, where data are created, either through experiment or extraction, and where data products are deployed. Related to philosophy, anthropology, law, business, and other fields focused on understanding human value.

In practice, these four areas are combined when applied to a specific domain (the "+1"), such as genomics, environmental sciences, financial trading, and any other imaginable vertical. When applied to a domain the "4" complement each other and often overlap.

4. AI from the Perspective of the 4 + 1 Model

4.1. *Data hardware and software systems*

The rise of AI is intimately linked to the amount and variety of digital data and the ability of systems to process and discover features within that data. Deep learning, in particular, consists of repetitive tasks on large amounts of data and hence is suited to large memory single instruction architectures. Enter the graphical processing unit (GPU) which is just that. Originally developed to support image processing as found in gaming, GPUs have propelled developments in deep learning. Combined with software developments, such as NVIDIA's CUDA which in turn led to PyTorch and TensorFlow, the stage was set to move deep learning, and AI more generally, into the mainstream. Combining GPUs and traditional CPUs provides a powerful computing environment, but where to compute? In the cloud, within the institution, or through a hybrid approach? A question that raises an interesting dilemma when training data scientists where the majority will go to the private sector. Certainly true of Masters in Data Science students which is where many data science programs have their roots. These students want access to cloud environments which run the full gamut of GPU/CPU capabilities in an elastic environment. Fine when cost is less of an issue, funding is continuous, and the culture is product oriented. All the things academia is not, with staggered funding models, limited funds, and an entrenched culture. Thus, when discussing systems to support AI, there is a tension between what systems the student needs to learn about and what might be available to perform the work.

When it comes to the systems component of data science, further tensions arise in the context of what is data science training versus what is data engineering training. By most definitions, both contain elements of AI, but data science contains more AI and less systems than data engineering which focuses on the pipelines used by data scientists, emphasizing data architectures, databases, and data warehousing.

4.2. *Data design*

From an AI perspective, data design relates to the ability of a human to determine what data make sense to study (data in) and the integrity of these data. How the results of that study (data out) are presented for interpretation by stakeholders in the study are the other end of that systems-based pipeline. Consider examples. A natural language processing study of medical literature in an effort to discover the side effects of a given drug could weight the authenticity of the literature under study. But how to arrive at the weighting scheme and what bias does it introduce? Combining data from clinical trials adds important input but also the concern of privacy which bleeds over into ethics and value. Not to mention trials that never get reported because they were unsuccessful adding further bias. Similarly, there are tools like Tableau that provide simple ways to manipulate data and report results in an easy interpretable visual way. Valuable, but subject to the "curse of the ribbon". Let us explain this metaphor. The molecular structures of proteins and DNA are represented by diagrams that look like intertwined ribbons. The DNA double helix is iconic in this regard. Yet, so ingrained are they that it is easy to believe that this is what a molecular structure is really like when in fact it is a highly volatile entity undergoing significant motion often to the point of disorder. The ribbon is both a blessing and a visual cue and limits our thinking. The same can be said of how we visualize the outcomes of any AI analysis. We must teach our students to look beyond the ribbon to seek alternative forms of representation and to develop tools that do so for others.

4.3. *Data analysis and modeling*

Exactly this book's wheelhouse and well covered by others. Here, we simply make a few observations of AI relevant to the intersection with the broader field of data science and those studying it. We couch this reliance in the notion of responsible data science. This extends beyond data ethics and value that we will cover next but rather speaks to the limitations of AI and the limitations of those of us who study and teach it. Outside those who study and use it, AI is not well understood in terms of capabilities, limitations, and threats. It has already had a profound impact on all our lives, yet few understand the impending implications upon our society by technologies that are highly disruptive. Career displacement is well underway — traditional jobs replaced by AI and new jobs created because of it. This will rattle us as we address the following question: What does it mean to be human in a society where AI is better at many of the jobs that we used to do? An old argument that goes back to the Luddites but all the more profound when every aspect of what we do and how we live is disrupted. The psychological impact of AI on what it means to be human receives too little attention and we must train generations of data science researchers to ponder and address the implications. Fear of automation is one thing as it removes the need to undertake physical activity; taking away the mental need is something else altogether. They must start with an understanding of AI and the ability to communicate the strengths, weaknesses, opportunities, and threats of AI in a broadly accessible way. To date, this has been left to schools of engineering and information science where AI is studied. We would argue this has not gone as well as is needed, often taking a very secondary role and with insufficient qualified faculty to address the issues. Data science is a new opportunity as its practitioners reach broadly across the disciplines of policy, law, and the humanities which have so much to contribute to the discourse.

This understanding starts with a recognition that the *how* is the easy part and the *why* less so. That is how to collect appropriate data, define a set of features to explore, run a machine learning pipeline, and get a result are relatively easy. Why did you get that result less so? Consider an example. This year's Science magazine's breakthrough of the year was the work of DeepMind using an AI pipeline, AlphaFold, to effectively solve a problem molecular biologists regard as the holy grail of molecular biology. How to predict the 3-dimensional structure of a protein from its one-dimensional sequence? This is covered in detail elsewhere in this volume. The point here is we can predict the final outcome but not the process by which that folding occurs. We have effectively solved the protein structure predictions problem but not the protein folding problem. The latter requires understanding why AlphaFold works — explainable AI and an understanding of the biological processes that lead to the final folded state. Notwithstanding, knowing that final state has huge implications ranging from drug discovery to food production to energy production.

The why takes us into the realm of explainable AI. Explainable AI follows three principles: transparency, interpretability, and explainability. We come back to this, and first consider the fourth quadrant in our $4 + 1$ model — data ethics and value.

4.4. *Data ethics and value*

Just as broccoli is good for you, you know you need to study and think in terms of the ethical consequence of what you are undertaking and the value proposition that represents, but you do not like it. Not liking it really translates into not understanding it, at least in a normative sense. Ethics and value are typically not studied in detail as part of STEM education, just as the basics of AI may not be taught to an ethicist as part of a broader philosophy program. There lies the breakdown. A consequence of the current siloed education system. What is needed is more than the opportunity for the STEM student to take one or two ethics classes and vice versa for the ethicist. There needs to be a culture of integration which diffuses throughout both fields. As a School of Data Science, our approach to this is to look at all we teach and research through the lens of the 4 + 1 model and hence have data ethics and value as an integral part of everything, not just an afterthought. This is hard, takes time, and requires a different mindset. The difficulty is that at this time, we do not have enough mentors who are trained to think across this boundary between two traditionally separate fields. The first task must be to train such people and subsequently build a reputation that transcends the disciplines. At this time, too few ethicists would have knowledge of the leading AI researchers and what they do and vice versa. If one takes a particularly dystopian view, the future of our society may depend on it. All too often, the consequences of AI are appreciated after negative consequences have arisen, not before. We must educate the next generation of AI researchers and data scientists to be preemptive. Understandable AI is part of that mission.

5. Understandable AI

If the historical and functional origin of data science lies in the application of AI to big data and to extract value, then the task of developing an understandable AI applies to each of the core domains of the data science pipeline. Although the lion's share of attention has been paid to the black box nature of deep learning algorithms, and the ethical problems this creates when, e.g., data products such as facial recognition software are revealed to be racially biased [23], the problem of making AI understandable is much broader than this.

Just as data scientists have used AI to manage and leverage data impedance, so too has AI made use of big data to develop and perfect its models over the years. The majority of AI models, from classical machine learning to current deep learning, are made possible by the existence of massive datasets with which to train models and discover patterns.

It follows that to understand an AI solution involves exposing every component of the pipeline in detail, from the extraction and creation of datasets to the deployment of data products to users. Products such as ImagNet and BERT are characterized as much by their algorithmic design as by the specific datasets from which they are made. They are also defined by the database models used to structure the data that in turn train the models, as well as by the specific ways that models are deployed by people and organizations.

Explainability has two salient dimensions in this context. The first is epistemic, relating to knowledge, and the second is ethical, relating to justice. Scientists who make use of AI to advance knowledge, such as a deep learning model to predict protein folding, want to know what the model says about proteins that might be generalized into theoretical knowledge. They also want to know how to reproduce results to confirm theoretical claims. Citizens who are affected by the use of an AI product to surveil and influence their behavior or behavior toward them are entitled to know how the product actually works. They want to know whether the assumptions the product encodes are fair, aside from its performance.

Both epistemic and ethical concerns can be addressed by developing open procedures at each stage of the pipeline. Tools and methods for correcting and exposing the implicit models of deep learning are in development with promising results [24]. But the rest of the pipeline matters too. The methods employed in the discovery and acquisition of data should be documented. Raw datasets — data before they are altered by the data scientist — should be available for inspection. Databases ought to follow standards and be interoperable by linked open data standards. Data wrangling processes should identify the assumptions made and specific procedures followed to clean and shape the data as they are made to conform to the requirements of a model. Similarly, the specifications of a data product and its role in decision-making should be documented and made available to all stakeholders.

Ultimately, a genuinely explainable AI will rely on the development of practices among data scientists to codify their work.

6. Conclusion

AI is driven by large amounts of digital data. In a generic sense, the science behind these data coupled with its exploration in every imaginable domain naturally enough has become known as data science. AI can be considered as a set of analytical techniques applied within data science and here we cast AI in that broader framework. We provide one interpretation of that framework, the $4 + 1$ model, which is in active use by our own School of

Data Science at the University of Virginia. Part of our work over the next few years within our fledgling school is to evaluate the applicability of the model to research, education, and service. The model is predicated on a data pipeline which predates data science as a field and which is tried and true. What has changed is the volume and complexity of the data entering the pipeline and hence the computer infrastructure, tools, methods, and indeed the number of people engaged in the field as it becomes increasingly central to our society.

This centrality is both an opportunity and a threat and certainly disruptive as we are already experiencing. Like prior disruptions, the popular literature and media seem to focus on the nefarious aspects of AI. As practitioners, we have an obligation to learn enough and to communicate a more balanced view. Data science provides a broader context to support that view and here we provide one approach to that broader context. It is what we teach our students so that they might practice and communicate what offers so much to our collective futures.

References

[1] M. D. Wilkinson, M. Dumontier, I. Aalbersberg *et al.* (2016). The FAIR Guiding Principles for scientific data management and stewardship. *Scientific Data*, *3*(1), Article no. 1. doi: 10.1038/sdata.2016.18.

[2] S. Galloway (2020). Higher education needs an overhaul. *Insider*, 2 December 2020. https://www.businessinsider.com/scott-galloway-how-to-make-higher-education-more-accessible-2020-12.

[3] P. Naur (1966). The science of datalogy. *Communications of the ACM*, *9*(7), 485. doi: 10.1145/365719.366510.

[4] P. Naur (1974). *Concise Survey of Computer Methods*, 1st edn. New York: Petrocelli Books.

[5] M. W. Kirby (2008). Operations research in World War Two: Its role in RAF Fighter Command. *Military Operations Research*, *13*(1), 65–72.

[6] C. Hayashi (1998). Data science, classification, and related methods. In *Proceedings of the fifth Conference of the International Federation of Classification Societies (IFCS-96)*, Kobe, Japan, March 27–30, 1996. Kobe: Springer.

[7] N. Ohsumi (1994). New data and new tools: A hypermedia environment for navigating statistical knowledge in data science. In *New Approaches in Classification and Data Analysis*. Berlin: Springer-Verlag, pp. 45–54.

[8] C. F. J. Wu (1997). Statistics = Data Science? https://www2.isye.gatech.edu/~jeffwu/presentations/datascience.pdf.

[9] W. S. Cleveland (2001). Data Science: An action plan for expanding the technical areas of the field of statistics. *International Statistical Review/Revue Internationale de Statistique*, *69*(1), 21–26. doi: 10.2307/1403527.

[10] D. Donoho (2017). 50 years of Data Science. *Journal of Computational and Graphical Statistics*, *26*(4), 745–766. doi: 10.1080/10618600.2017.1384734.

[11] J. Hammerbacher (2009). Information platforms and the rise of the Data Scientist. In *Beautiful Data: The Stories Behind Elegant Data Solutions*. Sebastopol, CA: O'Reilly Media, pp. 73–84.

[12] S. Zuboff (2019). *The Age of Surveillance Capitalism: The Fight for a Human Future at the New Frontier of Power*, 1st edn. New York: PublicAffairs.

[13] N. Yau (2009). Google's Chief Economist Hal Varian on statistics and data. *FlowingData*, 25 February 2009. https://flowingdata.com/2009/02/25/goog les-chief-economist-hal-varian-on-statistics-and-data/ (accessed 4 October 2020).

[14] N. Yau (2009). Data is the new hot, drop-dead gorgeous field. *FlowingData*, 7 August 2009. https://flowingdata.com/2009/08/07/data-is-the-new-hot-drop-dead-gorgeous-field/ (accessed 3 October 2020).

[15] N. Yau (2009). Rise of the Data Scientist. *FlowingData*, 4 June 2009. https://flowingdata.com/2009/06/04/rise-of-the-data-scientist/ (accessed 31 August 2020).

[16] M. Loukides (2010). What is data science? *O'Reilly Radar*, 10 June 2010. http://radar.oreilly.com/2010/06/what-is-data-science.html.

[17] T. H. Davenport and D. J. Patil (2012). Data Scientist: The sexiest job of the 21st century. *Harvard Business Review*, 1 October 2012. https:// hbr.org/2012/10/data-scientist-the-sexiest-job-of-the-21st-century (accessed 11 February 2017).

[18] H. R. Varian (2009). Hal Varian on how the web challenges managers. *McKinsey & Company*, 1 January 2009. https://www.mckinsey.com/ industries / technology - media - and - telecommunications / our - insights / hal-varian-on-how-the-web-challenges-managers (accessed 4 October 2020).

[19] J. Toonders (2014). Data is the new oil of the digital economy. *WIRED*, July 2014. https://www.wired.com/insights/2014/07/data-new-oil-digital-economy/ (accessed 16 January 2022).

[20] K. Bhageshpur (2019). Data is the new oil – And that's a good thing. *Forbes*, 15 November 2019. https://www.forbes.com/sites/forbestechcouncil/2019/ 11/15/data-is-the-new-oil-and-thats-a-good-thing/ (accessed 16 January 2022).

[21] R. Wirth and J. Hipp (1999). CRISP-DM: Towards a standard process model for Data Mining. http://cs.unibo.it/~danilo.montesi/CBD/Beatriz/10.1.1.1 98.5133.pdf.

[22] H. Mason and C. Wiggins (2010). A taxonomy of Data Science. *Dataists*, 25 September 2010, https://sites.google.com/a/isim.net.in/datascience_ isim/taxonomy (accessed 3 February 2023).

[23] S. U. Noble (2018). *Algorithms of Oppression: How Search Engines Reinforce Racism*. New York, NY: New York University Press.

[24] S. Palacio, A. Lucieri, M. Munir *et al.* (2021). XAI Handbook: Towards a unified framework for explainable AI. ArXiv210506677 Cs, May 2021. http://arxiv.org/abs/2105.06677 (accessed 16 January 2022).

© 2023 World Scientific Publishing Company
https://doi.org/10.1142/9789811265679_0005

Chapter 5

AlphaFold — The End of the Protein Folding Problem or the Start of Something Bigger?*

David T. Jones[†,§] and Janet M. Thornton[‡,¶]

[†]*Department of Computer Science, University College London,
Gower Street, London, UK*
[‡]*European Molecular Biology Laboratory —
EMBL's European Bioinformatics Institute (EMBL-EBI),
Wellcome Genome Campus, Hinxton, Cambridgeshire CB10 1SD, UK*
[§]*d.t.jones@ucl.ac.uk*
[¶]*thornton@ebi.ac.uk*

1. Introduction

In December 2020, a London-based AI company called DeepMind, now part of Google, made the following announcement about the long-standing protein folding problem: "In a major scientific advance, the latest version of our AI system AlphaFold has been recognized as a solution to this grand challenge by the organizers of the biennial Critical Assessment of protein Structure Prediction (CASP)". This bold claim, if really true, would of course have many implications for both experimental and computational structural biology, so here we try to put these new results in context and try to provide a perspective on the way forward.

DeepMind addressed this venerable challenge using almost all of our existing knowledge of protein structures, accumulated over 50 years, to train their powerful machine learning algorithms, some of which had already been used in the form of a program called AlphaGo to beat the best human Go players. The paper describing their model was published in Nature in July 2021, along with full working source code, which was a very welcome surprise to the scientific community. Figure 1 shows the "worst and the

---

*This chapter is an update of an article originally published in the March 2021 edition of *Crystallography News*.

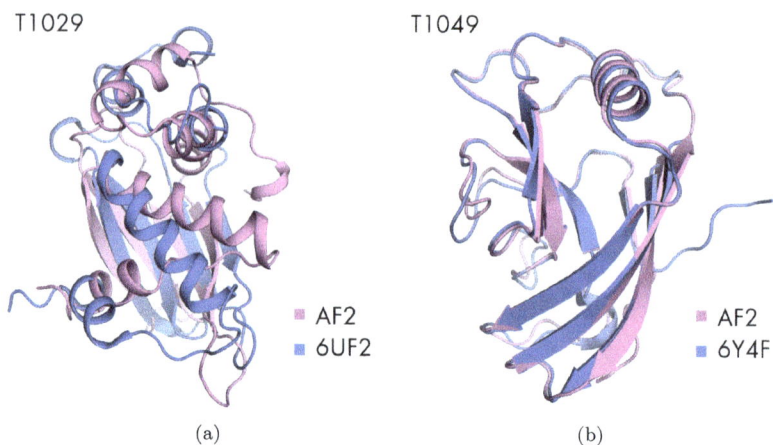

Fig. 1.   The "worst" and "best" of AlphaFold *de novo* models. The figures show the
superposition of the predicted model and the experimental structure determined later.
Target T1029 shows that there can still be issues to resolve in terms of multimeric
structures or large conformational changes, but target T1049 shows a more typical
case, and how good AlphaFold can be at modeling domains with no available template
information.

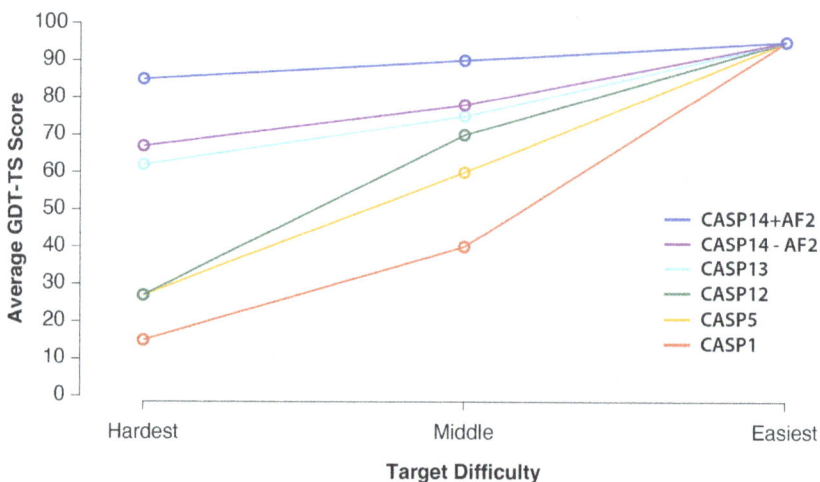

Fig. 2.   A comparison of pooled results from CASP experiments since CASP1 held
in 1993 to the recent CASP14 held in 2020. Targets are divided into the hardest (*de
novo* targets), middle, and easiest (simple homology modeling targets). For CASP14,
the results are shown with and without the results from AlphaFold. Data from
https://predictioncenter.org/casp14.

best" of AlphaFold *de novo* models. Here, we hope to give a balanced overview of what at least we know so far and try to put the results in the context of experimental structural biology going forward.

2. Background

Proteins are the workhorses of molecular biology — doing most of the biochemistry, immunology, structure building, and decoding of DNA in all living organisms. These polymers, built as chains of amino acids, have incredible properties, of which perhaps the most important and amazing is that they spontaneously fold into unique 3D structures, which determine their biological functions. Humans have just over 20,000 different proteins, not counting the wider proteome from alternative splicing, each performing a specific role. Currently, complete experimental structures (>90% of protein) have been determined for only ~2% of all human proteins, while partial structures are available for almost 22% of these proteins. Modeling, based on the structure of a relative from another species, has provided relatively reliable partial models for about 75% of human proteins. For most other organisms, the structural coverage is smaller. Having the protein structures contributes to our understanding of how the protein performs its biological function and is essential, for example, for drug and vaccine design. Thus, despite efforts from many crystallography laboratories around the world, there are still many, many proteins (UniProt now holds almost 210 million sequences) for which 3D structures are not available, in some cases because crystallization proves difficult.

Ever since the first structure of a protein (myoglobin) was solved by Kendrew in 1958 and the realization from Anfinsen that simple proteins folded up spontaneously in the right environment, there have been many attempts to predict the three-dimensional structure of a protein from its amino acid sequence. In 1969, the first homology model[1] was built manually in David Phillips' lab, using the recently determined lysozyme structure to model the structure of the related alpha-lactalbumin. Most commonly, however, attempts to predict protein structure from sequence have relied on computational methods ranging from simple statistical methods to advanced hardware-based molecular dynamics simulators.

The emergence of machine learning has had a large impact on many different scientific fields. In fact, machine learning has been used in structure prediction for almost 30 years, but now, extremely powerful machine learning methods, called deep learning, are available as a result of both new

---

[1]An homology model is a model built by comparing the sequences of two closely related proteins, where one already has a known 3-D structure and the other doesn't.

algorithm development and also efficient and relatively cheap accelerator hardware. In many ways, the protein folding problem is a perfect arena in which to test machine learning technology — it is complex; the data are well organized, freely available, and massive; there are well-tested scoring criteria for success (allowing results-oriented learning); the CASP experiment provides an independent assessment process; and there is a large community of people working on it. However, machine learning on such large datasets consumes large amounts of computational resources, especially in the training stages.

The challenge of how to predict protein structure from sequence has engaged many scientists over the years, to the extent that every two years there has been an independent assessment of our current ability to get the right answer — the CASP (Critical Assessment of Techniques for Protein Structure Prediction) meeting. This experiment has been coordinated by John Moult and colleagues (and funded mainly in the US) since its inception in 1993 and has had a profound influence on the field. Every two years, sequences are made available to the predictors, proposed by crystallography labs worldwide, before the structure is determined or at least before the structure has been submitted for publication. The predictors deposit their model coordinates and once the experimental structure is determined, the predictions are assessed by independent assessors — usually different experts each year. The results are then presented and discussed at the CASP meeting, and then publications from the most successful groups follow about 9 months later. At the most recent experiment (CASP14), over 200 groups deposited results and 67976 predictions were assessed for 84 targets. To date, targets in CASP have always been predominantly based on single domains rather than whole chains, but the definition of domains is done *post hoc*, with predictors not being given any information on the domain boundaries beforehand. Assessment, on the other hand, is solely based on individual domains. The target domains are divided into categories according to the difficulty of the challenge, initially judged by sequence similarity to any available template structures in PDB and later on during the final assessment according to structural similarity.

Over the years, CASP has accumulated a wide variety of unique metrics to assess the quality of the predictions, which has without a doubt made the results harder to understand by people outside the immediate CASP community. At first, CASP made use of well-known metrics, such as RMSD, where the root mean square deviation of the model from the experimental structure is calculated, either on just $C\alpha$ atoms or all heavy atoms. One of the issues with RMSD is that it is oversensitive to arguably less important differences in structure, e.g., in flexible regions, such as in long loops or at the termini. RMSD remains the best measure for relatively close predictions, but for *de novo* methods, useful cases where methods had managed to capture at least the correct fold were missed when judged by RMSD alone. Consequently, the CASP organizers developed more forgiving metrics that worked across the range of model quality, i.e., from "correct fold level" to "close to native structure". The main metric in CASP has become the GDT score or more precisely the Global Distance Test-Total Score (GDT-TS score). Briefly, the GDT score is based on the fraction of Cα positions that can be superposed to the experimental structure within a particular distance threshold. Rather than choosing a single threshold, however, GDT-TS makes use of four thresholds (1, 2, 4, 8 Å) and an average is taken. So, if you have a poor model where all the Cα atoms can only be superposed to between 4 and 8 Å, which would be more or less random, you would get a GDT-TS score of just 25%, but if all Cα atoms can be superposed to less than 1 Å, then you would get a perfect 100% score. A score of somewhere between 40 and 50 generally indicates that a correct fold has been produced. This means that a model with a GDT-TS score of 100 would at least have all its Cα atoms within 1 Å of the equivalent atoms in the experimental structure, but it doesn't necessarily mean perfect agreement. This is certainly a fairly generous metric compared to things like all-atom coordinate error in crystallography, but nonetheless, it provides a good way of comparing both hard *de novo* models and easier homology-based models on the same scale.

3. Results

To see both how structure prediction at CASP has evolved over time and what AlphaFold's contribution has been, Figure 2 shows some of the trends. This plot is a simplified version of a plot shown by John Moult at the CASP14 meeting. The lines show the mean GDT-TS score performance of the groups in various CASP experiments for targets ranging from easy homology modeling targets to hard *de novo* modeling targets. The lowest line shows the state of play at the very first CASP in 1993. One thing that is apparent is even then it was possible to produce excellent models for the easy targets by homology modeling. This is not really surprising, as sequence alignment alone will get you pretty much the right answer for those targets. This doesn't mean that the side chains are correctly placed, of course, and although not discussed here, this certainly has improved across the years that CASP has been running.

The first significant progress that took place in CASP was in the middle of the difficulty range. Methods like hidden Markov approaches to improve sequence alignment, fold recognition to identify distant relatives, and fragment assembly methods to identify fragments of a known fold and stitch them together had a major impact. This progress more or less stalled between CASP5 and CASP12, however. Also during this time, at least some of the hardest targets remained intractable for all groups until CASP13 in

2018. Two things contributed to this big jump in accuracy. First, with the rapid growth in sequence data banks, amino acid covariation methods had begun to be used in CASP to pick up correlated mutations in multiple sequence alignments. These evolutionary constraints identify amino acids which are close together in the 3D structure and allowed even some hard targets to be modeled accurately. The second development that appeared somewhere between CASP12 and CASP13 is that groups started to make use of deep learning methods to get more accurate information from this evolutionary information. AlphaFold is essentially the pinnacle of both of those advances along with some new ones of its own.

Figure 2 shows the impact that AlphaFold had in CASP14. The top line shows the average performance of all groups in CASP14, and the next line shows the same but with AlphaFold's models excluded. It's quite clear that AlphaFold alone has produced another step change in our ability to model protein domain folds. It was also very consistent, producing a model with a GDT score of 90 or more for two-thirds of the targets, with a median score of 92.4 for all targets and a median of 87 even for the hardest targets; it also produced the best model for over 90% of the targets. That's remarkable. Of course, it might be tempting to be critical of the fact that AlphaFold never produces a GDT score of exactly 100 and so clearly doesn't reach the accuracy expected of good crystal structures. However, that would be a naïve view. As a good topical example, Figure 3 shows DeepMind's model for ORF8 of SARS-Cov2 compared to Chain A of PDB entry 7jtl, which was the official target structure in CASP14. It's clear that AlphaFold has done a very good job here, with a GDT score of 87 and a Cα RMSD of 1.84 Å. At first sight, it would appear that the model, while very good, could have been better. But to put this in context, there is now a second higher resolution crystal structure available for ORF8 with PDB code 7jx6. The resolutions for 7jtl and 7jx6 are 2.04 and 1.61 Å, respectively. AlphaFold's model still only has a GDT score of 87 for this new structure, which may not be surprising, but what is surprising is that the maximum GDT score *between the two crystal structures* is also only 87. So, despite the low coordinate error we would expect for structures at this resolution, which conformation is the correct one? Can we call AlphaFold's model incorrect when two independently solved structures of the same small protein do not agree? Now, inspection of all these structures clearly shows that the differences in this case come down to the large loop between residues 44 and 68 (visible at the top left of Figure 3), which is probably flexible and perhaps only adopts a stable conformation when bound to its correct ligand. It's also possible that the loop in the two crystal structures is distorted by different crystal contacts. AlphaFold's model may in fact be a better unbiased estimate of the confirmation that the loop adopts in free solution. We don't know.

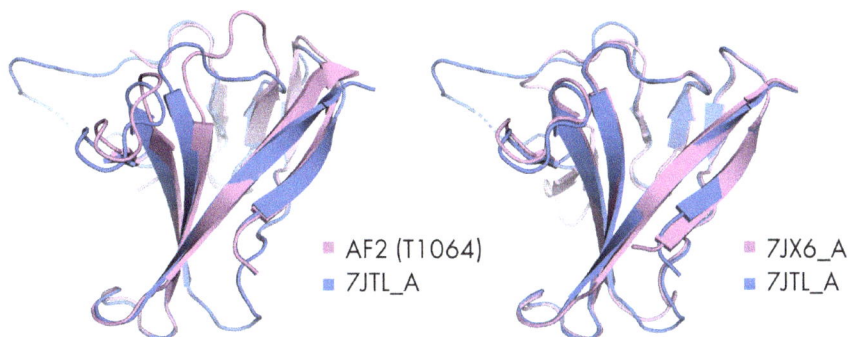

Fig. 3. AlphaFold's prediction for SARS-Cov2 ORF8. This is clearly a good model, but there are differences between the model (AF2) and two independently solved crystal structures (PDB structures 7JTL and 7JX6 A chains).

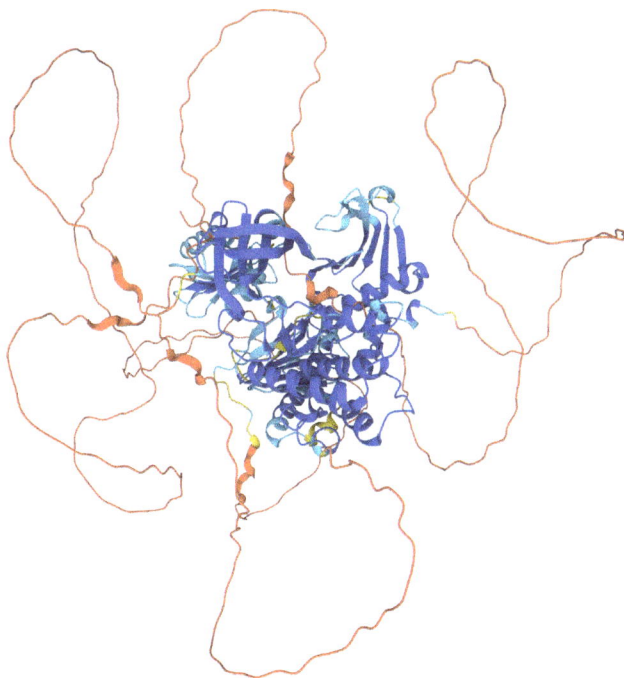

Fig. 4. A typical AlphaFold prediction for a human protein sequence (serine/threonine-protein kinase PLK4), taken from the EBI AlphaFold Model Database. The coloring is according to model confidence, with red colors indicating low confidence predictions.

One very interesting result in CASP14 was that for 3 or 4 structures, which the crystallographers were struggling to solve, the AlphaFold models were sufficiently accurate to produce a molecular replacement solution. One such protein was target T1100 (Archaeal Transmembrane Receptor Af1503), provided by one of the CASP14 assessors, Andrei Lupas (Max Planck Institute for Developmental Biology). This protein had been sitting "in a drawer" since 2010 with native diffraction data available at 3.5Å, but despite there being a reasonable template available in PDB, no phasing model had ever succeeded in producing a solution. The submitted AlphaFold models, however, produced a clear hit and allowed the structure to be determined. This case is interesting because while the domain folds of target T1100 were not in doubt, and many groups produced quite reasonable models, the details of the model clearly were important. As one of the assessors, Nick Grishin, joked, what AlphaFold got right in this case that nobody else did, were the details. This is evident by the fact that the all-atom RMSD for DeepMind's best model for the complete chain was 2.0 Å, compared to 4.7 Å for the next best group, which is even more impressive when you realize that T1100 is a homodimer (a protein structure made up of two identical copies of the same protein chain) and AlphaFold only submitted a single chain model.

4. How Did DeepMind Win CASP?

In more general terms, what DeepMind did that separated them from the chasing pack was that they took the whole CASP prediction process and numerically optimized the whole thing. This approach is commonly known as differentiable programming and in this specific application is called *end-to-end protein structure prediction*. Basically, the whole process of competing in 1 CASP was captured in a single neural network system, from extracting contact and distance information from the sequence alignments, through the steps of producing an approximate fold (which is where most of us in CASP stop), and finally through to the very difficult process of refining that approximate fold into an accurate all-atom model and in fact, all the way to calculating a final RMSD for all of the models generated. Each of these steps is usually treated as a separate part of the CASP experiment, but here, it was implemented in the form of a set of linked neural networks, which made the *whole process fully differentiable*. In other words, they simply did gradient descent on the whole CASP experiment and were able to come up with an unbeatable system by simply training the system to win CASP. They built a modeling system that had the *theoretical* capability of predicting protein structure at high levels of accuracy, if the optimum parameter settings could be found, and then they basically let the system evolve until it reached the highest level of accuracy. Simple it might sound, and others have proposed more limited approaches along similar lines, but getting all of that to work is still a hugely impressive engineering feat. However, even beyond the engineering challenge, the sheer amount of parameter searching needed is probably way beyond the computational resources available to typical academic researchers, though as computational power becomes cheaper, this may change.

The final publication of the AlphaFold2 paper [1] offered up answers to a lot of unanswered questions that were hanging in the air after the CASP14 meeting was over. The talks by DeepMind at the meeting gave some insight into the workings of the model but left a lot of gaps so that researchers enjoyed speculating about what was missing. The basics were obvious from the start. AlphaFold2 was constructed as a set of transformer models using the concept of attention [2].

Transformer models have been extremely successful in tackling natural language processing problems, for example, machine translation. The basic function of a transformer is to compute a string of new vectors from a string of input vectors. In the case of human language, these vectors initially represent different words e.g., "red" or "apple", but in AlphaFold, these vectors initially represent the 20 different amino acids that make up proteins. A description of how a transformer works is beyond the scope of this article, but basically, it means that vectors representing input tokens (for example, amino acids) are transformed into new representation vectors based on a weighted average of the original vectors. The weighting comes from the degree of attention (really just similarity) calculated between all pairs, either from pairs of vectors from different inputs or from the same input (called self-attention). Each transformer layer therefore can produce more meaningful representations based on the contexts of the input set of vectors. In the case of a natural language model, with enough transformer layers, English word vectors might end up being transformed into Italian word vectors, simply by training the model on texts taken from the two languages. In the case of AlphaFold, vectors representing amino acids are simply transformed into vectors that represent positions of atoms in 3-D space.

For AlphaFold, the overall system architecture had two main tracks, with the inputs to one track representing the rows and columns of a multiple sequence alignment (MSA), and those of the other track essentially representing the distances between each amino acid in the model. The MSA path allows the network to keep track of amino acid conservation and covariation features, while the distance matrix provides the 3-D spatial information for the amino acids. Information is exchanged between these two tracks, which means that the MSA is reinterpreted as the distance information is improved. Similarly, the distance maps can be improved as the MSA is reinterpreted. In the end, information from the two tracks is fed into the so-called structure module, which embeds the representations in 3-D space, i.e., generates a set of atomic coordinates. The job of the structure module is not just to produce a single set of coordinates but also to make improvements to the initial set of coordinates, again using an attention mechanism, though using a special geometric representation that is invariant to rotations and translations. Here again, it was speculated that DeepMind had made use of some new developments in geometric machine learning, called SE(3) equivariant attention, but in reality, the rotational and translational invariance was achieved using an old trick from structural bioinformatics, where individual local coordinate frames are defined for each residue based on the invariant backbone geometry of amino acids.

In some respects, seeing the final complete description of the method was seen as a little disappointing by some, after the anticipation that built up following the CASP meeting. Not because the method wasn't clever but simply because there appeared to be no radical new insights that were key to addressing the problem. In many respects, AlphaFold is "just" a very well-engineered system that takes many of the recently explored ideas in both the bioinformatics and machine learning field, such as methods to interpret amino acid covariation, and splices them together seamlessly using attention processing.

5. The AlphaFold Protein Structure Database[2]

In July 2021, DeepMind, in collaboration with EMBL-EBI, released the AlphaFold predicted structures of the human proteome and the most popular model organisms in the AlphaFold Database [3]. The structures are available open access to all (CC BY-4.0 license) and the data are available for bulk download via FTP.[3] The database is well structured, easy to use by a non-expert, and includes a good 3D viewer. Since then, two more releases have been made: one covering all the annotated protein sequences in UniProt (SwissProt) and most recently (in January 2022) the sequences of organisms on the World Health Organization's list of "Neglected Tropical Diseases" and organisms responsible for AMR (AntiMicrobial Resistance). In total, there are now about 1 million structures in the database, covering sequences from 49 organisms. It is anticipated that models for all the sequence entries in UniProt will be made available during 2022, totaling more than 100 million structures. By April 2022, the database was accessed by over 46,000 unique users located worldwide generating 1.5 million page views, illustrating the interest of biologists in the wider biological scientific

---

[2]https://alphafold.ebi.ac.uk/.
[3]ftp://ftp.ebi.ac.uk/pub/database/alphafold.

community in protein models. It will clearly have an impact in the coming years on our understanding of how life works at the molecular level.

6. Did AlphaFold Actually Solve the Protein Folding Problem?

In truth, the protein folding problem has never been a thing that can really ever be solved in one go. There are many layers to it, including how a protein fold changes when the ambient conditions are varied or when the sequence is mutated or when other molecules interact with it. It is very different from mathematical problems, which are expected to have definitive solutions that are immediately recognized by everyone. Without a doubt, however, AlphaFold's results in CASP14 were remarkably good and certainly represented a major leap forward in the field of protein modeling. Nevertheless, the approach still has some obvious limitations. CASP is a very limited experiment, where tests are only possible on structures solved experimentally in a relatively small window of time (about six months). It therefore has to be borne in mind that CASP only looks at a relatively small sample of test proteins. These proteins are selected not because they cover a wide range of problem cases but simply because they happen to be being solved during the CASP experiment timeline. Given the time constraints, results do not sample important classes of proteins sufficiently to say whether or not AlphaFold is likely to work on that class of protein.

The models that have been made available via the EBI AlphaFold Database do give us a wider view as to the capabilities of the method, but with those models, we generally don't know the correct answers to compare against. Nevertheless, if we look at the models generated for the 20,000 or so genetically encoded human proteins, then a few observations can be made. First, there are many regions in those proteins where AlphaFold is producing essentially random output (see Figure 4). Perhaps rather unwisely, the database was populated by taking each full-length unprocessed protein sequence and feeding it to the neural network. Those of us who have spent a lot of time analyzing the human proteome already know that a large fraction of those sequences are disordered and/or low-complexity sequence regions, and it is clear that AlphaFold has really no better idea of what to do with those regions than any previous method. It simply outputs long stretches of "random coil" with extremely low confidence scores. Given how little experimental data are available for those regions, that's perhaps all we could expect it to do. Not all of the strange-looking artifacts produced by AlphaFold can be attributed simply to intrinsically disordered regions. Quite a number of the badly modeled regions will be down to multimeric interactions with either other chains or homomeric interactions with copies of the same chain. *The AlphaFold source code*[4] and *Colab notebook*[5] have been made available and have recently been updated to support predicting multimeric structures.

The program also has no way to take account of ligand binding, either small molecules or biological polymers (such as with DNA/RNA/sugars or lipids).[6] In some cases, somewhat surprisingly, a ligand-binding site is correctly modeled, but this can be attributed simply to the fact that the majority of structures in PDB will have that ligand present in their crystals and so the neural networks will have been trained mostly on the "holo" form of the structure and are simply reproducing the (useful) biases in the original training data. For example, zinc-binding sites (which are very common in protein structures) are often almost identical in the models to an occupied zinc-binding site from the PDB, although no zinc is present in the model. From a physical perspective, this does not make sense, since the positive charge on the zinc ion clearly stabilizes the observed conformation. Without it, the conformation would not be energetically stable. As noted on the website: "AlphaFold is trained to predict the structure of the protein *as it might appear in PDB*".

Certainly, where ligands and their binding to the same protein family are highly variable, immunoglobulin-antibody binding being the most prominent example, AlphaFold does not produce useful results.

There are now many examples of researchers creating "add-ons" and building tools based on AlphaFold. For example, researchers at the Netherlands Cancer Institute have created *AlphaFill*,[7] which adds missing ligands and co-factors to AlphaFold protein structure predictions by using data from related proteins in the PDB [4]. Similarly, Agirre and colleagues have added carbohydrate chains to AlphaFold predicted structures [5].

Another fundamental limitation that perhaps has not been emphasized enough is that AlphaFold is dependent on having a reasonably good multiple sequence alignment as input. There is no evidence that (unlike real proteins) it can fold up a single amino acid sequence but rather that, like previous methods, it is exploiting evolutionary information for its predictions. From a purely practical perspective, especially given the rate at which genome sequencing is taking place, this may not be so important, but there will always be niche proteins for which only one or

---

[4]https://github.com/deepmind/alphafold/.

[5]https://colab.research.google.com/github/deepmind/alphafold/blob/main/notebooks/AlphaFold.ipynb.

[6]A ligand is any other molecule that can bind to a protein. This includes ions (e.g., Zinc), small molecules (e.g., ATP), other proteins (including the same or different proteins), nucleic acids, and sugars. Experimental structures in the PDB often contain such ligands, which may or may not be relevant to their biological function.

[7]https://alphafill.eu/.

maybe several related sequences can be found. Then, there is the problem of modeling the effects of mutations on protein structures, where AlphaFold generally produces the same answer as it does for the wild-type protein. The consequence is that it cannot distinguish benign and pathogenic variants.

Although there was a lot of surprise at how much computational time DeepMind had used to make their CASP models, in practice, it seems that the model doesn't require such extreme resources to produce at least acceptable models. Indeed, the pipeline has been streamlined to the point where models can be generated by any user, using Google's free CoLab web service, usually in less than half an hour for small to medium-sized proteins. The very best results still require additional processing time to either sample different multiple sequence alignments or allow further stochastic searching of the output models, but still, for typical models, AlphaFold requires about the same amount of computational time as other popular protein modeling methods.

So, to address the main question, we have to conclude that AlphaFold has not solved the protein folding problem but certainly has gotten closer than any other method to date. It may be the case that there can never be a definitive single solution to every question that arises from the folding and stability of protein molecules in cells, but for now at least, the challenge remains open.

7. Implications for Experimental Structural Biologists

So, what are the implications of this breakthrough for labs currently involved in experimental structure determination? Reactions on social media from crystallographers ranged from the almost ridiculously enthusiastic to something close to panic. Some clearly think that no prediction can ever replace an experimental structure. Some simply do not believe the results or at least don't believe that they are representative of the problems they are currently working on. At the extreme end is the worry that some may be out of a job. We don't feel that any of these positions make sense. First, AlphaFold certainly represents a step change in our ability to predict the structures of proteins from amino acid sequences. Any biologist who currently uses any kind of protein modeling or structure prediction tool today is only likely to benefit from these new technological developments.

The first challenge for crystallographers will be to test the accuracy of these predictions through a wide range of appropriate test cases. We need to quantify better the accuracy of the predictions and the limitations of the method. Second, many crystallographers have unresolved datasets in a drawer like the aforementioned target T1100 — which might find a solution with a more accurate model for molecular replacement.

Approaching DeepMind for predictions may well help to resolve many of these structures — using a combination of experimental data and predicted models.

The other big challenge is of course studying protein interactions with all sorts of ligands. Without such knowledge, the interpretation of how the structure performs its function becomes very difficult. The hope is that progress towards improving our ability to predict such interactions using machine learning will also be made using similar techniques to AlphaFold. Currently, accurate placement of ligands remains challenging, although it is possible in some situations.

At a broader level, in principle, we need to work together towards complete structural coverage of the proteome at least for the model organisms and of course those bacteria and parasites that cause diseases. The combination of predicted and experimental data will surely move us more rapidly towards this goal. One approach (mirroring the Structural Genomics Initiatives of the 90s) would be to have available structures for all identified domains, which are common throughout life. Such an encyclopedia would accelerate our ability to interpret genomes, proteomes, and their biological functions and longer-term empower cellular tomography to improve our understanding of the proteome content and its distribution throughout all types of cells.

From our perspective, the most exciting thing about this achievement is that this isn't the end of anything but is really the beginning of many new things. We are convinced that this will enable the field of structural biology to grow and contribute even more to our understanding of life at the molecular level.

References

[1] J. Jumper, R. Evans, A. Pritzel *et al.* (2021). Highly accurate protein structure prediction with AlphaFold. *Nature, 596*(7873), 583–589.

[2] A. Vaswani, N. Shazeer, N. Parmar *et al.* (2017). Attention is all you need. *Advances in Neural Information Processing Systems, 30*, 5998–6008.

[3] K. Tunyasuvunakool, J. Adler, Z. Wu *et al.* (2021). Highly accurate protein structure prediction for the human proteome. *Nature, 596*(7873), 590–596.

[4] M. L. Hekkelman, I. de Vries, R. P. Joosten *et al.* (2021). AlphaFill: Enriching the AlphaFold models with ligands and co-factors. *bioRxiv.* https://doi.org/10.1101/2021.11.26.470110.

[5] H. Bagdonas, C. A. Fogarty, E. Fadda *et al.* (2021). The case for post-predictional modifications in the AlphaFold Protein Structure Database. *Nature Structural & Molecular Biology, 28*, 869–870. https://doi.org/10.1038/s41594-021-00680-9.

© 2023 World Scientific Publishing Company
https://doi.org/10.1142/9789811265679_0006

Chapter 6

Applications of AI in Astronomy

S. G. Djorgovski*,§, A. A. Mahabal*,¶, M. J. Graham*,‖, K. Polsterer†,**,
and A. Krone-Martins‡,††

*California Institute of Technology, Pasadena, CA 91125, USA
†Heidelberg Institute for Theoretical Studies,
69118 Heidelberg, Germany
‡University of California, Irvine, CA 92697, USA
§djorgovski@caltech.edu
¶aam@astro.caltech.edu
‖mjg@caltech.edu
**kai.polsterer@h-its.org
††algol@uci.edu

1. Introduction and Background

Astronomy entered the era of big data with the advent of large digital sky surveys in the 1990s, which opened the TB-scale regime. Sky surveys have been the dominant source of data in astronomy ever since, reaching the multi-PB scale by the late 2010s; see, e.g., [1] for a review. This stimulated the creation of the Virtual Observatory (VO) framework [2,3], which has now evolved into a global data grid of astronomy (see https://ivoa.net), providing access to data archives from both ground-based observatories and surveys, and the space-based missions.

This wealth and growth of data rates, volumes, and complexity demanded applications of automated data processing and analysis tools. While VO and the individual archives provide data access and some tools, most of the remaining astronomical cyberinfrastructure and data analytics tools have been developed by the individual research groups, captured under the Astroinformatics umbrella. Today, applications of

Machine Learning (ML) and other AI methods are becoming common-place and growing rapidly. During 2021, according to the Astrophysics Data System (ADS; https://ui.adsabs.harvard.edu), there were about 1000 astronomy/astrophysics papers that involved ML or AI, and their numbers are growing exponentially, with a doubling time of about 20 months. AI is now a standard part of the astronomical toolkit.

ML/AI methods are used to create value-added higher-level data products for follow-up research and may include source detection and segmentation tasks, structural and morphological classification, as well as all kinds of ordinary classification and regression tasks. While supervised classification tools are by construction unable to detect any new types of objects that are not present in the training datasets, unsupervised clustering offers a possibility of discovering previously unknown classes and enables the detection of rare, unusual, or even previously unknown types of objects as outliers in some feature space.

Given the vast scope of the field, the goal of this chapter is not to provide a comprehensive review but rather to give some illustrative examples where ML/AI has enabled significant advances in astronomy.

A useful didactic overview is by [4]. The monograph [5] gives an extensive and practical coverage of the subject. For some recent examples, see [6].

2. Early Applications: Digital Sky Surveys

While there have been some early experiments in the early 1990s, the use of ML/AI in astronomy really started growing in the mid-1990s, with the advent of the first large digital sky surveys [7,8]. The initial applications were to automate repetitive tasks that were previously done by humans. A good example is the star-galaxy separation for the catalogs of objects detected in sky surveys. Following the image segmentation that identifies individual sources, several tens to hundreds of morphological and structural parameters are evaluated for each one, thus forming feature vectors that can be analyzed using ML tools. Essentially, first terabytes and now petabytes of images are converted into database catalogs of many millions to billions of feature vectors, each representing an individual detected source, in data spaces of hundreds of dimensions, or even thousands once multiple catalogs are combined.

In the visible, UV, and IR wavelength regimes, the first-order classification is between the unresolved sources ("stars") and resolved ones ("galaxies"), based purely on the image morphology. Supervised classification methods, such as the Artificial Neural Networks (ANNs) or Decision Trees (DTs), were used effectively for this task; see, e.g., [9,10].

Morphological classification can be used to identify and remove a variety of instrumental artifacts that may appear as outliers in the feature space, [11]. The physical classification as objects of different types, e.g., galactic stars vs. quasars, different types of galaxies, and different types of stars, requires additional data in a subsequent analysis.

Digital sky surveys opened a new, highly effective mode of astronomical discovery. Traditional mode of pointed observations focuses on the individual objects or small samples of objects. Sky surveys may detect billions of sources, and ML can be used to select and prioritize the most interesting targets for the follow-up with large and/or space-based telescopes, thus optimizing the use of these scarce resources. Applying supervised classifiers or cuts in the feature space informed by the domain expertise has been proved to be very effective in finding well-defined samples of relatively rare types of objects, such as high-redshift quasars or brown dwarfs [12–14].

3. Increasing Challenges: Time-Domain Astronomy

Improvements in the size, quality, and cost of astronomical detectors enabled much larger format imaging cameras, which in turn enabled the rise of the synoptic sky surveys, where large areas of sky are surveyed repeatedly. This opening of the Time Domain enabled systematic, scaled-up studies of various temporal phenomena, including variability of stars and active galactic nuclei, cosmic explosions of all kinds (e.g., many types of supernovae, gravitational wave events, etc.), moving objects such as the potentially hazardous asteroids, etc. Time Domain — essentially a panoramic cosmic cinematography — touches all fields of astronomy, from the Solar System to cosmology.

This opens new scientific opportunities but also brings new challenges in addition to those posed by the traditional sky surveys, by adding the variability information to the classification tasks, and often time-criticality due to the transitive nature of the observed events: the potentially most interesting ones have to be identified in real time, as they must be followed up before they fade away [14–19,63,64]. Figure 1 shows a conceptual illustration of some of these challenges.

In addition to the full electromagnetic (EM) spectrum, gravitational wave, high-energy cosmic rays, and neutrino observatories are also now providing copious amounts of data, opening the field of Multi-messenger Astronomy. In general, the events detected by these non-EM channels have a very poor angular resolution and directionality but identifying their EM counterparts is essential for their physical interpretation. This leads to large area searches for counterparts, with many potential candidates. ML methods can be used to classify the possible candidate counterparts, e.g.,

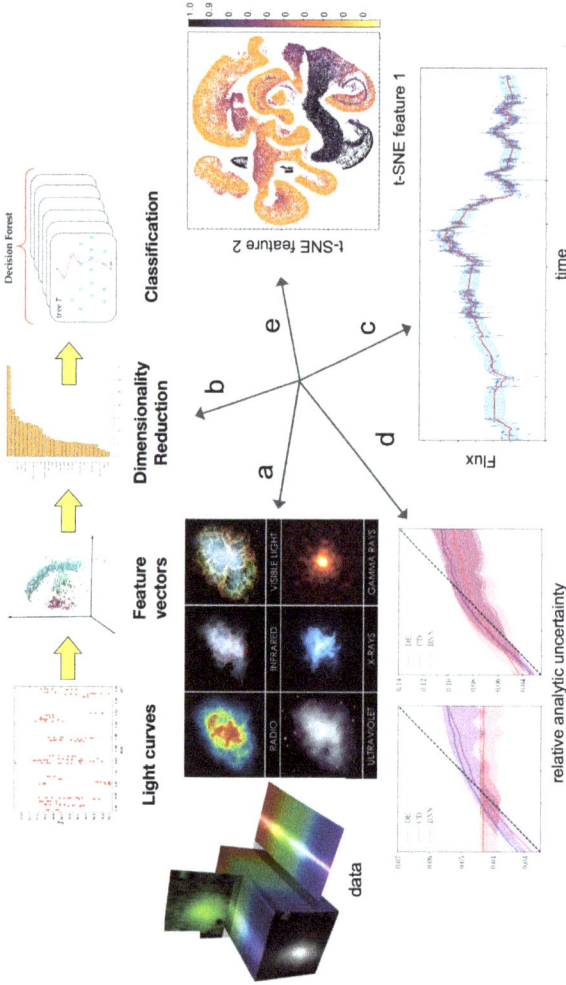

Fig. 1. The five major challenges facing TDA today: (a) a representation of a data cube signifying multiple wavelengths and multiwavelength observation of the Crab Nebula, (b) multiplicity of data features, (c) GPRs as a way to bridge gaps in observing, (d) understanding effect of noise on objects (from [29]), and (e) detecting anomalies (from [30]). Image credits: Stephen Todd, ROE and Douglas Pierce-Price, JAC for datacube; NASA/AUI and M. Bietenholz; NRAO/AUI and J. M. Uson, T. J. Cornwell (radio); NASA/JPL-Caltech/R. Gehrz/University of Minnesota (infrared); NASA, ESA, J. Hester and A. Loll/Arizona State University (visible); NASA/Swift/E. Hoversten, PSU (ultraviolet); NASA/CXC/SAO/F. Seward et al. (X-rays); NASA/DOE/Fermi LAT/R. Buehler (gamma rays) for Crab Nebula images.

[20,63,65,66], and other ML methods are being used to scrutinize and classify the non-EM signals themselves, e.g., [21,22].

One critical issue in classification in general is the poor scaling of the classification algorithms with the dimensionality of the feature space. This is especially important in the Time Domain; some approaches have been discussed by [23,24]. Feature dimensionality from several tens to few hundreds is now routine. Not all of these are independent (orthogonal) and some even add to noise for specific classes, making dimensionality reduction a critical need. For multiclass classification, disambiguating features that are important for one class but not another can be non-trivial. An example is the use of binary classifiers for the Zwicky Transient Facility (ZTF) [25]. Tools like DNN and XGBoost can be also used to identify the top features. When external features (e.g., from crossmatches to other surveys) are being incorporated, there can be missing features, which further complicates the use of some of the ML techniques. Techniques like Data Sheets [26] and Model Cards [27] can be used to standardize dataset creation and lead to reusable models [28].

Predicting the value of a time series between measurements is a common problem, particularly with multidimensional time series where values for all quantities at all timestamps are not available. In astronomy, this can pertain to prioritizing follow-up observations for interesting transient events. In the absence of a good theoretical model for the underlying process, a variety of interpolation schemes can be employed. However, these can also be a source of additional systematic errors.

An alternative is to adopt a probabilistic approach and regard the observed time series as a single draw from a multivariate Gaussian distribution fully characterized by a mean (normally assumed to be zero or constant) and a covariance function. Predicted points then just represent a subsequent draw and can be calculated with an associated uncertainty. Gaussian process regression (GPR) [31] uses the observed data to learn the hyperparameters of the underlying covariance kernel (and mean function if present). The form of the kernel function is a choice for the user but specific properties of the underlying process, such as stationarity, autoregressive behavior, or a spectral density representation, are easily represented. In fact, there is a theoretical duality between certain GPR kernels and neural network architectures [32], and neural networks can also be employed directly as kernels in some GPR implementations.

The main issue in using GPR, particularly with large multidimensional datasets with thousands of data points and/or comprising thousands of samples, is the speed of fitting since this typically involves extensive matrix inversion. Certain GPR implementations have achieved good performance by making very specific decisions on the functional form of the kernel function, e.g., it only uses exponential terms and optimizes accordingly, but this is not a global solution [33].

It is also unclear how good GPR is at forecasting data. There is a tendency with non-periodic kernels to regress to the mean with increasing time past the last observed data point and increasing uncertainty. Recurrent neural networks seem to show better performance [34], but they have also been used more in forecasting the next data point rather than data over an extended period of time. Obviously, if the underlying process is nonlinear, then forecasting presents a much bigger problem and more advanced deep learning architectures may be required.

Incorporating error bars in ML analysis is a notoriously non-trivial challenge. That fact, combined with classifying objects near the detection limit, raises a very different kind of a challenge. Observing ever-fainter objects helps push the science into newer areas, but at the same time, it comes with a greater risk of such objects turning out to be false positives (e.g., short-lived transients that are below the quiescent limit that brighten into observable range for a short duration). Uncertainty quantification, e.g., [35], combined with emulators and simulators [29], along with models based on Bayesian techniques may be needed [36].

Looking for anomalies, i.e., objects or events that do not seem to belong to any of the known classes, poses additional challenges. It is difficult to define what an anomaly is in the first place: Is it an out-of-distribution object, a completely independent or new class? Will more observations favor one interpretation or the other, and what kind of observations will be required? Active learning where newer observations are iteratively used to improve classification routinely indicates the requirement to revise classifications at the boundaries of ambiguity. However, the follow-up resources are limited, and with the ever-growing data rates, it becomes critical to optimize their use. Some early efforts in this arena include [30,37–40] and others.

4. A Growing Applications Landscape

While classification and outlier search remain a staple of survey-based astronomy, there is now a much broader range of ML/AI applications.

One application area of ML tools is the estimation of photometric redshifts (photo-z's). In cosmology, redshift, reflecting the increase in the scale of the universe since the light was emitted by some distant object, due to the cosmic expansion is a measure of distance and thus necessary in determining the physical parameters of distant galaxies and quasars, such as their luminosities and masses. Traditionally, redshifts are measured spectroscopically, which is observationally expensive. Photo-z's are a way of estimating the redshifts from the multicolor photometry, which is observationally much cheaper, and thus can be done for vastly larger numbers of objects. This is a use case where ML has enabled significant advances and savings of observing time, by including instrumental characteristics and physical models implicitly expressed through the data. There is an extensive literature on this subject with a wide variety of ML methods [41–50] and many others. One important conceptual change was to replace a single number representation of an estimated photo-z with a probability density distribution.

ML has been also used as a method for the discovery of gravitational lenses, operating both on the images from sky surveys [51] and time series of quasar variability [52]. Such large, systematically selected samples of gravitational lenses can be used as probes of dark matter and the expansion rate of the universe.

In addition to the data obtained through observations, the output of large numerical simulations is another large source of data calling for an automated analysis. Current developments led to hybrid approaches of classically computing physical models in combination with ML models. By doing so, time-consuming calculations can be replaced through very quick ML models that act as a surrogate with a similar accuracy as the original code. Thereby, larger volumes, with higher spatial and temporal resolution, can be computed without requiring more resources. Another aspect is that critical branching conditions can be detected, and the resolutions of the simulation can be adaptively changed, ensuring that those details are not lost or overseen while simulating. Some examples include [53–56] and others.

This is just a small sampling of the examples of the diverse, growing, and creative uses of AI/ML in astronomy.

5. Concluding Comments and Future Prospects

While the range and diversity of AI applications in astronomy continue to grow, most applications so far have been focused on the analysis of already acquired datasets and their derived data products, such as the tables of pre-extracted and expert-engineered features. However, the landscape of ML/AI applications is also changing rapidly, affecting different stages of a data-centric approach, data acquisition, processing, and analysis.

The acquisition stage covers the process of planning and performing observations. For the most part, this process was done by the individual experts, but based on specified quality criteria, AI systems can learn to perform this planning automatically. Based on the quick analysis of the initial data, instrument setup, exposure times, etc. can be used to close the loop between choosing the right observational setup and getting high-quality science data. This kind of fast, AI-based observation planning and control system will likely replace the current way of planning, scheduling, and observing, leading to an improved scientific outcome, both in the quality and quantity of the observations. This will be critical in the arena of Time-Domain and Multi-Messenger Astronomy, where transient events may be detected and followed up by a number of different surveys and facilities, and their prioritization for the follow-up would be essential.

Incorporation of domain knowledge into ML/AI analysis, such as the "physics-based" AI, is an active area of research, with many outstanding challenges remaining. Some examples include [57,58] and others.

Besides the analysis of scientific data, ML methods get utilized to access complex scientific content like scientific publications or to realize a natural language and chat-based access to data stored in catalogs. ML and AI-based systems may transform the way of finding and accessing data soon. Likewise, ML can be used to sort through the literature given a set of user preferences; an example is http://www.arxiv-sanity.com/.

Another novel direction is in using AI not just to map the data spaces and find interesting objects but to discover potentially interesting relationships that may be present in the data. One approach is to use symbolic regression, e.g., [59,60]. A related technique uses memetic regression [61,62].

As the data complexity continues to increase, the use of AI to detect interesting patterns or behaviors present in the data, that may elude humans, e.g., due to the hyper-dimensionality of the data, will keep on increasing. The interpretation of such AI-based discoveries still rests with the humans, but there is a possibility that some of them may simply exceed the human cognitive capabilities. We may increasingly see more examples of a collaborative human–AI discovery.

References

[1] S. G. Djorgovski, A. A. Mahabal, A. Drake *et al.* (2012). Sky surveys. In H. Bond (ed.), *Astronomical Techniques, Software, and Data.* Planets, Stars, and Stellar Systems, Vol. 2, ser. ed. T. Oswalt. Dordrecht: Springer, pp. 223–281.

[2] R. J. Brunner, S. G. Djorgovski, and A. S. Szalay (2001). *Virtual Observatories of the Future.* A.S.P. Conf. Ser., Vol. 225. San Francisco: Astronomical Society of the Pacific.

[3] S. G. Djorgovski and the NVO Science Definition Team (2002). *Towards the National Virtual Observatory.* Washington, DC: National Science Foundation. https://www.nsf.gov/mps/ast/sdt_final.pdf.

[4] D. Baron (2019). *Machine Learning in Astronomy: A Practical Overview.* https://arxiv.org/abs/1904.07248.

[5] Ž. Ivezić, A. Connolly, J. VanderPlas *et al.* (2020). *Statistics, Data Mining, and Machine Learning in Astronomy: A Practical Python Guide for the Analysis of Survey Data.* Princeton: Princeton University Press.

[6] I. Zelinka, M. Brescia, and D. Baron (eds.) (2021). *Intelligent Astrophysics.* Emergence, Complexity and Computation, 39. London: Springer Nature.

[7] N. Weir, U. Fayyad, S. G. Djorgovski *et al.* (1995a). The SKICAT system for processing and analysing digital imaging sky surveys. *Publications of the Astronomical Society of the Pacific, 107,* 1243–1254.

[8] U. Fayyad, P. Smyth, N. Weir *et al.* (1995). Automated analysis and exploration of image databases: Results, progress, and challenges. *Journal of Intelligent Information Systems, 4,* 7.

[9] N. Weir, U. Fayyad, and S. G. Djorgovski (1995b). Automated star/galaxy classification for digitized POSS-II. *The Astronomical Journal, 109,* 2401–2414.

[10] S. Odewahn, R. de Carvalho, R. Gal *et al.* (2004). The Digitized Second Palomar Observatory Sky Survey (DPOSS). III. Star-Galaxy separation. *The Astronomical Journal, 128,* 3092–3107.

[11] C. Donalek, A. Mahabal, S. G. Djorgovski *et al.* (2008). New approaches to object classification in synoptic sky surveys. *AIP Conference Proceedings, 1082,* 252–256.

[12] S. G. Djorgovski, A. Mahabal, R. Brunner *et al.* (2001a). Searches for rare and new types of objects. In R. Brunner, S. G. Djorgovski, and A. Szalay (eds.), *Virtual Observatories of the Future,* A.S.P. Conf. Ser., *225,* 52–63.

[13] S. G. Djorgovski, R. Brunner, A. Mahabal *et al.* (2001b). Exploration of large digital sky surveys. In A. J. Banday *et al.* (eds.), *Mining the Sky.* ESO Astrophysics Symposia. Berlin: Springer, pp. 305–322.

[14] S. G. Djorgovski, A. Mahabal, R. Brunner *et al.* (2001c). Exploration of parameter spaces in a virtual observatory. In J.-L. Starck and F. Murtagh (eds.), *Astronomical Data Analysis. Proceedings of SPIE, 4477,* 43–52.

[15] A. Mahabal, S. G. Djorgovski, A. Drake *et al.* (2011). Discovery, classification, and scientific exploration of transient events from the Catalina Real-Time Transient Survey. *Bulletin of the Astronomical Society of India, 39,* 387–408.

[16] S. G. Djorgovski, A. Mahabal, A. Drake *et al.* (2012a). Exploring the time domain with synoptic sky surveys. In E. Griffin *et al.* (eds.), *Proceedings of the IAU Symposium 285: New Horizons in Time Domain Astronomy.* Cambridge: Cambridge University Press, pp. 141–146.

[17] S. G. Djorgovski, A. Mahabal, C. Donalek *et al.* (2012b). Flashes in a star stream: Automated classification of astronomical transient events. *Proceedings of the IEEE e-Science 2012* (IEEE Press), 6404437.

[18] M. Graham, S. G. Djorgovski, A. Mahabal *et al.* (2012). Data challenges of time domain astronomy. *Distributed and Parallel Databases, 30,* 371–384.

[19] M. Graham, A. Drake, S. G. Djorgovski *et al.* (2017). Challenges in the automated classification of variable stars in large databases. In M. Catelan

and W. Gieren (eds.), *Wide-Field Variability Surveys: A 21st Century Perspective*, EPJ Web of Conferences, Vol. 152, 03001.

[20] I. Andreoni, M. Coughlin, E. Kool *et al.* (2021). Fast-transient searches in real time with ZTFReST: Identification of three optically discovered gamma-ray burst afterglows and new constraints on the kilonova rate. *The Astrophysical Journal, 918*, 63.

[21] M. Cabero, A. Mahabal, and J. McIver (2020). GWSkyNet: A real-time classifier for public gravitational-wave candidates. *The Astrophysical Journal Letters, 904*, L9. doi: 10.3847/2041-8213/abc5b5 *[arXiv:2010.11829 [gr-qc]]*.

[22] T. C. Abbott, E. Buffaz, N. Vieira *et al.* (2022). GWSkyNet-Multi: A machine learning multi-class classifier for LIGO-Virgo Public Alerts. https://arxiv.org/abs/2111.04015.

[23] C. Donalek, A. Kumar, S. G. Djorgovski *et al.* (2013). Feature selection strategies for classifying high dimensional astronomical data sets. In *Scalable Machine Learning: Theory and Applications, IEEE BigData 2013*, New York: IEEE Press, pp. 35–40.

[24] A. D'Isanto, S. Cavuoti, M. Brescia *et al.* (2016). An analysis of feature relevance in the classification of astronomical transients with machine learning methods. *Monthly Notices of the Royal Astronomical Society, 457*, 3119–3132.

[25] J. van Roestel, D. A. Duev, A. A. Mahabal *et al.* (2021). *The Astronomical Journal, 161*, 267.

[26] T. Gebru, J. Morgenstern, B. Vecchione *et al.* (2021). Datasheets for datasets. *Comm. ACM, 64*(12), 86–92.

[27] M. Mitchell, S. Wu, A. Zaldivar, *et al.* (2019). Model cards for model reporting. In *FAT* *'19: Conference on Fairness, Accountability, and Transparency*, New York: ACM Press, pp. 220–229.

[28] A. Mahabal, T. Hare, V. Fox *et al.* (2021). In-space data fusion for more productive missions. *Bulletin of the AAS, 53*(4), 500.

[29] J. Caldeira and B. Nord (2020). Deeply uncertain: Comparing methods of uncertainty quantification in deep learning algorithms. *Machine Learning: Science and Technology, 2*(1), 015002.

[30] J. R. Martínez-Galarza, F. B. Bianco, D. Crake *et al.* (2021). *Monthly Notices of the Royal Astronomical Society, 508*, 5734.

[31] C. Rasmussen and C. Williams (2006). *Gaussian Processes for Machine Learning*. Cambridge, MA: MIT Press.

[32] J. Lee, Y. Bahri, R. Novak *et al.* (2017). Deep neural networks as Gaussian processes. https://arxiv.org/abs/1711.00165.

[33] D. Foreman-Mackey, E. Agol, S. Ambikasaran *et al.* (2017). Fast and scalable Gaussian process modeling with applications to astronomical time series. *The Astronomical Journal, 154*, 220.

[34] Y. Tachibana, M. Graham, N. Kawai *et al.* (2020). Deep modeling of quasar variability. *The Astrophysical Journal, 903*, 17.

[35] M. Abdar, F. Pourpanah, S. Hussain *et al.* (2021). A review of uncertainty quantification in deep learning: Techniques, applications and challenges. *Information Fusion, 76*, 243–297.

[36] M. Walmsley, L. Smith, C. Lintott *et al.* (2020). Galaxy Zoo: Probabilistic morphology through Bayesian CNNs and active learning. *Monthly Notices of the Royal Astronomical Society*, *491*, 1554–1574.

[37] S. Webb, M. Lochner, D. Muthukrishna *et al.* (2020). *Monthly Notices of the Royal Astronomical Society*, *498*, 3077.

[38] V. A. Villar, M. Cranmer, E. Berger *et al.* (2021). A deep-learning approach for live anomaly detection of extragalactic transients. *The Astrophysical Journal Supplement Series*, *255*, 24.

[39] E. E. O. Ishida, M. V. Kornilov, K. L. Malanchev *et al.* (2021). Active anomaly detection for time-domain discoveries. *Astronomy & Astrophysics*, *650*, A195–A204.

[40] M. Lochner and B. Bassett (2021). ASTRONOMALY: Personalised active anomaly detection in astronomical data. *Astronomy and Computing*, *36*, 100481.

[41] N. Ball, R. Brunner, A. Myers *et al.* (2008). Robust machine learning applied to astronomical data sets. III. Probabilistic photometric redshifts for galaxies and quasars. *The Astrophysical Journal*, *683*, 12–21.

[42] O. Laurino, R. D'Abrusco, G. Longo *et al.* (2011). Astroinformatics of galaxies and quasars: A new general method for photometric redshifts estimation. *Monthly Notices of the Royal Astronomical Society*, *418*, 2165–2195.

[43] M. Brescia, S. Cavuoti, R. D'Abrusco *et al.* (2013). Photometric redshifts for quasars in multi-band surveys. *The Astrophysical Journal*, *772*, 140.

[44] M. Carrasco Kind and R. Brunner (2014). Exhausting the information: Novel Bayesian combination of photometric redshift PDFs. *Monthly Notices of the Royal Astronomical Society*, *442*, 3380–3399.

[45] S. Cavuoti, M. Brescia, G. Longo *et al.* (2012). Photometric redshifts with the quasi-Newton algorithm (MLPQNA): Results in the PHAT1 contest. *Astronomy & Astrophysics*, *546*, A13.

[46] S. Cavuoti, V. Amaro, M. Brescia *et al.* (2017). METAPHOR: A machine-learning-based method for the probability density estimation of photometric redshifts. *Monthly Notices of the Royal Astronomical Society*, *465*, 1959–1973.

[47] A. D'Isanto and K. Polsterer (2018). Photometric redshift estimation via deep learning. Generalized and pre-classification-less, image based, fully probabilistic redshifts. *Astronomy & Astrophysics*, *609*, A111.

[48] M. Salvato, O. Ilbert, and B. Hoyle (2019). The many flavours of photometric redshifts. *Nature Astronomy*, *3*, 212–222.

[49] S. J. Schmidt, A. I. Malz, J. Y. H. Soo *et al.* (2020). Evaluation of probabilistic photometric redshift estimation approaches for The Rubin Observatory Legacy Survey of Space and Time (LSST). *Monthly Notices of the Royal Astronomical Society*, *499*, 1587–1606.

[50] O. Razim, S. Cavuoti, M. Brescia *et al.* (2021). Improving the reliability of photometric redshift with machine learning. *Monthly Notices of the Royal Astronomical Society*, *507*, 5034–5052.

[51] A. Krone-Martins, L. Delchambre, O. Wertz *et al.* (2018). Gaia GraL: Gaia DR2 gravitational lens systems. I. New quadruply imaged quasar candidates around known quasars. *Astronomy & Astrophysics, 616*, L11.

[52] A. Krone-Martins, M. Graham, D. Stern *et al.* (2022). Gaia GraL: Gaia DR2 gravitational lens systems. V. Doubly-imaged QSOs discovered from entropy and wavelets. https://arxiv.org/abs/1912.08977.

[53] H. Kamdar, M. Turk, and R. Brunner (2016). Machine learning and cosmological simulations — II. Hydrodynamical simulations. *Monthly Notices of the Royal Astronomical Society, 457*, 1162–1179.

[54] Y. Ni, Y. Li, P. Lachance *et al.* (2021). AI-assisted superresolution cosmological simulations — II. Halo substructures, velocities, and higher order statistics. *Monthly Notices of the Royal Astronomical Society, 507*, 1021–1033.

[55] C. Lovell, S. Wilkins, P. Thomas *et al.* (2022). A machine learning approach to mapping baryons on to dark matter haloes using the EAGLE and C-EAGLE simulations. *Monthly Notices of the Royal Astronomical Society, 509*, 5046–5061.

[56] J. Chacón, J. Vázquez, and E. Almaraz (2022). Classification algorithms applied to structure formation simulations. *Astronomy and Computing, 38*, 100527.

[57] G. Karniadakis, I. Kevrekidis, L. Lu *et al.* (2021). Physics-informed machine learning. *Nature Reviews Physics, 3*(6), 422–440.

[58] Z. Liu, Y. Chen, Y. Du *et al.* (2021). Physics-augmented learning: A new paradigm beyond physics-informed learning. https://arxiv.org/abs/2109.13901.

[59] M. Graham, S. G. Djorgovski, A. Mahabal *et al.* (2013). Machine-assisted discovery of relationships in astronomy. *Monthly Notices of the Royal Astronomical Society, 431*, 2371.

[60] S.-M. Udrescu and M. Tegmark (2020). AI Feynman: A physics-inspired method for symbolic regression. *Science Advances, 6*, 2631.

[61] H. Sun and P. Moscato (2019). A memetic algorithm for symbolic regression. In *2019 IEEE Congress on Evolutionary Computation (CEC)*. New York: IEEE Press, pp. 2167–2174.

[62] P. Moscato, H. Sun, and M. Haque (2021). Analytic continued fractions for regression: A memetic algorithm approach. *Expert Systems with Applications, 179*, 115018.

[63] S. G. Djorgovski, M. Graham, C. Donalek *et al.* (2016). Real-time data mining of massive data streams from synoptic sky surveys. *Future Generation Computer Systems, 59*, 95–104.

[64] S. G. Djorgovski, A. Mahabal, C. Donalek *et al.* (2014). Automated real-time classification and decision making in massive data streams from synoptic sky surveys. In C. Medeiros (ed.), *Proceedings of the IEEE e-Science 2014* (IEEE Press), pp. 204–211.

[65] A. Mahabal, K. Sheth, F. Gieseke *et al.* (2017). Deep-learnt classification of light curves. In *2017 IEEE Symp. on Computational Intelligence (SSCI)*, pp. 2757–2764.

[66] A. Mahabal, U. Rebbapragada, R. Walters *et al.* (ZTF Team) (2019). Machine learning for the Zwicky transient facility. *Publications of the Astronomical Society of the Pacific*, *131*, 038002.

© 2023 World Scientific Publishing Company
https://doi.org/10.1142/9789811265679_0007

Chapter 7

Machine Learning for Complex Instrument Design and Optimization

Barry C. Barish[*], Jonathan Richardson[†], Evangelos E. Papalexakis[‡], and Rutuja Gurav[§]

University of California, Riverside CA, USA
[*]barry.barish@ucr.edu
[†]jonathan.richardson@ucr.edu
[‡]epapalex@cs.ucr.edu
[§]rutuja.gurav@email.ucr.edu

1. Introduction

In the era of large-scale scientific experiments, big data management and high-performance computing have become indispensable for the fast storage, retrieval, and analysis of the vast amounts of data generated. At the same time, there has been a growing interest in using advanced machine learning (ML) techniques for data analysis to make scientific discoveries. However, the potential of ML to accelerate scientific discovery is not limited to the analysis of an experiment's main data products. Frontier experimental apparatuses like the Large Hadron Collider (LHC), Laser Interferometer Gravitational-Wave Observatory (LIGO), and Electron-Ion Collider (EIC) are highly complex instruments with hundreds of degrees of freedom stabilized by cross-coupled feedback servos and with thousands of auxiliary sensors. The 4 km long detectors of LIGO, illustrated in Figure 1, consist of six coupled laser cavities formed by dozens of mirrors suspended from quadruple-stage pendula and mounted on active seismic isolation platforms. LIGO's main data product is the *strain*[1] which is used by astrophysicists to search for gravitational-wave signals. In addition to the main strain

---

[1] *Strain* is the fractional space change across a 4 km long arm of the interferometer relative to the total length of the arm.

Fig. 1.   Inside the control room of the Laser Interferometer Gravitational Observatory (LIGO) in Livingston, Louisiana. Image credit: Amber Stuver/Wikimedia Commons [https://commons.wikimedia.org/wiki/File:LLO_Control_Room.jpg].

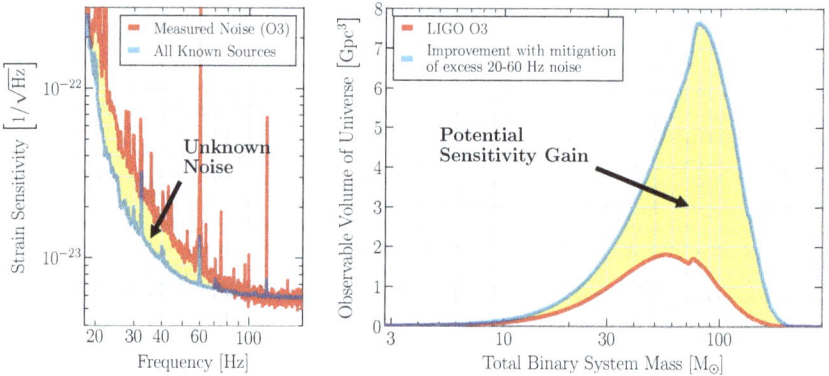

Fig. 2.   *Left:* Noise floor of the LIGO Hanford gravitational-wave detector during the O3 observing run (red), compared to the budgeted detector noise (blue). As shown, most of the noise in the 20–60 Hz band remains unidentified. *Right:* Projected improvement in the observable volume of the Universe for equal-mass binary black hole mergers, as a function of the total mass (in the source frame) of the binary, if this excess noise were identified and fully mitigated.

channel, each LIGO detector records over 10,000 channels monitoring the operation of each subsystem and the seismic, acoustic, and electromagnetic environment (for an overview of LIGO's environmental monitoring system, see [26]). The complexity of large scientific instruments, with their vast quantities of auxiliary data, presents an emerging opportunity to use ML more broadly to learn about the instrument itself.

Leveraging ML tools to diagnose performance limitations, such as poorly understood instrumental noise or control instabilities, and to identify more optimal designs could lead to big scientific returns through improved sensitivity, operational up-time, and data quality. As one example, nonlinear, or non-stationary, noise couplings of mostly unknown origin now limit the Advanced LIGO detectors in several ways. In particular, most of the detector noise in a band of key scientific interest, 20–60 Hz, remains unidentified altogether. The unidentified excess noise is shown in the left panel of Figure 2, indicated by the shaded region. The right panel of Figure 2 shows the impact of this noise on a key astrophysical metric. As shown, identifying and mitigating this noise would significantly enlarge both the volume of the universe and the astrophysical mass range accessible to gravitational-wave science, including enabling observations of mergers of the most massive stellar-origin black holes.

The unidentified excess noise in the LIGO detectors is believed to originate through nonlinear mechanisms because it does not exhibit high coherence with any of the multitudes of auxiliary signals. For this reason, it has proven very difficult to pinpoint the origins of nonlinear noise in Advanced LIGO using traditional (linear time-invariant) system identification techniques. However, such challenges are far from being specific to LIGO. In fact, they are common to complex actively controlled instruments, with another example being particle accelerators. In accelerators, ML can be used to optimize the performance of colliding beams, reduce beam losses, and steer the beam.

Developing new tools and approaches for understanding instrumental noise, as well as other operational anomalies, is thus critical to the future of complex instruments such as LIGO, the LHC, and the EIC. New unsupervised ML methods to model and analyze the multitude of auxiliary signals recorded in the detectors, over extended periods of time, offer an emerging opportunity to generate *actionable insights* that will guide instrument commissioning efforts and future design decisions. Previous applications of ML in complex systems like LIGO (for a through review, see [6]) or accelerators [9] overwhelming employ a supervised learning paradigm, where the desired input–output behavior of a system is known and is being approximated by a ML model (e.g., estimating the masses of the two colliding black holes in an observed gravitational wave). In many of the problems encountered within complex instrument operations, such supervision is scarce or non-existent, calling for the development of novel ML methods to tackle them.

Similar challenges also arise in the operation of large complex systems in general [20], so advances in this area will open opportunities for unsupervised and explainable knowledge discovery at large.

In the remainder of this chapter, we first discuss the key challenges and requirements for developing unsupervised learning models for complex instruments. This section also introduces ML terminology and concepts on which the later sections of this chapter will rely. We then discuss the potential of ML as a tool for diagnosing and optimizing the operational performance of an experimental apparatus, using the LIGO detectors as an illustrative case study. Finally, we discuss the prospect of using ML for instrument design, with applications to optimizing existing accelerators like the LHC as well as the ground-up design of future frontier accelerators such as the EIC.[2]

2. Machine Learning Challenges and Requirements

In adapting or developing new ML methods for complex instrument operations management and design, there are a number of fundamental challenges that must be addressed. We provide a brief overview of those challenges in the following. Although they are presented in a serial and independent manner, typically a combination of them manifests in any problem we may encounter.

2.1. *Weak or limited supervision*

Supervision is a key aspect of machine learning, and the paradigm of *supervised learning* is, most likely, the one to which most readers would have already been exposed: there is an abundance of (input data, desired output) pairs (e.g., an image and its associated label), and the task is to learn a model that maps a representation of the input to the desired label in a manner that *generalizes* to unseen inputs. However, a vast number of problems in the context of instrument diagnostics and design cannot afford the amount of human annotations necessary to train such models. For instance, when predicting operational failures, the annotations that would be most desirable would be ones which would characterize the parts of the instrument which are responsible for the failure. Unfortunately, this presents a *Catch-22*, since those annotations are the knowledge which we seek to extract from our application of machine learning. In such a case, we may resort to *proxy data* which can be obtained cheaply, does not require extensive human annotation, and may help us train models which can shed some light on the ultimate intractable task. We may use the presence or absence of instrument failure as a coarse label that indicates normal or abnormal operation, in hopes that the model that is able to successfully predict such a coarse label is capturing useful information that can enable exploratory analysis to further characterize such a failure.

---

[2]Find more information about the EIC here — https://www.bnl.gov/eic/.

Finally, this challenge is compounded by the fact that, even though the amounts of data generated by an instrument are massive, typically when creating ML-friendly datasets from which a model can learn meaningful and generalizable patterns, there is significant cleaning, down-selecting of channels and time periods, and other forms of pre-processing involved, which result in substantially reduced sizes for available curated datasets. This makes learning more challenging.

2.2. *Explainable models*

Machine learning models which are tasked with mapping input feature representations (e.g., sensor readings that monitor the state of the instrument for a certain time window) to a desired prediction (e.g., failure at time t_f) can take many different forms, all the way from classification trees and parametric equations to deep neural networks. As we mentioned above, a fundamental requirement for any such model is to generalize well to unseen examples. However, this is only one of the dimensions in which one can examine machine learning models. A dimension that is vital to many problems encountered in the context of this chapter is *explainability*, which measures the degree to which a human can readily understand the reasoning behind the model's decision and attribute such decision to different parts of the input data (in our running example, such attribution could be highlighting different sensors and temporal windows as bearing most of the weight of the prediction of a failure). Simple linear models or tree-based models lend themselves directly to such explanations (a linear model assigns different weights to inputs, and a tree can provide a set of rules based on the inputs which led to the decision). As machine learning models move towards highly overparametrized deep neural networks, the ability to generalize successfully increases. However, the ability to provide such explanations and attributions to the input becomes increasingly more challenging. Thus, there is an active research area within machine learning which is concerned with different paradigms and methods of explainability, ranging from readily explainable models to models for which only *post hoc* explanations can be provided [15]. In our context, any such form of explanation can be crucially important: coupled with the challenge of weak supervision described above, imbuing explainability to a model tasked with predicting an auxiliary target (e.g., whether a failure occurred) can shine light on parts of the data which can then be further examined systematically by domain experts. In this way, we may gain insight into potential physical mechanisms that can be responsible for the observed outcome (e.g., instrument failure).

2.3. Theory/physics-guided models

A major promise of modern deep learning models is their purported ability to capture arbitrarily nonlinear functions between input and output. However, such a statement, generic as it is, highly depends on a vast number of factors and problem parameters, such as the amount and quality of data available to us, the inherent hardness of the predictive task at hand, and the quality of the supervision, just to name a few. As a result, this promise is not always realized, and in practice, successfully training a model that reaches that ideal requires copious amounts of experimentation with different hyperparameters and design choices. Thus, an emerging area in machine learning research is the one of theory-guided, or *physics-guided*, modeling [18]. It aims to leverage well-understood information from a particular scientific domain of interest, incorporating that in the design or the training of the model such that models which are consistent with what theory dictates are preferred over models that are inconsistent (with a varying degree of strictness, depending on how such guidance is incorporated). Doing so may imbue stability and efficiency in how the model is able to perform and generalize, thus making such guided approaches very appealing. In our scenarios, one may envision identifying parts of the instrument whose operation is well understood and potentially expressed by precise equations and enforcing consistency of the trained model with respect to those equations. The intended by-product of this action is that the model learned will capture phenomena (both documented and unknown) in the data with higher fidelity, even though full *a priori* modeling of all phenomena may be infeasible or impossible.

2.4. Human (expert)-in-the-loop & active learning

The typical view of supervision in machine learning considers the process of obtaining human annotations as an offline, slow, and tedious process. However, an emerging trend in machine learning is to blur the boundaries between those two processes by introducing "human-in-the-loop frameworks", where a model is being continually refined according to human feedback. Key challenges in doing so include the determination of when and how often to solicit feedback, the form of the feedback itself (e.g., it may be easier for a human labeler to identify whether or not two data points are of the same type than to provide a type for a single data point [22]), and in what ways the model should adapt to the new feedback provided by the human. Human-in-the-loop analytics and learning, albeit an active and emerging field, is related closely with ideas previously developed within the field of information retrieval (studying and developing algorithms for efficient search and retrieval of information) and the area of relevance feedback [30]. Furthermore, parts of the desiderata in a human-in-the-loop framework are also the subject of the area of active learning [31], where the objective is to solicit new annotations for a limited number of data points such that the new model's performance is maximized. Active learning has found applications to science problems, such as anomaly detection in astronomy [17]. In realizing an end-to-end human-in-the-loop framework, however, more advances are necessary in a number of areas including scalability and visualization/human–computer interaction [10,38,40].

3. Optimizing Instrument Operational Performance

Optimal instrument performance is critical for achieving the scientific goals of a large-scale experiment. However, the complexity of large instruments often makes it difficult to identify the *root cause* of errors encountered during operation. Normal operation typically involves controlling many coupled degrees of freedom simultaneously, with a multitude of potential points of failure and entry for noise. Using instrumental data to identify poor operating conditions and diagnose errors thus requires monitoring many interacting subsystems. Even so, modeling of the instrument, or even individual subsystems, often fails to capture enough realistic detail to reproduce operational errors because (1) the number of possible failure modes is vast and unknown and (2) the state of the instrument and all of its subcomponents, at any moment, is also not fully known. Thus, the best prospect for uncovering root causes of anomalous operations or failures lies in mining time series from the large number of diagnostic channels,[3] various subsets of which may be non-trivially correlated, for *interesting* patterns.

Among patterns of interest are the so-called anomalies; they are outliers in the data that potentially hint towards processes that might be disrupting nominal operation of the instrument. In Ref. [9], the authors present a use case of modern particle accelerators, a poster child for a large-scale complex instrument, and cite that various anomaly detection techniques have been used at the LHC for identifying bad readings from beam position monitors and to assist in automated collimator alignment [36]. A key challenge for human operators is selecting a small subset of relevant channels for investigation from a vast number of channels which record the dynamics of the instrument. In this section, we broadly describe two machine learning pipelines to aid the diagnosis of two types of operational issues:

---

[3]A set of channels used for performing instrument diagnostics, primarily consisting of sensor readout or other quantities related to instrument control.

1. transient noise and 2. control failures. We will first briefly introduce these operational issues and then present detailed real-world examples of these issues encountered in a *state-of-the-art* complex instrument: ground-based gravitational-wave detectors.

3.1. *Transient noise*

Can contaminate the main data product of an experiment and thus lower its quality. For an active instrument, like a particle accelerator, this means repeating the experimental run which is costly but possible. For a passive observatory, like the ground-based gravitational-wave detectors at LIGO, such transient noise can lead to a missing part or whole of a unique astrophysical event that is impossible to observe again. Figure 4 shows the now-famous example of a loud noise transient corrupting a portion of the signal from the first ever binary neutron star merger detected by LIGO. Thus, it is critical to understand sources of such noise to potentially eliminate it with upgrades. Using archived data and machine learning methods, we can identify *witnesses* to noise artifacts by looking for correlations between transients in a set of diagnostic channels.[3] A subset of these diagnostic channels termed as *witness channels* can then be used to categorize, locate, and potentially eliminate the *root cause* of certain noise transients.

3.2. *Control failures*

Render the instrument unable to operate in a nominal state and thus reduce the duty cycle. This operational issue has a relatively larger impact than the **transient noise** issue as no science data can be produced while the instrument is recovering. Diagnosing the causes of control failures is crucial to mitigate future adverse events. Such failures are relatively easy to mitigate as they are occurring in real time but a key task is to *predict* an impending failure. We can address this task with machine learning by using data preceding failure events from a set of diagnostic channels to identify *precursors* to these failure events. In Ref. [11], the authors explore the use of deep neural networks[4] for predicting operational failures at a particle accelerator facility by modeling precursors to a failure from a set of diagnostic channels.[3] *Limited Supervision [2.1]:* The machine learning problem is formulated as a binary classification task where data points corresponding to failures (positive class) and nominal behavior (negative class) can be automatically labeled without manual human effort.

---

[4]A class of supervised machine learning models that are particularly good at learning complex, nonlinear functions of the input that map it to the prediction target.

Explainable Models [2.2]: Since deep neural networks are often black box models, the authors employ an explanation technique, layer-wise relevance propagation [2], to highlight a subset of diagnostic channels[3] that are relevant to failures.

Before presenting real-world examples of the two aforementioned operational issues in the context of our complex instrument of choice, LIGO, let us walk through the generic machine learning pipeline (shown in Figure 3 (*top row*)). Raw data from a data archive are processed with a domain expert's guidance to create a *task-specific dataset*. This task-specific dataset is then used to train an appropriate *machine learning model*. The model's performance is tested on a holdout set of data points that are not part of the model's training for *generalization* ability — a key expectation from any machine learning model. Finally, the *validation* of the model output is done using domain expert-defined tests which are often necessary for the downstream application of the model.

3.3. *Effect of noise transients on gravitational-wave searches*

For LIGO's online astrophysical search pipelines, one class of nonlinear noise artifact is particularly problematic: transient noise bursts, of largely unknown origin, known as *noise glitches* [3,4]. Multiple glitches occur during a typical hour of observation. Glitches contaminate the astrophysical data streams (see, for example, Figure 4), confusing burst-source gravitational-wave searches and hindering the timely issuance of real-time alerts for electromagnetic follow-up. By introducing a long non-Gaussian tail in the instrumental noise background, glitches also raise the statistical threshold for detecting true astrophysical events. Reducing the frequency of glitches will improve detection rates for all types of events but most especially for high-mass binary black hole mergers, whose signal-to-noise ratio is the poorest.

In Ref. [16], we use matrix and tensor factorization [21] to automatically identify relevant subsets from the set of diagnostic channels that are believed to be potential witnesses to *glitches* present in LIGO data in a five-day period from the third observing run. Figure 3 (*middle row*) shows an end-to-end pipeline for this task. We select a set of diagnostic channels and a set of *glitches* from LIGO's main channel where gravitational waves are observed. We then construct the *task-specific dataset* in the form of a 3-mode tensor[5] where mode-1 corresponds to the *glitches* in the main channel, mode-2 corresponds to diagnostic channels selected for this analysis, and mode-3 corresponds to features (e.g., duration, peak frequency,

---

[5]In the context of machine learning, a tensor is a multidimensional array.

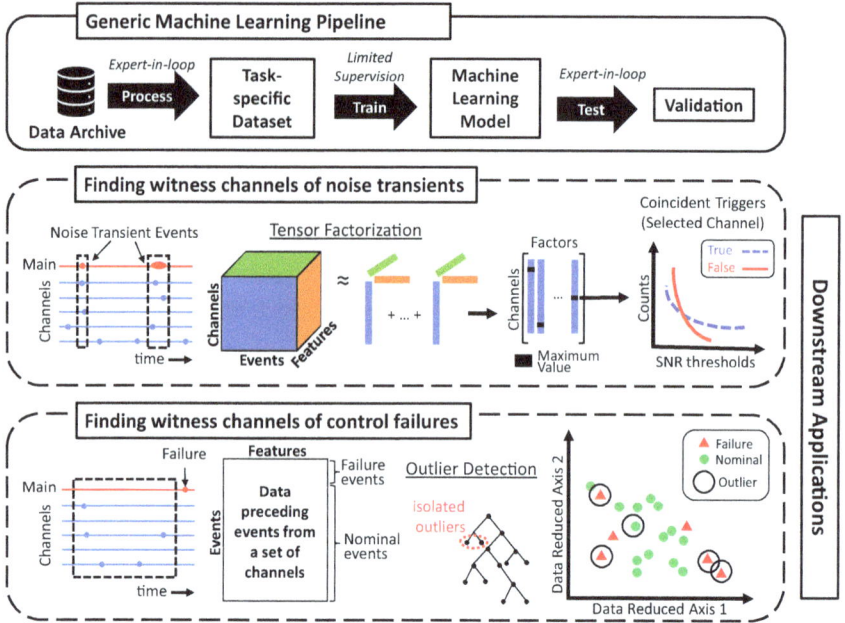

Fig. 3.   *Top row:* A generic machine learning pipeline typically has four stages starting at task-specific dataset creation to validation of the modeling output. *Middle row:* End-to-end pipeline for finding witnesses to noise transients that can potentially help diagnose sources of noise relies on selecting transient events of interest from the *main* channel and finding coincidences in a set of diagnostic channels. *Bottom row:* End-to-end pipeline for finding precursors of control failure events relies on isolating data from a set of witness channels preceding such events as outliers.

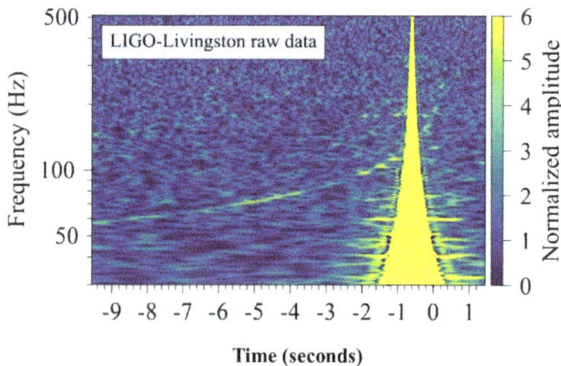

Fig. 4.   Time–frequency representation of the gravitational-wave event GW170817, as observed by the LIGO Livingston detector. Moments before merger, a noise glitch 1,000 times louder than the gravitational-wave signal occurred. Image reproduced courtesy of LIGO/Caltech/MIT.

bandwidth, and signal-to-noise ratio) of the *glitches* found in the diagnostic channels that are coincident with the main channel *glitches* within a short window around a main channel *glitch*. This tensor essentially encodes the presence or absence of a *glitch* in a diagnostic channel *"coincident"* with a *glitch* in the main channel. The *machine learning model* of choice is tensor factorization. We factorize this tensor into N factors and obtain factor matrices corresponding to the latent space representations of each mode. We use the factor matrix corresponding to the "diagnostic channels" mode to select N channels (one per factor), see Figure 5. We *validate* the channels thus selected as potential witnesses to the main channel *glitches* in the

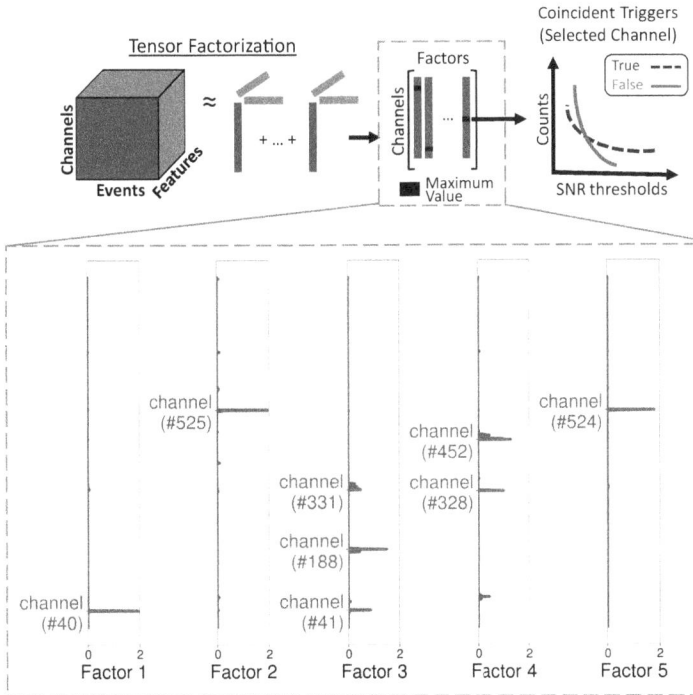

Fig. 5. *Finding witness channels to noise transients: Witness Selection* Factors corresponding to diagnostic channels of a $n = 5$ component tensor factorization of *channels* × *events* × *features* tensor that encodes the presence or absence of coincident noise transients in diagnostic channels. They show high magnitude values in a factor for a few out of the approx. 900 channels used for this analysis. For example, Factor 1 shows a high magnitude value for channel #40 which is then selected as a witness.

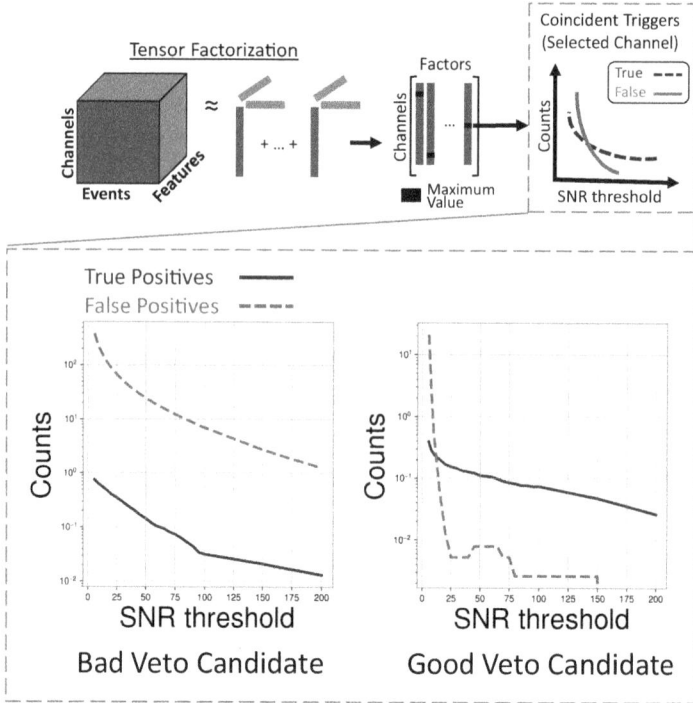

Fig. 6. *Finding witness channels of noise transients: Witness Validation* Two different channels selected using factors of the *channels × events × features* tensor show differing true vs false positive characteristics. *Left:* The selected channel has a high false positive rate at increasing SNR thresholds compared to the true positive rate suggesting that it might just be an inherently noisier diagnostic channel and thus cannot be used to veto science data segments for downstream gravitational-wave search pipelines as it will result in large loss of science data. *Right:* There is a sharp drop-off in the false positive rate of the selected channel above SNR threshold of 25 while the true positive rate remains relatively stable. We can use this selected channel to veto coincident noise transients in the science data.

dataset by examining the true positive rate[6] and false positive rate[7] of each selected witness channel for increasing values of signal-to-noise (SNR) thresholds, see Figure 6. The channels deemed *good veto candidates* by this validation step can then be considered for downstream applications like, for example, using the channel to veto and remove data segments from the main channel before searching for gravitational-wave signals.

---

[6]Number of times there was a coincident *glitch* in a selected witness channel and the main channel divided by the number of total *glitches* in the witness channel.

[7]Number of times there was a *glitch* in a selected witness channel but no coincident *glitch* in the main channel divided by the number of total *glitches* in the witness channel.

3.4. *Effect of control failures on gravitational-wave detector duty cycle*

Achieving resonance in the full LIGO system is a complex process (see, e.g., [33]) typically requiring 30 minutes to complete. Control failure occurs when a disturbance, either internal or external, causes the laser cavities to become "unlocked" from their resonant operating points. This type of control failure is termed as *lock loss*. Due to the frequency of lock losses, all three LIGO-Virgo detectors (LIGO Livingston, LIGO Hanford, and Virgo) were running at the same time only about 50% of the time during the third observing run. The majority of lock losses have no readily identifiable environmental cause [29] so may too be triggered by non-Gaussian noise events. Identifying and eliminating triggers of lock loss could potentially make a big improvement in the fraction of calendar time all three detectors are data taking, increasing the number of triple-coincident gravitational-wave detections. Observations by multiple detectors with different antenna patterns are critical for precise sky localization, as needed for targeted electromagnetic follow-up of potential multi-messenger events.

Figure 3 (*bottom row*) shows a pipeline that formulates the problem of diagnosing control failures as an anomaly detection task where the *task-specific dataset* is constructed by obtaining data preceding control failures from a set of diagnostic channels. We also obtain data during nominal operation periods from these channels. Thus, we do not need any explicit *supervision* as we have automatic *ground truth (labels)* for the data-points in our dataset as either *failure* or *nominal* events. We hypothesize that data preceding failure events in a subset of channels will have anomalies which might be precursors to the failures. The *machine learning model* of choice here is an unsupervised, tree-based Outlier Detection algorithm called Isolation Forest [23] that partitions the dataset using a tree structure and *isolates* anomalies as outliers. We validated the events deemed as anomalies by the algorithm by comparing them against the ground truth, see Figure 7.

There are some key challenges worth highlighting in the machine learning pipelines described in Sections 3.1 and 3.2. First, we assume a preprocessing step of creating the task-specific datasets from the massive amounts of raw, archived time series data. This step has an inevitable need for domain expertise as there can be potentially tens of thousands of diagnostic channels to choose from only a subset of which may be relevant to the task and these channels are often sampled at different rates capturing various phenomena occurring at different time and frequency scales. Beyond the selection of a set of diagnostic channels for any given analysis, the *"features"* engineered from the raw data streams can be explicitly hand-crafted to be semantically meaningful to the domain expert

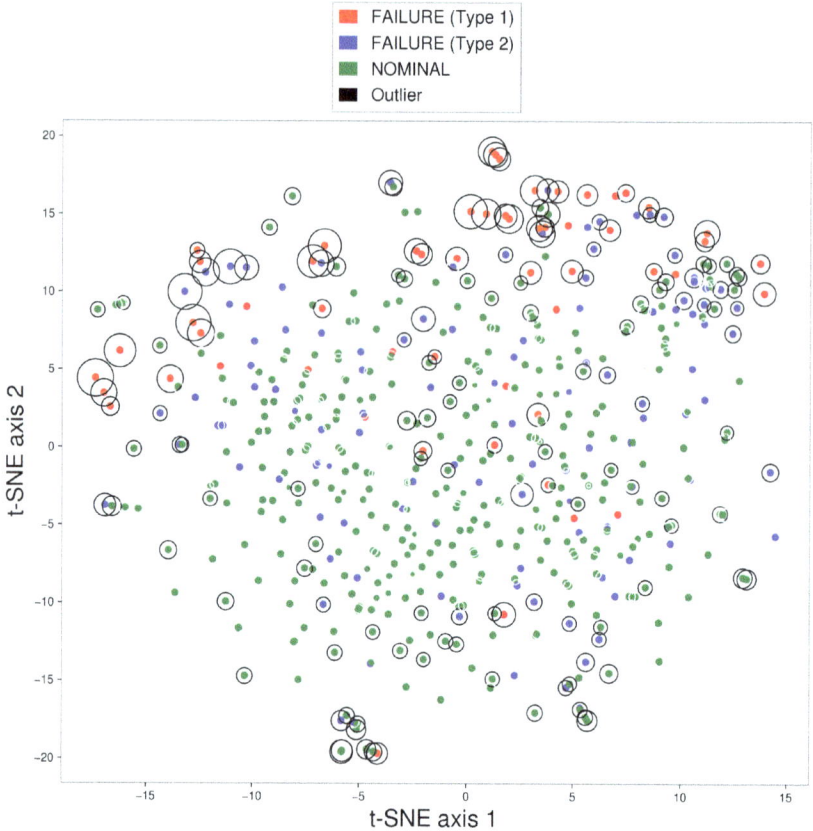

Fig. 7. *Finding witness channels of control failures:* (Note: The figure above shows a 2-D projection of the m-dimensional data ($m \gg 2$) using t-Distributed Stochastic Neighbor Embedding (t-SNE) [37] that tries to preserve distances in the higher-dimensional space for the purpose of visualization only). We obtain k features from segments of data preceding two types of control failures (*red and blue*) from a set of n diagnostic channels ($m = k \times n$). To complete the dataset, we also sample data segments during nominal operation (*green*). The outlier detection algorithm is fully unsupervised and does not use the ground-truth labels for the events in the dataset (failure or nominal) to isolate certain events as outliers (*circled in black*). We can see that instances of data preceding control failures (*red, blue*) are identified as outliers. The diameter of the black circle in this plot corresponds to an outlier score (larger score = bigger outlier) and this score can potentially be used as a threshold for reducing false positives (nominal events that are identified as outliers but with a relatively smaller outlier score).

or they can be implicitly learned by the machine learning model. Implicit feature representations of our data, like the ones learned by black box models like deep neural networks, reduce the burden of hand-crafting good enough features but make the output of our pipelines less interpretable. Moreover, at the end of the pipeline, we also seek expert guidance for creating validation tests that examine the utility of the machine learning model's output for downstream diagnostic applications.

3.5. *Public datasets*

Most real-world complex instruments have large quantities of raw archival operational data, as described in this section, that are not readily available to be used for training machine learning models. Therefore, machine learning applications use smaller benchmark datasets curated from the data archive or create synthetic datasets for *proof-of-concept*.

Following are some LIGO-specific public datasets available for machine learning in complex instruments' diagnostics.

(1) **LIGO Gravity Spy:** This dataset, as described in [39], consists of time–frequency spectrogram images of various noise transients in the main data product of LIGO. The machine learning task is to classify these images into a set of classes using state-of-the-art deep learning models like convolutional neural networks. The sample dataset is available here — https://zenodo.org/record/1476551#.YjoQ-3XMKV5.

(2) **LIGO diagnostic channel's dataset:** This is a multivariate time series dataset consisting of a three-hour period centered on a real gravitational-wave event, GW170814, from approx. 1,000 LIGO diagnostic channels. This dataset can be used for identifying noise transient's witness channels as described in this section or for subtracting noise from the main data product. The dataset can be found at the Gravitational Wave Open Science Center webpage — https://www.gw-openscience.org/auxiliary/GW170814/.

4. Optimizing Instrument Design

A fundamental requirement in instrument design is the ability to accurately and efficiently simulate different scenarios for a variety of instrument configurations, in pursuit of configurations which optimize a certain target physical quantity. In this section, we first provide a brief overview of the traditional simulation and optimization pipeline, and subsequently, we review an emerging machine learning breakthrough which has the potential to revolutionize instrument design.

4.1. *Current simulation & optimization tools*

Traditionally, the instrument design pipeline is roughly divided into two parts: simulation, where the behavior of an instrument (or one of its components) is estimated by software, and optimization, where the designer seeks to identify the best combination of parameters that satisfies a set of requirements for the component in question.

4.1.1. *Simulation*

Simulation is the process of estimating the response of an instrument or one of its components through software, thus eliminating the need to fabricate and physically experiment with that component. Such simulators have been widely used by both accelerators [1] and gravitational-wave detectors [12]. Typically, during simulation, the user/designer specifies a thorough description of the component that is being simulated and provides as input the environmental conditions (e.g., a certain event of interest) for which the component's response is needed. In turn, the simulator computes the response of that component, usually by numerically solving for the equations which govern that component's response. Finally, the last step in the pipeline takes as input the response/state of the component and outputs a reconstruction of a quantity of interest, which is used as an evaluation metric (e.g., energy).

4.1.2. *Optimization*

During a single run of the simulator, the parameters of the design to be simulated are user-defined. However, manually iterating over different designs in pursuit of one or more designs which satisfy the chosen criteria can be extremely inefficient and incomplete. To that end, in addition to simulators, effective design uses optimizers which are given a user-specified objective to optimize for (e.g., energy) and their goal is to effectively navigate the search space of designs and identify one or more that achieve the optimal objective. Ocelot [34] is such a general-purpose optimization tool which has been very popular in accelerator design. Interestingly, there are connections between optimization tools in instrument design and tools used in modern machine learning to fine-tune the design parameters (also called hyperparameters) of a large model, such as Bayesian optimization [25,35].

4.2. *Generative models for instrument simulation*

Despite the existence of efficient optimizers, whose goal is to minimize the number of times the simulation must be run, simulation in itself is a very computationally intensive and slow process. Furthermore, in order for a simulation to be accurate, it is typically restricted to very specific components of a larger instrument. As a result, simulating an instrument end-to-end would require the combination of a large number of specialized simulators, which are not necessarily designed to be compatible with each other. Thus, such an endeavor may be technically challenging or even intractable.

On the other hand, machine learning models, and especially deep neural networks, can be used as cheap, generic nonlinear function approximators. They have been studied for "data analysis" of an instrument's main data products (e.g., using deep neural networks to quickly estimate astrophysical parameters of a gravitational wave signal in real time, instead of carrying out the exact numerical calculations [13]). However, an emerging trend in instrument design is to replace traditional simulators with deep learning models, specifically leveraging recent advances in generative adversarial networks (GANs) [14].

A GAN is a machine learning model that itself consists of two sub-models: the *generator* and the *discriminator*. Typically, those two models are neural network-based, so the term "network" is commonly used when referring to them. The generator takes as input a vector, typically drawn at random from a Gaussian distribution, and it is tasked with outputting a data point (e.g., an image or the output of an instrument simulator) that is "realistic". The discriminator, on the other hand, takes two inputs: a "real" data point" (e.g., an actual image in our dataset or an actual output of an instrument simulator) and a "generated data point" (the output of the generator), and its task is to determine which data point is real and which is fake. During training, those two networks are engaged in a two-player game, where, as the generator gets better at producing realistic outputs, the discriminator improves its ability to detect fake data, and vice versa. At the end of the training process, the generator will ideally produce data indistinguishable from "real data" while effectively providing a means of sampling from the distribution of "real data".

The most well-known use case and success story of GANs are in the generation of images and videos that look extremely realistic [19]. However, the success of GANs extends far beyond this use case, with successful applications in drug discovery [24] and material design [7]. Very recently, there have been successful attempts at using GANs for the simulation of complex scientific instruments, as applied specifically to the simulation of

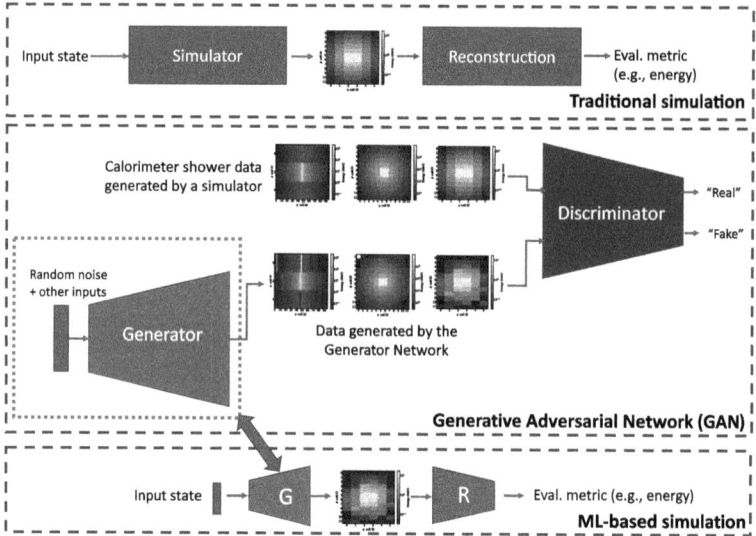

Fig. 8.   *Top row:* An illustration of the "traditional" simulation pipeline. *Middle row:* Illustration of a Generative Adversarial Network (GAN): The generator network is taking as input random noise and additional information about the state to be simulated and generates "fake" data. The discriminator network takes as input "real" data (as simulated by a traditional simulator such as Geant4) and "fake" data generated by the generator and determines which data point is fake or real. *Bottom row:* In the ML-based simulation pipeline, the simulator is replaced by the GAN generator and a "Reconstruction" neural network is replacing the analytical reconstruction process, which transforms the simulation output to a quantity of interest (e.g., energy). (Data figures show simulated and generated calorimeter showers and are adapted from Ref. [28].)

accelerator calorimeters [8,27,28]. Figure 8 provides an illustrative example. These recent attempts clearly demonstrate the feasibility and potential of harnessing the power of GANs for complex instrument design.

Despite early success in the calorimeter application, broad application of GANs to the problem of instrument simulation and design poses fascinating interdisciplinary research challenges. Those challenges pertain to ensuring that the generated data are of high quality, both as it pertains to how realistic they are as well as to the diversity of generated data points (a known mode of failure for GANs is the memorization of the training set or generation of very similar data points) [32]. Advances in the following areas, outlined in Section 2, can pave the way for tackling those challenges:

(a) *Physics-guided models:* In order to ensure that the generator will obey physical constraints and laws governing the instrument that it models, a physics-guided approach can incorporate this information in the design or training stages of the model. In Paganini *et al.* [28], the proposed GAN takes such a physics-guided approach, by modifying the loss function that is being optimized during training.

(b) *Limited supervision*: Training data for the GAN come from very expensive simulations. Thus, it may be infeasible to create very large training datasets, a challenge which may amplify issues such as the memorization of the training set by the GAN. Thus, designing solutions that work with limited supervision is imperative.

(c) *Expert-in-the-loop*: A big advantage of applying GANs to instrument simulation is that the definition of "realistic" is objective and can be analytically measured. This is in contrast to the original application of GANs, where judging the realism of a generated face or natural image can be subjective. However, when judging the diversity of generated data, the involvement of human experts can be crucial.

In addition to the immediate efficiency gains of substituting an inefficient simulator with a highly efficient neural network, a major promise of machine learning-driven instrument design is flexibility and modularity: once every component of an instrument can be efficiently simulated by a neural network, this can facilitate the simulation of increasingly larger portions of an instrument, ideally all the way to end-to-end simulation and design.

4.3. *Public datasets*

Three datasets used in [5] for simulating particle showers using GANs at the ATLAS detector at the LHC are hosted here — https://opendata.cern. ch/record/15012.

5. Conclusion

Instruments at the frontiers of science are becoming increasingly complex and data-intensive. There is a need for intelligent automation to tame this complexity, increase reliability, and push the limits of these technological marvels to make new scientific discoveries. This chapter explored the emerging application of machine learning for complex instrument operation's management and design. The current state of the art demonstrates very promising results, with machine learning methods empowering early detection of failures, diagnosing noise sources, and enabling the flexible simulation of different components of an instrument — tasks which may have previously been extremely tedious or downright impossible to do well by hand. There exist a number of fundamental challenges within machine learning research to successfully apply these techniques to solving issues of complex instruments, like the need for explainable and theory-guided modeling. Successful application of these techniques can pave the way for a new generation of complex instruments.

References

[1] S. Agostinelli, J. Allison, K. Amako *et al.* (2003). Geant4-a simulation toolkit. *Nuclear Instruments and Methods in Physics Research Section A: Accelerators, Spectrometers, Detectors and Associated Equipment, 506*(3), 250–303.

[2] S. Bach, A. Binder, G. Montavon *et al.* (2015). On pixel-wise explanations for non-linear classifier decisions by layer-wise relevance propagation. *PloS One, 10*(7), e0130140.

[3] L. Blackburn, L. Cadonati, S. Caride *et al.* (2008). The LSC glitch group: Monitoring noise transients during the fifth LIGO science run, *Classical and Quantum Gravity, 25*(18), 184004. https://doi.org/10.1088/0264-9381/25/18/184004.

[4] M. Cabero, A. Lundgren, A. H. Nitz *et al.* (2019). Blip glitches in advanced LIGO data. *Classical and Quantum Gravity, 36*(15), 155010. https://doi.org/10.1088/1361-6382/ab2e14.

[5] ATLAS Collaboration (2021). Atlfast3: The next generation of fast simulation in atlas. *arXiv preprint arXiv:2109.02551.*

[6] E. Cuoco, J. Powell, M. Cavaglià *et al.* (2020). Enhancing gravitational-wave science with machine learning. *Machine Learning: Science and Technology, 2*(1), 011002.

[7] Y. Dan, Y. Zhao, X. Li *et al.* (2020). Generative adversarial networks (GAN) based efficient sampling of chemical composition space for inverse design of inorganic materials. *NPJ Computational Materials, 6*(1), 1–7.

[8] L. de Oliveira, M. Paganini, and B. Nachman (2017). Learning particle physics by example: Location-aware generative adversarial networks for physics synthesis. *Computing and Software for Big Science, 1*(1), 1–24.

[9] A. Edelen, C. Mayes, D. Bowring *et al.* (2018). Opportunities in machine learning for particle accelerators. *arXiv preprint arXiv:1811.03172* https://arxiv.org/pdf/1811.03172.pdf.

[10] A. Endert, M. S. Hossain, N. Ramakrishnan *et al.* (2014). The human is the loop: New directions for visual analytics. *Journal of Intelligent Information Systems, 43*(3), 411–435.

[11] L. Felsberger, A. Apollonio, T. Cartier-Michaud *et al.* (2020). Explainable deep learning for fault prognostics in complex systems: A particle accelerator use-case. In *International Cross-Domain Conference for Machine Learning and Knowledge Extraction* (Springer), pp. 139–158.

[12] A. Freise, D. Brown, and C. Bond (2013). Finesse, frequency domain interferometer simulation software. *arXiv preprint arXiv:1306.2973.*

[13] D. George and E. A. Huerta (2018). Deep learning for real-time gravitational wave detection and parameter estimation: Results with advanced Ligo data. *Physics Letters B*, *778*, 64–70.

[14] I. Goodfellow, J. Pouget-Abadie, M. Mirza *et al.* (2020). Generative adversarial networks. *Communications of the ACM*, *63*(11), 139–144.

[15] R. Guidotti, A. Monreale, S. Ruggieri (2018). A survey of methods for explaining black box models. *ACM Computing Surveys (CSUR)*, *51*(5), 1–42.

[16] R. Gurav, B. Barish, G. Vajente *et al.* (2020). Unsupervised matrix and tensor factorization for ligo glitch identification using auxiliary channels. In *AAAI 2020 Fall Symposium on Physics-Guided AI to Accelerate Scientific Discovery*.

[17] E. E. Ishida, M. V. Kornilov, K. L. Malanchev *et al.* (2019). Active anomaly detection for time-domain discoveries. *arXiv e-prints*, *arXiv–1909*.

[18] A. Karpatne, G. Atluri J. H. Faghmous *et al.* (2017). Theory-guided data science: A new paradigm for scientific discovery from data. *IEEE Transactions on Knowledge and Data Engineering*, *29*(10), 2318–2331.

[19] T. Karras, S. Laine, and T. Aila (2019). A style-based generator architecture for generative adversarial networks. In *Proceedings of the IEEE/CVF Conference on Computer Vision and Pattern Recognition*, pp. 4401–4410.

[20] S. Khan and T. Yairi (2018). A review on the application of deep learning in system health management. *Mechanical Systems and Signal Processing*, *107*, 241–265. https://www.sciencedirect.com/science/article/pii/S0888327017306064.

[21] T. G. Kolda and B. W. Bader (2009). Tensor decompositions and applications. *SIAM Review*, *51*(3), 455–500.

[22] R. K. Vinayak and B. Hassibi (2016). Crowdsourced clustering: Querying edges vs triangles. *Advances in Neural Information Processing Systems*, *29*, 1316–1324.

[23] F. T. Liu, K. M. Ting, and Z.-H. Zhou (2008). Isolation forest. In *2008 Eighth IEEE International Conference on Data Mining* (IEEE), pp. 413–422.

[24] L. Maziarka, A. Pocha, J. Kaczmarczyk *et al.* (2020). Mol-cyclegan: A generative model for molecular optimization. *Journal of Cheminformatics*, *12*(1), 1–18.

[25] M. McIntire, T. Cope, S. Ermon *et al.* (2016). Bayesian optimization of FEL performance at LCLS. In *Proceedings of the 7th International Particle Accelerator Conference*.

[26] P. Nguyen, R. M. S. Schofield, A. Effler *et al.* (2021). Environmental noise in Advanced LIGO detectors. *Classical and Quantum Gravity*, *38*(14), 145001. https://doi.org/10.1088/1361-6382/ac011a.

[27] ATLAS collaboration (2020). Fast simulation of the ATLAS calorimeter system with generative adversarial networks. ATLSOFT-PUB-2020-006. https://cds.cern.ch/record/2746032.

[28] M. Paganini, L. de Oliveira, and B. Nachman (2018). Accelerating science with generative adversarial networks: An application to 3D particle showers in multilayer calorimeters. *Physical Review Letters*, *120*(4), 042003.

[29] J. Rollins (2017). Machine learning for lock loss analysis. LIGO Technical Report LIGO-G1701409.

[30] G. Salton and C. Buckley (1990). Improving retrieval performance by relevance feedback. *Journal of the American Society for Information Science*, *41*(4), 288–297.

[31] B. Settles (2009). Active learning literature survey. University of Wisconsin Report. https://minds.wisconsin.edu/bitstream/handle/1793/60660/TR1648.pdf.

[32] K. Shmelkov, C. Schmid, and K. Alahari (2018). How good is my GAN? In *Proceedings of the European Conference on Computer Vision (ECCV)*, pp. 213–229.

[33] A. Staley, D. Martynov, R. Abbott *et al.* (2014). Achieving resonance in the advanced LIGO gravitational-wave interferometer. *Classical and Quantum Gravity*, *31*(24), 245010. https://doi.org/10.1088/0264-9381/31/24/245010.

[34] S. Tomin, G. Geloni, I. Agapov *et al.* (2017). On-line optimization of European XFEL with ocelot. In *Proceeding 16th International Conference on Accelerator and Large Experimental Control Systems (ICALEPCS'17)*, pp. 1038–1042.

[35] R. Turner, D. Eriksson, M. McCourt *et al.* (2021). Bayesian optimization is superior to random search for machine learning hyperparameter tuning: Analysis of the black-box optimization challenge 2020. *arXiv preprint arXiv:2104.10201*.

[36] G. Valentino, R. Bruce, S. Redaelli *et al.* (2017). Anomaly detection for beam loss maps in the large hadron collider. In *Journal of Physics: Conference Series*, Vol. 874 (IOP Publishing), p. 012002.

[37] L. van der Maaten and G. Hinton (2008). Visualizing data using T-SNE. *Journal of Machine Learning Research*, *9*(86), 2579–2605. http://jmlr.org/papers/v9/vandermaaten08a.html.

[38] D. Xin, L. Ma, J. Liu *et al.* (2018). Accelerating human-in-the-loop machine learning: Challenges and opportunities. In *Proceedings of the Second Workshop on Data Management for End-to-end Machine Learning*, pp. 1–4.

[39] M. Zevin, S. Coughlin, S. Bahaadini *et al.* (2017). Gravity spy: Integrating advanced ligo detector characterization, machine learning, and citizen science. *Classical and Quantum Gravity*, *34*(6), 064003.

[40] Y. Zhang, F. Zhang, P. Yao *et al.* (2018). Name disambiguation in aminer: Clustering, maintenance, and human in the loop. In *Proceedings of the 24th ACM SIGKDD International Conference on Knowledge Discovery & Data Mining*, pp. 1002–1011.

© 2023 World Scientific Publishing Company
https://doi.org/10.1142/9789811265679_0008

Chapter 8

Artificial Intelligence (AI) and Machine Learning (ML) at Experimental Facilities

J. A. Sethian[*,†,‡,**], J. J. Donatelli[†,‡,††], A. Hexemer[‡,§,‡,‡],
M. M. Noack[†,‡,§§], D. M. Pelt[‡,¶,¶¶], D. M. Ushizima[†,‡,‖‖],
and P. H. Zwart[‡,‖,***]

[*]*Department of Mathematics, University of California,
Berkeley, USA;*
[†]*Department of Mathematics,
Lawrence Berkeley National Laboratory, USA*
[‡]*Center for Advanced Mathematics for Energy Research Applications,
Lawrence Berkeley National Laboratory, USA*
[§]*Advanced Light Source,
Lawrence Berkeley National Laboratory, USA*
[¶]*Leiden Institute of Advanced Computer Science (LIACS),
Netherlands*
[‖]*Molecular Biophysics and Integrated Bioimaging,
Lawrence Berkeley National Laboratory, USA*
[**]*sethian@math.berkeley.edu*
[††]*jjdonatelli@lbl.gov*
[‡‡]*ahexemer@lbl.gov*
[§§]*MarcusNoack@lbl.gov*
[¶¶]*d.m.pelt@liacs.leidenuniv.nl*
[‖‖]*dushizima@lbl.gov*
[***]*phzwart@lbl.gov*

1. The Rapid Evolution of Experimental Facilities

Large experimental facilities are undergoing a profound transformation. As examples, at light, neutron, and electron sources, increases in spatial and temporal resolution stemming from advances in detectors and coherence are peering into some of the smallest scales and fastest processes to inspect physical and biological mechanisms and help accelerate the design of new materials, understand biological processes, and explain complex physical principles.

The results of these experiments, as well as the way in which scientific facilities are utilized, are also changing:

- In some areas, due to automation, experiments can be set up and performed far more rapidly, bringing the challenge of deciding which experiments to be performed in what order.
- In other areas, there is limited experimental availability, and experiments are so complex that one must carefully choose which experiments to perform.
- The spectrum of possible configurations for an experiment is growing, representing a vast increase in the dimensionality of input space, which means that many more things can be tested, making the task of understanding dependencies and correlations both more difficult and more critical.
- Vast amounts of data are produced, both from individual experiments and from combining data from different experiments, offering tremendous opportunities and challenges associated with efforts to extract coherent understanding and information.

What is critically needed are new advances that can address multiple opportunities, including the following:

1.1. *Guiding scientific inquiry*

Algorithms to suggest new experiments, such as different samples, different experimental parameters, and different imaging modalities, and help guide discovery. How can we build models that point to new things to investigate? Testing everything is impractical — How can we incorporate goals into the search process to help suggest new experiments? Imagine algorithms that can accelerate a material's design process in which search through a high-dimensional parameter space is greatly enhanced by using results from previous and available experimental data to point to new configurations to test.

Building such algorithms will require incorporating known physics, biology, chemistry, etc. into mathematical algorithms that optimize desirable properties.

1.2. *Self-driving laboratories*

Optimizing the turnaround time and efficiency of experiments: A common experimental procedure is to set up an experiment, wait hours/days/weeks for it to finish, and then manually interpret the results to help decide which experiment to perform next. Imagine instead fast and automatic analysis of experimental results, aided by a vast library of accessible related experiments, to quickly interpret the output, and then augment computational models to lead to the next experiment. Ultimately, these algorithms should pave the way toward faster and more efficient experimentation.

Building such algorithms will require an entire infrastructure/ecosystem of cross-application algorithms, standardized data formats, readability across compute platforms, and access to compute resources from edge computing at the equipment, remote workflow execution at clusters and high-performance architectures, etc.

1.3. *Analyzing noisy and complex data*

As experiments generate results at the finest scales, new mathematical algorithms are needed to reconstruct models from highly complex experiments revolving around probabilistic information, delicate correlations, and multiscale dependencies, as well as a host of experiment-generated issues, including dropout, alignment, registration, and low signal-to-noise ratios. Good examples in recent years include correlation methods for X-ray free electron lasers, coherent surface scattering imaging (CSSI), and X-ray photon correlation spectroscopy (XPCS).

Developing this new mathematics requires bridging multiple fields, including computational harmonic analysis, dimensional reduction, Bayesian probabilities, and discrete graph methods, just to name a few.

1.4. *Detecting patterns across experiments*

Discovered patterns can help formulate new models, new predictive capabilities, and ultimately new theories. When viewed across experiments, patterns in data can emerge which may not be readily apparent in the context of a single or few isolated experiments. Algorithms, as well as shared communication systems, that can take an integrated approach to detect shared patterns and discover correlations, will be invaluable in building powerful new predictive models and theories.

Developing these new approaches will require wholly new mathematical and statistical methods, coupled to resources that can perform computations across a range of scales.

1.5. *Tuning and optimizing experiments*

As experimental equipment becomes more complex, understanding performance and guaranteeing stability, reproducibility, and robustness are key issues. For example, tuning the large number of parameters, magnets, and configurations to ensure beam stability is a major challenge. Algorithms that can both initially optimize experimental configurations, and, in real time, detect and correct perturbations will be invaluable.

These techniques will require close coupling of design and performance considerations and fast, real-time approaches.

In recent years, applications of AI techniques have led to significant breakthroughs in tackling these challenges in the context of light and neutron sources, as well as across other imaging modalities. In the rest of this brief paper, we discuss fundamental ideas behind AI, point out some particular challenges associated with applying AI to experimental data, and provide case studies of several ongoing efforts applying AI to a large light source and other facilities. Finally, we end with some comments, suggestions, and priorities for future work.

2. What is "Artificial Intelligence"?

The idea of "Artificial Intelligence" excites its proponents and may give pause to more traditional scientists. One view is that AI will allow machines, armed with data, no body of scientific knowledge, and free from biases, to find correlations without explicit models and, in an oracle-like fashion, predict results and outcomes far beyond our current abilities. In contrast, detractors argue that producing output that matches observations is not understanding, and that, without such understanding, one can neither extrapolate with confidence to new regimes nor safely trust what is being predicted.

This tension is unnecessary. Science has always relied on the back-and-forth between data and theory, and it is fair to say that theory has often lagged behind data analysis and empirical models.

Part of this tension stems from the phrase "artificial intelligence" itself: it is both purposefully and unnecessarily provocative. It sidesteps defining "intelligence" while emphasizing "artificial" as something new and alien, managing to be both scary and patronizing at the same time.

However, and more reassuringly, AI and ML are, broadly speaking, building on well-established (as well as rapidly evolving) branches of mathematics. For example, supervised ML firmly rests on mathematical approximation theory, which focuses on the simply stated question: "If you know something at some places, can you say anything about what happens at other places?" The simplest measurements gave way to linear, quadratic, least-squares models to estimate values, using known information to build these models.

Continuing the example of supervised ML, over the past few decades, applications of approximation theory, in tandem with new contributions from set theory, topology, geometry, linear algebra, and discrete mathematics, have exploded, due to the confluence of vast treasure troves of data, significant leaps in mathematical algorithms to build models based on this data, and the advent of large computers able to execute these algorithms quickly on immense datasets.

These applications of both classical and newly developed mathematics, statistics, and computer science have allowed us to greatly expand the mathematical toolbox, to include data with uncertainty, far more sophisticated causal and correlative relationships, probabilistic understanding, and reduced modeling. These advances have both opened up a startling new spectrum of applications as well as driven fundamental theoretical advances in the many subfields that contribute to these new technologies.

More broadly, machine learning has been labeled by some as equivalent to AI. Our view is that core mathematics coupled to modern-day data underlies ML and that connecting these methods to hardware (instruments, robots, etc.) creates AI.

Altogether, these advances are sometimes lumped together as "artificial intelligence". Richard Feynman's Lectures on Computation [1] begin with a wise perspective on a still-young field, and replacing "computer science" with "artificial intelligence" does not detract from Feynman's insight:

> *Computer science [Artificial intelligence] also differs from physics in that it is not actually a science. It does not study natural objects. Neither is it, as you might think, mathematics; although it does use mathematical reasoning pretty extensively. Rather, computer science [AI] is like engineering — it is all about getting something to do something, rather than just dealing with abstractions...*
>
> *But this is not to say that computer science [AI] is all practical, down to earth bridge-building. Far from it. Computer science [AI] touches on a variety of deep issues. It has illuminated the nature of language, which we thought we understood: early attempts at machine translation failed because the old-fashioned notions about grammar failed to capture all the essentials of language. It naturally encourages us to ask questions about the limits of computability, about what we can and cannot know about the world around us. Computer science [AI] people spend a lot of their time talking about whether or not man is merely a machine, whether his brain is just a powerful computer that might one day be copied; and the field of "artificial intelligence" — I prefer the term 'advanced applications' — might have a lot to say about the nature of "real" intelligence, and mind.*

Throughout the rest of this review, we will use the phrase AI/ML to represent these advances and focus on some of their contributions to analyzing results from experiments in synchrotron science.

3. Challenges in Applying AI/ML to Experimental Science

How can these mathematical advances in AI/ML be brought to experimental, scientific data? Here, it is important to underscore some additional challenges associated with bringing AI/ML to experiment.

3.1. Limited training data

Some of the most successful applications of AI/ML supervised learning have been in commerce, image and signal recognition, language translations, etc. Part of the reason for this is the wealth of "training data"— data that are tagged, annotated, and available as (input/output) pairs for building interpolations. In contrast, while there may be a large amount of data in a particular scientific application, it most often is not annotated or marked and hence of little use in an initial training stage. While there are many so-called "bootstrapping" methods to grow a dataset, these may not significantly increase the breadth of training data.

3.2. Interpolation vs. extrapolation

Most supervised AI/ML methods work through interpolation. The more an algorithm has seen and successfully classified data close to an unseen input, the higher the chances of making an accurate prediction. Yet, scientific examination is often most interested in extrapolation, in which the interesting cases/possible fruitful new arenas lie outside the training set. Current AI/ML methods typically are only blindly applied outside the training set, often with less than desirable results.

3.3. Incorporating scientific knowledge

It is clearly advantageous to build scientific domain knowledge into AI/ML methods. Physical principles, such as conserved properties and equivariant transformations, are all part of our deep understanding of scientific formulations. Yet, although there are multiple efforts in this direction, much needs to be done.

3.4. *Robustness, explainability and reliability*

How does one know when an AI/ML method is giving reliable information? When can one trust a result? When methods are trained on millions of data points with millions of free parameters, it is hard to know what is going on.

Paradoxically, because scientific AI/ML is often trained on far less data, it might be easier to determine the validity of such a method, although we are still a long way off. A model needing many more free parameters than available data often leads to ill-posedness and poor or false convergence.

Ultimately, the challenge in the application of AI/ML to scientific data comes down to a fundamentally different issue. Unlike some of the well-known successes in such fields as language translation and detecting commerce patterns, where the price of being wrong is small, in science applications, the price of being wrong can be high. Predicting a wrong drug or building an unstable large structure can have disastrous consequences.

4. Case Studies

Next, we turn to some current examples of meeting these challenges, drawn from applying AI/ML to information from synchrotron light sources.

4.1. *Case Study 1: AI/ML and optimized self-driving experiments*

4.1.1. *Overview*

Imagine probing a material in a synchrotron experiment by systematically measuring the effect of changing input parameters and configurations, such as temperature or pressure.[1] In a typical experiment, one of the two approaches is taken: either (1) a sequence of measurements is chosen in advance and executed in order or (2) an experiment is performed, and then a decision is made, based on expert human intuition, as to which experiment to perform next.

Neither of these approaches is efficient: the first approach may waste instrument time by collecting possibly redundant data, while the second approach relies on waiting for a human to make a decision, which may itself reflect bias or subjective decision-making. In high-dimensional spaces, the first approach is infeasible and the experimenter is often stuck with trying to make decisions based on intuition.

---

[1]Much of the description of this case is taken from [2–5].

Instead, a preferable approach analyzes the result of an experiment as soon as it is performed and then integrates those findings into an evolving model derived from previous experiments. Such a "surrogate model" serves as a low-order approximation to the high-dimensional response surface. This sparsely sampled surface and its uncertainties then act as a guide to suggest the next experiment, which might be in unexplored parts of the high-dimensional parameter space or in regimes where particularly interesting results are occurring.

More sophisticated and current active areas of research involve versions of these ideas that (a) couple the generation of this surface with optimization functions to steer the input parameters and (b) perform simulations to build and refine models that match the data as they are collected.

4.1.2. *Example: gpCAM*

One illustration of these ideas is provided by the gpCAM mathematical, algorithmic, and software environment (see Figure 1). As data are collected, they are first sent through a preprocessing procedure, which identifies key feature vectors and performs dimensionality reduction. This can include AI/ML techniques for image segmentation, structure extraction, and classification (see Case Study 2).

From the analyzed data, the Gaussian process-based autonomous experiment algorithm creates a prior probability density function by finding the possibly anisotropic and non-stationary variations of data with distance. Conditioning the prior yields posterior mean and covariance functions, which, combined with the trained prior, are used to define an acquisition function whose maxima (or minima) represent points of high-value measurements.

In more detail, given measurements $D = \{(\mathbf{x}_1, y_1), \ldots, (\mathbf{x}_N, y_N)\}$, our goal is to build a function $y_i = f(\mathbf{x}_i) + \epsilon(\mathbf{x}_i)$, where f is the unknown latent function and $\epsilon(\mathbf{x})$ is the noise.

- We start with a Gaussian probability density function (prior) defined over all possible model functions: here, the model functions are defined over the parameter space: all possible combinations of measurement outcomes (position, temperature, etc.))

$$p(\mathbf{f}) = \frac{1}{\sqrt{(2\pi)^N |\mathbf{K}|}} \exp\left[-\frac{1}{2}(\mathbf{f} - \boldsymbol{\mu})^T \mathbf{K}^{-1}(\mathbf{f} - \boldsymbol{\mu})\right], \qquad (1)$$

  where μ is the mean of the prior Gaussian probability density function (PDF) and K_{ij} is the covariance, defined via kernel functions, i.e., $K_{ij} = k(\mathbf{x}_i, \mathbf{x}_j)$.

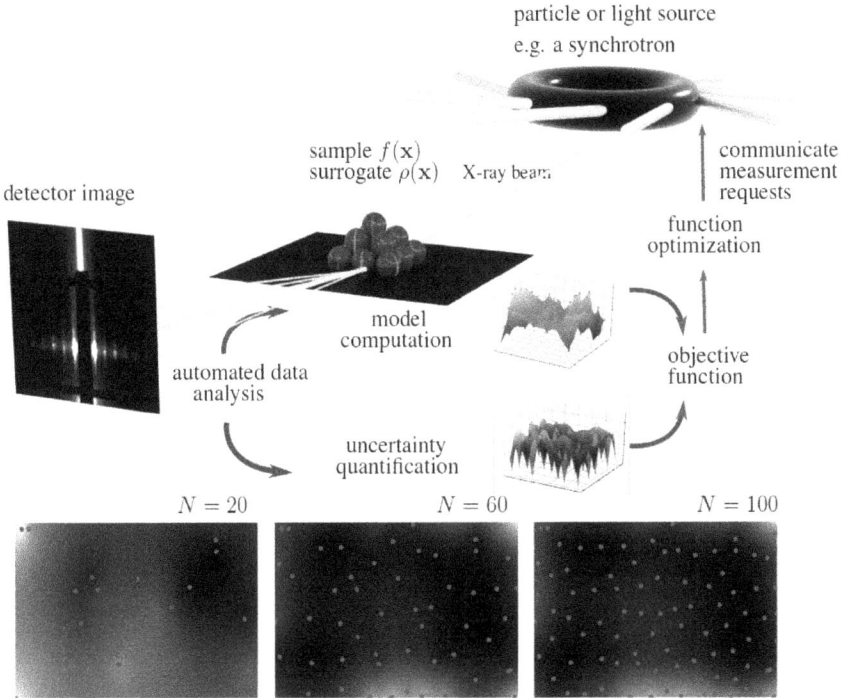

Fig. 1. Top: Execution sequence for gpCAM autonomous self-driving experiments at a synchrotron radiation beamline. Bottom: Sequence of approximations of an example response surface evolving with the number of measurements N is increased: points chosen based on the maximum posterior variance, guaranteed to be placed in areas of high uncertainty and clustering is therefore naturally avoided [top image from [3], bottom from [5]]. The same principle can be used to find material characteristics of interest.

- To cast this into a Bayesian framework, we define the likelihood as

$$p(\mathbf{y}) = \frac{1}{\sqrt{(2\pi)^N |\mathbf{V}|}} \exp\left[-\frac{1}{2}(\mathbf{y} - \mathbf{f})^T \mathbf{V}^{-1}(\mathbf{y} - \mathbf{f})\right], \qquad (2)$$

marginalize over $\mathbf{f}$ and condition on the data. The resulting posterior represents the probability distribution of the latent function at a set of positions $\mathbf{x}$.

- Kernels are symmetric and positive semi-definite functions: one common choice is the Matérn kernel class. This kernel class allows the user to change the order of differentiability which offers one of the simplest ways to include domain knowledge into the function approximation.

- Hyperparameters affecting the kernels and the prior mean function are then found by maximizing the marginal log-likelihood $\text{argmax}_{\phi\mu}\big(\log(L(D;\phi,\mu(\mathbf{x})))\big)$, where $\log(L(D;\phi,\mu(\mathbf{x}))) = -\frac{1}{2}(\mathbf{y} - \boldsymbol{\mu})^T(\mathbf{K}(\phi) + \mathbf{V})^{-1}(\mathbf{y} - \boldsymbol{\mu}) - \frac{1}{2}\log(|\mathbf{K}(\phi) + \mathbf{V}|) - \frac{\dim}{2}\log(2\pi)$.

This optimization can be augmented through constraints that allow more domain knowledge to be included. The trained prior and the GP posterior mean and variance functions are combined to form the acquisition function that will be used to find the next optimal measurements.

4.1.3. *Results*

The autonomous framework gpCAM has been applied to dozens of large autonomous experiments at light and particle sources around the world. All were steered without human guidance; instrument utilization has been increased by up to 400% and total experiment time was often decreased 10–50-fold (see Table 1 and Figure 2). AI/ML plays key roles in many stages of gpCAM's workflow loop, including the determination of appropriate surrogate structures, determination of feature vectors and quantities, and optimization steps.

4.2. *Case Study 2: AI/ML for limited scientific training data*

4.2.1. *Overview*

Typical ML algorithms for image analysis, recognition, and classification rely on vast databases of annotated and tagged images, often numbering in the tens of millions. ML algorithms, such as convolutional neural networks, assemble a network of a large number (often millions) of simple functions with very few parameters and then "train" the interconnected network by using energy minimization algorithms to converge to choices for these millions of parameters.

Networks requiring millions of training data are typically complicated and are prone to overfitting and convergence to non-optimal local minima. Nonetheless, such techniques are remarkably powerful and have led to an explosion in highly effective signal and image recognition schemes.

However, in scientific applications, especially using complex imaging equipment, it can be expensive to produce image data, hence relatively few images are available. More problematically, these images are seldom tagged or annotated and hence require time-consuming human analysis in order to be useful as training data.

Table 1. A selected subset of some large-scale experiments that were steered by CAMERA's *gpCAM* algorithm for autonomous data acquisition.

Experiment	Benefit
Autonomous X-ray Scattering Mapping [4–6], National Synctroron Light Source (NSLS-II)	Identifying ROIs quickly, beam utilization increased 15% to >80%, six-fold red in a number of measurements
Autonomous Synchrotron Infrared Mapping [7], Advanced Light Source (ALS)	Identifying ROIs quickly, no human biases, 10–50 times fewer data needed, beam utilization increased, enabling higher time resolution [7,8]
Autonomous Discovery of Correlated Electron Phases [9], ALS	Dataset size decreased to <10%
Inelastic Neutron Scattering [in prep.], Institut Laue-Langevin (ILL) (France)	No human intervention, experiment time decreased from several days to one night, hit rate inside the ROIs is twice as high
Autonomous SAXS Exploration of Nanoscale Ordering in a Blade-Coated Polymer-Grafted Nanorod Film, NSLS-II, and Air Force Research Lab (AFRL)	Dataset size reduced to 15%
Defect Identification through Autonomous Scanning Tunneling Spectroscopy [10], Molecular Foundry	Dataset size reduced to 4%, data acquisition time reduced to 35 hours from 1 month
Autonomous exploration of multidimensional material state-spaces underlying self-assembly of copolymer mixtures [in prep.], Center for Functional Nanomaterials (CFN)	First time optimally sampling 5d space, data need reduced to ≈ 6%
Autonomous Discovery of Optimal DNA-Origami Superlattice Assembly Pathways [in prep.], Columbia U., NSLS-II	Dimensionality first time > 2d leads to unseen science

This points to a key issue with applying AI/ML to experimental applications. One of the main tenets of AI/ML as presently framed is that "more data means better results". For scientific applications, it is important to rethink this tenet and explore other directions.

4.2.2. *Example: Mixed-scale dense networks*

"Mixed-Scale Dense Convolutional Neural Networks" [11] are an example of rethinking this view and building AI/ML for limited scientific data.

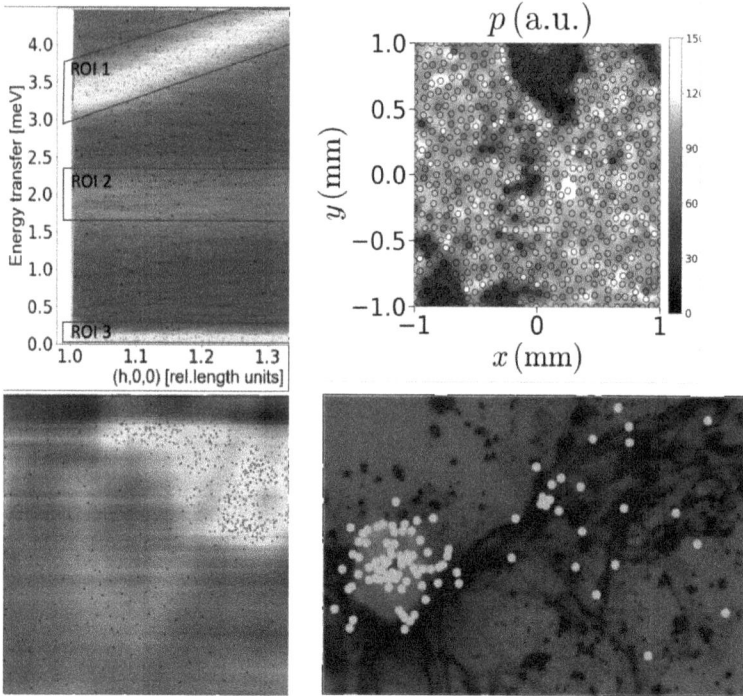

Fig. 2. A small subset *gpCAM* applications. *Top left*: A targeted autonomous experiment acquiring neutron-scattering data at the ThALES instrument in Grenoble, France. *gpCAM* can confidently place most points in regions of interest as soon as they are supported by the collected data. *Top right*: The result of an autonomous x-ray scattering experiment at NSLS-II. While the points seem randomly distributed, each and every data point is actually carefully chosen to maximally minimize the uncertainty of the model function. *Bottom left*: Autonomous angle-resolved photo-emission spectroscopy at ALS. Once again, points are largely places in the regions of interests (in yellow). *Bottom right*: Autonomous infra-red spectroscopy at ALS. The algorithm pursues a particular molecule characterized by a reference spectrum.

Typical "deep convolutional neural networks" (DCNN) add downscaling and upscaling operations to intermediate layers connected through convolution operations between input and output images to capture features at various image scales.

Instead, "Mixed-Scale Dense (MSD)" networks are built on a different network architecture. They calculate dilated convolutions as a substitute for scaling operations to capture features at various spatial ranges as well as at multiple scales within a single layer. This means that all layers have elements of the same size and all intermediate images can be densely connected together. MSD networks require far fewer images and intermediate parameters and hence have less of a risk of converging to non-optimal minima.

In a bit more detail, a standard convolutional neural network builds a sequence of functions $z_i * j = \sigma(g_{ij}(z_{i-1}) + b_{ij})$, where $z_i * j$ is the output layer i of a single channel j, with bias b_{ij}. Here, g convolves each channel with a different filter and sums the resulting images pixel-by-pixel, thus

$$g_{ij}(z_{i-1}) = \sum_{k=0}^{c_{i-1}} C_{h_{ijk}} z_{i-1}^k. \tag{3}$$

Here, σ is a nonlinear operation, typically a form of rectified linear unit (ReLU), and $C_g\alpha$ is a 2D convolution of image α with filter g. These filters are typically small (3x3 pixels), and the goal is to train these filters from the available data.

In contrast, Mixed-Scale Dense Networks associate convolutions with dilated stencil operators and then link all scales together. In this view, the channel operators and the convolution operators are of the form

$$z_i^j = \sigma\left(g_{ij}(\{z_0, \dots, z_{i-1}\})\right) + b_{ij})$$

$$g_{ij}(\{z_0, \dots, z_{i-1}\}) = \sum_{l=0}^{i-1} \sum_{k=0}^{c_{i-1}} D_{h_{ijkl}, s_{ij}} z_l^k \tag{4}$$

where the dilated convolution $D_{h,s}$ uses a dilated filter h that is only non-zero at distances that are a multiple of s pixels from the center.

In this view, since the stencil operators perform upscaling and downscaling, all layers can be connected, with the benefit that if a feature is detected early in the architecture, it does not need to be recomputed/rediscovered by other layers. This then means that fewer images, fewer parameters, and fewer iterations are required to converge to a predictive model. An architecture schematic is shown in Figure 3. For details, see [11,12].

4.2.3. *Results*

As an example, Figure 4 shows the application of MSD to the segmentation of cryo-electron tomography images. Here, the goal is to extract, analyze, and classify various structures from tomograms. These are time-consuming images to produce: it takes (a) several hours to grow the cells and extract the parasites under consideration, (b) several hours to plunge freeze the samples, (c) one hour to collect a single tilt series, and (d) one hour to process the raw data to obtain a 3D tomographic reconstruction. It then takes 30 minutes to manually annotate each slice, requiring 10 hours to annotate 20 slices, manually identifying nine different structures required for training. All told, it is a highly time-consuming and labor-intensive process to produce only a handful of training images, making standard AI/ML methods out of reach.

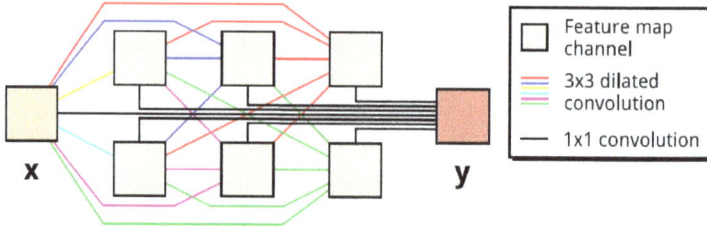

Fig. 3. Schematic representation of an MS-D network with $w = 2$ and $d = 3$. Colored lines represent 3–3 dilated convolutions, with each color representing a different dilation. Note that all feature maps are used for the final output computation. Figure taken from [11].

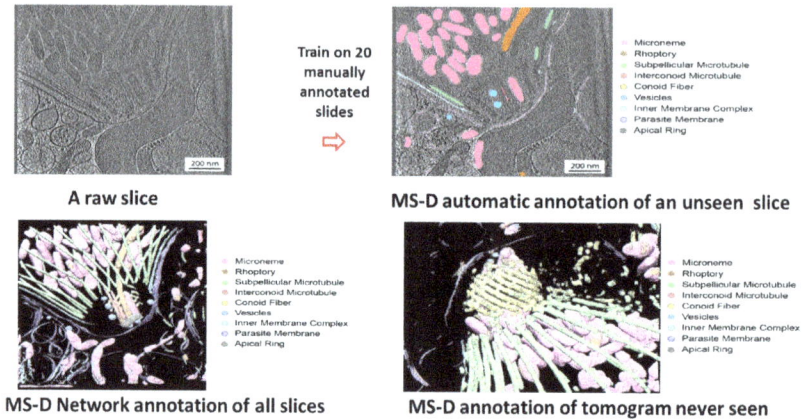

Fig. 4. Application of MSD networks to cryo-electron tomography imaging of Toxoplasma gondii, extracting and classifying multiple 3D structures using only 20 2D manually annotated training slices. (See [13] for a detailed discussion of the biological issues and contributors.)

Figure 4 shows the application of MSD networks to this limited image set, successfully training and extracting structures across a full range of tomograms, training on only 20 2D manually annotated slices.

4.3. *Case Study 3: AI/ML for automated high-throughput data analysis*

4.3.1. *Overview*

As experiments increase in rapidity and complexity, automated, high-throughput data analysis is required to keep pace. As data are collected,

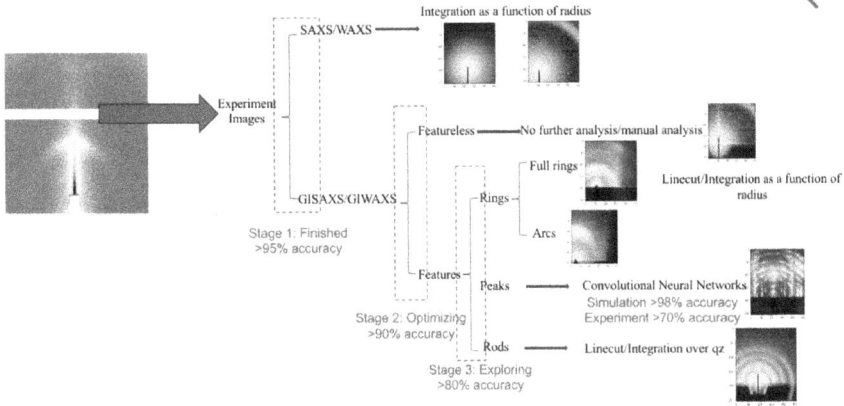

Fig. 5.   Application of CNN to X-ray scattering patterns using a layered classification scheme: Stage 1 splits patterns into two major classes, SAXS/WAXS and GISAXS/ GIWAXS, Stage 2 splits patterns into Featureless and with Features, and Stage 3 splits patterns into one of the three most characteristics features: rings, peaks, and rods. [14]

a key step is to use previously gathered data and information to help categorize and classify new results. Doing so will allow us to capitalize on previous models and information, both by quickly identifying patterns and principles at work across collected data and by refining proposed models with new results.

Imagine collecting a large number of scattering patterns from a synchrotron experiment. Typical experiments include four main types, namely small- and wide-angle X-ray scattering (SAXS and WAXS) and their respective surface-sensitive variation due to grazing incidence known as GISAXS and GIWAXS.

During a high-throughput, single experiment, these modes can be used interchangeably, thus sorting is difficult because the instrument seldom includes labels indicating the acquisition mode utilized. One might want to automatically compare the images collected to those in a previously generated library, to both determine the type of experiment and to find patterns that closely match or are similar to scattering patterns from previously known materials (see Figure 5). In these applications, a large number of tagged and annotated images may be readily available, and AI/ML identification techniques can be a powerful approach.

4.3.2. *Example: pyCBIR for Content-Based Image Retrieval*

pyCBIR [15,16] is a high-throughput image recommendation system built to quickly analyze patterns and compare them to a host library. First, each pattern undergoes featurization using one or more CNN architectures, extracting key feature vectors; additionally, pyCBIR also enables feature extraction using methods based on histogram analysis, which can be tuned to features inherent to the scattering patterns. Next, feature vectors are compared and images are sorted by similarity.

In order to deliver image recommendations, further research inspected the use of CNNs for the classification of images containing features such as rings, peaks, and arcs, as illustrated in Figure 5. Preliminary results showed high performance on classification tasks of GISAXS, using the information at different scales and varying levels of noise [14].

As a follow-up, current pipelines can also use pattern features from one or more CNN architectures, such as VGG-16, VGG-19, ResNet-50, Xception, and Inception ResNet, as input to AutoML, an automated paradigm for classification and performance evaluation. By interfacing with pyCBIR, that suite of AI/ML tools increases the availability of classifiers for predictions and includes random forests and a set of decision-tree-based methods that learn conditions for predictions, such as Lightgbm, XGBoost, Extra Trees, and Catboost [16].

4.3.3. *Results*

Working with a library database consisting of 3,512 GISAXS, 746 GIWAXS, 746 WAXS, and 645 SAXS images, pyCBIR [16] was used to identify and classify images from experiments. Figure 6 shows results with 99.11% accuracy.

4.4. *Case Study 4: Setting the stage: AI/ML for complex inverse problems*

4.4.1. *Overview*

The central challenge in inverse problems is to determine the input to a function/process given the output. This function/process can be straightforward, or highly complex, with a large number of unknown, hidden parameters. Which inversion techniques to use depends on the nature of the problem, Figure 7 shows three layers of complexity, from direct inversion on through to reconstructive approximations from known values.

Rather than using only one approach, there are in fact opportunities to weave all three together by breaking complex inversion problems into smaller pieces, each solved by the appropriate flavor of the above.

With the advent of more advanced AI/ML, this interplay can be greatly enhanced. To set the stage, in this case study, we give an example of a current powerful framework ripe for incorporating and exploiting AI/ML.

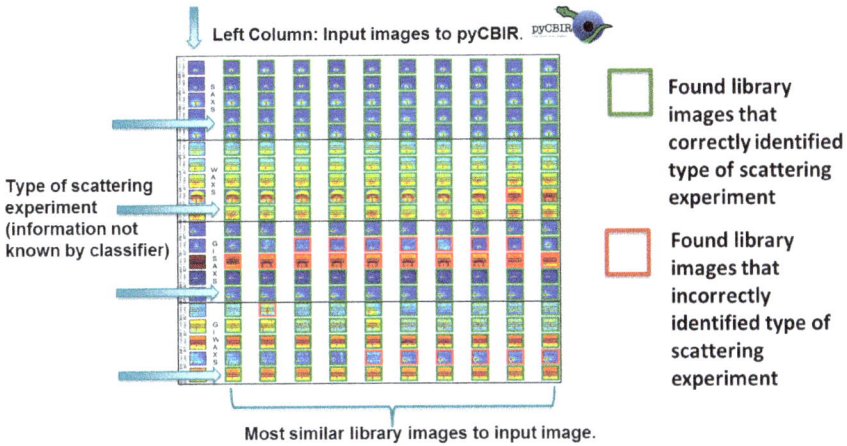

Fig. 6. Scattering patterns identified by pyCBIR. Left-most column shows individual images submitted to the image recommendation system while other columns indicate results of image retrieval by similarity, sorted from most similar to less similar as illustrated in a row from left to right. If the type of experiment is known, then the recommendation systems will show green bordered images corresponding to found similar images with correct classification of type of experiment.

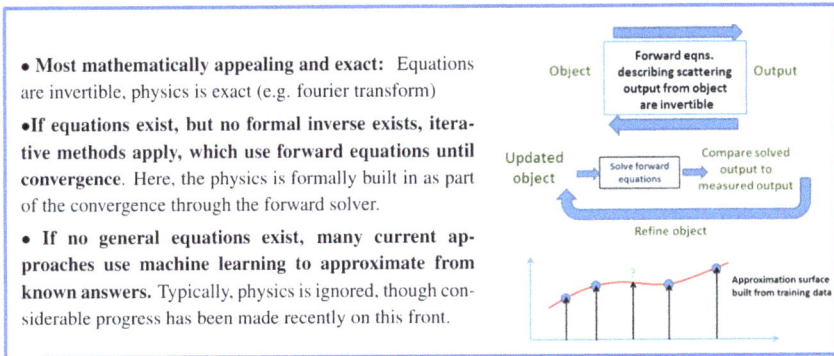

Fig. 7. Different ways to approach inverse problems: direct mathematical inversion (top), iteration with forward solvers (middle), and approximation from known answers (bottom).

4.4.2. *Example: Multi-Tiered Iterative Projections (M-TIP)*

Recently, a new mathematical and computational approach, known as Multi-Tiered Iterative Projections (M-TIP) [17,18], has been developed to tackle complex inverse problems. The fundamental idea is to break a complex problem into subparts, using the best inversion you can for each subpart, and iterate through subparts until convergence. These individual substeps can include exact inversion, pseudoinversion, and repeated forward iteration to reduce residuals. The data itself, as well as relevant physical principles (conservation, non-negative quantities, symmetries, etc.), are enforced within the projection operators.

Here, we consider a large class of inverse problems where the forward model $F(M) = D$, relating the physical model M to the data D, can be broken up into series of simpler, but possibly non-invertible, mathematical operations $F_1, \ldots, F_N$ and intermediate model quantities $w_1, \ldots, w_{N-1}$ via

$$w_1 = F_1(M), \quad w_2 = F_2(w_1), \quad \ldots, \quad D = F_N(w_{N-1}). \quad (5)$$

Common examples for the F_i include linear transformations, elementary functions, nonlinear products, etc. Also, the model M may need to satisfy additional constraints, e.g., positivity, symmetry, or compactness.

For each tier in Eq. (5) and model constraint, a projection operator is derived, which computes the minimum perturbation from a previous estimate to make it consistent with a given constraint. For example, to project w_{i-1} to be consistent with w_i (or $w_N = D$) and Eq. (5) and project M to satisfy constraint C, we compute

$$P_{w_i} w_{i-1} = \operatorname*{arg\,min}_{F_i(w)=w_i} ||w - w_{i-1}||, \quad P_C M = \operatorname*{arg\,min}_{\tilde{M} \text{ satisfies } C} ||\tilde{M} - M||. \quad (6)$$

For any constraint in Eq. (6) that cannot be satisfied, the projection instead computes a least squares solution.

M-TIP applies the projections in Eq. (6) in an iteration that converges to a model consistent with all constraints and data. Specifically, we initialize with random values $M^{(0)}$ and $w_i^{(0)}$ and iteratively compute

$$w_1^{(n)} = F_1(M^{(n-1)}), \ w_2^{(n)} = F(w_1^{(n)}), \ldots, w_{N-1}^{(n)} = F(w_{N-2}^{(n)}),$$

$$z_{N-1}^{(n)} = P_D w_{N-1}^{(n)}, \ z_{N-2}^{(n)} = P_{z_{N-1}^{(n)}} w_{N-2}^{(n)}, \ldots, z_1^{(n)} = P_{z_2^{(n)}} w_1^{(n)}, \quad (7)$$

$$M^{(n)} = P_C P_{z_1^{(n)}} M^{(n-1)},$$

where the z_i are intermediate projections of w_i (see Figure 8). This process is repeated until convergence to a fixed point consistent with the data and constraints. Equation (7) can be generalized to prevent stagnation in local minima by using negative feedback and can treat noise in the data by enforcing statistical constraints.

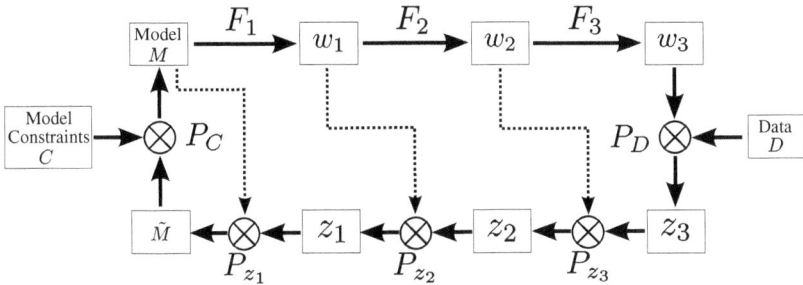

Fig. 8. Flowchart description of M-TIP. Bold arrows indicate the order of operations, dashed lines indicate dependencies, and circled crosses indicate inputs and outputs for a projection operator.

By exploiting the decomposition in Eq. (5), M-TIP can leverage optimal solutions for the subproblems via the projections in Eq. (6), which in many cases can be computed very efficiently, e.g., using numerical linear algebra, convex optimization, or even through simple analytic expressions for the projections.

4.4.3. *Results*

As an example, M-TIP was applied to the problem of reconstructing 3D macromolecular structure from fluctuation X-ray scattering (FXS) experiments conducted at X-ray free-electron lasers. In this experiment, biological particles (e.g., a virus) are launched through a hydrodynamic jetting process and intercepted by a very bright X-ray laser. This creates a two-dimensional scattering pattern measured by a detector, but each pattern is the superposition of the scattering from all of the particles in the beam at random orientations. It can be shown that angular cross-correlations of the patterns, summed over a large number of images, contain a unique fingerprint for the 3D structure of the imaged particles. However, solving the inverse problem of reconstructing 3D structure from these correlations had been an open problem since FXS was first proposed in the 1970s.

The FXS reconstruction problem is very challenging, as it is a high-dimensional, nonlinear, and non-convex optimization problem where the forward relation between the structure and data is very mathematically complex. These properties prevent traditional optimization methods, such as steepest descent and reverse Monte Carlo, from working well as they tend to get trapped in local minima, become unstable, or are unable to efficiently scale to the required problem sizes.

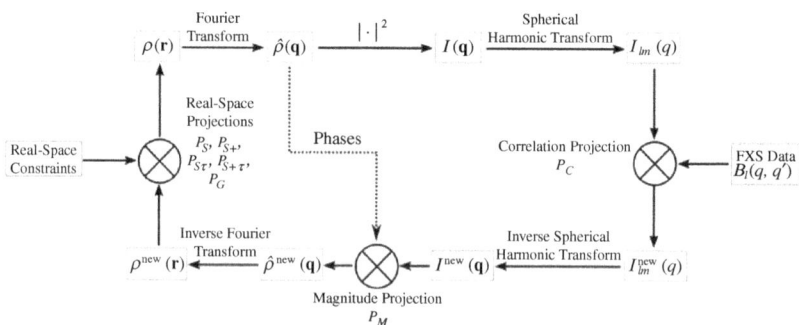

Fig. 9. Flowchart of M-TIP for FXS reconstruction via an iterative application of forward and projection operators.

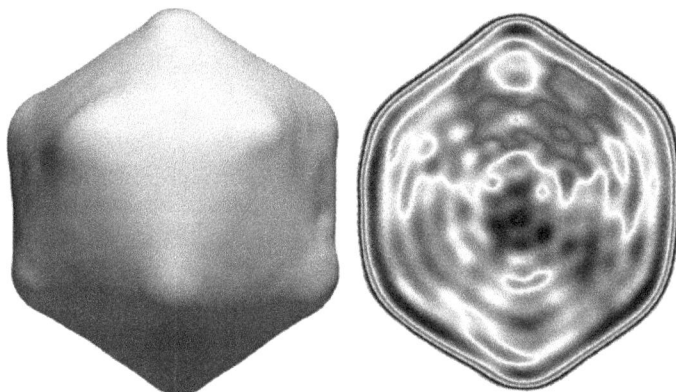

Fig. 10. PBCV-1 virus particle shell (left) and a 2-D slice through its center (right) depicting various densities (red, high; yellow and green, medium; blue, low), reconstructed using M-TIP.

The M-TIP approach provided the first reliable technique to reconstruct such data by optimally exploiting the mathematical substructures of the problem through an iterative application of carefully designed projection operators, which can be computed efficiently and robustly using recent advances in computational harmonic analysis, optimization theory, and numerical linear algebra. The flow diagram breaking the problem into iterative subparts is given in Figure 9.

The first successful 3D reconstruction from experimental FXS data was of a PBCV-1 virus using the M-TIP algorithm (see Figure 10).

In the case of FXS reconstruction, the projection operators used in M-TIP (see Figure 9) consist of well-understood mathematical operations and inversion using computational harmonic analysis, optimization theory, and numerical linear algebra. However, an exciting potential is that flexible modular frameworks like M-TIP could be leveraged to solve even more complex problems where the mathematical operations are either unknown or do not have efficient ways to calculate, by using AI/ML to learn efficient representations of the forward and projection operators for subparts of the problem. This would provide a seamless approach to combine both AI/ML and optimization that could combine their strengths and reduce their individual limitations, as we will describe in later sections.

5. Future Opportunities for AI/ML in Experiment and Computation

There are several opportunities for AI/ML to make profound contributions in both accelerating and fundamentally contributing to scientific progress.

For the most part, the sequence of experiments performed to obtain understanding are often decoupled from computations, which are either aimed at verifying or understanding experimental measurements or proceed independently and are linked later. Instead, there is tremendous benefit to be gained from having them proceed together. Imagine performing an experiment, obtaining partial results, and then learning from these results to then perform a complex simulation to refine a given model based on these experimental results, which then suggest further experiments. Here, AI/ML can be the driver that connects the two worlds.

We can think of connecting these worlds at multiple points, including the following:

- **AI/ML for Designing Materials:** Proposing new materials and solutions.
- **AI/ML Experiments to Advance Simulations and Theory:** Provide targeted insight that advances our abilities to compute and model fully-realized, complex mechanisms.
- **AI/ML for Optimizing, Self-Driving Experiments:** Efficient, autonomous experiments to optimize the use of limited resources.
- **AI/ML to Make Sense of Complex Data:** Solving inverse problems to extract meaning from measurements.
- **AI/ML for Discovering and Understanding the Scientific Land-scape:** Assembling disparate sources of information, experiments, simulations, and theory to build integrated understanding.

These steps are highly intertwined: here, we expand upon some of these ideas:

5.1. *AI/ML for designing materials*

Given a design goal of finding a new material that with prescribed performance properties, longevity, etc., where does one begin to look? A vast library of cataloged materials with associated properties, determined either through the experiment or simulations, can act as input to AI/ML to suggest new possibilities.

As one example, mining phase space for desired structure–property relationships will accelerate the design of new materials. A smart recommendation system, with the knowledge of different experimental techniques and their accuracy, could further recommend the best measurement to most accurately verify the system. Ideally, this recommendation system will provide an optimized analysis workflow for the experiment as well.

5.2. *AI/ML experiments to advance simulations and theory*

One of the most challenging issues in modeling, computation, and simulation is the vast range of time and space scales involved in physical phenomena. As an example, analyzing the performance and failure mechanisms of a battery depends on physics, chemistry, and materials sciences from the atomic and molecular levels, up through electronic characteristics, on to mesoscale phenomena connecting discrete to continuum scales, fracture initiation and crack propagation, large-scale cycling dynamics, etc.

The challenge is that mechanisms, models, and equations have been worked out for individual scales, but connecting them together is extraordinarily difficult. Adequate spatial and temporal resolution required for one scale is prohibitively expensive to carry up to the next scale, hence we need mechanisms to somehow pass information across scales so that a full, "multiscale" simulation can be run.

The opportunities for AI/ML are profound and transformative. For example, imagine running detailed, highly resolved calculations of a two-scale model, and, armed with the data at both scales, learning how information from one scale is communicated to a scale above and/or below. A series of such learned models could be used to connect various different scales, and resolved calculations at each scale could then rely on the learned model to communicate various global and integrated quantities to the next level.

Augmented by the considerable mathematical modeling and mesoscale approximations needed to discover key variables and mechanisms, such an approach would provide significant advancements in computational simulations across a host of applications.

This use of AI/ML to provide coupling between scales is not limited to data from simulations — one can easily imagine experiments specifically designed to extract scale-coupling models. For example, subjecting a material to a range of stresses might provide input data that can couple microscale discrete models to larger-scale continuum models.

5.3. *Optimizing, self-driving experiments*

The work described above already points to the power of automated, self-driving experiments. For the most part, these have been done in the context of a single laboratory and a single experimental modality. The next step is to build the mathematics, algorithms, and workflow to realize cross-facility, cross-experiment, and cross-computing optimized, self-driving experiments that make use of a wide range of available previous experiments and information.

As an example, we might want to probe a material characteristic across experimental techniques, instruments, and even facilities. One could imagine the same material being investigated in the neutron scattering facility in France, a synchrotron radiation beamline in Brookhaven, and a microscope in Berkeley. A supercomputer, at the same time, could provide simulation results. All those data streams have to be collected, interpreted, and harvested as to what set of experiments and simulations to perform next, all with one scientific question in mind. We already have all the tools necessary to accomplish this goal but it takes a vast range of expertise to link everything and to find a useful application. One candidate for a decision-making engine could be a vector-valued stochastic process that can detect and exploit relations of data points within one data stream but also in between datasets from different instruments. A kernel-based stochastic process needs additional flexibility to detect relationships between different data streams and requires exascale computing to allow for real-time decision-making. At the same time, the elegant math of a stochastic process allows for hypothesis testing along the way, testing, verifying, or falsifying claims and using the information for steering.

5.4. *AI/ML to make sense of complex data*

One of the most central goals in all of the experiment is the inverse problem of constructing a viable input model that explains the measured output. Although traditional optimization approaches have had long-standing success in solving inverse problems from data, they are fundamentally limited to problems where the physics can be efficiently mathematically formulated, the available constraints are sufficient to make the problem well posed, and the data are completely characterized. ML approaches, such as neural networks, to solving inverse problems offer the potential to learn and incorporate the missing physics, constraints, and data features. However, for sufficiently complex high-dimensional inverse problems, standard network approaches based on directly learning the entire inverse operator typically require an intractable number of degrees of freedom and training data and are overly sensitive to noise and missing measurements.

A promising approach to overcoming these limitations is to combine both optimization and ML in a mathematical framework able to leverage the strengths of each approach while reducing their individual limitations. In particular, the M-TIP framework of tackling complex inversion by weaving together individual substeps offers a powerful perspective ripe for advanced AI/ML.

M-TIP provides a seamless approach for combining both optimization and neural networks that could learn efficient representations for any forward operator F_i or projection P_{w_i}, P_M that cannot be efficiently computed with available techniques. So, instead of needing to learn the entire inversion, the networks only need to solve much smaller simpler subproblems, which would massively decrease the number of parameters and training data needed. Furthermore, this provides a natural way to handle incomplete and missing data, as the forward operations can be used to fill in (or predict) missing data that get used in the pseudoinversion steps, and this process can be regularized through the enforcement of constraints on the physical model M.

Somewhat abstractly, Figure 11 shows how a complex problem may be broken into subparts containing multiple approaches.

6. AI/ML for Discovering and Understanding the Scientific Landscape

All told, we are collecting vast amounts of information from multiple sources, including experimental measurements from a spectrum of imaging technologies (such as light, neutron, and electron sources) and mathematical models and algorithms tackling a range of scales, models, and complexities. AI/ML can prove critical to helping see the common and similar patterns and linkages contained in information coming from these disparate sources. Sorting out correlations vs. causations, identifying missing gaps, and building probabilistic relationships are critically needed key AI/ML opportunities.

Meeting these opportunities requires attention to arguably the most challenging issue facing the application of AI/ML to scientific problems,

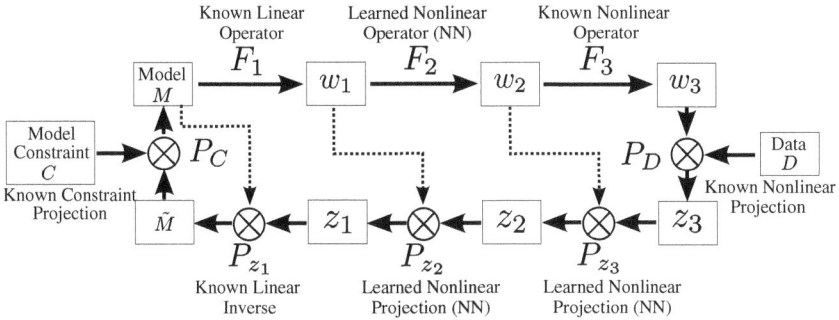

Fig. 11. Flowchart of ML-augmented M-TIP. Here, F_1 has fast linear forward and projection operators, F_2 has no known fast operators, F_3 has a fast nonlinear forward operator but no known fast projection, and F_4 has fast nonlinear forward and projection operators. Known fast operators are used where available, and NNs are used to learn and compute the remaining operators. Bold arrows indicate the order of operations, dashed lines indicate dependencies, and circled crosses indicate combining inputs in a projection operator.

namely building a coherent, smoothly integrated infrastructure. Indeed, we must make the transition from a one-off trained model test to a full deployment both within a facility and across facilities. Tracking and sharing of such AI/ML and analysis solution will be an integrated part of every experimental facility in the near future. This will require a fundamental shift in the way scientific knowledge is extracted from measurements.

Considerable progress is being made in these directions. The robustness of the AI/ML tools, data handling protocols, and associated infrastructure that has resulted from a global, multidisciplinary effort has laid a foundation for rapid deployment of bespoke solutions across many scientific disciplines that are featured within large-scale user facilities. Over the past years, an increased amount of automation and big-data type of experiments can now be performed within a home laboratory and the tools that have been developed for large scale facilities can be extended to be deployed at home.

The opportunities that come from sharing algorithms, data, compute resources, and optimally choosing efficient and targeted experiments rest on several key needs, including

- common formats,
- flexible and reconfigurable workflows and architectures,
- robust and reliable mathematical formulations, with algorithms written with more than one goal in mind,
- software that can meld these worlds together and coordinate multiple moving parts, capabilities, and objectives.

Altogether, these capabilities will enable and accelerate the fuller potential of AI/ML across many scientific disciplines.

References

[1] R. P. Feynman, T. Hey, and R. W. Allen (2018). *Feynman Lectures on Computation.* Boca Raton, London, New York: CRC Press.

[2] J. Yano, K. J. Gaffney, J. Gregoire *et al.* (2022). The case for data science in experimental chemistry: Examples and recommendations. *Nature Reviews Chemistry, 6,* 357–370.

[3] M. Noack, P. Zwart, D. Ushizima *et al.* (2021). Gaussian processes for autonomous data acquisition at large-scale synchrotron and neutron facilities. *Nature Review Physics, 3,* 685.

[4] M. M. Noack, K. G. Yager, M. Fukuto *et al.* (2019). A kriging-based approach to autonomous experimentation with applications to X-ray scattering. *Scientific Reports, 9,* 11809.

[5] M. M. Noack, G. S. Doerk, R. Li *et al.* (2020). Autonomous materials discovery driven by gaussian process regression with inhomogeneous measurement noise and anisotropic kernels. *Nature Scientific Reports, 10,* 17663.

[6] M. M. Noack, G. S. Doerk, R. Li *et al.* (2020). Advances in kriging-based autonomous X-ray scattering experiments. *Scientific Reports, 10,* 1325.

[7] E. Holman and M. Fang (2020). Autonomous adaptive data acquisition for scanning hyperspectral imaging. *Communication Biology, 3,* 684.

[8] P. M. Valdespino-Castillo, P. Hu, M. Merino-Ibarra *et al.* (2018). Exploring biogeochemistry and microbial diversity of extant microbialites in mexico and cuba. *Frontiers in Microbiology, 9,* 510.

[9] C. N. Melton, M. Noack, T. Ohta *et al.* (2020). K-means-driven gaussian process data collection for angle-resolved photoemission spectroscopy. *Machine Learning: Science and Technology, 1,* 2632–2153.

[10] J. C. Thomas, A. Rossi, D. Smalley *et al.* (2022). Autonomous scanning probe microscopy investigations over WS_2 and $Au\{111\}$. *NPJ Computational Materials, 8*(1), 1–7.

[11] D. Pelt and J. A. Sethian (2017). A mixed-scale dense convolutional neural network for image analysis. *Proceedings of the National Academy of Sciences, 115,* 254.

[12] D. M. Pelt, K. J. Batenburg, and J. A. Sethian (2018). Improving tomographic reconstruction from limited data using mixed-scale dense convolutional neural networks. *Journal of Imaging, 4*(11), 128.

[13] L. Segev-Zarko, P. Dahlberg, S. Sun *et al.* (2022). Cryo-electron tomography with mixed-scale dense neural networks reveals key steps in deployment of Toxoplasma invasion machinery, *PNAS Nexus, 1*(4), 183.

[14] S. Liu, C. N. Melton, S. Venkatakrishnan *et al.* (2019). Convolutional neural networks for grazing incidence X-ray scattering patterns: Thin film structure identification. *MRS Communications, 9,* 1–7.

[15] F. H. Araujo, R. R. Silva, F. N. Medeiros *et al.* (2018). Reverse image search for scientific data within and beyond the visible spectrum. *Expert*

Systems with Applications, *109*, 35–48. https://www.sciencedirect.com/science/article/pii/S0957417418302987.

[16] D. Ushizima, F. Araujo, R. Silva *et al.* (2021). Automated sorting of X-ray scattering patterns with convolutional neural networks. *Transactions on Computational Science & Computational Intelligence*, July.

[17] J. J. Donatelli, P. H. Zwart, and J. A. Sethian *et al.* (2015). Iterative phasing for fluctuation X-ray scattering. *Proceedings of the National Academy of Sciences*, *112*(33), 10286–10291. https://www.pnas.org/content/112/33/10286.

[18] J. J. Donatelli, J. A. Sethian, and P. H. Zwart *et al.* (2017). Reconstruction from limited single-particle diffraction data via simultaneous determination of state, orientation, intensity, and phase. *Proceedings of the National Academy of Sciences*, *114*(28), 7222–7227. https://www.pnas.org/content/114/28/7222.

© 2023 World Scientific Publishing Company
https://doi.org/10.1142/9789811265679_0009

Chapter 9

The First Exascale Supercomputer Accelerating AI-for-Science and Beyond

Satoshi Matsuoka[*], Kento Sato[†], Mohamed Wahib[‡], and
Aleksandr Drozd[§]

RIKEN Center for Computational Science, Kobe, Japan
[*]*matsu@acm.org*
[†]*kento.sato@riken.jp*
[‡]*mohamed.attia@riken.jp*
[§]*aleksandr.drozd@riken.jp*

1. Fugaku: The State-of-the-art CPU-based Supercomputer for Driving AI-for-Science

1.1. *Hardware*

Fugaku [1] is the flagship supercomputer hosted by RIKEN (R-CCS) in Japan. With the performance of 488 (double-precision) PFlops, Fugaku is the world's fastest supercomputer (leading the Top500 list [2]). Fugaku consists of 158,976 compute nodes that are each equipped with a Fujitsu A64FX CPU. A64FX provides 48 application CPU cores and is integrated with 32 GiB of HBM2 memory. The compute nodes are interconnected through the TofuD network. Each group of 16 compute nodes in Fugaku shares a 1.6 TB SSD storage, and all the nodes can access the global 150 PB Lustre file system. Figure 1 gives an overview of the design of Fugaku, from the racks and down to the individual cores.

1.2. *Software*

From the hardware specifications perspective, Fugaku is a fairly capable platform for running deep learning workloads. However, at the time Fugaku went into production, the software ecosystem for advanced AI methods was

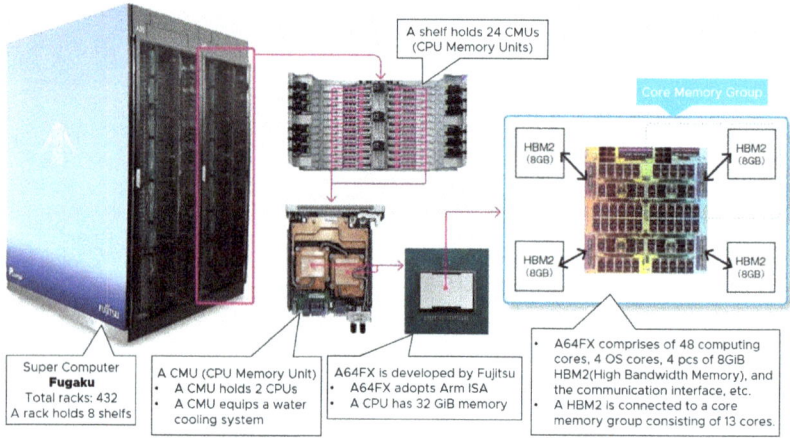

Fig. 1.   Illustration of Fugaku [3].

virtually not existent. This is because at the time Fugaku was designed (circa 2014), deep learning had not yet been a prominent workload.

1.2.1. *Deep learning software stack*

To work with deep learning methods, practitioners rely on *deep learning frameworks* — a specialized software which allows users to design and train Artificial Neural Networks (ANNs). Popular titles include PyTorch, TensorFlow, and MXNet among others. In summary, the frameworks allow users to (a) construct an ANN from basic tensor operations and a pre-defined set of basic building blocks (convolutional kernels, dense layers, recurrent units, various activation functions, etc.), (b) compute derivatives of the loss function for back-propagation, (c) execute forward and backward passes efficiently on a given hardware, and (d) provide additional helper functions for distributed training, data handling, etc.

Modern deep learning frameworks are extremely complicated software products and are typically designed in a hierarchical and modular fashion. Figure 2 outlines the stack of a DL framework. The user defines a computational graph of an ANN by using a domain-specific language or specialized API calls; this graph is optionally translated into an intermediate representation on which some optimizations could be performed. Individual basic building blocks are often isolated into reusable libraries of optimized deep learning primitives. Such libraries often target particular hardware platforms or in some cases a certain range of platforms. A thing to note is that for a particular platform, there are often multiple alternative

Models (ResNet50, BERT, CosmoFlow)	
Frameworks (Pytorch, TensorFlow, MXNet ...)	
IRs/ compilers (TVM, MLIR/XLA, ...)	Exchange formats (ONNX, NNEF ...)
DL-specific primitives (DNNL, cuDNN)	High-level comm libs (Horovod, DDP ...)
BLAS/FFT etc (OpenBLAS, cuBLAS ...)	Low-level comm libs (MPI, NCCL ...)
hardware (GPU, CPU, ASIC ...)	Fabric (infiniband, tofu)

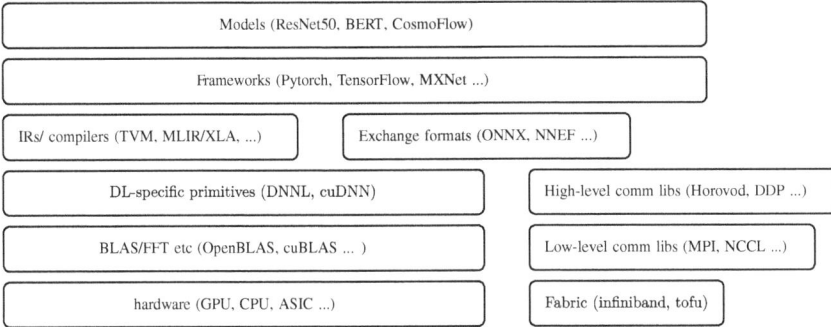

Fig. 2.   General overview of the software stack in deep learning frameworks.

libraries available. Finally, while for many of the basic building blocks the libraries provide custom implementations, in some cases, the computation is lowered to more conventional primitives and corresponding libraries, like BLAS or FFT, which in turn also could have multiple platform-specific implementations.

Thus, even within a single deep learning framework and a single chosen hardware platform, there are often multiple modes of execution available, including the choice of different back-ends/deep learning primitive libraries and underlying BLAS infrastructure. For instance, the popular PyTorch framework on conventional CPUs can work in define-by-run or JIT modes, and either use "native" back-end for computing ANN primitives, use oneDNN [4] with two possible tensor layouts ("native" and DNNL-specific), or be compiled with the TVM compiler.

1.2.2. *Deep learning on Fugaku*

The first objective in qualifying Fugaku for deep learning workloads was to determine on which level(s) of the software hierarchy to focus and if any of the existing solutions could have served as a good starting point. Studying the inner design of popular deep learning frameworks, surveying libraries of optimized primitives and related solutions was kick-started at RIKEN Center of Computational Science and continued in collaboration with industrial partners, namely Fujitsu Ltd, Arm Ltd, and Linaro. At the later stages, the engineering work on optimizing particular kernels was performed mostly at Fujitsu Ltd.

We have also explored promising candidates for supporting the A64FX processor: cuDNN [5], TVM [6], ARM NN [7], and oneDNN [4]. Another alternative would be focusing on "native" implementations that most of the deep learning frameworks have, especially for CPU platforms, and to contribute the optimized code there. The problem with the latter approach is, naturally, its limited portability to the different deep learning frameworks.

Nvidia's cuDNN [5] is perhaps one of the most well-known libraries of optimized deep learning primitives. The source codes for this library are not openly available, and the architectural target is constrained to NVIDIA GPUs. However, in a pilot study, we managed to create a mock GPU device and redirect corresponding API calls for several selected kernels (e.g., convolutions of common sizes without stride and dilation) to a simplistic BLAS-based implementation. The advantage of this approach is that deep learning frameworks tend to be heavily optimized for GPU targets, and this includes code outside of primitive libraries, e.g., support of asynchronous dispatch of kernels.

TVM [6] and ARM NN [7] have the advantage of explicitly supporting ARM CPUs, as a main target or as one of the possible targets. Both solutions, however, were focused predominantly on inference and had rudimentary support for training.

Finally, oneDNN was chosen as a base to enable performance portability of deep learning frameworks to the A64FX platform. Previously known as MKL DNN, this library was originally designed to target inference on Intel x86 CPUs but eventually evolved into an open-source project with a broader range of targets, for inference as well as training. Adding A64FX support to DNNL required first adding A64FX target to the Xbyak JIT assembler [8] and then writing custom implementations for individual kernels.

1.2.3. *Benchmarking deep learning on Fugaku*

To assess the progress of porting and optimizing deep learning frameworks to Fugaku, we have developed a custom solution called *benchmarker*. It can be used to evaluate the throughput of individual kernels as well as full models on small synthetic datasets. We had also joined the MLCommons organization [9], particularly MLPerf HPC working group to not only use MLPerf benchmarks but also to actively contribute to the development of this benchmarking suite.

The MLPerf HPC benchmarks are holistic in the sense that they capture critical features of emerging scientific machine learning workloads: massive data volume, large complex models, and training schemes that incorporate data parallelism, model parallelism, and hyper-parameter optimization. The MLPerf HPC benchmarks are also unique in that they offer performance characterization capability for state-of-the-art practices in scientific discovery. The emerging domain of coupling simulations with AI motivates the first two benchmarks included in the suite: CosmoFlow and DeepCAM. CosmoFlow model is a 3D convolutional network which is used to predict cosmological parameters in a large-scale simulation of mass distribution in an evolving universe. A total of 637 instances of CosmoFlow learning model were trained in 8 hours and 16 minutes: a rate of about 1.29 deep learning models per minute — 1.77 times faster than that of other systems [10]. Most notably, in a week scaling regime (measuring how many deep learning models can be trained per time unit) of the MLPerf HPC 1.0 benchmark (published November 17*th* 2021), Fugaku achieved unprecedented throughput [10].

Finally, although the main bulk of work on optimizing deep learning ecosystem for Fugaku is done, the development continues. The ongoing works target optimizing less commonly used primitives, networking, and IO.

2. AI-for-Science Applications — Case Studies

2.1. *Earth science, climate science*

2.1.1. *Remote sensing by Deep Learning from simulated data for flood and debris-flow mapping for flood disaster damage estimation*

Yokoyama *et al.* [11] proposed a framework that estimates the inundation depth (maximum water level) and debris-flow-induced topographic deformation from remote sensing imagery by integrating deep learning and numerical simulation. A water and debris-flow simulator generates training data for various artificial disaster scenarios. They showed that regression models based on Attention U-Net and LinkNet architectures trained on such synthetic data can predict the maximum water level and topographic deformation from a remote sensing-derived change detection map and a digital elevation model. The proposed framework has an inpainting capability, thus mitigating the false negatives that are inevitable in remote sensing image analysis.

2.1.2. *Clustering the weather patterns from a 1000-member ensemble simulation using the generative topographic mapping to investigate the potential factors that caused the July 2020 Kyushu heavy rain*

In the early July 2020, the Kyushu area in Japan has been experienced heavy rain with record-breaking rainfall amount at many sites. This caused severe damage and serious loss of life in two prefectures: Kumamoto and Kagoshima. In order to improve forecast systems in confronting with such events in future, it is desirable to understand the underlying mechanism. Duc *et al.* [12] have investigated the factors that could lead to this event by clustering a huge dataset consisting of 1000 potential 3-dimensional atmospheric states, which have been estimated from observations and a state-of-the-art numerical model. Using the generative topographic mapping technique, they classified these 1000 atmospheric states into 20 typical weather patterns. The cluster that yields the best match to the rainfall observations at Kyushu has been examined in detail. The July 2020 heavy rain is shown to be sensitive to the location of a mesoscale Baiu frontal depression along the Baiu front. This implies that observations over the east of China are important to reduce uncertainties in this case.

2.1.3. *High-resolution, real-time tsunami flood prediction through the use of AI*

Tohoku University, Earthquake Research Institute, the University of Tokyo, and Fujitsu Laboratories Ltd conducted a large number of high-resolution tsunami simulations using the world's fastest supercomputer Fugaku and constructed a new AI model using the offshore tsunami waveforms and flooding conditions in coastal areas obtained from the simulations as training data. By inputting the tsunami waveforms observed offshore at the time of an earthquake into the AI model, the flooding status of coastal areas can be predicted with a high spatial resolution of three-meter units before the tsunami arrives. This enables us to obtain detailed flooding forecast information for each section of land, such as the rise of a localized tsunami, taking into account the effects of buildings, structures, roads, and other social infrastructure in the coastal city area, thereby supporting more appropriate evacuation actions. The AI model learned in advance using "Fugaku" can be run on an ordinary PC in a few seconds, making it much easier to build a real-time flooding forecasting system, which previously required a supercomputer [13].

2.2. *Biomolecular science*

2.2.1. *Comprehensive gene network analysis by XAI for uncovering molecular mechanism of disease*

Gene regulatory network is crucial for understanding complex mechanisms of diseases because complex diseases (e.g., cancer) involve many genes connected in molecular networks rather than the abnormality of a single gene. The effectiveness of the networks-based analysis has been verified in various studies, e.g., drug combinations identification, cancer prediction, and protein–protein interaction [14–16]. Although various approaches were developed to gene network analysis, comprehensive interpretation of the massive networks remains a challenge. To settle on the issue, we considered the use of explainable artificial intelligence (XAI) approaches (i.e., DeepTensor and Tensor Reconstruction-based Interpretable Prediction (TRIP), proposed by Maruhashi *et al.* [17,18]), which are deep learning approaches based on tensor decomposition for learning multiway relations. Park *et al.* [19] then proposed a novel strategy for a comprehensive analysis of the massive gene networks. Their strategy is based on two stages, i.e., constructing sample-specific gene networks based on the kernel-based L1-type regularization and comprehensive analysis of the constructed multilayer networks by using the XAI, TRIP. The use of the XAI enables us to overcome the limitation of existing gene network analysis, i.e., narrow angle in the large-scale gene network analysis, and this leads to a better understanding of molecular interplay involved in disease. Their strategy was applied to analyze EMT-status-specific gene networks [20] and we uncovered the EMT markers. It can be seen through the literature that the identified markers have strong evidence as EMT markers, even though any biological knowledge about the identified genes was not incorporated in our analysis. It implies that our data-driven strategy based on XAI provides biologically reliable results for the large-scale gene network analysis.

2.3. Health and well-being

2.3.1. Discovering new insights into the influence relationship between genes leveraging explainable AI and causal discovery

Discovering new insights into the causal relationships by analyzing large-scale data is a critical issue in many fields such as medical research. Maruhashi *et al.* [21] developed TRIP, an Explainable AI by enhancing a tensor-based graph learning named DeepTensor introduced in Maruhashi *et al.* [22]. A set of large-scale graphs are represented as tensors, and TRIP decomposes these tensors so that high prediction accuracy is achieved by using the significance values of the components. TRIP was applied to the gene regulatory networks, i.e., causal relationships between genes, and discovered comprehensive insights into infiltration and metastasis that have been discovered in more than 10 years of research on epithelial cancer within a day by using the supercomputer Fugaku. Furthermore, the causal relationships should drastically differ depending on the organ and the individual and variations in gene expression, and the number of patterns combining expression levels of multiple genes exceeds 1,000 trillion. However, it spends over 4,000 years to compute all the causal relationships for each combinatorial pattern of expressions of 20,000 genes on an ordinary PC. To tackle the problem, we utilized Wide Learning, an Explainable AI that enumerates all possible hypotheses by the efficient algorithm for mining constrained patterns introduced by Iwashita *et al.* [23] and causal discovery technology on Fugaku. As a result, unknown causal relationships suggesting causes of resistance to lung cancer drugs in various expression patterns of multiple genes have been successfully extracted within a day.

2.3.2. *New technology for rapid discovery of unknown causal mechanisms related to drug resistance in cancer*

When molecularly targeted drugs for cancer continue to be administered to patients, cancer cells that have acquired resistance to the drugs may proliferate and relapse. Thus, precise data and analytical techniques are essential to elucidate the mechanism of cancer resistance acquisition, in which a group of cells that have acquired multiple driver mutations behave in a transformative and abnormal manner. Although there is technology to exhaustively extract conditions with characteristic causal relationships using "Wide Learning", an AI technology capable of explaining the basis of decisions and discovering knowledge, an exhaustive search for all 20,000 human genes was estimated to take more than 4,000 years on an ordinary computer. Therefore, speeding up the processing was a challenge. Fujitsu and Tokyo Medical and Dental University maximized the computational performance by parallelizing and implementing algorithms for conditional and causal searches to analyze all human genes in a practical time on the supercomputer "Fugaku", which features inter- and intraprocessor parallelism. Furthermore, by extracting promising gene combinations that could be conditions for producing drug resistance based on statistical information, we have developed a technology to achieve an exhaustive search in less than one day [24].

2.4. *Materials science and engineering*

2.4.1. *Facilitating ab initio configurational sampling of multicomponent solids using an on-lattice neural network model and active learning*

Kasamatsu *et al.* [25] proposed a scheme for *ab initio* configurational sampling in multicomponent crystalline solids using Behler–Parrinello-type neural network potentials (NNPs) in an unconventional way: the NNPs are trained to predict the energies of relaxed structures from the perfect lattice with configurational disorder instead of the usual way of training to predict energies as functions of continuous atom coordinates. Training set bias is avoided through an active learning scheme. This enables bypassing of the structural relaxation procedure which is necessary when applying conventional NNP approaches to the lattice configuration problem. This idea is demonstrated in the calculation of the temperature dependence of the degree of A/B site inversion in MgAl2O4, which is a multivalent system requiring careful handling of long-range interactions. The present scheme may serve as an alternative to cluster expansion for "difficult" systems, e.g., complex bulk or interface systems with many components and sublattices that are relevant to many technological applications today.

2.4.2. *Density functional theory from supervised learning*

Density functional theory (DFT) is the standard electronic structure theory and is widely used as a basis for materials design. DFT is based on the Hohenberg–Kohn theorem that there is a one-to-one correspondence between particle density and energy, a relationship that should be machine learnable, but the lack of this relationship makes the accuracy limited. Nagai *et al.* [26,27] recently proposed a method to establish this relationship using neural network methods. They found that the DFT developed in this study can improve the accuracy not only for molecular systems, for which the training set can be obtained by a very accurate quantum chemical method, but also for solids, for which the training set is unavailable but theoretically derived physical conditions work alternatively. This paves a systematic way for further accuracy and will serve as a tool for developing the ultimate material database.

2.4.3. *Nonlinear mode decomposition and reduced-order modeling of three-dimensional flow field using distributed machine learning on Fugaku for significantly reducing computational costs in high-precision simulations*

Nonlinear modes of the three-dimensional flow field were extracted by distributed machine learning on Fugaku. Mode decomposition is an approach used to decompose flow fields into physically important flow structures known as modes. Ando *et al.* [28] extended the convolutional neural network-based mode decomposition proposed by Murata *et al.* [29] to the three-dimensional flow field. However, because this process is costly in terms of calculation and memory usage for even a small flow field problem, the enormous computational and memory resources of the supercomputer Fugaku were employed. A hybrid parallelism method combining the distribution of network structure (model parallelism) and the training data (data parallelism) using up to 10,500 nodes on Fugaku was employed for learning. Furthermore, they constructed a reduced-order model to predict the time evolution of state variables in the reduced-order space (i.e., latent vector) using the long short-term memory networks.

Finally, they compared the reproduced flow field of the model with that of the original full-order model. In addition, they evaluated the execution performance of the learning process. Using a single core memory group, the whole learning process indicates a value of 129.50 GFLOPS being achieved, 7.57% of the single-precision floating-point arithmetic peak performance. Notably, the convolution calculation for backward propagation achieved 1103.09 GFLOPS, which is 65.39% of the peak. Furthermore, with the weak scaling test, the whole learning process indicates 72.9% with 25,250 nodes (1,212,000 cores) relative to 750 nodes. The sustained performance is 7.8 PFLOPS. In particular, the convolution calculation for backward propagation indicates a result of 113 PFLOPS (66.2% of the peak performance).

2.4.4. *A neural network-assisted genetic algorithm for multidisciplinary design optimization of an aerospace system*

To find an optimal design concerning several disciplines is the goal of every aerospace design optimization. Numerical design optimization has been a popular approach for efficiently solving it, thanks to the advancement of computing power. At its core, genetic algorithm (GA) is chosen as the optimizer since it features global optimization without requiring gradient information. However, it requires numerous evaluations that are often expensive. Hariansyah *et al.* [30] developed a surrogate-based optimization framework called Neural Network-Assisted Genetic Algorithm (NN+GA) that employs a multilayer perceptron (MLP) to substitute the expensive evaluations. The MLP is trained using initial samples obtained by the design of experiment method, i.e., Latin Hypercube Sampling (LHS). Besides the LHS, a novel method called deep convolutional generative adversarial network (DCGAN)-based sampling is also equipped in NN+GA to efficiently explore the design space and provide more informative data for MLP. The NN+GA has been applied to aerodynamic shape optimization of transonic airfoils [30] and structural layout optimization for composite aircraft wings [31]. The NN+GA outperforms a standalone GA in solving those optimization problems by cutting the required number of evaluations. The current challenge is to address the curse of dimensionality in high-dimensional problems. It is difficult to construct an accurate surrogate model in high-dimensional problems. Future research must make advancements in the method to efficiently explore the high-dimensional design space. One possible solution at hand is to employ a convolutional neural network (CNN)-based geometric filtering method to quickly detect shape abnormality so that only meaningful samples are used to train for the surrogate model. However, this method still requires further study as it only has limited applications.

2.5. *Astronomy and astrophysics*

2.5.1. *3D-spatiotemporal forecasting the expansion of supernova shells using Deep Learning toward high-resolution galaxy simulations*

Small-integration timesteps for a small fraction of short-timescale regions are bottlenecks for high-resolution galaxy simulations using massively parallel computing. For future higher-resolution galaxy simulations, Hirashima *et al.* [32] solved this problem. One possible way is an (approximate) Hamiltonian splitting method, in which only regions requiring small timesteps are integrated with small timesteps, separated from the entire galaxy. For hydrodynamics, the splitting is approximate since there are dissipations due to shocks. Since the smallest timestep is often necessary for gas affected by supernova (SN) explosions, they split these regions in our Hamiltonian splitting scheme. Suppose we use smoothed-particle hydrodynamics for galaxy simulations for the Hamiltonian splitting method. In that case, we need to pick up particles affected by an SN (the target particles) during the subsequent global step (the integration timestep for the entire galaxy) in advance. They, therefore, developed a deep learning model to predict a shell expansion after an SN explosion and an image processing algorithm to identify the target particles in the predicted regions. They confirmed that we can identify more than 95% of the target particles with our method, which is a better identification rate than using an analytic approach with the Sedov–Taylor solution. Combined with the Hamiltonian splitting method, our particle selection method using deep learning will improve the performance of galaxy simulations with extremely high resolution.

2.5.2. *Machine learning by neural network for quantum many-body solver and experimental data analysis*

Quantum many-body problems are known to show NP hard difficulty. Nomura *et al.* [33,34] and Yamaji *et al.* [35] have developed a solver by using Boltzmann machines to approximate solutions accurately and efficiently. It was applied to a challenging problem of a quantum spin model and established the existence of quantum spin liquid phase, which bears a long-ranged quantum entanglement. On another application of machine learning, they have extracted electron self-energy, which is hidden in the photoemission experimental data. It has established the existence of prominent resonance peaks which are responsible for the high-temperature superconductivity.

2.6. *Computer science and quantum computing*

2.6.1. *Compression of time evolutionary image data through predictive deep neural networks (2) for accelerating Big Data transfer*

Big data management is a critical mission for data-driven science. Major sources of big data include a large synchrotron radiation facility (SPring-8) which is expected to generate 1.3 EB of data per year. Data compression has been a popular approach for combating the explosive volume of image datasets by reducing the actual data size to be transferred. Rupak *et al.* [36] developed an efficient (de)compression framework called Time Evolutionary ZIP (TEZIP) that can support dynamic lossy and lossless compression of time evolutionary image frames with high compression ratio and speed. TEZIP employs PredNet to exploit the temporal locality of time evolutionary data, predict the next image frames, and derive the resulting differences between the predicted frame and the actual frame as a delta frame that is much more compressible. Next, they apply three encoding techniques to exploit the spatial similarities in the delta frames and then they apply lossless compressors to compress these encoded frames. Their evaluation on real-world time evolutionary data generated from SPring-8 showed that, in terms of compression ratio, TEZIP outperforms existing lossless compressors such as x265 by up to 3.2x and lossy compressors such as SZ by up to 3.3x.

2.6.2. *Quantum circuit encoding of classical data*

Although quantum computer can in principle treat an exponentially large amount of data, it is a major challenge in practice to represent classical data such as a classical image into a quantum circuit. Inspired by a tensor network method, Shirakawa *et al.* [37] have proposed a quantum-classical hybrid algorithm to construct an optimal quantum circuit for classical data that is represented as a quantum state by the amplitude encoding and employed classical computer to demonstrate the proposed algorithm.

3. Architectures for AI-for-Science — Past, Present, and Future

In this section, we discuss future architectures for AI-for-Science. As we know, Moore's law is ending and exploration of future computer architectures that will enable performance improvement around 2028–2030 is a critical research challenge. To do this, it is necessary to go back to the principles, analyze the current machines and future technologies, and

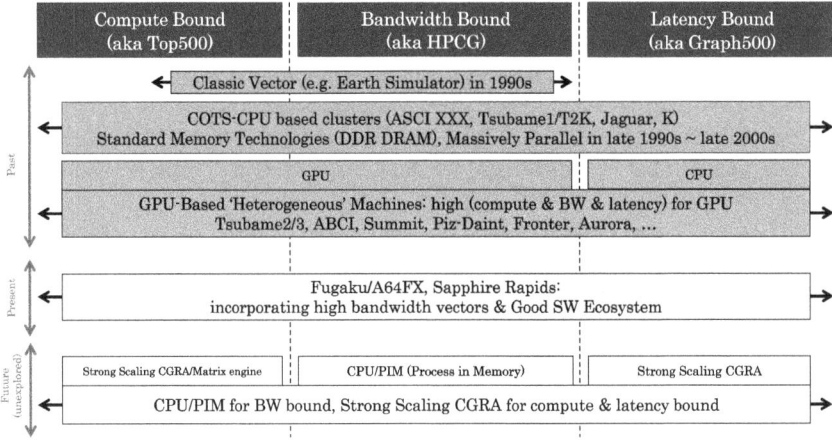

Fig. 3.   Application kernel categorization and architectures.

furthermore answer how applications compute, what the bottlenecks are, and how we can take advantage of the characteristics of future machines. When we look at the applications, there are three main types of kernels: compute-bound, bandwidth-bound, and latency-bound applications. In practice, the majority of applications are bandwidth-bound as represented by the HPCG benchmark and some are latency-bound as represented by the Graph500 benchmark. The classic vector machine like Earth simulator in 90s basically covered the bandwidth-bound applications and also compute-bound applications to some extent. The Earth simulator is sort of very specific to certain types of applications but this machine became No.1 on Top500.

Cost-based CPU clusters such as TSUBAME1, T2K, Jaguar, and the K computer emerged in the 1990s–2000s. They use standard memory technologies and basically attain performance with mass parallelism by lining all the processors up. They get performance for bandwidth/latency-bound applications by parallelism. We anticipated it will not scale and we started using GPUs. Such GPU-based heterogeneous machines became popular. These types of machines include TSUBAME2/3, ABCI, Summit, Frontier, Piz-Daint, and Aurora. In this case, GPUs would cover compute-bound and bandwidth-bound kernels, whereas CPUs cover latency-bound kernels.

What we did with Fugaku was to use design an architecture where the CPU, i.e., A64FX, would also behave like GPU cores to cover not only the bandwidth-bound kernels but also the compute-bound kernels by wide vectorization, i.e., SVE. What we haven't largely investigated is an architecture where CPU covers bandwidth-bound and latency-bound kernels and where GPU with tuned numerical libraries such as BLAS covers compute-bound kernels. Furthermore, we can use domain-specific accelerators in forms of either on-chip integration (SoC), multichip packaging, on-node accelerators, or specific accelerated nodes via interconnects. However, we would like to emphasize that accelerators are means to the end, not a purpose by itself.

Therefore, we need to analyze the effectiveness of domain-specific accelerators to figure out what the accelerator is good for, where it can be applied, and what are its shortcomings. But basically, we can see that very few codes rely on the GEMM kernels and many applications have a very low dependency on this linear algebra. In other words, if the performance of the GEMM kernels is infinite, even if you get a perfect speedup, you will only get a speedup of about 30% as a whole [38]. What we really need to do is to not only modestly increase FLOPS (e.g., with strong scaling CGRA/Matrix Engine) but also increase bandwidth (e.g., with general-purpose CPU and/or PIM) and reduce latency of the systems towards the next generation (e.g., with strong scaling CGRA).

References

[1] RIKEN Center for Computational Science. (2022). Fugaku supercomputer. [1 April 2022]. https://www.r-ccs.riken.jp/en/fugaku/.

[2] E. Strohmaier, J. Dongarra, H. Simon *et al.* (2021). TOP500. November. http://www.top500.org/.

[3] Nikkei XTech. (2022). Fugaku supercomputer. [1 April 2022]. https://xtech.nikkei.com/atcl/nxt/mag/nc/18/020600014/080600068/?P=2.

[4] Intel. (2022). oneAPI Deep Neural Network Library (oneDNN). [1 April 2022]. https://github.com/oneapi-src/oneDNN.

[5] S. Chetlur, C. Woolley, P. Vandermersch *et al.* (2014). CUDNN: Efficient primitives for deep learning. https://arxiv.org/abs/1410.0759.

[6] T. Chen, T. Moreau, Z. Jiang *et al.* (2018). TVM: An automated end-to-end optimizing compiler for deep learning. In *Proceedings of the 13th USENIX Conference on Operating Systems Design and Implementation*, ser. OSDI'18. USA: USENIX Association, pp. 579–594.

[7] L. Lai, N. Suda, and V. Chandra (2018). CMSIS-NN: Efficient neural network kernels for arm cortex-m cpus. https://arxiv.org/abs/1801.06601.

[8] Mitsunari Shigeo. Xbyak: A C++ JIT assembler for x86 (IA32), x64 (AMD64, x86-64). https://github.com/herumi/xbyak.

[9] P. Mattson, C. Cheng, G. Diamos *et al.* (2020). Mlperf training benchmark. In *Proceedings of Machine Learning and Systems*, I. Dhillon, D. Papailiopoulos, and V. Sze, (eds.), Vol. 2, pp. 336–349. https://proceedings.mlsys.org/paper/2020/file/02522a2b2726fb0a03bb19f2d8d9524d-Paper.pdf.

[10] S. Farrell, M. Emani, J. Balma *et al.* (2021). MLPERF HPC: A holistic benchmark suite for scientific machine learning on HPC systems. In *2021 IEEE/ACM Workshop on Machine Learning in High Performance Computing Environments (MLHPC)*. Los Alamitos, CA, USA: IEEE Computer Society, November, pp. 33–45. https://doi.ieeecomputersociety.org/10.1109/MLHPC54614.2021.00009.

[11] N. Yokoya, K. Yamanoi, W. He *et al.* (2022). Breaking limits of remote sensing by deep learning from simulated data for flood and debris-flow mapping. *IEEE Transactions on Geoscience and Remote Sensing, 60*, 1–15.

[12] L. Duc, T. Kawabata, K. Saito, and T. Oizumi (2021). Forecasts of the July 2020 Kyushu Heavy Rain Using a 1000-Member Ensemble Kalman Filter, SOLA, 2021, Vol. 17, pp. 41–47, Released on J-STAGE 8 March, 2021, Advance online publication 29 January, 2021, Online ISSN 1349-6476, https://doi.org/10.2151/sola.2021-007, https://www.jstage.jst.go.jp/article/sola/17/0/17_2021-007/_article/-char/en.

[13] Fujitsu leverages world's fastest supercomputer 'fugaku' and ai to deliver real-time tsunami prediction in joint project. (2022). https://www.fujitsu.com/global/about/resources/news/press-releases/2021/0216-01.html.

[14] M. Daoud and M. Mayo (2019). A survey of neural network-based cancer prediction models from microarray data. *Artificial Intelligence in Medicine, 97*, 204–214. https://www.sciencedirect.com/science/article/pii/S0933365717305067.

[15] F. Cheng, I. Kovács, and A. Barabási (2019). Network-based prediction of drug combinations. *Nature Communications, 10*(1), December, funding Information: The authors thank Yifang Ma, Marc Vidal, and Joseph Loscalzo for useful discussions on the manuscript. The authors thank Alice Grishchenko for polishing the figures. This work was supported by NIH grants P50-HG004233 and U01-HG001715 to A.-L.B. from NHGRI, and K99HL138272 and R00HL138272 to F.C. from NHLBI.

[16] A. Fout, J. Byrd, B. Shariat *et al.* (2017). Protein interface prediction using graph convolutional networks. In *Proceedings of the 31st International Conference on Neural Information Processing Systems*, ser. NIPS'17. Red Hook, NY, USA: Curran Associates Inc., pp. 6533–6542.

[17] K. Maruhashi, M. Todoriki, T. Ohwa *et al.* (2018). Learning multi-way relations via tensor decomposition with neural networks. In S. A. McIlraith and K. Q. Weinberger, (eds.), *AAAI*, AAAI Press, pp. 3770–3777. http://dblp.uni-trier.de/db/conf/aaai/aaai2018.html#MaruhashiTOGHIA18.

[18] K. Maruhashi, H. Park, R. Yamaguchi *et al.* (2020). Linear tensor projection revealing nonlinearity. *CoRR, abs/2007.03912.* https://arxiv.org/abs/2007.03912.

[19] H. Park, K. Maruhashi, R. Yamaguchi *et al.* (2020). Global gene network exploration based on explainable artificial intelligence approach. *PLOS ONE, 15*(11), 1–24 November. https://doi.org/10.1371/journal.pone.0241508.

[20] T. Shimamura, S. Imoto, Y. Shimada *et al.* (2011). A novel network profiling analysis reveals system changes in epithelial-mesenchymal transition. *PLOS ONE, 6*(6), 1–17, June. https://doi.org/10.1371/journal.pone.0020804.

[21] K. Maruhashi, H. Park, R. Yamaguchi *et al.* (2020). Linear tensor projection revealing nonlinearity. *CoRR, abs/2007.03912.* https://arxiv.org/abs/2007.03912.

[22] K. Maruhashi, M. Todoriki, T. Ohwa *et al.* (2018). Learning multi-way relations via tensor decomposition with neural networks. In S. A. McIlraith and K. Q. Weinberger (eds.), *Proceedings of the Thirty-Second AAAI Conference on Artificial Intelligence, (AAAI-18), the 30th innovative Applications of Artificial Intelligence (IAAI-18), and the 8th AAAI Symposium on Educational Advances in Artificial Intelligence (EAAI-18), New Orleans, Louisiana, USA, February 2–7, 2018*, AAAI Press, pp. 3770–3777.

[23] H. Iwashita, T. Takagi, H. Suzuki *et al.* (2020). Efficient constrained pattern mining using dynamic item ordering for explainable classification. *CoRR, abs/2004.08015.* https://arxiv.org/abs/2004.08015.

[24] Fujitsu and Tokyo medical and dental university leverage world's fastest supercomputer and AI technology for scientific discovery to shed light on drug resistance in cancer treatment. (2022). https://www.fujitsu.com/global/about/resources/news/press-releases/2022/0307-01.html.

[25] S. Kasamatsu, Y. Motoyama, K. Yoshimi *et al.* (2020). Enabling ab initio configurational sampling of multicomponent solids with long-range interactions using neural network potentials and active learning. https://arxiv.org/abs/2008.02572.

[26] R. Nagai, R. Akashi, and O. Sugino (2020). Completing density functional theory by machine learning hidden messages from molecules. *NPJ Computational Materials*, 6, 43, March. https://doi.org/10.1038/s41524-020-0310-0.

[27] R. Nagai, R. Akashi, and O. Sugino (2022). Machine-learning-based exchange correlation functional with physical asymptotic constraints. *Physical Review Research*, 4, 013106, February. https://link.aps.org/doi/10.1103/PhysRevResearch.4.013106.

[28] K. Ando, K. Onishi, R. Bale *et al.* (2021). Nonlinear mode decomposition and reduced-order modeling for three-dimensional cylinder flow by distributed learning on fugaku. In H. Jagode, H. Anzt, H. Ltaief and P. Luszczek (eds.), *High Performance Computing.* Cham: Springer International Publishing, pp. 122–137.

[29] T. Murata, K. Fukami, and K. Fukagata (2020). Nonlinear mode decomposition with convolutional neural networks for fluid dynamics. *Journal of Fluid Mechanics*, 882, A13.

[30] M. A. Hariansyah and K. Shimoyama (2021). On the use of a multilayer perceptron as an aerodynamic performance approximator in multi-objective transonic airfoil shape optimization. In *Proceedings of the 18th International Conference on Flow Dynamics*, pp. 754–763.

[31] Y. Inaba, S. Date, M. A. Hariansyah *et al.* (2021). Optimization of structural layout for composite aircraft wings. In *Proceedings of the 18th International Conference on Flow Dynamics*, pp. 793–795.

[32] K. Hirashima, K. Moriwaki, M. S. Fujii *et al.* (2022). Predicting the expansion of supernova shells for high-resolution galaxy simulations using deep learning. *Journal of Physics: Conference Series, 2207*(1), 012050, March. https://doi.org/10.1088/1742-6596/2207/1/012050.

[33] Y. Nomura, A. S. Darmawan, Y. Yamaji *et al.* (2017). Restricted Boltzmann machine learning for solving strongly correlated quantum systems. *Physical Review B, 96*, 205152, November.

[34] Y. Nomura and M. Imada (2021). Dirac-type nodal spin liquid revealed by refined quantum many-body solver using neural-network wave function, correlation ratio, and level spectroscopy. *Physical Review X, 11*, 031034, August.

[35] Y. Yamaji, T. Yoshida, A. Fujimori *et al.* (2021). Hidden self-energies as origin of cuprate superconductivity revealed by machine learning. *Physical Review Research, 3*, 043099, November 2021. https://gateway2.itc.u-tokyo. ac.jp/,DanaInfo=link.aps.org,SSL+doi/10.1103/PhysRevResearch.3.043099.

[36] R. Roy, K. Sato, S. Bhattachrya *et al.* (2021). Compression of time evolutionary image data through predictive deep neural networks. In *2021 IEEE/ACM 21st International Symposium on Cluster, Cloud and Internet Computing (CCGrid)*, pp. 41–50.

[37] T. Shirakawa, H. Ueda, and S. Yunoki (2021). Automatic quantum circuit encoding of a given arbitrary quantum state. *arXiv e-prints, arXiv:2112.14524*, December.

[38] J. Domke, E. Vatai, A. Drozd *et al.* (2021). Matrix engines for high performance computing: A paragon of performance or grasping at straws? In *2021 IEEE International Parallel and Distributed Processing Symposium, IPDPS 2021, Portland, Oregon, USA, 17–21 May 2021*, Portland, Oregon, USA, May, p. 10.

© 2023 World Scientific Publishing Company

https://doi.org/10.1142/9789811265679_0010

Chapter 10

Benchmarking for AI for Science

Jeyan Thiyagalingam*,¶, Mallikarjun Shankar†,‖,
Geoffrey Fox‡,**, and Tony Hey§,††

*Science and Technology Facilities Council, Rutherford Appleton
Laboratory, Harwell Campus, Ditcot, United Kingdom
†Oak Ridge National Laboratory, Oak Ridge, TN, USA
‡Computer Science and Biocomplexity Institute, University of Virginia,
Charlottesville, VA, USA
§Science and Technology Facilities Council, Rutherford Appleton
Laboratory, Harwell Campus, Didcot, United Kingdom
¶t.jeyan@stfc.ac.uk
‖shankarm@ornl.gov
**gcfexchange@gmail.com
††tony.hey@stfc.ac.uk

1. Introduction

The growth of Deep Learning (DL) within the broader field of Machine Learning (ML) in the last two decades has offered exciting possibilities for addressing a number of problems that have traditionally been associated with human intelligence, such as vision and natural language understanding. As such, these methodologies are finding applications in a wide variety of domains. Scientists and practitioners are rapidly expanding their areas where DL-based methodologies have offered several early successes, such as image processing and applications in high-resolution 2D and 3D data analysis. In addition to these early successes, DL-based techniques have also had a profound impact on finding innovative ways to tackle a number of grand challenges, including protein folding [1], improving the modeling of time evolution of a chemical system using molecular dynamics with machine learning-analyzed force fields [2], and in large language models (LLM) [3] that change the way we analyze and interpolate behaviors of complex systems.

While various ML techniques have been transformational in addressing a number of scientific problems, the measure of their success or suitability for various problems is still a dark art and mainly remains unmapped. This, indirectly, impedes scientific discoveries, whose central purpose is to develop an accepted understanding of the underlying structure in natural phenomena and behaviors of interest, which often requires identifying parsimonious and explainable principles and representations of the natural world so that the findings can be applied more broadly and continually validated by observations.

Thus, developing the notion of Benchmarking for AI for Science, a coherent method for comparing different ML/DL and AI for science algorithms and models against each other, is vital to accelerate the progress of AI-powered scientific discoveries. However, there are a number of challenges to overcome:

1. **Science Focus:** Conventional notions of benchmarking, particularly in computer science, are often considered to be time-performance-driven. As such, the goals have been focused on throughput and timing measurements. Examples include the number of floating point operations that can be performed in a second by an algorithm (floating point operations per second or FLOPs) and the number of outputs that can be produced by an algorithm every second. This notion has also been extended to subsystems, such as to measure interconnection performance (bandwidth or latency) or the number of bytes that can be read off a disk every second. In other words, the crucial metric of evaluation of these conventional benchmarks is time or a function of time. While this has been and is largely useful to measure the time responsiveness of algorithms, including that of machine learning algorithms (training and inference times), they do not measure the scientific merits of ML algorithms. This is acceptable when numerical performance (or numerical accuracies), which is often central to any algorithm, is considered to be fixed and uncompromisable. However, this may not be optimal, especially with different scientific challenges having different metrics for their success. Time-bound performance measurements may not capture the science focus very well. Instead, there is a need for AI benchmarking that maps different ML algorithms, a range of scientific problems, and their scientific merits.

2. **Taxonomy and Organization:** With several hundred (if not thousands) of ML/DL models and their variants, and with thousands of

domain-specific problems, assorted collections of science-focused benchmarks may soon become unusable and unintelligible. Ideally, benchmarks should serve as a blueprint for AI practitioners and scientists so that there are lessons for all concerned. This not only requires an acceptable level of taxonomy around these benchmarks so that relevant science cases are easily locatable but also careful organization of these (potentially overlapping) groups of benchmarks.

3. **Curation and Distribution:** These science-focused benchmarks, as highlighted in [4], will inherently rely on datasets and reference implementation(s) (which is an implementation of the solution to the scientific problem in question), often packaged as a suite. As such, the simple "download-and-fire" model does not work with a suite of benchmarks where datasets may have a considerable storage footprint. For public consumption, the suite, containing datasets, reference implementation(s), and even upcoming solutions must be maintained, curated, and distributed in a manner that is pragmatic.

4. **Evaluation Settings:** Results from a suite of benchmarks will not be credible unless they are obtained under controlled settings. As highlighted in [4], an evaluation framework is often essential for facilitating fair evaluation of these benchmarks.

5. **Cataloging of Results:** Although taxonomy and organization of benchmarks are crucial for facilitating the blueprinting agenda, the ultimate metric for scientists and practitioners is the relative benefit(s) of different ML algorithms for a given type of problem or family of problems. This relative measure is often provided by the science or performance metric (or the former normalized by the latter). This is likely to be served by a leader-board-like mechanism similar to traditional benchmarking pursuits.

6. **Staying Relevant:** Benchmarking for AI for Science must remain relevant to the conventional benchmarking community, where performance is the ultimate metric. The new initiative of Benchmarking for AI for Science must encompass performance as one of the auxiliary metrics to succeed.

There are several recent efforts around building AI Benchmarking [5–10]. While the majority of these are performance-focused, some of them attempt to look into the aspects of Benchmarking for AI for Science, namely Maelstrom [6], WeatherBench [7], and AI500 [10]. However, it is difficult to find a single effort that addresses all the challenges we outlined above. While traditional benchmarking aims to assess the performance of a system either with metrics such as raw performance or energy efficiency (see the Top500 efforts for High-Performance LINPACK or Green500 [11]), a growing class of benchmarks drive ML and AI performance and algorithmic innovation. The MLCommons effort has a benchmarking component including system performance and HPC considerations [12] and the Science working group [13] whose goals are most aligned with the objective of driving AI to enable Science. Mixed-precision application performance is assessed by the HPL-AI benchmark [14] which aims to understand the capability of systems to support the AI-oriented mixed-precision computational approach. Competition-style benchmarks [15,16] and goal or task-oriented benchmarks [17]** drive significant methodological innovation and the outcomes will then be precursors for use in scientific campaigns. In [4], a systematic assessment is conducted of benchmarking approaches, and we encourage the readers to consult that article for more detailed discussion and reviews around such initiatives.

In this chapter, we take one step further by discussing the broader set of issues around Benchmarking for AI for Science. The rest of this chapter is organized as follows: In Section 2, we discuss the role of AI in Science. With this section providing a broader context of the problem in line with the challenges we have outlined above, we then discuss how the overarching set of challenges can be addressed by the AI for Science community and potential benefits thereof in Section 4. We then conclude the chapter with key observations and directions for further research into this area in Section 5.

2. Role of AI in Science

To understand the implications of benchmarking the applicability of AI in facilitating scientific discovery, we make a distinction between the fundamental differences in the approach used by today's AI methodologies and that employed in science. The use of compact and generalizable representations of natural phenomena is the core building block of the scientific discovery process. In a scientific campaign, we aim to understand phenomena and describe them using the best of our understanding of relationships and rules stated in the language of mathematics. Validation of the relationships and rules with additional observational experiments gives us greater confidence that we have identified the underlying principles accurately. To focus on the role of AI in science campaigns, we differentiate between the discovery of parsimonious representations and their "forward applications" and AI-based approaches, and how and where they may apply within the campaign. The points of appearance and impact of AI methods within science are thus of interest and set the context for Benchmarking for AI for Science.

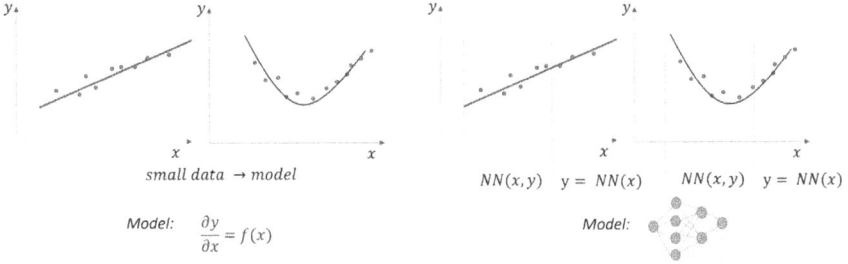

Fig. 1. Simplified view of the building block model in science and AI.

2.1. *Building blocks of scientific discovery and ML/DL models*

We illustrate the difference between scientific campaign formulation and AI-driven approaches by considering a rudimentary building block model of a subsystem, which characterizes data points on a two-dimensional plane. The scientific formulation of the building block model may represent the observed relationship in an elementary closed-form formula shown on the left of Figure 1, often making certain smoothness assumptions (or with defined statistical uncertainty). The ML/DL or AI model, shown on the right of Figure 1, in contrast, typically builds a "representation" of the data for interpolation purposes. Both approaches make certain assumptions about the distribution of the data.

The use and application of the two approaches, though, differ significantly. The building block science model is coupled with other building blocks to describe (i.e., model) complex systems in a predictive sense. Contemporary AI models, instead, target data-oriented interpolation. From the origins of ML (e.g., statistics) as well as the early AI techniques foreshadowing the methods in use today (such as learning with neural networks [18,19] and the Adaptive Linear Element model), the basic models to "learn" create the representation of the data relationships in the form of compositions of nonlinear mathematical operators. Deep neural networks (DNNs) over the ensuing four decades became powerful distributed representations [20] of the data. The DNNs in supervised mode are trained on a particular data domain, creating relationships in the form of the DNN representation $NN(x, y)$ on the right of Figure 1, and then the model operates in inference mode for new input data in the region $y = NN(x)$. The neural network may thus be thought of as an operator to convert system state to other representations. For classification, the operator would produce a category, for regression of a time series, it would classify (or produce) the next event, and so on. The scientific model accomplishes the same effect: converting the state to the resulting next state due to endogenous changes or exogenous inputs — the effects of which are captured by the basic building block models.

In computational science-driven discovery campaigns, building blocks representing component models may be assembled according to progressively broader accepted and understood principles into a complex set of dependencies — forming a larger model of the phenomena to be studied. These larger models may often not be "solved" by closed-form solutions or approximations but instead need large-scale simulations to execute the models. Figure 2 describes this structure in a grand challenge problem area: predicting weather and climate patterns.

This example of weather and climate science modeling and the use of AI is one of several called out in the U.S. Department of Energy AI for Science report [21]. Applications of AI methods for the Earth, environment, and climate research are growing rapidly as AI can enable optimization, data assimilation, data generation, clustering and dimensionality reduction, surrogate creation (and model emulation), and digital twin processing to alleviate the challenges of executing large interdependent models efficiently. AI, thus, operates in the interstices of the scientific models of today. These large complex models generate datasets which can be analyzed with AI methods to compare with observed data and validate the predictions obtained from the theoretical coupling of these models and their execution at higher and higher resolutions. Hybrid approaches that use the physics models together with AI modules interleaved are becoming the future of significant scientific discovery campaigns.

Traditional machine learning and algorithmic methods, including those employing sampling and probabilistic techniques, have offered performance bounds that may be used in quantifying the uncertainty and statistical variation in the outcomes. Current AI methods have gained tremendous success while operating in such a regime of estimation and model approximation. The bounds for properties, such as convergence and how it may depend on the distribution of the data, structure of the network, and associated hyperparameters, are only just being discovered [22]. The applicability of AI with insufficient guidelines and foundational recommendations for its use is one driver to develop robust procedures for Benchmarking for AI for Science. In the rest of this section, we highlight the design patterns for the use of AI in scientific campaigns and motivate our approach for Benchmarking for AI for Science.

2.2. Design patterns for AI in scientific campaigns

We list three example design patterns for the role of AI within scientific campaigns that offer context to benchmark the AI methods used for

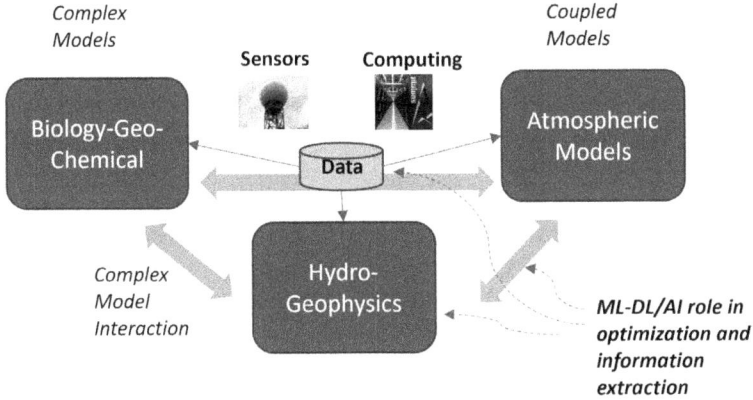

Fig. 2. Interacting models using observational data and computational modeling.

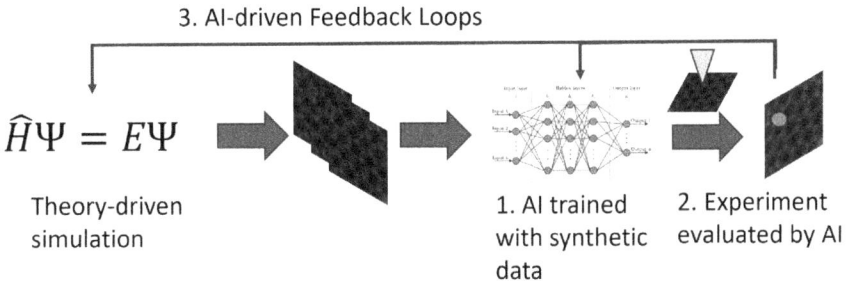

Fig. 3. AI training and automation with simulated scientific data.

scientific objectives. These design patterns represent versions of a generalized interleaving of the use of AI within expressions of first principles models — the physics of systems — to enable the improved understanding of a natural phenomenon.

2.2.1. *Simulation to generate data for training and use in inference*

An emerging design pattern in science is to help develop AI models with simulated data to, in turn, create models that can effectively classify observed behaviors during an experiment. These approaches are being employed in electron microscopy to help probe materials' structural parameters at atomic-scale (angstrom-scale) precision [23].

Figure 3 illustrates the workflow employed in these experiments. While machine learning analysis of the observed data can reveal specific properties of observational data, to employ deep learning effectively, the AI model must train on a significantly larger dataset. Here, the scientific model (typically, parsimoniously expressed) is computationally simulated to generate large amounts of data in the form of 2D and higher-dimensional structures that are used to train a convolutional neural network (CNN) which is highly effective for image analysis. The CNN can then rapidly process and categorize observational data from materials which would be significantly harder with traditional ML approaches. The AI model's classification performance and identification of expected variations in the material (such as defects) may be fed back into the theoretical model for further improvement of this feedback loop.

Extensions of this feedback loop to automate the microscope itself are further connecting the use of AI within the end-to-end feedback loop of scientific discovery [24].

2.2.2. Surrogate models to accelerate computational exploration

Another developing mode of integrating the power of AI methods within scientific campaigns is in their use as surrogates in large-scale simulation campaigns. For example, Monte Carlo simulations in quantum physics, nuclear physics, and materials science require targeted function evaluations (such as the energy potentials of a configuration of atoms) which may take significant time even for small systems of hundreds of atoms. Training an AI surrogate on detailed simulation models can give us a resulting model that can be extended to effectively "short-circuit" computationally intensive operations within larger campaigns.

This central idea may also be applied to digital twin scientific simulations. The digital representation of a scientific campaign (i.e., one with *a priori* known constituent models but with high complexity when put together with other models) can be simplified with surrogates that can take the place of computationally expensive models. The training time involved to achieve suitable accuracy of the AI model is trade-off that can influence the effectiveness of the use of the AI surrogate in the scientific campaign.

2.2.3. Generative models to augment contextual information

A powerful use of AI models trained on a certain domain data distribution is to use the AI models to generate data. This is complementary to the use of theory-based simulation data generation. Here, the AI emulates datasets that do not have explicit or obvious underlying first principles structures — such as images (n-dimensional) and sequences (e.g., signals and textual streams). These generative datasets may hold predictive value such as the use of transformers to generate the next state of the system.

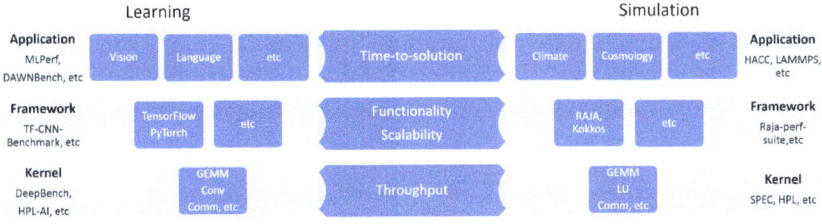

Fig. 4. Equivalences in the AI and Mod-Sim stacks (figure reproduced from [25]).

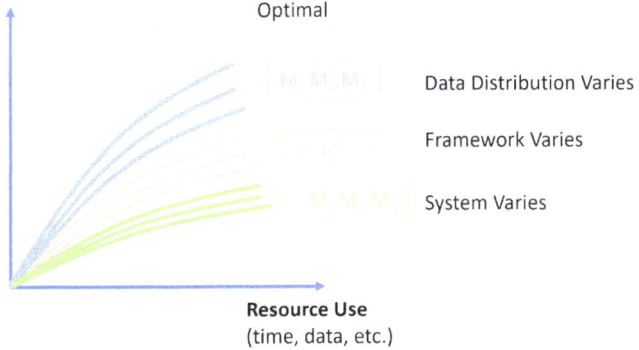

Fig. 5. AI Benchmarking dimensions.

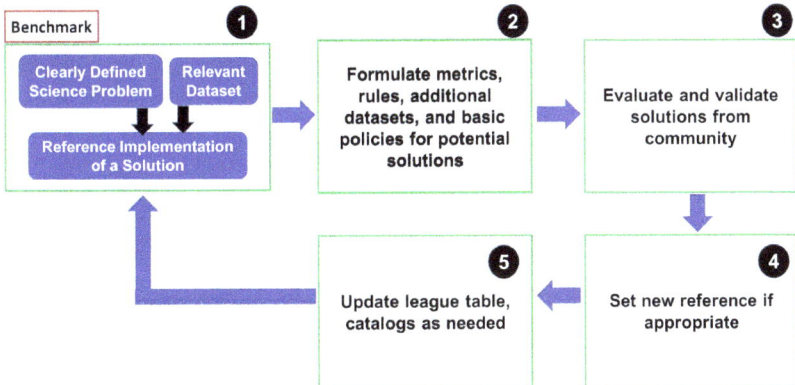

Fig. 6. A possible approach to implementing Benchmarking for AI for Science by working with the community.

Typically, these generative models may be used to fill in missing data, create enhanced representations of systems (e.g., in digital twins), and enable speculative exploration campaigns that may help steer a computational campaign.

2.3. Benchmarking for AI for scientific campaigns

Conventional notions of AI benchmarking measure performance of a system component, or of software or a particular method. These are typically quantified in the form of operations per second, throughput, latency, etc. Current benchmarking of AI systems and software also focuses on the effectiveness of the underlying hardware, software frameworks, and applications. Figure 4 shows parallels between the learning systems and the simulation (i.e., computational science) stacks with applications on top, relying on frameworks, and ultimately running on hardware operations at the lowest layer.

We argue that Benchmarking for AI for Science takes on a different form of work because of the differences in effectiveness of the AI methods and models themselves, and the wide range of hyper-parameter choices available to adapt the AI technique to the problem at hand. In addition, the choice of the AI method and its effectiveness to advance science may depend on the scientific domain's underlying assumptions and data of interest. This makes Benchmarking for AI for Science a question of improvement of methods and applicability for the nature of the scientific discovery, and less on system characteristics such as throughput (say, of images per second processed by a DL CNN model). Benchmarking for AI for Science must thus emphasize how well the scientific campaign is enabled by the AI technique at hand.

Established benchmark metrics to evaluate the performance of AI techniques include improving well-known statistics and machine learning metrics, such as classification accuracy, precision, recall, associated F1 scores, and receiver operating characteristic curves. However, as observed in Section 2.1, the patterns of use of AI are more varied than narrowly analyzing a set of data. For example, the use of AI as surrogates within a campaign depends not just on the accuracy of the trained model but on the trade-off in the time required for training and effectiveness of the surrogate — the time gained without losing resulting correctness — within the end-to-end campaign. The effectiveness of the same AI model may depend on the data regime it operates within — either in the context of training on simulation data (as in Section 2.2.1) or generating data through a GAN (as in Section 2.2.2).

The underlying hardware also determines the effectiveness of the AI method used. Today's GPU accelerators can execute matrix multiple operations for DL at much greater speeds than CPUs. A graph engine in the system architecture [26] may enable linked learning structures, thus providing better time to solution for one algorithm as compared to another. Note that while a graph neural network executing on a graph engine may not provide greater FLOPS as a platform, it may perform better in terms of supporting a graph-based AI method for the campaign. A similar argument applies to the software framework being used. In benchmarking methodologies, ideally, we keep all components in the comparison operation fixed while measuring the target metric while varying the one (or few) quantities under study. For Benchmarking for AI for Science, the variability of the AI techniques and their applicability requires us to constrain the nature of comparisons we should make. Figure 5 illustrates the broad scope that Benchmarking for AI for Science affords us. The M_1, M_2, and M_3 curves represent three AI models and methods that perform differently for the AI target metric of interest (the y-axis) depending on the campaign characteristics be it the underlying system, the software framework, the data distribution, etc.

In the next section, we discuss an approach to set up AI Benchmarks for science that aims to streamline how we may accomplish Benchmarking for AI for Science.

3. Approaches and Benefits

As highlighted in Section 2, AI can play a significant role in advancing the discovery process of various scientific problems. However, such a transition is unlikely to be made by a scientist or group of scientists alone. Instead, the overall solution is likely to be developed by a team of experts with differing sets of skills, covering domain-specific knowledge, machine learning, signal processing, mathematical optimization, statistics, Bayesian statistics, and research software engineering. To a certain extent, data science covers a number of these cross-cutting areas. Such a collaborative approach for developing unique solutions is not new for the scientific communities as has been demonstrated through various eScience projects [27]. However, it takes a considerable amount of time not only to develop such complex solutions from inception but also to settle for what is considered to be the best available solution.

3.1. *Structured approach for AI for Science Benchmarking advances*

The Benchmarking approach we outline here aims to bring together a community of people trying to address the challenge in return for the credit in addressing an important problem, academic dissemination, or securing an improved rank in the list of solutions outperforming what is considered a baseline solution. A coherent approach combining the scientific objective, AI methods of interest, and underlying system infrastructure is vital to ensure this approach succeeds. Using community-contributed competitions is not a new approach for finding the best possible solutions, such as in Kaggle competitions [15]. However, in our context, that of Benchmarking for AI for Science, it requires a set of carefully designed processes and a well-regulated flow of control among these processes. We depict our approach in Figure 6.

The AI for Science benchmark is made of two components: a reference implementation operating on a dataset and addressing a clearly defined scientific problem. This benchmark is then released to the community along with a basic set of rules and policies that the community must adhere to when producing solutions that can outperform the reference implementation. However, our interest is very much on science rather than system performance, the expectations from the community are more for methodological innovation driving to systematic improvements (even in aspects such as hyper-parameter tuning or model search). The policies may also include additional constraints, such as specifying which part of the reference implementation can be enhanced, whether a new solution can capture the whole end-to-end pipeline and the like. The community may also be given permission to use additional datasets, wherever possible. In a majority of the cases, if there is a framework, such as in SciMLBench [4,5], the framework itself will handle a number of these issues. The reported solutions have often to be peer reviewed, predominantly by the benchmark maintainers or problem originators. If the proposed solution outperforms the current reference implementation, the reference implementation will change to the new solution. This will entail updating of the performance table and catalog of techniques maintained in the benchmark database. Additionally, performance results of different solutions can also be compared against each other, and such evaluations can be automated, using containerized solutions, across a range of architectures.

There are several benefits to the community through this approach, including the following:

(1) The community has access to a wide range of solutions to a given type of problem. Although no two domains share the same problem, in a majority of the cases, techniques may be transferable.
(2) There is a healthy competition within the community that promotes the use of best techniques to stay relevant.
(3) With performance results reported as a secondary metric, the initiative is not distanced from the conventional benchmarking community.

As such, hardware vendors will be able to identify a number of use cases to focus on particular subsystems.

(4) This will provide a rich landscape of a mixed set of problems that leverages a variety of ML techniques and hence becomes a potential utility for testing various ML frameworks, platforms, and workflow models.

(5) The benchmark suite, problems, and solutions can easily serve as a learning platform for AI enthusiasts and practitioners.

(6) This is likely to encourage collaborations between disparate communities, such as signal processing and natural language processing.

These benefits are just a beginning or part of a larger set of benefits yet to be seen by the AI for Science community.

3.2. *Progress in AI for Science Benchmarks*

In recent months, the MLCommons Science working group and other research teams have come together to develop benchmarks with an approach as recommended above. The working group has created four science benchmarks with the characteristics discussed in Figure 6. These benchmarks have been described and published [28] and address the following four science domains with associated goals discussed in brief in the following:

- Cloud Mask — Develop a segmentation model for classifying the pixels in satellite images determining whether the given pixel belongs to a cloud or to a clear sky. The scope of the cloud-mask benchmark is to explore whether ML-driven algorithms can outperform or replace traditional Bayesian techniques.
- STEMDL — Provide a universal classifier for space group of solid-state materials and perform reconstruction of local electron density. Instead of relying on expensive simulations, the objective is to explore how ML/DL algorithms could perform advanced analysis of Convergent Beam Electron Diffraction.
- UNO — Predict tumor response to single and paired drugs, based on molecular features of tumor cells across multiple data sources. The ML component aims to predict the drug response values.
- Time Series Evolution Operator — Extract the evolution of a time series, exemplified using earthquake forecasting. The aim is to use ML not only for extracting the evolution but also to test the effectiveness using forecasting.

The domains here drive somewhat different approaches to address the scientific objective forcing domain-data characteristics with hard-to-label and typically non-human categorizable feature sets to improve the underlying AI methods to advance science.

4. Future Directions

In this chapter, we have introduced the notion of Benchmarking for AI for Science as different from AI Benchmarking of systems. Although the two do overlap, the motivations and potential outcomes are different. More specifically, the AI Benchmarking is purely focused on time-sensitive performance measures, whereas Benchmarking for AI for Science is focused on scientific metrics. However, this is not without challenges, and we have outlined the broader set of challenges we face as we embark on this endeavor. We have also presented design patterns in which scientific campaigns employ AI. These design patterns are a part of a larger and broader set of areas within which the AI for Science community is finding use for AI. We have also outlined potential approaches we can adopt for accelerating the pace at which we facilitate Benchmarking for AI for Science and hence accelerating the pace of obtaining scientific discoveries through the application of AI. We discuss the direct benefits of the Benchmarking for AI for Science initiative to the AI for Science practitioner community as well as to technology providers.

There are, however, a number of issues still to be addressed for this endeavor to be successful. Maintaining and sustaining a rich list of functional benchmarks over a period of time is a challenging task, demanding substantial investments and resources, which are impossible to meet without communities coming together with their efforts. These efforts can begin with a simple contribution of a problem or dataset to evaluating these benchmarks on a variety of hardware platforms. With frameworks like SciMLBench or MLCommons WG Benchmarks [13], we believe we will be able to convince the different communities and industries to work together for making a true impact on science.

Acknowledgments

This work was supported by Wave 1 of the UKRI Strategic Priorities Fund under the EPSRC grant EP/T001569/1, particularly the "AI for Science" theme within that grant, by the Alan Turing Institute, and by the Benchmarking for AI for Science at Exascale (BASE) project under the EPSRC grant EP/V001310/1, along with the Facilities Funding from Science and Technology Facilities Council (STFC) of UKRI, NSF Grants 2204115 and 2210266, and DOE Award DE-SC0021418. This manuscript has been jointly authored by UT-Battelle, LLC under Contract No. DE-AC05-00OR22725 with the U.S. Department of Energy. This research also used resources from the Oak Ridge Computing Facilities, which are DOE Office of Science user facilities, supported under contract DE-AC05-00OR22725, and from the PEARL AI resource at the RAL, STFC.

References

[1] J. Jumper, R. Evans, A. Pritzel *et al.* (2021). Highly accurate protein structure prediction with AlphaFold. *Nature*, *596*, 583–589. https://doi.org/10.1038/s41586-021-03819-2.

[2] H. Wang, L. Zhang, J. Han *et al.* (2018). DeePMD-kit: A deep learning package for many-body potential energy representation and molecular dynamics. *Computer Physics Communications*, *228*, 178–184. https://doi.org/10.1016/j.cpc.2018.03.016.

[3] T. B. Brown, B. Mann, N. Ryder *et al.* (2020). Language models are few-shot learners, Arxiv. https://doi.org/10.48550/arXiv.2005.14165.

[4] J. Thiyagalingam, M. Shankar, G. Fox *et al.* (2022). Scientific machine learning benchmarks. *Nature Reviews Physics*, *4*, 413–420. https://doi.org/10.1038/s42254-022-00441-7.

[5] J. Thiyagalingam, K. Leng, S. Jackson *et al.* (2021). SciMLBench: A benchmarking suite for AI for science. https://github.com/stfc-sciml/sciml-bench.

[6] The MAELSTROM Project. https://www.maelstrom-eurohpc.eu/.

[7] S. Rasp, P. D. Dueben, S. Scher *et al.* (2020). WeatherBench: A benchmark data set for data-driven weather forecasting. *Journal of Advances in Modeling Earth Systems*, *12*(11), e2020MS002203.

[8] C. Coleman, D. Narayanan, D. Kang *et al.* (2017). DAWNBench: An end-to-end deep learning benchmark and competition. https://dawn.cs.stanford.edu/benchmark/.

[9] T. Ben-Nun, M. Besta, S. Huber *et al.* (2019). A modular benchmarking infrastructure for high-performance and reproducible deep learning. In *2019 IEEE International Parallel and Distributed Processing Symposium (IPDPS)*, pp. 66–77. https://doi.org/10.1109/IPDPS.2019.00018.

[10] Z. Jiang, W. Gao, F. Tang *et al.* (2021). HPC AI500 V2.0: The methodology, tools, and metrics for benchmarking HPC AI systems. In *2021 IEEE International Conference on Cluster Computing (CLUSTER)*, Portland OR, USA, pp. 47–58. https://doi.org/10.1109/Cluster48925.2021.00022.

[11] https://www.top500.org/project/linpack/; https://www.top500.org/lists/green500/.

[12] https://mlcommons.org/en/groups/training-hpc/.

[13] MLCommons Science Working Group. https://mlcommons.org/en/groups/research-science/.

[14] https://hpl-ai.org/.

[15] Kaggle Competitions. https://www.kaggle.com/.

[16] Billion-scale approximate nearest neighbor search challenge. https://big-ann-benchmarks.com/.

[17] Beyond the Imitation Game: Quantifying and extrapolating the capabilities of language models. https://arxiv.org/abs/2206.04615; https://github.com/google/BIG-bench.

[18] W. S. Mcculloch and W. Pitts (1943). A logical calculus of the ideas immanent in nervous activity. *Bulletin of Mathematical Biophysics*, *5*, 115–133.

[19] F. Rosenblatt (1958). The perceptron: A probabilistic model for information storage and organization in the brain. *Psychological Review*, *65*(6), 386–408.

[20] D. Rumelhart, G. Hinton, and R. Williams (1986). Learning representations by back-propagating errors. *Nature*, *323*, 533–536. https://doi.org/10.1038/323533a0.

[21] R. Stevens, V. Taylor, J. Nichols *et al.* (2020). AI for Science: Report on the Department of Energy (DOE) Town Halls on Artificial Intelligence (AI) for Science. United States: N.p. Web. https://doi.org/10.2172/1604756.

[22] M. Jordan (2019). Artificial intelligence: The revolution hasn't happened yet. https://hdsr.mitpress.mit.edu/pub/wot7mkc1/release/10.

[23] M. P. Oxley, J. Yin, N. Borodinov *et al.* (2020). Deep learning of interface structures from simulated 4D STEM data: Cation intermixing vs. roughening. *Machine Learning: Science and Technology*, *1*, 04LT01.

[24] S. V. Kalinin, M. Ziatdinov, J. Hinkle *et al.* (2021). Automated and autonomous experiments in electron and scanning probe microscopy. *ACS Nano*, *15*(8), 12604–12627. https://doi.org/10.1021/acsnano.1c02104.

[25] J. Yin, A. Tsaris, S. Dash *et al.* (2021). Comparative evaluation of deep learning workload for leadership-class systems. *BenchCouncil Transactions on Benchmarks, Standards and Evaluations*, *1*(1), https://doi.org/10.1016/j.tbench.2021.100005.

[26] GNNerator: A hardware/software framework for accelerating graph neural networks. *arXiv:2103.10836*.

[27] T. Hey, S. Tansley, and K. Tolle *et al.* (2009). *The Fourth Paradigm: Data-Intensive Scientific Discovery*. Microsoft Research. https://www.microsoft.com/en-us/research/publication/fourth-paradigm-data-intensive-scientific-discovery/.

[28] J. Thiyagalingam *et al.* (2022). AI Benchmarking for Science: Efforts from the MLCommons Science Working Group. *ISC 2022, Workshop on HPC on Heterogeneous Hardware (H3)* — to appear in Springer LNCS.

Part C. Exploring Application Domains

ALMA astronomical interferometer in Chile with the Milky Way galaxy. Photographer credit: Sangku Kim/ESO. *Licensed under a Creative Commons Attribution 4.0 International License.*

Astronomy and Cosmology

© 2023 World Scientific Publishing Company
https://doi.org/10.1142/9789811265679_0011

Chapter 11

Radio Astronomy and the Square Kilometre Array

Anna Scaife

*Jodrell Bank Centre for Astrophysics, University of Manchester,
Manchester, UK*
anna.scaife@manchester.ac.uk

1. Modern Radio Astronomy and the Square Kilometre Array

In March 2019, representatives from seven different countries came together in Rome to sign a treaty convention that would bring into being the world's largest radio observatory: the Square Kilometre Array (SKA). In doing so, the international partners of the SKA project recognized not only the key scientific drivers that underpinned the design of the observatory but also the potential of astronomy for driving technological development and innovation. Ratified the following year, the SKA treaty created the first intergovernmental organization for radio astronomy and marked the formal creation of one of the world's largest scientific facilities.

The scientific drivers for the SKA span a wide range of key topics in modern astrophysics and in order to condense these science cases into technical requirements for the observatory, a prioritization exercise was carried out by the international radio astronomy community. One of the most prominent themes that emerged from this review was an ambition to detect and, furthermore, to *map* a period of cosmic history known as the Epoch of Reionization (EOR; [24]). The EoR represents the point in cosmic evolution when the very first stars and galaxies were born, emerging out of a dark Universe filled with almost nothing but neutral hydrogen. By mapping changes in the neutral hydrogen spectral emission line, the SKA will be able to determine exactly how and when these events took place, revolutionizing our understanding of how the Universe around us today was formed.

Another key science driver for the SKA is to test Einstein's theory of general relativity, which predicted the existence of gravitational waves propagating in space-time as a result of the motion or collapse of very massive objects. By very accurately measuring the regular radio pulses from a network of neutron stars known as pulsars, the SKA will be sensitive to gravitational waves at frequencies of nanohertz (nHz; [23]), which result from much more massive astrophysical events than those seen by Advanced LIGO (~100 Hz) or the European Space Agency spacecraft LISA (~mHz).

There is no space on these pages to explore the full science case for the SKA in detail, but in brief, it will significantly impact a broad range of open questions in modern astrophysics. These include understanding how galaxies form and evolve, how the first magnetic fields were generated, and of course, are we alone in the Universe. However, it is also of crucial importance to remember that with each new generation of astronomical observatory, it is not necessarily the manner in which they advance our current scientific understanding that becomes their most persistent legacy but rather the serendipitous discoveries that are made in the pursuit of that objective. In this era of big science and big data, where extracting scientific impact relies increasingly on algorithms rather than individuals, we must not automate out the potential for discovery.

At the time of writing, there are 15[1] countries involved in the design and construction of the SKA. Together, they will build not one but two telescopes in the first phase of the project. The reason for building two separate instruments lies in the differing technologies required to efficiently measure signals in different parts of the radio spectrum because for the SKA to achieve the scientific goals laid out in its requirements, the observatory needs to measure radio waves with frequencies all the way from the megahertz (MHz) to the gigahertz (GHz) regime.

While political and logistical considerations always play a part in the siting of new scientific facilities, in astronomy, a key element of this decision is also governed by the suitability of the local observing environment. For radio astronomy at SKA frequencies, the primary environmental factor is the density of radio frequency interference (RFI). RFI is a consequence of man-made electronic devices and, as such, its prevalence is strongly correlated with local population density across most of the world. For the SKA, the most suitable telescope locations were determined to be remote Western Australia, around 800 km north of Perth, part of the ancestral lands of the Wajarri Yamaji people, and the Karoo region in the Northern Cape of South Africa, where a substantial radio-quiet astronomy reserve has been created by the national government.

---

[1]Australia, Canada, China, France, Germany, India, Italy, Japan, the Netherlands, Portugal, South Africa, Spain, Sweden, Switzerland, and the UK.

The first of the SKA telescopes will operate at low radio frequencies (50–350 MHz) where radio signals have wavelengths of several meters. The preferred technology for receivers in this band is based on dipole antennas, arranged into groups known as stations and phased electronically to create a steerable reception pattern in the sky. In the first phase of the SKA, the SKA1-LOW telescope, as it will be known, will be comprised of 130,000 dipole antennas grouped into 512 stations, each with a diameter of 65 m. The SKA1-LOW telescope will be sited in Western Australia and its design is primarily driven by the Epoch of Reionization science case, see Figure 1.

The second of the SKA telescopes will operate in the mid-frequency radio band (350 MHz–1.7 GHz) where radio signals have wavelengths from around one meter to tens of centimeters. The technology for the SKA1-MID instrument will look more similar to many people's idea of a radio telescope and use dishes to receive incoming radio signals. This telescope will be sited in South Africa and, when complete, will comprise 197 individual radio dishes separated by distances of up to approximately 200 km, see Figure 2.

In order to create images of the sky, both telescopes will employ a technique known as radio interferometry or, more formally, Earth-rotation aperture synthesis. This technique correlates the signals from arrays of dishes or antennas in order to synthesize an aperture of equivalent size to the largest separation in the array, overcoming the physical limitations of building larger and larger single-dish telescopes. In this way, the resolution of radio telescopes, which in simple terms is governed by the number of wavelengths one can fit across the aperture, is now extremely flexible and can be tailored to a particular science case as part of array design.

To enable the required correlation, the signals from individual dishes in the case of SKA1-MID, and from antenna stations in the case of SKA1-LOW, need to be transported over significant distances to their respective central signal processing facilities in Perth and Cape Town. The data rate at this point in the signal chain is expected to be of order $\sim$10 Tb/s from each telescope. Following correlation, the signals will then be transmitted to a further processing facility, known as the science data processor, in order to be calibrated and for image formation to occur.

At the same time, time-domain signals will also be transported, processed, and calibrated in order to enable non-imaging science cases such as pulsar timing to take place. Together, when the telescopes become fully operational in 2027, it is anticipated that the output data products from the SKA will amount to approximately 300 PB per telescope per year.

2. The Big Data Challenge of the SKA: Why AI is Needed

Like many other fields, radio astronomy has been transformed over the past two decades by the availability of high-time-resolution digitization.

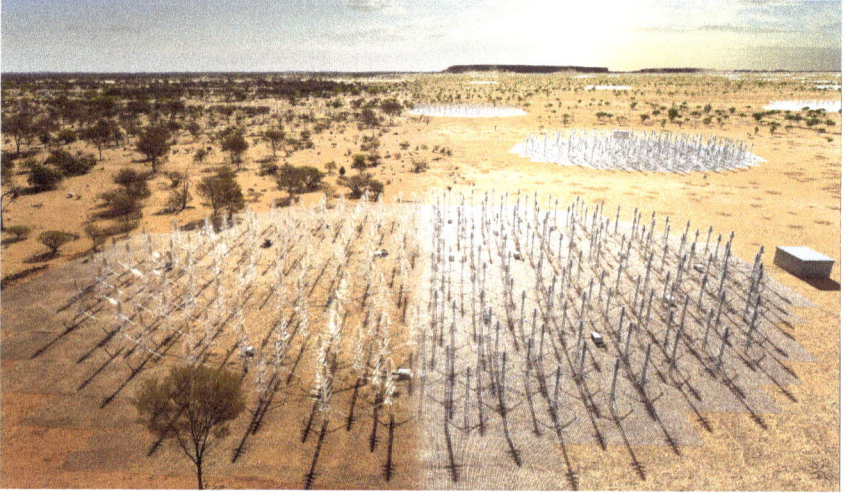

Fig. 1.   A composite image of the SKA-LOW telescope, blending the existing prototype station in Western Australia with an artist's impression of the future SKA-LOW stations. Image credit: SKAO.

Fig. 2.   Composite image of the SKA-MID telescope, blending the existing precursor MeerKAT telescope dishes already on site with an artist's impression of the future SKA dishes. Image credit: SKAO.

For radio astronomy, this has influenced the design and construction of radio telescopes in a number of specific ways. Perhaps, the most significant influence of this change has been to enable signal processing that was historically performed using physical radio-frequency (RF) hardware to be completed in software instead. This has led to substantial increases in spectral resolution and allowed arrays of radio receivers, i.e., radio interferometers, to scale in size in a manner not previously possible due to signal-processing limitations. As a consequence of early-stage digitization, it is now true to say that most modern radio telescopes are *software telescopes*, also benefiting in large part from the improved availability of digital processing technologies such as field-programmable gate arrays (FPGAs) and graphics processing units (GPUs) at different stages of the signal processing chain.

The increased flexibility and sensitivity that these advances have brought to radio astronomy also come with a cost: the data volume of standard astronomical datasets has increased significantly. Twenty years ago, a typical dataset from the Very Large Array (VLA) telescope would have been of order gigabytes in data volume; today, datasets from the upgraded Jansky VLA (JVLA), MeerKAT, or LOFAR telescopes have data volumes of order terabytes; and when the SKA telescope commences science operations later this decade, it will produce individual datasets that are on petabyte scales.

Just as in many other scientific fields, astronomers are learning to adapt to this new normal of big data. In particular, for the SKA, a network of regional data centers around the world are being developed to provide computing and storage so that individual astronomers can remotely access and process their data into final scientific outputs, see Figure 3. Such interventions on a national or regional scale are essential to enable the extraction of scientific impact from the telescope in a timely fashion, as well as allowing participation from as broad a cross-section of the scientific community as possible. However, in addition to the specific computing requirements of such analysis, a paradigm shift in analysis methodologies is also required. This paradigm shift is a consequence not only of the increased data volumes but also of the corresponding sensitivity improvements that those data volumes entail. Where historical radio surveys detected tens to hundreds of astronomical objects per square degree in the sky, the SKA and its precursor instruments will detect thousands to hundreds of thousands of sources in an equivalent area. Consequently, the big data challenge for the SKA is not simply processing the data volume itself but also processing the astronomical information contained *within* that data volume.

Much of modern astrophysics relies on population analysis to constrain physical models, and extracting these different populations from SKA data cubes will therefore be essential for addressing many of the science goals

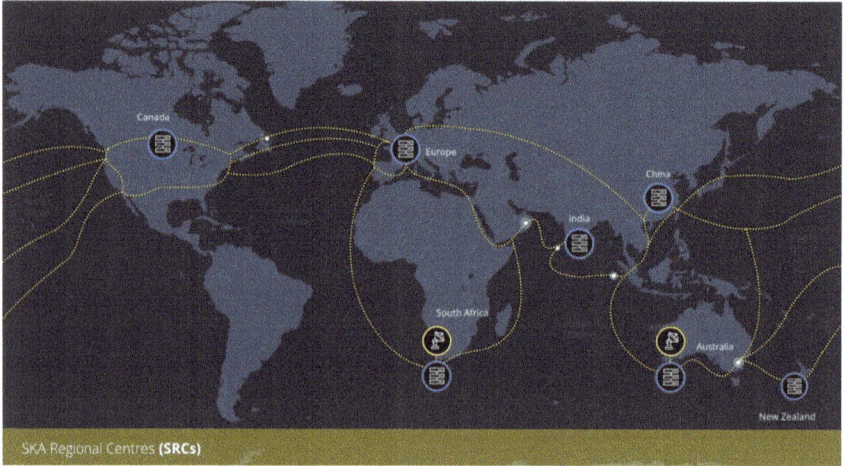

Fig. 3.   The proposed network of SKA Regional Centers will enable astronomers around the world to access data from the two telescopes. Image credit: AENEAS Project with funding from the European Union's Horizon 2020 Research and Innovation Programme under grant agreement 731016.

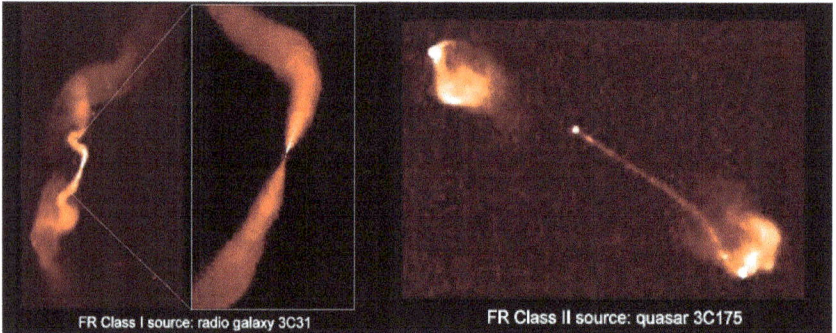

Fig. 4.   The radio galaxies 3C31 and 3C175 show the difference in morphology between the Fanaroff–Riley type I and Fanaroff–Riley type II classifications. Image credit: these images use data obtained with the Very Large Array (VLA) telescope of the National Radio Astronomy Observatory (NRAO) and are reproduced with permission from Alan Bridle's Image Gallery.

that have informed its design and construction. Moreover, given the data volumes associated with SKA data products, it is clear that the use of artificial intelligence will play a key role in identifying these populations; however, such analyses rely on a stringent estimation of bias and uncertainty arising from both intrinsic and observational, i.e., instrumental, selection effects. Therefore, astronomers must also be mindful of the biases and reliability associated with different AI implementations when these are introduced into the experiment.

3. AI for Image Analysis in Radio Astronomy

Unlike many other branches of astronomy that operate photon-based imaging systems, radio astronomy relies on the classical collection of radio waves. As a consequence, radio telescopes do not natively recover images of the sky but rather measure the amount of power inherent in the radio sky brightness distribution as a function of time, frequency, and angular scale. To form images from these data requires additional signal processing that typically relies on a spatial Fourier inversion. Although computationally expensive, for many branches of astrophysics that use radio data, this image formation process is a standard and necessary component of the data processing framework and results in the visualization of high-energy physical processes that would otherwise be invisible to the human eye.

Using AI for the imaging process itself is of increasing interest for the radio astronomy community, with applications now starting to emerge in the literature (e.g., [14,43]). The optimization approaches used to reconstruct images from discrete and inherently under-sampled radio measurements have a natural synergy with those used for training deep-learning models, and recent applications to radio data from SKA precursor telescopes are showing promising results from deep neural network-based approaches in terms of both scalability and performance [48]. Associated with the imaging process is the use of convolutional auto-encoders for denoising radio images in order to recover improved constraints on the identification and quantification of astrophysical structures, particularly with respect to the faint diffuse radio emission which traces the cosmic web of large-scale structure (e.g., [16,17]).

Once radio images are formed, the scientific investigation of their content uses many of the same signal processing techniques more widely applied across the physical sciences and in computer vision applications. And as the number of images from radio telescopes has increased, along with the multiplicity of structure within those images, artificial intelligence is increasingly being leveraged to extract and analyze this information in a timely fashion. Key applications in this area include deep learning approaches to object detection and morphological classification across a range of astrophysical system types. However, morphological classification in astronomy is in many cases rooted in phenomenology rather than an *a priori* physical understanding of astrophysical systems. This is of course a consequence of the nature of astronomy, perhaps the only branch of physics based entirely on inference: it is not possible for astronomers to change the underlying parameters that result in a particular astrophysical phenomenon but rather the nature and quantitative estimation of those parameters can only be inferred through observational measurement of a system beyond their control. More generally for classification, this means that target labels in astronomy do not necessarily align with truly discrete, separable populations but instead represent useful waypoints on a spectrum of morphology underpinned by a continuum of physical processes. Moreover, the subjective nature of historical by-eye labeling introduces additional biases into how these waypoints are defined. It is perhaps partly for these reasons, compounded further by intrinsic and observational selection effects in data collection and labeling, that supervised learning approaches for multiclass classification in radio astronomy are now accompanied by a diverse range of unsupervised and self-supervised approaches that aim to re-evaluate the manner in which we group astrophysical systems, provide a deeper physical understanding from these new ensembles, and identify new or unusual object types (e.g., [36,37]).

3.1. *Case study: Radio galaxy classification*

A canonical example of the use of AI for image-based classification in radio astronomy is that of radio galaxies. Radio galaxies are a form of *active* galaxy, characterized by the presence of large jets or outflows powered by accretion onto a central super-massive black hole. These largely relativistic outflows contain a plasma of ultra-relativistic electrons, accelerated by compressed magnetic fields to produce strong synchrotron emission that is visible in the radio band. Shortly after their discovery in the 1950s, it was identified that these synchrotron radio sources were associated with some of the most massive optical galaxies, which played *host* to the central black hole. Furthermore, the optical properties of those galaxies suggested that a significant fraction was disturbed or undergoing mergers, leading radio astronomers to suppose that the dynamics of these events in some way triggered the activity responsible for the large-scale radio emission. Today, it is possible to detect and image a large number of radio galaxies, in particular, due to the invention of the earth rotation aperture synthesis technique, recognized by the 1974 Nobel Prize in Physics, which allowed radio astronomy to overcome the resolution limitations inherent in long-wavelength observing when using a single antenna. Consequently, population studies have shown that radio galaxies fall into a variety of subclasses, and this categorization has evolved over the past 60 years to incorporate new information from other frequency bands (optical, infra-red,

X-ray, gamma-ray, etc.), as well as more detailed morphological information from successive generations of advanced radio observatories.

One of the most widely adopted and applied morphological classification schemes for radio galaxies is the Fanaroff–Riley (FR) classification [15]. Although this scheme was first introduced over four decades ago, it has persisted in the radio astronomy literature. The morphological divide seen in this classification scheme has historically been explained primarily as a consequence of differing jet dynamics. Fanaroff–Riley type I (FRI) radio galaxies have jets that are disrupted at shorter distances from the central supermassive black hole and are therefore centrally brightened, while Fanaroff–Riley type II (FRII) radio galaxies have jets that remain relativistic to large distances, resulting in bright termination shocks, see Figure 4.

The structural differences highlighted by the FR classification scheme may be related to the intrinsic power in the jets but could also be influenced by the characteristics of the environment local to individual galaxies, in particular, the density of the surrounding inter-galactic medium. However, for various reasons, disentangling the consequences of these intrinsic and environmental effects is difficult when using integrated electromagnetic properties alone [19]. Hence, radio galaxy morphology remains a crucially important piece of information for gaining a better physical understanding of the FR dichotomy and of the full morphological diversity of the radio galaxy population. Separating these effects, as well as constraining their impact on the different properties of radio galaxies, is crucial not only for understanding the physics of radio galaxies themselves and hence galaxy evolution more generally but also for other areas of astronomy and cosmology, which use radio galaxies over cosmological distances as probes of the wider Universe. While progress is still being made in this field, it is hoped that the new generation of radio surveys, such as those that will be made by the SKA with improved resolution, sensitivity, and dynamic range, will play a key part in finally answering these questions. However, given the huge numbers of radio galaxies expected to be detected by the SKA, and indeed its precursor instruments, current methods, which have relied heavily on *by eye* classification for individual galaxies, will no longer be a viable option for separating FRI- and FRII-type populations. Consequently, an increasing amount of work is being undertaken within the radio astronomy community to automate, using image-based deep learning methods, this perhaps once rather routine task of radio galaxy classification.

The groundwork in this field was done by Aniyan and Thorat [4] who made the first use of CNNs for the classification of Fanaroff–Riley (FR) type I and type II radio galaxies. This was quickly followed by other works involving the use of deep learning in source classification. Examples include Lukic *et al.* [27] who made use of CNNs for the classification of compact and extended radio sources from the Radio Galaxy Zoo catalog [6], the Classifying Radio Sources Automatically with a Neural Network (CLARAN [49]) model, which made use of the Faster R-CNN network to identify and classify radio sources; Alger *et al.* [3] made use of an ensemble of classifiers including CNNs to perform host (optical) galaxy cross-identification. Tang *et al.* [45] made use of transfer learning with CNNs to perform cross-survey classification. Capsule networks were explored as an alternative to CNNs, but no specific advantage was found compared to traditional CNNs [28]. As for many other fields, transformers have also been introduced within radio astronomy classification and Bowles *et al.* [12] showed that an attention-gated CNN could be used to perform FR classification of radio galaxies with equivalent performance to other models in the literature but using ∼50% fewer learnable parameters than the next smallest classical CNN in the field. More recently, Scaife and Porter [40] showed that using group-equivariant convolutional layers that preserved the rotational and reflectional isometries of the Euclidean group resulted in improved overall model performance and stability of model confidence for radio galaxies at different orientations, and Bastien *et al.* [7] generated synthetic populations of FR radio galaxies using structured variational inference.

4. AI for Time-domain Analysis in Radio Astronomy

While astronomy is often considered a particularly visual research field, the nature of radio data makes its spectral and temporal properties equally important for understanding the extreme physics taking place in the high-energy Universe. Dynamic spectra that show time–frequency behavior in the radio regime form a crucial part of many research fields: from understanding the Sun and magnetospheric activity on other planets within our own Solar System to cosmological studies of the wider Universe using the recently discovered enigmatic *fast radio bursts*, which are extremely short-lived (∼ millisecond), highly frequency-dispersed signals, the origin of which is not yet fully understood.

From a signal processing perspective, a crucial component of handling such dynamic spectra is the excision of man-made signals known as radio frequency interference (RFI). Such signals arise from a wide variety of sources, both terrestrial and satellite-based, and are consequently an unavoidable reality of modern radio astronomy in this digital age. The removal or separation of such RFI from radio datasets is not limited to radio astronomy; it is also a topic of interest for other industries, such as those using radar systems, but given the comparatively extremely faint nature of astronomical radio signals,[2] it is of particular importance in this field.

Consequently, the use of AI-based approaches for RFI excision and mitigation is of significant interest. Deep learning approaches, in particular using U-net architectures, have proved successful when compared to other more standard statistical analysis techniques used for RFI removal, although the degree of success varies across applications and datasets (e.g., [26,46]). Recently, these approaches have also been applied to separating RFI contamination from the radio *technosignatures* considered to be an indication of extraterrestrial life [39]. RFI is currently the most significant challenge in the detection of radio technosignatures, the identification of which is being actively pursued at a number of observatories around the world and forms part of the science case for the SKA.

A unifying circumstance in attempts to separate astronomical information in the time domain from its man-made contaminants is the high degree of class imbalance between true astrophysical signals and RFI, with a typical incidence of true signals being $\ll 0.1\%$. Consequently, although the term classification is often applied to such signal partition in the literature, the comparative rarity of true astronomical signals means that it is often better addressed as an outlier or out-of-distribution problem, using one-vs-rest classification or anomaly detection approaches.

4.1. *Case study: Pulsar classification*

Pulsars are rapidly rotating neutron stars that emit very precisely timed repeating radio pulses with periods of milliseconds to seconds. These objects are formed through the death of massive stars ($>8\,M_\odot$), which have collapsed masses that are insufficient to undergo complete gravitational collapse and form a black hole but are sufficiently massive that collapse causes their electrons to combine with protons and form neutrons, a process which continues until neutron degeneracy pressure is high enough to prevent further gravitational collapse. By the time this happens, such stars are almost exclusively comprised of neutrons, compressed into a sphere of approximately 20 km in diameter [29].

Finding and observing pulsars is a core science goal of the SKA, which intends to conduct a cosmic census of the pulsar population in order to address a number of key questions in modern physics. By their very nature, the mass of pulsars makes them unique laboratories of strong-field gravity,

---

[2]The standard unit of measurement in radio astronomy is the Jansky, where 1 Jansky = 10^{-26} Watts m^{-2} Hz^{-1}.

an environment that is impossible to replicate on Earth. Indeed, it was these extreme physical conditions that enabled pulsar astronomers to obtain the first observational evidence for the existence of gravitational waves, as predicted by Einstein's theory of general relativity, and this was recognized by the 1993 Nobel Prize in Physics. A related science driver for the SKA is to use the radio pulses from *thousands* of pulsars with millisecond spin periods in a coordinated experiment to map the passage of gravitational waves through our Galaxy as a disturbance in the regularity of these pulse arrival times [22]. This will open up a new gravitational wave regime, different from that detectable by, e.g., the LIGO experiment here on Earth (e.g., [1]). However, to conduct such an experiment, the SKA must first identify and map the location of thousands of previously unknown pulsars by separating their periodic signals from other contaminating data, in particular man-made radio frequency interference.

Unlike the radio galaxy classification problem, which will mainly be addressed through post-processing of off-line data products that are delivered by the SKA Observatory to data centers around the world, the output volume of observational data in the time domain will be so large that persistent storage solutions rapidly become impossible given current hardware and cost limitations. This is particularly problematic for pulsar hunting as, to date, the vast majority of new pulsars have been discovered through the offline reprocessing of archived data, sometimes years after it has been first observed. Consequently, the soft real-time constraint for identifying pulsars from SKA data represents a significant shift in approach for the radio astronomy community and as a result, the development of classification algorithms that will address this problem has become a subject of significant interest over the past few years.

The first application of AI to pulsar candidate selection was made by Eatough *et al.* (2010) using a multilayer perceptron model. In this original work, 12 numerical features were extracted from the time-domain data and, since then, the nature of such feature engineering in pulsar classification has become a recurrent theme throughout the literature (e.g., [8,35]). Lyon *et al.* [31] and [30] used an information theoretic approach to feature engineering rather than a physically motivated approach to implement rapid pulsar candidate classification using a method based on the Gaussian–Hellinger Very Fast Decision Tree (GH-VFDT). This method is also an example of an *incremental stream classifier*, designed directly to address the soft real-time requirements of the SKA as well as time-dependent changes in data distribution, see Figure 5. The stream-based method was shown to outperform batch-based static classifiers for the pulsar identification problem and further improvements to this method were also made by Tan *et al.* [44].

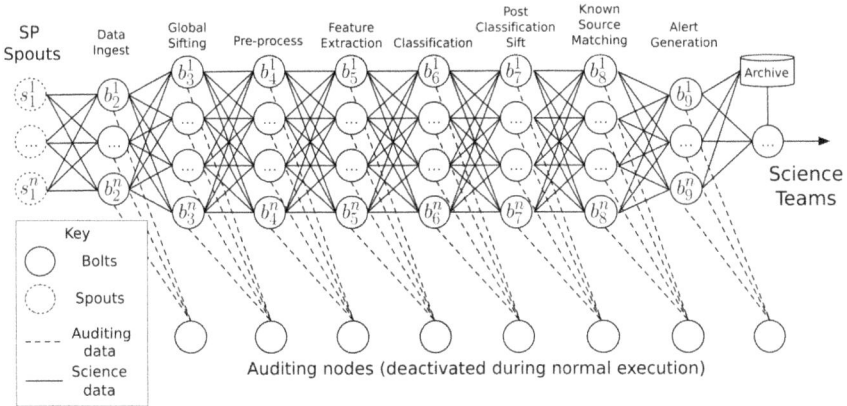

Fig. 5. Data processor topology for the incremental stream pulsar classifier from Ref. [30] utilizing the Apache Storm framework [21].

The issue of class imbalance for pulsar classification remains a key theme in this field, as does the associated issue of prior probability shift under variable observing conditions due to changes in RFI over short and long timescales. Yao *et al.* [50] addressed the issue of class imbalance between pulsars and non-pulsars by using an ensemble classifier with a weighted loss function, Bethapudi and Desai [10] explored minority class over-sampling approaches, and Agarwal *et al.* [2] demonstrated that using synthetic astronomy data to produce a balanced training set worked effectively when testing on real data. More recently, Kordzanganeh *et al.* [25] showed that the pulsar classification problem mapped well to the Bloch sphere using a single-qubit quantum neural network.

5. AI Challenges for the SKA

The application of artificial intelligence and in particular deep learning to radio astronomy comes with a number of challenges. While the data volumes and data rates for the SKA may themselves seem technically daunting, it is perhaps ensuring the scientific rigor required for SKA science that provides the biggest challenge to the operational implementation of AI for radio astronomy.

A key factor influencing this on many levels is a paucity of labeled data — ironically, although we have too much data, we also do not have enough. For example, while archival datasets for training radio galaxy classifiers are of comparable size to many of those used in computer vision (e.g., CIFAR, MNIST), with around 10^5 samples available, a fundamental difference is the sparsity of labels in those radio galaxy datasets, as only a small fraction of data points are labeled. This is largely due to the domain knowledge required for labeling, which incurs a high cost per label compared to typical benchmark datasets.

This is particularly a concern in radio astronomy where data are selected for labeling in a biased manner due to instrumental, observational, and intrinsic effects which favor, for example, particular flux density (brightness) and redshift (distance) ranges. This makes it difficult to know how representative our labeled or indeed unlabeled data are of the true generating distribution, and the consequent compounded effects of multiple dataset shifts on model performance are therefore not always clear *a priori*. As a result, the generalization performance of models trained using these data is questionable [9] and the potential for direct transfer learning may be limited [45]. Specific examples of how this is being addressed for machine learning applications in astronomy include the use of Gaussian process modeling to augment training data and make it more representative of test data in photometric classification [11] and in galaxy merger classification where domain adaptation techniques have also been explored [13]. However, in both of these cases, the solutions are tackling covariate shift between the labeled and test data and do not yet address more general or compound forms of dataset shift.

For supervised deep learning applications, this lack of labeled data also often creates the need to augment datasets. This practice has been raised as a concern for applications of Bayesian deep learning, where it has been suggested that unprincipled data augmentation may result in the likelihood of mis-specification and consequently be a significant factor in the widely observed cold posterior effect [47], where the Bayesian complexity term in the evidence lower bound objective (ELBO) function needs to be down-weighted with respect to the likelihood in order to achieve optimal performance. In radio astronomy specifically, the cold posterior effect has been observed in deep learning models for radio galaxy classification [33,34]; however, rather than data augmentation being the dominant factor, the use of average or consensus labeling in training data was raised as a more serious contribution. Since the labels for many training data sets in radio astronomy — and astronomy more widely — are currently taken from archival catalogs, where no individual labeling information is available, this suggests that a change is necessary going forward in the way we produce our catalogs.

A paucity of labeled data also suggests that unsupervised or semi-supervised learning methodologies may be a more efficient way to leverage the information currently available for radio astronomy. However, although many semi-supervised learning (SSL) algorithms are successful on standard benchmarking datasets in the regime of low data ($\sim[10, 10^3]$ data points), less work has been done to assess their robustness to various real-world problems. The shortcomings of SSL have previously been documented in this regard [38]. SSL implementations where both the labeled and unlabeled data are drawn from the same generating distribution have been shown to improve performance in pulsar classification for small labeled sets [5], but early applications to radio galaxy classification suggest that dataset shift between the labeled and unlabeled data pools when using truly unlabeled data is problematic and that the effectiveness of SSL may be limited without adaptation of existing methods [41,42].

Another challenge is that of artifacts, misclassified objects, and ambiguity arising from how the classes in radio astronomy datasets are defined. Underestimation and miscalibration of uncertainties associated with model outcomes for data samples that are peripheral to the main data mass are well documented in the machine learning literature, see, e.g., [18], and it has been demonstrated that out-of-distribution data points will be misclassified with arbitrarily high precision by standard neural networks [20]. While the use of probabilistic AI approaches that address these issues is undoubtedly a necessity for radio astronomy in the long term, the domain-specific literature in this area remains sparse. This is perhaps somewhat surprising given the large emphasis placed on statistical inference more widely in radio astronomy and cosmology analysis, as well as the early contributions to the field of Bayesian deep learning from the astronomy community (e.g., [32]). Moreover, the correct treatment of out-of-distribution samples is likely to be essential for preserving that most important scientific task of new astronomical observatories: *discovery*.

References

[1] B. P. Abbott and the LIGO Consortium (2016). Observation of gravitational waves from a binary black hole merger. *Physical Review Letter*, *116*, 061102. https://link.aps.org/doi/10.1103/PhysRevLett.116.061102.

[2] D. Agarwal, K. Aggarwal, S. Burke-Spolaor *et al.* (2020). FETCH: A deep-learning based classifier for fast transient classification. *Monthly Notices of the Royal Astronomical Society*, *497*(2), 1661–1674. https://doi.org/10.1093/mnras/staa1856, *arXiv:1902.06343 [astro-ph.IM]*.

[3] M. J. Alger, J. K. Banfield, C. S. Ong *et al.* (2018). Radio Galaxy Zoo: Machine learning for radio source host galaxy cross-identification. *Monthly Notices of the Royal Astronomical Society*, *478*(4), 5547–5563. https://academic.oup.com/mnras/article-pdf/478/4/5547/25204505/sty1308.pdf, https://doi.org/10.1093/mnras/sty1308.

[4] A. K. Aniyan and K. Thorat (2017). Classifying radio galaxies with the convolutional neural network. *The Astrophysical Journal Supplement*, *230*(2), 20. https://doi.org/10.3847/1538-4365/aa7333, *arXiv:1705.03413 [astro-ph.IM]*.

[5] V. Balakrishnan, D. Champion, E. Barr *et al.* (2021). Pulsar candidate identification using semi-supervised generative adversarial networks. *Monthly Notices of the Royal Astronomical Society*, *505*(1), 1180–1194. https://doi.org/10.1093/mnras/stab1308.

[6] J. K. Banfield, O. I. Wong, K. W. Willett *et al.* (2015). Radio Galaxy Zoo: Host galaxies and radio morphologies derived from visual inspection. *Monthly Notices of the Royal Astronomical Society*, *453*(3), 2326–2340. https://doi.org/10.1093/mnras/stv1688, *arXiv:1507.07272 [astro-ph.GA]*.

[7] D. J. Bastien, A. M. M. Scaife, H. Tang *et al.* (2021). Structured variational inference for simulating populations of radio galaxies. *Monthly Notices of the Royal Astronomical Society*, *503*(3), 3351–3370. https://doi.org/10.1093/mnras/stab588, *arXiv:2102.01007 [astro-ph.IM]*.

[8] S. D. Bates, M. Bailes, B. R. Barsdell *et al.* (2012). The High Time Resolution Universe Pulsar Survey — VI. An artificial neural network and timing of 75 pulsars. *Monthly Notices of the Royal Astronomical Society*, *427*(2), 1052–1065. https://doi.org/10.1111/j.1365-2966.2012.22042.x, *arXiv:1209.0793 [astro-ph.SR]*.

[9] B. Becker, M. Vaccari, M. Prescott *et al.* (2021). CNN architecture comparison for radio galaxy classification. *Monthly Notices of the Royal Astronomical Society*, *503*(2), 1828–1846. https://doi.org/10.1093/mnras/stab325, *arXiv:2102.03780 [astro-ph.GA]*.

[10] S. Bethapudi and S. Desai (2018). Separation of pulsar signals from noise using supervised machine learning algorithms. *Astronomy and Computing*, *23*, 15–26. https://doi.org/10.1016/j.ascom.2018.02.002, *arXiv:1704.04659 [astro-ph.IM]*.

[11] K. Boone (2019). Avocado: Photometric classification of astronomical transients with Gaussian process augmentation. *The Astronomical Journal*, *158*(6), 257. https://doi.org/10.3847/1538-3881/AB5182, https://iopscience.iop.org/article/10.3847/1538-3881/ab5182.

[12] M. Bowles, A. M. Scaife, F. Porter *et al.* (2021). Attention-gating for improved radio galaxy classification. *Monthly Notices of the Royal Astronomical Society*, *501*(3), 4579–4595.

[13] A. Ćiprijanović, D. Kafkes, S. Jenkins *et al.* (2020). Domain adaptation techniques for improved cross-domain study of galaxy mergers. In *Machine Learning and the Physical Sciences — Workshop at the 34th Conference on Neural Information Processing Systems (NeurIPS)*. http://arxiv.org/abs/2011.03591.

[14] L. Connor, K. L. Bouman, V. Ravi, and G. Hallinan (2022). Deep radio-interferometric imaging with POLISH: DSA-2000 and weak lensing. *Monthly Notices of the Royal Astronomical Society*, *514*(2), 2614–2626.

[15] B. L. Fanaroff and J. M. Riley (1974). The morphology of extragalactic radio sources of high and low luminosity. *Monthly Notices of the Royal Astronomical Society*, *167*, 31P–36P. https://doi.org/10.1093/mnras/167.1.31P.

[16] C. Gheller and F. Vazza (2021). Convolutional deep denoising autoencoders for radio astronomical images. *Monthly Notices of the Royal Astronomical Society*, *509*, 990–1009. https://doi.org/10.1093/mnras/stab3044.

[17] C. Gheller, F. Vazza, and A. Bonafede (2018). Deep learning based detection of cosmological diffuse radio sources. *Monthly Notices of the Royal Astronomical Society*, *480*, 3749–3761. https://doi.org/10.1093/mnras/sty2102.

[18] C. Guo, G. Pleiss, Y. Sun *et al.* (2017). On calibration of modern neural networks. In *International Conference on Machine Learning* (PMLR), pp. 1321–1330.

[19] M. J. Hardcastle and J. H. Croston (2020). Radio galaxies and feedback from AGN jets. *New Astronomy Reviews*, *88*, 101539. https://doi.org/10.1016/j.newar.2020.101539, *arXiv:2003.06137 [astro-ph.HE]*.

[20] M. Hein, M. Andriushchenko, and J. Bitterwolf (2018). Why relu networks yield high-confidence predictions far away from the training data and how to mitigate the problem. *CoRR*, abs/1812.05720. 1812.05720, http://arxiv.org/abs/1812.05720.

[21] A. Jain and A. Nalya (2014). *Learning Storm*. Packt Publishing, Birmingham, UK.

[22] G. Janssen, G. Hobbs, M. McLaughlin *et al.* (2015). Gravitational wave astronomy with the SKA. In *Advancing Astrophysics with the Square Kilometre Array (AASKA14)*, p. 37, *arXiv:1501.00127 [astro-ph.IM]*.

[23] E. Keane, B. Bhattacharyya, M. Kramer *et al.* (2015). A cosmic census of radio pulsars with the SKA. In *Advancing Astrophysics with the Square Kilometre Array (AASKA14)*, p. 40, *arXiv:1501.00056 [astro-ph.IM]*.

[24] L. Koopmans, J. Pritchard, G. Mellema *et al.* (2015). The cosmic Dawn and Epoch of reionisation with SKA. In *Advancing Astrophysics with the Square Kilometre Array (AASKA14)*, p. 1. https://doi.org/10.22323/1.215.0001, *arXiv:1505.07568 [astro-ph.CO]*.

[25] M. Kordzanganeh, A. Utting, and A. Scaife (2021). Quantum machine learning for radio astronomy. In *Machine Learning and the Physical Sciences — Workshop at the 35th Conference on Neural Information Processing Systems (NeurIPS)*. http://arxiv.org/abs/2112.02655.

[26] M. Long, Z. Yang, J. Xiao *et al.* (2019). U-NetIM: An improved U-net for automatic recognition of RFIs. In P. J. Teuben, M. W. Pound, B. A. Thomas and E. M. Warner (eds.), *Astronomical Data Analysis Software and Systems XXVII*, *Astronomical Society of the Pacific Conference Series*, Vol. 523, p. 123.

[27] V. Lukic, M. Brüggen, J. K. Banfield *et al.* (2018). Radio Galaxy Zoo: Compact and extended radio source classification with deep learning. *Monthly Notices of the Royal Astronomical Society*, *476*(1), 246–260. https://doi.org/10.1093/mnras/sty163, *arXiv:1801.04861 [astro-ph.IM]*.

[28] V. Lukic, M. Brüggen, B. Mingo *et al.* (2019). Morphological classification of radio galaxies: capsule networks versus convolutional neural networks. *Monthly Notices of the Royal Astronomical Society.* https://doi.org/10.1093/ mnras/stz1289.

[29] A. Lyne and F. Graham-Smith (2012). *Pulsar Astronomy.* Cambridge University Press, Cambridge, UK.

[30] R. Lyon, B. Stappers, L. Levin *et al.* (2019). A processing pipeline for high volume pulsar candidate data streams. *Astronomy and Comput-ing, 28*, 100291. https://doi.org/10.1016/j.ascom.2019.100291, https://www. sciencedirect.com/science/article/pii/S2213133718301343.

[31] R. J. Lyon, B. W. Stappers, S. Cooper *et al.* (2016). Fifty years of pulsar candidate selection: From simple filters to a new principled real-time classification approach. *Monthly Notices of the Royal Astronomical Soci-ety, 459*, 1104. https://doi.org/ 10.1093/mnras/stw656, *arXiv:1603.05166 [astro-ph.IM].*

[32] D. MacKay (1992). Bayesian model comparison and backprop nets. In J. Moody, S. Hanson and R. P. Lippmann (eds.), *Advances in Neural Infor-mation Processing Systems*, Vol. 4 (Morgan-Kaufmann). https://proceedings. neurips.cc/paper/1991/file/c3c59e5f8b3e9753913f4d435b53c308-Paper.pdf.

[33] D. Mohan and A. Scaife (2021). Weight pruning and uncertainty in radio galaxy classification. In *Machine Learning and the Physical Sciences — Workshop at the 35th Conference on Neural Information Processing Systems (NeurIPS).* http://arxiv.org/abs/2111.11654.

[34] D. Mohan, A. M. M. Scaife, F. Porter *et al.* (2022). Quantifying uncer-tainty in deep learning approaches to radio galaxy classification. *Monthly Notices of the Royal Astronomical Society, 511*(3), 3722–3740. https://doi.org/10.1093/ mnras/stac223, *arXiv:2201.01203 [astro-ph.CO].*

[35] V. Morello, E. D. Barr, M. Bailes *et al.* (2014). SPINN: A straightfor-ward machine learning solution to the pulsar candidate selection problem. *Monthly Notices of the Royal Astronomical Society, 443*(2), 1651–1662. https://doi.org/10.1093/mnras/stu1188, *arXiv:1406.3627 [astro-ph.IM].*

[36] R. I. J. Mostert, K. J. Duncan, H. J. A. Röttgering *et al.* (2020). Unveil-ing the rarest morphologies of the lofar two-metre sky survey radio source population with self-organised maps. https://doi.org/10.1051/0004-6361/202038500.

[37] K. Ntwaetsile and J. E. Geach (2021). Rapid sorting of radio galaxy mor-phology using haralick features. *Monthly Notices of the Royal Astronomical Society, 502*, 3417–3425. https://doi.org/10.1093/mnras/stab271.

[38] A. Oliver, A. Odena, C. Raffel *et al.* (2018). Realistic evaluation of semi-supervised learning algorithms. In *6th International Conference on Learning Representations, ICLR 2018 – Workshop Track Proceedings*, Vol. 2018, December.

[39] P. Pinchuk and J-L. Margot (2021). A machine-learning-based direction-of-origin filter for the identification of radio frequency interference in the search for techno signatures. *arXiv e-prints, arXiv:2108.00559 [astro-ph.IM].*

[40] A. M. M. Scaife and F. Porter (2021). Fanaroff-Riley classification of radio galaxies using group-equivariant convolutional neural networks. *Monthly Notices of the Royal Astronomical Society, 503*(2), 2369–2379. https://doi.org/10.1093/mnras/stab530, *arXiv:2102.08252 [astro-ph.IM]*.

[41] I. V. Slijepcevic and A. M. M. Scaife (2021). Can semi-supervised learning reduce the amount of manual labelling required for effective radio galaxy morphology classification? In *Machine Learning and the Physical Sciences — Workshop at the 35th Conference on Neural Information Processing Systems (NeurIPS)*. http://arxiv.org/abs/2111.04357.

[42] I. V. Slijepcevic, A. M. M. Scaife, M. Walmsley *et al.* (2022). Radio Galaxy Zoo: Using semi-supervised learning to leverage large unlabelled data-sets for radio galaxy classification under data-set shift. *Monthly Notices of the Royal Astronomical Society.* https://doi.org/10.1093/mnras/stac1135.

[43] H. Sun and K. L. Bouman (2020). Deep probabilistic imaging: Uncertainty quantification and multi-modal solution characterization for computational imaging. *arXiv:2010.14462arXiv:2010.14462 [cs.LG]*.

[44] C. M. Tan, R. J. Lyon, B. W. Stappers *et al.* (2017). Ensemble candidate classification for the LOTAAS pulsar survey. *Monthly Notices of the Royal Astronomical Society, 474*(4), 4571–4583. https://doi.org/10.1093/mnras/stx3047.

[45] H. Tang, A. M. M. Scaife, and J. P. Leahy (2019). Transfer learning for radio galaxy classification. *Monthly Notices of the Royal Astronomical Society, 488*(3), 3358–3375. https://doi.org/10.1093/mnras/stz1883, *arXiv:1903.11921 [astro-ph.IM]*.

[46] A. Vafaei Sadr, B. A. Bassett, N. Oozeer *et al.* (2020). Deep learning improves identification of Radio Frequency Interference. *Monthly Notices of the Royal Astronomical Society, 499*(1), 379–390. https://doi.org/10.1093/mnras/staa2724.

[47] F. Wenzel, K. Roth, B. Veeling *et al.* (2020). How good is the Bayes posterior in deep neural networks really? In H. D. III and A. Singh (eds.), *Proceedings of the 37th International Conference on Machine Learning, Proceedings of Machine Learning Research*, Vol. 119 (PMLR), pp. 10248–10259. https://proceedings.mlr.press/v119/wenzel20a.html.

[48] Y. Wiaux, F. Vazza, and A. Bonafede (2021). Radio-interferometric imaging with learned denoisers (airi). *Monthly Notices of the Royal Astronomical Society, 480*, 3749–3761. https://doi.org/10.1093/mnras/sty2102.

[49] C. Wu, O. I. Wong, L. Rudnick *et al.* (2019). Radio Galaxy Zoo: CLARAN — A deep learning classifier for radio morphologies. *MNRAS, 482*(1), 1211–1230. https://doi.org/10.1093/mnras/sty2646, *arXiv:1805.12008 [astro-ph.IM]*.

[50] Y. Yao, X. Xin, and P. Guo (2016). Pulsar candidate selection by assembling positive sample emphasized classifiers. In *2016 12th International Conference on Computational Intelligence and Security (CIS)*, pp. 120–124. https://doi.org/10.1109/CIS.2016.0036.

© 2023 World Scientific Publishing Company
https://doi.org/10.1142/9789811265679_0012

Chapter 12

AI for Astronomy: The Rise of the Machines

Andrew Connolly

Department of Astronomy, University of Washington
ajc@astro.washington.edu

1. Introduction

In the summer of 2024, after 10 years of construction, the Vera C. Rubin Observatory will enter operations and begin scanning the skies above northern Chile. With a 3.2 gigapixel camera (see Figure 1), each image from Rubin will cover about 10 square degrees so that every three nights Rubin will survey half of the sky. Each night Rubin will generate a stream of 10 million alerts for any source that has appeared, changed in brightness, or moved in the sky. Every year, all of the data accumulated up to that point will be reprocessed to generate deeper images and improved catalogs of sources. By the end of its 10-year survey (the Legacy Survey of Space and Time or LSST), Rubin is expected to have detected 37 billion stars and galaxies and for each of these sources to have ~1000 independent detections (a time series of observations covering the ultraviolet to the near-infrared). All data from Rubin will be released to the astronomical community and to the public as a whole.

The idea of building the Rubin Observatory was initially discussed in the late 1990s just as the first digital survey of the universe, the Sloan Digital Sky Survey (SDSS), was beginning operations. Funding was provided by philanthropists and foundations, including Charles and Lisa Simonyi and Bill Gates, to design and prototype the technologies for the wide field camera and 8.4m mirror that make up the heart of Rubin. Construction started, after numerous reviews, on the 1st August 2014 with funding from the National Science Foundation (NSF) and the Department of Energy (DOE).

Fig. 1.   The focal plane for the Rubin LSST camera. The camera comprises 189 sensors with a total of 3.2 billion pixels. Each image from the camera can be read out in two seconds and, combined with the Rubin telescope, covers approximately 10 square degrees of the sky (credit: Jacqueline Orrell/SLAC National Accelerator Laboratory).

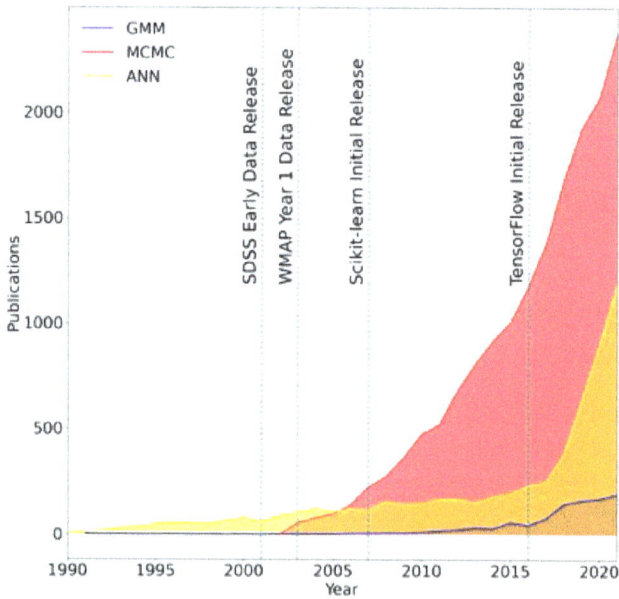

Fig. 2.   The number of papers that mention Markov Chain Monte Carlo (MCMC), Artificial Neural Networks (ANNs), or Gaussian Mixture Models (GMMs) as a function of year (measured from the SAO/NASA Astrophysics Data System Abstract Service). The dashed lines represent the release of the first SDSS data, the year one data release of the Wilkinson Microwave Anisotropy Probe (WMAP) cosmic microwave background observations, and the initial release of the open source machine learning libraries Scikit-learn and TensorFlow.

In comparison to this decades-long development process, over the same period of time, computer technologies have gone through numerous development cycles. Google was founded as a company in 1998 and now processes over 5 billion search queries a day. AlexNet heralded the emergence of deep neural networks in 2012 when it dramatically improved image classification performance in the ImageNet Large Scale Visual Recognition Challenge. Amazon launched Elastic Compute Cloud (EC2) in August 2006 and now accounts for about a third of a $40 billion cloud market and, by 2019, Netflix (which first offered a streaming option to its subscribers in 2007) was streaming more data every two hours than the total accumulated data expected from Rubin over its 10-year lifespan.

With large-scale astronomical facilities taking decades to design, construct, and operate, the science and the technology used to undertake that science will evolve dramatically from the concepts considered in the original proposals. The start of operations for a facility provides an opportunity for the astronomy community to rethink how they will access and make use of the data, to evaluate the capabilities of current approaches and methodologies, and to look at the computational needs of the community to support their science. In this article, I will look at how machine learning and the computational resources on which it relies have evolved over the last decade and the opportunities and challenges the astronomical community faces in realizing the scientific promise of the LSST.

2. The Emergence of Machine Learning in Astronomy

The definition of machine learning (ML) in the Oxford English Dictionary, "the capacity of computers to learn and adapt without following explicit instructions, by using algorithms and statistical models to analyze and infer from patterns in data", is well aligned with the scientific methods used to analyze and interpret large-scale astronomical survey data. New experiments, surveys, and instruments often drive the adoption of ML methodologies in astronomy. Figure 2 shows the rise in the use of techniques such as Markov Chain Monte Carlo (MCMC), Artificial Neural Networks (ANNs), and Gaussian Mixture Models (GMMs) and how their adoption by the astronomy community correlates with the release of new datasets or software libraries. As an example, the rapid adoption of MCMC as a method for estimating the posteriors on cosmological parameters coincided with the release of the Wilkinson Microwave Anisotropy Probe data that measured the fluctuations in the temperature of the Cosmic Microwave Background. The adoption of neural networks as a tool for classification dramatically increased when packages such as TensorFlow were made publicly available.

In the context of the LSST, the range of science that will be enabled means that we can expect the impact on ML methodologies and approaches to be broad. The four key LSST science drivers are cosmology (understanding the nature of dark energy and dark matter), Milky Way science (constraining the assembly history of our Galaxy), a census of the small bodies within the inner and outer Solar System, and characterizing the variable and transient sky. The science that will emerge from the LSST will clearly be much broader than just these research areas (as was found with the SDSS). Given the space available in this article, it is not possible to do justice to even one of these science themes. Instead, I will focus on one of the unique aspects of Rubin, its capacity to monitor the night sky, and how opening the exploration of the fourth dimension of the universe (i.e., time) might impact the development and advances in ML for time series data. I will consider the application of ML to both the real-time discovery of new astrophysical phenomena and the offline or batch processing of historical data to characterize the populations of variable sources within the universe.

While we think of ML as driving discoveries in astronomy, the application of ML techniques often comes at the end of the science workflow. Access to data both in terms of its availability and the tools with which we acquire it, software libraries that enable astronomers to implement statistical methodologies in a robust and reproducible manner, computational resources that can scale to the size of the data, and people trained to undertake and interpret these complex analyses must all be in place prior to the data exploration and discovery phase.

3. Open Data and Open Science

The widespread use of statistical and ML tools in astronomy coincided with a dramatic increase in the accessibility of data. The SDSS started this move to open data with a series of releases of calibrated images and spectra, together with catalogs of the properties of sources extracted from these spectra and images. This open data policy made the SDSS one of the most cited astronomical facilities in the world. By 2019, papers published using the SDSS data had surpassed 8000 and had amassed over 400,000 citations, a number which would put the SDSS in the top 20 cited authors in terms of h-index.

With surveys such as the LSST, data volumes from the first year of operations will exceed all the accumulated optical datasets collected prior to the start of the LSST. As with the SDSS, the LSST will release its accumulated data periodically over the length of the survey. Data availability is, however, only the first and potentially easiest component of open data. Rapid classification of astronomical alerts or transient events often requires merging multiple datasets (e.g., utilizing wide-field imaging to find counterparts to the gravitational wave signals from LIGO or spectroscopic follow-up of gamma-ray bursts). Joint processing of datasets that span the electromagnetic spectrum can remove degeneracies when modeling the physical properties of astronomical sources (e.g., improving photometric redshift distance estimates by combining near-infrared data from the Roman Space Telescope with optical data from the LSST). Interoperability between facilities will be critical to simplify the joint analysis of datasets. Part of this will come from data format and exchange standards through bodies such as the International Virtual Observatory Alliance (IVOA). Formats for sparsely sampled, multiband time series data are, however, only at an early stage with interest in columnar data storage formats such as Apache Parquet growing within the community [1]. Concepts such as data lakes with centralized repositories of structured and unstructured data and, in particular, implementations that share a common cloud-based infrastructure will play a role in simplifying access to data across observatories. In fact, with Rubin"s interim data facility being housed in the cloud, there is an opportunity to not just store data within the cloud but use this to transition astronomers to working in frameworks that make use of cloud resources including the elasticity of the compute resources as well as the availability of scalable machine learning frameworks (e.g., SageMaker and AutoML). This would increase the accessibility of survey astronomy datasets in a manner similar to that achieved by the SDSS (which transitioned the astronomy community to using databases) but only if the cost of entry when utilizing cloud resources can be kept low.

4. The Democratization of Machine Learning with the Emergence of Open Frameworks

If the early 2000's witnessed the impact of open data on research productivity, the 2010's was when access to open source software packages such as Astropy [2], scikit-learn [3], astroML [4], PyTorch [5], and TensorFlow [6] broadened the use of ML techniques in astronomy (see Figure 2). Looking forward, the development of science platforms for the analysis of astronomical data (e.g., the Rubin Science Platform) presents an opportunity to expand to an era where services (e.g., Science as a Service) can be made available to the research community as a whole. In this way, packages and software frameworks started by Astropy and scikit-learn can be extended to scale to the volume of Rubin data without requiring individual researchers to learn the many arcane practices of debugging distributed computing frameworks. This has the potential to accelerate science not just through access to the elastic computing capabilities of the cloud but also through community development of common tools.

Accomplishing such a vision will require the astronomy community to define appropriate and common interfaces to the data. Abstractions for parallelizing scientific data analysis in a way that is easily used by the majority of astronomers remain undefined (many ML applications do not work out-of-core or with distributed computation). The requirements for computationally demanding science use cases are just beginning to emerge through the development of science and software road maps by the LSST Science Collaborations and the creation of programs such as the LSST Interdisciplinary Network for Collaboration and Computing (LINCC) to support the development of the required software frameworks.

Many hurdles beyond the questions of abstraction stand in the way of making such an initiative a success and equitable. This includes how to provision resources on the cloud such that any researcher can access them, how to ensure that the cost models are consistent with research funding, and how to minimize the on-ramp for new users starting out in the cloud. Solutions to these challenges will need to be part computational (scaling algorithms to run on large distributed compute systems and defining the appropriate computational abstraction), part methodological (developing the right statistical techniques and approaches for noisy and incomplete data), and part sociological (enabling the astronomy community to share their tools and knowledge for the benefit of all).

5. The Challenge of Machine Learning for Streaming Data

While Rubin is often considered a time-domain survey with each part of the sky observed 1000 times, in reality, these time series data will be sparsely sampled, noisy, distributed across six separate filters or passbands, and will take 10 years to accumulate. Gaps between observations due to the survey strategy, weather, and the rise of the Sun mean that the data are unevenly as well as sparsely sampled. This introduces a number of interesting challenges for ML in astronomy. In the following sections, I consider two aspects of time-domain science, the real-time stream of events from Rubin (e.g., the detection of supernova see Figure 3) and the batch or offline processing of the accumulated time series data (e.g., to characterize the variability of astronomical populations).

One of the biggest advances in ML for real-time astronomy was not the creation of a classifier to detect unusual sources but the development of a set of methodologies, often referred to as real-bogus classifiers, that remove "junk" or artifacts within the data [7]. The first of these was developed for the Palomar Transient Factory (PTF). PTF surveyed the

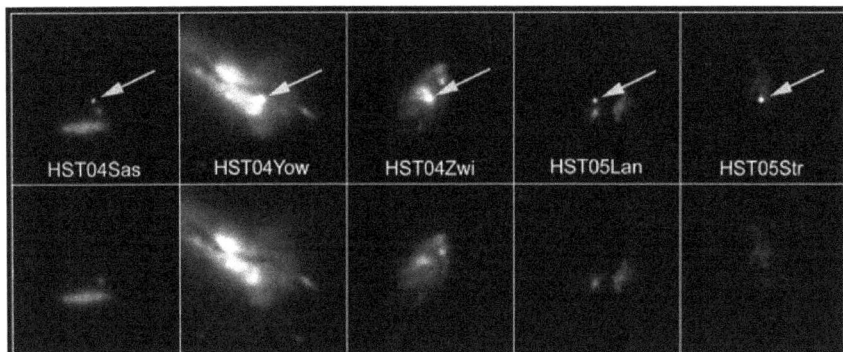

Fig. 3. A mosaic of images of galaxies with distant supernova observed by the Hubble Space Telescope. The bottom row shows the galaxies before (or after) the supernova. The top row shows the position of the supernova (the final stages of stellar evolution with the explosion of the progenitor star). For Type Ia supernova, the brightness of the supernova correlates with its distance and, with the detection of hundreds of thousands of these supernova with surveys such as the LSST, can be used to measure the expansion rate of the universe and constrain the properties of dark energy (credit: NASA, ESA, and A. Riess, Space Telescope Science Institute).

northern hemisphere using a small but wide field camera at a rate of about 3750 square degrees an hour. Images from each night were compared with composite images taken on earlier nights, often by digitally subtracting a pair of images and identifying the residual sources that might be indicative of a transient (e.g., a supernova) or variable (e.g., an RR Lyra star) source. Small inaccuracies in the alignment of the images or variations in the image quality between nights gave rise to false detections. Such were the magnitude of the false detections that their number could exceed the number of astronomical sources by two orders of magnitude. In a landmark paper, Bloom *et al.* [7] applied a random forest (an ensemble learning technique based on decision trees) that reduced the number of false positives by a factor of 10. This reduction in the background, essentially sifting the astronomical wheat from the chaff, did not in and of itself provide great scientific insight into the properties of the variable sources or the artifacts within the data. Its impact was in reducing the noise in the stream of alerts from PTF so that new astronomical sources could be identified including tidal disruption events [8] and the earliest identification of the onset of a Type Ia supernovae [9].

LSST will integrate real-bogus methodologies to reduce the number of false positives from its data stream but will still generate approximately 10^7 events per night. Providing access to these streams of alerts requires the development of infrastructure for sending and filtering alerts to the community. Open-source packages such as Apache Kafka, originally developed by LinkedIn as a distributed event streaming platform, can already scale to much higher data throughput than that generated by LSST and have now been adopted by the astronomical community. This has led to the concept of brokers, systems that connect to these event streams and filter sources in order to identify high-value objects that require follow-up observations from other telescopes [10]. Real-time or early detection of transients (i.e., within a few hours of the first observation) provides detailed insight into the physics of the transients. This includes the potential detection of the breakout of shocks from the surface of a star during the supernova explosion, which would provide a measure of the size and type of progenitor star. Without such capability, the physics of progenitors of supernovae and transients remains poorly understood.

Classification techniques adopted by brokers typically rely on feature extraction either from statistical representations of light curves or from the use of autoencoders to reduce the inherent dimensionality of the data. The state of the art is to pass these features to neural networks that have been trained on a set of label data. Recurrent neural networks (RNNs) and variants such as Long Short-Term Memory networks (LSTMs) outperform conventional convolutional neural networks [11] by utilizing connections between layers to encode the temporal aspect of the data. The success of RNNs in the early classification of time series data comes from their ability to preserve the information from previous epochs of data and to adapt to new online or streaming data. More recent applications of RNNs directly to the classification of sequences of images [12] offer the promise of alert classification that can incorporate the morphological properties of the sources and potentially their environment.

6. Physics-Driven Approaches to Machine Learning

With the increasing sophistication of deep networks in classifying and explaining complex processes (e.g., AlphaFold), can developments in AI and ML provide a framework for discoveries for the Rubin Observatory? As noted above, for earlier generations of sky surveys, ML has been instrumental in the classification of sources, weeding artifacts from the astrophysical signal, and measuring the statistical properties of astronomical objects (e.g., measures of large-scale clustering). Is it possible for these approaches to go beyond filtering and classification to provide insights into the physics of astronomical processes? As Jim Gray once asked, could ML uncover the Hertzsprung–Russell diagram, the tight relationship between the effective temperature and luminosity of stars that led to the development of stellar astrophysics? Could AI identify that relation from observational data and develop a theoretical model to explain the correlation? Given the current state of the art for ML, the answer is still probably no. There are, however, a number of recent approaches that could provide more theoretical insight into the physics by reducing the number of dimensions needed to represent the properties of astronomical sources — analogous in some ways to the role of phenomenology in advancing theory in high-energy physics.

One of the more interesting aspects of ML in astrophysics is not using AI to learn theory but the integration of physical models within the structure of the AI. The use of physical constraints or the recognition of symmetries within the data (e.g., by learning the structure of the data in the rest frame of the sources and then applying redshift and dimming as an afterburner to the trained networks) can reduce the dimensionality of the model that must be learned. Large, often noisy, and heterogeneous datasets can then be projected into a physically motivated subspace.

For surveys such as the LSST, the classification of supernovae and their use in observational cosmology provides one such example of the benefits of building AI applications within a physics framework. Our ability to discover dark energy arose when astronomers could identify candidate Type 1a supernovae (SN) sufficiently close to their explosion that large telescopes could follow up the detections to confirm the classifications and measure the supernova redshift. Because Type 1a SN act as standard candles (i.e., they have a constant brightness), their distance can be estimated and compared to their redshift to measure the expansion rate of the universe. One of the primary limitations for SN cosmology is accurately typing the SN to identify those that are Type Ia. Usually, we do this by taking a spectrum of the SN close in time to its explosion. Spectroscopic follow-up of SN is expensive, requiring large amounts of 10m class telescope time. While ~50 SN were used in the initial discovery of dark energy, surveys such as LSST will detect hundreds of thousands of SN. If we could classify Type Ia SN just from their light curves, we wouldn't need spectroscopic confirmation (we can always get the redshift of the SN from its host galaxy redshift at a later time).

Classification of supernova and by extension other transient sources based on their optical properties has, therefore, become one of the holy grails in supernovae cosmology. Machine learning data challenges (much like ImageNet and Kaggle) have emerged to encourage the development of new methodologies. One of the most successful of these was the PLASTICC data challenge [13] where over 1,089 teams competed to classify time series observations for a range of astrophysically variable sources. The winning approach utilized standard machine learning techniques including Gaussian processes to interpolate the poorly sampled light curves and boosted decision trees (LightGBM) to classify sources from features measured from the light curves [14]. The primary advance, however, came from the augmentation of the training data based on an understanding of how the physics changes the properties of the observations (i.e., time dilation and dimming due to the redshifting of astronomical sources) and matching the noise or uncertainties in the training data to those expected from the observations or test data. This augmentation addressed one of the challenges of training any machine learning algorithm — labeling the data is expensive in terms of telescope time, so training samples are often limited and not representative of the data at hand. Augmentation increased the training sample by a factor of 75 and improved the classification of Type Ia SN from 0.83 to 0.96 (in terms of the area under the curve) [14].

This recognition that symmetries exist within the data that we can exploit because we know how to model them led to the idea of separating the intrinsic unknowns or latent variables (for example, the variables that represent the variation in the spectral properties of a SN) from the physical processes that we know how to model (i.e., redshift, the response function of the filter curves through which the source will be observed, the properties of the dust within the host galaxy, and the sampling of the time series data). The complexity or dimensionality of the network needed to capture the diversity of SN is then substantially reduced [15], which leads to a reduction in the size of the required training set. The performance of such physics-based approaches using the benchmark data from the PLASTICC data challenge improved SN completeness by 10% over Boone [14] at a redshift $z = 0.4$ and by 50% by a redshift of one. For a fairer comparison (i.e., not using the data augmentation of the training sample used by Boone), the improvement increases to almost a factor of 2 at a redshift $z = 0.5$.

It is important to note that these improvements did not come from an advance in the complexity of the neural network architecture, they came more from a careful separation of what is known and what we want to learn. This separation reduces the need for the class labels of the training sample to be balanced or representative of the test sample as a whole, which has been a limitation for many machine learning approaches in the past. While such approaches offer a lot of promise for learning more about the physics of variable sources, there are many interesting challenges that remain to be addressed. How do we account for noise within the data? How do we express classifications in terms of a posterior distribution which is likely multimodal rather than current maximum likelihood or variational approaches? How do we interpret the models we fit, particularly when using many layers in deep networks, and understand the impact of sampling of the light curves on the inference we make? To address this will require advances in the theory of AI as well as the implementation of computationally efficient techniques.

7. Scalability of Machine Learning

Continuing the focus on how we represent information and the objective of reducing the computational complexity, we consider how physics-driven approaches might impact the ML frameworks we want to build to deliver science with the LSST data. Should we build scalable infrastructures that try to meet large swaths of the scientific needs of the community? Such systems take longer to develop and would be higher in cost but have the potential multiplexing advantage of producing a large amount of science. In other fields such as computational biology, this approach hasn't always been successful with systems being built that took years and millions of dollars to develop, but by the time they were ready, the science had moved on. Alternatively, we could create simplified infrastructure for running bespoke analyses for specific science questions. This would be more agile with rapid development but the applications would be limited. Is there a middle ground?

By reducing the size of the training sample, and the complexity of the model, we can often simplify the parallelization needed to scale an analysis (e.g., where each source or light curve can be analyzed independently). This simplification enables a broader range of computational tools to be utilized, from serverless approaches such as cloudknot [16] and lithops [17], which take Python functions and containerize them to work on cloud services, to the more traditional parallel analytics frameworks such as Apache Spark, Dask, and Ray.

An example of the use of industry-supported analysis tools in astrophysics is Astronomy Extensions for Spark (AXS) [1], which extends Apache Spark for astronomy applications by integrating a data partitioning scheme appropriate for sources distributed across the sky, adding a sort-merge-join optimization for cross-matching large astronomical catalogs, and providing efficient access to light curves using Apache Parquet. Spark provides a simple interface for writing user-defined functions that can encapsulate astrophysical applications used by astronomers when working with time series data. This enables large-scale analyses to be distributed across large numbers of cores with each light curve analyzed independently. In a recent example, AXS was used to search for unusual variability within light curves from the Zwicky Transient Facility. Processing and classifying 1.4 billion light curves took about 450 core hours (or 2 hrs on a cloud resource).

From this, we can see that the computational resources required to undertake an analysis comparable in scale to ones that astronomers will perform on LSST data can be relatively small. The reason for this is that research is often iterative in nature. As we undertake an exploration of a dataset, we search for the appropriate features needed to identify our signal, we identify and remove artifacts within the data that arise in the data processing, and we repeatedly reprocess or analyze the data to refine and downselect the data. The workflow for this classification can be treated as a hierarchical process, where simple filters can exclude the majority of the data and the smaller the size of the data, the more computationally complex the analyses we can afford to apply. Progressively pruning and downselecting candidate light curves as the analysis becomes more complicated limits the requirements on memory, simplifies the processing, and reduces the time spent debugging a distributed systems (a challenge when memory usage is high and the data are unstructured and heterogeneous).

8. Training and Software Engineering in the Sciences

As ML has emerged as a cornerstone of our astrophysical analyses (and the sciences in general), the need to train and educate the astronomical community in the underlying statistical and computational methods has grown. Significant developments have occurred in this area over the last five years with the creation of data science tracks in astronomy, the expansion of courses in statistics and machine learning to astronomical departments, the production of extensive educational material in books and online, and the hiring of faculty to teach in these areas. We are beginning to define curricula for teaching machine learning including Bayesian statistics, supervised and unsupervised learning, dimensionality reduction, sampling methods, clustering and density estimation techniques, and time series methodologies. These classes and options are typically available at larger universities and the challenge we still face is how to bring ML to smaller institutions (i.e., to make these resources available when the support structures such as programming and software engineering courses may not be readily available). Open curricula and course material could be part of the solution if they were designed to be modular, where students and teachers could build courses tailored to their needs without having to do so from scratch.

Developing a structure for how we, as a community, teach data science could address the needs of ML users but not necessarily those who will build and deploy new methodologies and software frameworks. For software to be sustainable over the lifetime of a project, we need software engineering practices to be in place that ensure code is tested, readable, and maintained. This challenge is not limited to astronomy. In a survey at the University of Washington in 2020, over 41% of respondents found it difficult to hire people with software engineering expertise despite having available funding. This was because funding for these software engineering positions was often tied to short-term grants or available in the form of fractional support which reduced the pool of applicants willing to take on the work. The solution to this problem was to hire a student ($>30\%$ of the respondents) or to use external consultants (15–20%) to meet their software needs. Hiring of students to perform software engineering tasks without the requisite training is clearly an inefficient approach and leads to well-known difficulties in building robust and reproducible software, not to mention the "misdirection" of the student from their primary educational goal. Reliance on external consultants is often expensive and hard to scale to the broader research community.

Training programs targeting students in astronomy and physics are needed on campus to provide the students with best practices and guidance in developing software. This could create a larger talent pool or pipeline of software development expertise that could meet the needs of data-intensive science over the next decade. Perhaps, most importantly, it would enable the creation of a community of practice for researchers who focus on software development and provide for continuing education, mentoring, and training so that we can retain this expertise on campus. Currently, researchers whose focus is software are often isolated, working as the sole software engineer in their lab, research group, or even department and are without a peer community. This structure differs dramatically from the software engineering teams that are typical in industry.

Universities have an advantage of scale that can help alleviate these issues but only if resources can be shared across researchers and research groups. Pools of software engineers drawn from academia and industry with a range of skills and levels of seniority could enable software engineers to embed within research groups to evaluate their needs and design and implement software solutions. This would enable research groups to work with software engineers without having to find long-term positions that are fully funded and would leverage the significant fractional funding currently available to support this work.

With a growing reliance on software engineering to develop and support our computational tools, a sign of success would be the removal of the semipermeable membrane that exists between industry and academia where when someone takes a job in industry, the path to return to academia is often closed off. With the need for more software engineering talent and experience within astronomy, we have the opportunity to break these barriers and enable researchers to return to astronomy with their new software skills (even if only for a number of years before moving back to industry) and provide a more natural flow of talent. This would deepen the pool of talent in astronomy and provide a means of bootstrapping software engineering education.

9. The Challenges and Opportunities Ahead

However we approach ML and scalable software in this new era, discoveries will be made and a deeper understanding of the universe will emerge. As in the past, astronomers will adapt to the resources that are made available to them and work around the limitations of statistical methodologies. The challenge we face is whether we can make use of our earlier experiences to limit our missteps over the next decade.

While we typically speak of the volume of data from the LSST, it is not so much the size of the data that we must address rather it is the complexity of the scientific analyses. A survey of Rubin's science collaborations identified multiple science cases that would each require 100k–3M CPU hours for completion (for science in the first year of Rubin operations). Scaling this science is more than just providing more computational hardware. Tools, even industry tools, don't always exist that are robust enough to scale for a typical science analysis or have the required functionality. For example, many of the scalable analysis frameworks assume scientists work independently (i.e., they do not deal with multitenancy applications) which is not how astronomers typically work (we run different algorithms across the same dataset many times over). This means, we need to extend the functionality of large open source analysis frameworks (e.g., Spark, Dask, and Ray). The skills to accomplish this are often beyond those of a typical graduate student. We need to train or bring in these skills to astronomy.

Extending existing (industry and academic) analysis frameworks and infrastructure to meet our science requirements will mean upstreaming extensions to existing code bases. This requires significant software engineering skills. The AXS extensions described above have still not been integrated into Spark's master branch and so its developers must maintain and support a separate fork of the code. An opportunity exists to identify what software infrastructure is needed by researchers across all of the sciences, to develop a road map for addressing common computational needs, and to identify the resources needed to support the development of these code bases and services. If we look at how our science questions map to software requirements as a whole, we might find that the software infrastructure we need to develop is common to multiple science domains. This could reduce the resources needed to scale existing and new tools to enable the discoveries we expect from the LSST but only if we approach this question as a community and not as individual researchers.

References

[1] P. Zečević, C. T. Slater, M. Jurić *et al.* (2019). AXS: A framework for fast astronomical data processing based on Apache Spark. *Astronomical Journal*, *158*(1), 37. https://doi.org/10.3847/1538-3881/ab2384, *arXiv:1905.09034 [astro-ph.IM]*.

[2] Astropy Collaboration, A. M. Price-Whelan, B. M. Sipöcz *et al.* (2018). The Astropy project: Building an open-science project and status of the v2.0 core package. *Astronomical Journal*, *156*(3), 123. https://doi.org/10.3847/1538-3881/aabc4f, *arXiv:1801.02634 [astro-ph.IM]*.

[3] F. Pedregosa, G. Varoquaux, A. Gramfort *et al.* (2011). Scikit-learn: Machine learning in Python. *Journal of Machine Learning Research*, *12*, 2825–2830.

[4] J. VanderPlas, A. J. Connolly, Z. Ivezic *et al.* 2012. Introduction to astroml: Machine learning for astrophysics. In *CIDU*. IEEE, ISBN 978-1-4673-4625-2, pp. 47–54, ISBN 978-1-4673-4625-2.

[5] A. Paszke, S. Gross, F. Massa *et al.* (2019). Pytorch: An imperative style, high-performance deep learning library. In H. Wallach, H. Larochelle, A. Beygelzimer, F. d'Alché-Buc, E. Fox and R. Garnett (eds.), *Advances in Neural Information Processing Systems 32*. Curran Associates, Inc., pp. 8024–8035.

[6] M. Abadi, A. Agarwal, P. Barham *et al.* (2015). TensorFlow: Large-scale machine learning on heterogeneous systems. https://www.tensorflow.org/, software available from tensorflow.org.

[7] J. S. Bloom, J. W. Richards, P. E. Nugent *et al.* (2012). Automating discovery and classification of transients and variable stars in the synoptic survey era. *Publications of the Astronomical Society of the Pacific*, *124*(921), 1175. https://doi.org/10.1086/668468, *arXiv:1106.5491 [astro-ph.IM]*.

[8] S. Cenko, J. Bloom, S. Kulkarni *et al.* (2012). Ptf10iya: A short-lived, luminous flare from the nuclear region of a star-forming galaxy. *Monthly Notices of the Royal Astronomical Society*, *420*(3), 2684–2699. https://doi.org/10.1111/j.1365-2966.2011.20240.x

[9] P. E. Nugent, M. Sullivan, S. B. Cenko *et al.* (2011). Supernova SN 2011fe from an exploding carbon-oxygen white dwarf star. *Nature*, *480*(7377), 344–347. https://doi.org/10. 1038/nature10644, *arXiv:1110.6201 [astro-ph.CO]*.

[10] T. Matheson, C. Stubens, N. Wolf *et al.* 2021. The ANTARES astronomical time-domain event broker. *Astronomical Journal*, *161*(3), 107. https://doi.org/10.3847/1538-3881/abd703, *arXiv:2011.12385 [astro-ph.IM]*.

[11] D. Muthukrishna, G. Narayan, K. S. Mandel *et al.* (2019). RAPID: Early classification of explosive transients using deep learning. *Publications of the Astronomical Society of the Pacific*, *131*(1005), 118002. https://doi.org/10.1088/1538-3873/ab1609, *arXiv:1904.00014 [astro-ph.IM]*.

[12] R. Carrasco-Davis, G. Cabrera-Vives, F. Förster *et al.* (2019). Deep learning for image sequence classification of astronomical events. *Publications of the Astronomical Society of the Pacific*, *131*(1004), 108006. https://doi.org/10.1088/1538-3873/aaef12, *arXiv:1807.03869 [astro-ph.IM]*.

[13] R. Hložek, K. A. Ponder, A. I. Malz *et al.* 2020. Results of the Photometric LSST Astronomical Time-series Classification Challenge (PLAsTiCC). *arXiv e-prints, arXiv:2012.12392 [astro-ph.IM]*.

[14] K. Boone (2019). Avocado: Photometric Classification of Astronomical Transients with Gaussian process augmentation. *Astronomical Journal, 158*(6), 257. https://doi.org/10.3847/1538-3881/ab5182, *arXiv:1907.04690 [astro-ph.IM]*.

[15] K. Boone (2021). ParSNIP: Generative models of transient light curves with physics-enabled deep learning. *Astronomical Journal, 162*(6), 275. https://doi.org/10.3847/1538-3881/ac2a2d, *arXiv:2109.13999 [astro-ph.IM]*.

[16] A. R. Halford and A. Rokem (2018). Cloudknot: A Python library to run your existing code on AWS batch. In F. Akici, D. Lippa, D. Niederhut and M. Pacer (eds.), *Proceedings of the 17th Python in Science Conference*, pp. 8–14. https://doi.org/10.25080/Majora-4af1f417-001.

[17] J. Sampe, P. Garcia-Lopez, M. Sanchez-Artigas *et al.* (2021). Toward multicloud access transparency in serverless computing. *IEEE Software, 38*(1), 68–74, 3029994. https://doi.org/10.1109/MS.2020.

Climate Change

© 2023 World Scientific Publishing Company
https://doi.org/10.1142/9789811265679_0013

Chapter 13

AI for Net-Zero

Alberto Arribas*,‖, Karin Strauss†,**, Sharon Gillett‡,††,
Amy Luers§,‡‡, Trevor Dhu¶,§§, Lucas Joppa§,¶¶,
Roy Zimmermann†,‖‖, and Vanessa Miller§,***

*Environmental Sustainability, Microsoft, Reading, United Kingdom
†Microsoft Research, Microsoft, Redmond, USA
‡Microsoft Research, Microsoft, Cambridge, USA
§Environmental Sustainability, Microsoft, Redmond, USA
¶Environmental Sustainability, Microsoft, Canberra, Australia
‖aarribas@microsoft.com
**kstrauss@microsoft.com
††sharon.gillett@microsoft.com
‡‡amyluers@microsoft.com
§§trevor.dhu@microsoft.com
¶¶lujoppa@microsoft.com
‖‖royz@microsoft.com
***vanessa.miler-fels@se.com

1. Introduction

"The evidence is irrefutable: greenhouse gas emissions are choking our planet and putting billions of people at immediate risk"; these are the words of Antonio Guterres, UN Secretary-General during the presentation of the Intergovernmental Panel on Climate Change (IPCC) report in 2021. The world has already warmed by about $1.1°C$ and avoiding catastrophic climate change (unprecedented extreme changes from global temperature increasing above $1.5°C/2°C$) requires halting the accumulation of greenhouse gases (GHGs) from human activities in the atmosphere — i.e., reaching net-zero. Net-zero is achieved when, overall, anthropogenic GHG emissions are balanced by anthropogenic GHG removals. GHGs include carbon dioxide

(CO_2), methane (CH_4), nitrous oxide (N_2O), and fluorinated gases, but CO_2 emissions are the most common due to fossil fuels and their effects are among the longest lasting.

Achieving net-zero is an urgent challenge. As shown by the IPCC, limiting global temperature increases to $1.5°C$ requires reaching net-zero CO_2 emissions by 2050. This means reducing CO_2 emissions from around 50 gigatons per year (Gt/year) to approximately 5–10 Gt/year in less than 30 years and, in addition, removing those remaining 5–10 Gt/year. However, transformations affecting entire infrastructure systems, as needed to achieve net-zero, typically take longer than 30 years to deploy [1]. The complexity of the net-zero challenge is increased because there is not only a need to balance GHG reductions and removals over multidecadal timescales but to do so in alignment with socio-economic (e.g., social justice and economic growth) and ecological requirements (e.g., water conservation, and biodiversity). This demands improving governance, accountability, and reporting mechanisms, which are currently inadequate [2]. Therefore, achieving net-zero is a complex challenge that requires both improved capabilities for carbon accounting and improved capabilities for decarbonizing all sectors of the global economy, including removing CO_2 from the atmosphere. The good news is that technological progress can enable the capabilities we need.

AI is a key technology to accelerate and achieve the required transformations because of its proven ability to process large datasets from heterogeneous sources (e.g., satellites, sensors, mobile phones, or written reports), to improve optimization and automation (e.g., helping to increase the availability of renewable energy), and to accelerate scientific discovery (e.g., facilitating the development of carbon-free materials). In addition, AI has been proven to be scalable — it can be applied globally — and successful at helping to solve a wide range of complex problems [3–5]. However, it is worth remembering that, beyond R&D, the world also needs more practical experience in testing and deploying new technologies and business strategies at scale [1].

In general, no single domain offers greater opportunities for deep decarbonization than electric power [1] but there are many other areas where AI can help carbon accounting and decarbonizing the economy. Indeed, one of the most exciting aspects of AI is its potential to enable advances made by experts in other fields who can adopt AI for their own purposes [6]. As is shown in this chapter, direct measuring of GHG emissions and materials engineering are two critical knowledge gaps where AI can make a significant impact to achieve net-zero.

This chapter is structured as follows: Section 2 presents how AI can rapidly improve the accounting of carbon and the reduction and removal of

GHG emissions to decarbonize the economy. It discusses how to overcome existing limitations and analyses the most relevant knowledge gaps where AI can make an impact.

Section 3 explains the need to ensure AI itself is environmentally sustainable.

Finally, AI does not exist in a vacuum. Section 4 discusses how AI must be integrated within people, processes, and policy systems to accelerate the progress towards net-zero.

2. AI for Net-Zero

Achieving net-zero requires improved capabilities for accounting, reducing, and removing GHG emissions. This section provides an estimate of the magnitude of the challenge before briefly describing how AI has already been successfully used (Table 1). Finally, this section identifies and discusses the key research challenges where AI can significantly accelerate and improve the accounting, reducing, and removing of GHG emissions (Table 2).

2.1. *What is the magnitude of the challenge?*

It is worth starting by providing an estimate of the magnitude of the net-zero challenge. In this chapter, the term "accounting" is used to include the direct measurement of GHG emissions, the estimation of emissions (e.g., via emissions factors), and, finally, the monitoring and balancing of those emissions in adequate ledgers. To achieve net-zero, it is necessary to account for all of the approximately 50 Gt/year GHG emissions that happen today and to track progress towards reducing these emissions to about 5–10 Gt/year by 2050. The accounting challenge also includes the need to measure and verify the removal of the remaining 5–10 Gt/year.

Decarbonizing the economy requires reductions and removals of GHG emissions. In terms of reductions, it is useful to consider some of the key sectors and the fraction of GHG emissions that these sectors represent:

– electricity generation ~25% of global GHG emissions,
– transport ~14% of global GHG emissions,
– manufacturing (industrial processes) ~21% of global GHG emissions,
– buildings ~6% of global GHG emissions,
– land use ~24% of global GHG emissions.

Data from *Contribution of Working Group III to the Fifth Assessment Report of the Intergovernmental Panel on Climate Change*, 2014 (IPCC).

Table 1. Summary and examples of previous uses of AI for net-zero.

	Reducing					Removing	
	Accounting	Electricity generation	Transport	Manufacturing (and buildings)	Land sector	NbS	Tech
Size of the challenge[a]	~50Gt/year GHG emissions in 2021	~25% of GHG emissions	~14% of GHG emissions	~27% of GHG emissions	~24% of GHG emissions	~5–10Gt from 2050	~5–10Gt/yr from 2050
State-of-art examples*	Detection of emitting infrastructure / tracking of emissions / detection of GHG leaks / monitoring of emissions from land-use	Balancing variable generation / dynamic scheduling and pricing / local-grid management and optimisation	Efficiency of transport system / modal shift / alternative fuels research	Real-time management of buildings / carbon-free materials research	Irrigation management / crop yield prediction / monitoring of emissions	Monitoring of emissions	Materials research / identification of storage locations
Data sources	Remote sensing / in-situ sensors / census and reports data	In-situ sensors / remote sensing /	Vehicle sensors / mobile phones / remote sensing	In-situ sensors / remote sensing / mobile phones / real-state data	In-situ sensors / remote sensing / UAV	Remote sensing / in-situ sensors / UAV	In-situ sensors
Relevant AI tools currently used*	Computer vision / data fusion / computation fluid dynamics / NLP / transfer learning	Computer vision / unsupervised learning / reinforcement learning / generative models / causality / transfer learning	Computer vision / unsupervised learning / reinforcement learning	Computer vision / data fusion / NLP / computation fluid dynamics / reinforcement learning / unsupervised learning / transfer learning / causality	Computer vision / reinforcement learning / transfer learning / causality	Computer vision / reinforcement learning / learning	Computer vision / data fusion / unsupervised learning /

Notes: *From Rolnick *et al.* 2019 "Tackling Climate Change with Machine Learning". For specific references see text.

[a] Estimations from IPCC are: electricity systems responsible for 25% GHG emissions / Estimation from IPCC: Transport accounts for ~25% of energy-related CO_2 emissions / Estimation from IPCC: energy consumed in Buildings accounts for ~25% of energy-related emissions.

Table 2. Key knowledge gaps and AI tools to address them.

	Reducing					Removing	
	Accounting	Electricity generation	Transport	Manufacturing (and buildings)	Land sector	NbS	Tech
Size of the challenge[a]	~50Gt/year GHG emissions in 2021	~25% of GHG emissions	~14% of GHG emissions	~27% of GHG emissions	~24% of GHG emissions	~5–10Gt from 2050	~5–10Gt/yr from 2050
Areas of impact from direct measuring & material science knowledge gaps	Direct measuring of GHG for reliable accounting systems direct measuring for reducing error bars from land sector and Methane	Material science for energy storage	Material science for sustainable fuels	Material science for carbon-free materials (e.g. cement, steel, semiconductors	Direct measuring of CO_2 and CH_4	Direct measuring – verification and leakage	Material science for sorbent materials
Key AI and computing tools for direct measuring & material science knowledge gaps	Computer vision, multi-sensor data fusion, computational fluid dynamics	Life cycle analysis, material design, reinforcement learning, inference, NLP, computational fluid dynamics	Life cycle analysis, material design, reinforcement learning, inference, NLP, computational fluid dynamics	Life cycle analysis, material design, reinforcement learning, inference, NLP, computational fluid dynamics	Computer vision, multi-sensor data fusion, computational fluid dynamics	Computer vision, multi-sensor data fusion, computational fluid dynamics	Life cycle analysis, material design, reinforcement learning, inference, NLP, computational fluid dynamics

Electricity generation offers the greatest opportunities for deep decarbonization. As described by IPCC, "the pervasive use of carbon-free electricity could cover more than half the GHG reductions needed to achieve net-zero", but for that to happen, low-carbon technologies to generate electricity need to increase from approximately one-third today to 80% by 2050 [1].

Transport accounts for approximately one-quarter of all energy-related CO_2 emissions (IPCC), but despite the opportunity for electrification, much of the sector (e.g., freight transportation represents half of transport emissions) is hard to decarbonize because of the difficulty of replacing the high-energy density of fossil fuels used in aviation and shipping.

Manufacturing has been estimated to account for slightly over 20% of global GHG emissions (IPCC). Industrial processes and building materials are the leading causes of difficult-to-eliminate emissions [7], and high-heat industrial processes such as steel, cement, and refining oil account for approximately 25% of the global energy use [1]. As an illustration, if it were a country, the cement industry would be the third larger emitter of GHG after China and USA [8]. In addition, the energy consumed in buildings is responsible for approximately one-quarter of the global energy-related emissions (IPCC), but with the right combination of design and management, it is possible for buildings to consume almost no energy [9].

Finally, the land sector has been estimated to be responsible for about a quarter of global GHG emissions (IPCC) and this may well be an underestimate [10] because the largest uncertainties — over 20% [11] — in GHG emissions are in the land-use sector. Additional emissions come from climate change accelerating processes such as forest fires and permafrost melting. According to some estimates [12], better land management and agricultural practices could account for a third of the global GHG reductions needed.

In terms of removing GHG emissions, the challenge is to eliminate about 5–10 Gt/year from the atmosphere by 2050 using a mixture of nature-based, technology-based, and hybrid approaches. It should be noted that the carbon removal industry is still in its infancy, particularly the development of technology-based solutions. A non-comprehensive summary of nature-, technology-based, and hybrid approaches to carbon removal follows. For a more in-depth discussion, see [13].

Nature-based solutions involve mostly terrestrial ecosystems and soils, and it includes land-use practices that enhance carbon storage in plants, trees, soils, and soil ecosystems (microbes and fungi). Technology-based solutions and Hybrid solutions include the following: Direct air capture (chemical processes by which CO_2 is captured from ambient air and geologically sequestered and stored); BiCRS (biomass carbon removal and storage); BECCS (bioenergy with carbon capture and sequestration, or electricity, liquid fuels or heat production using biomass where the CO_2 produced is captured and sequestered); and Carbon mineralization (processes by which CO_2 forms a chemical bond with a reactive mineral, which can occur at the surface and subsurface level).

2.2. *What has been done already?*

The use of AI for Climate has been an active area of research during the last few years. AI has been successfully applied in various projects related to the accounting of carbon and the decarbonization of the economy by helping to reduce and remove GHG emissions. A summary of representative projects, data sources, and AI tools is presented in Table 1 (see [3] and ClimateChange.ai for a more comprehensive listing of recent applications of AI for climate). As an illustration, a few practical examples are briefly described in the following.

2.2.1. *Accounting of GHG emissions*

AI, specifically computer vision tools, has been used to process remote sensing data to monitor and estimate the amount of carbon sequestered by forests and peatlands [14]. AI has also been used to detect GHG emitting infrastructure by processing high-resolution satellite data available globally to generate building footprints at national scale (e.g., Microsoft's computer-generated building footprints for USA: https://github.com/Microsoft/USBuildingFootprints). In addition to the use of satellite or LiDAR data, Natural Language Processing tools have been applied to real estate records to predict building heights [15], which is a useful proxy to estimate their energy consumption and emissions. The use of NLP on written records is important as it illustrates how AI could improve the traditional process of recording and accounting for GHG emissions in national or non-estate actors' inventories.

Despite these successes, there is still much to be done and limitations in data availability and knowledge need to be overcome for AI to have a significant impact on the reporting of GHG emissions. For example, satellites can measure concentrations of GHGs with global coverage, but CO_2's long lifespan and high background baseline concentration make it difficult for the current generation of satellites to pinpoint any new CO_2 emissions from a specific building or factory. In addition, current satellite data have a coarse spatial resolution and large temporal and spatial gaps, particularly in hyperspectral data, making them unsuitable for the precise tracking of emissions.

It should be noted that the biggest gap in knowledge and the largest uncertainties — larger than 20% for both China and USA and over 60% for Brazil [11] — in measuring CO_2 emissions are related to land sector. There are also big uncertainties in the direct measuring of emissions (and the estimation of related emissions factors) for methane and nitrous oxide.

2.2.2. *Decarbonizing the economy — reduction of GHG emissions*

In electric power generation, a major transformation is already underway. Successful examples of the use of AI include improving the forecasting of renewable energy generation (solar [16], wind [17]); the balancing of production and demand [18]; the design of real-time pricing strategies [19]; and the design of materials for batteries [20]. It can be argued that technological progress in clean electricity has already set off a virtuous circle, with each innovation creating more political will to do even more [1]. Replicating this in other sectors is essential.

For transport, successful AI use examples include the optimization of logistic decisions [21], increased efficiency of public transport by learning the behavior of users [22], and improved scheduling of charging electric vehicles [23]. For Manufacturing (and buildings), successful examples include the use of ML to develop structures that require less raw material [24] and the real-time management of buildings and infrastructure — e.g., using intelligent control systems, algorithms can allow devices and systems to adapt to usage and occupancy in residential buildings [25] and IT datacenters (DeepMind AI Reduces Google Data Centre Cooling Bill by 40%). AI can also help to improve the maintenance of buildings and infrastructure [26] and facilitate grid balancing [27]. For the land sector, successful examples include improved irrigation, disease detection, crop yield prediction [28], and the monitoring of emissions from peatlands and forests [29].

Despite the evident progress and significant potential for AI to reduce GHG emissions and accelerate the transition to net-zero, there are still limitations that need to be overcome. These include the following: data availability (e.g., one of the challenges for AI-driven material science is coping with small or moderate size datasets); practical and interdisciplinary experience deploying new technologies in complex systems (the electricity grid and manufacturing are examples of vast and complex physical infrastructure); and policy and economic incentives (these are mature and complex markets with a large number of customers).

2.2.3. *Decarbonizing the economy — removal of GHG emissions*

AI has been used to help monitor emissions from nature which can enable nature-based Solutions. Also, AI could be used to accelerate materials discovery to improve sorbents, increasing their efficiency to capture carbon and reducing their degradation over time [30], and to help identify potential storage locations for carbon in the same way as oil and gas companies have used Machine Learning and subsurface images/data to identify oil and gas reservoirs [31].

Carbon removal is an emerging area and there is much to be done. AI could have a significant impact on the removal of GHG emissions, but similarly to the case for reducing, it requires overcoming limitations in data, knowledge, practical interdisciplinary experience in deploying new technologies in complex systems, and policy/economic incentives.

2.3. What are the key limitations and the key knowledge gaps where AI could make a significant impact to achieve net-zero?

Its proven ability to process large datasets from heterogeneous sources, its scalability, and its applicability to a wide range of complex problems make AI a critical technology to accelerate the transformation required to achieve net-zero. However, given the need for a radical and simultaneous transformation of multiple complex systems (electricity generation, transport, manufacturing, and land-sector) in a short period of time (less than 30 years), making AI effective for net-zero needs a more fundamental change than simply developing and transferring technology.

For AI to be effective, it must be applied in a way that incorporates and expands the substantial body of knowledge that already exists [4], and AI must be integrated within people, processes, and policy systems.

As shown in Figure 1, there are three common factors currently limiting the impact of AI for accounting and decarbonizing the economy (i.e., reducing and removing GHG emissions): policy, economic, and skills incentives; multidisciplinary experience deploying new technology in complex systems; and data quality and availability.

How to overcome these limitations to enable AI to have a significant impact for net-zero is discussed below.

2.3.1. *Limitations in policy, economics, and skills*

Making AI effective requires a multilevel and multidisciplinary view of the problem, a system dynamic approach recognizing interdependencies and feedback loops, and a focus around the concerns, interests, and values of users [5]. That requires appropriate incentives in policy, economics, and education.

For example, the necessary AI technology to improve the charging and efficiency of electric vehicles largely exists, but it requires complementary assets such as policies to increase adoption (e.g., banning the sale of fossil

NET ZERO

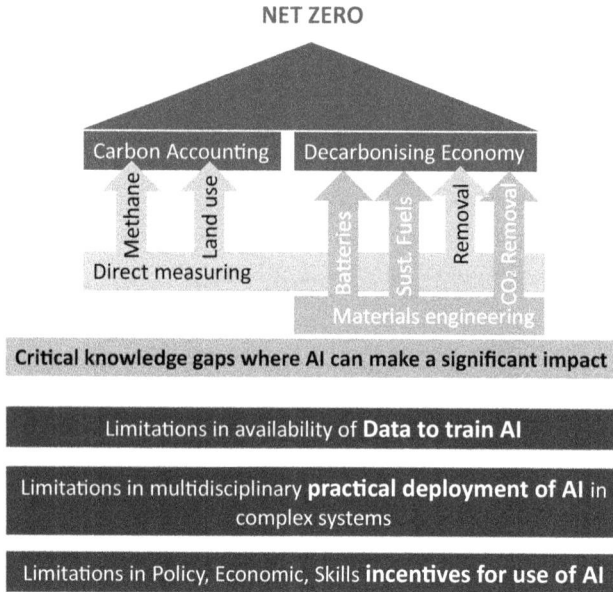

Fig. 1.   Schematic describing current limitations and critical knowledge gaps where AI could enable and accelerate the transition to net-zero.

fuel engines) and economic incentives and urban planning to provide access to charging points. Similarly, AI can make a significant and rapid impact reducing the energy consumption and emissions of buildings. However, given their long lifespan, buildings will often need the retrofitting of solutions, which requires policy and economic incentives to increase the adoption of AI solutions.

It is also important to realize that, for AI to fulfill its potential to achieve net-zero, there is also a need to address current skill shortages. For example, the "Understanding the UK AI labour market" report completed by the UK government in 2020 found that approximately 50% of organizations were affected by a lack of candidates with the right skills. In addition, a lack of diversity and social inequity in AI was also found, an important issue that needs addressing.

Net-zero is an active area of policy development. For example, the European Union's Green Deal is not only intended to address climate change but to act as the key economic growth strategy for Europe. The "Carbon Border Adjustment Mechanism" (a measure within the Green Deal designed to ensure that imported goods pay a price for their carbon emissions that is comparable to the price paid by EU domestic producers) is an example of a policy designed to help reduce manufacturing's large carbon footprint. These types of policies are important to incentivize and accelerate transformation and AI adoption. Otherwise, and particularly in the case of manufacturing given the substantial investment required in physical infrastructure, organizations often adopt low-risk and change-averse strategies.

AI can help the design of effective policies and incentives: causality frameworks and agent-based modeling offer an opportunity to evaluate different options and optimize policies while balancing trade-offs.

2.3.2. *Limitations in multidisciplinary deployment of new technology in complex systems*

The development of appropriate policy and economic incentives is not the only issue: the world also needs to rapidly acquire more practical experience in deploying and testing new technologies and business strategies at scale [1].

As described in Section 2.2, AI technologies already exist to account for carbon and help decarbonize economic sectors; the issue is how to deploy them faster and better to help transform and optimize the existing systems. For example, the more a power grid relies on renewables, the more frequently the supply may not match the demand [1]. AI algorithms can help by optimizing for system goals (e.g., simultaneously optimize for scheduling, pricing, and minimize emissions [32]). Critically, balancing the grid requires significant improvements from operators, but, also, AI needs to incorporate domain-specific knowledge because much of previous work used domain-agnostic approaches.

In order to deploy new technologies into complex systems, there is already a large amount of knowledge available in the field of Operations Research that AI can further improve on. For example, the use of AI and digital twins can enable the testing of processes and equipment prior to its physical implementation and enable predictive maintenance of machinery after implementation. This offers enormous possibilities to reduce costs and risks. Equally, AI can be used to enable efficiencies across the energy-transport-manufacturing nexus (e.g., by identifying optimal locations for manufacturing facilities, taking into account the availability of carbon-free energy, and transport networks).

2.3.3. *Limitations in data*

The ongoing progress to address limitations in policy and overcome challenges in practical deployment needs to be complemented with a fundamental ingredient to unlock the potential of AI: data. Current limitations in data availability affect the appropriate accounting of carbon and the effective reduction and removal of GHG emissions to decarbonize the economy.

A critical source of data for AI is remote sensing. Many of today's satellites measuring GHG (GOSAT, OCO, and CAMS; see Report on GHG Monitoring from Space (wgicouncil.org) for a comprehensive inventory) are equipped with hyperspectral cameras that can measure the interaction of GHG with sunlight and estimate their concentrations [14]. However, although satellites can measure concentrations of GHGs with global coverage, CO_2's long lifespan and the high background baseline concentration make it difficult for the current generation of satellites to pinpoint any new CO_2 emissions from a specific building or factory. Also, current satellite data have a coarse spatial resolution and large temporal and spatial gaps, particularly in hyperspectral data, making them unsuitable for the precise tracking of emissions.

Luckily, new satellite missions are already scheduled for launch (see Report on GHG Monitoring from Space (wgicouncil.org)) and will generate datasets with an improved range of spatial, temporal, and spectral resolutions or scales. In addition, AI can use standard satellite imagery (high-res RGB images) to fill the gaps in hyperspectral data. Beyond remote sensing data, mobile phones, drones, and *in situ* sensors are also increasing the amount of data available to directly measure GHG emissions but some of these data sources (e.g., mobile phones) pose potential challenges around privacy and data management. Finally, remote sensing and sensor data need to be combined with data already existing from national and non-state actors' inventories (e.g., as done in projects such as Global Carbon Project) and other data sources such as real-estate or industry databases (e.g., the Materials Project (materialsproject.org) and the UCI Machine Learning Repository for material discovery). However, much of the necessary data can be proprietary, low quality, or representative only of some specific assets or processes, making it difficult to use (e.g., it is estimated that 60–70% of industrial data go unused; see Factory Records: GE Providing Procter & Gamble Greater Access to the Cloud for Analyzing Manufacturing Data | GE News).

Data are absolutely critical and the trend to make data available is positive, but for AI to fulfill its potential for net-zero, it is also necessary to continue improving quality control, standards, and data licensing so all required data can be used to train AI algorithms. Pioneering projects such as Climate TRACE, Global Carbon Project, Carbon Monitor, and Terrain AI are exploring AI methodologies and partnerships to overcome data challenges and provide near-real-time measuring of global GHG emissions. Recent initiatives such as Carbon Call (carboncall.org) are tackling inefficiencies and problems in current ledger systems which do not provide the accountability needed for nations and organizations.

2.3.4. *Critical knowledge gaps*

As shown, rapid progress is taking place to address limitations in policy, practical deployment, and data quality and availability. However, there is a final limitation in need of addressing: knowledge. Specifically, there are two critical knowledge gaps for achieving net-zero where AI can have a significant impact:

– direct measuring of GHG emissions,
– science discovery for engineering carbon-free materials.

As shown in Table 2 and Figure 1, these two critical knowledge gaps map into all areas of carbon accounting and decarbonizing the economy. Although it is difficult to make a precise quantitative assessment of their impact, their qualitative importance for achieving net-zero is easy to demonstrate:

The direct measurement of GHG emissions (CO_2, CH_4, and N_2O) is crucial for the proper accounting of carbon (a 50 Gt/year challenge), which requires reliable and interoperable accounting systems with accountability that current GHG ledgers do not provide (carboncall.org). Also, direct measurement is needed for reducing GHG emissions from the land sector (which has the largest uncertainties and is responsible for $\sim$24% of global emissions, including most methane emissions) and finally, for unlocking the use of nature-based solutions for carbon removal ($\sim$5–10 Gt/year challenge).

Science discovery, specifically materials engineering, is critical for the decarbonization of the economy, including for the reduction of GHG emissions by enabling the storage of carbon-free energy, enabling sustainable fuels required for aviation and shipping (freight is responsible for 50% of transport emissions), and enabling carbon-free manufacturing (embodied carbon in, e.g., steel, cement, or semiconductors). Materials discovery is also critical for tech-based carbon removal (estimated to be 5–10 Gt/year from 2050). Finally, as will be discussed in Section 3, material discovery may also be necessary to reduce embodied carbon in IT infrastructure.

How AI can help address these two critical knowledge gaps is discussed in the following.

2.3.5. *The first knowledge gap relates to the direct measurement of GHG emissions*

AI enables the combination of multiple data sources to provide better estimations of GHG emissions. For example, Climate TRACE and Carbon Monitor use *in situ* measurements (highly accurate from sources such as sensors and vessels' locations but not fully available or covering every country, sector, or asset), remote sensing imagery (from public and private satellites and from visible and other spectrums), and additional data sources such as corporate disclosures (often estimated using emission factors). Working with a coalition of partner organizations (such as WattTime, OceanMind, and BlueSky Analytics in the case of Climate TRACE), these data are used to train and continuously improve AI algorithms to estimate where emitting assets are located, when emissions happen, and how much emissions take place.

AI can also be used to address the specific challenge of reducing the error bars in emissions from land sector. For example, Terrain AI [Terrain- AI —Uncovering new insights to support effective climate change decision making (terrainai.com)] establishes fully instrumented benchmark test sites (covering grasslands, croplands, forestry, wetlands, peatlands, and urban areas) and uses Machine Learning algorithms to generate suitable information for sustainable management and policy development. Carbon Plan has used satellite imagery to identify locations experiencing forest losses due to deforestation and estimated the amount of carbon removed from the forest, and Synthetaic has used High-Performance Computing, generative AI, and deep Neural Networks to map concentrated animal feeding operations (that are a major source of methane emissions) from satellite imagery.

An active area of research is the use of Transfer Learning to generalize the application of AI algorithms developed in rich-data settings to low-data settings. A practical example has been demonstrated in the use of AI to estimate the height of trees or the thickness of peat from LiDAR's data to assess the carbon stock, which then has been generalized to regions where LiDAR data were not available by using AI to predict LiDAR's measurements from satellite imagery [33], enabling global scaling.

The use of AI to improve the direct measuring of GHG emissions globally can significantly improve and accelerate the use of nature-based solutions for carbon removal by addressing critical issues such as verification and leakage. For example, AI can improve the development of policy incentives [34] (e.g., to encourage farmers to adopt practices that sequester carbon and reduce emissions as intended in EU's agricultural policies) and make possible farming practices that allow farmers to work at scale while adapting local land's needs (FarmBeats: AI, Edge & IoT for Agriculture - Microsoft Research is a pioneering example). Finally, AI can enable the engineering of biological fertilizers that could replace chemical ones, reducing costs and facilitating carbon sequestration in soils. The use of AI for biology is a nascent but promising area of research.

2.3.6. *The second knowledge gap relates to carbon-free materials*

In general terms, the process of discovering new materials is slow and difficult but AI can help the decarbonization of the economy by optimizing R&D, reducing costs, and accelerating the development of carbon-free materials [6]. The use of AI to develop new materials will require making data available from experiments (small data) and real-world implementations.

For example, supervised learning and generative models can be used to develop storage batteries using natural resources. Similarly, AI can improve the development of alternative fuels and reduce their current green premium. Biofuels have the potential to serve as low-carbon drop-in fuels that retain the properties of fossil fuels (high energy density) while retaining compatibility with existing infrastructure [35]. Also, hydrogen — if produced using carbon-free electricity — can be used as a sustainable fuel and as energy storage because it can be stored at lower cost than electricity. Hydrogen can be used to decarbonize manufacturing processes requiring high heat.

AI can help us to model and design carbon-free construction materials. For example, Reinforcement Learning has been used to propose novel, low-emission formulas for concrete that could satisfy desired structural characteristics [36].

Finally, the transition to carbon-free electricity (which needs to rapidly increase from one-third today to approximately 80% by 2050) will also require the use of Carbon Capture and Storage technologies where AI can help by developing new materials and by optimizing processes. AI can also improve carbon removal in technology-based approaches such as Direct Air Capture (e.g., by improving materials for sorbent reusability and CO_2 uptake or by developing corrosion-resistant components able to withstand high temperatures [37]) and help identify and monitor sequestration sites [38].

3. Net-Zero for AI

Artificial intelligence plays a dual role: it can help achieve net-zero, but it also generates GHG emissions. As with any other IT-related activity,

AI depends on computational resources, such as processors, memory, and networks. The implication of this dependency is that GHG emissions from AI have two sources: the embodied carbon in the manufacturing of the infrastructure required and the direct energy consumption to use that infrastructure to train and deploy AI.

All forms of computing, including AI, are growing rapidly because they are useful tools for society, including for tackling the net-zero challenge. Accordingly, its energy use is also increasing and it has been estimated that in 2018 the energy use in datacenters had grown to be 1% of global electricity consumption [39]. However, it should be noted that thanks to energy efficiency improvements, the increase in datacenter energy use has grown much more slowly than the number of datacenters and the equipment they house. Expressed as energy per compute instance, the energy intensity of global datacenters has decreased by 20% annually since 2010 [39].

Despite the improvements in energy efficiency, there is no reason for complacency: recently, a rapid acceleration in AI resource consumption has been observed, driven by increases in the scale of deep learning AI models and the breadth of their application [40]. This rapid growth of AI has raised concerns around AI's carbon footprint [41] and brought attention to the importance of getting AI itself to net-zero.

Typically, the development cycle of an AI model can be described in four phases (Data Processing/Experimentation/Training/Inference) and, until recently, the focus for each of these phases has been on performance, with little consideration for improving environmental efficiency. Getting AI to net-zero will require a widespread shift to focus on environmental efficiency for all four phases of the model development cycle and, also, for the complete life cycle of the underlying infrastructure, from manufacturing to decommissioning.

Some shifts are already underway. The most important change towards reducing carbon emissions that have been implemented so far is the widespread use of carbon-free electricity. For example, Facebook AI reports that in 2020, renewable energy powered all of its operational use of AI, reducing its total carbon footprint by roughly two-thirds [40], and all major cloud providers (including Microsoft Azure, Amazon Web Services, and Google Cloud) are either already powering their datacenters with 100% carbon-free energy or have roadmaps to do so by 2030.

Powering datacenters with carbon-free energy needs to be done as part of a bigger drive to increase the overall availability of carbon-free energy globally — for uses such as transport and manufacturing — and, also, for computing and machine learning that happens outside datacenters. For example, on-device AI learning is becoming more ubiquitous and offers privacy advantages. Estimations of federated learning in devices have shown that its carbon footprint is comparable to that of training an orders-of-magnitude larger model in a centralized setting [40] and renewable energy is typically far more limited for client devices than for datacenters.

In terms of embodied carbon, a key issue that has been identified for datacenters is semiconductors, which account for approximately a third of the total embodied carbon. With regard to devices, it has been estimated that embodied carbon accounts for 74% of the total footprint of client devices (e.g., Apple's environmental report for iPhone 11). Therefore, the previous analysis about science discovery for carbon-free materials is also extremely relevant to reduce AI's carbon footprint.

Moving forward, it is necessary to shift the focus of AI development towards environmental efficiency. The development of simplified and standardized environmental efficiency measurements is needed to prioritize the highest-impact optimizations. Iterative engineering improvements, based on a combination of hardware and software innovations, need to continue happening to make learning models run more efficiently. In addition, it is necessary to prioritize the use of less compute- and memory-intensive AI methods, address on-device learning efficiency, develop more efficient techniques for the re-use of expensive models already trained, and transfer knowledge about efficiency advancements from deep learning research into practice.

4. Conclusion and Vision for Future

Avoiding catastrophic climate change requires halting the accumulation of greenhouse gases from human activities in the atmosphere — i.e., reaching net-zero. Achieving net-zero is a complex and urgent challenge that requires improved capabilities for carbon accounting for decarbonizing (by reducing and removing GHG emissions) all sectors of the global economy. The good news is that technological progress can enable the improved capabilities we need.

AI is a key technology to achieve the required transformations because of its proven ability to scale and solve a wide range of problems [3–5] by processing large datasets from heterogeneous sources (e.g., satellites, sensors, mobile phones, or written reports), improving optimization and automation (e.g., helping to increase the availability of renewable energy), and enabling R&D to address knowledge gaps.

This chapter has presented examples of how AI has already been successfully used (Table 1) before analyzing how AI can enable net-zero and how AI itself can become environmentally sustainable. Although not the focus of this chapter, it should be noted that AI can also help increase resilience to climate change by facilitating adaptation, and the assessment and management of climate risk.

Three common factors currently limiting the impact of AI for carbon accounting and decarbonizing (reducing and removing GHG emissions) the economy have been identified (Figure 1):

- incentives (policy, economic, skills) for AI use,
- practical deployment of AI in complex systems,
- data quality and availability.

As it has been shown, rapid progress is taking place to address limitations in all of them. Achieving net-zero requires further progress and simultaneous action — which AI can enable and further accelerate — across all those dimensions. Furthermore, there is still a critical knowledge gap in two key areas:

- direct measuring of GHG emissions,
- science discovery for materials engineering.

Direct measuring of GHG emissions and material engineering are critical for achieving net-zero (see Figure 1 and Table 2) because of their importance for accounting carbon (reducing the currently large uncertainties from land sector and addressing critical GHG such as methane), reducing emissions (across energy, transport, manufacturing, and land sector), and removing emissions (for both, nature- and technology-based solutions).

AI can play a fundamental role to accelerate R&D and address these two knowledge gaps.

For the direct measuring of GHG emissions, key data enabling the use of AI include remote sensing, *in situ* sensors, mobile data, and administrative records (e.g., real estate records). Key AI approaches and computational tools include computer vision, multisensor data fusion, and computational fluid dynamics.

For materials engineering, key data enabling the use of AI include the following: materials and fabrication properties; chemical property databases, synthesizability data, and supply chain data. Key AI approaches and computational tools include Life Cycle Analysis, material design, reinforcement learning, inference, NLP, and computational fluid dynamics.

In addition, it should be noted that these two critical knowledge gaps are not currently receiving the level of investment required. As shown in a recent analysis of investment in climate technology (PwC State of Climate Tech 2021), the share of climate tech venture investment in manufacturing, agri-food, and built environment is approximately 25% of the total venture capital investment, despite the emissions from these three sectors representing approximately 70% of the global GHG emissions. By contrast, transport accounts for over 60% of venture capital investment. Therefore, there is a strong case to focus investment on these knowledge gaps.

By focusing on addressing the two fundamental knowledge gaps of direct measuring of GHG and materials engineering, AI can enable proper accounting (including reducing existing big uncertainties from land sector and methane emissions) and accelerate the decarbonization of the economy by facilitating GHG reductions (energy storage, sustainable fuels, and carbon-free materials) and enabling carbon removals (by addressing limitations in nature-based solutions such as verification and leakage and making tech-based solutions cost-effective).

References

[1] I. Azevedo, M. R. Davidson, J. D. Jenkins *et al.* (2020). The paths to net zero: How technology can save the planet. *Foreign Affairs*, *99*(3), 18–27.

[2] S. Fankhauser, S. M. Smith, M. Allen *et al.* (2022). The meaning of net zero and how to get it right. *Nature Climate Change*, *12*, 15–21.

[3] D. Rolnick, P. L. Donti, L. H. Kaack *et al.* (2019). Tackling climate change with machine learning. arXiv.org.

[4] S. W. Fleming, J. R. Watson, A. Ellenson *et al.* (2022). Machine learning in Earth and environmental science requires education and research policy reforms. *Nature Geoscience*, *15*, 878–880.

[5] R. Nishant, M. Kennedy, and J. Corbetta (2020). Artificial intelligence for sustainability: Challenges, opportunities, and a research agenda. *International Journal of Information Management*, *53*, 102104.

[6] K. T. Butler, D. W. Davies, H. Cartwright *et al.* (2018). Machine learning for molecular and materials science. *Nature*, *559*, 547–555.

[7] S. J. Davis, N. S. Lewis, M. Shaner *et al.* (2018). Net-zero emissions energy systems. *Science*, *360*, 6396.

[8] J. Lehne and F. Preston (2018). *Making Concrete Change, Innovation in Low-Carbon Cement and Concrete*. Chatham House Report, Energy Environment and Resources Department, London, pp. 1–66.

[9] M. Olsthoorn, J. Schleich, and C. Faure (2019). Exploring the diffusion of low-energy houses: An empirical study in the European union. *Energy Policy*, *129*, 1382–1393.

[10] N. M. Mahowald, D. S. Ward, S. C. Doney *et al.* (2017). Are the impacts of land use on warming underestimated in climate policy? *Environmental Research Letters*, *12*(9), 094016.

[11] E. McGlynn, S. Li, M. F. Berger *et al.* (2022). Addressing uncertainty and bias in land use, land use change, and forestry greenhouse gas inventories. *Climatic Change*, *170*(5), 5.

[12] P. Hawken (2018). *Drawdown: The Most Comprehensive Plan Ever Proposed to Reverse Global Warming*. Penguin. London, United Kingdom.

[13] L. Joppa, A. Luers, E. Willmott *et al.* (2021). Microsoft's million-tonne CO2 removal purchase — Lessons for net zero. *Nature, 597*, 629–632.

[14] B. Minasny, B. I. Setiawan, S. K. Saptomo *et al.* (2018). Open digital mapping as a cost-effective method for mapping peat thickness and assessing the carbon stock of tropical peatlands. *Geoderma, 313*, 25–40.

[15] F. Biljecki, H. Ledoux, and J. Stoter (2017). Generating 3D city models without elevation data. *Computers, Environment and Urban Systems, 64*, 1–18.

[16] C. Voyant, G. Notton, S. Kalogirou *et al.* (2017). Machine learning methods for solar radiation forecasting: A review. *Renewable Energy, 105*, 569–582.

[17] A. M. Foley, P. G. Leahy, A. Marvuglia *et al.* (2012). Current methods and advances in forecasting of wind power generation. *Renewable Energy, 37*, 1–8.

[18] H. S. Hippert, C. E. Pedreira, and R. C. Souza (2001). Neural networks for short-term load forecasting: A review and evaluation. *IEEE Transactions on Power Systems, 16*(1), 44–55.

[19] S. D. Ramchurn, P. Vytelingum, A. Rogers *et al.* (2011). Agent-based control for decentralised demand side management in the smart grid. *10th International Conference on Autonomous Agents and Multiagent Systems, 1*, 5–12.

[20] K. Fujimura, A. Seko, Y. Koyama *et al.* (2013). Accelerated materials design of lithium superionic conductors based on first-principles calculations and machine learning algorithms. *Advanced Energy Materials, 3*(8), 980–985.

[21] Y. Bengio, A. Lodi, and A. Prouvost *et al.* (2018). Machine learning for combinatorial optimization: A methodological tour d'Horizon. arXiv.org.

[22] X. Dai, L. Sun, Y. Xu (2018). Short-term origin-destination based metro flow prediction with probabilistic model selection approach. *Journal of Advanced Transportation*.

[23] E. S. Rigas, S. D. Ramchurn, and N. Bassiliades (2015). Managing electric vehicles in the smart grid using artificial intelligence: A survey. *IEEE Transactions on Intelligent Transportation Systems, 16*(4), 1619–1635.

[24] R. H. Kazi, T. Grossman, H. Cheong *et al.* (2017). Early stage 3D design explorations with sketching and generative design. In *UIST '17: Proceedings of the 30th Annual ACM Symposium on User Interface Software and Technology*. New York: ACM Press, pp. 401–414. https://doi.org/10.1145/3126594.3126662.

[25] D. Urge-Vorsatz, K. Petrichenko, M. Staniec *et al.* (2013). Energy use in buildings in a long-term perspective. *Environmental Sustainability, 5*(2), 141–151.

[26] F. Jia, Y. Lei, J. Lin *et al.* (2016). Deep neural networks: A promising tool for fault characteristic mining and intelligent diagnosis of rotating machinery with massive data. *Mechanical Systems and Signal Processing, 72*, 303–315.

[27] F. Burlig, C. R. Knittel, D. Rapson *et al.* (2017). *Machine Learning From Schools About Energy Efficiency*. National Bureau of Economic Research. Working Paper Series 23908. doi: 10.3386/w23908, http://www.nber.org/papers/w23908.

[28] J. You, X. Li, M. Low *et al.* (2017). Deep Gaussian process for crop yield prediction based on remote sensing data. In *Thirty-First AAAI Conference on Artificial Intelligence*. San Francisco, 2017.

[29] H. Joosten, M. Tapio-Biström, and S. Tol (2012). *Peatlands: Guidance for Climate Change Mitigation Through Conservation, Rehabilitation and Sustainable Use*. Food and Agriculture Organization of the United Nations.

[30] V. B. Cashin, D. S. Eldridge, A. Yu *et al.* (2018). Surface functionalization and manipulation of mesoporous silica adsorbents for improved removal of pollutants: A review. *Environmental Science: Water Research & Technology*, *4*(2), 110–128.

[31] M. Araya-Polo, J. Jennings, A. Adler *et al.* (2018). Deep-learning tomography. *The Leading Edge*, *37*(1), 58–66.

[32] P. L. Donti, B. Amos, and J. Z. Kolter (2017). Task-based end-to-end model learning in stochastic optimization. *Advances in Neural Information Processing Systems*, 5484–5494.

[33] P. Rodríguez-Veiga, J. Wheeler, V. Louis *et al.* (2017). Quantifying forest biomass carbon stocks from space. *Current Forestry Reports*, *3*(1), 1–18.

[34] C.-H. Chen, H.-Y. Kung, and F.-J. Hwang (2019). Deep learning techniques for agronomy applications. *Agronomy*, *9*(3).

[35] L. H. Kaack, P. Vaishnav, M. G. Morgan *et al.* (2018). Decarbonizing intraregional freight systems with a focus on modal shift. *Environmental Research Letters*, *13*(8), 083001.

[36] X. Ge, R. T. Goodwin, J. R. Gregory *et al.* (2019). Accelerated discovery of sustainable building materials. arXiv.org.

[37] G. Holmes and D. W. Keith (2012). An air–liquid contactor for large-scale capture of CO_2 from air. *Philosophical Transactions of the Royal Society A: Mathematical, Physical and Engineering Sciences, 370*(1974), 4380–4403.

[38] B. Chen, D. R. Harp, Y. Lin *et al.* (2018). Geologic CO_2 sequestration monitoring design: A machine learning and uncertainty quantification based approach. *Applied Energy*, *225*, 332–345.

[39] E. Masanet, A. Shehabi, N. Lei *et al.* (2020). Recalibrating global data center energy-use estimates. *Science*, *367*, 984–986.

[40] C.-J. Wu, R. Raghavendra, U. Gupta *et al.* (2022). Sustainable AI: Environmental implications, challenges and opportunities. arXiv.org.

[41] E. Strubell, A. Ganesh, and A. McCallum (2019). Energy and policy considerations for deep learning in NLP. arXiv.org.

© 2023 World Scientific Publishing Company
https://doi.org/10.1142/9789811265679_0014

Chapter 14

AI for Climate Science

Philip Stier

Department of Physics, University of Oxford, UK
philip.stier@physics.ox.ac.uk

1. Introduction

While the introduction of AI has been a recent step change in many areas of science, the beginnings of AI in climate research are much less well defined. This is because climate research is by scale inherently big data intensive so that its research community had to develop automated tools for prediction and statistical data analysis from the onset, without knowledge that these approaches will be considered as AI or Machine Learning (ML, application of AI to learn from data without instruction) in the future (or even without being aware now). For example, regression and clustering have been applied for decades to understand associations between climate variables in observational and modeling data. Probabilistic methods and Bayes' theorem have been widely used to tackle inverse problems in the inference of climate parameters from Earth observations, as, e.g., in optimal estimation retrievals of atmospheric properties (e.g., temperature, clouds, and composition) from satellite data [2]. Clustering techniques, such as k-means, have been widely used to identify and attribute weather patterns and cloud regimes [3]. Causal attribution techniques have been developed to isolate anthropogenic climate signals from natural variability, generally requiring significant dimensionality reduction, e.g., through Principal Component Analysis [4].

Building on this early work, recent advances in AI are now transforming climate science, across all fields, which we will investigate in the following. The focus of this chapter is less on the specific AI/ML methods applied to each problem — there are plenty of choices, they are rapidly evolving, and there generally exists limited consensus on the optimal method for each task — but rather on the key application areas and opportunities for AI/ML to transform climate science.

2. Climate Modeling

Climate models span a wide range of complexities, from simple zero-dimensional energy balance models with analytical solutions to complex numerical Earth System Models predicting the transient evolution of the key Earth system components. In the following, we will be focusing on the latter type of model with an emphasis on the physical climate system. A climate model can be generalized as a map C, mapping the climate state vector $\mathbf{x}(t)$, from its initial state $\mathbf{x}(t_0)$ through time t, typically with prescribed spatiotemporally varying boundary conditions, such as natural (e.g., volcanic emissions and solar radiation) and anthropogenic (e.g., concentrations of CO_2, aerosols, and land use) perturbations, represented here as vector $\mathbf{b}(t)$. C includes structural (due to the formulation of the underlying equations representing climate processes) and parametric (due to inexact knowledge of parameters $\boldsymbol{\theta}$ in these equations) uncertainties:

$$\mathbf{x}(t) = C(\mathbf{x}(t_0), \mathbf{b}(t), \boldsymbol{\theta})$$

C here represents a wide range of complex physical and, in Earth System Models, bio-chemical processes. A climate model generally discretizes Earth, and spatially (e.g., structured or unstructured grids and spherical harmonics) and physical conservation laws (of momentum, energy, and mass), represented as systems of coupled partial differential equations, are numerically integrated forward in time. However, to maintain numerical stability [5], this time integration must be performed with short integration timesteps; for a typical climate model with 1 degree × 1 degree (approximately 100 km) resolution, the timestep is typically O(10 min), which has to be further reduced for higher spatial resolutions as will be discussed in the following. For a typical transient climate simulation from the year 1700 to 2100, this requires O(10^7) time-integration steps solving a complex set of equations for O(10^6) grid points. Note that climate models effectively integrate random manifestations of weather over time and are structurally often very similar to weather forecasting models so that many applications of AI discussed in the following apply to both domains.

However, key climate processes occur on small scales that cannot be explicitly resolved in such climate models. For example, clouds form droplets microscopically on a scale of O(10^{-6} m), which grow by diffusion and collisions to form precipitation of O(10^{-3} m). Macroscopically, clouds typically occur on scales of O(10^2 m) to O(10^5 m). As it is computationally not possible to globally resolve all of these scales, such processes are *parametrized*, i.e., approximated from the explicitly resolved large-scale climate variables. While tremendously successful in weather and climate prediction, such simplified parametrizations introduce structural deficiencies by construction, which contribute significantly to the remaining overall model uncertainty.

Another, often overlooked, problem is that climate models contain many such parameterizations to represent, e.g., clouds, radiation, turbulence, gravity waves, and oceanic mesoscale eddies. Due to the underlying complexity, these are generally solved sequentially via operator splitting, separately computing the solution for each, and combining these separate solutions to calculate the overall tendency for each variable that is then integrated forward in time. In fact, typical climate models have three operator-split parameterizations for clouds alone: (i) calculating the cloud amount, (ii) the convective transport of momentum, water, and tracers, and (iii) the cloud microphysics, i.e., the evolution of droplets of crystals.

Physical climate modeling has pushed the envelopes of supercomputing from its inception; hence, it is not surprising that the climate modeling community now embraces the opportunities provided by the advancement of AI and machine learning as we will discuss in the following.

2.1. *Emulating climate model parameterizations*

Based on a long heritage of climate model development, most AI applications in climate modeling have focused on the emulation of climate model parameterizations *in existing climate modeling frameworks* with two main objectives:

(i) Speedup, implementing emulators of existing parameterizations for reduced computational cost. Applications include the following:
  – Emulation of atmospheric radiative transfer using neural networks: it has been demonstrated that a neural network emulation of a longwave radiation code in a climate model achieved a speedup of 50–80 times faster than the original parameterization [6], an approach which has subsequently been extended to the shortwave radiation and improved in accuracy [7].
  – Emulation of aerosol microphysics: testing various ML approaches, such as neural networks, random forests, and gradient boosting: it has been shown that a neural network can successfully emulate an aerosol microphysics module in a climate model, including physical constraints, with a speedup of over 60 times than the original model [8].

(ii) Accuracy: the speedup provided by AI/ML allows for replacing (computationally affordable) simplified parameterizations with emulations of (previously computationally unaffordable) higher-accuracy reference models. Applications include the following:
  – Replacement of uncertain atmospheric convective cloud parameterizations with neural networks, e.g., emulating 2D cloud-resolving models for each column (superparameterization). Rasp *et al.* [9] use a nine-layer deep, fully connected network with 256 nodes in each layer with around 0.5 million parameters to successfully replace the convection scheme in a climate model with multiyear simulations closely reproducing the mean climate of the cloud-resolving simulation as well as key aspects of variability. Interestingly, their neural network conserves energy approximately without incorporating this as a physical constraint during the training. Remaining problems with stability can be overcome by the explicit incorporation of physical constraints [10].
  – Emulation of gravity wave drag parameterizations: training on an increased complexity version of an existing scheme, emulators have been built that produce more accurate weather forecasts than the operational version while performing 10 times faster on GPUs than the existing scheme on a CPU [11].
  – Representation of unresolved ocean mesoscale eddies: computationally efficient parameterizations of ocean mesoscale eddies have been developed based on relevance vector machines and convolutional neural networks from high-resolution simulations [12]. Physical constraints are explicitly embedded in the design of the network: the architecture forms the elements of a symmetric eddy stress tensor so that exact global momentum and vorticity conservation can be achieved, and the results are interpretable.

Based on the long heritage of specialized parameterization development, it is not entirely surprising that current approaches primarily focus on the speedup and improvement of parameterization in existing structural frameworks. However, the incorporation of AI/ML provides significant opportunities to overcome structural limitations of current climate models.

First, key climate processes are coupled on timescales much faster than the climate model integration timestep, e.g., the interaction between aerosols and clouds. However, under current operator splitting approaches, these processes can only interact with every host model timestep, typically O(10 min). AI/ML offers the *opportunity to emulate such coupled processes jointly*, eliminating structural operator splitting errors — an opportunity that has not yet been widely capitalized on. Second, AI/ML also provides an opportunity to develop entirely new parameterizations, under the incorporation of observational constraints, as we will now discuss.

2.2. *Development of new climate model parameterizations*

The development of climate model parameterizations generally combines theory with either detailed process or high-resolution modeling or observed relationships between small-scale processes and resolved scale variables (e.g., cloud fraction parameterized as a function of grid-scale atmospheric humidity [13]). However, the *systematic* incorporation of observational constraints in the parameterization development has remained challenging. Consequently, observations are often primarily used for model evaluation and parameter tuning *after the structural model development* and often only based on aggregate statistics, such as gridded monthly means of satellite observations. It is surprising — and concerning — that current climate model development and evaluation make use of only a small fraction of the information content from an unprecedented amount of Earth observations available.

However, new approaches to systematically incorporate observations and high-resolution simulations in the development of parameterizations are being developed. A framework for machine learning-based parameterizations to learn from Earth observations and targeted high-resolution simulations has been outlined [14]. In this framework, parameters and parametric functions of parameterizations are learned by minimizing carefully chosen (yet still subjective) objective functions that penalize the mismatch between the simulations and observations or between the simulations and targeted high-resolution simulations. It should be noted that such methods still incorporate structural errors introduced by the specific formulation of the parametrization itself and its spatiotemporal coverage. For example, current convection parameterizations in climate models suffer from their restriction to a single model column, which makes it difficult to accurately represent larger organized cloud systems.

A particular challenge for observation-data-driven approaches in climate modeling is that, by construction, we expect the climate system to change between the training period, for which observations are available, and under future climate change. Reliable satellite-based Earth observations are available from about 1980 to the present day, i.e., from a period that has already undergone significant climate change. Such dataset shifts arising from non-stationarity of the climate processes differ from most traditional machine learning applications, for which the underlying distributions are assumed to remain the same between training and test sets. In addition, there exists a risk of introducing selection biases due to the incompleteness of Earth observations.

Machine learning strategies to limit the impact of dataset shifts from non-stationarity include active learning [15], querying for additional constraints from observations, or process modeling when dataset shifts are detected [14]. Common approaches based on feature dropping, i.e., removing features underlying the dataset shifts, are undesirable in the presence of real physical shifts in the distribution of climate state variables under climate change. Beucler *et al.* [16] develop "climate-invariant" mappings of thermodynamic variables in the emulation of subgrid scale processes by physically rescaling the inputs and outputs of ML models to facilitate their generalization to unseen climates. However, it is not yet entirely clear how such methods generalize to state-dependent and potentially discontinuous feedback process, such as phase-dependent cloud feedbacks [17] or potential bifurcation points [18].

2.3. *Calibration of climate and climate process models*

Climate models contain a significant number of uncertain model parameters θ. For example, the convective rate of mixing of clouds with their environment is highly uncertain, due to the large uncertainty associated with small-scale turbulent processes, but has a profound impact on upper tropospheric humidity, cloudiness, and ultimately climate sensitivity [19]. During the model development phase, such climate model parameters are generally tuned *ad hoc* to minimize biases against a subset of present-day observations. However, it is possible to create climate model variants with different parameter combinations that evaluate reasonably against present-day observations and still simulate very different climate sensitivity [20]. Perturbed Parameter Ensembles (PPEs), varying climate model parameters within their uncertainty bounds, have been proposed as a way to probe the full parametric uncertainty [21]. However, due to the large number of uncertain climate model parameters — e.g., 47 key parameters have been identified in the HadGEM3 climate model [22] — a very large number of simulations would be required to probe uncertainty in this 47-dimensional parameter space. This approach has been pioneered in the citizen-science project climateprediction.net [19,21] based on the distributed computing power provided by a large number of volunteers. However, the computational demand limits application to lower-resolution models of limited complexity or requires reducing the number of parameters through sensitivity analysis (e.g., [22]).

The availability of AI/ML-based emulation of climate model outputs provides an alternative approach for uncertainty estimation and calibration for climate models. A Bayesian framework for the calibration of numerical models with atmospheric applications has been introduced [23], based on

Gaussian Processes [24]. In this framework, an ensemble of climate model simulations is performed that probe the parametric uncertainty in all parameter dimensions. Latin hypercubes [25] provide an efficient sampling of the parameter space, reducing the number of simulations to perform. Emulation, e.g., using Gaussian Processes, is performed on a set of model outputs both for observational constraint, as well as to assess the impact of this constraint on key climate metrics, such as radiative perturbations to the global energy balance. Calibration of the model corresponds to the inverse problem of finding the optimal combination of parameters θ that best match a set of observations corresponding to the emulated model output, which can be densely sampled (as opposed to the sparsely performed climate model simulations). Due to structural model uncertainties and representation errors, a model will never exactly match a comprehensive set of observations. Hence, the goal of calibration is generally to minimize a suitably chosen objective function, commonly some form of distance metrics between the model output and corresponding observations taking into account observational errors, such as those used in history matching [26] using techniques, such as Approximate Bayesian Computation (ABC) or Markov Chain Monte Carlo (MCMC). These approaches to climate model calibration have been pioneered in the context of constraining the highly uncertain effect of aerosols (air pollution particles) on clouds and climate [27].

Open-source tools providing a general workflow for emulating and calibrating climate models with a wide range of heterogeneous observations are now becoming available [28].

2.4. *Digital Twin Earths*

Through confluence of advances in high-performance computing and efficient computational solvers for non-hydrostatic equations of fluid flow at small scales, it is now possible to numerically simulate the global Earth's atmosphere at cloud-resolving kilometer scales [29]. Combination with Earth observations at similar scales would allow us to exploit a much larger fraction of the information content from observations than previously possible and to avoid key structural deficiencies associated with parameterizations, in particular for deep convective clouds or ocean mesoscale eddies, that can be removed as the associated flows are now explicitly resolved. The computational challenge is immense: e.g., the ICON model with 2.5 km resolution has 84×10^6 grid columns with 90 levels and, for numerical stability, requires integration over climatological timescales in 4.5 s timesteps. Storage of just 10 climate variables approaches 1 Tb per output timestep [29] and several Pb per day. Novel AI-based approaches for data compression, e.g., using autoencoders learning the underlying physics, encoding the data to a lower-dimensional space for output and subsequent decoding during the analysis, could make data analysis tractable again [30].

The entrance of models with superior physical realism opens the doors for the development of *digital twins* of Earth [31]. Digital Twin Earths combine coupled physical and biogeochemical models of Earth system components, such as the atmosphere, oceans, the carbon cycle, or even the biosphere, with Earth observations using data assimilation. Data assimilation aims for the optimal combination of observations with simulations in a physically consistent framework, which allows us to compensate for observational gaps, while observations constrain model uncertainties due to remaining structural and parametric errors. Such Twin Earths will allow us to timely assess the impacts of societal decisions under the impacts of climate change over timescales from days to decades.

While broad agreement currently exists that a solid physical basis is a precondition for the interpretability and trustworthiness of Digital Twin Earths [32], AI/ML will have a big part to play in their development. Key applications will include the emulation of remaining subgrid scale parameterizations (e.g., turbulence, cloud microphysics, radiation), data-driven development of new parameterizations and model components as well as tools to analyze and query the vast datasets created by such models.

In the longer-term future, progress in physics-constrained machine learning and explainable artificial intelligence (XAI) could lead to a paradigm shift away from computationally expensive numerical integration in short timesteps — but this will require a step change in trustworthy AI and its broader perception.

3. Analysis of Climate Model Data

3.1. *Emulation*

Current climate model intercomparisons create vast amounts of data, so big that they can no longer simply be queried to provide guidance to policy-makers. The sixth phase of the Coupled Model Intercomparison Experiment (CMIP6) [33], the main international climate modeling exercise, includes several ten thousand simulation weeks from individual climate models; the size of its output is estimated to be around 18 Pb [34]. Consequently, current climate model ensembles can only explore a very limited subset of the socio-economic scenarios [35] available to policymakers. Therefore, key policy decisions are generally based on simple global-mean climate parameters, most famously the goal to "limit global warming to well below 2, preferably to 1.5 degrees Celsius, compared to pre-industrial levels" in the Paris Agreement. Real-time information for policymakers, e.g., during United Nations Conference of the Parties (COP) negotiations, is generally provided by reduced complexity Integrated Assessment Models (e.g., [36]). While such models can be physically consistent and evaluated against complex climate models, they by construction neglect the complex regional variations of climate change and its impacts.

The availability of AI/ML techniques for the emulation of large-scale datasets provides opportunities to develop a new generation of reduced complexity climate model emulators for key climate parameters. These tools remain fully traceable to the output of large ensembles of complex climate models, e.g., CMIP6, and predict the global patterns of regional climate change.

From an AI/ML perspective, the emulation of climate model output is not dissimilar from climate modeling itself. Such an emulator can be generalized as a map E, mapping the climate state vector $\mathbf{x}(t)$, through time t in dependence of transient boundary conditions $\mathbf{b}(t)$.

$$\mathbf{x}(t) = E(\mathbf{b}(t), \theta_{ml})$$

However, there exist a few conceptual differences: because E is learning the machine learning model parameters θ_{ml} from the fitting of a precalculated training dataset $\mathbb{X}$ (the climate model output), no explicit integration in time is necessary. Furthermore, because climate is defined as the longer-term average of individual weather patterns, it is generally possible to aggregate over larger temporal timescales, such as annual or even decadal means, although it may be desirable to also emulate the seasonal cycle as well as shorter-term extremes or even full probability distributions. Finally, the primary application as a decision-making tool for choices of socio-economic scenarios means that boundary conditions, such as CO_2 emissions, can generally be aggregated to global means. However, it should be kept in mind that this may limit the applicability to, e.g., regional precipitation response to short-lived climate forcers, such as aerosols, for which the emission location impacts the response [37].

A benchmarking framework based on CMIP6 [33], ScenarioMIP [35], and DAMIP [38] simulations performed by a full complexity climate model has been developed [39], combined with a set of machine learning-based models. A range of emulators based on Gaussian Processes [24], Random Forests [40], long short-term memory (LSTM) [41], neural networks as well as Convolutional Neural Networks (CNNs) [42] are available in a common framework suitable for emulation of Earth System components [28]. These emulators can predict annual-mean global distributions of key climate parameters, including extreme values, given a wide range of emissions pathways, and allow us to efficiently probe previously unexplored scenarios, a concept that could become invaluable in (computationally expensive) Digital Twin Earths.

3.2. Downscaling

The resolution of global climate models is generally too coarse to predict local climate impacts on scales of relevance, e.g., for critical infrastructure, such as solar or wind power plants, or for river catchment areas, for the assessment of flood risk. Such higher resolution predictions have traditionally been made using regional climate models, which simulate regional climate in high resolution based on the boundary conditions from global climate models or using statistical downscaling, developing statistical relationships between resolved scale coarse climate variables and local or regional climate variables of interest [43,44].

Treating a two-dimensional climate dataset as an image, the downscaling problem is closely related to the concept of super-resolution in machine learning, aiming to generate consistent high-resolution images from low-resolution input images. While this is in principle an ill-posed problem, machine learning-based super-resolution methods take advantage of prior knowledge about the structure of the high-resolution images and have achieved remarkable accuracy. For climate downscaling, prior knowledge about high-resolution orography (in particular, for precipitation, often triggered by flow over mountains) and surface characteristics (in particular, for temperature, as it affects the absorption of sunlight and surface fluxes) are expected to improve the prediction. These and other physical constraints can be included explicitly or implicitly as part of high-resolution training datasets.

In supervised super-resolution downscaling, a machine learning model is trained using high-resolution climate datasets from observations (e.g., precipitation data from radar networks or high-resolution models to predict high-resolution climate data from low-resolution inputs, such as low-resolution climate models). Successful applications include the following: the use of CNNs for continental-scale downscaling of temperature and precipitation [45,46] and the use of Generative Adversarial Networks (GANs) to downscale wind velocity and solar irradiance outputs from global climate models scales representative for renewable energy generation [47].

However, reliable high-resolution training datasets do not exist for all applications. For example, the assessment of climate impacts over Africa is of crucial societal importance but very limited observational networks exist that could be used as high-resolution training data. Hence, the development of unsupervised downscaling methods has a large potential. Groenke et al. [48] treat downscaling as a domain alignment problem and develop an unsupervised model to learn a mapping between two random variables based on their shared structure with a predictive performance comparable to existing supervised methods.

4. AI for Earth Observations in Climate Science

Observations have played a key role in the discovery and our understanding of key climate processes ever since the discovery of the importance of water vapor and carbon dioxide for atmospheric radiation by Eunice Foote [49]. Robust constraints from Earth observations are of vital importance for trust in climate models and their predictions. Today, with an unprecedented amount of Earth observation data available from spaceborne and ground-based observing systems, the role of observations in climate science is becoming increasingly limited by our ability to extract the relevant information content at scale.

For decades, the exploitation of Earth observations for climate science has focused on pixel-by-pixel retrievals of relevant climate parameters, such as temperature profiles, atmospheric composition, and cloud properties, primarily from spectral radiance measurements. This approach has been tremendously successful but rejects a significant fraction of the information content available in Earth observations arising from spatio-temporal structures beyond the single pixel. The advent of reliable and scalable AI/ML for feature detection and classification provides a unique opportunity to explore the full potential of Earth observations to increase our understanding of climate process as well as for climate model constraint and evaluation.

4.1. *Remote sensing retrievals*

The retrieval of climate-relevant parameters, represented as a state vector $\mathbf{x}$, from remote sensing observations is an inverse problem for which often no unique solutions exist. Generally, a forward radiative transfer model $\mathbf{F}(\mathbf{x})$ is used to simulate observations $\mathbf{y}$ of spectral radiances (passive instruments) or backscatter (active instruments) in the presence of measurement errors ε under the assumption of prior knowledge $\mathbf{x_a}$ about the state vector. The retrieval aims to minimize the difference, generally expressed as cost function comprising of a data-fit term measuring the fit between the forward model $\mathbf{F}(\mathbf{x})$ and the observation $\mathbf{y}$, and a regularizer measuring the fit between the best estimate of the state vector $\hat{\mathbf{x}}$ and the prior $\mathbf{x_a}$. Such retrievals, often performed in the Bayesian framework of Optimal Estimation [2], have been successfully deployed in satellite remote sensing of climate parameters, such as temperature and humidity profiles, cloud properties, and atmospheric composition, and allow to systematically take into account multiple error sources [50]. However, significant uncertainties remain in the estimation of fundamental climate parameters; in fact, the uncertainty in our estimates of total ice water in the atmosphere is nearly as large as the total amount itself [51], as well as of associated cloud properties, such as the cloud droplet number concentration [52], severely limiting our ability to constrain current climate models. There remains significant potential to advance on current retrievals using AI, including multisensor fusion and the use of invertible neural networks. However, it should be noted that the retrieval problem is generally highly under-constrained. See further details in Chapter 17.

4.2. *Feature detection and tracking*

Driven by a vast number of commercial applications, the availability of large-scale labeled training datasets (e.g., ImageNet [53]) as well as of open source platforms for machine learning, and the development of robust and reliable machine learning models, the detection and classification of features in images has rapidly advanced and now influences most aspects of modern life.

Maybe surprisingly, the use of observable features from Earth observations, such as cloud patterns or ocean eddies, has so far remained a niche area for the systematic evaluation and constraint of climate models. One reason is that current low-resolution climate models have, by construction, limited skill in simulating such small-scale features and are therefore primarily evaluated based on aggregate statistics. But equally, the task may have simply felt too daunting as manual detection of features in vast Earth observation datasets is simply not practical, except for low-frequency events, such as tropical cyclones.

However, the availability of reliable and scalable AI/ML-based feature detection (detecting objects) and semantic segmentation (classifying each pixel) techniques has started to rapidly transform the analysis of Earth observations for climate science, as evident from the following examples centered on the role of clouds for climate, noting that there are similar applications across many areas of climate research:

Quasi-linear tracks from well-defined pollution sources, such as ships, volcanoes, cities, or industrial areas, have been extensively used to study the effect of air pollution to brighten clouds [54] — but their manual detection has remained challenging. Deep convolutional neural networks with skip connection architecture (U-Net) have been trained based on hand-labeled ship-track data from the MODIS satellite instrument [55] and applied in a case study for the stratocumulus cloud deck off the coast of California. Applying a similar technique, it has recently been possible to catalog all ship tracks globally since 2002 and find marked reductions under emissions control regulations introduced in 2015 and 2020 [56]. Such AI-based approaches allow the global assessment and continuous monitoring of anthropogenic climate perturbations.

Cloud feedbacks are the dominant contributors of inter-model spread in climate sensitivity among current climate models [57] and often involve subtle transitions between cloud regimes and morphologies that are difficult to simulate and need to be observationally constrained:

Low stratocumulus clouds scatter sunlight back to space, have large cloud fractions, and therefore cool the Earth. It is therefore important to understand the transition from stratocumulus clouds to cumulus clouds with lower cloud fraction and therefore a weaker cooling effect and how this might be affected by climate change. Such transitions can occur as a pocket of open cells (POCs) in a closed stratocumulus cloud field and the effect of air pollution on this process had been hypothesized to have a significant effect on climate. However, such prior work was limited to case studies with a small number of POC occurrences. Training a modified ResNet-152 which has been pre-trained on ImageNet, it has been possible to analyze a 13-year satellite record to identify >8,000 POCs globally [58]. This allowed for the first time to conclude that the overall radiative effect of POCs on climate is small.

To understand cloud feedbacks, it is key to understand which environmental factors control cloud regimes and morphology. A labeled dataset of mesoscale cloud organization crowd-sourced from the Zooniverse platform [59] has been used [60] to train deep learning algorithms for object detection (Resnet [61]) and subsequent image segmentation (Unet [62], from fastai library). The application to an 11-year satellite dataset then allowed us to derive heat maps for individual cloud morphologies and to link them to the presence of their physical drivers, which may change under climate change.

However, the vast scale of climate datasets often makes hand-labeling impossible, so the development and deployment of unsupervised classification techniques have great potential. An unsupervised classification scheme for mesoscale cloud organization based on the ResNet-34 CNN residual network feeding the produced embeddings into a hierarchical clustering algorithm has been developed and trained on and applied to GOES-16 satellite images [63]. It was shown that the derived cloud clusters have distinct cloud structures and radiative and morphological properties with unique physical characteristics.

4.3. *Extreme event and anomaly detection*

While much of the attention to climate change focuses on global mean temperature rise, the most severe impacts occur through the associated shift in the likelihood and strength of extreme events, such as heatwaves, flooding, synoptic storms, tropical cyclones, or droughts.

It would therefore seem expected that reliable objective techniques for the detection, quantification, and prediction of extreme events were readily available. However, this is not the case, as illustrated in the case of observed changes in heavy precipitation shown in Figure 1. In fact, for large parts of the globe, including most of Africa and South America, there exists limited data or literature to even quantify observed changes, let alone robust methodologies. The selection of extreme weather events to be attributed to climate change [64,65] has been generally performed heuristically, with the potential to introduce selection biases (and potentially ignoring less-developed and less-observed parts of the world). The secretary-general of the United Nations, António Guterres, has tasked the World Meteorological Organization in 2022 "to ensure every person on Earth is protected by early warning systems within five years" [66].

The capability of AI to detect changes in large-scale datasets provides an opportunity to transform our ability to detect, quantify, and predict changes in extreme climate events.

As a first step, AI is now being used to objectively detect weather patterns associated with extreme events, such as the detection of tropical cyclones, atmospheric rivers (as a cause of heavy precipitation), or the detection of fronts, primarily using supervised or semi-supervised machine learning methods [67,68]. Such methods rely on training datasets and toolkits are being developed to curate expert-labeled datasets for tropical cyclones and atmospheric rivers based on high-resolution model simulations [69].

However, such curated datasets remain limited in scope and only capture a limited subset of extreme event types. They currently do not capture key sources of extreme weather in the developing world, such as mesoscale convective systems and associated dust storms.

The significant potential of AI to develop unsupervised techniques for the objective detection and classification of extreme events and in particular of their response to a changing climate remains underexplored.

4.4. *Learning relationships between climate variables and climate processes*

Traditionally, the vast majority of use cases of Earth observations in climate science have focused on specific climate variables. However, key climate processes involve multiple variables so methods to discover and exploit the relationship between such variables could provide additional, and potentially more direct, constraints on the underlying physical processes.

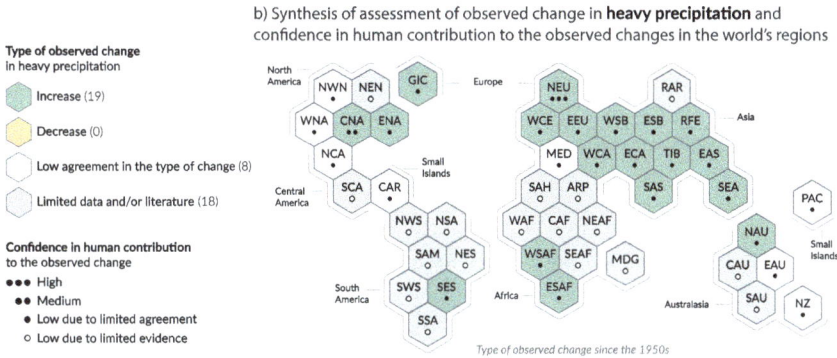

Fig. 1. Intergovernmental Panel on Climate Change synthesis of current assessment of observed changes in heavy precipitation and confidence in human contribution to these changes (IPCC AR6 Summary for Policymakers [1]).

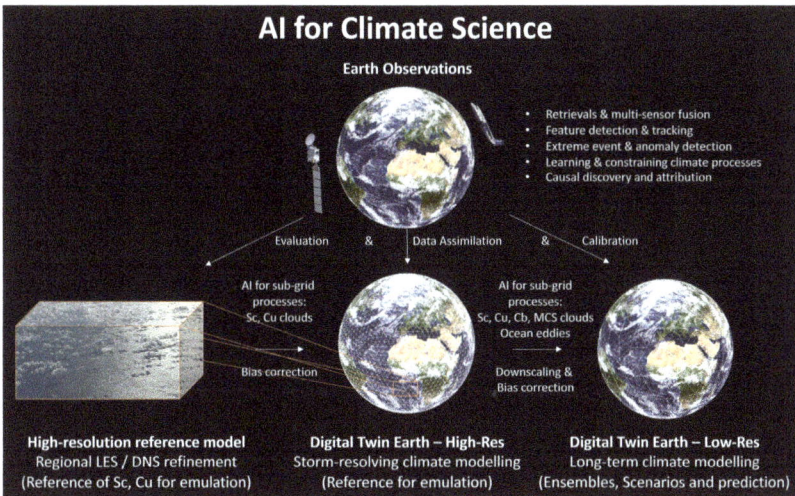

Fig. 2. Applications of AI for Climate Science in the context of Digital Twin Earths.

For example, the linear ML method of ridge regression has been used to quantify how clouds respond to changes in the environment from Earth observations and climate model simulations [70]. This allows the identification of key processes underlying cloud feedbacks and to provide a tighter constraint on the amplifying effect of clouds on global warming. Using a wider range of cloud controlling factors and a nonlinear approach based on gradient boosting decision trees (LGBM [71]), regimes of cloud controlling environmental variables from Earth observations have been identified [72] that provide a new constraint on the representation of clouds in global climate models.

However, it should be noted that the climate system is a coupled dynamical system so care must be taken when evaluating statistical relationships between climate variables as correlation does not necessarily imply causation.

4.5. Causal discovery and attribution

In a large-scale dynamical system such as the Earth, inevitably many climate variables are coupled. Consequently, when observing relationships between climate variables, e.g., through regression or correlation, it is generally not clear which relationships are causal and which are driven by a common driver (confounder) [73].

In climate modeling, mechanism denial, perturbed parameter ensembles, or adjoint methods are widely used to identify and quantify causal relationships related to the importance of specific processes.

Optimal fingerprinting methods have been developed for the detection of climate impacts and their attribution to specific anthropogenic forcers [4]. This typically involves comparison of model-simulated spatio-temporal patterns of the climate response to external forcings to the observational record in a reduced dimensional space, e.g., from Principal Component Analysis. Both simulated and observed responses are normalized by internal variability to improve the signal-to-noise ratio. The observed climate change is regarded as a linear combination of signals from climate forcers, such as greenhouse gases or air pollution, and the internal climate variability and the magnitude of the response to each forcing are estimated using linear regression (cf. [74]). However, such fingerprinting methods rely on climate models accurately representing the key climate processes.

Hence, methods that allow for causal discovery and attribution solely from observations are required. As it is generally not desirable to conduct large-scale control experiments with the climate system, there exists significant potential for advanced statistical and AI causal methodologies. Recent advances in causal inference based on graph-based structural causal models, where climate variables are the nodes, edges indicate causal connections, and arrows include causal directions, are now being increasingly applied in climate science (cf. [75]). New methods combining conditional independence tests (to identify potential causal links) with a causal discovery algorithm (to remove false positive links) have been developed to estimate causal networks from large-scale time-series datasets [76]. However, it is worth pointing out that many climate observations are discontinuous. For example, most satellite-based Earth observations stem from sun-synchronous polar orbiting satellites with a fixed overpass time, generally providing only one measurement per day (for retrievals relying on solar wavelengths) so with a temporal resolution that is lower than, e.g., the lifetime of most individual clouds. New causal inference methods suitable for discontinuous observations based on causal forests and neural networks are being developed in the context of the effect of air pollution on clouds and climate [77].

5. How AI/ML Will Transform Climate Science

Climate change is one of the greatest challenges facing Planet Earth. Achieving the goals of the Paris Agreement requires the fastest transformation of the world's economy that has ever been attempted. It is therefore vital that the underpinning scientific evidence is robust, interpretable, and trustworthy. Physical understanding will always remain at its core.

At the same time, advances in climate research are held back by our ability to simulate climate at sufficiently small scales that resolve key processes explicitly, as well as by our ability to interpret the vast amount of data from climate models and Earth observations. It is becoming increasingly clear that AI and machine learning will make transformational contributions to both areas — with the challenge to deliver physically constrained, trustworthy, and explainable results.

For climate modeling, it seems inconceivable that anything else than hybrid models, combining numerical solutions of fundamental physical equations with faster and/or more accurate AI components, will dominate the short- to medium-term future. And AI will dominate for heuristic model components for which no closed set of physical questions exists, such as models of biogeochemical cycles and ecosystems. The question remains primarily what fraction of the physical climate models will ultimately be replaced by AI, which in turn depends on its physical consistency and interpretability, underpinning trust. Challenges include the optimal incorporation of physical constraints; the development of climate invariant model components to deal with non-stationarity as the climate system will change between the training period and future climate; and, importantly, interpretability: as the climate system does not allow for control experiments, it is fundamental that climate predictions remain interpretable as a basis for trust. In addition to speed up by fast emulation, specific opportunities to improve climate models with AI include the following: the emulation of parameterizations from more accurate reference models and observations; the possibility to avoid operator splitting between different climate processes by emulating multiple climate model components together; the potential to overcome locality of current parameterizations through consideration of non-local inputs to the emulation [78]; the potential to introduce memory through approaches such as LSTM, e.g., for convection parameterizations; as well as exploiting the opportunities provided by the coevolution of AI-based and reduced-precision climate model components [79].

Already, AI is transforming our ability to analyze the vast output of climate model simulations and this impact is only going to increase in the future. AI-based emulation of climate model scenarios will provide easily accessible spatio-temporal guidance to policymakers that remains fully traceable to the underpinning complex climate model simulations. Future opportunities include the emulation of the full probability distribution of climate variables to flexibly assess extreme events as well as the inclusion of regional emission variations in the emulators to provide guidance on their regional and global impacts. Combination of emulation of climate model output with AI-based downscaling techniques as well as further advances in unsupervised downscaling techniques could ultimately provide accessible high-resolution data on climate change and impacts on local and regional decision-making.

While much of the current attention on AI in climate science focuses on modeling, AI will entirely transform our ability to interpret Earth observations to exploit the full information content available. This is not without challenges: climate observations are heterogeneous, discontinuous, on non-Euclidean spaces, and big — with each snapshot being vastly bigger than typical image resolutions used in standard machine learning applications and total data volumes increasing by many Pb each year. The general presence of a multitude of confounding factors makes causal attribution from observations alone challenging. However, future opportunities are plentiful: AI will make it possible to detect, track, and label climate phenomena all the way to individual clouds or ocean eddies. Combination with causal discovery tools will allow identification and quantification of key drivers of climate change. It will facilitate the objective detection of climate impacts and changing extreme events, e.g., flooding, wildfires, droughts, and heatwaves, across the full observational record and its attribution to anthropogenic activities, e.g., replacing prevailing linear methods with nonlinear neural networks in detection and attribution applications.

Ultimately, the challenge will be to optimally combine physical models and Earth observations with AI to accelerate climate science.

For the foreseeable future, the $O(1\,\mathrm{km})$ resolution of even storm-resolving Digital Twin Earths currently in planning will not be sufficient to resolve key processes, such as low-cloud feedbacks that dominate current climate model uncertainty so they will need to be informed, possibly by AI, by even higher-resolution Large Eddy Simulation (LES) or Direct

Numerical Simulation (DNS) models. Likewise, it will not be possible to routinely run storm-resolving Digital Twin Earths for a large number of scenarios over the wide parameter space explored in current climate model intercomparisons so they may need to be complemented with low-resolution twins for long-term climate scenario simulations. Biases introduced by the low-resolution twin parameterizations could be systematically corrected using ML-learned correction terms derived from the high-resolution twins, as has been recently successfully demonstrated [80]. And data from the high-resolution twins could be used as training data for supervised super-resolution downscaling of low-resolution twins to predict climate impacts and in particular extreme events on scales relevant for decision-making. Such a vision of twin Digital Twin Earths (let's call it DTE^2) is presented in Figure 2 and would not be possible without AI for climate science.

References

[1] V. Masson-Delmotte, P. Zhai, A. Pirani *et al.* IPCC, 2021: Summary for policymakers. In *Climate Change 2021: The Physical Science Basis. Contribution of Working Group I to the Sixth Assessment Report of the Intergovernmental Panel on Climate Change*, In Press: Cambridge University Press.

[2] C. D. Rodgers (1976). Retrieval of atmospheric-temperature and composition from remote measurements of thermal-radiation (in English). *Reviews of Geophysics*, *14*(4), 609–624. doi: 10.1029/RG014i004p00609.

[3] C. Jakob and G. Tselioudis (2003). Objective identification of cloud regimes in the Tropical Western Pacific (in English). *Geophysical Research Letters*, *30*(21). doi: 10.1029/2003GL018367.

[4] K. Hasselmann (1993). Optimal fingerprints for the detection of time-dependent climate-change (in English). *Journal of Climate*, *6*(10), 1957–1971. doi: 10.1175/1520-0442(1993)006<1957:OFFTDO>2.0.CO;2.

[5] R. Courant, K. Friedrichs, and H. Lewy (1928). Über die partiellen Differenzengleichungen der mathematischen Physik. *Mathematische Annalen*, *100*, 32–74. doi:10.1007/BF01448839.

[6] V. M. Krasnopolsky, M. S. Fox-Rabinovitz, and D. V. Chalikov (2005). New approach to calculation of atmospheric model physics: Accurate and fast neural network emulation of longwave radiation in a climate model (in English). *Monthly Weather Review*, *133*(5), 1370–1383. doi: 10.1175/Mwr2923.1.

[7] V. M. Krasnopolsky, M. S. Fox-Rabinovitz, Y. T. Hou *et al.* (2010). Accurate and fast neural network emulations of model radiation for the NCEP coupled climate forecast system: Climate simulations and seasonal predictions (in English). *Monthly Weather Review*, *138*(5), 1822–1842. doi: 10.1175/2009mwr3149.1.

[8] P. Harder, D. Watson-Parris, P. Stier *et al.* (2022). Physics-informed learning of aerosol microphysics. *Environmental Data Science*, *1*, E20.

[9] S. Rasp, M. S. Pritchard, and P. Gentine (2018). Deep learning to represent subgrid processes in climate models (in English). *Proceedings of the National Academy of Sciences of the United States of America, 115*(39), 9684–9689. doi: 10.1073/pnas.1810286115.

[10] J. Yuval, P. A. O'Gorman, and C. N. Hill (2021). Use of neural networks for stable, accurate and physically consistent parameterization of subgrid atmospheric processes with good performance at reduced precision (in English). *Geophysical Research Letters, 48*(6). doi: 10.1029/2020GL091363.

[11] M. Chantry, S. Hatfield, P. Dueben *et al.* (2021). Machine learning emulation of gravity wave drag in numerical weather forecasting (in English). *Journal of Advances in Modeling Earth Systems, 13*(7). ⟨GotoISI⟩://WOS: 000682994000010.

[12] L. Zanna and T. Bolton (2020). Data-driven equation discovery of ocean mesoscale closures (in English). *Geophysical Research Letters, 47*(17). ⟨GotoISI⟩://WOS:000572406100081.

[13] H. Sundqvist, E. Berge, and J. E. Kristjansson (1989). Condensation and cloud parameterization studies with a Mesoscale Numerical Weather Prediction Model (in English). *Monthly Weather Review, 117*(8), 1641–1657. doi: 10.1175/1520-0493(1989)117<1641:Cacpsw>2.0.Co;2.

[14] T. Schneider, S. W. Lan, A. Stuart *et al.* (2017). Earth System Modeling 2.0: A blueprint for models that learn from observations and targeted high-resolution simulations (in English). *Geophysical Research Letters, 44*(24), 12396–12417. doi: 10.1002/2017gl076101.

[15] B. Settles (2009). Active Learning Literature Survey in "Computer Sciences Technical Report" University of Wisconsin–Madison, Wisconsin–Madison, Vol. 1648.

[16] T. Beucler, M. Pritchard, J. Yuval *et al.* (2021). Climate-invariant machine learning. doi: 10.48550/arXiv.2112.08440.

[17] I. Tan, T. Storelvmo, and M. D. Zelinka (2016). Observational constraints on mixed-phase clouds imply higher climate sensitivity (in English). *Science, 352*(6282), 224–227. ⟨GotoISI⟩://WOS:000373681600046.

[18] T. M. Lenton, H. Held, E. Kriegler *et al.* (2008). Tipping elements in the Earth's climate system (in English). *Proceedings of the National Academy of Sciences of the United States of America, 105*(6), 1786–1793. ⟨GotoISI⟩:// WOS:000253261900005.

[19] D. A. Stainforth, T. Aina, C. Christensen *et al.* (2005). Uncertainty in predictions of the climate response to rising levels of greenhouse gases (in English). *Nature, 433*(7024), 403–406. doi: 10.1038/nature03301.

[20] T. Mauritsen, B. Stevens, E. Roeckner *et al.* (2012). Tuning the climate of a global model (in English). *Journal of Advances in Modeling Earth Systems, 4.* doi: 10.1029/2012ms000154.

[21] M. Allen (1999). Do-it-yourself climate prediction (in English). *Nature, 401*(6754), 642. doi: 10.1038/44266.

[22] D. M. H. Sexton, C. F. McSweeney, J. W. Rostron *et al.* (2021). A perturbed parameter ensemble of HadGEM3-GC3.05 coupled model projections: Part 1: Selecting the parameter combinations (in English). *Climate Dynamics, 56*(11–12), 3395–3436. doi: 10.1007/s00382-021-05709-9.

[23] M. C. Kennedy and A. O'Hagan (2001). Bayesian calibration of computer models (in English). *Journal of the Royal Statistical Society B, 63*, 425–450. doi: 10.1111/1467-9868.00294.

[24] C. E. Rasmussen and C. K. I. Williams (2006). *Gaussian Processes for Machine Learning* (Adaptive Computation and Machine Learning). Cambridge, Massachusetts: MIT Press, p. xviii, 248 pp.

[25] M. D. Mckay, R. J. Beckman, and W. J. Conover (1979). A comparison of three methods for selecting values of input variables in the analysis of output from a computer code (in English). *Technometrics, 21*(2), 239–245. doi: 10.2307/1268522.

[26] I. Vernon, M. Goldstein, and R. G. Bower (2010). Galaxy formation: A Bayesian uncertainty analysis rejoinder (in English). *Bayesian Analysis, 5*(4), 697–708. doi: 10.1214/10-Ba524rej.

[27] L. A. Lee, K. J. Pringle, C. L. Reddington *et al.* (2013). The magnitude and causes of uncertainty in global model simulations of cloud condensation nuclei (in English). *Atmospheric Chemistry and Physics, 13*(18), 9375–9377. doi: 10.5194/acp-13-9375-2013.

[28] D. Watson-Parris, A. Williams, L. Deaconu *et al.* (2021). Model calibration using ESEm v1.1.0-an open, scalable Earth system emulator (in English). *Geoscientific Model Development, 14*(12), 7659–7672. ⟨GotoISI⟩://WOS: 000731831100001.

[29] B. Stevens, M. Satoh, L. Auger *et al.* (2019). DYAMOND: The DYnamics of the Atmospheric general circulation Modeled On Non-hydrostatic Domains (in English). *Progress in Earth and Planetary Science, 6*(1). doi: 10.1186/s40645-019-0304-z.

[30] B. Stevens. Faster Faster — Machine learning our way to a new generation of storm-resolving Earth system models. United Nations ITU. https://aifor good.itu.int/event/ai-and-climate-science-bjorn-stevens/ (accessed 2022).

[31] P. Bauer, P. D. Dueben, T. Hoefler *et al.* (2021). The digital revolution of Earth-system science. *Nature Computational Science, 1*, 104–113. doi: 10.1038/s43588-021-00023-0.

[32] M. Reichstein, G. Camps-Valls, B. Stevens *et al.* (2019). Deep learning and process understanding for data-driven Earth system science (in English). *Nature, 566*(7743), 195–204. doi: 10.1038/s41586-019-0912-1.

[33] V. Eyring, S. Bony, G. A. Meehl *et al.* (2016). Overview of the Coupled Model Intercomparison Project Phase 6 (CMIP6) experimental design and organization (in English). *Geoscientific Model Development, 9*(5), 1937–1958. doi: 10.5194/gmd-9-1937-2016.

[34] V. Balaji, K. E. Taylor, M. Juckes *et al.* (2018). Requirements for a global data infrastructure in support of CMIP6 (in English). *Geoscientific Model Development, 11*(9), 3659–3680. doi: 10.5194/gmd-11-3659-2018.

[35] B. C. O'Neill, C. Tebaldi, D. P. van Vuuren *et al.* (2016). The Scenario Model Intercomparison Project (ScenarioMIP) for CMIP6 (in English). *Geoscientific Model Development, 9*(9), 3461–3482. doi: 10.5194/gmd-9-3461-2016.

[36] R. J. Millar, Z. R. Nicholls, P. Friedlingstein *et al.* (2017). A modified impulse-response representation of the global near-surface air temperature

and atmospheric concentration response to carbon dioxide emissions (in English). *Atmospheric Chemistry and Physics*, *17*(11), 7213–7228. ⟨GotoISI⟩://WOS:000403779200004.

[37] P. Stier, S. C. V. d. Heever, M. Christensen *et al.* (2022). Multifaceted aerosol effects on precipitation. *Nature Geoscience*, EGU22, the 24th EGU General Assembly, held 23–27 May, 2022 in Vienna, Austria; id.EGU22-2856. doi: 10.5194/egusphere-egu22-2856.

[38] N. P. Gillett, H. Shiogama, B. Funke *et al.* (2016). The Detection and Attribution Model Intercomparison Project (DAMIP v1.0) contribution to CMIP6 (in English). *Geoscientific Model Development*, *9*(10), 3685–3697. doi: 10.5194/gmd-9-3685-2016.

[39] D. Watson-Parris, Y. Rao, D. Olivié *et al.* (2022). ClimateBench: A benchmark dataset for data-driven climate projections. *Journal of Advances in Modeling Earth Systems*, *14*, doi: 10.1029/2021MS002954.

[40] T. K. Ho (1995). Random decision forests. In *Proceedings of 3rd International Conference on Document Analysis and Recognition*. IEEE, pp. 278–282.

[41] S. Hochreiter and J. Schmidhuber (1997). Long short-term memory. *Neural Computation*, *9*(8), 1735–1780. doi: 10.1162/neco.1997.9.8.1735.

[42] Y. L. Cun, B. Boser, J. S. Denker *et al.* (1990). Handwritten digit recognition with a back-propagation network. In *Advances in Neural Information Processing Systems 2*. D. Touretzky (ed.). Denver, USA: Morgan Kaufmann Publishers Inc., pp. 396–404.

[43] T. M. L. Wigley, P. D. Jones, K. R. Briffa *et al.* (1990). Obtaining sub-grid-scale information from coarse-resolution general-circulation model output (in English). *Journal of Geophysical Research: Atmospheres*, *95*(D2), 1943–1953. doi: 10.1029/JD095iD02p01943.

[44] G. Burger, T. Q. Murdock, A. T. Werner *et al.* (2012). Downscaling extremes — An intercomparison of multiple statistical methods for present climate (in English). *Journal of Climate*, *25*(12), 4366–4388. doi: 10.1175/Jcli-D-11-00408.1.

[45] J. Bano-Medina, R. Manzanas, and J. M. Gutierrez (2020). Configuration and intercomparison of deep learning neural models for statistical downscaling (in English). *Geoscientific Model Development*, *13*(4), 2109–2124. doi: 10.5194/gmd-13-2109-2020.

[46] T. Vandal, E. Kodra, S. Ganguly *et al.* (2017) DeepSD: Generating high resolution climate change projections through single image super-resolution, *arXiv:1703.03126*. doi: 10.48550/arXiv.1703.03126.

[47] K. Stengel, A. Glaws, D. Hettinger *et al.* (2020). Adversarial super-resolution of climatological wind and solar data (in English). *Proceedings of the National Academy of Sciences of the United States of America*, *117*(29), 16805–16815. doi: 10.1073/pnas.1918964117.

[48] B. Groenke, L. Madaus, and C. Monteleoni (2020). ClimAlign: Unsupervised statistical downscaling of climate variables via normalizing flows. doi: 10.48550/arXiv.2008.04679.

[49] E. Foote (1856). Circumstances affecting the heat of the Sun's rays. *The American Journal of Science and Arts*, *22*(66), 383–384.

[50] C. D. Rodgers (2000). *Inverse Methods for Atmospheric Sounding* (Series on Atmospheric, Oceanic and Planetary Physics, no. 2). Singapore: World Scientific.

[51] O. Boucher, D. Randall, P. Artaxo *et al.* (2013). Clouds and aerosols. In S. Fuzzi, J. Penner, V. Ramaswamy, *et al.* (eds.), *Working Group I Contribution to the Intergovernmental Panel on Climate Change Firth Assessment Report* (Climate Change 2013: The Physical Science Basis). Geneva: Cambridge University Press.

[52] D. P. Grosvenor, O. Sourdeval, P. Zuidema *et al.* (2018). Remote sensing of droplet number concentration in warm clouds: A review of the current state of knowledge and perspectives (in English). *Reviews of Geophysics*, *56*(2), 409–453. doi: 10.1029/2017rg000593.

[53] J. Deng, W. Dong, R. Socher *et al.* (2009). ImageNet: A large-scale hierarchical image database. In *2009 IEEE Conference on Computer Vision and Pattern Recognition*, 20–25 June 2009, pp. 248–255. doi: 10.1109/CVPR.2009.5206848.

[54] M. Christensen, A. Gettelman, J. Cermak *et al.* (2021). Opportunistic experiments to constrain aerosol effective radiative forcing. *Atmospheric Chemistry and Physics Discussions*, *2021*, 1–60. doi: 10.5194/acp-2021-559.

[55] T. L. Yuan, C. Wang, H. Song *et al.* (2019). Automatically finding ship tracks to enable large-scale analysis of aerosol-cloud interactions (in English). *Geophysical Research Letters*, *46*(13), 7726–7733. ⟨GotoISI⟩:// WOS:000476960100074.

[56] D. Watson-Parris, M. W. Christensen, A. Laurenson, *et al.* (2022). Shipping regulations lead to large reduction in cloud perturbations. *Proceedings of the National Academy of Sciences*, *119*(41), e2206885119.

[57] M. D. Zelinka, T. A. Myers, D. T. Mccoy *et al.* (2020). Causes of higher climate sensitivity in CMIP6 models (in English). *Geophysical Research Letters*, *47*(1). doi: 10.1029/2019GL085782.

[58] D. Watson-Parris, S. A. Sutherland, M. C. Christensen *et al.* (2021). A large-scale analysis of pockets of open cells and their radiative impact (in English). *Geophysical Research Letters*, *48*(6). doi: 10.1029/2020GL092213.

[59] B. Stevens, S. Bony, H. Brogniez, *et al.* (2020). Sugar, gravel, fish and flowers: Mesoscale cloud patterns in the trade winds. *Quarterly Journal of the Royal Meteorological Society*, *146*(726), 141–152. https://www.zooniverse. org/projects/raspstephan/sugar-flower-fish-or-gravel.

[60] S. Rasp, H. Schulz, S. Bony *et al.* (2020). Combining crowdsourcing and deep learning to explore the mesoscale organization of shallow convection (in English). *Bulletin of the American Meteorological Society*, *101*(11), E1980– E1995. ⟨GotoISI⟩://WOS:000598066100007.

[61] T.-Y. Lin, P. Goyal, R. Girshick *et al.* Focal loss for dense object detection. *arXiv:1708.* (02002). https://ui.adsabs.harvard.edu/abs/ 2017arXiv170802002L.

[62] O. Ronneberger, P. Fischer, and T. Brox. U-Net: Convolutional networks for biomedical image segmentation, *arXiv:1505.04597.* https://ui.adsabs. harvard.edu/abs/2015arXiv150504597R.

[63] L. Denby (2020). Discovering the importance of mesoscale cloud organization through unsupervised classification (in English). *Geophysical Research Letters*, *47*(1). ⟨GotoISI⟩://WOS:000513983400007.

[64] M. Allen (2003). Liability for climate change (in English). *Nature*, *421*(6926), 891–892. ⟨GotoISI⟩://WOS:000181186900017.

[65] World Weather Attribution. https://www.worldweatherattribution.org (accessed 07/04/2022).

[66] World Meteorological Organization (2022). *Early Warning Systems Must Protect Everyone within Five Years*. Geneva: World Meteorological Organization.

[67] E. Racah, C. Beckham, T. Maharaj *et al.* ExtremeWeather: A large-scale climate dataset for semi-supervised detection, localization, and understanding of extreme weather events, *arXiv:1612.02095*. https://ui.adsabs.harvard.edu/abs/2016arXiv161202095R.

[68] Y. Liu, E. Racah, Prabhat *et al.* Application of deep convolutional neural networks for detecting extreme weather in climate datasets, *arXiv:1605.01156*. https://ui.adsabs.harvard.edu/abs/2016arXiv160501156L.

[69] Prabhat, K. Kashinath, M. Mudigonda *et al.* (2021). ClimateNet: An expert-labeled open dataset and deep learning architecture for enabling high-precision analyses of extreme weather (in English). *Geoscientific Model Development*, *14*(1), 107–124. ⟨GotoISI⟩://WOS:000608796300001.

[70] P. Ceppi and P. Nowack (2021). Observational evidence that cloud feedback amplifies global warming (in English). *Proceedings of the National Academy of Sciences of the United States of America*, *118*(30). doi:10.1073/pnas.2026290118.

[71] G. Ke, Q. Meng, T. Finley *et al.* (2017). LightGBM: A highly efficient gradient boosting decision tree. https://proceedings.neurips.cc/paper/2017/file/6449f44a102fde848669bdd9eb6b76fa-Paper.pdf.

[72] A. Douglas and P. Stier (May 2022). Defining regime specific cloud sensitivities using the learnings from machine learning. In *EGU General Assembly Conference Abstracts*, pp. EGU22-8848.

[73] H. Reichenbach (1956). *The Direction of Time*. Berkeley: University of California Press (in English).

[74] G. Hegerl and F. Zwiers (2011). Use of models in detection and attribution of climate change (in English). *WIREs Climate Change*, *2*(4), 570–591. doi:10.1002/wcc.121.

[75] J. Runge, S. Bathiany, E. Bollt *et al.* (2019). Inferring causation from time series in Earth system sciences (in English). *Nature Communications*, *10*. ⟨GotoISI⟩://WOS:000471586600001.

[76] J. Runge, P. Nowack, M. Kretschmer *et al.* (2019). Detecting and quantifying causal associations in large nonlinear time series datasets (in English). *Science Advances*, *5*(11). ⟨GotoISI⟩://WOS:000499736100002.

[77] A. Jesson, P. Manshausen, A. Douglas *et al.* Using non-linear causal models to study aerosol-cloud interactions in the Southeast Pacific. *arXiv:2110.15084*. https://ui.adsabs.harvard.edu/abs/2021arXiv211015084J.

[78] P. Wang, J. Yuval, and P. A. O'Gorman. Non-local parameterization of atmospheric subgrid processes with neural networks, *arXiv:2201.00417*. https://ui.adsabs.harvard.edu/abs/2022arXiv220100417W.

[79] P. D. Dueben, J. Joven, A. Lingamneni *et al.* (2014). On the use of inexact, pruned hardware in atmospheric modelling (in English). *Philosophical Transactions of the Royal Society A*, *372*(2018). doi: 10.1098/rsta.2013.0276.

[80] C. S. Bretherton, B. Henn, A. Kwa *et al.* (2022). Correcting coarse-grid weather and climate models by machine learning from global storm-resolving simulations (in English). *Journal of Advances in Modeling Earth Systems*, *14*(2). doi: 10.1029/2021MS002794.

Energy

© 2023 World Scientific Publishing Company
https://doi.org/10.1142/9789811265679_0015

Chapter 15

Accelerating Fusion Energy with AI

R. Michael Churchill*, Mark D. Boyer†, and Steven C. Cowley‡

Princeton Plasma Physics Laboratory
*rchurchi@pppl.gov
†mboyer@pppl.gov
‡scowley@pppl.gov

1. Introduction

Fusion energy offers the promise of a clean, carbon-free baseload energy source to power the future. One line of fusion research uses magnets to confine plasmas at millions of degrees Celsius to produce fusion power. The science and engineering of magnetic-confinement fusion has progressed sufficiently to the point that devices currently being built are expected to reach a milestone in fusion energy development: a device where the self-heating of the plasma by the fusion reaction itself exceeds the external heating — the "burning plasma" regime. One such device is ITER, a large multinational machine being built in the south of France. Several privately funded companies are also aggressively developing and building machines, such as the SPARC tokamak being built by Commonwealth Fusion Systems in Massachusetts. The field of fusion energy is reaping the benefits of decades of scientific research enabling the creation of these devices on the path to commercial fusion power plants.

Scientists and engineers face a number of challenges in designing, building, and operating these fusion devices. Fusion plasmas must be heated and confined sufficiently long for economical power plants but also avoid instabilities and elevated heat transport loss that can arise in operating these machines at the edge of peak performance. Many disparate diagnostics are employed on these devices, but the harsh conditions of fusion plasmas make complete understanding using diagnostics alone impossible. Models

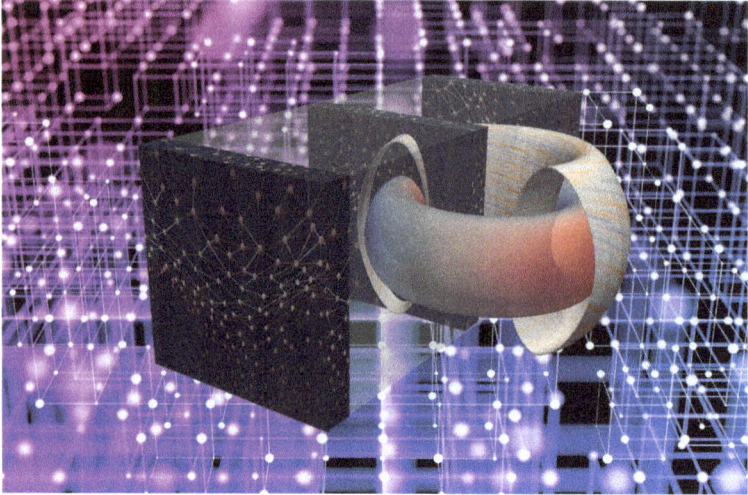

Fig. 1. Depiction of fusion research on a doughnut-shaped tokamak enhanced by artificial intelligence. Image courtesy of Eliot Feibush/PPPL and Julian Kates-Harbeck/Harvard University.

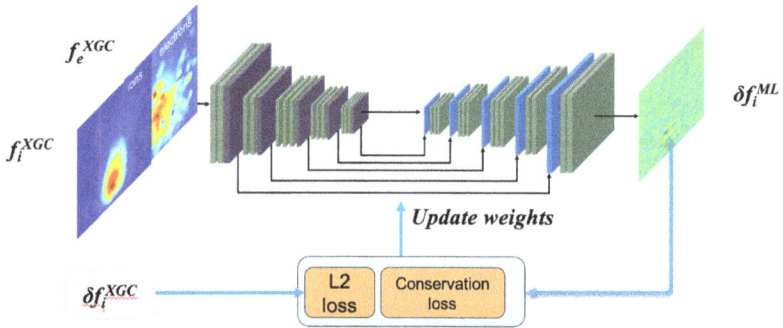

Fig. 2. Encoder–decoder neural network used to accelerate a targeted collision kernel inside a larger gyrokinetic turbulence code XGC.

and simulations are therefore heavily relied on in fusion energy research to understand the plasma dynamics and enable extrapolation to new devices.

As in many other science areas, fusion energy has seen an increased interest in leveraging AI/ML tools to aid in facing these challenges [1], covering a range of fusion research activities from machine control to large-scale simulation (see Figure 1 for an artistic depiction). This chapter will contain a description of some of the key challenges in magnetic confinement fusion for which AI/ML will be a critical part of the solution. Particular attention will be paid to aspects of these challenges that have unique and interesting features from an AI/ML perspective.

2. Challenges in Fusion Reactor Operations and Control

Magnetic confinement fusion reactors are large-scale and complex physical systems with subsystems that must be precisely orchestrated to achieve and maintain the extreme conditions needed to produce fusion. Within the core of the reactor, hydrogen isotopes are heated to millions of degrees forming a toroidal plasma confinement by magnetic fields. The dynamic behavior of fusion plasmas is highly nonlinear and spans a vast range of temporal and spatial scales. ITER, for example, will be a torus with a major radius of 6.2 meters, with experimental shots lasting up to 10 minutes, yet physical phenomena such as turbulence (a dominant driver of transport in tokamaks) have millimeter length scales and characteristic fluctuations with microsecond time periods. Surrounding the core, there are superconducting magnetic coils requiring power supplies and cryogenics, vacuum systems and gas injection systems to maintain the density of the plasma, neutral beam injectors that accelerate particles to fuel and heat the plasma, and RF systems used to help heat and stabilize the plasma. Hundreds of diagnostics are employed, including systems for measuring magnetic fields, the interaction of the plasma with lasers, and the X-rays and neutrons generated by the plasma. These systems all have engineering limits that must be accounted for during operations to protect the capital investment and avoid extended downtime. Additionally, while there is no chance for an event analogous to a fission meltdown in fusion reactors, there are numerous plasma instabilities that must be avoided during operations. These instabilities can lead to reduced performance or even rapid termination of the plasma. The latter not only decreases the uptime and therefore power generation efficiency of the reactor but also is accompanied by large forces and heat loads that could potentially damage reactor components.

2.1. *Experiment design and exploration*

Present-day experiments aim to establish the physics and technological basis for demonstration reactors. There are only a handful of major experiments in the world, and operation time is limited, while there is a vast range of phenomena to be studied. It is critical to make efficient use of each experimental plasma discharge, and as we move toward operation of bigger, more expensive devices, like ITER, efficiency and safety of exploration of the experimental operating space become even more critical. Between shots, decision-making has typically relied heavily on the plans made days in advance by experimentalists or the experience of operators. There is, however, a vast amount of empirical data, computational analysis, and predictive simulation capability that could be used to actively inform the exploration of the operating space. The main challenges to making use of this information are the volume of data and the computational expense of simulations. AI represents an opportunity to merge historical data and simulations into an assistive tool for operators to efficiently explore the operating space.

High-fidelity simulations have been studied for use in actuator trajectory optimization [2] but have computational times that are far too long to be used between shots or even between days of operation. On the other hand, approaches based on very reduced or empirical models, while much faster, may lack the fidelity or generalizability required to achieve high performance [3]. Recent approaches aim to use machine learning to accelerate high-fidelity physics codes to real-time relevant timescales and to augment these with empirical-data-driven models for phenomena lacking well-validated physics models [4–6]. By quantifying the uncertainty of the machine learning models through ensemble methods or other means, the model predictions could be used to propose actuator trajectories optimized for performance, robustness of predictions, or informativeness [7]. The model predictions and results of new experiments could also be used to propose new high-fidelity simulations to augment the training data for accelerated models. In this active-learning approach to reactor operation, the time trajectories of a large number of actuators must be optimized. This will require novel strategies, like the development of efficient methods for high-dimensional and multifidelity Bayesian optimization [8,9]. As experiments move toward reactor scale devices, the forces, heat loads, and radiation hazards increase, so optimization and active learning strategies must be developed consistent with use in a safety-critical, nuclear-regulated environment.

2.2. *Real-time control, monitoring, and protection*

In order to maintain plasma stability and optimal performance in response to changing device conditions, active control systems are required. The complexity of the system motivates the use of model-based control techniques rather than manually tuned control algorithms. Most control systems rely on linear control methods targeting specific operating points, however, the nonlinear and complexity of tokamak plasmas motivate the development of nonlinear control schemes that can handle the changes in system response as operating conditions change and can actively avoid or trigger changes in regime or events (e.g., transitions from low-confinement to high-confinement mode and flushing impurities from the plasma by triggering edge-localized modes).

Application of nonlinear model-based control design techniques requires reduced predictive models of reactor evolution with execution times appropriate for faster-than-real-time forecasting or real-time linearization around the present operating point at intervals fast enough to keep up with changes in operating conditions. As noted in previous sections, AI/ML approaches can enable acceleration of first-principles models and offline or online learning of empirical response models. For use in control design (especially considering the safety-critical nature of reactor operations), these models must come with efficiently computed and well-calibrated uncertainty estimates [10–12]. As new machines are developed and operating spaces are explored, the models may be asked to make predictions outside the training domain, so techniques for detecting out-of-distribution samples and regularizing predictions outside the training domain must be developed and applied. To efficiently commission new reactors, techniques for transfer learning must be developed so that models trained on data from previous devices can quickly adapt based on a small number of samples from the new device.

Key to enabling high-performance real-time control is estimating the state of the plasma from available measurements. While typical control systems in present-day experiments make use of hundreds of sensors at submillisecond sample times, there are many diagnostic systems that provide important information about the plasma behavior that have sample times or resolutions that make real-time analysis a challenge. Recent AI/ML hardware and software developments provide tools that can enable edge processing of high-resolution diagnostics to provide a featurized dataset to the decision-making processes in the control system [13]. AI/ML models can also be trained to assess the behavior of fusion plasmas and make decisions directly from the high-dimensional data. A key challenge to decision-making based on high-resolution data is dealing with the multiscale behaviors. This is studied in [14] through the use of specialized convolutional neural networks.

Beyond feedback stabilization and active regulation of operating scenarios, the real-time control system must maintain robust control by monitoring the proximity of the operating point to unsafe regions of operating space that could either directly damage the device (due to forces or heat loads) or lead to uncontrollable instabilities that rapidly terminate the plasma (referred to as disruptions). When possible, the operating scenario must be altered to maintain a safe distance from unsafe regions, and, if avoiding the boundaries becomes unavoidable, safe ramp-down scenarios must be initiated. Similarly, the health and status of reactor components must be actively monitored so that operation can be safely maintained, altered, or stopped when a diagnostic, actuator, or other reactor component is compromised.

Disruptions are a major concern for reactors, since the large forces and heat load could cause damage to the device leading to costly downtime and repairs. However, while understanding and simulating the physics of these events is an active area of research, theory-based prediction of the onset of disruptions has not yet demonstrated the accuracy and reliability required for avoiding disruptions in reactor operations. AI/ML has emerged as a powerful tool for developing disruption predictions based on empirical databases of disruptive plasmas [15–17], however, there are three major challenges to the application of these methods that are active areas of research. There is the need for interpretability (to understand the cause of a disruption so that specialized response strategies can be developed), generalizability/transferability (to transfer models from small experiments to reactor scale devices), and the development of strategies to train these models within a safety critical environment (how do we learn operational limits without crossing them very frequently or at all?).

Initial success in the development and application of reinforcement learning has mostly been in games with well-defined and observable environments, however, there have been recent successes in video games with continuous, high-dimensional states and actions, and only partial observation of the states, e.g., [18]. Developing learning-based policies like these for reactor control is an active area of research that could be a key approach to dealing with the complex decision-making required to respond to disruption warnings and the potential combinatorial explosion of exception handling. Just this year, deep reinforcement learning policies for controlling the tokamak plasma shape were successfully demonstrated on the TCV experiment, in collaboration with DeepMind [19]. A simulation environment based on a free-boundary Grad–Shafranov equation solver was used to train a policy (a multilayer perceptron) using maximum *a posteriori* policy optimization, an actor-critic algorithm. With a 1–3 day training time per target plasma evolution and using 5000 parallel actors, the approach was shown to stabilize a range of unique plasma shapes. While the shape control problem can be accurately simulated with computationally cheap models, the ability of the trained policies to perform well on the actual device is a key demonstration of clearing the "sim2real" gap for a fusion application. For other tokamak control problems, there remains a significant gap between the predictions of available models and experimental behavior, as well as a steep computational cost for most models. Development of more capable and more efficient simulations, as well as approaches to learn from multifidelity models, will be critical to expanding reinforcement learning to other areas of tokamak control. It will also be essential to develop methods for learning and deploying policies in a safety-critical environment, including providing performance guarantees to make this approach compatible with nuclear regulations.

3. Acceleration and Validation of Simulation

Due to the multiscale and multiphysics nature of fusion plasmas, along with their harsh environment, simulation and modeling play an important role in interpreting and predicting the behavior of fusion devices, not only for current devices but also in designing next-generation machines. These simulations range from simple, fast analytical physics models to complex, first-principles codes that require the largest supercomputers in the world to run. In addition, often several models are integrated together in order to cover varying physics and temporal scales for better whole-device modeling. While great strides have been made in developing simulations which correctly reproduce certain parts of real experiments, there still exists a substantial "sim2real" gap, where even the most sophisticated simulations cannot replicate all important aspects of all fusion experimental discharges, again due to the complicated dynamics arising from the multiscale, multiphysics nature of these plasmas. It is therefore particularly important to validate such simulations on a wide range of experimental discharges, to determine where such simulations can fall apart, and guide scientists to the holes in our modeling understanding. While there is often a trade-off between speed and physical realism of a simulation, for purposes of plasma control, machine operation, or model-based design optimization, where time is of the essence, we need to maximize physics fidelity of these simulations, while meeting the time-to-solution requirements of the various use cases fusion scientists have.

Naturally, AI/ML techniques for accelerating simulations are being pursued by the fusion community, as in many other scientific communities. The range of techniques being used and the type and scale of simulations they are being applied to vary widely, with many more opportunities opening to include inductive biases in the machine learning models that enable more faithful reproductions of the physics included in these simulation codes.

3.1. *AI/ML challenges and opportunities for acceleration and validation of simulation*

3.1.1. *AI/ML acceleration of simulation*

One of the central challenges faced by fusion scientists in applying machine learning to simulation is to determine at what level of the simulation to incorporate the machine learning model. The right tool for the job is important, and some use cases can easily treat the entire simulation as a black box, requiring minimal outputs, while other use cases may necessitate a more targeted kernel acceleration due to simulation complexity or data size.

3.1.2. *Complete replacement of simulation, "black box"*

An example of complete replacement of a simulation by neural networks is found in work from the General Atomics group, on accelerating the Trapped Gyro-Landau Fluid (TGLF) reduced quasilinear turbulence model [20]. Despite being a reduced model (TGLF is tuned using a database of first-principles gyrokinetic turbulent simulations), TGLF's runtime of order tens of minutes can be a hindrance in steady-state integrated modeling scenarios which iterate a number of times to find self-consistent solutions of the tokamak core particle and energy transport. TGLF outputs a range of physics quantities, but the most important for these iterative modeling scenarios are the turbulent transport fluxes. Multilayer perceptron neural networks were trained to take in 10 different scalar quantities representing the magnetic geometry and gradients in the plasma composition (density and temperature) and output four scalar quantities of predicted transport fluxes. The network was not large but performed sufficiently well for the needs of accurately predicting the fluxes to converge to a steady-state solution, while being 10^6 times faster [21].

3.1.3. *Targeted kernel acceleration*

Many other simulations are complex, first-principles codes which may not conveniently reduce to simple scalar inputs and outputs but nevertheless can be accelerated with more sophisticated neural networks or have targeted kernels of the code accelerated by machine learning. An example is the XGC code [22], a massively parallel, gyrokinetic particle-in-cell code for studying turbulence in the difficult edge region of fusion devices. This code is a hybrid Lagrangian code, pushing marker particles in a Lagrangian sense, with self-consistent electric field calculations, but then interpolating these markers to an Eulerian grid each timestep for calculation of source contributions (neutrals, collisions, heating, etc.). Unlike the above TGLF example, it is computationally infeasible to generate a large dataset of averaged turbulent fluxes under varying input conditions, as XGC requires significant computing resources. However, acceleration of the XGC code has been achieved by targeting a kernel and calculating the effect of collisions. Inputs to the collision kernel are two-dimensional particle distribution functions, $f(v_\perp, v_\parallel) \in \mathbb{R}^2$, and the output is the change in these distribution functions due to collisions, $\delta f(v_\perp, v_\parallel) \in \mathbb{R}^2$. This problem then can be treated similar to a semantic segmentation problem often seen in computer vision, where each pixel is classified as belonging to an object of a certain class, except in this case, the target was a regression problem, with the output being continuous. An encoder–decoder architecture was used (ReSeg), with the encoder a CNN and the decoder consisting of four RNNs to capture a more global structure [23]. When this network was trained on millions of XGC examples and then embedded into the C++ codebase of XGC, speedups of ~5x were found for collision-dominated XGC simulations.

The loss used includes physics-based constraints and therefore deserves further discussion as many scientific fields require simulation solutions which follow physical conservation laws (to desired numerical accuracy). The governing PDE, the Fokker–Planck collision operator in Landau form, has conservation laws associated with it, reflecting the fact that these plasma particle collisions conserve particle, momentum, and energy. These terms were added as "soft constraints", as regularization terms in the loss in addition to the traditional L_2 loss, i.e., $L_{total} = L_2 + \sum_i \lambda_i |\delta x_i / x_i|$, where x_i is the normalized integral moments of the distribution functions f and δf represents the conservation constraints normally used as convergence constraints in the traditional iterative numerical solver. Using these constraints in the loss improved the neural network accuracy by two orders of magnitude and a further two orders of magnitude improvement when using a stochastic augmented Lagrangian technique to dynamically adjust the λ_i regularization coefficients. This level of accuracy is needed in long time simulations to ensure the accumulation of errors won't ruin the final solutions.

Beyond constraints added to the loss, in the last few years, there has been rapid progress in the area of ensuring physical constraints are met with deep neural networks, for example, in many implementations of equivariant neural networks [24] that ensure certain symmetries are respected in the output solutions. In addition, various works have implemented deep neural networks which learn the operator instead of a function map directly [25], potentially better capturing symmetries and other characteristics of the underlying governing equations. This allows in addition for better generalization to changing simulation meshes and/or boundary conditions.

Nevertheless, challenges remain in using machine learning to replace targeted kernels. In particular, generalization and long-term stability of solutions of the entire simulation are of primary concern and importance.

3.1.4. *Numerical PDE solver acceleration*

A different tactic can be used to avoid some of the potential issues with generalization and long-term stability of black-box treatment of entire simulations or targeted kernels, and that is of using machine learning to replicate or improve the actual numerical solvers used inside the simulation. This can come in various forms, some examples of which we give here being pursued inside the fusion energy community and elsewhere. First, machine learning can be applied to accelerate iterative solvers such as GMRES, by providing better initial guesses to the solver [26]. This was applied to an implicit PIC simulation of electron plasma wave oscillations, where a neural network learned from many simulations to suggest a vector space $\mathcal{V}$ such that an initial guess of the linear equation solution $A^{-1}b$ lies closely in the span of $\mathcal{V}$. Initial work gave a modest decrease of 25% in the number of GMRES iterations needed to converge to a solution. Other ongoing research is looking at using ML to produce better preconditioners for matrix solvers used in radio-frequency wave propagation in plasmas. Another area of current research looks at using differentiable simulations and using neural networks in effect to learn subgrid models for kinetic simulations, enabling stable, long-time simulations with a reduced number of mesh points (inspired by work from Google with weather prediction [27]).

These methods are particularly beneficial as they in principle have the benefits of the traditional numerical solver (stability, accuracy guarantees). Some applications can accept a trade-off of reduced accuracy for increased speed, but in cases which absolutely must meet accuracy constraints, these methods closer to the numerical solver machinery may be critical.

3.1.5. *Validation of simulation with experiment*

Simulation and modeling need experimental validation to gain full confidence in predictions for future devices. AI/ML can provide several benefits in this process that are beginning to be leveraged in the fusion energy field. Bayesian inference is often performed using synthetic diagnostic forward models to extract physics parameters from actual experimental diagnostic data (often called "Integrated data analysis" in the fusion energy field). But the sequential sampling algorithms typically used, such as Markov Chain Monte Carlo (MCMC), are too slow to perform the statistical inference on the many time points from experimental discharges. Neural networks have recently been used in fusion energy experiments to learn the inverse mapping performed by statistical inference, providing fast inference which can reasonably keep up with the experimental output [28]. Related, simulation-based inference (also variously called likelihood-free inference) techniques using machine learning methods such as normalizing flows are being used to directly compare simulation and experiment, providing uncertainties on simulation inputs required to match experiment [29]. AI/ML enables these more principled statistical inference techniques to be applied broadly for fusion energy simulation/modeling to experiment comparisons.

4. Design Optimization

Scientists designing the next fusion machines typically turn to computational methods, taking into account engineering and physics constraints in an iterative optimization loop to determine the placement of magnets and subsystems for maximum fusion performance. This is critically important in an advanced fusion machine design called the stellarator, which uses complicated, non-planar magnets to confine the plasma. The stellarator optimization process typically consists of calculating desired magnetic fields optimized based on multiple physics and engineering constraints and then optimizing the magnetic coils' structures which produce these fields [30]. Current work has applied methods to improve and make possible gradient-based optimization of coil structures, including using adjoint methods [31] and the use of automatic differentiation [32]. Simple proxy functions are often used for calculating the physics constraints, to avoid costly physics simulators. As seen in the previous section, ML is a natural fit for creating accurate surrogate models from simulators and so is beginning to be applied to those models used in stellarator optimization. Here again, structure in the machine learning models to ensure the conservation of physical quantities is important for physical realism. Given the importance of gradient-based optimization with the complicated workflows composing the stellarator optimization process, future work in fully end-to-end differentiable workflows could prove beneficial.

5. AI and the Future of Fusion

The field of fusion energy is benefiting from the use of AI/ML to realize the promise of fusion energy for society. Many other research areas beyond the brief examples presented here are beginning or are ripe for research into how to best leverage AI/ML tools. The targeted customers range from fusion scientists trying to interpret experimental data with their models, to machine operators and engineers seeking to guarantee robust control and safe operation of machines. By working with fusion scientists and engineers, those with expertise in AI/ML can greatly contribute to tackling the many unique science and engineering challenges on the road to realizing the promise of fusion energy.

Acknowledgments

Funding for these various works was provided through the U.S. Department of Energy Office of Fusion Energy Sciences and Scientific Discovery through Advanced Computing (SciDAC) program by the U.S. Department of Energy Office of Advanced Scientific Computing Research.

References

[1] D. Humphreys, A. Kupresanin, M. D. Boyer *et al.* (2020). *Advancing Fusion with Machine Learning Research Needs Workshop Report.* Springer US, Vol. 39, no. 4. https://doi.org/10.1007/s10894-020-00258-1.

[2] W. Wehner, E. Schuster, M. Boyer *et al.* (2019). Transp-based optimization towards tokamak scenario development. *Fusion Engineering and Design,* *146,* 547–550. sI:SOFT-30. https://www.sciencedirect.com/science/article/pii/S0920379619300274.

[3] J. Barton, M. Boyer, W. Shi *et al.* (2015). Physics-model-based nonlinear actuator trajectory optimization and safety factor profile feedback control for advanced scenario development in DIII-d. *Nuclear Fusion, 55*(9), 093005, July. https://doi.org/10.1088/0029-5515/55/9/093005.

[4] M. Boyer, S. Kaye, and K. Erickson (2019). Real-time capable modeling of neutral beam injection on NSTX-u using neural networks. *Nuclear Fusion, 59*(5), 056008, March. https://doi.org/10.1088/1741-4326/ab0762.

[5] S. M. Morosohk, M. D. Boyer, and E. Schuster (2021). Accelerated version of NUBEAM capabilities in DIII-D using neural networks. *Fusion Engineering and Design, 163*(August 2020), 112125. https://doi.org/10.1016/j.fusengdes.2020.112125.

[6] M. D. Boyer and J. Chadwick (2021). Prediction of electron density and 19 pressure profile shapes on NSTX-U using neural networks. *Nuclear Fusion, 61,* 046024.

[7] M. Boyer (2020). Toward fusion plasma scenario planning for NSTX-U using machine-learning-accelerated models. In *Proceedings of the 2nd Conference on Learning for Dynamics and Control,* ser. Proceedings of Machine Learning Research, A. M. Bayen, A. Jadbabaie, G. Pappas, P. A. Parrilo, B. Recht, C. Tomlin, and M. Zeilinger, Eds., Vol. 120. PMLR, 10–11 June, pp. 698–707. https://proceedings.mlr.press/v120/boyer20a.html.

[8] K. Kandasamy, A. Krishnamurthy, J. Schneider *et al.* (2018). Parallelised Bayesian optimisation via Thompson sampling. In *Proceedings of the 21st International Conference on Artificial Intelligence and Statistics,* ser. Proceedings of Machine Learning Research, A. Storkey and F. Perez-Cruz, Eds., Vol. 84. PMLR, 09–11 April, pp. 133–142. https://proceedings.mlr.press/v84/kandasamy18a.html.

[9] K. Kandasamy, G. Dasarathy, J. Schneider *et al.* (2017). Multi-fidelity Bayesian optimisation with continuous approximations. In *International Conference on Machine Learning,* pp. 1799–1808. PMLR.

[10] B. Lakshminarayanan, A. Pritzel, and C. Blundell (2017). Simple and scalable predictive uncertainty estimation using deep ensembles. *Advances in Neural Information Processing Systems*, *30*.

[11] Y. Chung, W. Neiswanger, I. Char *et al.* (2020). Beyond pinball loss: Quantile methods for calibrated uncertainty quantification. *arXiv preprint arXiv:2011.09588*.

[12] W. Neiswanger, C. Wang, and E. Xing (2014). Asymptotically exact, embarrassingly parallel MCMC. Technical Report. https://arxiv.org/pdf/1311.4780.pdf.

[13] A. C. Therrien, R. Herbst, O. Quijano *et al.* (2019). Machine learning at the edge for ultra high rate detectors. In *2019 IEEE Nuclear Science Symposium and Medical Imaging Conference (NSS/MIC)*, pp. 1–4.

[14] R. M. Churchill, B. Tobias, and Y. Zhu (2020). Deep convolutional neural networks for multi-scale time-series classification and application to tokamak disruption prediction using raw, high temporal resolution diagnostic data. *Physics of Plasmas*, *27*(6), 062510.

[15] C. Rea, K. J. Montes, A. Pau *et al.* (2020). Progress toward interpretable machine learning–based disruption predictors across Tokamaks. *Fusion Science and Technology*, *76*(8), 912–924.

[16] J. Kates-Harbeck, A. Svyatkovskiy, and W. Tang (2019). Predicting disruptive instabilities in controlled fusion plasmas through deep learning. *Nature*, *568*(7753), 526–531. http://dx.doi.org/10.1038/s41586-019-1116-4.

[17] Y. Fu, D. Eldon, K. Erickson *et al.* (2020). Machine learning control for disruption and tearing mode avoidance. *Physics of Plasmas*, *27*(2), 022501.

[18] O. Vinyals, I. Babuschkin, W. M. Czarnecki *et al.* (2019). Grandmaster level in StarCraft II using multi-agent reinforcement learning. *Nature*, *575*(7782), 350–354. http://dx.doi.org/10.1038/s41586-019-1724-z.

[19] J. Degrave, F. Felici, J. Buchli *et al.* (2022). Magnetic control of tokamak plasmas through deep reinforcement learning. *Nature*, *602*(7897), 414–419, February. https://doi.org/10.1038/s41586-021-04301-9.

[20] J. E. Kinsey, G. M. Staebler, and R. E. Waltz (2008). The first transport code simulations using the trapped gyro-Landau-fluid model. *Physics of Plasmas*, *15*(5), 055908, May. http://aip.scitation.org/doi/10.1063/1.2889008.

[21] O. Meneghini, G. Snoep, B. C. Lyons *et al.* 2020. Neural-network accelerated coupled core-pedestal simulations with self-consistent transport of impurities and compatible with ITER IMAS. *Nuclear Fusion*, *61*(2), 026006, December, publisher: IOP Publishing. https://doi.org/10.1088/1741-4326/abb918.

[22] S. Ku, R. Hager, C. Chang *et al.* (2016). A new hybrid-Lagrangian numerical scheme for gyrokinetic simulation of Tokamak edge plasma. *Journal of Computational Physics*, *315*, 467–475. http://linkinghub.elsevier.com/retrieve/pii/S0021999116300274.

[23] M. A. Miller, R. M. Churchill, A. Dener *et al.* 2021. Encoder–decoder neural network for solving the nonlinear Fokker–Planck–Landau collision operator in XGC. *Journal of Plasma Physics*, *87*(2), April, publisher: Cambridge University Press. https://www.cambridge.org/core/journals/journal-of-plasma-physics/article/abs/encoderdecoder-neural-network-for-solving-the-

nonlinear-fokkerplancklandau-collision-operator-in-xgc/A9D36EE037C1029 C253654ABE1352908.

[24] R. Wang, R. Walters, and R. Yu (2020). Incorporating symmetry into deep dynamics models for improved generalization. *arXiv:2002.03061v4*, February. https://arxiv.org/abs/2002.03061v4.

[25] Z. Li, N. Kovachki, K. Azizzadenesheli *et al.* (2021). Fourier neural operator for parametric partial differential equations. *arXiv:2010.08895 [cs, math]*, May, *arXiv: 2010.08895*. http://arxiv.org/abs/2010.08895.

[26] R. Kube, R. M. Churchill, and B. Sturdevant (2021). Machine learning accelerated particle-in-cell plasma simulations. *NeurIPS Machine Learning for Physical Sciences Workshop*, p. 8.

[27] D. Kochkov, J. A. Smith, A. Alieva *et al.* (2021). Machine learning accelerated computational fluid dynamics. *Proceedings of the National Academy of Sciences*, *118*(11). *arXiv:2102.01010 [physics]*, January, http://arxiv.org/abs/2102.01010.

[28] A. Pavone, J. Svensson, A. Langenberg *et al.* (2019). Neural network approximation of Bayesian models for the inference of ion and electron temperature profiles at W7-X. *Plasma Physics and Controlled Fusion*, *61*(7), April, IOP Publishing. https://iopscience.iop.org/article/10.1088/1361-6587/ab1d26.

[29] C. Furia and M. Churchill. (2021). Likelihood-free inference using normalizing flows for experiment and simulation comparison. In *Bulletin of the American Physical Society*, Vol. 66, No. 13. American Physical Society. https://meetings.aps.org/Meeting/DPP21/Session/JP11.86.

[30] L.-M. Imbert-Gerard, E. J. Paul, and A. M. Wright (2020). An introduction to stellarators: From magnetic fields to symmetries and optimization. *arXiv:1908.05360 [physics]*, August. http://arxiv.org/abs/1908.05360.

[31] E. J. Paul, M. Landreman, A. Bader *et al.* (2018). An adjoint method for gradient-based optimization of stellarator coil shapes. *Nuclear Fusion*, *58*(7), 076015, May, IOP Publishing. https://doi.org/10.1088/1741-4326/aac1c7.

[32] N. McGreivy, S. R. Hudson, and C. Zhu (2021). Optimized finite-build stellarator coils using automatic differentiation. *Nuclear Fusion*, *61*(2), 026020, February. http://arxiv.org/abs/2009.00196.

© 2023 World Scientific Publishing Company
https://doi.org/10.1142/9789811265679_0016

Chapter 16

Artificial Intelligence for a Resilient and Flexible Power Grid

Olufemi A. Omitaomu[*,‡], Jin Dong[†,§], and Teja Kuruganti[*,¶]

[*]*Computational Sciences and Engineering Division, Oak Ridge National Laboratory, Oak Ridge, Tennessee, USA*
[†]*Electrification and Energy Infrastructure Division, Oak Ridge National Laboratory, Oak Ridge, Tennessee, USA*
[‡]*omitaomuoa@ornl.gov*
[§]*dongj@ornl.gov*
[¶]*kurugantipv@ornl.gov*

1. Introduction

The nation's electric grid is an extensive infrastructure that has fueled economic growth for the last century. However, the needs of the 21st century necessitate transformational change in the grid to address decarbonization and resilience. The goal of a smart grid is to transition the electric power grid from an electromechanically controlled system into an electronically controlled system, moving from a reactive system to a proactive system. According to the US Department of Energy's Smart Grid System Report [1], smart grid systems consist of information management, control technologies, sensing, communication technologies, and field devices that coordinate multiple processes to successfully generate, transmit, and deliver electricity to end users. These smart grid technologies have changed conventional grid planning and operation problems in at least three key areas with the ability to (1) monitor or measure processes, communicate data back to operation centers, and often respond automatically to adjust a process; (2) share data among devices and systems; and (3) process, analyze, and help operators access and apply the data coming from digital technologies throughout the grid. Some of the related problem spaces in smart grids include load forecasting, power grid stability assessment, fault detection, and smart grid security. These key elements enable the collection of significant amounts of high-dimensional and multitype data from electric power grid operations. However, the traditional modeling, optimization, and control technologies have many limitations in processing these datasets.

Faster information processing for smart grid technologies is becoming increasingly important as the traditional power grid is instrumented with digital devices that transform the collection and dissemination of information to decision makers, industry stakeholders, and electrical consumers. Compared to legacy electric grid operations, the smart grid provides new functionalities, such as support for clean and decentralized power generation and storage capabilities, accommodation of changing demand patterns with vehicle electrification, and implementation of demand-side management strategies. Unlike the legacy power grid, the smart grid allows for customer participation in grid operations: consumers will not only consume electrons and generate data but can also respond to the dynamic processes in the system, delivering flexibility, as decision makers in various contexts — including in demand response (DR) programs.

Therefore, improved communication and data processing functionalities are essential for successful smart grid operations. Information systems that support the smart grid are expected to be more reliable and flexible to accommodate many sophisticated analysis and control algorithms. In addition, customer participation requires utilities to distribute data and results of analyses to a diverse group of users and third-party service providers. Currently, power grid data collection and processing use a centralized approach in a client–server model with just a few servers running data collection, storage, access, and analysis and visualization applications. Although this model was sufficient for the legacy electric grid operation system, it has significant drawbacks for a smart grid system.

With the modernization of the power grid, power grid information can be classified into the following layers [2]:

- The **Physical Layer** represents the traditional electrical services and consists of generation, transmission, and distribution infrastructure, which was predominantly a one-way communication layer. With the emergence of the smart grid, this layer now includes distributed energy resources (DERs), such as wind and solar generation, as well as auxiliary devices, such as smart meters, phasor measurement units, and electric vehicles.

- The **Sensor Layer** consists of a sensor infrastructure deployed on the physical layer for monitoring operation and performance. This layer can also be considered the data layer and provides the much needed data that will transform the electromechanically controlled system into an electronically controlled system. However, the deployment of sensors *only* cannot achieve a true smart grid. This layer generates a massive amount of data and information that must be analyzed to be of significant use.

- The **Analytics Layer** supports resilient and flexible power grid operations using artificial intelligence (AI) techniques. Without an efficient and effective analytics layer, a true smart grid is not feasible. AI will play a significant role to analyze the data and information generated by the sensor layer.
- The **Market Layer** provides brokerage services for buying and selling electricity. The traditional market layer will need to undergo modification to allow for added sublayers that enable customers to sell their DERs and enable cloud services to satisfy the needs of producers, customers, and other users in the smart grid system.

Given the massive amounts of data and information expected to flow through power utility companies with the implementation of smart grid technologies, the need to apply AI techniques in the smart grid becomes more apparent. AI techniques use massive amounts of data to create and train intelligent algorithms to handle tasks that would otherwise require human intelligence and intervention. Although machine learning (ML) is often used interchangeably with AI, it is just one of the ways to achieve AI systems. Other methods used in AI systems include neural networks, robotics, expert systems, fuzzy logic, and natural language processing. Overall, AI techniques enable decision-making with speed and accuracy. In smart grid applications, AI can be defined as *the mimicking of grid operators' cognitive functions by computers to achieve self-healing capabilities*. However, AI might not be able to replace grid operators in some cases. Although AI systems can be more precise, reliable, and comprehensive, many challenges remain in applying AI techniques to the smart grid. Two types of AI systems are possible in smart grid: *Virtual AI* and *Physical AI*. Virtual AI systems include informatics that assist grid operators in performing their jobs. Physical AI systems include self-aware AI systems that can optimize and control specific grid operations with or without human intervention. Furthermore, AI systems in the smart grid can be further divided into artificial narrow intelligence (ANI) and artificial general intelligence (AGI). ANI refers to AI systems developed for a specific task with applicable requirements and constraints (e.g., an AI system that performs load forecasting using different datasets). AGI, on the other hand, refers to AI systems developed to learn and evolve autonomously — just like humans do. The development of AGI systems could help realize true smart grid systems in the future.

Research for AI-based smart grid applications has increased significantly in the past decade. Similarly, in the last 4 years, some of these studies have been revisited in more recent work [3–7]. In this chapter, we explore the roles of AI in power grids in terms of virtualization of power grid operations, human–machine collaboration for efficient grid operations, and DERs for efficient grid services.

2. Virtualization of Power Grid Operations

Some of the smart grid requirements highlighted in Section 1 may be better satisfied using AI applications that implement functionalities as services in the cloud rather than using the traditional client–server models. Some potential cloud models are listed in the following [8]:

- An **Infrastructure-as-a-Service (IaaS)** model offers virtualized resources to users directly on an as-needed basis. This is comparable to a car rental service. Users choose the resources they need and use them as desired, but the resources are not theirs, and they are returned after the specified rental period.
- A **Platform-as-a-Service (PaaS)** model offers a programmable environment for developers to construct applications directly in the cloud. This service level is analogous to a taxi service, in which the users specify their unique destination or end goal, and the environment constructs the application using the platform.
- A **Software-as-a-Service (SaaS)** model offers finished production software delivered to users through cloud portals. This service is equivalent to a bus service. The software has a predetermined set of applications, and users share the same software. Thus, users shift from locally installed software to online software services with the same functionality. SaaS may be the most appropriate model for power utility companies with limited in-house resources to develop internal AI applications. However, most of the power grid data collection and analysis applications may have to undergo a redesign to fully leverage the elasticity, scalability, and reliability of SaaS. Given the diversity of AI techniques, the new system should be developed to accommodate multiple, diverse smart grid applications.

These cloud services will enable utilities to try different computational methods, algorithms, and models to determine the most appropriate one for their use case. These readily available services will also accelerate the adoption of data analytics applications for better decision-making without the significant initial investment associated with infrastructure procurement and technical personnel acquisition and training.

For power grid applications, the technical requirements for these cloud services should mimic the requirements laid out by Duvvuri [9], including (1) **reusability** — AI algorithms and AI systems must serve numerous and diverse applications for the grid operators; (2) **scalability** — the services should meet the vertical (e.g., adding additional RAM and CPU resources) and horizontal (e.g., adding more machines and/or users) scalability needs; (3) **decentralized** — the services should run algorithms/models near the data location to mimic the distributed nature of grid operations; (4) **online** — the services must feature real-time and near real-time processing of operations data to meet the operators' needs; (5) **offline** — services must accommodate data and models for forensic analysis; and (6) **security** — the services must protect the grid data, models, and outputs against malicious access, alterations, and/or theft to maintain operations integrity.

Based on these requirements, the traditional methods for grid applications may need to be modified for a cloud computing platform. Some studies in this area are emerging. Zhou *et al.* [10] proposed a PaaS platform for smart grids. This platform leverages the rich sensing devices and information networks found in smart grids for anomaly detection. Specifically, the authors used the data stream from the power grid to perform a two-class classification of residential data to detect normal and abnormal customer activity. Prompt and real-time detection and diagnosis of equipment failures in the power grid are an integral part of a smart grid. Recently, a fault detection method for a power grid cloud platform was proposed [11]. The approach consists of three layers — a device layer, a field layer, and a cloud center layer — and uploads the data collected by the various monitoring systems at the device layer to the field layer for data preprocessing. The cloud center layer has IaaS, PaaS, and SaaS services and uses previously stored data in the field layer to train an ML model and classify equipment faults. Zhang *et al.* [12] explored a cloud computing platform for a power grid dispatching and control applications. The proposed platform monitors the power grid through the cloud terminal, which calls various services and displays the results. According to the authors, the proposed platform "improves global perception, global analysis, and global control of the large power grid dispatching and control system ability". Furthermore, Zhang *et al.* [13] proposed and implemented a serverless platform and dispatch communication system to ensure operation continuity regardless of the local infrastructure's availability and accessibility. These studies serve as exemplary frameworks for other grid operators to secure their cloud services.

Following is a list of problems that these services could help mitigate:

- **Protecting the Grid Data and AI Models:** Traditionally, individual utility companies collect, store, and protect their data internally and develop their AI/ML models. With the significant amount of data collected, these tasks require significant investments in infrastructure and personnel. Furthermore, the power grid's increasingly digital and interconnected landscape makes managing the vulnerabilities of the grid data and AI models uniquely challenging from a cybersecurity perspective. Although AI promises to enhance the security of grid data and AI models, the computing cost is significant — even for large utility companies. However, the adoption of these cloud services could help alleviate this issue and even help small- and medium-sized utility companies benefit from AI in their operations. Thus, these capabilities are needed to secure the grid data while also allowing for industry-wide sharing of data and AI models.

- **AI Technologies for Grid Resilience:** The changing global climate is leading to more frequent droughts, excess rainfall patterns, more extreme weather events, and increased wildfire activity. All these extreme events impact power generation, transmission, and distribution. AI models are needed to better forecast weather patterns for multiple days ahead of an event and estimate its potential impacts on grid operations to minimize unplanned outages and achieve faster restoration of grid services. Furthermore, there is an increasing need to understand the risks of cascading failures from sequential or concurrent extremes that could propagate through the power grid. Cloud services could help scale the existing AI models and develop new scalable AI models.

- **AI for Grid-Integrated Smart Communities:** Our communities, like the power grid, are transitioning into smart communities by using digital devices and sensors (e.g., Internet of Things [IoT]) to collect data and manage assets and/or services efficiently. On the one hand, individual homes are increasingly being instrumented with sensors and digital devices to monitor activities, control appliances, and reduce waste. Many of these homeowners are also transitioning from purely electrical consumers to electrical prosumers (i.e., customers with the ability to generate and consume electricity), which increases the complexities in the modeling of their daily activities. On the other hand, cities and counties are being instrumented with smart devices for efficient service control and resource management. Furthermore, new infrastructures are being deployed to cater for the emerging smart transportation era, including charging stations for electric vehicles and infrastructure-readiness technologies for autonomous vehicles. At the center of these emerging smart communities is a reliable and resilient power supply. AI/ML algorithms can assist with the complex optimization of this interdependent system-of-systems (power grid, smart homes, and smart communities) for seamless implementation and increased likelihood of success.

3. Human–Machine Collaboration for Efficient Grid Operations

Generally, one can assume that AI systems can think, learn, and understand the information presented to them in the context of power grid operations, when given the appropriate datasets and algorithms, just as humans in power grid operating rooms. However, AI algorithms suffer from the so-called *black box* problem in which the algorithms do not provide justification or rationale for their output. According to Wenskovitch and North [14], this is only half of the problem, and there is another black box: human cognition. On one hand, there is no justification by the algorithms for their output; therefore, the users of these algorithms or the AI systems built using them are faced with the decision of whether to accept the results at face value without the ability to question or understand the underlying processes. On the other hand, the human (i.e., the power grid operators') mind is a black box to the algorithms. This is the essence of the two-black-boxes problem [14]. For AI systems to be more effective and actionable, the algorithms that drive the systems must be able to learn from humans. The AI systems can efficiently discover hidden patterns and implicit knowledge in big data, and humans are known for conducting cognitive sensemaking, such as performing abductive reasoning, drawing inferences, making judgments, and bringing domain expertise to bear. The collaboration of these two entities is required to achieve a true smart grid. This collaboration is not a single technology, but it is a group of powerful technologies including AI, ML, natural language processing, and cognitive science. Thus, some researchers are advocating for the phrase *Amplified Intelligence* to account for the human elements in the collaboration.

In power grid applications, a cognitive system is a paradigm that capitalizes on information technology, AI, and human cognition to enhance grid operations. Thus, in the future, humans and AI are expected to play a combined role in a grid operation's decision-making processes. Recent experimental results suggest that when humans and AI work together, they outperform the AI or humans working alone on the same task [15]. Interestingly, the combined performance improved only in one direction; i.e., performance improved when the AI delegated work to humans but not when humans delegated work to the AI; this is probably because humans do not delegate well [15] or because of the black-box nature of human cognition to the AI algorithms.

Following is a list of grid problems that this collaboration could help mitigate:

- **Control Rooms Operations:** The power grid is operated from utility control rooms. The interfaces in these control rooms enable operators to track the status of covariates through indicators located at different control desks within the control room. Alarms indicate the occurrence of any abnormal conditions in one or more subsystems. From the control room, the operators should be able to change the system's operational conditions at any time. Grid operators monitor huge amounts of data, and their job is becoming more complicated as utilities add more renewable energy, storage, and demand-side resources to the grid. This deviation from the monolithic style of power generation is expanding, thus adding new layers of complexity to control room operations. These new layers are add-ons to the existing control room configuration, which sometime makes coupling difficult. Thus, the situational awareness (SA) of the operators becomes important; i.e., the operators' mental awareness of the current process state and ability to anticipate future process states based on experience and training. The ability of an operator to maintain the highest SA possible always depends on the task workload, information rate, system design, and complexity of tasks [16]. Monitoring and quickly processing large amounts of real-time data is a potential AI application in control room operations.
- **Power Grid Observability and Operations:** Power grids generate a large and growing amount of data through traditional and newer sensor technologies, although only a fraction of data available today are actionable. Moreover, a growing queue of sensor technologies await computational innovation to transform novelty into application. Traditionally, operating system data from supervisory control and data acquisition (SCADA) systems were collected from distributed locations back to a central control room. Asset health sensors collect and transmit data in a similar fashion, although some devices are configured to collect data locally and retain only a window of time, and an engineer must visit a field location to manually retrieve the data. Data are typically archived using a data historian or database and subsequently analyzed to serve functions in planning, visualization, and operations. Often, scan rates for the devices are limited owing to storage/communication restrictions. Performing analytics using AI — especially at a position closer to the data (i.e., at the edge) — will enable grid operations to leverage the large amount of sensor data as real-time actionable information to improve operational efficiency. AI can be performed on the data at the data sources (Edge AI) or at a centralized data storage location. Edge AI will accelerate the evolution of sensing capabilities, communication strategies, network optimizations, and application scenarios. Thus, there

is an opportunity for the power industry to embrace the exciting era of edge AI. However, edge AI will cause task-oriented data traffic flow over communication networks, for which disruptive communication techniques, efficient resource allocation methods, and holistic system architectures must be developed. The challenges for building edge AI ecosystems are multidisciplinary and span wireless communications, ML, operations research, grid applications, regulations, and ethics.

Despite the immense benefits of implementing AI in the power grid, this effort is not without challenges:

- **Acceptance of machines in the human–machine collaboration:** If AI algorithms are to become an integral part of power grid operations, the power grid operators must be willing to accept the AI-based insights with similar weight as those of humans in the decision-making process. Reportedly, humans have an aversion to AI algorithm insights in other applications [17]; specifically, the insights from machines are either ignored or given lesser weight. For this collaboration to become a reality in power grid operations, it is important to ask (1) if grid operators are comfortable with machine involvement; (2) what grid tasks and/or level of involvement are the operators comfortable with; (3) how should insights from machines be integrated into the decision-making process; and (4) how should continuous integration of machine insights be evaluated over time.

  One way to improve operators' confidence is through a cooperative learning loop [14] in which both human and machine must remain close to each other to foster an improved understanding. This is achieved through an iterative learning process. The objective of the learning loop is to fully open the black boxes by addressing how to extract critical information from the AI, how to present that information in an actionable manner to the human, how to extract cognition from the human, and how to present that cognition in a meaningful way to the AI [14].

- **Balancing responsibility for decision-making:** Balancing responsibility is another challenge to making human–machine collaboration a reality. As explained by Fügener *et al.* [15], the human–machine collaboration is more productive only in one direction: when a machine delegates work to a human. Therefore, some of the related questions to ask include the following: (1) are grid operators willing to accept task delegation from machines; (2) how does one best handle the division of labor between human and machine to achieve improved performance; and (3) what is needed to achieve the same level of performance with humans delegating tasks to machines?

In this context, delegation is the act of successfully executing a grid operation task via AI by giving the AI system full autonomy over the task. Delegation in a project management context has been studied, and some of those strategies could be adapted for human–machine collaboration. Some delegation-related questions include the following: (1) what factors influence human–machine collaboration success; (2) what factors are critical for the delegation process to be successful; (3) what delegation strategies are most effective for the collaboration; and (4) is there a relationship between task complexity and delegation strategy?

- **Integration of human cognition into AI algorithms:** In traditional grid operations, operators usually make use of notes and diagrams, externalized knowledge, and recall information in their decision-making process. Converting these industry artifacts into a digital form will provide a window into the operators' thought process. The challenge is modeling the human cognition. According to Wenskovitch and North [14], semantic relationships, trees, and related hierarchical structures such as file systems can enable humans to externalize their cognition. However, the externalization of operator cognition is not useful if it cannot be converted into a form and context understandable by a machine.

4. Distributed Energy Resources for Efficient Grid Services

The distribution grid has evolved rapidly in various aspects in the past two decades, including in terms of generation, demand, and control. Inspired by the widespread penetration of DERs, the integration of renewable energy resources (RES) is essential for decarbonizing the grid and making the distribution system more flexible and active [18]. On the generation side, the deployment of distributed generators — such as photovoltaics, wind turbines, and microturbines — has been increasing in distribution systems in recent decades [19]. Meanwhile, on the load side, residential and commercial customers are becoming more involved in grid services, including DR and ancillary services. On the one hand, the intermittency and uncertainty of RES have brought tremendous challenges to the operations and control of the distribution grid. On the other hand, the advanced metering infrastructure (e.g., the bilateral smart meter) and smart inverters facilitate the information exchange between DERs and the distribution system operator (DSO) [20]. Therefore, the development of advanced DER intelligence and data-driven control techniques is imperative to transforming the passive distribution system into an active system that can achieve optimal efficiency and reliability.

AI could help ensure a flexible and reliable distribution grid in two significant categories:

- **DER intelligence for DSO:** Emerging technologies, such as IoT, edge computing, real- time monitoring and control, peer-to-peer (P2P) energy, DERs, and DR, have the potential to transform the distribution grid into a more efficient, flexible, reliable, resilient, and sustainable infrastructure [21]. Conventionally, a SCADA system is used to handle energy resources, but this centralized architecture is not amenable or scalable to the growing deployment of DERs. The system-level distribution-grid intelligence includes advanced monitoring and control devices throughout the distribution system that actively respond to the information and actuations from the end users. Traditional model-based solutions require complete and accurate distribution network models (in a distribution circuit) and online solutions for a challenging non-convex optimization problem (i.e., optimal power flow problem), which prevent its wide adoption in real-world feeders [22]. Hence, various DER intelligence models have been proposed to enhance the DSO operation using operational data. The overarching goal is to simplify and accelerate the management algorithms while delivering comparable or better performance compared with the model-based solution.

  Instead of modeling the feeder's detailed voltage drop, Gao *et al.* [22] developed a decentralized reinforcement learning (RL)-based volt/volt-ampere reactive control to adjust the tap positions of the on-load tap changers based on the operational data. For a similar voltage regulation problem, Xu *et al.* [23] developed a safe off-policy RL algorithm to avoid voltage violation while minimizing network losses. Zhou *et al.* [24] proposed using AI or RL to design the optimal pricing signal by assuming community P2P energy trading is a Markov decision process. Similarly, Eck *et al.* [25] remarked that AI can support distribution grid operators in handling high DER penetration based on a local energy market.

- **DER intelligence for end-use customers:** As distribution networks transition from passive components of the power system to active players in the electricity market, new opportunities are opening for consumers to participate in the local electricity market and reduce the overall operation cost. Modern home energy management systems and smart devices enable the deployment of intelligent devices at the grid's edge. For instance, an artificial neural network algorithm was developed for a demand-side management system for smart consumers [26]; a deep deterministic policy gradient algorithm was utilized to optimally select the setpoint of a multizone residential heating, ventilation, and air conditioning (HVAC) system to minimize energy consumption while accounting for comfort [27]; and a deep RL-based algorithm was developed to control the building HVAC systems [28]. All these algorithms have shown that the proposed AI techniques can improve the grid efficiency and flexibility while delivering the desired indoor environment. More recently, a comparison study [29] revealed that the computational burden of the data-driven approach is much smaller than the model-based approach. Therefore, the learning-based approach is more suitable for online deployment for the residential DR programs.

Despite AI's promise in tackling DER integration challenges, several concerns for both the DSOs and end users do exist:

- **Modeling — Lack of safety and model constraints derived from the physical environment:** A shared assumption of the RL success relies heavily on the intrinsic state-action relationship being able to sufficiently learn via many samples. However, (1) this does not necessarily hold true for a full-blown model of the distribution grid, in which the sample collection is limited by real-time operations, and physical model constraints are difficult to represent efficiently (i.e., they rely purely on data); (2) to guarantee safe grid operation, certain physical criteria must be always satisfied: the generation must match demand and voltage/frequency must fall into a prescribed range. This basically raises one more critical safety/stability requirement for the AI algorithms (i.e., all AI solutions must guarantee the feasibility of the distribution grid operation).

   Developing hybrid or physics-informed models that can integrate domain information and physical knowledge with the learning techniques [30,31] might be worth investigating to address the safety concerns and model-constraint incompatibility concerns faced by data-driven learning algorithms.

- **Control — Go beyond off-the-shelf RL-based management:** Most of the RL-based energy management systems focus on applications of an off-the-shelf RL algorithm for the DER integration problem without diving into the analysis of convergence to an optimal policy. Unfortunately, such a policy search procedure is equivalent to solving hard non-convex optimization problems in which solutions are prone to getting stuck in local suboptimal points instead of global optimal points [32]. Hence, tailored RL or alternative AI algorithms [33] are required to deliver better control policy with faster convergence for specific distribution grid applications.

   Furthermore, the existing RL-based algorithms focus primarily on direct load dispatch of DERs and the wholesale electricity market, whereas little attention has been given to the price-based control in the distribution market. How to efficiently exploit the potential of DERs for a distribution market based on pricing strategies, such as distribution locational marginal price (DLMP), remains an open question to be answered. Considering the complex dynamics of real-world distribution circuits and customer responses, a model-free DLMP model is needed for aggregators to manage the individual residents and to minimize the electricity payment as well as maintain the secure and economic operation of the distribution system.

- **Deployment — Lack of deployable algorithms for multiagent learning and sequential decision-making problems:** Despite huge potential for DER integration, the current cloud computing service architecture hinders the wide deployment of DER intelligence in the distribution grid. Owing to the exponential increase in the full discrete action space, it is becoming almost prohibitive to apply RL to coordinate the operation of DERs in a distribution grid. Thus, edge computing [34], which can realize these services using resources at the network's edge near the data sources, has emerged as a desirable solution. Moreover, owing to the complex interaction between the DSO and customers, conducting an accurate sensitivity analysis to identify the influence of rewards on customer response as well as design optimal control for multiagent systems remains challenging for distribution networks. Q-learning is a model-free RL algorithm to learn the value of an action in a particular state. A multiagent Q-learning-based approach could deliver better control performance with reduced electricity costs and accelerated computational speed when making control decisions at the edge devices.

5. Summary

The emerging smart grids will help achieve a fully self-learning system that will be responsive, adaptive, self-healing, fully automated, and cost-effective [35]. AI/ML technologies could help achieve true smart grids by addressing issues in several areas:

- **Cloud Services to Eliminate Barriers to AI Adoption:** To achieve a fully self-learning smart grid system, the integration of AI with cloud computing — which can enhance security and robustness and minimize outages — will play a more important role in smart grid systems.
- **Data Preprocessing for AI Using Fog Computing:** Fog computing facilitates the operations of edge computing by preprocessing raw grid data locally rather than forwarding the raw data to the cloud. By providing on-demand resources for computing, fog computing has numerous advantages (e.g., energy efficiency, scalability, and flexibility). Some studies [36–39] have conducted tentative research for integrating fog computing into the smart grid, and fog computing will play a bigger role as the amount of data in the future smart grid increases.

- **Knowledge Enhancement through Transfer Learning:** The lack of labeled data is still a challenge for some smart grid applications. Thus, the concept of transfer learning in which knowledge gained while solving one problem can be applied to a different but related problem can be useful. Transfer learning reduces the requirements of training data, which motivates researchers to use them to overcome insufficient data. In recent years, deep transfer learning tasks [40] have received more attention, and they could have widespread applications in smart grid applications.

- **Consumer Behavior Prediction and/or Optimization in a Smart Cities Context:** With the emergence of smart cities and the evolution of the 5G network and IoT, demand-side management is becoming a vital task for managing the participation of users and producers in power systems. Learning patterns of consumer behavior and power consumption can contribute to DR tasks on the consumer side.

- **Amplified Intelligence for Optimal Smart Grid Operations:** The collaborative human and machine system has emerged to combine the expertise of humans and AI technologies for more efficient control room operations. Understanding the optimal strategy for delegating tasks between humans and machines could lead to a more human-centered approach to AI design.

Thus, the following are some suggested follow-on research areas:

- **Incorporating DERs for carbon reduction with AI:** In the United States, buildings account for 35% of total energy-related carbon dioxide emissions, making them top candidates for decarbonization. Considering the intermittent renewable generation, carbon intensities in the power grid are time-varying and can fluctuate significantly within hours, so using AI to dispatch building loads in response to the carbon intensities could lead to lower carbon emissions for the overall building operation.

- **Investigating integrated AI design:** Instead of single objective study, integrated AI with multiobjectives should be investigated, which will enable better designs of the control rules to achieve synergetic emission, energy, resilience, and cost reduction goals.

- **Delegating grid tasks between human and machines:** To eliminate the subjective in delegating tasks to machines, advanced AI approaches in the context of game-theoretic framework should be investigated for identifying optimal strategy for delegating tasks among human and machines.

- **Analyzing human factor issues in control rooms:** As control rooms become more sophisticated, the study of human factor issues in control rooms is even more important. Traditional approaches for studying human factor issues are subjective, cumbersome, and usually not scalable. The feasibility of using AI as a gaming agent in a virtual environment to evaluate human factor issues should be investigated.

References

[1] Smart Grid System Report, U.S. Department of Energy (2018). https://www.energy.gov/sites/prod/files/2019/02/f59/Smart%20Grid%20Report%20November%202018_1.pdf (accessed 15 January 2021).

[2] H. M. Meza and M. Rodriguez-Martinez (2017). Cloud-based and Big Data-enabled brokerage system for smart grids. In *2017 IEEE International Congress on Big Data (BigData Congress)*. IEEE, June 2017, pp. 502–506.

[3] O. A. Omitaomu and H. Niu (2021). Artificial intelligence techniques in smart grid: A survey. *Smart Cities*, *4*(2), 548–568.

[4] P. Verma, K. Sanyal, D. Srinivasan *et al.* (2018). Computational intelligence techniques in smart grid planning and operation: A survey. In *2018 IEEE Innovative Smart Grid Technologies-Asia (ISGT Asia)*. IEEE, May 2018, pp. 891–896.

[5] B. K. Bose (2017). Artificial intelligence techniques in smart grid and renewable energy systems—Some example applications. *Proceedings of the IEEE*, *105*(11), 2262–2273.

[6] S. S. Ali and B. J. Choi (2020). State-of-the-art artificial intelligence techniques for distributed smart grids: A review. *Electronics*, *9*(6), 1030.

[7] M. D. Lytras and K. T. Chui (2019). The recent development of artificial intelligence for smart and sustainable energy systems and applications. *Energies*, *12*(16), 3108.

[8] O. A. Omitaomu, A. Sorokine, and V. Chandola (2015). Virtualization of the evolving power grid. *IEEE Smart Grid Newsletters*. https://smartgrid.ieee.org/component/content/article/176-composite-loads-in-stand-alone-inverter-based-microgrids.

[9] V. Duvvuri (2020). Minerva: A portable machine learning microservice framework for traditional enterprise SaaS applications. https://arxiv.org/pdf/2005.00866.pdf (accessed 15 December 2021).

[10] M. Zhou, J. Li, W. Geng *et al.* (2021). IAPSG: A novel intelligent application platform for smart grid. *IOP Conference Series: Earth and Environmental Science*, *632*(4), 042055.

[11] W. Li, Y. Li, J. Shi *et al.* (2021). Power grid fault detection method based on cloud platform and improved isolated forest. In *2021 IEEE 5th Advanced Information Technology, Electronic and Automation Control Conference (IAEAC)*. IEEE, March 2021, Vol. 5, pp. 864–867.

[12] L. Zhang, L. Zhang, M. Liu *et al.* (2020). Cloud terminal for bulk power grid dispatching system. In *2020 IEEE 4th Conference on Energy Internet and Energy System Integration (EI2)*. IEEE, pp. 3625–3630.

[13] S. Zhang, X. Luo, and E. Litvinov (2021). Serverless computing for cloud-based power grid emergency generation dispatch. *International Journal of Electrical Power & Energy Systems, 124*, 106366.

[14] J. Wenskovitch and C. North (2020). Interactive artificial intelligence: Designing for the "Two Black Boxes" problem. *Computer, 53*(8), 29–39.

[15] A. Fügener, J. Grahl, A. Gupta *et al.* (2022). Cognitive challenges in human-artificial intelligence collaboration: Investigating the path toward productive delegation. *Information Systems Research, 33*(2), 678–696.

[16] H. V. P. Singh and Q. H. Mahmoud (2020). NLP-based approach for predicting HMI state sequences towards monitoring operator situational awareness. *Sensors, 20*(11), 3228.

[17] T. Haesevoets, D. Cremer, K. Dierckx *et al.* (2021). Human-machine collaboration in managerial decision making. *Computers in Human Behavior, 119*, 106730.

[18] L. Bai, Y. Xue, G. Xu *et al.* (2017). Distribution locational marginal pricing (DLMP) for congestion management and voltage support. *IEEE Transactions on Power Systems, 33*(4), 4061–4073.

[19] X. Wang, F. Li, J. Dong *et al.* (2021). Tri-level scheduling model considering residential demand flexibility of aggregated HVACs and EVs under distribution LMP. *IEEE Transactions on Smart Grid, 12*(5), 3990–4002.

[20] R. R. Mohassel, A. Fung, F. Mohammadi *et al.* (2014). A survey on advanced metering infrastructure. *International Journal of Electrical Power & Energy Systems, 63*, 473–484.

[21] I. Antonopoulos, V. Robu, B. Couraud *et al.* (2020). Artificial intelligence and machine learning approaches to energy demand-side response: A systematic review. *Renewable and Sustainable Energy Reviews, 130*, 109899.

[22] Y. Gao, W. Wang, and N. Yu (2021). Consensus multi-agent reinforcement learning for volt-var control in power distribution networks. *IEEE Transactions on Smart Grid, 12*(4), 3594–3604.

[23] H. Xu, A. Domínguez-García, and P. Sauer (2019) Optimal tap setting of voltage regulation transformers using batch reinforcement learning. *IEEE Transactions on Power Systems, 35*(3), 1990–2001.

[24] S. Zhou, Z. Hu, W. Gu *et al.* (2019). Artificial intelligence based smart energy community management: A reinforcement learning approach. *CSEE Journal of Power and Energy Systems, 5*(1), 1–10.

[25] B. Eck, F. Fusco, R. Gormally *et al.* (2019). AI modelling and time-series forecasting systems for trading energy flexibility in distribution grids. In *Proceedings of the Tenth ACM International Conference on Future Energy Systems*, June 2019, pp. 381–382.

[26] M. N. Macedo, J. Galo, L. A. L. De Almeida *et al.* (2015). Demand side management using artificial neural networks in a smart grid environment. *Renewable and Sustainable Energy Reviews, 41*, 128–133.

[27] Y. Du, H. Zandi, O. Kotevska *et al.* (2021). Intelligent multi-zone residential HVAC control strategy based on deep reinforcement learning. *Applied Energy, 281*, 116117.

[28] T. Wei, Y. Wang, and Q. Zhu (2017). Deep reinforcement learning for building HVAC control. In *Proceedings of the 54th Annual Design Automation Conference 2017*, pp. 1–6.

[29] X. Kou, Y. Du, F. Li *et al.* (2021). Model-based and data-driven HVAC control strategies for residential demand response. *IEEE Open Access Journal of Power and Energy*, *8*, 186–197.

[30] J. Z. Kolter and G. Manek (2019). Learning stable deep dynamics models. *Advances in Neural Information Processing Systems*, *32*.

[31] Y. Chen, Y. Shi, and B. Zhang (2018). Optimal control via neural networks: A convex approach. *arXiv preprint arXiv:1805.11835.*

[32] M. Fazel, R. Ge, S. Kakade *et al.* (2018). Global convergence of policy gradient methods for the linear quadratic regulator. In *International Conference on Machine Learning*. PMLR, July 2018, pp. 1467–1476.

[33] D. P. Kingma and J. Ba (2014). Adam: A method for stochastic optimization. *arXiv preprint arXiv:1412.6980.*

[34] C. Feng, Y. Wang, Q. Chen *et al.* (2021). Smart grid encounters edge computing: Opportunities and applications, *Advances in Applied Energy*, *1*(Feb), Art. no. 100006.

[35] S. S. Ali and B. J. Choi (2020). State-of-the-art artificial intelligence techniques for distributed smart grids: A review. *Electronics*, *9*(6), 1030.

[36] M. A. Ferrag, M. Babaghayou, and M. A. Yazici (2020). Cyber security for fog-based smart grid SCADA systems: Solutions and challenges. *Journal of Information Security and Applications*, *52*, 102500.

[37] G. M. Gilbert, S. Naiman, H. Kimaro *et al.* (2019). A critical review of edge and fog computing for smart grid applications. In *International Conference on Social Implications of Computers in Developing Countries*. Springer, Cham, May 2019, pp. 763–775.

[38] S. Zahoor, S. Javaid, N. Javaid *et al.* (2018). Cloud–fog–based smart grid model for efficient resource management. *Sustainability*, *10*(6), 2079.

[39] B. Tang, Z. Chen, G. Hefferman *et al.* (2017). Incorporating intelligence in fog computing for big data analysis in smart cities. *IEEE Transactions on Industrial Informatics*, *13*(5), 2140–2150.

[40] C. Tan, F. Sun, T. Kong *et al.* (2018). A survey on deep transfer learning. In *International conference on artificial neural networks*. Springer, Cham, October 2018, pp. 270–279.

Environmental Science

© 2023 World Scientific Publishing Company
https://doi.org/10.1142/9789811265679_0017

Chapter 17

AI and Machine Learning in Observing Earth from Space

Jeff Dozier

University of California, Santa Barbara, USA
dozier@ucsb.edu

1. Introduction

The launches of Sputnik 1 in 1957 and Explorer 1 in 1958 were driven more by Cold War politics than by scientific curiosity. Nevertheless, these early observations began the study of *Earth Observations from Space* [1], the title of a U.S. National Academies report that documented critical scientific discoveries in the half-century following the launch of the first U.S. satellite. Detectors on three satellites launched in 1958 — Explorer 1, Explorer 3, and Pioneer 3 — identified powerful radiation belts, later known as the Van Allen belts, extending 10^5 km from Earth, a quarter of the way to Earth's Moon [2]. Subsequently, satellites in the Television Infrared Observation Satellite (TIROS) series measured Earth's albedo and emitted thermal infrared radiation to begin studies of our planet's radiation balance [3]. Similar measurements continue today to document the imbalance that causes Earth to warm, along with measurements of other changes at the global scale, such as sea level rise [4].

"Observing Earth from space" in this chapter's title depends on the ability to sense signals that propagate over long distances with no help from a transmitting medium. Two forces — electromagnetic radiation and gravity — meet this criterion. Most sensors deployed in remote sensing measure electromagnetic radiation in wavelengths from the ultraviolet ($<0.4\,\mu$m) through the microwave (>2 mm). *Passive* remote sensing measures radiation in the environment, either reflected from sunlight, emitted by Earth's surface and atmosphere, or reflection or transmission from "signals of opportunity" from sources such as communication or global positioning satellites. *Active* remote sensing includes both the sensor and the source for the radiation in the case of "radar" or "lidar" (radio or light detecting and ranging). The measurement of Earth's spatiotemporally varying gravity field yields information about the displacement of water, in liquid or solid form, between groundwater, oceans, and ice sheets [5].

The importance of "observing Earth from space", in the context of this book, lies in the recognition that Earth's climate system includes the dynamic interplay between the atmosphere and the ocean and land surface; the surface does not simply provide a static lower boundary condition.

2. AI and Machine Learning in Remote Sensing

In combination, the roles of "artificial intelligence and machine learning" in the context of observing Earth from space lie in the need to analyze large volumes of multidimensional data (2D or 3D spatially plus time and wavelength and perhaps polarization) that are sometimes noisy, account for the problem that other factors besides the variables of interest affect the signal, mitigate the computational complexity of the equations that govern the behavior of absorption and scattering by individual particles and their assemblages, and address the issue that inversion of the signal to recover the governing input variables sometimes has multiple local solutions.

In an interview for IEEE, "Stop calling everything AI" [6], computer scientist and statistician Michael Jordan praises computers' capability for "low-level pattern-recognition capabilities that could be performed in principle by humans but at great cost" and goes on to point out that such "systems do not involve high-level reasoning or thought". This chapter there considers machine learning as a sophisticated process of supervised or unsupervised classification that uncovers statistical relationships or clustering between observations and information, which can be subsequently used to provide information from very large volumes of observations. Examples of applications of machine learning in remote sensing are emerging; the existing literature that assesses different methods is insightful (e.g., [7]).

Examples of AI in remote sensing are harder to find unless one broadens the definition of AI. Otherwise, as Jordan [8] asserts, "Most of what is labeled AI today ⋯ is actually machine learning", as evident in papers published in special issues of the journals *Sensors* [9] and *Remote Sensing* [10]; titles of papers in these contain the word "intelligence" but their content applies more to machine learning. This chapter instead presents some examples of problems where AI might be able to help.

A commonly hard-to-achieve objective, "explainable" AI or machine learning, emphasizes the need in science to get the right answers for the right reasons [11]. Prediction itself is not the only goal. Statistical predictions that do not lead to the understanding of a process may be intriguing but run the risk of missing the responsible mechanisms.

3. Objectives for Observations

This chapter's discussion of Observing Earth from Space focuses on quantitative measurements of variables that affect "Earth System Science", a term coined in the 1980s to consider global change on time scales of decades to centuries driven by interactions between the physical climate system, biogeochemical cycles, and the solid Earth, all connected through the hydrologic cycle [12,13]. This perspective drove the development and implementation of EOS, the U.S. Earth Observing System [14], a sequence of four satellites launched from 1997 to 2004. Of the four, three continue to operate in 2022, well beyond their design life.

EOS implemented two data practices that we now take for granted but which were innovative at the time: (1) investigators created estimated values of scientifically important global variables from the measurements of top-of-atmosphere signals so that other scientists could analyze processes without having to go through the arcane transformations of the electromagnetic radiation or gravitational variation needed to retrieve state variables; (2) the data products from EOS were made freely available to any user, anywhere, with no proprietary embargo period nor any cost beyond that of reproduction and delivery. This policy was developed before the Internet was widely available, so the cost to the users for reproduction and delivery has turned out to be zero.

This perspective on observing Earth for Earth System Science leads to a focus on retrieving quantitative geophysical and biological variables, as distinctive from classification in the usual image processing sense. Much of the literature on AI and machine learning in image processing seems to stem from the computer vision discipline (e.g., [15]), medical imaging [16], and, to a lesser known extent, the classified intelligence community [17]. Although recognition of objects has a place in Earth System Science, e.g., in discrimination between snow and clouds [18], the more pressing problem lies in the measurement of important variables.

4. Radiative Transfer, AI, and Machine Learning

4.1. *Absorption and scattering of radiation*

As radiation passes through a medium, absorption and scattering affect its propagation, and the absorption of the energy in turn leads to emission. Applying to disciplines such as astrophysics, climate science, and remote sensing [19], the radiative transfer equation has analytic solutions for simple configurations, but usually numerical methods are needed. A variety of solution methods exist, some depending on simplifying assumptions; about two dozen codes are publicly available [20].

Moreover, the characterization of the "medium" depends on the relationship between the sizes of absorbing and scattering particles — e.g., cloud droplets, leaves, soot, algae, or dust — and the wavelength of the radiation. In situations where the wavelength is small compared to the size of particles and the spacing between them, we can treat the problem as a medium, usually air, which absorbs some wavelengths but is also populated by particles. In opposite situations where the wavelength is large compared to the sizes of the particles and their spacing, we might treat the whole assemblage as the medium. Take snow as an example. The wavelengths of the solar spectrum at Earth's surface (0.28–2.5 µm) are smaller than the effective radius of grains in a snowpack (50–1,200 µm), so we consider the absorption and scattering properties of the grains in the radiative transfer calculations and neglect absorption by air in the short distances between them [21]. If we instead consider the snowpack's reflection of a radar signal at a wavelength between 2 cm and 1 m, then the medium is the air–snow mixture. The possible presence of liquid water in the snowpack complicates the response. In the solar wavelengths, the complex refractive indices (the fundamental optical property of a bulk material) of ice and water are similar [22,23], and the water's main effect is to cause the snow grains to cluster [24]. In the radar wavelengths, indeed in the microwave spectrum generally, water is ∼ 80× more absorptive than ice [25].

Efficient numerical solutions to the appropriate equations are available but nevertheless challenge computing over large datasets. Gustav Mie [26] developed equations for scattering and absorption by a single spherical particle early in the 20th century, but effectively fast computational solutions came seven decades later [27,28], along with equations for non-spherical or coated particles [29]. Similar computational intensity exists in the microwave regime, whereby snow, soils, and forests are each considered as a medium with bulk optical properties and 3D heterogeneity [30].

4.2. AI, machine learning, and the inversion problem

Inverting a measured electromagnetic signal to recover the geophysical or biological properties that govern scattering, absorption, and emission — from the atmosphere, water column, snowpack, forest, etc. — multiplies the computation. Inversion involves minimization of characteristics of a modeled solution compared to the measurement, and finding a minimum requires estimates of gradients or other approaches, which involve multiple radiative transfer calculations. The inversion especially consumes cycles when the image data are spectroscopic, typically with several hundred wavelength bands.

By brute force, the computation can be beaten down by massive parallelism, taking advantage of the fact that the spectral signatures of each pixel can be analyzed independently. Machine learning can offer a less costly alternative: choose a sample of the pixels that covers the span of likely properties, run the inversion routines on those, and use machine learning as a supervised problem to estimate the properties of interest on whole images or even whole sets of images. Strategies to sample include uniqueness with a tolerance. At full precision, the set of unique pixels is hardly any smaller than the complete set of pixels, but using a unique-within-tolerance filter enables the selection of sets of pixels that are spectrally similar. Alternatively, oversegmentation with superpixels can reduce noise and effectively cover the range of conditions that affect the variables being retrieved [31]. In this case, AI could be explored to best select the characteristics of the imagery and the underlying drivers of the properties of interest.

4.3. *Uncertainty in illumination geometry in mountains*

In some disciplines such as hydrology and ecology, mountains play important roles. Worldwide, two billion people depend on spring and summer snowmelt for their water supply [32], and in the lower and middle latitudes, most snow falls in the mountains. For example, 24% of North America is mountainous, but those areas account for 60% of the precipitation, much of it as snow [33]; similar statistics probably apply worldwide, but the data to assess such proportions are sparser [34]. Similarly, most large wildfires occur in the mountains [35]. One can argue, therefore, that plausible changes in climate will have their greatest importance in mountain ranges that supply water resources and whose forests are susceptible to fire. Mountainous terrain affects remotely sensed observations through their influence on illumination geometry, specifically angles of solar illumination and view and the fraction of the overlying hemisphere open to the sky.

Evaluations of the quality of globally available digital elevation models (DEMs) seem to focus on errors in the elevations themselves. However, the use of DEMs in remote sensing lies largely in the need to match illumination angles with their corresponding pixels in images, for both passive [36] and active [37] remote sensing, hence the need to account for errors in the resulting calculations of illumination geometry. The differencing operations to calculate slope and aspect from digital data amplify relative errors in the elevations, and the analyses of elevation errors (e.g., [38]) do not apparently discuss the correlation of errors. That is, if the RMS error of a typical global dataset is $\sim$8 m, are the uncertainties of the elevations 1 arcsec apart

($\sim$30 m) uncorrelated? If so, the uncertainty in the difference in elevation between the points translates to a large uncertainty in slope. The variance of the normal difference distribution [39] is the sum of the variances of the distributions of each, so in this case, the RMS error of the difference in elevation would be 11 m if the errors are uncorrelated.

In retrieving the geophysical properties of a surface that control its reflectance, we distinguish between the intrinsic reflectance, which one would observe on a flat open area, and the apparent reflectance measured by a sensor looking downward [41]. Modeling the effect of the terrain explains the difference, assuming that the representation of the terrain is correct. Figure 1 illustrates the consequences of likely incorrect calculation of the illumination geometry. The scatter diagram shows the cosine of the local illumination angle on the x-axis and the brightness in Landsat OLI (Operational Land Imager) band 5 (851–879 nm, where diffuse solar irradiance is small) on the y-axis. Indeed, a relationship should exist, but it should not be perfect because the intrinsic albedo of the surface also varies. The problematic values in the upper left part of the graph show very bright but poorly illuminated pixels, hence the calculation of the illumination angles must be wrong, owing to incorrect gradients of the terrain calculated from the DEM. The values in the lower right corner of the scatter plot are also possibly problematic. These very dark pixels are allegedly well illuminated; they could be intrinsically dark, or the illumination cosines are incorrect.

Potentially, AI could help inform a retrieval algorithm. Correctly incorporating the physical processes that drive the reflectance enhances the accuracy of the retrieval but only if the perceived illumination geometry is correct.

4.4. *Ambiguity in inversions of radiative transfer*

A pernicious problem in inverting the radiative transfer equation stems from the possibility that different combinations of input values can produce calculations of the electromagnetic signal whose differences are below the noise level of the signal itself. Twomey's [42] classic work, *Introduction to the Mathematics of Inversion*, illustrated atmospheric sounding as one of two canonical examples of the problem: from spectroscopic infrared measurements from satellite, the task is to retrieve atmospheric profiles of temperature and humidity. Even if the problem is linear, i.e., $\boldsymbol{Af} = \boldsymbol{g}$, the problem of solving for $\boldsymbol{f}$ from measurements $\boldsymbol{g}$ can give incorrect results because matrix $\boldsymbol{A}$ can be nearly singular or of low rank. The solution for $\boldsymbol{f}$ therefore depends on additional knowledge. For example, is it smooth, can

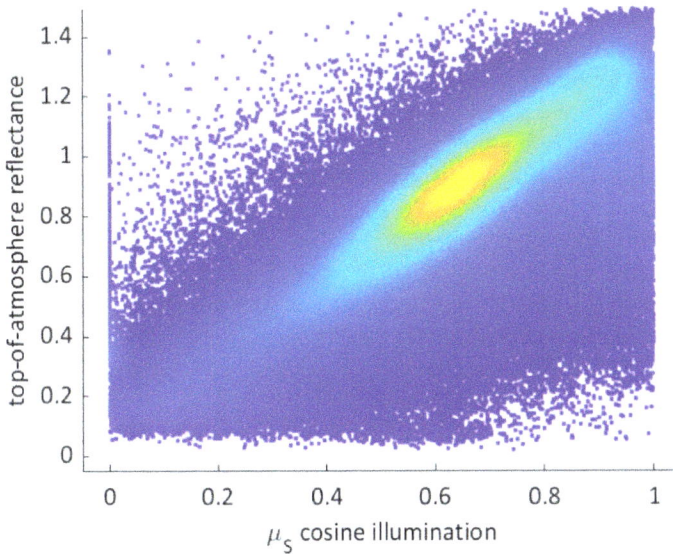

Fig. 1. Landsat 8 OLI image reflectance in the Indian Himalaya, 22 February 2016 versus cosine of local illumination angle computed from Cartosat [40] digital elevation data.

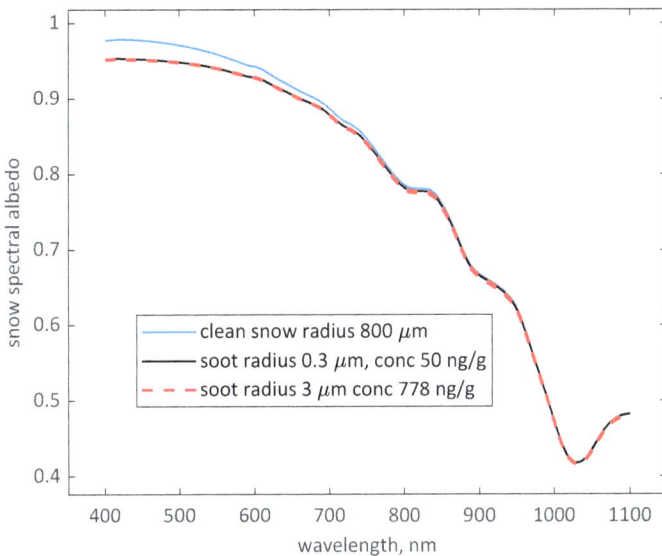

Fig. 2. Retrieval of black carbon content in snow, depending on the grain size of the snow itself (800 µm, blue line, clean snow) and the size and concentration of these light-absorbing particles (black and red lines).

we estimate a distribution or mean value, and do we have a time series so we can consider prior values?

In many regions, the albedo of snow is degraded by light-absorbing impurities such as soot or dust [43], resulting in snow disappearing earlier, snowmelt runoff peaking higher, and glaciers receding because the ice, which is darker than the winter snow, melting more in the summer season. Figure 2 shows a spectroscopic retrieval of soot concentration in typical snow in the melt season. The blue line shows the albedo of clean snow, and the red and black lines show the albedo of snow with black carbon (soot). The red and black lines are on top of one another, yet they represent concentrations of the absorbing impurities that are an order of magnitude different, $50\,\mathrm{ng/g}$ versus $778\,\mathrm{ng/g}$. This situation is an example of a problem that AI could help solve, by considering how other information could be brought to bear to distinguish whether the contamination results from local sources, in which case the sizes of the particles could be large, or from long-distance transport, in which case the sizes must be small.

5. Examples of Machine Learning in Interpreting Remotely Sensed Imagery

Some examples illustrate progress and ideas for future development: fluxes of water, energy, and carbon derived from remote sensing; socioeconomic and environmental information even in resource-constrained institutions; information about snow properties derived retrospectively but needed in April, not July.

5.1. *Fluxes of water, energy, and carbon*

Alemohammad *et al.* [44] describe WECANN (Water, Energy, and Carbon with Artificial Neural Networks), a suite of remotely sensed measurements to estimate global spatial and seasonal values of three variables: sensible heat exchange, latent heat exchange (and thus evaporation), and gross primary productivity, the energetic difference between photosynthesis and respiration. They use data products from a suite of sources to assemble the drivers of the surface energy balance: net radiation, air temperature, soil moisture, precipitation, snow, growth rates, photosynthesis, and respiration. Some measurements were available from multiple sources, hence independently estimating their values. To get information about photosynthesis, they measure solar-induced fluorescence from the GAME-2 satellite (Global Ozone Monitoring Experiment). To distinguish fluorescence from solar radiation during daylight, when the reflected solar radiation would overwhelm the fluorescence, the sensor measures in a very narrow (0.3 nm) Fraunhofer band where the Sun's atmosphere absorbs much of the radiation.

The investigation employed a feed-forward neural network, trained on data from 2008 through 2010, assessed with data from 2011, validated results using other satellite data products and flux measurements from towers, and carried through 2015 for discussion of the findings about the fluxes. The training by design implicitly couples the three output variables, rather than defining their physical relationships. R^2 statistics were 0.95 for latent heat exchange, 0.89 for sensible heat exchange, and 0.90 for gross primary productivity. The scatter plots indicate that the high correlations result partly from many corresponding values of low magnitudes.

5.2. *Socioeconomic and environmental conditions in remote or data-poor regions*

MOSAIKS [45], Multitask Observation using Satellite Imagery and Kitchen Sinks, enables users with only laptop computing access to use remotely sensed data to estimate socioeconomic and environmental conditions that affect human welfare. Using the Google Static Maps API (3 spectral bands, ~4 m spatial resolution), they extracted features from each image that reduced the data volume by a factor of 8. Although this step is computationally intensive, it needs to be done just once, so MOSAIKS acts as an unsupervised classifier that can help unlock satellite imagery for a more diverse and larger audience than supervised approaches have done to date. The variables of interest include forest cover, population density, nighttime lights, household income, length of the road network, and housing prices normalized by size. These were then regressed against the unsupervised features extracted by MOSAIKS for a subset of the images and then evaluated and validated against images not used in the training. The processing is extensible; users can regress their own ground data against image features; simple linear regression or ridge regressions are recommended. Once the regression coefficients are established, the analyses can be repeated for different images in separate locations or as the landscape changes with newly acquired image features.

The regression step does not tax computing resources, so MOSAIKS scales across users and tasks for which the same extracted features are appropriate. R^2 values for statistical fits in their U.S.-wide analysis range from 0.91 for forest cover, 0.73 for population density, to 0.45 for household income. At the scale of the planet, household income and housing prices were not considered because their relationship with quality of life varies so much in different countries. Similar statistical performance was achieved with R^2 values of 0.85 for forest cover and 0.62 for population density.

The analysis indicates that resource-constrained governments could use such techniques to survey their citizens.

5.3. *Snow water equivalent in mountains*

Remotely sensing the spatiotemporal distribution of *snow water equivalent* (SWE = depth × density) is the biggest unsolved problem in mountain hydrology. Dozier *et al.* [46] explain the difficulties in retrieving SWE from any electromagnetic signal, noting that the importance of snow as a water resource requires forecasts of snowmelt runoff during the winter and spring before the snow melts. One way to estimate SWE distribution to use to train a machine learning approach is through reconstruction. Sensors in the optical part of the solar spectrum can retrieve information about the presence or absence of snow, along with its albedo but not its depth or SWE. However, using such information can provide the remotely sensed date of disappearance of snow from each pixel, and that finding can be combined with a calculation of melt to reconstruct the accumulated SWE for each day back to the last significant snowfall [47].

With this method, the snow resource can only be assessed retroactively after snow disappears, but the SWE values thereby obtained can be used to train a model that then uses remotely sensed data during the snow season to enable snowmelt runoff forecasts. Bair *et al.* [48] evaluated this approach in the Sierra Nevada of California, where surface measurements are available to validate the retrievals, and then demonstrated the value in the Hindu Kush range of Afghanistan, showing that the 2011 drought could have been predicted in time for international agencies to marshal humanitarian aid. The machine learning model incorporated snow cover retrieved from optical sensors, passive microwave brightness temperature, and historical patterns of snow accumulation also derived from reconstruction.

6. Concluding Remarks

Scientists with expertise in Earth science, radiative transfer, computing, and statistics tend to reside in different camps, thereby failing mostly to combine the knowledge that would enhance the benefits of AI and machine learning to observations of Earth from space [49]. A long-standing recommendation, dating back to the publication of *Computing the Future* [50], identified the difference between computational science and computer science, the former requiring collaborative expertise to best take advantage of algorithms, data management, and computing resources to solve scientific problems.

An observation that might apply is that the choice of the training data matters more than the machine learning method. For example, Bair *et al.* [48] showed that bagged regression trees and feed-forward neural networks produced nearly identical results, with the neural networks returning the occasional troubling outlier. My own experiments using MATLAB's Machine Learning App or Amazon's Sagemaker showed that applying multiple methods — Gaussian process regression, neural network fitting, and boosted regression — to the same imaging spectroscopy datasets of large size produced similar statistical performance. I tend to favor Gaussian process regression because the training is faster than neural network fitting in MATLAB's Deep Learning Toolbox, but utilizing a system with a GPU could remove that advantage.

My assertion — the choice of the training data matters more than the machine learning method — affects our approach to employing AI and machine learning in observing Earth, but I recognize the observation is based on my limited experience. The current decade will see the launch of several spaceborne imaging spectrometers that will produce high data volumes. The use of AI and machine learning to analyze those images will require exploration of the ways they can be selected for investigation, but such analyses will be fruitful in using these data for understanding Earth's processes. The task will be to select the independent variables in ways that relate to the geophysical and biological processes involved, to thereby avoid overtraining and spurious correlation.

References

[1] National Research Council (2008). *Earth Observations from Space: The First 50 Years of Scientific Achievement.* Washington, D.C.: National Academies Press, 144 pp.

[2] J. A. Van Allen and L. A. Frank (1959). Radiation around the Earth to a radial distance of 107,400 km. *Nature, 183,* 430–434. doi: 10.1038/183430a0.

[3] T. H. Vonder Haar and V. E. Suomi (1969). Satellite observations of the Earth's radiation budget. *Science, 163,* 667–668. doi: 10.1126/science.163.3868.667.

[4] E. C. Weatherhead, B. A. Wielicki, V. Ramaswamy *et al.* (2018). Designing the climate observing system of the future. *Earth's Future, 6,* 80–102. doi: 10.1002/2017EF000627.

[5] B. D. Tapley, M. M. Watkins, F. Flechtner *et al.* (2019). Contributions of GRACE to understanding climate change. *Nature Climate Change, 9,* 358–369. doi: 10.1038/s41558-019-0456-2.

[6] K. Pretz (2021). Stop calling everything AI, machine-learning pioneer says. *IEEE Spectrum,* 21 March 2021. https://spectrum.ieee.org/the-institute/ieee-member-news/stop-calling-everything-ai-machinelearning-pioneer-says.

[7] J. Ball, D. Anderson, and C. S. Chan (2017). Comprehensive survey of deep learning in remote sensing: Theories, tools, and challenges for the community. *Journal of Applied Remote Sensing*, *11*, 042609. doi: 10.1117/1.JRS.11.042609.

[8] M. I. Jordan (2019). Artificial intelligence — The revolution hasn't happened yet. *Harvard Data Science Review*, *1*. doi: 10.1162/99608f92.f06c6e61.

[9] M Graña, M. Wozniak, S. Rios *et al.* (2020). Computational intelligence in remote sensing: An editorial. *Sensors*, *20*, 633. doi: 10.3390/s20030633.

[10] G. Jeon (2021). Editorial for the special issue "Advanced Artificial Intelligence and Deep Learning for Remote Sensing". *Remote Sensing*, *13*, 2883. doi: 10.3390/rs13152883.

[11] J. W. Kirchner (2006). Getting the right answers for the right reasons: Linking measurements, analyses, and models to advance the science of hydrology. *Water Resources Research*, *42*, 03S04. doi: 10.1029/2005WR004362.

[12] F. P. Bretherton (1985). Earth system science and remote sensing. *Proceedings of the IEEE*, *73*, 1118–1127. doi: 10.1109/PROC.1985.13242.

[13] W. Steffen, K. Richardson, J. Rockström *et al.* (2020). The emergence and evolution of Earth System Science. *Nature Reviews Earth & Environment*, *1*, 54–63. doi: 10.1038/s43017-019-0005-6.

[14] G. Asrar and J. Dozier (1994). *EOS: Science Strategy for the Earth Observing System*. Woodbury, NY: American Institute of Physics, 119 pp.

[15] D. M. Pelt and J. A. Sethian (2018). A mixed-scale dense convolutional neural network for image analysis. *Proceedings of the National Academy of Sciences of the United States of America*, *115*, 254. doi: 10.1073/pnas.1715832114.

[16] J. Saltz (2023). AI and medical imaging. In A. Choudhary, G. Fox, and T. Hey (eds.), *Artificial Intelligence for Science: A Deep Learning Revolution*.

[17] T. Hitchens (2020). NRO Taps AI For future 'hybrid architecture'. Breaking Defense. https://breakingdefense.com/2020/08/nro-taps-ai-for-future-hybrid-architecture/.

[18] T. Stillinger, D. A. Roberts, N. M. Collar *et al.* (2019). Cloud masking for Landsat 8 and MODIS Terra over snow-covered terrain: Error analysis and spectral similarity between snow and cloud. *Water Resources Research*, *55*, 6169–6184. doi: 10.1029/2019WR024932.

[19] S. Chandrasekhar (1960). *Radiative Transfer*. New York: Dover Publications, Inc., 393 pp.

[20] K. Stamnes, G. E. Thomas, and J. Stamnes (2017). *Radiative Transfer in the Atmosphere and Ocean*, 2nd edn. Cambridge, U.K.: Cambridge University Press, 528 pp.

[21] S. G. Warren (1982). Optical properties of snow. *Reviews of Geophysics*, *20*, 67–89. doi: 10.1029/RG020i001p00067.

[22] G. M. Hale and M. R. Querry (1973). Optical constants of water in the 200-nm to 200-µm wavelength region. *Applied Optics*, *12*, 555–563. doi: 10.1364/AO.12.000555.

[23] S. G. Warren and R. E. Brandt (2008). Optical constants of ice from the ultraviolet to the microwave: A revised compilation. *Journal of Geophysical Research*, *113*, D14220. doi: 10.1029/2007JD009744.

[24] S. C. Colbeck (1979). Grain clusters in wet snow. *Journal of Colloid and Interface Science*, *72*, 371–384. doi: 10.1016/0021-9797(79)90340-0.

[25] W. J. Ellison (2007). Permittivity of pure water, at standard atmospheric pressure, over the frequency range 0-25 THz and the temperature range 0-100°C. *Journal of Physical and Chemical Reference Data*, *36*, 1–18. doi: 10.1063/1.2360986.

[26] G. Mie (1908). Beiträge zur Optik trüber Medien, Speziell Kolloidaler Metallösungen. *Annals of Physics*, *25*, 377–445. doi: 10.1002/andp.19083300302.

[27] H. M. Nussenzveig and W. J. Wiscombe (1980). Efficiency factors in Mie scattering. *Physical Review Letters (USA)*, *45*, 1490–1494. doi: 10.1103/PhysRevLett.45.1490.

[28] W. J. Wiscombe (1980). Improved Mie scattering algorithms. *Applied Optics*, *19*, 1505–1509. doi: 10.1364/AO.19.001505.

[29] C. F. Bohren and D. R. Huffman (1983). *Absorption and Scattering of Light by Small Particles*. New York: John Wiley and Sons, 530 pp.

[30] C. Elachi and J. J. van Zyl (2021). *Introduction to the Physics and Techniques of Remote Sensing*, 3rd edn. New York: John Wiley & Sons, 560 pp.

[31] M. S. Gilmore, D. R. Thompson, L. J. Anderson *et al.* (2011). Superpixel segmentation for analysis of hyperspectral data sets, with application to Compact Reconnaissance Imaging Spectrometer for Mars data, Moon Mineralogy Mapper data, and Ariadnes Chaos, Mars. *Journal of Geophysical Research*, *116*, E07001. doi: 10.1029/2010JE003763.

[32] J. S. Mankin, E. Viviroli, D. Singh *et al.* (2015). The potential for snow to supply human water demand in the present and future. *Environmental Research Letters*, *10*, 114016. doi: 10.1088/1748-9326/10/11/114016.

[33] M. L. Wrzesien, M. T. Durand, T. M. Pavelsky *et al.* (2018). A new estimate of North American mountain snow accumulation from regional climate model simulations. *Geophysical Research Letters*, *45*, 1423–1432. doi: 10.1002/2017GL076664.

[34] M. L. Wrzesien, T. M. Pavelsky, M. T. Durand *et al.* (2019). Characterizing biases in mountain snow accumulation from global datasets. *Water Resources Research*, *55*, 9873–9891. doi: 10.1029/2019WR025350.

[35] P. E. Dennison, S. C. Brewer, J. D. Arnold *et al.* (2014). Large wildfire trends in the western United States, 1984–2011. *Geophysical Research Letters*, *41*, 2928–2933. doi: 10.1002/2014GL059576.

[36] J. Dozier (1989). Spectral signature of alpine snow cover from the Landsat Thematic Mapper. *Remote Sensing of Environment*, *28*, 9–22. doi: 10.1016/0034-4257(89)90101-6.

[37] S. Manickam and A. Barros (2020). Parsing synthetic aperture radar measurements of snow in complex terrain: Scaling behaviour and sensitivity to snow wetness and landcover. *Remote Sensing*, *12*, 483. doi: 10.3390/rs12030483.

[38] E. Uuemaa, S. Ahi, B. Montibeller *et al.* (2020). Vertical accuracy of freely available global digital elevation models (ASTER, AW3D30, MERIT,

TanDEM-X, SRTM, and NASADEM). *Remote Sensing*, *12*, 3482. doi: 10.3390/rs12213482.

[39] E. W. Weisstein (2022). Normal difference distribution. Wolfram Math World. https://mathworld.wolfram.com/NormalDifferenceDistribution. html.

[40] ISRO (2011). *Evaluation of Indian National DEM from Cartosat-1 Data*, Indian Space Research Organization, Hyderabad. http://bhuvan.nrsc.gov.in/ data/download/tools/document/CartoDEMReadme_v1_u1_23082011.pdf.

[41] E. H. Bair, J. Dozier, C. Stern *et al.* (2021). Divergence of apparent and intrinsic snow albedo over a season at a sub-alpine site with implications for remote sensing. *Cryosphere*, *16*, 1765–1778. doi: 10.5194/tc-2021-361.

[42] S. Twomey (1977). *Introduction to the Mathematics of Inversion in Remote Sensing and Indirect Measurements* (Developments in Geomathematics). Amsterdam: Elsevier, 243 pp.

[43] S. M. Skiles, M. Flanner, J. M. Cook *et al.* (2018). Radiative forcing by light-absorbing particles in snow. *Nature Climate Change*, *8*, 964–971. doi: 10.1038/s41558-018-0296-5.

[44] S. H. Alemohammad, B. Fang, A. G. Konings *et al.* (2017). Water, Energy, and Carbon with Artificial Neural Networks (WECANN): A statistically based estimate of global surface turbulent fluxes and gross primary productivity using solar-induced fluorescence. *Biogeosciences*, *14*, 4101–4124. doi: 10.5194/bg-14-4101-2017.

[45] E. Rolf, J. Proctor, T. Carleton *et al.* (2021). A generalizable and accessible approach to machine learning with global satellite imagery. *Nature Communications*, *12*, 4392. doi: 10.1038/s41467-021-24638-z.

[46] J. Dozier, E. H. Bair, and R. E. Davis (2016). Estimating the spatial distribution of snow water equivalent in the world's mountains. *WIREs Water*, *3*, 461–474. doi: 10.1002/wat2.1140.

[47] K. Rittger, E. H. Bair, A. Kahl *et al.* (2016). Spatial estimates of snow water equivalent from reconstruction. *Advances in Water Resources*, *94*, 345–363. doi: 10.1016/j.advwatres.2016.05.015.

[48] E. H. Bair, A. A. Calfa, K. Rittger *et al.* (2018). Using machine learning for real-time estimates of snow water equivalent in the watersheds of Afghanistan. *Cryosphere*, *12*, 1579–1594. doi: 10.5194/tc-12-1579-2018.

[49] D. Thompson and P. G. Brodrick (2021). Realizing machine learning's promise in geoscience remote sensing. *Eos*, *102*. doi: 10.1029/2021EO160605.

[50] National Research Council (1992). *Computing the Future: A Broader Agenda for Computer Science and Engineering*. Washington, D.C.: National Academies Press, 288 pp.

© 2023 World Scientific Publishing Company
https://doi.org/10.1142/9789811265679_0018

Chapter 18

Artificial Intelligence in Plant and Agricultural Research

Sabina Leonelli[*,‡] and Hugh F. Williamson[†,§]

*Exeter Centre for the Study of the Life Sciences & Institute for Data
Science and Artificial Intelligence, University of Exeter, Exeter, UK
†DIGIT Lab, Business School, University of Exeter, Exeter, UK
‡s.leonelli@exeter.ac.uk
§h.williamson@exeter.ac.uk

1. Introduction

Artificial Intelligence (AI) offers great potential towards the development
of plant and agricultural research and its application to social and environmental problems on a global scale, including — but not limited to — climate
change, biodiversity conservation, food security, and drug development.
This potential is only beginning to be adequately explored, however, due
to the relatively inefficient cooperation between experts with required
and complementary skills and the constraints on infrastructures that can
systematically inform such AI efforts. This chapter starts with a brief review
of the prospects and promises of AI in this domain, focusing particularly
on machine learning (ML) applications, as this has been the area of AI that
has been most developed in plant science [1]. We then analyze three sets of
challenges — and related opportunities —peculiar to plant and agricultural
research: (1) the need to tackle diverse biological phenomena which are
highly susceptible to changing environmental conditions; (2) the ways in
which the various stakeholders of relevance to agricultural development,
including both public and private sectors, need to be organized and
coordinated to ensure appropriate use of the technology; and (3) the
requirements posed by the vast ecosystem of data types and infrastructures
relevant to crop science. We conclude that AI can best fulfill its promise
when it is developed through extensive transdisciplinary collaborations
across the many stakeholders involved, thus acting as a platform for a

revitalized, meaningful, and impactful engagement around what is meant by agricultural development and how technology can best support its achievement for the benefit of humanity as a whole.

2. Prospects and Promises

Following wider trends in biosciences, both basic and applied plant sciences have increasingly emphasized data-intensive modes of research over the last two decades. The capacity to measure biological complexity at the molecular, organismal, and environmental scales has increased dramatically, as demonstrated by the following: advances in high-throughput genomics and norms and tools that have supported the development of a commons of publicly shared genomic data; the development of platforms for high-throughput plant phenotyping in the laboratory, the greenhouse, and the field; and the proliferation of remote sensing devices on-farm [2–4]. Such platforms and associated data generation have contributed to a booming AI industry in commercial agriculture, focused on the delivery of "precision" farming strategies: Reports have estimated that the market for AI in agriculture was worth $330 million in 2018 and could reach $1,550 million in 2025 [5]. Indeed, AI applications in plant research and agriculture have so far primarily benefited large-scale industrial farming [6], with R&D investment focused on commodity crops such as wheat, rice, and maize; high-value horticultural crops such as soft fruits; and intensively managed environments such as orchards and vineyards. In addition to this, however, the amount and type of data being collected, alongside advancements in AI methods, offer the opportunity to ask and address new questions of fundamental importance to plant scientists and agricultural stakeholders around the world, with transformative implications for current approaches to planetary health [7]. In this chapter, we primarily focus on machine learning (ML) applications, as this has been the area of AI that has been most developed in plant science with applications ranging from sequence analysis to genomic selection and phenotyping [1].

Four key areas of innovation in this domain can be singled out:

1. elucidating and managing the complexity of biological data, organisms, and systems,
2. tackling changing environmental and climatic conditions to foster planetary health,
3. supporting conservation and the sustainable exploitation of biodiversity,
4. improving food security to address the ongoing demographic explosion.

Using AI to acquire a better understanding of biological systems is a fundamental step towards all four of these goals. Researchers in the plant sciences have harnessed ML methods to understand biological complexity at several levels, from the molecular through to the physiological. At the molecular level, they include inferring the regulatory networks that control gene expression and other tasks that have proved insurmountable without the support of advanced computing [8,9]. At the phenotypic level, the use of ML in image-based analysis of plants in the lab or the field (phenomics) offers many opportunities to better understand plant growth and environmental responses in detail and use non-destructive means [2]. Deep supervised Convolutional Neural Networks (CNNs) for instance are revolutionizing the scale and accuracy of field evaluation, agricultural monitoring, and the study of plant properties [10–12]. These technologies also facilitate the integration of high throughput phenotyping data with other forms of research data, including genomic, field evaluation, and climatic data. Together, these approaches to genomics, phenomics, and the domains that bridge them hold great potential to improve our understanding of the complex interactions between plant genotypes, environments, and management strategies (G × E × M interactions) that determine crop growth and performance in agriculture [13] — and thereby enable research and interventions on plants on a global scale.

This research directly underpins the second area of innovation, which involves understanding and responding to the impacts of our changing global climate and environments, in order to preserve and if possible enhance the conditions of existence on this planet. Better understanding of the performance of different plants under a variety of environmental stressors — and the molecular systems that underpin this — will enhance plant breeders' ability to adapt new crop varieties to changing agricultural conditions. At the same time, ML itself can increase the efficiency of breeding, e.g., in identifying gene editing targets [13] or in prediction-based Genomic Selection methods [14]. Complementary to our understanding of plant biological systems, ML can also be used to augment longstanding statistical methods of *in silico* crop modeling. This allows researchers to predict the performance of different crop varieties/genotypes across a much wider range of environmental conditions (including predicted future environmental conditions) than it would be feasible to conduct field trials under [15].

The ability to respond to changing environmental conditions is predicated on access to the broadest possible range of plant biodiversity, as a source of new genetic material for breeding and as research objects to increase our understanding of plant biology and ecology [16]. Large quantities of biodiversity are already held in digital collections and seed banks around the globe, but making these usable for research remains a significant hurdle. ML can contribute to unlocking these collections, e.g., by supporting the digitalization of plant specimen information [17] and providing automatic identification of species and traits [18]. These advancements can foster the discovery of valuable material and inform the study of evolutionary dynamics and changing species distribution relative to environmental change [19].

Together, these applications strengthen and enhance our systems of agricultural research and development, which is vital to ensure global food security in the face of climate change and the massive demographic growth predicted for the twenty-first century. ML also promises to support farmers and food production directly, e.g., in the growing field of smartphone-based apps that use computer vision to provide plant disease detection and diagnostic services to farmers in locations where access to agricultural advisory services may be lacking, such as PlantVillage Nuru [20]. Realizing the full potential of innovation in these interlinked domains will depend, however, on overcoming major challenges, to which we now turn.

3. Biological Challenges

The first set of challenges are biological, in terms of both the nature of plant biological systems and the structure of biological research. As the above examples of ML applications indicate, one of the distinctive tasks for the plant sciences is to understand the complex gene-environment interactions that influence plant biology and span multiple scales: from the molecular and cellular, through the microbiome and soil, and up to climate systems. On top of these are human management practices in agricultural and other cultivation settings, which have long affected the conditions for plant life and must therefore be factored in. Understanding these interactions requires understanding not only of plants but also of the wide range of species that populate the environment, from bacteria and viruses through fungi and animals, and the biological systems that they participate in, including soil composition and the effects of chemical interventions such as the use of fertilizers and pesticides. Accordingly, as computational capacity increases relative to such complexity, examples of useful applications of AI to plant science contexts are increasing, with the COVID-19 pandemic crisis further accelerating interest in this approach [21].

One of the most ambitious applications of ML is the effort by several Australia-based researchers to develop a suite of models for predicting key traits of agronomic importance (including yield, protein content, and flowering time), across several different plant species, based on vast quantities of data collected as part of the Australian National Variety Trials [22]. By integrating field trial data with satellite images, weather data, soil sample tests, agrochemical application, and other agronomic management data, the researchers were able to generate accurate predictive models that were not simply "black boxes", as many ML models are, but indicated causal pathways for scientists to investigate. While their models were focused on capturing environmental interactions, the authors highlight the potential for ML to capture interactions across other levels as well, including the molecular. Achieving such multiscale predictive modeling is one of the key aspirations for AI/ML in plant and crop science.

While advances in digital data analysis present many new opportunities, ensuring that data, models, and other outputs link back to the material samples with which data are associated (seeds, germplasm, and other biological sources) is vital to ensure that those outputs can be effectively interpreted and reused [3]. Unlike fundamental research on model organisms, the value of plant science to practical applications in agriculture and other domains is predicated on the understanding and manipulation of plant biological diversity, including variation within as well as between species [16]. This can include the discovery of genetic traits in wild crop relatives that are of potential use in crop breeding, such as traits for disease resistance or resilience under certain climatic conditions, or the identification of biological compounds of pharmaceutical value, among other activities. Given the central place of diversity and variation, clear and consistent reporting on the material samples to which data and models refer is necessary, first, in order to understand the latter's scope of relevance and, second, because the utility of digital data (e.g., genomic sequences) is often limited without access to the original samples. To take an example, in Genomic Selection methods, statistical and ML models trained with detailed genotypic and phenotypic data can be used to predict the value of individual plants as parents in breeding programs, based only on genotypic data taken from the plant [14]. This can reduce the time and increase the accuracy of crop breeding, but it is dependent on using models trained with very closely related plant populations to those being analyzed [23]. To ensure the validity of predicted breeding values, it is necessary to know precisely which populations were used for training and their relation to the breeding population, thus also requiring detailed pedigree data.

4. Governance Challenges

The second set of challenges that we would identify are those related to the governance of data in plant and agricultural science. Governance in plant and agricultural research is made especially complex by the multiplicity of different stakeholders in the domain, stretched across a range of sites from scientific research through the diverse networks of food systems. Each of these stakeholders has his/her own distinct relationship to data: plant breeders pursue data on socio-economic and environmental conditions in tightly defined target markets while generating large-scale experimental data of their own; farmers produce a wide variety of data of potential research interest as part of their everyday work but may be ambivalent about sharing these and unaware of how to use existing data sources to inform their own planning and production strategies; and many agritech companies now produce sensing devices for farms or collect data directly from proprietary farm equipment, often providing a range of commercial services off the back of these data. Moreover, there is a large divergence between the emphasis on molecular data within academic plant science and the equally strong emphasis on (phenotypic) field evaluation data favored in applied domains such as breeding. Ongoing efforts to bridge this gap, such as integrating genomic data in breeding, are still limited in their reach, which points to the difficulties of translating plant research into agronomic spaces, especially at the global level [24]. Developing governance strategies for plant data sharing and use that take into account the complicated social, legal, and political dynamics of the field is a significant challenge with major implications for how and to what extent AI and ML technologies can be implemented in the field [25].

Ongoing questions about access to samples and related data present a further challenge. Several international agreements for access and benefit sharing (ABS) are now in force that govern the global exchange of important plant materials, specifically the International Treaty on Plant Genetic Resources for Food and Agriculture (ITPGRFA) and the Nagoya Protocol of the UN's Convention on Biological Diversity. ABS agreements mandate that any benefits accruing from the use of selected plant material be shared with the nation or community from which it was sourced and make this a condition of access to the original material. This has led to ongoing debates about the status of data generated from samples covered by ABS regimes, as the open sharing of data is perceived by some as a threat to the integrity of ABS principles and structures [26]. While data are not yet subject to ABS requirements, attempts to determine future policy directions on this subject are underway [27] as are attempts to improve linkage and identification of datasets derived from ABS-regulated materials through the Global Information System (GLIS) of the ITPGRFA [28]. The potential for increased regulation of plant data may hold large implications for ML applications, where datasets can play a very important role in training, e.g., even in the absence of material samples on which to perform experiments or validate outputs. Similarly, what status ML models and outputs may have in regard to requirements for benefit sharing, where those outputs have been generated from regulated data, remains an open question. Both the access and the benefit-sharing questions may contribute significantly to shaping the future landscape of ML in the plant sciences, with significant opportunities for AI to take such issues on board and contribute to their solution.

A case in point is the protection of sensitive data, especially data collected from farms, e.g., data that include locations or information about crop production. In biomedicine, the creation of large-scale data resources from the Human Genome Project onwards has been accompanied by the development of strong governance regimes, legislation, and ethics protocols for data sharing, protection, and use [29]. These may well provide a model for plant science, and an area where AI could support the development of data mining tools that mitigate the sensitivities associated with providing access to raw data — for instance by focusing on running algorithms across existing databases with no need for direct data access. To take one recent example, the CGIAR international agricultural research network is implementing a system modeled on the OpenSAFELY platform for the analysis of sensitive biomedical data within its GARDIAN data ecosystem [30]. This platform allows analytical code to be taken to data, which is held in a secure repository and not made directly available to researchers, rather than researchers downloading data on which they can then run their own analyses. The use of such platforms is entirely voluntary for the moment and currently targeted towards increasing access to commercially sensitive data that corporate actors may be disinclined to share. This also points to one of the key differences in the governance arena between biomedicine and plant science, namely that where human biomedical data comes under the legally protected category of personal data (at least in jurisdictions such as the European Union), much of the data utilized in plant and agricultural research is covered by contract law and thereby reduced to a problem of commercial ownership and use [31]. Without sustained efforts to address data sensitivity issues beyond commercial sensitivity, challenges such as the reluctance of farmers to share on-farm data will persist and limit the possibilities for data-intensive research beyond experimental sites [32].

5. Data Challenges

Following from the biological and governance issues we mentioned, the third set of challenges concerns the development and implementation of effective and reliable data management strategies for AI and ML. Given the complexity of biological systems, biological research tends to be very fragmented compared with other sciences, and biological data are highly heterogeneous as a result [3,33,34]. Biodiversity thus encourages the production of research methods and instruments specifically tailored to the organisms and systems in question, with different laboratories producing data in a wide variety of ways. Having validated, meaningful, and usable ways to integrate large, multidimensional datasets from different sources and scientific approaches is therefore of critical importance if AI is to become a routine component of plant and agricultural science.

Central to this is the establishment of a favorable data landscape for AI, consisting of the networks and practices of sourcing, managing, and maintaining data (for a synoptic view, see Table 1). This is important both for resource-intensive commercial sites, whose often secretive data practices can limit productive exchange and reciprocal learning across relevant industries and sectors, and for research undertaken within small-to-medium enterprises and publicly funded bodies, including research in and for the Global South. Identifying the primary challenges faced by users and would-be users of AI in the contemporary data landscape of plant science is necessary to understand the possibilities and limitations afforded by AI for public as well as private plant and agricultural research. This might range from recognizing the differing priorities and interests of plant scientists vis-à-vis computer scientists [35] to explicitly tackling large concerns and ongoing controversies around data generation, ownership, and governance, a particularly difficult task given the multitude of stakeholders and differences in resources, power, and visibility.

There are problems of data management that most stakeholders experience and whose recognition and resolution can help bring together this field. One such problem concerns the difficulties in evaluating data quality and securing robust reference (ground truth) data for model training and validation. For the development of models of field-level crop growth and agricultural systems, detailed data are required on a combination of variables ranging from the growth of plants themselves through soil conditions and water flows, and this in turn requires extensive and usually expensive monitoring systems. These are occasionally available from purpose-built platforms at dedicated sites, such as the increasing number of high-throughput plant phenotyping facilities being constructed by both academic and commercial researchers around the world, but more usually have to be obtained directly from data holders at local, regional, or global scales. The high value of such data means that they are frequently subject to restrictions on access or expensive licensing agreements that can lock users out. Moreover, datasets are often generated in formats that are not machine-readable and are not labeled using appropriate data and metadata standards, which in turn greatly constrains the applicability of ML. Where this issue has been tackled head-on, for instance, through investment in data curation [36] and in extensive stakeholder consultations around semantic standards for plant and agricultural data [37], the results have been notable, with responsible data governance going hand-in-hand with effective data

Table 1. Synoptic view of the data challenges, possible solutions, and what can be lost and gained by investment in those areas. Extracted from Williamson *et al.* (2021) (licensed as CC-BY).

Data challenges	Solutions	Risks	Payoff
Heterogeneity of data types and sources in biology and agriculture	Implementing FAIR principles for all data types Acknowledging and rewarding data sources	Inconsistent standardization between domains and communities	New possibilities for multiscale analysis integrating diverse data types
Selection and digitization of data that are viable for AI applications	Clear and accessible guidance on data requirements for AI New procedures for priority setting and selecting data	High labor costs of digitization and analysis on resources that may not prove to be significant	AI tools and outputs that push forward the cutting edge of plant science research
Ensuring sufficient linkage between biological materials and data used for AI applications	Clear documentation of material provenance when producing data and throughout analytical workflows	Increased documentation costs Exposure of commercially or otherwise sensitive materials	Clear understanding of the biological scope of AI tools
Standardization and curation of data and related software to a level appropriate for AI applications	Development and use of shared semantic standards Standardization of data at the point of collection	Potential to lose system-specific information that does not fit common standards	Reusable multisource datasets Easier validation and sharing between groups
Obtaining training and adequate ground truth data for model validation and development	Ensuring that data quality benchmarking is tailored to analytical purposes Expanded collections of ground truth and training datasets	Data quality assessment requires error estimates and information on data collection, which are often lacking	Reproducible and sound inferences with clear scope of validity

(Continued)

Table 1. (*Continued*)

Data challenges	Solutions	Risks	Payoff
Access to computing and modeling platforms, and related expertise	Making software and models open and adaptable where appropriate and/or having clear documentation on their scope Provide researchers with full workflows, not only software	Software used outside its range of proven usefulness Danger of extrapolation and overfitting	A suite of tools with clearly marked utility and relevance for a wide range of analytical tasks in the plant sciences
Improving responsible data access	Opening access to datasets held by government and research institutions Implementation of data governance regimes to protect sensitive data and ensure benefit sharing	"Digital feudalism"; unequal distribution of benefits from public or personal data	Greater data resources of direct relevance to agricultural and other plant science applications
Engagement across plant scientists, data scientists, and other stakeholders	Investment in and promotion of data services for plant scientists Promotion of plant science problems, especially GxE interactions, to ML researchers Identification of and investment in grand challenges and engagement	High cost with potentially limited impact unless closely targeted to needs and interests of researchers and wider stakeholders	Greater community participation in the development of ML as a resource for plant science

sharing strategies and appropriately curated data supporting the design and application of AI. Nevertheless, there has yet to be a dedicated push to extend this work to the semantic needs of ML technologies, and many research funders and institutions do not provide targeted incentives to make data publicly available [4], with data infrastructures aimed to fill this gap (such as the aforementioned GARDIAN ecosystem of the CGIAR) still at a nascent stage. As a result of these data challenges, validating models across a range of field environments becomes a limiting factor on the meaningful extension of ML technologies across the agricultural domain.

6. Conclusion: AI as Engagement Platform for Agricultural Development

AI has the potential to expand horizons of research and development in plant science and agriculture and contribute to tackling the major challenges of the twenty-first century, climate change, and new demands for food security in the face of a rapidly expanding global population. Much progress has been made by experts in biosciences and computer science towards developing new techniques and methods that respond to key research problems and by experts in the commercial sector working to improve precision and efficiency in agriculture. These are not mere technical fixes: AI is providing novel ways to imagine and achieve agricultural development, biodiversity conservation, and planetary health, through the application of tools that affect all human interactions with plants — from conservation management to environmental monitoring, from the identification of climate-resistant crops to the fight against plant pathogens, from the use of fertilizers and pesticides to the seed trade, and from the design of agricultural machinery to the skills of farmers.

Given the transformative nature of this potential impact, it is crucial to extend engagement with AI technologies beyond the sphere of professional scientists to include other stakeholders in food systems, including farmers, agronomic advisors, plant breeders, food manufacturers and suppliers, nutritionists, and others. Without dialog with and among stakeholders, it will be difficult to identify the priority areas where there is the greatest opportunity for AI applications to achieve environmental and socio-economic impact and to develop technology, standards, and infrastructures that can be sustainably used around the world without unintentionally causing harm. Wide and sustained engagement among stakeholders is necessary to tailor technologies to the challenges posed by the "green" sector and the role of plants in relation to food systems and environmental sustainability, rather than letting technology dictate the direction of travel. As things stand, and despite the substantial developments we have described, the opportunities currently available in terms of AI applications may not necessarily be those most useful for plant research and agronomy. Further work and investment are needed not only to identify those priority areas but also to structure the field to best respond to them and maximize the ways in which AI can support sustainable agricultural development. Existing communities of practice, such as the Improving Global Agricultural Data group of the Research Data Alliance (comprising working groups on wheat, rice, semantic standards, metrics, and capacity development) and the ELIXIR Plant Science Community (focused on the whole plant data workflow within Europe), provide valuable sources of expertise and collaboration and need to be placed at the center of technological and political visions for AI roadmaps to planetary health [25].

Last but not least, improvements in data management may help identify and account for ethical and societal issues of relevance to agronomy and food production. There has been widespread concern that the adoption of ML tools implies a decrease in the oversight and control retained by humans on the interpretation of results, including the assessment of the potential implications of any resulting actions for stakeholder communities such as farmers, breeders, and consumers. This has been flanked by worry around documenting the provenance of data and rewarding the efforts involved in generating the materials and conditions for data collection, especially where results are extracted from farming communities in deprived areas. Practical solutions to these concerns require concerted effort from data producers and curators, research institutions, data infrastructures, and international governance. For instance, the impact of specific crop varieties on diverse landscapes is considered by digital infrastructures developed by the CGIAR, while the allocation of ownership claims and rewards attached to discovery is incorporated into the Global Information System (GLIS) of the International Treaty on Plant Genetic Resources for Food and Agriculture. Thus, data management strategies can help us to ensure that consideration and participative evaluation of the environmental, social, and economic impact of AI tools lie at the core of all future AI initiatives.

7. Competing Interests

No competing interests were disclosed.

8. Grant Information

H. F. W. and S. L. were funded via the "From Field Data to Global Indicators" project from the Alan Turing Institute, under EPSRC grant EP/N510129/1. S. L. was funded by ERC grant number 101001145 and the Wissenschaftskolleg zu Berlin, which provided the ideal space to complete this manuscript.

References

[1] H. F. Williamson, J. Brettschneider, M. Caccamo *et al.* (2021). Data management challenges for artificial intelligence in plant and agricultural research [version 1; peer review: 1 approved, 1 approved with reservations]. *F1000Research*, *10*(324). https://f1000research.com/articles/10-324.

[2] F. Tardieu, L. Cabrera-Bosquet, T. Pridmore *et al.* (2017). Plant phenomics: From sensors to knowledge. *Current Biology*, *27*(15), R770–R783. https://doi.org/10.1016/j.cub.2017.05.055.

[3] S. Leonelli (2016). *Data-Centric Biology: A Philosophical Study*. Chicago, IL: University of Chicago Press.

[4] S. Leonelli, R. P. Davey, E. Arnaud *et al.* (2017). Data management and best practice in plant science. *Nature Plants*, *3*, 17086. https://doi.org/10.1038/nplants.2017.86.

[5] Market Reports (2019). *Global Artificial Intelligence (AI) in Agriculture Market Size, Status and Forecast 2019–2025*, 26 March 2019. https://www.marketreportsworld.com/TOC/13268433#TOC.

[6] I. M. Carbonell (2016). The ethics of big data in big agriculture. *Internet Policy Review*, *5*(1). https://doi.org/10.14763/2016.1.405.

[7] T. Tsiligiridis and K. Ainali (2018). Remote sensing Big AgriData for food availability. In *Proceedings of the SPIE 10836, 2018 International Conference on Image and Video Processing, and Artificial Intelligence*, no. 108361G, 29 October 2018. https://doi.org/10.1117/12.2327014.

[8] K. Mochida, S. Koda, K. Inoue *et al.* (2018). Statistical and machine learning approaches to predict gene regulatory networks from Transcriptome Datasets. *Frontiers in Plant Science*, *9*(1770). https://doi.org/10.3389/fpls.2018.01770.

[9] J. Sperschneider (2020). Machine learning in plant-pathogen interactions: Empowering biological predictions from field scale to genome scale. *New Phytologist*, *22*(1), 25–41. https://doi.org/10.1111/nph.15771.

[10] A. Dobrescu, M. V. Giuffrida, and S. A. Tsaftaris (2020). Doing more with less: A multitask deep learning approach in plant phenotyping. *Frontiers in Plant Science*, *11*, 141. https://doi.org/10.3389/fpls.2020.00141.

[11] M. P. Pound, J. A. Atkinson, A. J. Townsend *et al.* (2017). Deep machine learning provides state-of-the-art performance in image-based plant phenotyping. *Gigascience*, *6*(10), 1–10. https://doi.org/10.1093/gigascience/gix083.

[12] J. Gao, A. P. French, M. P. Pound *et al.* (2020). Deep convolutional neural networks for image-based *Convolvulus sepium* detection in sugar beet fields. *Plant Methods*, *16*(29). https://doi.org/10.1186/s13007-020-00570-z.

[13] H. Wang, E. Cimen, N. Singh *et al.* (2020). Deep learning for plant genomics and crop improvements. *Current Opinion in Plant Biology*, *54*, 34–41. https://doi.org/10.1016/j.pbi.2019.12.010.

[14] A. L. Harfouche, D. A. Jacobson, D. Kainer *et al.* (2019). Accelerating climate resilient plant breeding by applying next-generation artificial

intelligence. *Trends in Biotechnology*, *37*(11), 1217–1235. https://doi.org/10.1016/j.tibtech.2019.05.007.

[15] C. Folberth, A. Baklanov, J. Balkovič *et al.* (2019). Spatio-temporal downscaling of gridded crop model yield estimates based on machine learning. *Agricultural and Forest Meteorology*, *264*, 1–15. https://doi.org/10.1016/j.agrformet.2018.09.021.

[16] M. B. Hufford, J. C. Berny Mier y Teran, and P. Gepts (2019). Crop biodiversity: An unfinished magnum opus of nature. *Annual Review of Plant Biology*, *70*, 727–751. https://doi.org/10.1146/annurev-arplant-042817-040240.

[17] P. S. Soltis (2017). Digitization of herbaria enables novel research. *American Journal of Botany*, *104*(9), 1281–1284. https://doi.org/10.3732/ajb.1700281.

[18] S. Younis, C. Weiland, R. Hoehndorf *et al.* (2018). Taxon and trait recognition from digitized herbarium specimens using deep convolutional neural networks. *Botany Letters*, *165*(3–4), 377–383. https://doi.org/10.1080/23818107.2018.1446357.

[19] P. L. M. Lang, F. M. Willems, J. F. Scheepens *et al.* (2019). Using herbaria to study global environmental change. *New Phytologist*, *221*(1), 110–122. https://doi.org/10.1111/nph.15401.

[20] L. M. Mrisho, N. A. Mbilinyi, M. Ndalahwa *et al.* (2020). Accuracy of a smartphone-based object detection model, PlantVillage Nuru, in identifying the foliar symptoms of the viral diseases of Cassava — CMD and CBSD. *Frontiers in Plant Science*, *11*(590889). https://doi.org/10.3389/fpls.2020.590889.

[21] B. King (2020). Inaugural Address, CGIAR Big Data Convention 2020. https://bigdata.cgiar.org/blog-post/2020-convention-session-welcome-opening-keynote-computational-sustainability/

[22] S. J. Newman and R. T. Furbank (2021). Explainable machine learning models of major crop traits from satellite-monitored continent-wide field trial data. *Nature Plants*, *7*, 1354–1363. https://doi.org/10.1038/s41477-021-01001-0.

[23] J. E. Spindel and S. R. McCouch (2016). When more is better: How data sharing would accelerate genomic selection of crop plants. *New Phytologist*, *212*(4), 814–826. https://doi.org/10.1111/nph.14174.

[24] X. Delannay, G. McLaren, and J. M. Ribaut (2012). Fostering molecular breeding in developing countries. *Molecular Breeding*, *29*, 857–873. https://doi.org/10.1007/s11032-011-9611-9.

[25] H. F. Williamson and S. Leonelli (eds.) (2022). *Towards Responsible Plant Data Linkage: Global Challenges for Agricultural Research and Development*. Cham: Springer.

[26] S. Aubry (2019). The future of digital sequence information for plant genetic resources for food and agriculture. *Frontiers in Plant Science*, *10*(1046). https://doi.org/10.3389/fpls.2019.01046.

[27] E. Morgera, S. Switzer, and M. Geelhoed (2020). *Possible Ways to Address Digital Sequence Information–Legal and Policy Aspects*. Study for the European Commission. Strathclyde Centre for Environmental Law

and Governance. https://ec.europa.eu/environment/nature/biodiversity/international/abs/pdf/Final_study_legal_and_policy_aspects.pdf.

[28] D. Manzella, M. Marsella, P. Jaiswal *et al.* (2022). Digital sequence information and plant genetic resources: Global policy meets interoperability. In H. F. Williamson and S. Leonelli (eds.), *Towards Responsible Plant Data Linkage: Global Challenges for Agricultural Research and Development.* Cham: Springer.

[29] S. Hilgartner (2017). *Reordering Life: Knowledge and Control in the Genomics Revolution.* Cambridge, MA: MIT Press.

[30] CGIAR Platform for Big Data in Agriculture webinar (2021). OpenSAFELY for sensitive agricultural data, 9 December 2021. https://bigdata.cgiar.org/blog-post/webinar-opensafely-for-sensitive-agricultural-data/.

[31] L. Wiseman, J. Sanderson, and L. Robb (2018). Rethinking AgData ownership. *Farm Policy Journal, 15*(1), 71–77.

[32] L. Wiseman, J. Sanderson, A. Zhang *et al.* (2019). Farmers and their data: An examination of farmers' reluctance to share their data through the lens of the laws impacting smart farming. *NJAS–Wageningen Journal of Life Sciences, 90–91*(100301). https://doi.org/10.1016/j.njas.2019.04.007.

[33] T. Hey, S. Tansley, and K. Tolle (eds.) (2019). *The Fourth Paradigm: Data-Intensive Scientific Discovery.* Redmond, WA: Microsoft Research.

[34] V. Marx (2013). The big challenges of big data. *Nature, 498*, 255–260. https://doi.org/10.1038/498255a.

[35] S. Tsaftaris and H. Scharr (2019). Sharing the right data right: A symbiosis with machine learning. *Trends in Plant Science, 24*(2), 99–102. https://doi.org/10.1016/j.tplants.2018.10.016.

[36] S. J. Newman and R. T. Furbank (2021). A multiple species, continent-wide, million-phenotype agronomic plant dataset. *Nature Scientific Data, 8*(116). https://doi.org/10.1038/s41597-021-00898-8.

[37] E. Arnaud, M. A. Laporte, S. Kim *et al.* (2020). The ontologies community of practice: A CGIAR initiative for Big Data in Agrifood systems. *Patterns, 1*(7), Article no. 100105. https://doi.org/10.1016/j.patter.2020.100105.

Health

© 2023 World Scientific Publishing Company
https://doi.org/10.1142/9789811265679_0019

Chapter 19

AI and Pathology: Steering Treatment and Predicting Outcomes

Rajarsi Gupta, Jakub Kaczmarzyk,
Soma Kobayashi, Tahsin Kurc, and Joel Saltz

*Department of Biomedical Informatics, Renaissance School
of Medicine at Stony Brook University, Stony Brook, NY, USA*

1. Introduction

The human body is constructed from over 10^{13} cells organized in complex patterns of hierarchical organization. Each cell carries out its own metabolism. During various portions of the human lifespan, different types of cells replicate, differentiate, migrate, and sometimes die. The combination of AI, high-end computing capabilities, and improvements in sensor and molecular characterization methods are making it possible to analyze humans and other animal and plant life forms in a quantitative granular, multiscale, cell-based fashion.

In this chapter, we focus on a particular class of targeted human tissue analysis — histopathology — aimed at quantitative characterization of disease state, patient outcome prediction, and treatment steering. During the past 150 years, much of anatomic pathology consisted of characterization and diagnostic recognition of visually identifiable morphological patterns seen in tissue. Over the past few decades, molecular characterizations have become increasingly important in anatomic pathology. The advent of AI and ubiquitous high-end computing are enabling a new transition where quantitatively linked morphological and molecular tissue analyses can be carried out at a cellular and subcellular level of resolution. Along with quantitative assessments of predictive value and reproducibility of traditional morphological patterns employed in anatomic pathology, AI algorithms are enabling exploration and discovery of novel diagnostic biomarkers grounded in prognostically predictive spatial and molecular patterns.

2. Digital Histopathology: A Brief Background

Histopathology is best defined by understanding its two root words: *histology* — the microscopic study of tissue structures — and *pathology*— the study of diseases. Histopathology thus involves the microscopic analysis of patient tissue specimens and changes in tissue structure to understand disease causes and mechanisms. Pathologists analyze clinical tissue specimens under powerful microscopes to evaluate changes in tissue structure. Based on their evaluation, they diagnose, subtype, determine prognosis, and help guide treatment decisions of patients. Acquisition of tissue samples is the first step of this process and is largely performed from organ sites with active disease. Some examples are tissue taken directly from cancer or from intestinal regions affected with inflammatory bowel disease. Several additional steps are taken before collected tissue is ready for microscopic evaluation. The first involves fixation, either in formalin or by freezing, to preserve the tissue and structural architecture. Fixed tissues are sliced into thin sections of several microns in thickness onto glass slides. Finally, the tissue sections are treated by a process called staining that allows structures to be more emphasized and visible to the human eye. Hematoxylin and Eosin (H&E) staining, for example, reveals features such as organization, texture, and morphology of cell nuclei and the multicellular tissue structures they form together. Cancer can be diagnosed by the replacement of expected cell types with aberrant-appearing cancer cells and the disruption of typical organ-specific multicellular organization. For certain diagnoses, the spatial distribution of molecular markers is crucial. Another type of staining, called Immunohistochemistry (IHC), applies antigen-specific antibodies that target specific markers within tissue specimens. This identifies the presence or absence of microscopic protein targets in the tissue. Both structural and molecular information are employed in determining cancer subtype and in guiding treatment.

A pathologist's examination of a tissue slide under a microscope is a *qualitative* process. The pathologist will use their experience and pathology knowledge to classify tissue using complex classification criteria developed over the years by both the pathology and the broader medical community [1]. The classifications evolve over time in response to a combination of observational clinical studies and clinical trials. The interpretive process is subjective [2–4]; different pathologists who examine the same specimen may not classify the tissue in the same way.

Digital histopathology facilitates *quantitative* analyses of tissue specimens. Tissue acquisition and preparation processes (tissue fixation and staining protocols) are the same as in traditional pathology. A glass tissue slide with H&E or IHC staining is placed in a digital microscopy instrument with state-of-the-art imaging sensors. These instruments capture an image of the tissue specimen like a digital camera but at much higher resolution to generate whole slide images (WSI) that can be more than $100{,}000 \times 100{,}000$ pixels in size. WSIs can be generated at different levels of resolution; a pixel will commonly represent a 0.25–1 micron tissue region.

Digital microscopy instruments have improved remarkably over the past 20 years. Scanning a tissue specimen at 0.5 micron per pixel resolution used to require several hours. Modern instruments can output WSIs at 0.25 micron per pixel resolution in approximately one minute. They have advanced focusing mechanisms and automated trays which can hold hundreds of glass slides, enabling high throughput generation of WSIs in a pathology lab or a tissue bank. These systems have increasingly become ubiquitous in research settings and are now being widely adopted for clinical use [5,6]. As the digital microscopy instruments get faster, higher resolution, and more cost effective, we expect tissue banks and pathology labs at research and clinical institutions will be able to scan hundreds of thousands of glass slides per year in the not-too-distant future. Indeed, the BIGPICTURE project of the EU Innovative Medicines Initiative will collect millions of digital slides for the development of AI methods as well as AI applications in pathology research [7].

GLOBOCAN 2020 [8] estimates cancer incidence and mortality produced by the International Agency for Research on Cancer. Worldwide, there is an estimated 19.3 million new cancer cases (18.1 million excluding non-melanoma skin cancer). The number of slides examined per patient depends on the nature of the cancer, local treatment practices, and available resources. Worldwide, a conservative estimate of five to ten pathology tissue slides per new cancer patient yields a rough worldwide estimate of 100–200 million tissue specimens created per year. Many additional slides are generated in diagnostic workups that do not lead to a cancer diagnosis and in assessment of cancer recurrences and metastases.

3. Applications of AI in Digital Histopathology

Gigapixel resolution WSIs offer a rich landscape of data that can be leveraged by computation to improve diagnostic reproducibility, develop high-resolution methods for predicting disease outcome and steering treatment, and reveal new insights to further advance current human understanding of disease. In this chapter, we look at the applications of AI in three important tasks that support these goals. The first task is the extraction of quantitative features from WSIs. Quantitative imaging features can enable novel insights into pathophysiological mechanisms at disease onset, progression, and response to treatment. This task generally involves the process of detecting, segmenting, and classifying objects (e.g., nuclei and cells), structures (e.g., stroma), and regions (e.g., tumor regions) within a WSI. Figure 1 shows an example of a breast tissue specimen being segmented into regions with invasive breast cancer and normal tissue. Figure 2 shows the results of a model that segments invasive cancer and regions with infiltrating immune cells. The second task is the classification of WSIs. Classifications in pathology are complex and nuanced with hierarchies consisting of tens of thousands of subcategories. The third and overarching task is to predict patient outcome and to assess the impact of different treatments on a patient's disease course. This task differs from the first two as it involves prediction of intrinsically uncertain future events. While predictions can be carried out with digital pathology information alone, in a broad sense, the best predictions are likely to require integrated analysis of microscopic tissue images, radiology images, and clinical and molecular information.

3.1. *Computer science challenges*

Viewed from a computer science perspective, computer vision tasks in digital pathology include (1) detection and segmentation of objects in high-resolution image data, (2) assignment of a class label to each image in an image collection, and (3) predictions from a combination of image and other data sources. The work on panoptic segmentation [9] abstracts key requirements associated with many digital pathology segmentation-related tasks. In some cases, object detection and quantification rather than segmentation are all that an application requires. The computer vision community has developed a variety of algorithms to address such problems; see for instance [10]. Nevertheless, segmentation is a challenging task in digital pathology because the tissue landscape is highly heterogeneous and complex. There are hundreds of thousands of cells and nuclei and thousands of micro-anatomic structures and regions in a typical tissue specimen. The texture, shape, and size properties of cells, nuclei, and structures can vary significantly across tissue specimens (depending on the cancer type/subtype and stage) and even within the same tissue. The task of assigning a class label to images in a collection is extremely well recognized in the computer vision community; there has been transformative progress in this area over the past decade. Digital pathology image classification problems are challenging as they typically involve gigapixel resolution images and frequently include classifications with substantial nuance. Creation of fine-grained training data is difficult, time consuming, expensive, and requires expert clinician insight. A major challenge is thus to train classification models using sparse, weakly annotated training data.

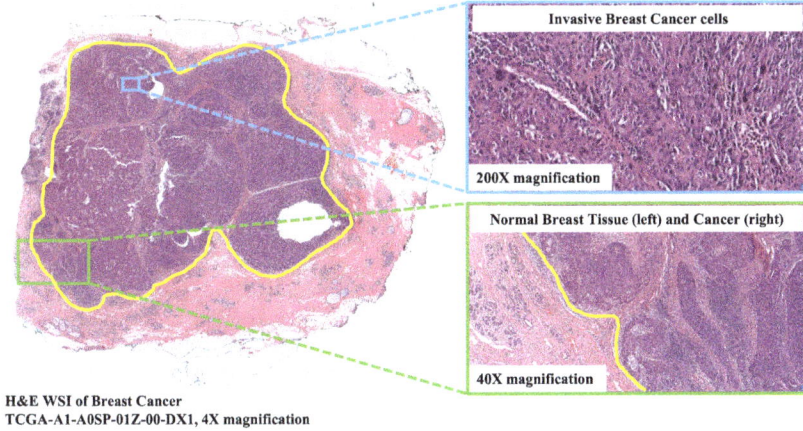

H&E WSI of Breast Cancer
TCGA-A1-A0SP-01Z-00-DX1, 4X magnification

Fig. 1. H&E WSI of breast cancer tissue sample from the Cancer Genome Atlas (TCGA). Insets show invasive breast cancer cells shown at 200× and a representative area showing the invasive margin between cancer and normal tissues delineated by the solid yellow line.

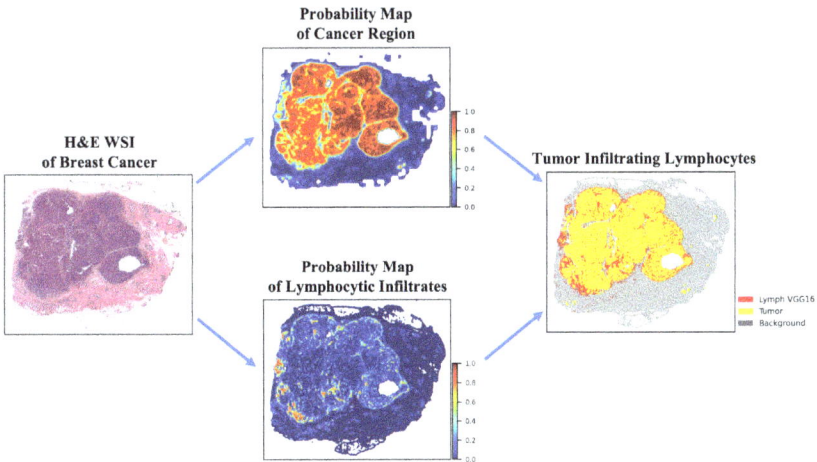

Fig. 2. Segmentation and classification of breast cancer tissue and TILs. Breast cancer tissue segmentation is indicated by the yellow color, where superimposed red color shows the presence and spatial distribution of TILs at 50 μm resolution. H&E WSI from TCGA Breast Cancer (BRCA) collection, specimen TCGA-A1-A0SP-01Z-00-DX1.

Prediction-related tasks include (1) prediction of which patients will develop a given disease, (2) prediction of how quickly and in what ways a given disease will progress, and (3) prediction of how given patients will respond to a particular treatment. Predictions can be made using pathology images alone yet will likely need to progress to integrate analysis of temporal sequences of combined clinical observations, clinical notes, radiology imaging, pathology images, molecular data, and treatment data. There are many different ways prediction problems can be formulated and solved with myriad computational and mathematical challenges associated with the coupled analyses of highly interrelated but structurally disparate imaging, genomic, and clinical datasets.

3.2. *Tools and methodology*

A wide spectrum of deep learning methods, such as convolutional neural networks (CNNs), multi-instance learning (MIL), attention mechanisms, recurrent neural networks (RNNs), and transformers, have been developed by the data analytics community [11,12]. Digital pathology has adapted many of them. CNNs, e.g., are routinely employed in the WSI segmentation and classification tasks described above. Multiresolution analysis and MIL methods are frequently employed to carry out WSI classification. Transformers are being leveraged to generate image representations that can be incorporated into downstream classification and segmentation tasks. Development and application of AI methods for digital pathology image analysis is a highly active area of research. In the next sections, we provide examples of how AI has been applied in the three tasks described above. We refer the reader to excellent survey papers for a more comprehensive coverage (e.g., [13–15]).

3.3. *Detection, segmentation, and characterization of microanatomic structures*

Tissue is made up of micro-anatomic structures such as cells, ducts, stromal regions, and glands. The nucleus is a core micro-anatomic structure that harbors cellular DNA and plays a central role in disease diagnosis and prognosis. A telltale sign of cancer, e.g., is abnormal nuclei. Cancer causes visible changes in the shape, size, and texture of the nucleus (e.g., cancerous nuclei are generally larger and more irregularly shaped). Quantitative features computed from nuclei could provide novel biomarkers to study the pathophysiology of cancer and better understand its mechanisms. Cooper *et al.*, for instance, used the shape and texture features of nuclei to create morphology-driven clusters of glioblastoma cases [14]. They observed correlations between the clusters and cancer subtypes and genomic signatures, indicating the diagnostic and prognostic power of quantitative nuclear features. In another study, Yu *et al.* computed thousands of features from segmented nuclei and cells from lung cancer cases [15]. A downstream machine learning analysis using the features showed correlations with patient outcome.

The process of extracting quantitative nuclear features from tissue images requires the detection, segmentation, and classification of nuclei. This can be a challenging task because of the volume and morphological variability of nuclei in tissue images. For example, lymphocyte nuclei are dark, round, and small with 8-micron diameter on average. The nuclei of cancer cells, on the other hand, are generally larger than 10 microns in diameter and irregular in shape. Moreover, nuclei may touch or overlap each other without easily distinguishable boundaries. Figure 3 shows an example of nucleus segmentation and classification in a WSI. Kumar *et al.* developed a nucleus segmentation pipeline with a CNN architecture consisting of multiple convolutions and fully connected layers [16]. They labeled pixels in the training dataset with one of the three classes: inside a nucleus, outside a nucleus, and boundary pixel. They introduced the boundary pixel label to train a model that can separate touching nuclei. Their segmentation model was effectively a three-class pixel-level classifier. They determined the number of convolution and fully connected layers empirically by testing different configurations. After input images were processed by the CNN model to label nuclei and their contours, a region-growing method was applied to the output to finalize the boundaries of nuclei. In a more recent work, the top-scoring participants of a digital pathology challenge proposed a multistep deep learning pipeline for nucleus segmentation [17]. The

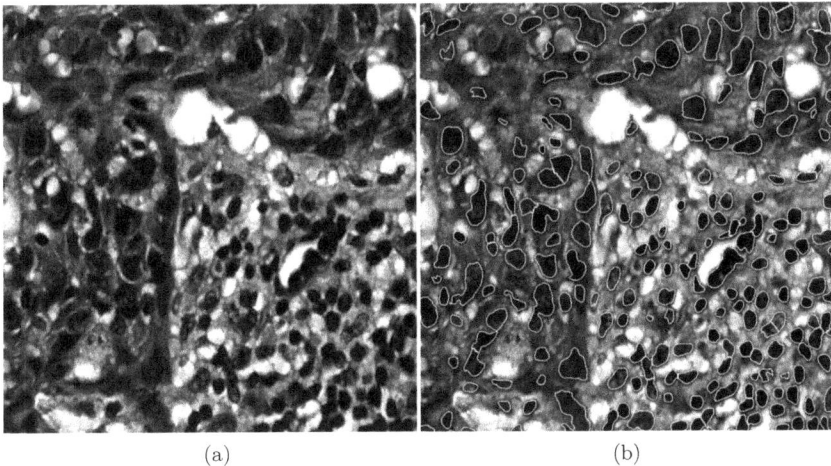

(a) (b)

Fig. 3.   An example of nucleus segmentation: (a) an image patch with tissue and nuclei; (b) nuclei segmented in the patch are shown in blue polygons.

pipeline trained two CNNs to detect blobs of nuclei and their boundaries to generate blob and border masks. The masks were then used in the next step of the pipeline to separate nucleus boundaries by dilating the border mask and subtracting it from the blob mask. In the final stage, a watershed algorithm was used to identify individual nuclei.

In many works, classification of nuclei into classes (such as malignant epithelium, lymphocyte, and endothelial) is handled as a post-processing step after nuclei are segmented and a set of features are computed. Graham et al. proposed a novel CNN architecture, called HoVer-Net, to both segment and classify nuclei in a single method [18]. The proposed architecture includes a feature extraction module with layers of residual units to extract deep features from input images. The features are then input into three CNN branches for segmenting individual nuclei and classifying them. These branches predict (1) if a pixel is part of a nucleus or not, (2) the horizontal and vertical distances of identified nucleus pixels to their centers of mass (for the purpose of separating touching nuclei), and (3) the type of nucleus for each nucleus pixel. The branches consisted of upsampling layers, which restore image resolution reduced in the feature extraction module, and densely connected layers for predicting nucleus pixels and boundaries. In an experimental comparison to other nucleus segmentation methods, HoVer-Net achieved state-of-the-art results in multiple accuracy metrics.

Deep learning methods require large amounts of high-quality training data to train accurate and generalizable models. This has been an ongoing challenge in nucleus segmentation work. It is time consuming to manually segment individual nuclei, and this process often requires input from expert pathologists to ensure nuclei and their boundaries are correctly identified. A number of projects have implemented crowd-sourcing and semi-automated mechanisms to increase training dataset sizes [19,20]. Another approach is to use synthetic datasets [21,22]. Hou et al. proposed a synthetic data generation and segmentation workflow which included a generative adversarial network (GAN) architecture and a nucleus segmentation CNN [21]. The workflow creates an initial set of synthetic tissue image patches and segmentation masks and then refines them using the GAN, while training a U-Net [23] segmentation model. The U-net model is trained with synthetic data with a training loss that is re-weighted over the synthetic data. This minimizes the ideal generalization loss over the real data distribution to improve the accuracy of the segmentation model. The authors demonstrated the efficacy of this approach by training a multicancer segmentation model and applying it to over 5,000 images from 10 cancer types [24]. In another recent work, Krause et al. used conditional GAN architectures to synthesize images with and without microsatellite instability in colorectal cancer [25].

In addition to the morphological properties of individual nuclei and other micro-anatomic structures, spatial relationships between nuclei and tumor regions also play a critical role in cancer prognosis. For example, studies have shown correlations between the amount of lymphocyte infiltration in tumor regions and clinical outcome [26]. If the main objective is to quantitate such spatial interactions, patch-based methods can provide an approximation of what can be computed by pixel-level nuclei and region segmentations. Training data generation is generally less time consuming with patch-based methods; the annotator only has to label a patch as class-positive or -negative (e.g., tumor-positive to indicate the patch is in or intersects a tumor region or lymphocyte-positive to indicate the patch contains lymphocytes) instead of painstakingly tracing the boundaries of individual nuclei and tumor regions. Le *et al.* employed a patch-based approach for segmentation and classification of spatial patterns of tumor regions and tumor-infiltrating lymphocytes (TIL) in breast cancer WSIs [27]. Each WSI was partitioned into a grid of patches, and tumor and TIL models were trained to predict if a patch was positive. That is, in the case of tumor segmentation, the tumor model predicted if the patch intersected a tumor region, and in the case of lymphocyte classification, the TIL model predicted if the patch contained lymphocytes. The authors showed that the predicted tumor infiltration (i.e., the ratio of lymphocyte patches intersecting tumor patches to the total number of tumor patches) correlated with survival rates.

3.4. *Image-level classification*

WSI-level or patient-level annotations are an important source of training information for image-level classifications. For example, a biopsy to diagnose cancer will simply be attributed a "benign" or "malignant" label without pixel-level annotations. Such annotations are generated by pathologists when diagnosing the disease and in the course of providing patient care; pathologists are also typically able to quickly generate WSI-level annotations. Classification of WSIs using WSI-level annotations can be formulated as a multi-instance learning (MIL) problem to identify salient image regions. MIL methods generally partition a WSI into patches and execute an iterative two-stage approach consisting of patch-level predictions carried out using a neural network followed by a data integration and image-level prediction phase.

Patch voting has been commonly used to attribute the most common predictions made at the patch level to the WSI. Korbar *et al.* trained a ResNet-based architecture to predict between hyperplastic polyp, sessile serrated polyp, traditional serrated adenoma, tubular adenoma, and

tubulovillous/villous adenoma on patches extracted from an H&E-stained
WSI of colorectal biopsy specimens [28]. WSIs were then assigned a label
according to the most common patch-level prediction, provided that the
prediction was made on at least five patches. Patch-level predictions can also
be aggregated by a machine learning classifier to make WSI-level inferences.
Li *et al.* trained two ResNet-50 networks as feature extractors on patches
of different sizes from breast cancer WSIs [29]. The authors utilized smaller
128×128-pixel patches to capture cell-level features and larger 512×512-pixel patches for tissue morphology and structure information. K-means
clustering was performed on extracted patch feature representations to
identify discriminative patches, of which histograms were generated for
each WSI. An SVM then classified each WSI as normal, benign, *in situ*,
or invasive using these histograms. Hou *et al.* utilized an expectation-
maximization (EM) MIL approach to train models for the classification
of glioma and non-small cell lung carcinoma subtypes [30]. The authors
assumed a hidden variable is associated with each patch that determines
whether the patch is discriminative for the WSI-level label. EM was utilized
to estimate this hidden variable and iteratively identify discriminative
patches. Notably, to address patches close to decision boundaries that may
be informative, the authors trained two CNNs at different scales in parallel
and averaged their predictions.

Campanella *et al.* developed a patch-ranking-based approach [31]. A
ResNet-34 model was trained with the MIL assumption that a WSI
predicted as positive has at least one patch classified as cancer. For
every positive WSI, extracted patches are ranked by predicted cancer
probability. As such, patches most discriminative of WSI-level positivity
are iteratively learned to train the patch-based model. For WSI-level
inference, the model performs predictions on extracted patches. The top
S most suspicious patches for cancer undergo feature extraction and are
then passed onto an RNN for WSI-level prediction. One downside to
ranking patches by prediction probability is that this operation is not
trainable. As an alternative, the MIL problem can also be viewed from
the perspective of assigning weights to patches based on their importance
to the WSI label. Ilse *et al.* proposed a two-layer attention mechanism
that provides weighted averages of input patch representations to provide
trainable MIL pooling [32]. The authors utilized a breast cancer dataset,
where WSIs were labeled positive if at least one breast cancer cell existed,
and a colon cancer dataset, where positive WSIs contained at least one
epithelial nuclei. For both tasks, the attention mechanism outperformed
the traditional max and mean MIL pooling operations. Although trainable,
Zhao *et al.* note that the weighted average approach is a linear combination
operation and propose the incorporation of graph convolutional networks

to generate WSI-level representations for predicting lymph node metastasis in colorectal adenocarcinoma patients [33]. Here, image patches from a WSI are each considered graph nodes. Should distances calculated between extracted features of these image patch nodes be less than a predetermined threshold, an edge is constructed. Thus, graph construction allows for the generation of WSI representations that capture inter-patch relationships in a structured format.

More recently, groups have begun to incorporate RNN and Long-Short Term Memory (LSTM) networks for this final WSI inference step. To classify gastric and colonic epithelial tumors, Iizuka *et al.* trained the Inception-V3 model on non-neoplastic, adenoma, and adenocarcinoma image patches [34]. The trained model was used as a patch-level feature extractor. Sequences of patch features were inputted to train an RNN with two LSTM layers to predict at the WSI level. To account for the sequence dependence of RNN-based networks, patch feature sequences were randomly shuffled during training.

3.5. *Prediction of patient outcome and treatment response*

Survival analysis is an important part of the process of predicting clinical outcomes and response to treatment for a patient or a group of patients. It aims to predict the duration of time before an event occurs such as disease remission or patient death. In the context of cancer patient survival, for example, it is used to predict the probability that a patient or a group of patients will be alive X number of months (or years) after they have been diagnosed with cancer. A variety of AI methods have been applied to survival analysis in digital pathology either using tissue images only or by integrating tissue image data and other data types.

WSISA developed by Zhu *et al.* is an example of the methods that use tissue images only [35]. It adaptively sampled patches from the entire WSI to train CNNs. The authors argued that sampling patches from the entire image instead of annotated regions was more likely to capture and incorporate heterogeneous patterns and would provide additional information for better survival prediction. The selected patches were clustered with a K-means algorithm. Multiple CNN-based survival models were trained with patches from each cluster in order to select clusters with better prediction accuracy. The selected clusters are then aggregated via fully connected neural networks and the boosting Cox negative likelihood method. Wulczyn *et al.* proposed a deep learning-based analysis pipeline that transformed the survival regression problem into a classification problem. The approach divided survival time into survival intervals and predicted to which interval(s) a patient would be assigned [36]. In the analysis pipeline, each WSI was partitioned into patches randomly sampled from tissue areas. Image features were extracted from the patches through CNNs. The patch-level features were then averaged and input to a fully connected layer to classify an input image into the survival intervals. Chen *et al.* devised a graph-based representation of a WSI in which graph nodes are image patches and edges connect adjacent patches [37]. A graph convolutional neural network was trained with this representation of WSIs to learn hierarchical image features. The features were pooled to create WSI-level embeddings and train a model with Cox proportional loss function [38] for survival analysis. Chang *et al.* developed a deep learning network, called hybrid aggregation network, which aggregated data from multiple whole slide images belonging to a patient [39]. In this approach, image features are extracted at the patch level from whole slide images using a CNN, creating whole slide feature maps. The resulting feature maps are aggregated via two aggregation components. One component was designed to aggregate features such that informative features are abstracted to region representations. The second component combined the region representations from multiple whole slide images from the same patient to predict survival rates.

Some projects combined tissue image data with other data modalities [40–44]. Mobadersany *et al.* proposed a method to integrate tissue image data and genomic biomarkers in a single framework to predict outcomes [42]. In this method, regions of interest were annotated in WSIs, and patches were sampled from the annotated regions. Patch-level deep features were extracted via convolutional layers. The deep features and genomic variables were then input to fully connected layers, which are connected to a Cox proportional hazards layer that models survival output. Their evaluation with lower-grade glioma and glioblastoma cancer cases showed that integration of image data and genomics resulted in much better performance. Chen *et al.* used attention mechanisms in a multimodal deep learning framework, called Multimodal Co-attention Transformer [43]. This network learns to map image and genomic features in a latent feature space. The authors demonstrated with cases from lung, breast, brain, and bladder cancers that attention-guided integration of imaging and genomic features in a deep learning framework led to better survival prediction accuracy. Vale-Silva and Rohr developed MultiSurv, which integrates representations from clinical, imaging, and omics data modalities for cancer survival prediction [44]. MultiSurv uses submodels trained for specific data modalities to generate feature representations. The feature representations are integrated into a single representation via a data fusion layer. The integrated representation is processed by another deep learning network to output survival probabilities for a set of pre-defined time intervals. The authors used ResNext-50 CNN [45] for image data and fully connected networks for the other modalities and the integrated feature representation. The authors applied MultiSurv to 33 cancer types and showed that it produced accurate survival predictions.

4. Conclusions

Image analysis techniques based on traditional machine learning or statistical approaches suffered from their dependence on hand-crafted features and the need to fine-tune many method-specific input parameters. While a traditional method might have performed very well on a specific dataset, it in many cases failed to easily and effectively generalize to other datasets without substantial fine-tuning. For example, the organizers of the 2018 Data Science Bowl used traditional methods in CellProfiler [46] for a reference baseline against AI methods [47]. Even when the traditional methods were fine-tuned by experts, AI methods outperformed them by a significant margin. Similarly, evaluations done by Kumar *et al.* [16] showed similar trends — CNN models surpassed the performances of traditional methods in CellProfiler and Fiji [48]. With their superior performance and better generalizability, AI methods show tremendous potential for more successful applications of tissue image analysis in research and clinical settings. As a result, the landscape of medicine is being transformed by the rapid development of new AI technologies.

4.1. *Clinical and research implications*

In digital pathology, deep learning methods are being used to carry out nuanced computational multiresolution tissue analyses. The goals of these analyses are to identify building blocks that can be used to create new methods for steering treatment and to act as decision support aids for improving precision and reproducibility of diagnostic classification. These methods are advancing rapidly and an ecosystem of companies are swiftly developing; in our view, over the coming decade, these methods will transform clinical and research histopathology. Nevertheless, there are challenges to be overcome in order to realize this transformation and more effectively integrate AI into clinical practice.

One of the most important challenges is the development of interpretable and explainable AI. Implementation of AI methods is still as much an art as it is engineering and science, and many AI methods are black boxes from clinicians' and biomedical researchers' perspectives. It is critical to understand how an AI model has arrived at a particular set of results in order to reliably employ AI in the decision-making process. Several research projects have started looking at explainable AI for histopathology [49,50]. Biological and environmental differences between patient cohorts can limit the generalizability of conclusions reached and tools developed. Quantification of accuracy, reproducibility, and generalizability of AI-based outcome predictions is an open question that needs to be further explored.

Initially, clinical decision support software that guides clinicians through recommendations in the form of predictions and prediction confidences may serve as a practical introduction to AI approaches in clinical settings. Kiani *et al.* developed a deep learning assistant that provides pathologists with predicted probabilities of liver cancer subtypes for hepatic tumor resections [51]. Although correct predictions significantly increased pathologist accuracy, incorrect predictions significantly decreased accuracy. As such, proper delineation of physician liability and safeguards to protect patient safety will also be of critical importance in the future integration of AI into patient care. An additional consideration centers on the capacity of AI to build upon newly acquired data. Healthcare systems are inundated with patient data on a daily basis. Regulatory mechanisms allowing for continuous learning and improvement of AI on real-time patient data need to be approached with tremendous care but are an integral step in unlocking the full potential of AI in healthcare. The FDA has already been exploring the adoption of a total product lifestyle regulatory oversight to AI-based software as medical devices [52].

4.2. *Frontiers in algorithm and tool development*

The complexities and types of deep learning networks are increasing — new architectures include transformers and graph networks. Some of these architectures are observed to be difficult to train, requiring large training datasets and substantial computational power. In this vein, Bommasani *et al.* have introduced the concept of foundation models that are trained on extremely high quantities of data and then adapted towards varieties of tasks [53]. Analogous to BERT being trained on vast corpuses to learn an implicit representation of language for use in downstream tasks, one could imagine training a foundation model on a wide range and variety of images or histological specimens to be fine-tuned for specific applications. Feature extraction would focus more on the implicit properties of data rather than the selection of those effective for the task at hand. With less dependence on task-specific loss functions, foundation model-derived representations have the potential to be fine-tuned for a significant range of applications — e.g., different computer vision tasks, diseases, and organ sites. Additionally, the reduced task-specific biases of these learned representations may offer benefits in problems that require integration of temporal or multimodal data. Input specimens can be considered within reduced-bias manifolds built upon vast quantities of training data to probe relationships with and effects of data from other modalities.

In an increasing number of application areas, pre-trained models (also referred to as foundation models [53]) and domain adaptation and transfer learning methods are becoming more widely used to overcome the network complexity and computation challenges. We expect that these strategies will make their way into digital histopathology. Even now, networks pre-trained on ImageNet are widely used to speed up convergence [54]. Moreover, synthetic data generation techniques and federated training approaches could augment these strategies. With federated training, histopathology teams will have access to vast quantities of well-distributed, multicenter data even if they cannot exchange image data because of regulatory concerns as well as the high cost of data exchange and storage. This shift from smaller datasets annotated for specific tasks will allow for the training of more robust and accurate models. The generation of these models will invite an exciting period gearing towards practical implementation of these methodologies into clinical care with increased emphasis on logistics, regulations, risk, and most importantly, true benefit to patient health.

References

[1] V. Kumar, A. K. Abbas, and J. C. Aster (2014). *Robbins and Cotran Pathologic Basis of Disease*. Amsterdam: Elsevier Science Health Science Division. ISBN 978-0323531139 10th Edition.

[2] S. H. Yoon, K. W. Kim, J. M. Goo *et al.* (2016). *European Journal of Cancer*, *53*, 5.

[3] J. B. Sørensen, F. R. Hirsch, A. Gazdar *et al.* (1993). *Cancer*, *71*, 2971.

[4] D. Muenzel, H.-P. Engels, M. Bruegel *et al.* (2012). *Radiology and Oncology*, *46*, 8.

[5] B. F. Boyce (2017). *Biotechnic & Histochemistry*, *92*, 381.

[6] A. J. Evans, T. W. Bauer, M. M. Bui *et al.* (2018). *Archives of Pathology & Laboratory Medicine*, *142*, 1383.

[7] BIGPICTURE (2021). https://bigpicture.eu.

[8] H. Sung, J. Ferlay, R. L. Siegel *et al.* (2021). *CA Cancer Journal for Clinicians*, *71*, 209.

[9] A. Kirillov, K. He, R. Girshick *et al.* (2019). *Proceedings of the IEEE/CVF Conference on Computer Vision and Pattern Recognition*, pp. 9404–9413.

[10] S. Abousamra, M. Hoai, D. Samaras *et al.* (2021). *AAAI.*

[11] M. Z. Alom, T. M. Taha, C. Yakopcic *et al.* (2019). *Electronics*, *8*, 292.

[12] D. W. Otter, J. R. Medina, and J. K. Kalita (2021). *IEEE Transactions on Neural Networks and Learning Systems*, *32*, 604.

[13] C. L. Srinidhi, O. Ciga, and A. L. Martel (2021). *Medical Image Analysis*, *67*, 101813.

[14] S. Deng, X. Zhang, W. Yan *et al.* (2020). *Frontiers of Medicine, 14*, 470.

[15] D. Ahmedt-Aristizabal, M. A. Armin, S. Denman *et al.* (2022). *Computerized Medical Imaging and Graphics, 95*, 102027.

[16] N. Kumar, R. Verma, S. Sharma *et al.* (2017). *IEEE Transactions on Medical Imaging, 36*, 1550.

[17] Q. D. Vu, S. Graham, T. Kurc *et al.* (2019). *Frontiers in Bioengineering and Biotechnology, 7*.

[18] S. Graham, Q. D. Vu, S. E. A. Raza *et al.* (2019). *Medical Image Analysis, 58*, 101563.

[19] M. Amgad, L. A. Atteya, H. Hussein *et al.* (2021). *arXiv* [cs.CV].

[20] S. Graham, M. Jahanifar, A. Azam *et al.* (2021). *Proceedings of the IEEE/CVF International Conference on Computer Vision*, pp. 684–693.

[21] L. Hou, A. Agarwal, D. Samaras *et al.* (2019). *Proceedings of the IEEE Computer Society Conference on Computer Vision and Pattern Recognition, 2019*, 8533.

[22] X. Gong, S. Chen, B. Zhang *et al.* (2021). *Proceedings of the IEEE/CVF Winter Conference on Applications of Computer Vision*, pp. 3994–4003.

[23] O. Ronneberger, P. Fischer, and T. Brox (2015). Lecture Notes in Computer Science 234.

[24] L. Hou, R. Gupta, J. S. Van Arnam *et al.* (2020). *Scientific Data, 7*, 185.

[25] J. Krause, H. I. Grabsch, M. Kloor *et al.* (2021). *Journal of Pathology, 254*, 70.

[26] M. Amgad, E. S. Stovgaard, E. Balslev *et al.* (2020). *NPJ Breast Cancer, 6*, 16.

[27] H. Le, R. Gupta, L. Hou *et al.* (2020). *American Journal of Pathology, 190*, 1491.

[28] B. Korbar, A. M. Olofson, A. P. Miraflor *et al.* (2017). *Journal of Pathology Informatics, 8*, 30.

[29] Y. Li, J. Wu, and Q. Wu (2019). Classification of breast cancer histology images using multi-size and discriminative patches based on deep learning. *IEEE Access, 7*, 21400–21408.

[30] L. Hou, D. Samaras, T. M. Kurc *et al.* (2016). *Proceedings of the IEEE Computer Society Conference on Computer Vision and Pattern Recognition, 2016*, 2424.

[31] G. Campanella, M. G. Hanna, L. Geneslaw *et al.* (2019). *Nature Medicine, 25*, 1301.

[32] M. Ilse, J. Tomczak, and M. Welling (2018). In J. Dy and A. Krause (eds.), *Proceedings of the 35th International Conference on Machine Learning* (PMLR, 10–15 Jul 2018), pp. 2127–2136.

[33] Y. Zhao, F. Yang, Y. Fang *et al.* (2020). In *Proceedings of the IEEE/CVF Conference on Computer Vision and Pattern Recognition*, pp. 4837–4846.

[34] O. Iizuka, F. Kanavati, K. Kato *et al.* (2020). *Scientific Reports, 10*, 1504.

[35] X. Zhu, J. Yao, F. Zhu *et al.* (2017). In *Proceedings of the IEEE Conference on Computer Vision and Pattern Recognition*, pp. 7234–7242.

[36] E. Wulczyn, D. F. Steiner, Z. Xu *et al.* (2020). *PLoS One, 15*, e0233678.

[37] R. J. Chen, M. Y. Lu, M. Shaban *et al.* (2021). *Medical Image Computing and Computer Assisted Intervention–MICCAI 2021* (Springer International Publishing), pp. 339–349.

[38] S. G. Zadeh and M. Schmid (2021). *IEEE Transactions on Pattern Analysis and Machine Intelligence*, *43*, 3126.

[39] J.-R. Chang, C.-Y. Lee, C.-C. Chen *et al.* (2021). Hybrid aggregation network for survival analysis from whole slide histopathological images. In *Medical Image Computing and Computer Assisted Intervention–MICCAI 2021*, pp. 731–740.

[40] R. J. Chen, M. Y. Lu, J. Wang *et al.* (2020). Pathomic fusion: An integrated framework for fusing histopathology and genomic features for cancer diagnosis and prognosis. *IEEE Trans. Med. Imaging*, *41*(4), 757–770.

[41] S. Agarwal, M. Eltigani Osman Abaker, and O. Daescu (2021). Survival prediction based on histopathology imaging and clinical data: A novel, whole slide CNN approach. In *Medical Image Computing and Computer Assisted Intervention–MICCAI 2021*, pp. 762–771.

[42] P. Mobadersany, S. Yousefi, M. Amgad *et al.* (2018). *Proceedings of the National Academy of Sciences of the United States of America*, *115*, E2970.

[43] R. J. Chen, M. Y. Lu, W.-H. Weng *et al.* (2021). In *Proceedings of the IEEE/CVF International Conference on Computer Vision*, pp. 4015–4025.

[44] L. A. Vale-Silva and K. Rohr (2021). Long-term cancer survival prediction using multimodal deep learning. *Scientific Reports*, *11*(1), 13505.

[45] S. Xie, R. Girshick, P. Dollár *et al.* (2017). In *Proceedings of the IEEE Conference on Computer Vision and Pattern Recognition*, pp. 1492–1500.

[46] A. E. Carpenter, T. R. Jones, M. R. Lamprecht *et al.* (2006). *Genome Biology*, *7*, R100.

[47] J. C. Caicedo, A. Goodman, K. W. Karhohs *et al.* (2019). *Nature Methods*, *16*, 1247.

[48] J. Schindelin, I. Arganda-Carreras, E. Frise *et al.* (2012). *Nature Methods*, *9*, 676.

[49] A. B. Tosun, F. Pullara, M. J. Becich *et al.* (2020). *Advances in Anatomic Pathology*, *27*, 241.

[50] M. Amgad, L. Atteya, H. Hussein *et al.* (2021). Explainable nucleus classification using decision tree approximation of learned embeddings. *Bioinformatics*, *38*(2), 513–519.

[51] A. Kiani, B. Uyumazturk, P. Rajpurkar *et al.* (2020). *NPJ Digital Medicine*, *3*, 23.

[52] www.fda.gov (2021).

[53] R. Bommasani, D. A. Hudson, E. Adeli *et al.* (2021). *arXiv* [cs.LG].

[54] K. He, R. Girshick, and P. Dollár (2019). In *Proceedings of the IEEE/CVF International Conference on Computer Vision*, pp. 4918–4927.

© 2023 World Scientific Publishing Company
https://doi.org/10.1142/9789811265679_0020

Chapter 20

The Role of Artificial Intelligence in Epidemiological Modeling

Aniruddha Adiga[*,¶], Srinivasan Venkatramanan[*,‖],
Jiangzhuo Chen[*,**], Przemyslaw Porebski[*,††], Amanda Wilson[*,‡‡],
Henning Mortveit[*,†,§§], Bryan Lewis[*,¶¶], Justin Crow[‡,‖‖],
Madhav V. Marathe[*,§,***], and NSSAC-BII team[*]

[*]*Biocomplexity Institute, University of Virginia*
[†]*Engineering Systems and Environment, University of Virginia*
[‡]*Division of Social Epidemiology, Virginia Department of Health*
[§]*Department of Computer Science, University of Virginia*
[¶]*aniruddha@virginia.edu*
[‖]*srini@virginia.edu*
[**]*jc3qw@virginia.edu*
[††]*pjp2b@virginia.edu*
[‡‡]*alw4ey@virginia.edu*
[§§]*hsm2v@virginia.edu*
[¶¶]*brylew@virginia.edu*
[‖‖]*justin.crow@vdh.virginia.gov*
[***]*marathe@virginia.edu*

1. Introduction

An *epidemic* refers to a widespread occurrence of cases of an infectious illness, specified health behavior, or other health-related event that is clearly in excess of normal expectancy. A *pandemic* is an epidemic on a global scale. Epidemics are as old as documented human history — from the plagues in Roman times and the Middle Ages, the fall of the Han empire in the third century in China, and the defeat of the Aztecs in the 1500s due to a smallpox outbreak [1]. The 1918 influenza pandemic caused significant social disruption and was responsible for more than 50 million deaths worldwide. In the 21st century alone, we have seen significant epidemics, including the H5N1 pandemic, the H1N1 pandemic, SARS and MERS pandemics, the Cholera outbreak in Yemen, and the Ebola and Zika epidemics. The ongoing COVID-19 pandemic has caused significant social, economic, health, and political disruptions and has reminded us that, in spite of significant technological and public health advances, pandemics will continue to occur.

For ethical and practical reasons, controlled experiments in epidemiology that are used to understand scientific phenomena are more complex, and often impossible, to conduct. As a result, computational models play an important role in elucidating the space-time dynamics of epidemics. They also serve an essential role in evaluating various intervention strategies, including pharmaceutical and non-pharmaceutical interventions. The role of individual behavior and public policies are critical for understanding and controlling epidemics, and computational techniques can provide powerful tools for studying these problems.

In this chapter, we discuss the development and use of data-driven Artificial Intelligence (AI) techniques to support real-time epidemic science. We had already supported real-time decision-making at the federal level during the H1N1 pandemic [2,3] and also supported the Department of Defense (DoD) during the Ebola epidemic [4–6]. Here, we describe our efforts during the ongoing COVID-19 pandemic; while COVID-19 required us to address challenges identified during the H1N1 and Ebola outbreaks, this pandemic also brought forth an entirely new set of questions and challenges. We will describe these aspects herein.

1.1. *An AI perspective*

We first began to work on this class of problem over 20 years ago. Our goal was to identify new computational techniques for studying large complex socio-technical systems and to develop tools to support policymakers in planning responses to pandemics as well as human-initiated bioterrorism events. Solutions to these problems required us to borrow ideas from diverse areas in science and engineering, including network science, high-performance computing, urban planning, economics, nonlinear systems, algorithmics, statistics, etc. Over time, it became increasingly clear that an AI perspective on complex socio-technical systems was valuable; several ideas and concepts in AI proved to be the conceptual glue critical for developing an integrated solution. This includes traditional AI topics, such as multiagent systems representing large complex populations, causality, reasoning and inference in complex systems, and human–computer interactions. However, they also bring forth some of the new ideas in AI, including explainability, fairness and biases in AI systems, digital twins, and deep learning. Furthermore, two important concepts have emerged over the course of the ongoing COVID-19 pandemic: (i) real-time analysis and (ii) operationally relevant AI. We have tried to highlight this perspective throughout this chapter.

Varied uses of models and the role of data. Different kinds of models are appropriate at different stages during the response phase of a pandemic. Data-driven machine learning models are helpful for forecasting and short-term projections. For longer-term projections and understanding the effects of different kinds of interventions and counterfactual (what if) analysis, mechanistic models are usually more helpful. As COVID-19 evolved, models have evolved as well. Compartmental models were able to adapt relatively quickly to changes in epidemic dynamics. However, assessing detailed interventions and representing behavior is better done using detailed agent-based models.

As with any mathematical modeling effort, data play a significant role in the utility of such models. Before the COVID-19 pandemic, obtaining timely disease surveillance data was challenging; COVID-19 was a watershed event in this sense. Curated data regarding confirmed cases, hospitalizations, human mobility, deaths, and various social interventions are now available for all of the United States (US) at a county-level resolution. This has made real-time modeling possible. Even so, gaps exist. Data continues to be noisy, and its coverage in terms of geography, time, and social groups is frequently less than complete.

2. Modeling Approaches

Epidemiological models fall into two broad classes: statistical models that are largely data-driven and mechanistic models that are based on underlying theoretical principles on how the disease spreads. We discuss five types of models in this chapter; the first four would be classified as mechanistic models, while the last model comprises data-driven statistical and machine learning methods.

2.1. *Compartmental models*

Infectious disease dynamics have been modeled over the past century using various mathematical and computational abstractions. Depending on the question of interest, these model structures may incorporate various statistical and mechanistic aspects and have different computational and data requirements. One of the earliest and most successful modeling frameworks are compartmental models [7] which divide the overall population into different disease *compartments* (also referred to as *disease states*) and capture the transitions between these using differential or difference equations. For instance, the most common such model is the SIR model (Susceptible–Infected–Recovered) whose state transitions are represented by the following equation:

$$\dot{S} = -\beta SI, \quad \dot{I} = \beta SI - \gamma I \quad \dot{R} = \gamma I \tag{1}$$

where β is referred to as the *transmission rate* and γ as the *recovery rate*. Further refinements of this model include (i) incorporating contact matrices for age stratification, (ii) additional compartments to capture more complex disease progressions, and (iii) metapopulation structures to capture spatially explicit dynamics. Through the COVID-19 pandemic, these models have been widely used and are very instrumental in influencing policy. This is due to their flexibility in answering different questions, their ability to work under data-poor conditions, and their computational ease for running large experiment designs across parameters to capture underlying uncertainty or potential scenarios. We have employed variations of this framework since February 2020 to run various scenario-based projections for the state and federal agencies in the United States. Here, we describe how the model structure was adapted for different questions and time points in the pandemic and highlight the importance of a data-driven responsive pipeline to support policymakers.

2.2. *Metapopulation models*

Metapopulation models serve as a good trade-off between Ordinary Differential Equation (ODE) and network models and are well suited to capture spatial heterogeneity in disease dynamics. The population of interest is divided into spatially distinct *patches*, and within each patch, the disease dynamics are simulated with a homogeneous mixing assumption. The patches are also connected to each other through a weighted directed network capturing the movement of individuals between the patches. The movement is often representative of *commuting* (as opposed to *migration*), thus preserving the home population counts of each patch. While the disease evolution resembles a homogeneous ODE model within a single patch, the mobility network generates heterogeneity and longer hops between the spatial subpopulations. PatchSim is a deterministic implementation of this approach. More details of this modeling framework are available in [8].

2.3. *Adaptive compartmental models*

The simulation model used for producing disease outcomes has evolved over the past two years in response to policy needs, biological and social aspects, and changing data availability. The adaptive modeling framework has been operational since September 2020. In essence, it is a discrete time *Susceptible–Exposed–Infectious–Recovered* (SEIR) compartmental model with modeled *Vaccination*. The model is instantiated and calibrated using real-world datasets. The basic model structure and its extensions have been used for supporting the *Scenario Modeling Hub* for over one year and reflect common assumptions made by the teams to account for incomplete, missing, or delayed aggregate data [9].

We begin with the slightly modified SEIR dynamics to account for vaccination and waning of immunity. We also capture presymptomatic infectiousness and asymptomaticity using additional parameters. While vaccinations are parameterized using real-world uptake datasets and projections using vaccine acceptance estimates [10], the waning of immunity due to natural infection and vaccination is parameterized using the latest estimates from the literature. Variants are parameterized using growth rates and onset times. Furthermore, subsequent variants require capturing additional dynamics, such as cross-variant protection and variant-specific vaccine efficacies. This has resulted in a more complex immune-tiered multistrain implementation.

The model is calibrated to observed confirmed cases. Due to high reporting bias and underreporting, we use seroprevalence estimates [11] to derive infection counts via a case-ascertainment rate. Hospitalizations and deaths are obtained using an age-stratified post-processing module that accounts for vaccine uptake and time-varying case-hospitalization (CHR) and case-fatality (CFR) rates. Case data are augmented by 1-week-ahead forecasts from a statistical ensemble before calibration. The calibration process results in time-varying transmissibility (β), which is then projected under various conditions of vaccine uptake and/or variant prevalence to produce scenario-based projections.

2.4. *Agent-based models*

Agent-based networked models (sometimes referred to as *agent-based models*) extend metapopulation models further by explicitly capturing the interaction structure of the underlying populations. Such models are often resolved at the level of single individual entities (animals, humans, etc.). In this class of models, the epidemic dynamics can be modeled as a diffusion process on a specific undirected contact network $G(V, E)$ on a population V – each edge $e = (u, v) \in E$ implies that individuals (also referred to as nodes) $u, v \in V$ come into contact.[1] Let $N(v)$ denote the set of neighbors of

---

[1] Note that while edge e is represented as a tuple (u, v), it actually denotes the set $\{u, v\}$, as is standard in graph theory.

v. The SIR model on the graph G is a dynamical process in which each node is in one of the S, I, or R states. Infection can potentially spread from u to v along edge $e = (u, v)$ with a probability of $\beta(e, t)$ at time instant t after u becomes infected, conditional on node v remaining uninfected until time t — this is a discrete version of the rate of infection for the ODE model discussed earlier. We let $I(t)$ denote the set of nodes that become infected at time t. The (random) subset of edges on which the infections spread represents a disease outcome and is referred to as a *dendrogram*. This dynamical system starts with a configuration in which there are one or more nodes in state I and reaches a fixed point in which all nodes are in state S or R.

Such a network model captures the interplay between the three components of computational epidemiology: (i) individual behaviors of agents, (ii) unstructured, heterogeneous multiscale networks, and (iii) the dynamical processes on these networks. It is based on the hypothesis that a better understanding of the characteristics of the underlying network and individual behavioral adaptations can give better insights into contagion dynamics and response strategies. Although computationally expensive and data-intensive, agent-based models for epidemiology alter the types of questions that can be posed, providing qualitatively different insights into disease dynamics and public health policies.

2.5. *Data-driven models*

The purely data-driven approaches mostly apply statistical models to the data, determine patterns in the data, and/or unearth patterns in data sources and have been particularly effective in forecasting over relatively short horizons. *Statistical models* determine statistical properties from the observed data and leverage it for forecasting. Some of the popular methods employed in infectious disease forecasting are auto-regressive (AR) models [12–17] and filtering methods (Kalman filters, particle filters, etc.) [18–21]. Due to the highly non-stationary data, statistical models have not been effective for COVID-19 data forecasting. *Deep learning* (DL) models and deep neural networks (DNNs) are also popular choices, and several architectures have been considered for extracting patterns in the observed time series, such as feed forward networks [22–24]), long short-term networks [25,26], attention-based long short-term memory (LSTM) models [27–29], and graph-based spatio-temporal models [30–32]. The deep learning models require substantial training data and are susceptible to overfitting; in addition, they also lack *explainability*. *Hybrid models* are an emerging class of models which are an amalgamation of theory-based mechanistic models with DL models and have been employed in influenza forecasting [33–35] and COVID-19 forecasting [36–38].

3. Applications

In the previous section, we described some of the modeling approaches we have used in our COVID-19 research. In this section, we go into more detail on how these approaches were applied to specific applications.

3.1. *Scenario modeling*

Multimodel approaches have been very useful for supporting policymakers during the pandemic. While the short-term forecasting efforts (Centers for Disease Control and Prevention (CDC) Forecasting Hub) build upon nearly a decade of experience in seasonal influenza forecasting, a similar effort for scenario-based projections for COVID-19 was started in January 2021 (https://covid19scenariomodelinghub.org/viz.html). Following the support for multimodel frameworks in other domains and early success found during the COVID-19 pandemic [39], the Scenario Modeling Hub (SMH) has been regularly updated since then for over 12 separate rounds [9]. These rounds have studied the impact of varying levels of non-pharmaceutical interventions (NPIs), vaccine uptake, and variant parameters. One of the advantages of this framework is the coordination across teams in the experiment design while maintaining model diversity and entertaining long-term uncertainty in pandemic trajectories.

For instance, Round 5 of the SMH focused on a 2×2 design to study the impact of vaccine uptake and NPI relaxations. There was significant uncertainty in the actual uptake of vaccines since, by May 2021, they were widely available and all adults 18 years and older were eligible. While the Census Household Pulse Survey conducted in March 2021 estimated acceptance at around 68%, a more optimistic estimate of 83% emerged from Facebook surveys. Furthermore, given the CDC recommendations, mask-wearing levels were decreasing, but the level of reduction in NPI compliance was unclear. Thus, the scenarios considered a moderate relaxation (50% over six months) versus a faster relaxation (80% over six months). In the Adaptive framework, the vaccine acceptance estimates were used to generate future uptake schedules, and the NPI scenarios were used to modulate the projected transmissibility over the next six months. Figure 1 shows the simulated runs across various scenarios along with the ensemble obtained across models. It shows how the moderate NPI scenarios captured the trajectory better while also highlighting the need to update scenarios at regular intervals (e.g., the Delta surge that was not anticipated in May 2021).

3.2. Weekly projection modeling

Since the beginning of the pandemic, we have provided weekly scenario-based model projections at the state and federal levels. In particular, the weekly updates for the Virginia Department of Health (VDH) have been operational since April 2020 and have spanned different counterfactual conditions pertaining to non-pharmaceutical interventions, vaccinations, seasonality, novel variants, etc. We have used both the metapopulation framework (Section 2.2) and the Adaptive compartmental modeling framework (Section 2.3) at different stages of the pandemic.

The model we began using for simulating COVID-19 dynamics within Virginia is based on a similar implementation at a national scale for studying the spatio-temporal spread of seasonal influenza in the United States [8]. It is a mechanistic metapopulation modeling framework, representing SEIR dynamics within and across spatial units, aka *patches* (e.g., 133 counties/independent cities in VA), as described in Section 2.2. The model assumed homogeneous mixing within each patch and inter-patch mixing modulated by commuter traffic. Disease dynamics were instantiated using preliminary best guess estimates, and disease parameters (specifically the transmissibility and infectious duration) of the model were calibrated to confirmed cases at the county level. We follow a Bayesian model calibration approach similar to [5] and use a multivariate Gaussian to model the observation error with respect to the logarithm of the cumulative counts. Starting from a uniform prior, we run a sequential Markov chain Monte Carlo (MCMC) (Metropolis–Hastings) to obtain posterior distribution for the disease parameters. These are used to provide uncertainty bounds around our projections. Severe outcomes (such as hospitalizations, ICU admissions, and ventilator needs) were obtained by post-processing the simulated incidence curves with appropriate delays and scaling parameters. Using estimated durations of stay for these severe outcomes and available bed capacities, deficits are computed at suitable levels of aggregation (e.g., Virginia Healthcare Alerting and Status System (VHASS) regions). We initially modeled five projection scenarios: one based on the limited effect of social distancing (depicting the worst case) and four others based on different durations and intensities for social distancing impact. In the setup, we assumed that intense social distancing began on March 15, 2020, based on the Virginia State of Emergency Executive order. The scenarios are based on 25% and 50% reduction in transmissibility (mixing rates within the metapopulation) lasting until April 30, 2020, and June 10, 2020, respectively. We did not assume any role of seasonality in reducing the transmissibility during the summer. Initial estimates can be seen in Figure 2.

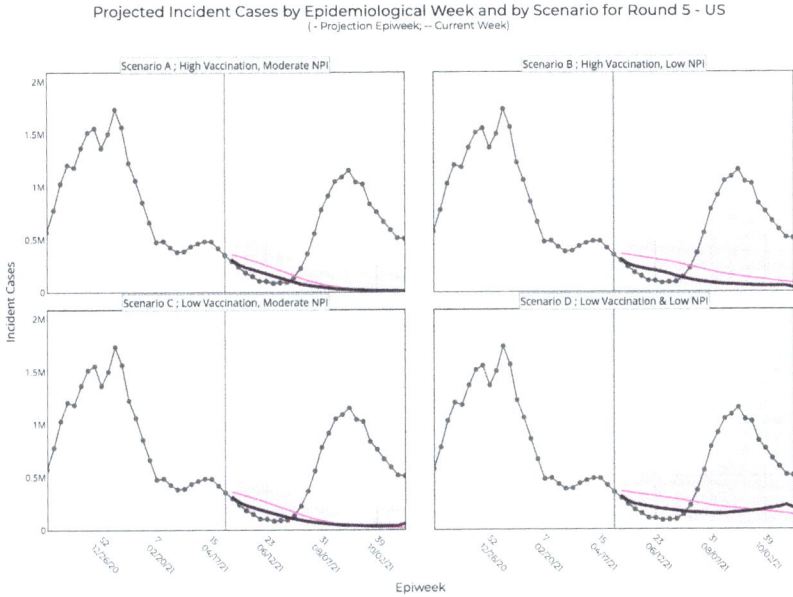

Fig. 1.   Long-term scenario projections using Adaptive framework under different vaccine and NPI conditions during Round 5 of Scenario Modeling Hub. The Ensemble projection across multiple models is shown in black, while the Adaptive framework is shown in pink. The ground truth is marked with black circles, with the vertical line representing the projection timepoint. (Screenshot from https://covid19scenariomodelinghub. org/viz.html.)

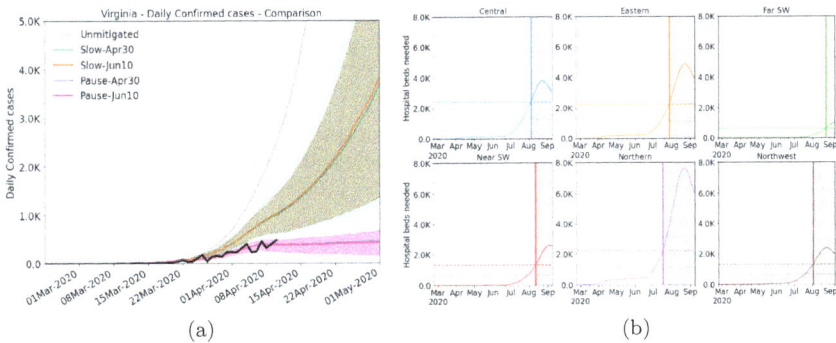

Fig. 2.   Sample projections for initial metapopulation runs (12 April 2020).

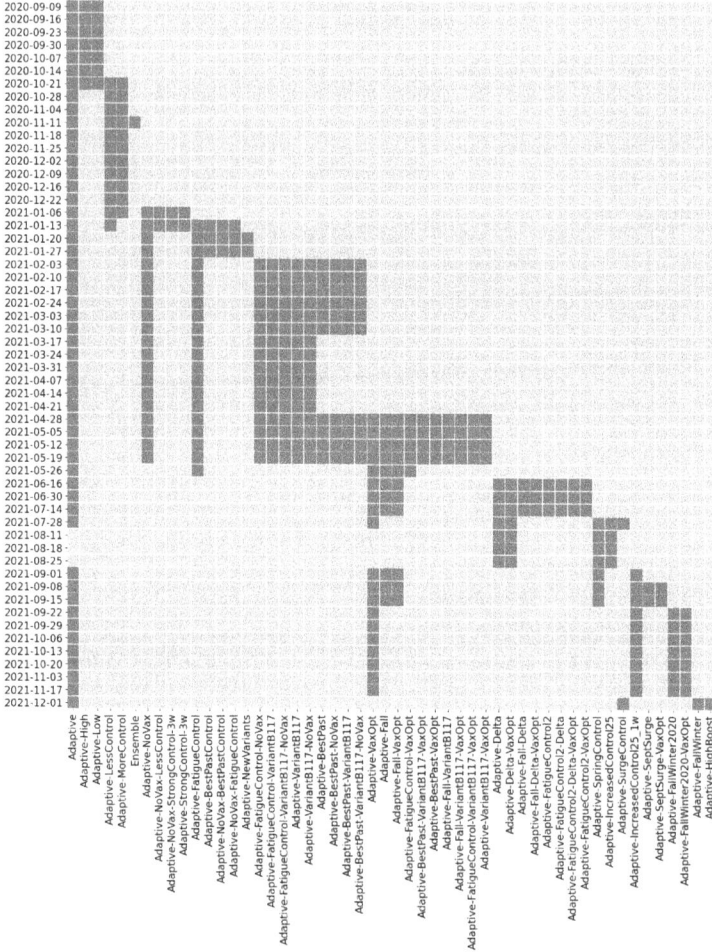

Fig. 3. Various scenarios for weekly projections using the Adaptive framework from September 2020 to December 2021. Solid gray shading indicates that a particular scenario was included in that week's projections.

Since September 2020, we have been using the Adaptive modeling framework for weekly projections. As described in Section 2.3, while the framework lacks spatial connectivity, it is significantly enhanced by additional datasets in terms of vaccination and variants and is better calibrated to confirmed cases. Various scenarios run under this framework are listed in Figure 3. As one might notice, these scenarios range from NPI counterfactuals (scenario names including "Control" and "Surge"),

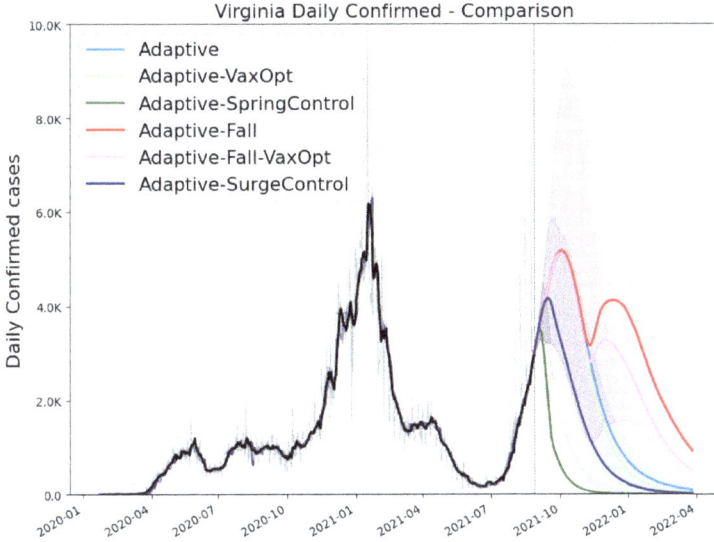

Fig. 4.   Sample projections produced during September 2021.

seasonal variations (scenario names with "Fall" and "FallWinter"), variant introductions (scenarios with "Delta" and "VariantB117"), and vaccine uptake ("NoVax", "VaxOpt", and "HighBoost"). Different scenarios are of interest during various phases of the pandemic, and some scenarios are used for longer periods (e.g., NoVax/VaxOpt) to highlight the impact of past decisions (scenarios with no vaccinations) and for encouraging public action (optimistic uptake of vaccines). For instance, Figure 4 shows a combination of scenarios that considered different levels of control (NPI similar to Spring 2021 versus adaptations following a Surge) and vaccine uptake (status quo versus optimistic uptake). In these settings, the vaccine acceptance levels were informed using the COVID-19 Trends and Impact Survey (CTIS).

3.3.   *Forecasting*

Forecasting epidemics is a crucial task in the effective control of disease spread and for understanding disease dynamics. Accurate and timely forecasting is the goal but is complicated due to the co-evolution of epidemics, individual and collective behavior, viral dynamics, and public policies. Some of the critical challenges are related to data, the existence of multiple targets, multiple model evaluation metrics, and socio-economic and political dependencies.

As discussed in Section 2, several classes of models exist for understanding disease prevalence through several *targets*. While compartmental models predict the disease dynamics and derive the *targets* as the outcome, statistical and machine learning methods model the data without considering the disease dynamics. No single class of model is shown to be the best, especially as seen during the COVID-19 pandemic. However, it has been observed that forecasts from an ensemble of models tend to have better performance when compared to individual forecasts [40], even a relatively simple ensemble model such as the median of forecasts (https://viz.covid19forecasthub.org/). The applicable variety of models can be described through an example of a real-time COVID-19 forecasting model.

3.3.1. *An example of a multimethod ensemble model*

The multiclass ensemble model consists of statistical (autoregressive (AR), autoregressive integrated moving average (ARIMA), and Kalman filter), deep learning (LSTM), and compartmental (SEIR) models where the models themselves were deliberately kept simple to ensure ease of model training. Although simple, the models have been adapted to forecast a highly non-stationary time series. We considered a Bayesian Model Averaging Ensemble (BMA) model [41], which considers the performance of the individual models during the training regime, unlike the median-based ensemble, and assigns weights to individual model forecasts. This model has been employed for providing cases and hospitalization forecasts at multiple resolutions; a detailed description of the BMA-based forecasting framework is provided in [42].

3.3.2. *Observations*

Forecasts and weights distribution. We have observed spatio-temporal variability in the distribution of weights through the framework. Figure 5(a) depicts the variability through choropleth maps whose colors indicate the dominant methods (i.e., methods with the highest weight). In August 2020, we observed a nearly uniform distribution of weights, while in November 2020, ARIMA appeared to dominate, and in December 2020, the SEIR model is dominant.

Forecast performance of individual methods. We evaluated 22 weeks of forecast data starting from the first week of August 2020 to the second week of January 2021 for all 3142 counties of the US. The performance across 1- to 4-week-ahead targets (horizon) is evaluated separately. The Mean Absolute

(a)

(b)

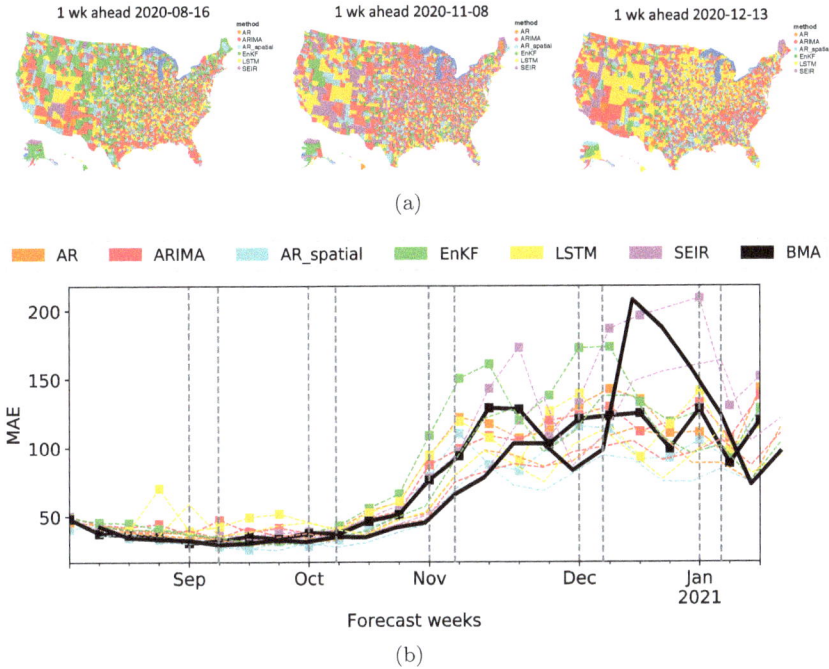

Fig. 5. Understanding the time-varying importance of models through weights distribution and forecast performances: (a) Spatial distribution of methods with the highest weights per county displayed across three different forecast weeks. (b) Performance of BMA and the individual models across various forecast weeks since August 2020. The performance of individual models varies across weeks, while BMA shows relatively lower variation across weeks. The legend is common to both the figures.

Error (MAE)[2] was used for comparing the point forecasts. The overall performance of each method was computed as the MAE across all the forecast weeks and counties and indicates that the average performance of individual models is similar. Also, the performance of the BMA ensemble is comparable to, if not better than, the best performing model, which is in accordance with previous observations made in [43]. The average performance of the methods across all counties for each forecast week is shown in Figure 5(b), and it can be observed that, in comparison to most methods, the BMA has a lower variation.

The BMA ensemble and the individual methods focus on each location or region independently. However, epidemic dynamics in a region are

---

[2]If $\{\hat{y}_i\}_{i=1}^N$ are the N forecasts and $\{y_i\}_{i=1}^N$ the ground truth values, MAE $= \frac{1}{N}\sum_{i=1}^N |y_i - \hat{y}_i|$.

influenced by the dynamics of its neighbors. It is important to incorporate the spatial dependencies into the model, and a natural approach is to employ network-based methods such as the meta-population models (cf. 2.2). These models depend on accurate networks for calibrating the conventional network-based model parameters, and constructing such networks is often a challenge due to a lack of data. Recently, Graph Neural Network models (GNNs) have been shown to learn patterns in graph data that can describe the relationship between the input graphs and output, but, like most DL models, they require large datasets to train. Hybrid models have addressed the issue of training DNNs using limited data by incorporating the underlying causal mechanisms into the training [44]. Some of the GNN-based hybrid models have shown promising results in epidemic forecasting [31,37,45]; in the next section, we summarize one such forecasting model for COVID-19 case counts.

3.3.3. *An example of hybrid GNN models*

The causal-based neural network model referred to as CausalGNN attempts to jointly learn embeddings related to the spatio-temporal data (i.e., dynamic graphs) and the causal model (referred to as *epidemiological context* henceforth) represented by all the parameters and features corresponding to the disease models (e.g., S, E, I, R, and other disease parameters). Specifically, the framework has the following characteristics: (i) An attention-based dynamic GNN module embeds spatial and temporal signals from disease dynamics using a connectivity network. (ii) A causal module encodes the single-patched compartmental model signals to provide epidemiological context. Unlike traditional network-based compartmental models, in this approach, the patches are connected via a learned GNN, and the calibration is done through computationally efficient GNN training. (iii) To ensure the flow of spatio-temporal information into the epidemiological model and vice versa, we allow for interaction between the causal and GNN modules. This is realized using a causal encoder which encodes causal features through node embedding. Similarly, the causal decoder is used to infer causal model parameters. A detailed description of the modules, encoding mechanisms, optimization strategies, and the architecture is provided in [46].

Major observations. The experimental results shown in the original paper [46] indicate that CausalGNN performs consistently better than the baselines across multiple scales and with increasing horizons. Two possible reasons for the better performance are the following: (i) the attention-based GNN architecture processes spatial and temporal signals efficiently and (ii) the method handles epidemiological context via an SIRD model (an SIR model with an additional compartment for Deaths) at the node level.

In the realm of spatio-temporal forecasting models, the forecasts from the CausalGNN model explicitly designed for epidemic forecasting improve performance over other hybrid model forecasts (discussed in [46]). The CausalGNN has superior performance when compared to SIR and PatchSEIR, especially for long-term forecasting. The vanilla recurrent neural network (RNN), gated recurrent unit (GRU), and LSTM models perform well for shorter forecast horizons; however, for longer horizons, their performance diminishes. This highlights the importance of capturing spatial disease transmission patterns in the input data for long-term forecasting. This demonstrates the ability of DNNs in modeling nonlinear patterns for achieving good forecasting performance. We also conducted an ablation study on three critical components of our CausalGNN framework: the causal module, graph structure, and attention mechanism. The results show that all three components play essential roles in improving our model's performance.

4. Decision Support Tools

In this chapter, we have discussed how AI guided the development of modeling and simulation platforms for predicting COVID-19 prevalence under various conditions, including the emergence of novel variants, differing vaccination strategies, and NPIs such as social distancing, mask-wearing, and school closures. While these platforms provide significant insights into the pandemic and mitigating strategies, communicating these results to the policymakers with the authority to recommend or enable change is key to changing epidemic trends. Results can be communicated via talks and articles, but with so many sources of information, sometimes conflicting, it may be difficult for policymakers, analysts, and the general public to draw meaningful conclusions.

To this end, one way to communicate the results of predictions and analyses in a way people may more easily understand is through *decision support tools*. Decision support tools provide visualizations and other analytical capabilities to help viewers get a broader understanding about some aspects of the pandemic, such as COVID-19 infections, hospitalizations, vaccinations, or deaths. Visualizations often allow people to quickly assess current trends and evaluate the impact that different strategies would have on these trends, such as how increased mask-wearing might flatten the pandemic curve.

The COVID-19 pandemic gave rise to a variety of such dashboard applications. One of the first web-based tools released during the pandemic was the COVID-19 Dashboard by the Center for Systems Science and

Engineering (CSSE) at Johns Hopkins University (JHU) [47]. This tool provides visualizations of where COVID-19 infections and deaths are occurring, along with data that other researchers could use in their case studies. Similarly, the CDC COVID Data Tracker [48] provides similar visualizations on case counts, hospitalizations, and deaths, both surveillance data and forecasts; furthermore, it provides general guidance to help people protect themselves, as well as localized guidance based on trends at the state and county level. The Institute of Health Metrics and Evaluation (IHME) has a COVID-19 Projections website [49] offering reports, viewed either in Map format or as time series charts, that illustrate cumulative deaths, daily deaths, hospitalizations, vaccinations, infections, testing, mask use, and social distancing; like CDC's tool, it provides both surveillance counts as well as projections dependent on different scenarios, such as 80% mask usage. This tool also offers mechanisms for comparing statistics across regions. The COVID-19 Mobility Impact Dashboard was developed using a combination of SafeGraph patterns data, US Census data, and a mobility-based model to allow policymakers and public health officials to assess the impact that reducing or increasing foot traffic by Place of Interest (POI) categories would have on pandemic spread [50]. These are but a few of several web applications, each developed to allow officials to make informed decisions.

In addition to statistical dashboards like the ones described above, other applications developed during the pandemic serve different purposes. COVIDWise is a mobile phone app launched by VDH that uses Bluetooth connections to perform anonymous contact tracing between users. That way, if a user tests positive for COVID-19, an alert can be sent through the app to let contacts know that they have been exposed [51]; in addition, VDH can use this information for data analysis to help them do resource planning. EXperiments in Computational Epidemiology for Action and Decision Support (EXCEADS) is an application we developed that is a web-based epidemic simulation tool. Users can develop disease models and run experiments to see how the disease as designed would perform under differing initialization and intervention conditions; it relies on EpiHiper, an implementation of agent-based models described earlier in Section 2.4 and used for many COVID-19 response studies (e.g., [52,53]), to run its simulations. Unlike the other tools mentioned here, the VDH Mobile Vaccine Site Recommendation pipeline has no user interface but still provides decision support. The pipeline uses SafeGraph weekly patterns mobility data, US Census data, and vaccination data provided by VDH to advise local health officials on where to stand up local vaccination sites in order to target under-vaccinated demographic groups [54].

As illustrated above, many kinds of decision support tools were inspired by the COVID-19 pandemic. In the following section, we describe one such web-based decision support tool in more detail.

4.1. *COVID-19 surveillance dashboard*

Early in the pandemic, it quickly became evident that both experts and the general public needed a way to assess the COVID-19 situation at a glance. Although several organizations started web dashboards to help people understand the situation on the ground (including JHU's dashboard [47], described above), these dashboards often focused on niche areas of interest, such as covering specific regions or a particular aspect of the pandemic. In order to facilitate decision support, our goal was to release a dashboard that was more universal and general in its coverage so that policymakers and the public could have a more comprehensive and accurate view of what was happening on the ground.

We released the COVID-19 Surveillance Dashboard [55] on February 3, 2020, or just 12 days after the first case was identified in the United States. In the two years since its inception, the dashboard's coverage has been extended to provide country-level surveillance globally; state/province-level data for 20 countries, including China; and county-level data for the US. Furthermore, the feature set was similarly extended to offer better visualizations and analytical capabilities. As of March 8, 2022, the dashboard has been visited by approximately 1.2 million users from over 220 countries; at its peak usage in April 2020, when fewer dashboards were available, it saw 80,000 views and 50,000 unique users per day [56]. The dashboard can be viewed at https://nssac.bii.virginia.edu/covid-19/dashboard/.

4.1.1. *Applicability to AI*

In addition to its variety of visualizations and visual analytics, this tool delivers real-time assessments of the situation on the ground. This can only be done through daily data updates. We depend on multiple data streams, and coordinating these updates requires a pipeline of steps to read the data, convert it to the proper format, perform validation, and calculate augmented surveillance data, including estimated active and recovered cases. This pipeline is illustrated in Figure 6.

Also, the Analytics tab uses Natural Language Processing (NLP) to answer user questions using visual analytics. A user types in a question, like "current top 10 countries active", and the dashboard uses NLP methods to

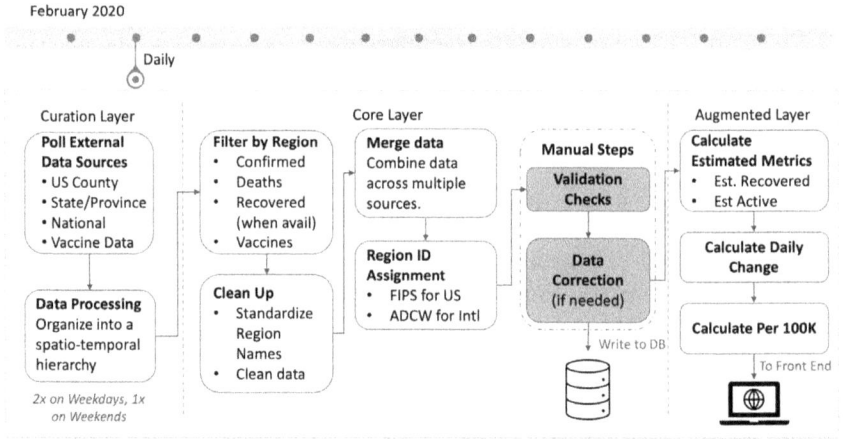

Fig. 6. COVID-19 Surveillance Dashboard deployment: In order to provide real-time data visualizations, the dashboard's underlying dataset is updated twice a day on weekdays and once a day on weekends. The process steps can be divided into three layers: *Curation*, where data are polled from many external data sources (currently 12); *Core*, where the data are collated and validated; and *Augmented*, where derived data are calculated from the core dataset.

interpret the question and plot the answer on a graph; users can download those answers in various formats.

5. Discussion and Concluding Remarks

In this chapter, we have described the use of data-driven AI models for real-time epidemic science. The applications of these techniques were illustrated by describing our efforts during the evolving COVID-19 pandemic over the past two years. As discussed earlier, the development of such models was based on several traditional AI methods. However, as the pandemic evolved, the response efforts required the inclusion of several contemporary solutions, including graphical models, explainable AI, deep learning, and AI for Social Good. A number of topics were not considered in this chapter, primarily because of space considerations. We discuss them briefly in the following — subsequent papers will cover them in-depth. First, AI methods were used to analyze (social) media to uncover issues related to misinformation, memes, and other social phenomena that played a significant role during the pandemic [57,58]. For instance, vaccine hesitancy, fake news, and political polarization influenced pandemic outcomes. Second, AI techniques were used to develop innovative contact tracing apps. These apps showed promise early on but had mixed uptake [59,60] which limited their effectiveness. Third, AI techniques were used to explore vaccination in terms of effective distribution strategies. For example, the selection of which subpopulations should be vaccinated first when the supply is limited can have a significant impact on overall outcomes. Fourth, AI techniques in the area of computational chemistry and biology guided drug discovery and repurposing during the ongoing pandemic [61,62]. Fifth, researchers have begun exploring reinforcement learning techniques to model adaptive human behavior and intervention policies [63]. Finally, AI techniques assisted in the discovery and identification of emerging variants [64].

Acknowledgments

We thank the members of the Biocomplexity COVID-19 Response Team and the Network Systems Science and Advanced Computing (NSSAC) Division of the University of Virginia for their thoughtful comments and suggestions on epidemic modeling response support. The NSSAC-BII team is Aniruddha Adiga, Amanda Wilson, Srinivasan Venkatramanan, Jiangzhuo Chen, Andrew Warren, Bryan Lewis, Parantapa Bhattacharya, Stefan Hoops, Brian Klahn, Joseph Outtten, Przemyslaw Porebski, Benjamin Hurt, Gursharn Kaur, Lijing Wang, Henning Mortveit, Dawen Xie, Stephen Eubank, Christopher L. Barrett, and Madhav V. Marathe.

This work has been partially supported by the University of Virginia Strategic Investment Fund award number SIF160, VDH Grant PV-BII VDH COVID-19 Modeling Program VDH-21-501-0135, NSF XSEDE Grant TG-BIO210084, NSF OAC-1916805 (CINES), NSF CCF-1918656 (Expeditions), CNS-2028004 (RAPID), OAC-2027541 (RAPID), and CNS-2041952 (PREPARE).

References

[1] F. Brauer, P. van den Driessche, and J. Wu (2008). *Mathematical Epidemiology, Springer Verlag, Lecture Notes in Mathematics*, Vol. 1945. Springer.

[2] C. Barrett, K. Bisset, J. Leidig *et al.* (2010). An integrated modeling environment to study the co-evolution of networks, individual behavior and epidemics. *AI Magazine, 31*(1), 75–87.

[3] K. R. Bisset, J. Chen, S. Deodhar *et al.* (2014). Indemics: An interactive high-performance computing framework for data-intensive epidemic modeling. *ACM Transactions on Modeling and Computer Simulation (TOMACS), 24*(1), 1–32.

[4] S. Venkatramanan, B. Lewis, J. Chen *et al.* (2018). Using data-driven agent-based models for forecasting emerging infectious diseases. *Epidemics, 22,* 43–49.

[5] A. Fadikar, D. Higdon, J. Chen *et al.* (2018). Calibrating a stochastic, agent-based model using quantile-based emulation. *SIAM/ASA Journal on Uncertainty Quantification, 6*(4), 1685–1706.

[6] M. M. Waldrop (2017). News feature: Special agents offer modeling upgrade. *Proceedings of the National Academy of Sciences, 114*(28), 7176–7179.

[7] R. M. Anderson and R. M. May (1992). *Infectious Diseases of Humans: Dynamics and Control.* Oxford: Oxford University Press.

[8] S. Venkatramanan, J. Chen, A. Fadikar *et al.* (2019). Optimizing spatial allocation of seasonal influenza vaccine under temporal constraints. *PLoS Computational Biology, 15*(9), e1007111.

[9] R. K. Borchering, C. Viboud, E. Howerton *et al.* (2021). Modeling of future COVID-19 cases, hospitalizations, and deaths, by vaccination rates and nonpharmaceutical intervention scenarios–united states, April–September 2021. *Morbidity and Mortality Weekly Report, 70*(19), 719.

[10] J. A. Salomon, A. Reinhart, A. Bilinski *et al.* (2021). The US COVID-19 trends and impact survey: Continuous real-time measurement of COVID-19 symptoms, risks, protective behaviors, testing, and vaccination. *Proceedings of the National Academy of Sciences, 118,* 51.

[11] F. P. Havers, C. Reed, T. Lim *et al.* (2020). Seroprevalence of antibodies to sars-cov-2 in 10 sites in the United States, 23 March–12 May 2020. *JAMA Internal Medicine, 180*(12), 1576–1586.

[12] S. Yang, M. Santillana, and S. C. Kou (2015). Accurate estimation of Influenza epidemics using Google search data via ARGO. *Proceedings of the National Academy of Sciences, 112*(47), 14473–14478.

[13] P. Rangarajan, S. K. Mody, and M. Marathe (2019). Forecasting Dengue and Influenza incidences using a sparse representation of Google trends, electronic health records, and time series data. *PLoS Computational Biology, 15*(11), e1007518.

[14] S. Kandula, D. Hsu, and J. Shaman (2017). Subregional nowcasts of seasonal Influenza using search trends. *Journal of Medical Internet Research, 19*(11), e370.

[15] Z. Wang, P. Chakraborty, S. R. Mekaru *et al.* (2015). Dynamic Poisson autoregression for Influenza-like-illness case count prediction. In *Proceedings of the 21th ACM SIGKDD International Conference on Knowledge Discovery and Data Mining,* pp. 1285–1294.

[16] A. F. Dugas, M. Jalalpour, Y. Gel *et al.* (2013). Influenza forecasting with Google Flu Trends. *PLoS One, 8*(2), e56176.

[17] J. M. Radin, N. E. Wineinger, E. J. Topol *et al.* (2020). Harnessing wearable device data to improve state-level real-time surveillance of Influenza-like illness in the USA: A population-based study. *The Lancet Digital Health, 2*(2), e85–e93.

[18] W. Yang, A. Karspeck and J. Shaman (2014). Comparison of filtering methods for the modeling and retrospective forecasting of Influenza epidemics. *PLoS Computational Biology, 10*(4), e1003583.

[19] J. Shaman and A. Karspeck (2012). Forecasting seasonal outbreaks of Influenza. *Proceedings of the National Academy of Sciences, 109*(50), 20425–20430.

[20] J. Shaman, A. Karspeck, W. Yang *et al.* (2013). Real-time Influenza forecasts during the 2012–2013 season. *Nature Communications*, *4*, 2837.

[21] W. Yang, B. J. Cowling, E. H. Lau *et al.* (2015). Forecasting Influenza epidemics in Hong Kong. *PLoS Computational Biology*, *11*(7), e1004383.

[22] O. Wahyunggoro, A. E. Permanasari and A. Chamsudin (2013). Utilization of neural network for disease forecasting. In *59th ISI World Statistics Congress*. Citeseer, pp. 549–554.

[23] H. M. Aburas, B. G. Cetiner and M. Sari (2010). Dengue confirmed-cases prediction: A neural network model. *Expert Systems with Applications*, *37*(6), 4256–4260.

[24] Q. Xu, Y. R. Gel, L. L. Ramirez *et al.* (2017). Forecasting Influenza in Hong Kong with Google search queries and statistical model fusion. *PloS One*, *12*(5), e0176690.

[25] S. Volkova, E. Ayton, K. Porterfield *et al.* (2017). Forecasting Influenza-like illness dynamics for military populations using neural networks and social media. *PloS One*, *12*(12), e0188941.

[26] S. R. Venna, A. Tavanaei, R. N. Gottumukkala *et al.* (2019). A novel data-driven model for real-time Influenza forecasting. *IEEE Access*, *7*, 7691–7701.

[27] X. Zhu, B. Fu, Y. Yang *et al.* (2019). Attention-based recurrent neural network for Influenza epidemic prediction. *BMC Bioinformatics*, *20*(18), 1–10.

[28] B. Adhikari, X. Xu, N. Ramakrishnan *et al.* (2019). EpiDeep: Exploiting embeddings for epidemic forecasting. In *Proceedings of the 25th ACM SIGKDD International Conference on Knowledge Discovery & Data Mining*, pp. 577–586.

[29] A. Ramchandani, C. Fan, and A. Mostafavi (2020). DeepCOVIDNet: An interpretable deep learning model for predictive surveillance of COVID-19 using heterogeneous features and their interactions. *arXiv preprint arXiv:2008.00115*.

[30] L. Wang, A. Adiga, S. Venkatramanan, *et al.* (2020). Examining deep learning models with multiple data sources for COVID-19 forecasting. In *Proceedings of the IEEE International Conference on Big Data*.

[31] S. Deng, S. Wang, H. Rangwala *et al.* (2020). Cola-GNN: Cross-location attention based graph neural networks for long-term ILI prediction. In *Proceedings of the 29th ACM International Conference on Information & Knowledge Management*, pp. 245–254.

[32] A. Kapoor, X. Ben, L. Liu *et al.* (2020). Examining COVID-19 forecasting using spatio-temporal graph neural networks. *arXiv preprint arXiv:2007.03113*.

[33] L. Zhao, J. Chen, F. Chen *et al.* (2015). Simnest: Social media nested epidemic simulation via online semi-supervised deep learning. In *2015 IEEE International Conference on Data Mining*. IEEE, pp. 639–648.

[34] T. Hua, C. K. Reddy, L. Zhang *et al.* (2018). Social media based simulation models for understanding disease dynamics. In *Proceedings of the 27th International Joint Conference on Artificial Intelligence, IJCAI-18*. International Joint Conferences on Artificial Intelligence Organization, pp. 3797–3804.

[35] L. Wang, J. Chen, and M. Marathe (2019). DEFSI: Deep learning based epidemic forecasting with synthetic information. In *Proceedings of the AAAI Conference on Artificial Intelligence*, Vol. 33, pp. 9607–9612.

[36] R. Dandekar, C. Rackauckas, and G. Barbastathis (2020). A machine learning-aided global diagnostic and comparative tool to assess effect of quarantine control in COVID-19 spread. *Patterns*, *1*(9), 100145.

[37] J. Gao, R. Sharma, C. Qian *et al.* (2021). STAN: Spatio-temporal attention network for pandemic prediction using real-world evidence. *Journal of the American Medical Informatics Association*, *28*(4), 733–743.

[38] E. L. Ray, L. C. Brooks, J. Bien *et al.* (2021). Challenges in training ensemble to forecast COVID-19 cases and deaths in the United States. *International Institute of Forecasters*. https://forecasters.org/blog/2021/04/09/chall enges-in-training-ensembles-to-forecast-covid-19-cases-and-deaths-in-the-united-states/ (accessed 21 November 2022).

[39] K. Shea, M. C. Runge, D. Pannell *et al.* (2020). Harnessing multiple models for outbreak management. *Science*, *368*(6491), 577–579.

[40] N. G. Reich, L. C. Brooks, S. J. Fox *et al.* (2019). A collaborative multiyear, multimodel assessment of seasonal Influenza forecasting in the United States. *Proceedings of the National Academy of Sciences*, *116*(8), 3146–3154.

[41] T. K. Yamana, S. Kandula, and J. Shaman (2017). Individual versus superensemble forecasts of seasonal Influenza outbreaks in the United States. *PLoS Computational Biology*, *13*(11), e1005801.

[42] A. Adiga, L. Wang, B. Hurt *et al.* (2021). All models are useful: Bayesian ensembling for robust high resolution COVID-19 forecasting. In *KDD '21: Proceedings of the 27th ACM SIGKDD Conference on Knowledge Discovery & Data Mining*, pp. 2505–2513.

[43] T. K. Yamana, S. Kandula, and J. Shaman (2016). Superensemble forecasts of Dengue outbreaks. *Journal of The Royal Society Interface*, *13*(123), 20160410.

[44] A. Karpatne, G. Atluri, J. H. Faghmous *et al.* (2017). Theory-guided data science: A new paradigm for scientific discovery from data. *IEEE Transactions on Knowledge and Data Engineering*, *29*(10), 2318–2331.

[45] Y. Wu, Y. Yang, H. Nishiura *et al.* (2018). Deep learning for epidemiological predictions. In *The 41st International ACM SIGIR Conference on Research & Development in Information Retrieval*. ACM, pp. 1085–1088.

[46] L. Wang, A. Adiga, J. Chen *et al.* (2022). CausalGNN: Causal-based graph neural networks for spatio-temporal epidemic forecasting. In *Proceedings of the 36th AAAI Conference in Artificial Intelligence (to appear)*. AAAI Press.

[47] E. Dong, H. Du, and L. Gardner (2020). An interactive web-based dashboard to track COVID-19 in real time. *The Lancet Infectious Diseases*, *20*(5), 533–534.

[48] Center for Disease Control and Prevention, CDC covid data tracker (2022). https://covid.cdc.gov/covid-data-tracker (accessed 8 March 2022).

[49] Institute for Health Metrics and Evaluation, COVID-19 projections. (2022). https://covid19.healthdata.org/ (accessed 8 March 2022).

[50] S. Chang, M. L. Wilson, B. Lewis *et al.* Supporting COVID-19 policy response with large-scale mobility-based modeling. In *Proceedings of the 27th ACM SIGKDD Conference on Knowledge Discovery & Data Mining*, pp. 2632–2642. doi: 10.1145/3447548.3467182.

[51] Virginia Department of Health, Covidwise app — Save lives, download covidwise. (2022). https://www.vdh.virginia.gov/covidwise/ (accessed 9 March 2022).

[52] P. Bhattacharya, D. Machi, J. Chen *et al.* (2021). AI-driven agent-based models to study the role of vaccine acceptance in controlling COVID-19 spread in the us. In *2021 IEEE International Conference on Big Data (Big Data)*, pp. 1566–1574.

[53] S. Hoops, J. Chen, A. Adiga *et al.* (2021). High performance agent-based modeling to study realistic contact tracing protocols. In *2021 Winter Simulation Conference (WSC)*, pp. 1–12.

[54] Z. Mehrab, M. L. Wilson, and S. Chang (2021). Data-driven real-time strategic placement of mobile vaccine distribution sites. *medRxiv*.

[55] Biocomplexity Institute at University of Virginia. (2022). COVID-19 surveillance dashboard. https://nssac.bii.virginia.edu/covid-19/dashboard/ (accessed 8 March 2022).

[56] A. S. Peddireddy, D. Xie, P. Patil *et al.* (2020). From 5vs to 6cs: Operationalizing epidemic data management with COVID-19 surveillance. *MedRxiv : the preprint server for health sciences*, https://doi.org/10.1101/2020.10.27.20220830.

[57] I. A. Scott and E. W. Coiera (2020). Can AI help in the fight against COVID-19? *Medical Journal of Australia*, *213*(10), 439–441.

[58] A. I. Bento, T. Nguyen, C. Wing *et al.* (2020). Evidence from Internet search data shows information-seeking responses to news of local COVID-19 cases. *Proceedings of the National Academy of Sciences*, *117*(21), 11220–11222.

[59] A. Akinbi, M. Forshaw, and V. Blinkhorn (2021). Contact tracing apps for the COVID-19 pandemic: A systematic literature review of challenges and future directions for neo-liberal societies. *Health Information Science and Systems*, *9*(1), 1–15.

[60] V. Colizza, E. Grill, R. Mikolajczyk *et al.* (2021). Time to evaluate COVID-19 contact-tracing apps. *Nature Medicine*, *27*(3), 361–362.

[61] G. Arora, J. Joshi, R. S. Mandal *et al.* (2021). Artificial Intelligence in surveillance, diagnosis, drug discovery and vaccine development against COVID-19. *Pathogens*, *10*(8), 1048.

[62] Y. Zhou, F. Wang, J. Tang *et al.* (2020). Artificial Intelligence in COVID-19 drug repurposing. *The Lancet Digital Health*, *2*(12), e667–e676.

[63] R. Capobianco, V. Kompella, J. Ault *et al.* (2021). Agent-based Markov modeling for improved COVID-19 mitigation policies. *Journal of Artificial Intelligence Research*, *71*, 953–992.

[64] T. T. Nguyen, Q. V. H. Nguyen, D. T. Nguyen *et al.* (2020). Artificial Intelligence in the battle against coronavirus (COVID-19): A survey and future research directions. *arXiv preprint arXiv:2008.07343*.

Life Sciences

© 2023 World Scientific Publishing Company
https://doi.org/10.1142/9789811265679_0021

Chapter 21

Big AI: Blending Big Data with Big Theory to Build Virtual Humans

Peter Coveney*,†,‡ and Roger Highfield¶,§

*Centre for Computational Science, Department of Chemistry and
Advanced Research Computing Centre, University College London,
London, UK
†Institute for Informatics, Faculty of Science, University of Amsterdam,
The Netherlands
¶Science Museum, Exhibition Road, London, UK
‡p.v.coveney@ucl.ac.uk
§roger.highfield@sciencemuseum.ac.uk

1. Introduction

Computational scientists hope one day to forecast the health of an individual patient from mathematical models of the body primed with that person's data, just as current weather forecasting relies on a supercomputer running a mathematical model updated with data from meteorological stations, satellites, and an array of other instruments. The data and models that reproduce fundamental aspects of living processes are already being woven together by teams around the world to simulate cells, tissues, and organs on high-performance computers. One day, the hope is that "virtual humans" based on these functional models will deliver a new generation of healthcare (Figure 1) [1,2].

AI will play an important role in this effort to create digital twins of the human body to deliver a new generation of truly personalized and predictive medicine. AI, notably machine learning, ML, is already being successfully used in medicine in a variety of contexts. When it comes to virtual human research, the most mature application can be found in computer-aided drug discovery, where virtual screening of libraries of millions of candidate drugs is routinely performed. A full account of the state of the art in this domain can be found in our forthcoming book [4].

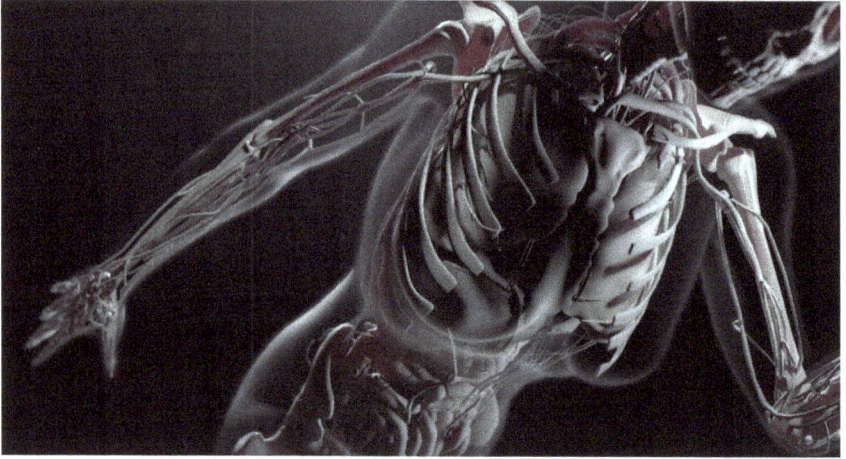

Fig. 1.   A virtual human. Barcelona Supercomputing Centre/CompBioMed [3].

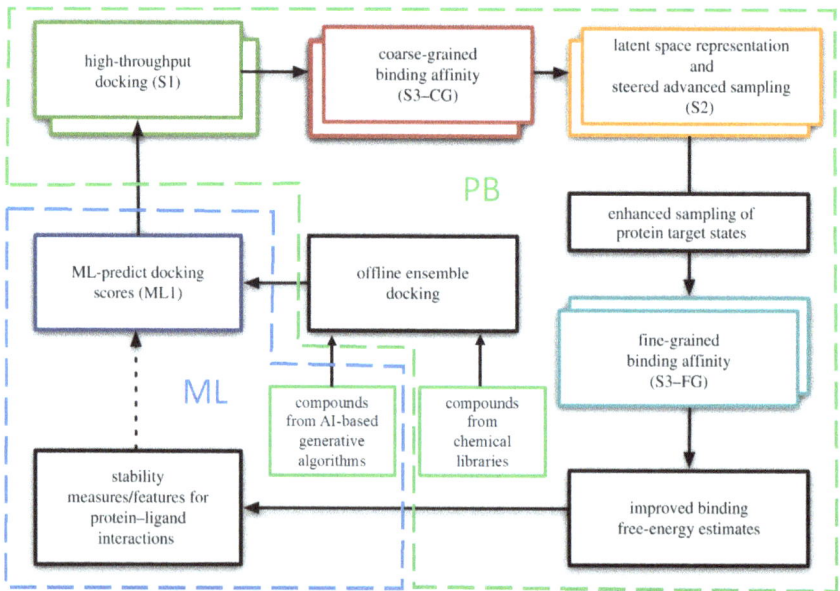

Fig. 2.   The pipeline for Big AI virtual drug development. The pipeline combines ML (blue dashes) and PB (green dashes) into a unified workflow, allowing both upstream and downstream exchange of information in the iterative loop [42].

However, there are plainly limits to what ML can do. For understandable reasons, the applications where ML disappoints or fails do not attract the same interest and publicity as the successes. In this chapter, we argue that ML is necessary but not sufficient to advance medicine. However, we do believe that a blend of AI and mechanistic understanding — what we call "Big AI" — is more powerful, where AI hypotheses can be tested in physics-based (PB) simulations, and the results of physics-based methods can be used to train AI. By setting up an iterative cycle this way, the impact of AI could be transformed, not least in healthcare applications, such as the virtual human project. This idea has gained traction in recent years and in diverse fields, such as earth systems, climate science, turbulence modeling, quantum chemistry, materials science, and hydrology [5].

While iterations between physics-based and machine learning offer one kind of Big AI, another kind can be found in the guise of what is called a "physics-informed neural network", or PINN, a deep learning algorithm developed by George Karniadakis and colleagues which is both trained and must satisfy a set of underlying physical constraints, such as the laws of motion, symmetry, energy conservation, and thermodynamics. PINNs can answer questions when very little data are available and infer unknown parameters [6]. In short, a PINN uses theory to fill gaps in data and understanding, an approach that has been used in fluid dynamics and to improve COVID-19 prediction models, for example, [7].

2. Traditional, "Narrow", AI

While in practice we gather relatively little patient data, in theory, a bewildering variety is now available to inform doctors, from scans of the heart and other organs to whole-body imaging and the reading of various -omes, whether detailed DNA sequences — the genome — and associated transcriptomics — the transcriptome — or features of metabolism — the metabolome — or indeed the entire complement of proteins — the proteome. Many efforts have long been underway to correlate these data and, one hopes, make sense of them. Because genomes do not tell the whole story, genomics pioneer Craig Venter combined DNA analyses with whole-body MRI scan, metabolomics screening, heart monitoring, pedigree analysis, microbiome sequencing, and other laboratory tests in one precision medicine initiative to proactively screen for disease risk [8]. In another initiative, Leroy Hood of the Institute for System Biology, Seattle, gathered a plethora of data from patients for five years to create what he calls "personal health clouds". Analysis of these clouds reveals signals of what he calls "pre-pre-disease" that doctors could use to anticipate problems and then intervene to maintain health. Hood envisages a "P4" future, where treatments can be predictive, preventive, personalized, and participatory [9].

A great deal of hope and expectation is placed on what artificial intelligence can deliver when unleashed on big data in healthcare. As a subfield of AI, Deep Learning (DL) has one key difference from machine learning — the manner the representations of data being learnt. Unlike the hand-crafted representations in ML, they are learnt automatically as part of the learning process in DL. Deep learning refers to the use of artificial neural networks which have many more than the minimum of three layers, along with many more parameters to tune. The outcome is, as expected, an improved ability to match training data but, as we will see, there are significant drawbacks.

Examples of the rise of ML in medicine abound. Combined with advanced imaging, ML offers a way to aid diagnosis. Early efforts to use computer-aided detection of breast cancer showed no extra benefit [10]. By 2020, however, there was a glimpse that AI could outperform radiologists [11]. AI has been leveraged to improve the detection of cervical precancer [12]. AI has also been used to find treatments for children with brain cancer [13].

Recently, DeepMind's AlphaFold made important progress in protein structure prediction [14] and holds out the prospect of making reliable predictions of many 3D protein structures which have not been solved experimentally — offering a dramatic acceleration in the rate at which such structures can be assessed and integrated into many research projects, notably drug discovery. This represents a remarkable advance, though it is important to point out that these structures are static "snapshots", limited in the sense that they are primarily derived from x-ray crystallography, rather than those derived from nuclear magnetic resonance spectroscopy conducted on samples at normal body temperature. Many proteins co-exist in multiple conformational states *in vivo* but the methodology currently cannot accommodate these differences. The advance, spectacular though it undoubtedly is, essentially offers a lookup table for 3D protein crystal structures in given conformations in a kind of take-it-or-leave manner. While it will certainly accelerate much work in molecular biology, the advance does little to assist ongoing research to unlock the science — the essential biology, chemistry, and physics — of *how and why* proteins fold into these structures.

But amid all the hyperbole accompanying successful applications, we should not forget the many examples when machine learning has failed to deliver. As one example, though there are signs of promise in using AI to aid the diagnosis of COVID-19 [15], a survey of more than 300 machine learning models described in scientific papers in 2020 concluded that none of them were suitable for detecting or diagnosing COVID-19 from standard medical imaging, due to biases, methodological flaws, lack of reproducibility, and "Frankenstein datasets" [16]. We will return to the reasons why ML fails, from the assumptions sometimes used to the old saw that correlation does not mean causation.

Despite these caveats, narrow AI already shows huge promise when it comes to accelerating research. In the case of the COVID-19 pandemic, as perhaps the most topical example of many, AI could be used in many ways: for tracking the spread of the virus, which should help governments and public health officials to coordinate a rapid response, to accelerate drug discovery and vaccine design [17], and to propose drug combinations for the treatment of COVID-19 [18]. However, though important, AI alone is not enough to accelerate progress in these applications.

3. How Far Can We Go with AI?

Confidence in AI is rising. There are those who believe that, thanks to AI, we no longer need to simulate the molecular dynamics of interactions between potential drugs and targets in the body and that AI can simply "learn" how to find new pharmaceuticals. This has been reflected in the agenda of companies, such as Benevolent AI, Exscientia, Valence Discovery, and Phenomic, and partnerships, such as AION Labs, which aims to adopt AI and computational discoveries to accelerate drug discovery and was formed from the alliance of four pharmaceutical companies, AstraZeneca, Merck KGaA, Pfizer, and Teva Pharmaceutical Industries — and a hi-tech and biotech investment firm — Amazon Web Services and the Israel Biotech Fund. Exscientia and Evotec claimed that EXS21546, an A2a receptor antagonist for adults with advanced solid tumors, marked the first AI-designed molecule for immuno-oncology to enter human clinical trials and was discovered in just eight months [19].

ML is indeed very effective at predicting docking scores, which assess how well a potential drug fits a target protein, and can now do this by a form of surrogate learning that is much faster than docking itself [20]. But linking docking scores with binding affinities, that is the ability of the drug to adhere to the active site, has not proved easy to do: there is no simple correlation established between the scoring function and binding affinities. Physics-based simulations must be employed here to obtain sufficient ensembles of conformations for accurate binding affinity prediction.

In general, the physical data in real-world applications are insufficient for the training of machine learning when it comes to chaotic systems: the size of the dataset required grows exponentially with the number of variables in play. ML methods will always be limited by their training data and, when it comes to complex real-world environments, obtaining data that are big enough to reliably train an ML will always be an issue. This means that "smart" methods of handling data reduction that still reliably cover the parameter space will be essential.

Despite these shortcomings, some go even further when it comes to the potential of ML. They believe we do no longer need theoretical understanding or underpinning at all. One popular commentator even predicted the rise of machine learning methods would herald the end of theory and the scientific method [21]. This would mark a profound change in the way science is done, from today's blend of empiricism and reason to a "pre-Baconian" variety that relies on data alone [22,23]. We do not agree with this view, not least because of the pervasive influence of theory, which is used to curate and guide the way that data are gathered. However, the motivation for adopting this view is understandable: biomedical and life sciences do not submit easily to mathematical treatment because they deal with such complex systems.

It is precisely because we live in the era of "Small Theory" in biomedicine that current Big Data approaches are so seductive: they offer an alternative that produces "results" quickly. The problem with this, of course, is that science is not purely empirical: while machine learning offers the equivalent of a lookup table based on its training, the scientific method is a synthesis of data and *understanding* and this can be seen most vividly in simulations, where computers can blend theory and data to make predictions.

4. The Problem with Traditional AI

Though AI can be powerful, reliance on big data and machine learning alone can be problematic. As mentioned earlier, overfitting is one possible shortcoming, where ML is highly reliable when confronted with its training data but can be confounded by novel datasets [24]. The ratio of false to true correlations soars with the size of the dataset. Indeed, there can be too much data to produce correlations to any degree of confidence.

When using machine learning, assumptions are baked into the underlying learning algorithms which frequently do not apply to complex systems — they assume the smoothness of the curves that join data points, that data distributions follow Gaussian statistics, and so on. But nonlinear systems frequently display discontinuities and, because they can be correlated over considerable distances in space and time, are often non-Gaussian [25]. And there is perhaps the best known and most infamous fallacy of all, that the correlations identified by these learning systems imply causal connections. Without deeper theoretical understanding to curate and limit them, AI methods are simply "black boxes" that reveal little about their inherent limitations, inbuilt assumptions, and intrinsic biases.

No wonder, then, that bodies such as the EU and UN are concerned about overreliance on AI. The latter has called for a moratorium [26]. The former has published a draft law to regulate artificial intelligence [27]. The EU Artificial Intelligence Act (AIA) is notable for its expansive definition of AI systems, and the imposition of extensive documentation, training, and monitoring requirements on AI tools that fall under its purview. Any company with EU market exposure that develops or wants to adopt machine-learning-based software will be affected by this development.

The need for reliable, reproducible, and understandable forecasts will be paramount when virtual humans are used to make predictions about how a patient will respond to a treatment, how a virtual population will respond to a deadly disease, or indeed any forecast which could lead to a drastic change in the way we live [28]. We need to be more confident than ever that we can trust computers — and the people who program and train them — because, as efforts to model the COVID-19 pandemic have shown, that future is already upon us.

To make progress in this era of Big Data, the answer is to get the best of both worlds by combining AI with physics-based (PB) modeling in what we call "Big AI". Though crude, one can already see this approach being successfully used in one of the more mature aspects of virtual human research: customizing drugs to suit a given patient.

5. The Rise of Big AI

Big AI marks an important extension of conventional AI in drug discovery. The use of AI — for the prediction of binding affinities using, say, a deep neural network — has already been an active research area. In fluid dynamics, for example, the so-called hybrid modeling — combining physics-based and data-driven modeling — has shown advantages over using pure physics-based or machine learning models [29].

In the area of drug design, the approach has been used, for instance, in predicting antimicrobial resistance [30], classifying kinase conformations [31], modeling quantitative structure-activity relationships [32], and predicting contact maps in protein folding [33]. One study of free energy calculations using a hybrid ML/MM (molecular mechanics) model claimed chemical accuracy in modeling protein-ligand binding affinities [34]. There has been important progress but, of course, we remain some way from developing personalized treatments this way.

Drug discovery is in urgent need of fresh thinking, however. The COVID-19 pandemic, where vaccine development outpaced the effort to develop novel antivirals, is the latest reminder that current methods of drug design are cumbersome, taking about 10 years and $1–3 billion to develop a single marketable drug molecule [35]. The huge investment of time and expense required to develop novel pharmaceuticals encourages conservatism and, by the same token, discourages innovation. To allow pharma to become more creative, the process has to become more efficient and quicker. Because of the vast number of potential ligands (ranging from a few hundred million to billions), it is clearly not possible to synthesize them in wet laboratories nor is it desirable given, when it comes to COVID-19, that most of them are not going to bind with SARS-CoV-2 proteins at all. This is where AI can play an important role.

ML methods are today invariably waiting in the wings to replace slower and more compute-intensive HPC-based simulations with ML-based predictions. For example, molecular dynamics, or MD, is a popular approach for the simulation of protein–drug combinations including conformational sampling which is derived from Newtonian equations of motion and the concepts of statistical thermodynamics. MD-based free energy calculation methods have been widely applied for predicting protein–ligand binding affinities and are subject to extensive experimental validation [36–41]. There are many such free energy methods, some "approximate", others more "accurate".

Big AI can be seen in the use of active learning, which incorporates common machine learning, wet-lab experimentation, and human feedback iteratively to improve its predictions (Figure 2). Here, one can glimpse an element of Big AI, which we believe will be key to its future success: physics-based modeling and its study through computer simulation. Using this approach, the hypotheses generated from the ML component may be used to plan and execute physics-based simulations and wet-lab experiments, and the data collected from the simulations and experiments are used to further train the ML model.

For a drug discovery project, the active learning can iteratively update the model by defining and screening the most interesting chemical space and then guide subsequent experiments to verify the hypotheses. Recent developments in ML allow the generation of novel drug-like molecules *in silico*. These methods use "generative" AI. The so-called generative adversarial networks, or GANs, which consist of one network to create drug-like molecules and a "critic" network to check their promise. These two neural networks fight each other — hence adversarial — in the sense that one attempts to con the other into thinking its creations are genuinely part of the dataset of which the other is a custodian. Over time, GANs allow AI to produce increasingly "convincing" drug molecules. This kind of approach allows us to sample a more sizeable fraction of the chemical space of relevance (estimated to be about 10^{68} compounds) than has been the case hitherto. However, the reliability of such methods is very much dependent on providing GANs with the right data.

6. Coping with Chaos

There is, however, a deeper issue to negotiate in drug design. Ever since the 1960s, when Edward Lorenz discovered that tiny rounding errors can lead to chaotic fluctuations (the "butterfly effect"), we have known that care must be taken with systems that have strong sensitivity to rounding or inaccuracies. Based on simulation data, some extravagant claims have been made about the potential of ML in drug design but such approaches can face particular problems, as a result of chaos, in the sensitivity of these simulations to training data. Here, even PINNS runs into difficulty.

When it comes to physics-based modeling, however, there is a way to cope with chaos [38]. In the last decade or so, ensemble simulation-based methods have been proposed — and successfully used in fields such as weather forecasting — which overcome the issue of variability in predictions from MD-based methods due to their extreme sensitivity to simulation initial conditions which also leads to non-Gaussian statistics. In particular, two methods — enhanced sampling of MD with the approximation of continuum solvent (ESMACS) [38] and thermodynamic integration with enhanced sampling (TIES) [43] — have been shown to deliver accurate, precise, and reproducible binding affinity predictions within a couple of hours.

Another important factor affecting the reliability of results is the extent of statistical sampling achieved by MD simulations. Various other so-called "enhanced sampling" methods have also been developed so as to supposedly better sample the phase space based on forms of replica exchange visited in single trajectory simulations [44]. No doubt to the surprise of many, when studied more closely in terms of their statistical robustness through the use of ensembles, such oft-touted methods may be found to cause degradations, as opposed to improvements, in their predictions [45].

Even when done carefully, these *in silico* methods are computationally demanding and are unable to explore the vast chemical space relevant for drug molecule generation. To focus on the hunt, they require human insight, but this takes time and slows the process of drug discovery by delaying the pipeline of candidate ligands to wet laboratories for testing. Even if this step is accelerated, another bottleneck in drug design looms because there is a limit to the number of compounds that can be studied experimentally.

7. Big AI in Drug Discovery

As already mentioned, the most potential to accelerate drug discovery comes from Big AI, which means curating Big Data with Big Theory. ML is constrained by theoretical understanding [22] of the kind used in physics-based methods, which involve *ab initio* as well as semi-empirical methods which are fully or partially derived from firm theoretical foundations. The strengths and weaknesses of ML and PB methods complement each other and so it makes sense to couple them in Big AI for drug discovery. In the past few years, several attempts have been made to create synergies between ML and PB methods in order to get favorable outcomes. Robust predictive mechanistic models are of particular value for constraining ML when dealing with sparse data, exploring vast design spaces to seek correlations, and, most importantly, testing if correlations are causal [28].

In recent work with a large, international team, we have presented a novel *in silico* blueprint for drug design by using PB methods in combination with ML ones to make the former "nimbler" and the latter "smarter" [20]. Potential candidates are selected from the output of an ML algorithm and they are scored using PB methods to calculate binding free energies, exactly as described in Figure 2. This information is then fed back to the ML algorithm to refine its predictions. This loop proceeds iteratively involving a variety of PB scoring methods with increasing levels of accuracies at each step ensuring that the DL algorithm gets progressively more "intelligent".

We attempt to generate ligand structures with improved binding potency towards a given target protein using an iterative loop with both upward and downward exchange of information at each step — this approach, we believe, has not been attempted before. This integration of PB- and ML-based methods can substantially improve the efficacy of the exploration of chemical libraries for lead discovery. We have used our workflow for the analyses of several million compounds from a set of orderable compound libraries and have applied it for drug repurposing to find candidates that bind to SARS-CoV-2 main protease with thus far encouraging results [46]. We obtained binding affinities agreeing well with experimental measurements and also gained detailed energetic insight into the nature of drug–protein binding that would be useful in drug discovery for the target studied. Our coauthor, Rick Stevens, has led an American team that has used a similar Big AI approach, harnessing the US super-computer infrastructure to sift 6.5 million molecules to find a compound called MCULE-5948770040, a promising inhibitor of the protease [47].

Using large-scale supercomputing infrastructure, these methods can scale to the vast number of calculations required to provide input to the ML models. Equally important, our methods are designed to provide key uncertainty quantification, a feature vital to our goal of using active learning to optimize campaigns of simulations to maximize the chance that predictive ML models will find promising drug candidates. Not only will the exploitation of AI ensure that the best use is made of medicinal chemists for drug discovery, but it also helps counter any bias from chemists during the exploration of the chemical space. By being more efficient, they will encourage a wider and deeper search for useful compounds. Carefully trained ML algorithms may be expected to reach regions of the extensive chemical space that could remain untouched — or perhaps "unthought of" — by humans.

8. Big AI in the Virtual Human

The human body is the ultimate multiscale, multiphysics system where another promising application of Big AI is found in speeding up slower simulations and improving load balancing on large supercomputers through providing "surrogate models" (sometimes called "model order reduction"). Surrogates are designed to behave like components of a complex multiscale, multiphysics system, such as a cell, organ, or the whole human body, so that such systems can be more efficiently simulated. Efficiency can be improved by replacing compute-intensive fine-grained models with a much less compute-intensive machine-learned surrogate model. Given the uncertainties in these complex simulations, the use of surrogates is gaining traction.

Here, aspects of the full physics of a highly detailed multiscale model can be replaced with machine-learned behaviors that act in the same way so that complex partial differential equations do not have to be solved regularly. As one example of this approach, used to understand liquid water and ice at the atomic and molecular level, ML first learns quantum mechanical interactions between atoms so that it can make speedy predictions about the energy and forces for a system of atoms, bypassing the need to perform computationally expensive quantum mechanical calculations [48]. A key ingredient of success is to use Big AI and ensure ML is constrained by real physics — such as the law of conservation of energy — to ensure that it does not produce implausible answers when it hits a situation that is sufficiently different from its training dataset. These surrogate models are only as good as the data used to train them and the theory used to constrain them.

Physics-based models can be replaced with pure ML only in cases where enough data can be or have been collected to train the algorithms or in cases where there are clear and simple rules and a well-defined final goal (like DeepMind's AlphaGo, which can learn from training games played against itself to continually improve; its training does not depend on records of games by human players). In most cases, however, AI/ML exploits data brought together from multiple sources, including data collected in real world and generated from physics-based computer simulation.

ML-driven, physics-based simulations have enabled one team to understand how potentially correlated conditions may affect a particular patient with a coarctation of the aorta, a birth defect in which a part of the aorta is narrower than usual. Capturing all possible combinations of factors with simulations is intractable without the help of ML. They validated blood flow simulations against *in vitro* measurements in 3D-printed phantoms representing the patient's vasculature and then used simulations to develop a framework to identify the minimal training set required to build a predictive model on a per-patient basis, to improve treatments of congenital heart disease [49].

This is analogous to the use of ML for nowcasting, in well-understood circumstances. Google's deep learning models can predict short-term weather, nowcasting, better and faster than traditional simulations. The ML models use 2D radar images, in which the geography may not be taken into account sufficiently. This means that longer timescale predictions will be less accurate as the effects of the geography become more important. For example, the models trained using USA data cannot be used directly in the UK. In contrast with such an ML approach, a PB model can use 3D data in which the geography is built into the parameters used in the model.

While we have focused on the use of Big AI for the more fine-grained, molecular, aspects of the virtual human project, machine learning is also making an impact at higher levels. Just as multiscale modeling seeks understanding in an ocean of experimental data, so machine learning will provide invaluable tools to preprocess these data, help understand poorly framed problems, aid the construction of models, and analyze all the data to arise from multiscale modeling of the human body, for instance, to understand the emergence of function and distinguish correlation from causation [47].

To move from atomic structures to proteins, tissues, and heartbeats, manifested as gradients of electrical activity in simulated tissue, high-performance computers were enlisted by Colleen Clancy and Igor Vorobyov at the University of California, Davis, and colleagues to make a direct comparison between the electrocardiograms of the simulated tissue and electrocardiograms from patients that have taken various drugs. They studied the human Ether-à-go-go-Related Gene (hERG) potassium channel and were able to simulate how the drugs diffuse across membranes, interact with hERG, and explored emergent properties in a fiber of 165 virtual heart cells, 5 cm by 5 cm of virtual ventricular tissue and an *in silico* wedge of left ventricular tissue. With multiscale computer simulation data, aided by machine learning, they were able to work out necessary and sufficient parameters that predict vulnerability to arrhythmia and, with enough high-performance computing, they used this multiscale model to distinguish drugs that prolong the QT interval, such as dofetilide, from those that are harmless, such as moxifloxacin [50].

Machine learning has also contributed to the Virtual Brain, an open-source simulation platform that blends experimental brain data from a wide range of sources to improve the understanding of the brain's underlying mechanisms. The virtual brain models are capable of simulating human brain imaging that is routinely carried out in hospitals, such as EEG, MEG, SEEG, and fMRI. One example of how the virtual brain can be used is in dealing with epilepsy, notably in those cases where seizures cannot be controlled by drugs and the only option is for surgeons to remove the epileptogenic zone. To help clinicians plan this difficult surgery, the virtual brain team creates personalized brain models of patients and simulates the spread of abnormal activity during seizures [51].

9. The Future of Big AI

Big AI represents a milestone that lies somewhere between the current generation of AI, which has superhuman abilities for very narrow applications, and a future of general artificial intelligence, when an AI agent is able to understand or learn any intellectual task that a human being can.

To enter the era of Big AI, we need theory to be as pervasive in biology and medicine as in physics. This will not be straightforward. The prevailing view is that the complexities of life do not easily yield to theoretical models. Clinicians are understandably daunted by the prospect of trying to deliver truly actionable predictions in medicine and translating innovations from the laboratory to the clinic. Some biologists regard the use of mathematical theory as irrelevant to their field [52]. Leading biological and medical journals publish little theory-led, let alone purely theoretical, work. Research that lies at the interface between experiment and theory can "fall between the cracks". As a result of the well-established phenomenon of confirmation bias [53], peer review in journals that specialize in biology and medicine tends to maintain the status quo — and that means the current emphasis on observations and experiments. Too few biology or bioinformatics students are trained to understand the theory of dynamical systems needed to describe biological processes. Many biologists and clinicians remain content with *post hoc* rationalizations and "predictions" based on how cohorts of similar patients have behaved in the past.

As we have shown with a diverse range of examples, from PINNs to predictions that harness physics as well as machine learning, more attention

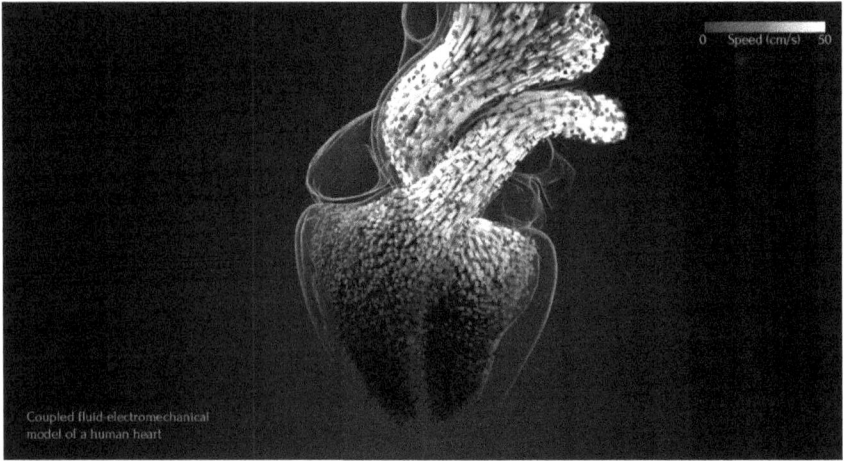

Fig. 3.   Virtual heart. Barcelona Supercomputing Centre/CompBioMed.[3]

needs to be given to theory in biology if Big AI is to succeed. We are not alone in thinking that theory is necessary to make sense of the deluge of data in the biosciences [54] and enable us to "see the wood for the trees". More funding that is dedicated to gathering and processing data should be diverted towards efforts to discern the laws of biology. AI needs to be better integrated into the scientific endeavor. When it comes to the remarkable potential of the virtual human and digital twins, the fields of Big Data and AI are important but their potential to transform healthcare will be diminished without melding AI and theory together in Big AI.

When the era of Big AI is upon us, we expect it to have an impact far beyond the virtual human, where it will help build more precise models of cells, organs (such as the heart shown in Figure 3), and organ systems and, through surrogates constrained by physics, accelerate the development of drugs, surgery, and treatments. AI, curated by theory, will have huge implications across science and mark an important advance towards the goal of general artificial intelligence.

Acknowledgment

We are grateful to Dr Shunzhou Wan for his assistance in editing the later stages of this chapter.

References

[1] P. Hunter, T. Chapman, P. V. Coveney *et al.* (2013). A vision and strategy for the virtual physiological human: 2012 update. *Interface Focus, 3*, 20130004.

[2] J. W. S. McCullough and P. V. Coveney (2021). High fidelity blood flow in a patient-specific arteriovenous fistula. *Scientific Reports, 11*, 22301.

[3] The virtual human project — YouTube. https://www.youtube.com/watch?v=1ZrAaDsfBYY.

[4] P. V. Coveney and R. R. Highfield (2023). *Virtual You: How Building Your Digital Twin will Revolutionize Medicine and Change Your Life.* Princeton: Princeton University Press.

[5] J. Willard, X. Jia, S. Xu *et al.* (2022). Integrating scientific knowledge with machine learning for engineering and environmental systems. *ACM Computing Surveys, 55*(4), 1–37. https://doi.org/10.1145/3514228.

[6] M. Raissi, P. Perdikaris, and G. E. Karniadakis *et al.* (2019). Physics-informed neural networks: A deep learning framework for solving forward and inverse problems involving nonlinear partial differential equations. *Journal of Computational Physics, 378*, 686–707.

[7] E. Kharazmi, M. Cai, X. Zheng *et al.* (2021). Identifiability and predictability of integer- and fractional-order epidemiological models using physics-informed neural networks. *Nature Computational Science, 1*, 744–753.

[8] B. A. Perkins, C. Thomas Caskey, P. Brar *et al.* (2018). Precision medicine screening using whole-genome sequencing and advanced imaging to identify disease risk in adults. *Proceedings of the National Academy of Sciences of the United States of America, 115*, 3686–3691.

[9] L. Hood (2013). Systems biology and p4 medicine: Past, present, and future. *Rambam Maimonides Medical Journal, 4*, e0012–e0012.

[10] C. D. Lehman, R. D. Wellman, D. S. M. Buist *et al.* (2015). Diagnostic accuracy of digital screening mammography with and without computer-aided detection. *JAMA Internal Medicine, 175*, 1828–1837.

[11] S. M. McKinney, M. Sieniek, V. Godbole *et al.* (2020). International evaluation of an AI system for breast cancer screening. *Nature, 577*, 89–94.

[12] L. Hu, D. Bell, S. Antani *et al.* (2019). An observational study of deep learning and automated evaluation of cervical images for cancer screening. *Journal of the National Cancer Institute, 111*, 923–932.

[13] D. M. Carvalho, P. J. Richardson, N. Olaciregui *et al.* (2022). Repurposing Vandetanib plus Everolimus for the treatment of ACVR1-mutant diffuse intrinsic pontine glioma. *Cancer Discovery, 12*, 416–431.

[14] J. Jumper, R. Evans, A. Pritzel *et al.* (2021). Highly accurate protein structure prediction with AlphaFold. *Nature, 596*, 583–589.

[15] X. Mei, H.-C. Lee, K.-Y. Diao *et al.* (2020). Artificial intelligence–enabled rapid diagnosis of patients with COVID-19. *Nature Medicine, 26*, 1224–1228.

[16] M. Roberts, D. Driggs, M. Thorpe *et al.* (2021). Common pitfalls and recommendations for using machine learning to detect and prognosticate for COVID-19 using chest radiographs and CT scans. *Nature Machine Intelligence, 3*, 199–217.

[17] H. Lv, L. Shi, J. W. Berkenpas *et al.* (2021). Application of artificial intelligence and machine learning for COVID-19 drug discovery and vaccine design. *Briefings in Bioinformatics, 22,* bbab320.

[18] W. Jin, J. M. Stokes, and R. T. Eastman (2021). Deep learning identifies synergistic drug combinations for treating COVID-19. *Proceedings of the National Academy of Sciences of the United States of America, 118,* e2105070118.

[19] A. Payne, P. Fons, I. Alt *et al.* (2021). EXS21546, a non-CNS penetrant A 2A R-selective antagonist for anti-cancer immunotherapy. *American Association for Cancer Research (AACR) Annual Meeting.*

[20] A. P. Bhati, S. Wan, D. Alf *et al.* (2021). Pandemic drugs at pandemic speed: Infrastructure for accelerating COVID-19 drug discovery with hybrid machine learning- and physics-based simulations on high-performance computers. *Interface Focus, 11,* 20210018.

[21] C. Anderson (2008). The end of theory: The data deluge makes the scientific method obsolete. *Wired Magazine, 16,* 1–2.

[22] P. V. Coveney, E. R. Dougherty, and R. R. Highfield (2016). Big data need big theory too. *Philosophical Transactions of the Royal Society, 374,* 20160153.

[23] S. Succi and P. V. Coveney (2019). Big data: The end of the scientific method? *Philosophical Transactions of the Royal Society, 377,* 20180145.

[24] D. M. Hawkins (2004). The problem of overfitting. *Journal of Chemical Information and Computer Sciences, 44,* 1–12.

[25] S. Wan, A. P. Bhati, S. J. Zasada *et al.* (2020). Rapid, accurate, precise and reproducible molecule-protein binding free energy prediction. *Interface Focus, 10,* 20200007.

[26] United Nations (2021). Urgent action needed over artificial intelligence risks to human rights. *UN News.* https://news.un.org/en/story/2021/09/1099972.

[27] Regulation of the European Parliament and of the Council — Laying down harmonised rules on Artificial Intelligence (Artificial Intelligence Act) and amending certain union legislative acts (2021). *EUR-Lex.* https://eur-lex.europa.eu/legal-content/EN/TXT/?qid=1623335154975&uri=CELEX%3A52021PC0206.

[28] P. V. Coveney and R. R. Highfield (2021). When we can trust computers (and when we can't). *Philosophical Transactions of the Royal Society A: Mathematical, Physical and Engineering Sciences, 379,* 20200067.

[29] O. Erge and E. van Oort (2022). Combining physics-based and data-driven modeling in well construction: Hybrid fluid dynamics modeling. *Journal of Natural Gas Science and Engineering, 97,* 104348.

[30] J. J. Davis, S. Boisvert, T. Brettin *et al.* (2016). Antimicrobial resistance prediction in PATRIC and RAST. *Scientific Reports, 6,* 27930.

[31] D. I. McSkimming, K. Rasheed, and N. Kannan (2017). Classifying kinase conformations using a machine learning approach. *BMC Bioinformatics, 18,* 86.

[32] J. Gomes, B. Ramsundar, E. N. Feinberg *et al.* (2017). Atomic convolutional networks for predicting protein-ligand binding affinity. *arXiv* 1703.10603.

[33] S. Wang, S. Sun, Z. Li *et al.* (2017). Accurate de novo prediction of protein contact map by ultra-deep learning model. *PLOS Computational Biology*, *13*, e1005324.

[34] D. A. Rufa, H. E. Bruce Macdonald, J. Fass *et al.* (2020). Towards chemical accuracy for alchemical free energy calculations with hybrid physics-based machine learning/molecular mechanics potentials. *bioRxiv*. doi: 10.1101/2020.07.29.227959.

[35] T. A. Sullivan (2019). Tough road: Cost to develop one new drug is \$2.6 billion; Approval rate for drugs entering clinical development is less than 12%. *Policy and Medicine*. https://www.policymed.com/2014/12/a-tough-road-cost-to-develop-one-new-drug-is-26-billion-approval-rate-for-drugs-entering-clinical-de.html.

[36] G. Fox, J. Qiu, D. Crandall *et al.* (2019). Contributions to high-performance Big Data computing. *Advanced Parallel Computing*, *34*, 34–81.

[37] S. Genheden and U. Ryde (2010). How to obtain statistically converged MM/GBSA results. *Journal of Computational Chemistry*, *31*, 837–846.

[38] S. Wan, A. P. Bhati, S. J. Zasada *et al.* (2017). Rapid and reliable binding affinity prediction for analysis of bromodomain inhibitors: A computational study. *Journal of Chemical Theory and Computation*, *13*, 784–795.

[39] D. W. Wright, S. Wan, C. Meyer *et al.* (2019). Application of ESMACS binding free energy protocols to diverse datasets: Bromodomain-containing protein 4. *Scientific Reports*, *9*, 6017.

[40] P. W. Fowler, K. Cole, N. Claire Gordon *et al.* (2018). Robust prediction of resistance to Trimethoprim in Staphylococcus aureus. *Cell Chemical Biology*, *25*, 339–349.e4.

[41] S. Wan, G. Tresadern, L. Pérez-Benito *et al.* (2020). Accuracy and precision of alchemical relative free energy predictions with and without replica-exchange. *Advanced Theory and Simulations*, *3*, 1900195.

[42] A. A. Saadi, D. Alfe, Y. Babuji *et al.* (2021). IMPECCABLE: Integrated Modeling PipelinE for COVID Cure by Assessing Better LEads. *ACM International Conference Proceeding Series* (Association for Computing Machinery).

[43] A. P. Bhati, S. Wan, and P. V. Coveney (2019). Ensemble-based replica exchange alchemical free energy methods: The effect of protein mutations on inhibitor binding. *Journal of Chemical Theory and Computation*, *15*, 1265–1277.

[44] Y. I. Yang, Q. Shao, J. Zhang *et al.* (2019). Enhanced sampling in molecular dynamics. *The Journal of Chemical Physics*, *151*, 70902.

[45] A. P. Bhati and P. V. Coveney (2022). Large scale study of ligand–protein relative binding free energy calculations: Actionable predictions from statistically robust protocols. *Journal of Chemical Theory and Computation*, *18*, 2687–2702.

[46] S. Wan, A. P. Bhati, A. D. Wade *et al.* (2022). Thermodynamic and structural insights into the repurposing of drugs that bind to SARS-CoV-2 main protease. *Molecular Systems Design and Engineering*, *7*, 123–131.

[47] M. Alber, A. B. Tepole, W. R. Cannon *et al.* (2019). Integrating machine learning and multiscale modeling — Perspectives, challenges, and opportunities in the biological, biomedical, and behavioral sciences. *NPJ Digital Medicine*, *2*, 1–11.

[48] B. Cheng, E. A. Engel, J. Behler *et al.* (2019). Ab initio thermodynamics of liquid and solid water. *Proceedings of the National Academy of Sciences of the United States of America*, *116*, 1110–1115.

[49] B. Feiger, J. Gounley, D. Adler *et al.* (2020). Accelerating massively parallel hemodynamic models of coarctation of the aorta using neural networks. *Scientific Reports*, *10*, 9508.

[50] P.-C. Yang, K. R. DeMarco, P. Aghasafari *et al.* (2020). A computational pipeline to predict cardiotoxicity: From the atom to the rhythm. *Circulation Research*, *126*, 947–964.

[51] S. Olmi, S. Petkoski, M. Guye *et al.* (2019). Controlling seizure propagation in large-scale brain networks. *PLoS Computational Biology*, *15*, e1006805.

[52] P. V. Coveney and R. R. Highfield (1991). *The Arrow of Time: The Quest to Solve Science's Greatest Mystery*. W.H. Allen, London.

[53] M. J. Mahoney (1977). Publication prejudices: An experimental study of confirmatory bias in the peer review system. *Cognitive Therapy and Research*, *1*, 161–175.

[54] P. Nurse (2021). Biology must generate ideas as well as data. *Nature*, *597*, 305.

© 2023 World Scientific Publishing Company
https://doi.org/10.1142/9789811265679_0022

Chapter 22

A Roadmap for Defining Machine Learning Standards in Life Sciences

Fotis Psomopoulos[*,‖], Carole Goble[†,**],
Leyla Jael Castro[‡,††], Jennifer Harrow[§,‡‡],
and Silvio C. E. Tosatto[¶,§§]

[*]*Institute of Applied Biosciences, Centre for Research and Technology
Hellas, Thessaloniki, Greece*
[†]*Department of Computer Science, The University of Manchester, Oxford
Road, Manchester, UK*
[‡]*ZB MED Information Centre for Life Sciences, Cologne, Germany*
[§]*ELIXIR Hub, Wellcome Genome Campus, Hinxton, UK*
[¶]*Department of Biomedical Sciences, University of Padua, Padua, Italy*
[‖]*fpsom@certh.gr*
[**]*carole.goble@manchester.ac.uk*
[††]*ljgarcia@zbmed.de*
[‡‡]*harrow@ebi.ac.uk*
[§§]*silvio.tosatto@unipd.it*

1. Introduction

Machine Learning (ML) is becoming increasingly popular in Life Sciences as an efficient mechanism to extract knowledge and new insights from the vast amounts of data that are constantly generated. Phrases like *"Analysis of big data by machine learning offers considerable advantages for assimilation and evaluation of large amounts of complex health-care data"* [1] and *"Protein engineering through machine-learning-guided directed evolution enables the optimization of protein functions"* [2] are indicative of a common theme; ML is recognized as a new tool in research and innovation in Life Sciences.

Of course, this is not really an unexpected development. Data Science is now an established field in its own right, with data scientists (typically bioinformaticians in a Life Science context) being one of the most sought out professions in research and industry groups alike. Bringing with it a full cadre of systematic tools and multidisciplinary methods from Computer Science, Applied Statistics, and Information Technologies, Data Science is considered to have brought forth the "fourth paradigm" of science [3], effectively transforming the way science is performed.

In this context, ML is also becoming prevalent in disciplines that, traditionally, have not dealt consistently with Artificial Intelligence (AI) and ML. Moving beyond the process where a human being is the main orchestrator of the methods that extract meaning and knowledge from data, ML focuses on techniques that enable machines to learn how to perform this by themselves, by building models (aka learning) from the provided data. This transition is clearly evidenced in the literary explosion of corresponding articles over the past decade, from around 500 publications around ML in 2010 to approximately 14k publications in 2020, an exponential increase that doesn't show any signs of slowing down in the short term.

These publications cover the entire breadth of ML methods and techniques from traditional decision trees and clustering methods to neural networks and deep learning, and with applications across almost all Life Science domains; from clinical text mining and real-life digital health data to medical imaging and integrated multiomics analyses. Of particular note is, of course, the protein structure prediction algorithm AlphaFold [4], published in 2021 and effectively solving a long-standing challenge in structural biology.

2. Challenges

The use of ML is clearly on the rise in Life Sciences. However, ML is not a one-solution-fits-all nor a magic wand that can address any challenge in Life Sciences and beyond. In this context, the increase in ML applications for Life Sciences highlights additional key challenges that are particularly relevant in this domain and beyond the traditional ones in the field of ML (such as efficiency, interpretability, federation, etc.), notably: reproducibility, benchmarking, fairness, and standardization.

Although each of these challenges brings its own complexities, they are all integrally linked to the quest for trusted ML models — with trust being the imperative word in Life Sciences [5].

2.1. *Reproducibility*

Reproducibility is usually the first issue raised when debating computational methods — and of course, ML tasks are clearly included here [6].

The question of a reproducibility crisis in science has been at the forefront of several discussions for at least half a decade, leading to several efforts in addressing it — including quantitative assessments of the overall situation [[7], p. 500] and opinion articles [8] that attempt to better frame the issue in the first place.

As a direct outcome of this challenge, many journals today expect authors to fill in checklists that cover key methodological issues, such as the steps used in data processing and statistical analysis. These are now considered fairly straightforward procedures and part of the effort to facilitate understanding and examination by readers and allow results to be replicated. The advance of ML techniques in the wider biomedical community, despite offering new solutions in tackling the inherently complex tasks within the domain, can also introduce new barriers to reporting and reproducibility. Overcoming these barriers requires a deep understanding of the intricacies of the ML methods themselves, as their power stems from highly complex model architecture, vast numbers of parameters, and massive, high-quality training data. In this context, substantial and accurate reporting of the ML process, as the first but crucial step towards effective reproducibility, remains an open challenge.

2.2. *Benchmarking*

Moving a step further from the process of applying ML, the outcome itself — and its evaluation — is still an open issue. Setting aside activities where the method is the main goal, the vast majority of ML-related publications in Life Sciences are far more interested in the practical applications of a constructed model or the new biological insights that the model might provide.

This focus inherently raises the question: "how can you ensure that the outcome of the ML method is indeed a valid one or an improvement over existing ones?" — in other words, the question can be reformulated as either "how is the model evaluated?" or "what are the corresponding benchmarks that this new ML method has been tested against?"

Despite the apparent simplicity of these two questions, answers to them are not guaranteed to be given. It is worth noting that due to the lack of expertise and/or understanding, nearly 20% of ML publications in Life Sciences over the past 10 years do not include any evaluation at all [9] — a number that rises as high as ∼34% when no computational co-authors were present. This is a very clearly captured, and rather worrying trend, that needs immediate attention by researchers and publishers alike. Inadequate explanations of the main parts of ML methods will not only lead to distrust of the results but will also block the transfer of the suggested approaches to an applied context (such as the clinic and patient care).

2.3. Fairness

It would be remiss not to highlight another element that has been often debated in ML solutions — fair (or unbiased) models. As it stands, the problem of algorithmic bias is both well known and well studied in ML. Simply put, if the data contain biases, such as skewed representation of certain categories or missing information, the application of ML can lead to discriminatory outcomes and propagate them into society — i.e., unfair or biased ML models. But even determining what "unfairness" should mean in a given context is non-trivial: there are many competing definitions, and choosing between them often requires a deep understanding of the underlying task.

This issue is one of the most critical in Life Sciences, especially when considering applications that have a direct consequence on human health. There are already enough examples where an ML model ended up reflecting the existing biases in society (such as the racial bias in a commercial algorithm of the U.S. healthcare system in 2019 [10]), even when using data that could be potentially assessed by a human expert in order to avoid such biases in the first place. In the biomedical field, where the vast amount of molecular data makes curating them virtually impossible, having an established process that can assess the fairness of the produced model is of paramount importance. Efficient data management protocols and platforms can facilitate the overall process of identifying potential biases in the involved data, but this is only the first step in tackling this challenge.

2.4. Standardization

Standards and best practices establish a regulatory network that can facilitate trustworthy and fair AI and ML while minimizing the inherent risks. Once again, this is not a new challenge. There have been several calls-to-arms, for "setting the standards for machine learning in biology" [11], in order to address essentially the challenges that have been listed so far: reproducibility, inherent bias, and reporting.

This doesn't mean, however, that there have been no efforts so far in attempting to set out guidelines. On the contrary, there are several publications that aim to provide context-specific solutions, such as the "Ten Quick Tips for Deep Learning in Biology" [12], the "Ten quick tips for machine learning in computational biology" [13], the "Guide to Machine Learning for Biologists" [14], and the "Data management challenges for artificial intelligence in plant and agricultural research" [15] However, community support is needed alongside rhetoric and guidelines to actually facilitate their application and essentially have a meaningful impact in the field.

3. Emerging Solutions

The challenges for the appropriate and successful application of ML in Life Sciences are hopefully clear by this point. We are also in a unique position in time — as a global community of researchers and citizen scientists — to really tackle them by offering concrete solutions.

3.1. *FAIR principles for machine learning*

First and foremost, there is now a global focus to ensure the FAIRness of digital objects of Science — data, software, workflows, and, indeed, models of all kinds. The FAIR Principles (Findable, Accessible, Interoperable, and Reusable), initially proposed for data [16], are now a staple concern across both domain-specific and domain-agnostic discussions. Moving beyond data, the FAIR Principles for Research Software [17] and the FAIR workflows [18] are proposals from their respective communities under the FAIR umbrella.

This global focus on FAIR also opens the way to FAIRness in Machine Learning. There is an ongoing debate across all domains on how the FAIR Principles may be re-interpreted for ML — whether that's the process itself or the actual model/outcome [19]. FAIRness in ML could pave the road to more open and reproducible methods, facilitating trust of the outcome by the involved stakeholders.

3.2. *Emerging community-based standards*

Which also brings the discussion to the support by the wider community with regard to standards and best practices in ML. One of the most recent achievements in this field are the DOME recommendations [20] (https://dome-ml.org/), a clear set of recommendations for reporting ML approaches used in Life Sciences that were produced by the ELIXIR Machine Learning focus group. Targeting four major aspects when reporting supervised machine learning applications: data, optimization, model, and evaluation. The recommendations have been implemented as an ML reporting checklist, consisting of questions to the author and designed to assist in writing and reviewing ML-related papers.

The DOME recommendations were designed as a community-based effort, involving researchers from multiple countries and institutes. Additionally, aiming to become a widely supported standard, and setting also an example for other standards to follow, they are fully open to community feedback and further improvement, with a distinct governance structure in place to support future revisions. Importantly, DOME encapsulates only the most essential requirements for sufficient and clear ML reporting in the life sciences, as a minimal standard, making them broadly applicable and adoptable. For instance, a DOME-based checklist could be used by publishers so authors, reviewers, and readers can clearly identify key elements for a published approach using ML. Table 1 shows the DOME recommendations and corresponding information that could be verified (first two columns). The third column goes one step further by specifying the nature of the requested data, information that could be used to define a structure metadata schema.

Table 1.   An overview of the DOME recommendations, listing the main components as well as the corresponding information expected to be captured in each case.

DOME dimension	Requested information	Type of data
Data	Dataset source	Link to data repository or archive
	Split of the training dataset	Array of numbers representing percentages (training, test, validation)
	Distribution of the training dataset	Number of positive and negative examples
	Independence	Explanatory text
Optimization	Algorithm	Text (e.g., neural network and random forest)
	Data transformation	Text (e.g., global features and sliding window)
	(hyper)Parameters	Parameter name-value pairs
	Features	Number and protocol used (text)
	Fitting strategy	Explanatory text
	Regularization	Yes/No
Model	Interpretability	Yes (with examples)/No
	Output	Text (e.g., binary classification and regression)
	Performance	Execution time and CPU/GPU needed
	Software	Link to code or code metadata (if not open)
Evaluation	Evaluation method	Text (e.g., cross-validation)
	Performance measures	Measure-value pair (e.g., accuracy)
	Comparison	List of related methods
	Confidence	Interval and statistical significance
	Availability	Yes/No

Ultimately, the objective of the DOME recommendations is to increase the transparency and reproducibility of ML methods for the reader, the reviewer, the experimentalist, and the wider community. Of course, these recommendations are not exhaustive and should be viewed as a consensus-based first iteration of a continuously evolving system of community self-review.

The development of a standardized approach for reporting ML methods has major advantages in increasing the quality of publishing ML methods. First, the disparity in manuscripts of reporting key elements of the ML method can make reviewing and assessing the ML method challenging. Second, certain key statistics and metrics that may affect the validity of the publication's conclusions are sometimes not mentioned at all. Third, there are unexplored opportunities associated with meta-analyses of ML datasets. Access to large sets of data can enhance both the comparison between methods and facilitate the development of better-performing methods while reducing unnecessary repetition of data generation. In this context, the DOME recommendations are the first step towards a standardized data structure to describe the most relevant features of the ML methods being presented.

3.3. *Lightweight machine-processable representations*

Although some features of DOME are exclusive to ML models, e.g., split of training sets, some common ones are shared with other software-based approaches. Therefore, it is possible to extend or build on work already developed by the Life Sciences community around machine-processable structured descriptions of resources. Bioschemas https://bioschemas.org/ provides usage guidelines, called profiles, for using the Schema.org vocabulary [21] to embed high-level, semantically interoperable, descriptions of Life Sciences resources including datasets (Dataset profile), software (ComputationalTool profile), and workflows (ComputationalWorkflow profile).

An ML Bioschemas profile could start with some core elements, e.g., DOME-based, with the possibility of being enriched to target community-based requirements. Table 1 can be used as a starting point for such a profile which would naturally connect to other Bioschemas specifications such as Dataset (to point to the dataset source) and ComputationalTool (to point to the software with the possibility to include also information about the algorithm and data transformation methods thanks to properties such as application category and subcategory). The Schema.org HowTo type (https://schema.org/HowTo) could be used as the basis for capturing the experimental parameters.

3.4. Community building

A top-down approach to tackling challenges is the usual practice in academia; getting together a group of leading experts in a room can allow for a razor-sharp focus on solutions. However, building trust around both the application of ML methods, as well as for the models themselves, requires stepping out of the ivory tower and really engaging across all relevant stakeholders. As such, one of the emerging efforts is around building dedicated communities across both academia and industry to address common challenges.

There are already several examples of such initiatives; for example, the Confederation of Laboratories for Artificial Intelligence Research in Europe [22] (CLAIRE) is such an academic-oriented network that encompasses multiple disciplines while working with key stakeholders to find mechanisms for citizen engagement and industry and public sector collaboration, looking at AI and ML challenges in health and sustainable agriculture among others.

Another, global-scale network focused exclusively on Life Sciences is the Pistoia Alliance [23]; established with the goal to facilitate collaboration across Industrial members, the network is organizing its efforts around projects designed to overcome common obstacles to innovation and to transform R&D — whether identifying the root causes of inefficiencies, working with regulators to adopt new standards, or helping researchers implement AI effectively. One of the more relevant projects under the Pistoia Alliance umbrella, and a great example of cross-sectoral community building, is the implementation of an AI and ML community [24] that currently has a focus on developing a Best Practices Toolkit for Machine Learning Ops [25] (MLOps) in life sciences, i.e., a set of practices that aim to reliably and efficiently deploy and maintain ML pipelines.

4. Opportunities

Taking these trends and milestones into consideration, we can also attempt to provide some context for the road ahead, by looking at the upcoming opportunities. Specifically, there are some key trends at the global level that will have a distinct impact on the way we perceive and effectively apply ML in Life Sciences.

4.1. Open science and machine learning

One of the more impactful movements recently is that of "Open Science". Open science in essence refers to the transformation that science is undergoing, and it is therefore very likely that in the long term, the adjective open should not even be necessary as science will be open by default [26]. Major funding agencies worldwide, such as the European Commission, are seeking to advance open science policy from its inception in a holistic and integrated way, covering all aspects of the research cycle from scientific discovery and review to sharing knowledge, publishing, and outreach.

Open Science also has a direct impact on the application and overall utilization of ML. Any ML method requires both data and software, so making these openly available, as part of the Open Science movement, will greatly facilitate further developments in the field. However, this also implies that any barriers to accessing the protocols and software tools of the ML process itself would also need to be removed, while at the same time ensuring that the knowledge and information necessary to adequately assess them are also available and clearly indicated.

This is of particular importance in Life Sciences, as clear understanding of the underlying assumptions, biases, and parameters used in the ML process is essential towards an effective assessment of the model's validity. However, Life Sciences bring their own challenges to the Open Science movement — although data need to be open, in a biomedical context, this is not always feasible or legal when protecting patient privacy. In that sense, new approaches in applying ML to sensitive data will need to be investigated, requiring Federated Learning [27] across distributed systems while preserving privacy.

4.2. *Machine learning as an infrastructure*

Another clear opportunity that Open Science brings is the need for open science platforms. Already, there is a global effort in establishing seamless and interoperable platforms around data and facilitating deposition, curation, discovery, and analysis (to name but a few). Such data infrastructures are already beyond the conceptual/design phase and are reaching an "established" status, making data accessible to the entire scientific community — and beyond.

There are several examples of such efforts and e-infrastructures specific to Life Sciences, from the European Open Science Cloud [28] and the data services associated with the European Health Data Space [29] to the NIH Data Commons [30] and the Australian BioCommons [31]. All of these share the same overarching goal and accelerate new biomedical discoveries by providing a cloud-based platform where researchers can store, share, access, and interact with digital objects (data, software, etc.) generated from biomedical research.

As all of these infrastructures mature, a new layer will emerge: the ML services (or artificial intelligence services if we want to generalize).

In Life Sciences, such a layer will really democratize the use and application of ML across all domains, from smart and scalable agribiotechnology studies to clinical research and diagnostic services. Of course, these are all intricately tied to the existence of standards in ML that will be essential in interconnecting the different ML components and producing an outcome, a model, that is trustworthy and unbiased. Therefore, and in order to pave the road to such a future, setting up standards that have the backing of both the community as well as of the domain experts is the first, critical step.

5. Conclusions

AI and ML are rapidly growing disciplines within the life sciences industry. The AI-associated healthcare market is expected to grow rapidly and reach USD 6.6 billion by 2021 corresponding to a 40% compound annual growth rate [32]. And almost half of global life sciences professionals are either using, or are interested in using, AI in some area of their work [33].

ML has the potential for transformative impact on Life Sciences. However, for ML models to become trusted by all, community-backed standards need to be established and scientists must prioritize openness in all aspects of the process itself. For example, third parties should be able to obtain the same results as the original authors by using their published data, models, and code. By doing so, researchers can ensure the accuracy of reported results and detect biases in the models [34].

Hopefully, here we have been able to highlight some of the key challenges and potential goals that we should aim for, as a community, to achieve this level of integration between ML and Life Sciences to "maximize the potential of ML in biology".

References

[1] K. Y. Ngiam and I. W. Khor (2019). Big data and machine learning algorithms for health-care delivery. *The Lancet Oncology, 20*(5), e262–e273. doi: 10.1016/S1470-2045(19)30149-4.

[2] K. K. Yang, Z. Wu, and F. H. Arnold (2019). Machine-learning-guided directed evolution for protein engineering. *Nature Methods, 16*(8), 687–694. doi: 10.1038/s41592-019-0496-6.

[3] T. Hey, S. Tansley, K. Tolle *et al.* (2009). *The Fourth Paradigm: Data-Intensive Scientific Discovery*. Redmond, Washington: Microsoft Research.

[4] J. Jumper, R. Evans, A. Pritzel *et al.* (2021). Highly accurate protein structure prediction with AlphaFold. *Nature, 596*(7873), 583–589. doi: 10.1038/s41586-021-03819-2.

[5] S. Whalen, J. Schreiber, W. S. Noble *et al.* (2022). Navigating the pitfalls of applying machine learning in genomics. *Nat Rev Genet.* *23*, 169–181. doi: 10.1038/s41576-021-00434-9.

[6] M. Hutson (2018). Artificial intelligence faces reproducibility crisis. *Science*, *359*(6377), 725–726. doi: 10.1126/science.359.6377.725.

[7] M. Baker (2016). 1,500 scientists lift the lid on reproducibility. *Nature*, *533*(7604), 452–454. doi: 10.1038/533452a.

[8] D. Fanelli (2018). Opinion: Is science really facing a reproducibility crisis, and do we need it to? *Proceedings of the National Academy of Sciences of the United States of America*, *115*(11), 2628–2631. doi: 10.1073/pnas.1708272114.

[9] M. Littmann, K. Selig, L. Cohen-Lavi *et al.* (2020). Validity of machine learning in biology and medicine increased through collaborations across fields of expertise. *Nature Machine Intelligence*, *2*(1), 18–24. doi: 10.1038/s42256-019-0139-8.

[10] Z. Obermeyer, B. Powers, C. Vogeli *et al.* (2019). Dissecting racial bias in an algorithm used to manage the health of populations. *Science*, *366*(6464), 447–453. doi: 10.1126/science.aax2342.

[11] D. T. Jones (2019). Setting the standards for machine learning in biology. *Nature Reviews Molecular Cell Biology*, *20*(11), 659–660. doi: 10.1038/s41580-019-0176-5.

[12] B. D. Lee, A. Gitter, C. S. Greene *et al.* (2021). Ten quick tips for deep learning in biology. *arXiv:2105.14372 [cs, q-bio]* (accessed 10 January 2022). http://arxiv.org/abs/2105.14372.

[13] D. Chicco (2017). Ten quick tips for machine learning in computational biology. *BioData Mining*, *10*(1), 35. doi: 10.1186/s13040-017-0155-3.

[14] J. G. Greener, S. M. Kandathil, L. Moffat *et al.* (2022). A guide to machine learning for biologists. *Nature Reviews Molecular Cell Biology*, *23*(1), 40–55. doi: 10.1038/s41580-021-00407-0.

[15] H. F. Williamson, J. Brettschneider, M. Caccamo *et al.* (2021). Data management challenges for artificial intelligence in plant and agricultural research. *F1000Res*, *10*, 324. doi: 10.12688/f1000research.52204.1.

[16] M. D. Wilkinson, M. Dumontier, I. J. Aalbersberg *et al.* (2016). The FAIR guiding principles for scientific data management and stewardship. *Scientific Data*, *3*(1), 160018. doi: 10.1038/sdata.2016.18.

[17] FAIR Principles for Research Software (FAIR4RS Principles). doi: 10.15497/RDA00065.

[18] C. Goble, S. Cohen-Boulakia, S. Soiland-Reyes *et al.* (2020). FAIR computational workflows. *Data Intelligence*, *2*(1–2), 108–121. doi: 10.1162/dint_a_00033.

[19] L. J. Castro, D. S. Katz, and F. Psomopoulos (2021). Working towards understanding the role of FAIR for machine learning. doi: 10.4126/FRL01-006429415.

[20] I. Walsh, D. Fishman, D. Garcia-Gasulla *et al.* (2021). DOME: Recommendations for supervised machine learning validation in biology. *Nature Methods*, *18*(10), 1122–1127. doi: 10.1038/s41592-021-01205-4.

[21] R. V. Guha, D. Brickley, and S. Macbeth (2016). Schema.org: Evolution of structured data on the web. *Communications of the ACM, 59*(2), 44–51. doi: 10.1145/2844544.

[22] CLAIRE. https://claire-ai.org/.

[23] Pistoia Alliance | Collaborate to Innovate Life Science R&D. https://www.pistoiaalliance.org/.

[24] Artificial Intelligence & Machine Learning Community — Pistoia Alliance. https://www.pistoiaalliance.org/.

[25] M. M. John, H. H. Olsson, and J. Bosch (2021). Towards MLOps: A framework and maturity model. In *2021 47th Euromicro Conference on Software Engineering and Advanced Applications (SEAA)*, Palermo, Italy, Sep. 2021, pp. 1–8. doi: 10.1109/SEAA53835.2021.00050.

[26] J. C. Burgelman, C. Pascu, K. Szkuta *et al.* (2019). Open Science, Open Data, and Open Scholarship: European policies to make science fit for the twenty-first century. *Frontiers in Big Data, 2*, 43.

[27] L. J. Dursi, Z. Bozoky, R. de Borja *et al.* (2021). CanDIG: Federated network across Canada for multi-omic and health data discovery and analysis. *Cell Genomics, 1*(2), 100033. doi: 10.1016/j.xgen.2021.100033.

[28] European Open Science Cloud. https://eosc.eu/.

[29] European Health Data Space. https://ec.europa.eu/health/ehealth-digital-health-and-care/european-health-data-space_en.

[30] NIH Data Commons. https://commonfund.nih.gov/commons.

[31] Australian BioCommons. https://www.biocommons.org.au/.

[32] Artificial intelligence in healthcare market to see 40% CAGR surge. https://healthitanalytics.com/news/artificial-intelligence-in-healthcare-market-to-see-40-cagr-surge.

[33] A. Bohr and K. Memarzadeh (2020). The rise of artificial intelligence in healthcare applications. *Artificial Intelligence in Healthcare*. Academic Press, pp. 25–60. doi: 10.1016/B978-0-12-818438-7.00002-2.

[34] B. J. Heil, M. M. Hoffman, F. Markowetz *et al.* (2021). Reproducibility standards for machine learning in the life sciences. *Nature Methods, 18*(10), 1132–1135. doi: 10.1038/s41592-021-01256-7.

Materials Science and Engineering

© 2023 World Scientific Publishing Company
https://doi.org/10.1142/9789811265679_0023

Chapter 23

Artificial Intelligence for Materials

Debra J. Audus*, Kamal Choudhary[†],
Brian L. DeCost[‡], A. Gilad Kusne[§],
Francesca Tavazza[¶], and James A. Warren[‖]

*Material Measurement Laboratory,
National Institute of Standards and Technology,
Gaithersburg, MD 20899, USA*
*debra.audus@nist.gov
[†]kamal.choudhary@nist.gov
[‡]brian.decost@nist.gov
[§]aaron.kusne@nist.gov
[¶]francesca.tavazza@nist.gov
[‖]james.warren@nist.gov

1. Introduction

Modern materials research and development (R&D) is the driving force behind new materials that transform our lives ranging from advances in battery technology to the nanoparticle technology behind messenger ribonucleic acid (mRNA) vaccines. It tackles grand challenges such as clean energy and a circular economy, as well as more mundane but important advances such as stronger glass for cell phones and warmer, less bulky clothing. It includes brand-new products never seen before, as well as incremental advances. However, it is also a slow process. For example, it took over half a century from when poly(lactic acid) was first discovered until it was regularly used in products such as compostable cups. To reduce the barriers, the Materials Genome Initiative (MGI) was established in 2011 in the United States where the goal is to bring materials to market twice as fast and at a fraction of the cost by making data accessible, leading a culture shift, training the next generation, and integrating experiment, computation, and theory [1]. Related efforts include the Findability, Accessibility, Interoperability, and Reusability (FAIR) Data Infrastructure (Europe, 2018), which encompasses the Novel Materials Discovery (NOMAD) data repository (Europe, 2014) and Material Research by Information Integration Initiative (Japan, launched in 2015, ended in 2020).

Since the initial launching of the MGI, artificial intelligence (AI), including machine learning (ML), has led to numerous, rapid advances in society including virtual assistants, image recognition, recommender systems, language translation, etc. It quickly became obvious that these concepts could also play a similarly transformative role in the materials domain. AI in material science starts to appear in comprehensive reports [2] a mere five years since the initial MGI strategy [1], which included the foundations such as accessible data but not AI explicitly.

To understand the power of AI in the materials domain, consider recent advances in the protein structure prediction problem. Specifically, this is an over 50-year-old grand challenge to predict the structure of a protein based on its sequence of amino acids that has spurred an enormous amount of research and, notably, a competition called Critical Assessment of protein Structure Prediction (CASP) that occurs every two years since 1994 to benchmark global advances. In 2020, AlphaFold [3], an AI entry from DeepMind, achieved an average error on the order of the size of a carbon atom and almost a factor of 3 less than the next closest entry. The reason why it is significant is not only that it made astonishing progress on a grand challenge but that it can often predict accurate structures with uncertainty in minutes as opposed to costly, time-consuming experiments that require specialized equipment and that both the model and a database of results were made available [4]. This subsequently enabled research in antibiotic resistance, investigations of severe acute respiratory syndrome coronavirus 2 (SARS-CoV-2) biology, and enzymes to break down plastics. However, there is still more progress to be made. Experiments will still be necessary for outliers, the architecture of AlphaFold is complex, and both why it works and the science behind it are still unknown.

AI can also catalyze similar advances within the more traditional materials domain. In the following, we highlight the rapid advances, outstanding challenges, and vision for the future in the field of materials AI; we also refer the reader to an excellent perspective [5]. In Section 2, we introduce the reader to AI for materials including the different types of tasks, models, and approaches that are commonly used. Particular attention is paid to recent advances. One of the largest barriers for widespread adoption of AI in materials is often the need for large, curated datasets. Fortunately, AI can be used to tackle this problem. Section 3 discusses how AI can be used for generation of data with a focus on simulation data, as well as unstructured text. As discussed in Section 4, AI can, in principle, plan and execute scientific experiments and simulations completely independently or with humans in the loop. Yet, for AI in materials to reach its full potential, it is not only the data scarcity problem that needs to be solved. Other challenges include the need for benchmarks, uncertainty quantification, interpretability, the need for semantic search, and further intertwining of experiment, simulation, theory, and data in the spirit of the MGI as discussed in Section 5. As detailed in Section 6, it is an exciting time in the field of materials and AI — there are both lots of exciting advances and lots of interesting problems still to solve. For readers new to the field, we recommend REsource for Materials Informatics (REMI) [6] and learning resources therein, as well as a best practices guide [7].

2. AI Allows You to Make a Material Model

The transformative value of adding AI approaches to the collection of tools already available to material scientists results from ML's capacity to accelerate, optimize, correlate, and discover many of the linkages between how a material is processed, the internal structures that are formed, and the resultant properties. This capacity reflects ML's ability to produce material models that, given specific inputs, quickly and reliably predict searched-for outputs.

The process of making ML models is a complex one, involving a series of steps, each one critical to the overall success. The process starts with data collection, often requiring a large, or relatively large, set of data. Luckily, in the last few years, many material properties' databases have been developed and continue to be developed, containing either computational or experimental data [8]. The next step is data curation, where any incorrect data are identified and eliminated, as well as areas of missing data are searched for and, if possible, corrected. The third step focuses on representing and preprocessing the data to facilitate machine learning use and maximize performance. This step may include data rescaling, normalization, binarization, and other data operations. A particular focus for supervised learning analysis is featurization, i.e., identifying which material properties need to be passed to the ML model as inputs. It is a key step, as the better the feature selection, the more effective the model. Often, domain knowledge is used in determining such features, but that is not the only approach. Other strategies include dimensionality reduction methods such as Principal Component Analysis (PCA), where low-dimensional properties-relevant features are extracted from high dimensional data based on data statistics. Another dimensionality reduction method represents a material in terms of a graph, with atoms as nodes and bonds as edges. This latter method is employed by graph neural networks algorithms. The next critical choice, which is tied to the featurization method, is the choice of the ML algorithm. A vast gamut of possibilities are available, and are currently used, in material science. The choice depends on the type of application. Materials property prediction, in particular, has seen wide use of ML and requires supervised learning, where the dataset has to contain both input and output data. Specifically, the prediction of continuous-value physical quantities, like electronic energy gaps or stress distributions, is called regression, while establishing discrete-value labeled groups is performing classification, as, for instance, when determining if a material is metallic or not. Conventional algorithms (decision trees, kernel methods, etc.) as well as deep learning methods are used to these ends. An example of a different use of supervised algorithms is Symbolic Regression, where ML is used to determine the best mathematical formula to express correlations between inputs and outputs, instead of evaluating a physical property. Regression and classification often focus on learning a surrogate ML function to map the input to output. The function is then used for predictions. Symbolic regression is used to find an interpretable model. A variation in the possible applications is the use of supervised ML to determine, or optimize, not specific physical quantities but parameters in functions, as it is the case when determining classical force fields [9]. Examples of all such applications will be discussed later in this section. While supervised learning is the AI type most used in materials science, it is not the only one. Examples of unsupervised learning can be found, for instance, in automatic terminology extraction (natural language processing [10]) for materials science, aimed at identifying information on material properties, microstructures, or process parameters currently disperse in unstructured sources. As the name says, unsupervised learning detects correlations/patterns between inputs with minimal external guidance and without being given any form of output. Phase mapping is another example where unsupervised learning has been used. In addition to supervised and unsupervised learning, material science's applications are also making use of semi-supervised learning [11], transfer learning [12], and representation learning [13]. The last steps in the making of an ML model are the validation and uncertainty quantification. A certain amount of the input data is always set aside for validation purposes, i.e., never enters into the training. These data are then used to quantify the performance of the model through the evaluation of statistical quantities like the mean average error (MAE) or the root mean square error (RMSE). Quantifying uncertainty for predictions is a significant challenge on its own. While probabilistic models natively output uncertainty, others may require additional processes such as varying parameters (and hyperparameters) of the machine learning model. Additionally, uncertainty can be quantified over collections of predictions using statistical measures such as the number of true positives, true negatives, etc. Uncertainty analysis is important for quantifying a model's performance, though it is commonly not included in published research.

Focusing on most current applications of supervised learning in material science, it is notable that one of its key strengths is its applicability to a variety of length scales. In the case of property prediction applications, for instance, ML has often been used at the atomistic level to substitute for high-fidelity, high-computational cost density functional theory (DFT) calculations. Specifically, many groups have taken advantage of the availability of vast and open sources of DFT databases and modeled material properties like stability, exfoliability, elastic behavior, electronic energy gaps, and optical properties, for ideal crystalline [14], molecular, and polymeric materials [15]. At the continuum level, it has been extensively used to model fracture propagation and other failure mechanisms [16]. In these applications, ML has taken the place of finite element modeling (FEM) and Finite-Discrete Element Modeling (FDEM). Even relatively new fields, like additive manufacturing, have made extensive use of ML techniques, often applied to the investigation of defect-related material behavior. For instance, the effect of surface roughness or of defect location, size, and morphology on the fatigue life of a laser melted alloy, such as those found in additive manufacturing, has been probed using deep learning [16]. Multiscale investigations have been pursued as well, as in the case of Hsu *et al.* [17], where a machine learning approach connecting molecular simulation into a physics-based data-driven multiscale model was utilized to predict fracture processes and toughness values. Within the polymer's domain [18], a major challenge that continues to progress is the representation of the polymer. However, with correct choices, exciting advances such as determining better materials for gas separation [19] are in the works.

Beyond property prediction, ML models have been extremely effective in model optimization and material discovery. One example of model optimization is the use of neural networks to accelerate the computation of classical force fields. Because of their numerically very accurate representation of high-dimensional potential-energy surfaces, they can provide energies and forces many orders of magnitude faster than *ab initio* calculations, thus enabling molecular dynamics simulations of large systems. Transferability may, though, be a problem, as ML does not extrapolate well. Including information on the physical nature of the interatomic bonding into a neural network potential is one possible solution to such a shortcoming, as proposed by the developers of the Physically Informed Neural Networks (PINNs) potential [20]. A different example of model optimization is the use of ML to develop exchange and correlation functionals for DFT [21]. DFT is the *ab initio* approach most frequently used when studying the electronic structure of materials at the atomic scale. While exact in principle, various approximations are required to perform DFT simulations in practice, among which the form of the exchange-correlation functional is, possibly, the most important, as it captures the electron-electron interaction. Traditionally built exchange-correlation functionals take a long time to be developed and, occasionally, have extremely complex analytical forms and are problematic in their accuracy and transferability for certain classes of materials. ML-built exchange-correlation functionals have the potentiality to improve over the traditional ones while being effective for solids and molecules alike.

3. Application Modalities

Well-curated datasets are necessary precursors to a supervised machine learning model. In materials informatics, data often include atomic structures and chemical formulae, images, spectra, point values, and texts such as peer-reviewed articles as shown in Figure 1. There have been numerous efforts for organizing the datasets. A complete list of such efforts can be found elsewhere [22–24]. In the following sections, we provide a few well-known example applications of the above modalities. Atomic structure data are usually obtained from quantum and classical mechanical methods such as DFT and molecular dynamics simulations. Recently, there has been a huge upsurge in specialty DFT-based datasets due to growing computational power. The physio-chemical information in atomistic structure data has been used in machine learning tasks through the use of Euclidean hand-crafted descriptors and non-Euclidean graph neural network frameworks. An example of converting the atomic structure into a graph is shown in Fig. 2. Some of the common material property models generated using atomistic data are for formation energy, total energy, bandgap, and modulus of elasticity. Such developed models have been used for materials screening purposes such as for alloy, energy, and quantum materials design. More details about such applications can be found elsewhere [23,25].

Some of the numerous, common imaging techniques (microscopy) for materials science include optical microscopy (OM), scanning electron microscopy (SEM), scanning probe microscopy (SPM), which includes scanning tunneling microscopy (STM) or atomic force microscopy (AFM),

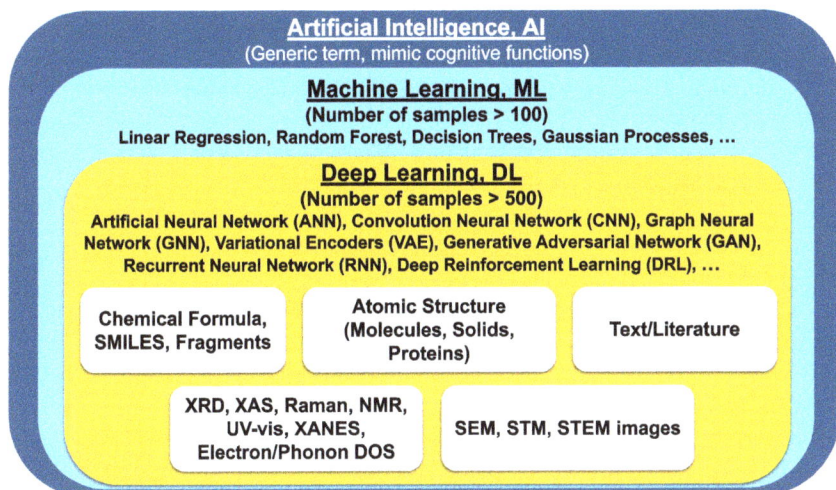

Fig. 1. Schematic showing an overview of Artificial Intelligence (AI), Machine Learning (ML), and Deep Learning (DL) methods and their applications in materials science and engineering (reprinted according to the terms of the CC-BY license [23]).

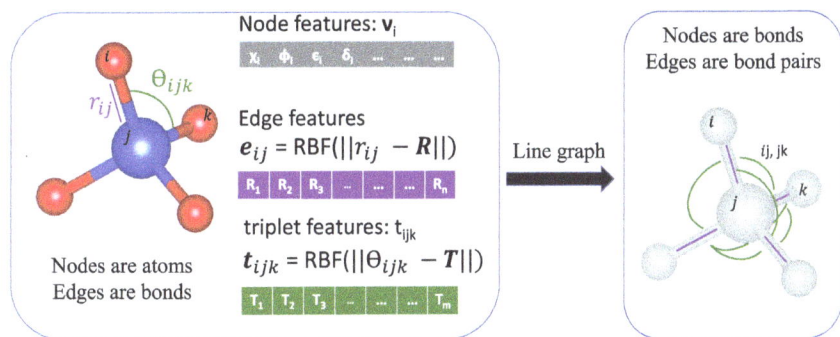

Fig. 2. Schematic representations of an atomic structure as a graph using Atomistic Line Graph Neural Network (ALIGNN) (reprinted according to the terms of the CC-BY license [26]).

and transmission electron microscopy (TEM) and its variants, such as scanning transmission electron microscopy (STEM). As applications of imaging techniques have become widespread, there is often a large amount of generated data which can be difficult to analyze manually. ML techniques are useful for automating and aiding manual work in tasks such as image classification of lattices, detecting defects, resolution enhancement, microstructure learning, image reconstruction, and making physics-based models using image data. A detailed review of ML for materials image data can be found elsewhere [23,27]. To give a few example works, in Ref. [28], the authors developed datasets and machine models for analyzing defects in graphene and FeTe systems. In Ref. [29], the authors developed semantic segmentation models for steel that can be used for accurately detecting damages. In Ref. [30], a computational STM image dataset was developed along with ML models to classify 2D materials lattice with up to 90% accuracy. In Ref. [31], the authors used a convolutional neural net (CNN) that was pre-trained on non-scientific images to perform microstructure reconstruction.

Spectral data such as X-ray and neutron diffraction (XRD, ND), X-ray absorption near edge structure (XANES), electron energy loss (EELS), infrared and Raman (IR/Raman), and ultraviolet and visible (UV-VIS) provide great insight into structural, composition, and dynamic behavior of materials. XRD is one of the widely used methods for developing large datasets for materials and training machine learning models. A detailed overview on such a topic can be found in Refs. [23,32]. To give a few example applications, Park *et al.* [33] used CNN for predicting structural properties of materials with up to 95% accuracy. Dong *et al.* introduced parameter quantification network (PQ-Net) to extract physio-chemical information from XRD data. Timoshenko *et al.* [34] used a neural network for XANES to predict coordination number of metal clusters. Liu *et al.* [35] used SVM and CNN methods to predict Raman spectra using a Raman spectra database. Fung *et al.* [36] used CNNs to predicting electronic density of states obtained from DFT.

The text data for materials are obtained from academic journal articles, preprint repositories such as arXiv, and crowd-sourced resources like Wikipedia. Compared to other applications, datasets for natural language processing are often scarce due to copyright restrictions and paywalls. Nevertheless, there has been substantial research in this field due to rapid developments in the field of sequence modeling. Such techniques are being used for automatically extracting relevant material property data from text to guide theoretical and experimental work such as material synthesis, magnetic phase transition temperature calibration, and designing batteries and solar cells [37–39].

4. Autonomous Science

Advances in technology often require the discovery and development of novel advanced materials. As a result, the search for advanced materials continually expands to materials of greater and greater complexity in both the number of chemical components and processing steps. However, with each new element or processing step, the number of potential materials to investigate grows exponentially (e.g., if 10 experiments are used to investigate the impact of one variable, 10^N experiments will be required to investigate the impact of N variables). Manual investigations rapidly become infeasible. High-throughput techniques [40] provide a short-term solution, making it possible to synthesize thousands of unique materials in a few hours and characterize these materials in rapid succession. Machine learning can then be used to reduce data analysis from weeks and months to seconds. Nevertheless, high-throughput methods do not provide the exponential scaling needed.

The last few years have seen the rise of autonomous materials research systems [41] – where machine learning controls experiment design, execution (both physical and *in silico*), and analysis in a closed loop. These systems use active learning, the machine learning field focused on optimal experiment design, to ensure that each subsequent experiment maximizes knowledge gained toward user-defined goals. Active learning allows users to balance two high-level goals: exploration and exploitation. Exploration seeks to gain global knowledge of the target material system, while exploitation uses past knowledge to hone in on possible optimal materials. Active learning on its own has been used to build research recommendation engines to advise scientists in the lab and *in silico* [42]. Autonomous systems combine the automated experiment and simulation tools of high-throughput science with active learning, guiding each study in the lab or *in silico* through the vast materials search space, accelerating the discovery and study of advanced materials.

The advent of autonomous systems does not mean that prior physical knowledge is thrown out. In fact, autonomous system performance improves by incorporating prior physical knowledge found in laws, heuristics, and databases. Scientific machine learning [2] is the AI subfield that focuses on incorporating prior physical knowledge into AI and ML. The goal is to design models and learning algorithms so that their inductive bias reflects physical principles. This promotes physically realistic predictions and provides opportunities for physically meaningful model interpretations. For instance, the Gibbs phase rule along with more general rules, such as a material can only be composed of a positive amount of constituent phases and materials of similar synthesis are more likely to have similar properties, have been used to improve phase map data analysis and prediction [43].

Autonomous measurement systems take the first step toward autonomous materials exploration and discovery. These systems guide each subsequent measurement experiment to obtain maximal information for the target sample. Parameters that are optimized include where on the sample to measure next, the temperature of the material, and measurement-specific parameters such as beam wavelength. For example, autonomous X-ray measurements were used to guide beam location to accelerate nano-particle density determination [44] and autonomous X-ray measurements were used to select subsequent sample compositions in the search for novel materials, resulting in a 10x acceleration toward the discovery of the new, best-in-class phase change memory material [45].

Success in autonomous chemistry preceded materials science, with systems that optimize molecular mixtures for applications such as chemical reaction optimization [46]. Accordingly, the majority of autonomous materials systems focus on "wet" synthesis such as optimizing quantum dots for emission energy [47]. More recently, closed-loop "dry" materials synthesis and characterization were exemplified for thin-film resistance optimization [48].

While active learning can be used to guide a researcher in which material to investigate next across a large design space, often the lab systems are limited in the number of variables that can be automated and machine learning controlled. For instance, sputtering systems are limited in the number of components that can be deposited at a time and control over the measurement beam path may be locked out for the users. Advances in autonomous physical science will require innovations in physical systems that will allow for greater autonomous control of experiments in the lab.

Additionally, machine learning for autonomous systems could also gain a great advantage from the large amount of prior knowledge of expert users. This requires the development of human-in-the-loop systems where the autonomous system is able to interact with and learn from expert users. This is also an ongoing area of research.

5. Challenges

At the time of writing, a robust discourse spanning the materials and chemistry fields has developed around constructing and deploying creative applications of ML methods to enable more efficient and scalable research and development. The value proposition and validity of ML-enabled scientific methodologies have been demonstrated many times over, and the education and training ecosystem in this subfield is rapidly maturing. Advancement of transformational ML applications in science now depends on addressing specific challenges in the scalability and generalization ability of ML systems, as well as their ease of integration into higher-level scientific workflows.

Availability of sufficiently large datasets for training ML systems is widely acknowledged as a challenge in the physical sciences, particularly where sample fabrication and characterization are time and cost-intensive.

Three general strategies are currently being pursued: investing in massive datasets through high-throughput experimentation and computation, deploying active learning and autonomous systems for targeted collection of high-value data, and improving the sample complexity of ML systems through algorithmic improvements. The preceding sections of this chapter outline the current progress along each of these axes. Continued innovation critically depends on the fields' ability to quantify, communicate, and mitigate dataset and annotation bias.

Progress in ML is historically enabled by clearly defined tasks, with robust performance measures that guide innovation. Failing to account for dataset bias can lead to benchmarks that reward memorization [49], making clear assessments of methodological innovation difficult. At present, many of the large materials datasets used in applied ML research have been repurposed from materials discovery efforts not directly motivated by ML applications. The resulting forms of dataset bias are acknowledged in the materials literature, but further detailed quantification and research into mitigation strategies will enable the community to develop more productive ML systems. This bias assessment covers not only the data themselves but extends to the framing of the ML task in the context of ultimate scientific goals. For example, DFT formation energy is a popular atomistic prediction target used throughout the literature to benchmark model quality, but thermodynamic stability is a much more relevant (and challenging) target for materials discovery and design applications [50]. This kind of investment into clearly defined ML tasks and well-designed benchmark datasets will help the materials community engage more effectively around concrete problems with the broader AI community. The Open Catalyst Challenge [51] provides an excellent example of this kind of clear problem framing and effective coordination of the general ML community.

High-quality and well-characterized datasets provide a foundation for the field to develop model introspection and interrogation tools that build and preserve confidence for ML-based decision-making in the sciences. These are of critical importance because scientific progress and discovery are often fundamentally at odds with a central assumption relied on by most ML systems: that data for which predictions are made are identically distributed to the training data. Machine learning systems, especially the overparameterized deep learning models popular in current research, can perform notoriously poorly when extrapolating with high confidence. The importance of principled uncertainty quantification for machine learning predictions is increasingly being emphasized in materials research, especially as more researchers adopt active learning methodologies that rely on well-calibrated measures of model confidence. More research is needed to decompose predictive uncertainty across multiple model and training components and to be able to propagate uncertainties of the underlying training data through the modeling pipeline as well.

Similarly, general-purpose ML model introspection and interpretability tools [52] are helping materials researchers to identify and explain trends in ML model behavior. Materials-specific adaptation of these methods, such as an additive modeling strategy to decompose the contribution of individual atoms in a crystal to a target property [53], can provide new ways of studying materials phenomena and for understanding how ML models form predictions. Progress in this direction will depend on greater adoption of standard model introspection tools in the materials community and an ongoing discourse of developing creative methods for critiquing ML models and predictions. These tools will be most effective in combination with ML systems designed from the ground up to incorporate and reflect physical principles so that ML models and their predictions can directly be interpreted in terms of physical insight [2].

Finally, there are important areas in which methodological innovation will substantially boost scientific progress. The subfield of scientific machine learning is rapidly developing creative modeling approaches that tailor the inductive biases of ML systems to reflect physical principles. For example, graph neural network architectures reflect well the local structure and permutation invariance in atomistic systems, and neural differential equations are enabling data-driven discovery of mechanistic models in mechanical and pharmacokinetic systems. There is a rich diversity of theoretical modeling approaches in materials science, and developing generalizable approaches for incorporating them into ML systems is an important and challenging task.

With respect to automated materials discovery and design, deep generative models have shown encouraging progress for molecular [54] and crystalline [55] systems. Important research directions include developing methods that go beyond structural prototype search, methods for using generative models for reaction engineering and synthesis planning, and developing a framework for connecting generative models to higher-level materials structures and models.

Curation of structured knowledge and, crucially, metadata will enable novel forms of ML application in materials science, such as semantic search, which incorporates specific domain knowledge into information retrieval. Automated literature mining to extract and link information to construct knowledge graphs is an active topic of research in the ML community. Specific materials science emphasis is needed to build on early work in chemical named entity recognition, information extraction from common graphical representations of measured materials properties, and extraction of material properties and synthesis protocols [56]. These tools and the resulting scientific knowledge graph and related infrastructure will create opportunities for integrating structured concepts into information retrieval, predictive modeling tools, and ML model interrogation and interpretability tools.

A final challenge area is the seamless integration of ML into larger materials design systems. This covers both multiple interacting ML-based systems as well as conventional computational materials science infrastructure. The long-standing multiscale modeling challenge provides many opportunities, for example, end-to-end learning in neural networks that parameterize physical simulations or performing coarse graining to connect classical modeling components. Finally, rigorous incorporation of scientific domain knowledge may require going beyond machine learning to identify opportunities for applications of broader artificial intelligence methodology, such as search-based techniques and symbolic reasoning [57].

6. Conclusion and Outlook

In this chapter, we have outlined the many ways that AI has the power to catalyze transformational advances in materials R&D. We have detailed the myriad ways that AI is and will continue to impact materials research, including in the predictions of materials properties, the influence of defects and dopants, and how materials fail. AI techniques can markedly accelerate the hunt for new materials with desirable properties, allowing for inverse design techniques that can zero in on the optimal processing techniques needed to obtain the desired materials performance.

Additionally, AI approaches can accelerate the characterization of materials systems, using the powerful image analysis/processing techniques that drove many of the notable breakthroughs in AI. Since materials can be characterized not just by images of their internal structure but also by patterns resulting from techniques such as X-ray and electron scattering, image processing techniques are especially potent.

It was noted that with the maturation of data gathering and improved data infrastructures, the raw materials for AI will be in increasingly greater and greater supply. This positive development is compounded by the advent of AI-driven, autonomous laboratory setups, where closed-loop experimental designs will enable the exploration of far wider processing and compositional parameter variations than we were previously practical, creating a virtuous feedback loop that could yield truly paradigm-shifting levels of data and, ultimately, knowledge about the existing and sought for materials.

We also spent some time addressing the challenges that must be overcome to realize the full potential of AI approaches. The required data (and metadata) infrastructures are still not there, and those that exist do not interoperate especially well. AI approaches have definite risks, and benchmarking efforts are needed to provide trust in these methods, and, where possible, uncertainty bounds provided. It is also desirable that AI methods incorporate the best available physical knowledge and insights, ensuring the algorithms respect known science and underlying symmetries.

We began our discussion by considering the success of the AlphaFold effort, which linked the fine structure of proteins (the amino acid sequence) to the ultimate conformation. This type of linkage is not analogous to materials R&D; it *is* materials R&D, albeit for a very specific research question. Perhaps one of the great stories of the success of AlphaFold was the CASP competition, which drove the protein folding research community forward for 30 years, long before AI techniques became commonplace in either biomedical or materials research. There is an enormous opportunity for the materials R&D community to create new "grand challenge" problems that are of the same magnitude as the protein folding problem and could result in materials that address many of the pressing concerns facing humanity today, including energy efficiency, climate change mitigation through carbon capture materials and cleaner energy production, enhanced recyclability and reduction in plastics pollution, and new biocompatible medical devices and implants. AI is poised to make these revolutions in the human condition achievable with a speed and expense that was, until very recently, unimaginable.

References

[1] J. P. Holdren, T. Kalil, C. Wadia *et al.* (2014). *Materials genome initiative strategic plan.* Washington D.C.: Office of Science and Technology Policy, Vol. 6.

[2] N. Baker, F. Alexander, T. Bremer *et al.* (2019). Workshop report on basic research needs for scientific machine learning: Core technologies for artificial intelligence. USDOE Office of Science (SC), Washington, D.C. (United States), Tech. Rep.

[3] J. Jumper, R. Evans, A. Pritzel *et al.* (2021). Highly accurate protein structure prediction with alphafold. *Nature, 596*(7873), 583–589.

[4] D. Hassabis (2021). Putting the power of alphafold into the world's hands. July, [posted 22 July 2021]. https://deepmind.com/blog/article/putting-the-power-of-alphafold-into-the-worlds-hands.

[5] D. M. Dimiduk, E. A. Holm, and S. R. Niezgoda (2018). Perspectives on the impact of machine learning, deep learning, and artificial intelligence on

materials, processes, and structures engineering. *Integrating Materials and Manufacturing Innovation, 7*(3), 157–172.

[6] https://pages.nist.gov/remi/ (accessed 22 March 2022).

[7] A. Y.-T. Wang, R. J. Murdock, S. K. Kauwe *et al.* (2020). Machine learning for materials scientists: An introductory guide toward best practices. *Chemistry of Materials, 32*(12), 4954–4965.

[8] Z. Song, X. Chen, F. Meng *et al.* (2020). Machine learning in materials design: Algorithm and application. *Chinese Physics B, 29*(11), 116103.

[9] Y. Zuo, C. Chen, X. Li *et al.* (2020). Performance and cost assessment of machine learning interatomic potentials. *The Journal of Physical Chemistry A, 124*(4), 731–745.

[10] F. Olsson (2009). A literature survey of active machine learning in the context of natural language processing. SICS, Tech. Rep. 2009:06.

[11] J. E. van Engelen and H. H. Hoos (2019). A survey on semi-supervised learning. *Machine Learning, 109*(2), 373–440.

[12] S. J. Pan and Q. Yang (2009). A survey on transfer learning. *IEEE Transactions on Knowledge and Data Engineering, 22*(10), 1345–1359.

[13] K. Bengio, A. Courville, and P. Vincent (2013). Representation learning: A review and new perspectives. *IEEE Transactions on Pattern Analysis and Machine Intelligence, 35*(8), 1798–1828.

[14] K. Choudhary, K. F. Garrity, A. C. Reid *et al.* (2020). The joint automated repository for various integrated simulations (jarvis) for data-driven materials design. *NPJ Computational Materials, 6*(1), 1–13.

[15] H. Doan Tran, C. Kim, L. Chen *et al.* (2020). Machine-learning predictions of polymer properties with polymer genome. *Journal of Applied Physics, 128*(17), 171104.

[16] H. Bao, S. Wu, Z. Wu *et al.* (2021). A machine-learning fatigue life prediction approach of additively manufactured metals. *Engineering Fracture Mechanics, 242*, 107508.

[17] Y.-C. Hsu, C.-H. Yu, and M. J. Buehler, (2020). Using deep learning to predict fracture patterns in crystalline solids. *Matter, 3*(1), 197–211.

[18] L. Chen, G. Pilania, R. Batra *et al.* (2021). Polymer informatics: Current status and critical next steps. *Materials Science and Engineering: R: Reports, 144*, 100595.

[19] J. W. Barnett, C. R. Bilchak, Y. Wang *et al.* (2020). Designing exceptional gas-separation polymer membranes using machine learning. *Science Advances, 6*(20), eaaz4301.

[20] G. P. P. Pun, R. Batra, R. Ramprasad *et al.* (2019). Physically informed artificial neural networks for atomistic modeling of materials. *Nature Communications, 10*(1).

[21] S. Dick and M. Fernandez-Serra (2020). Machine learning accurate exchange and correlation functionals of the electronic density. *Nature Communications, 11*(1), 1–10.

[22] C. Draxl and M. Scheffler (2018). Nomad: The fair concept for big data-driven materials science. *Mrs Bulletin, 43*(9), 676–682.

[23] K. Choudhary, R. Batra, R. Ramprasad *et al.* (2021). Recent advances and applications of deep learning methods in materials science. *arXiv preprint arXiv:2110.14820.*

[24] C. W. Andersen, R. Armiento, E. Blokhin *et al.* (2021). Optimade: An API for exchanging materials data. *arXiv preprint arXiv:2103.02068.*

[25] R. K. Vasudevan, K. Choudhary, A. Mehta *et al.* (2019). Materials science in the artificial intelligence age: high-throughput library generation, machine learning, and a pathway from correlations to the underpinning physics. *MRS Communications*, 9(3), 821–838.

[26] K. Choudhary and B. DeCost (2021). Atomistic line graph neural network for improved materials property predictions. *NPJ Computational Materials*, 7(1), 1–8.

[27] M. Ge, F. Su, Z. Zhao *et al.* (2020). Deep learning analysis on microscopic imaging in materials science. *Materials Today Nano*, 11, 100087.

[28] S. Somnath, C. R. Smith, N. Laanait *et al.* (2019). Usid and pycroscopy–open source frameworks for storing and analyzing imaging and spectroscopy data. *Microscopy and Microanalysis*, 25(S2), 220–221.

[29] B. L. DeCost, B. Lei, T. Francis *et al.* (2019). High throughput quantitative metallography for complex microstructures using deep learning: A case study in ultrahigh carbon steel. *Microscopy and Microanalysis*, 25(1), 21–29.

[30] K. Choudhary, K. F. Garrity, C. Camp *et al.* (2021). Computational scanning tunneling microscope image database. *Scientific Data*, 8(1), 1–9.

[31] X. Li, Y. Zhang, H. Zhao *et al.* (2018). A transfer learning approach for microstructure reconstruction and structure-property predictions. *Scientific Reports*, 8(1), 1–13.

[32] Z. Chen, N. Andrejevic, N. C. Drucker *et al.* (2021). Machine learning on neutron and X-ray scattering and spectroscopies. *Chemical Physics Reviews*, 2(3), 031301.

[33] W. B. Park, J. Chung, J. Jung *et al.* (2017). Classification of crystal structure using a convolutional neural network. *IUCrJ*, 4(4), 486–494.

[34] J. Timoshenko, D. Lu, Y. Lin *et al.* (2017). Supervised machine-learning-based determination of three-dimensional structure of metallic nanoparticles. *The Journal of Physical Chemistry Letters*, 8(20), 5091–5098.

[35] J. Liu, M. Osadchy, L. Ashton *et al.* (2017). Deep convolutional neural networks for Raman spectrum recognition: A unified solution. *Analyst*, 142(21), 4067–4074.

[36] V. Fung, G. Hu, P. Ganesh *et al.* (2021). Machine learned features from density of states for accurate adsorption energy prediction. *Nature Communications*, 12(1), 1–11.

[37] E. Kim, K. Huang, A. Saunders *et al.* (2017). Materials synthesis insights from scientific literature via text extraction and machine learning. *Chemistry of Materials*, 29(21), 9436–9444.

[38] C. J. Court and J. M. Cole (2018). Auto-generated materials database of curie and néel temperatures via semi-supervised relationship extraction. *Scientific Data*, 5(1), 1–12.

[39] S. Huang and J. M. Cole (2020). A database of battery materials auto-generated using chemdataextractor. *Scientific Data*, *7*(1), 1–13.

[40] M. L. Green, C. L. Choi, J. R. Hattrick-Simpers *et al.* (2017). Fulfilling the promise of the materials genome initiative with high-throughput experimental methodologies. *Applied Physics Reviews*, *4*(1), 011105.

[41] E. Stach, B. DeCost, A. G. Kusne *et al.* (2021). Autonomous experimentation systems for materials development: A community perspective. *Matter*, *4*(9), 2702–2726.

[42] D. Xue, P. V. Balachandran, J. Hogden *et al.* (2016). Accelerated search for materials with targeted properties by adaptive design. *Nature Communications*, *7*(1), 11241.

[43] S. Ament, M. Amsler, D. R. Sutherland *et al.* (2021). Autonomous materials synthesis via hierarchical active learning of non-equilibrium phase diagrams. *Science Advances*, *7*(51).

[44] M. M. Noack, K. G. Yager, M. Fukuto *et al.* (2019). A kriging-based approach to autonomous experimentation with applications to X-ray scattering. *Scientific Reports*, *9*(1), 11809.

[45] A. G. Kusne, H. Yu, C. Wu *et al.* (2020). On-the-fly closed-loop materials discovery via Bayesian active learning. *Nature Communications*, *11*(1), 5966.

[46] A.-C. Bédard, A. Adamo, K. C. Aroh *et al.* (2018). Reconfigurable system for automated optimization of diverse chemical reactions. *Science*, *361*(6408), 1220–1225.

[47] R. W. Epps, M. S. Bowen, A. A. Volk *et al.* (2020). Artificial chemist: An autonomous quantum dot synthesis bot. *Advanced Materials*, *32*(30), 2001626.

[48] R. Shimizu, S. Kobayashi, Y. Watanabe *et al.* (2020). Autonomous materials synthesis by machine learning and robotics. *APL Materials*, *8*(11), 111110.

[49] I. Wallach and A. Heifets (2018). Most ligand-based classification benchmarks reward memorization rather than generalization. *Journal of Chemical Information and Modeling*, *58*(5), 916–932.

[50] C. J. Bartel, A. Trewartha, Q. Wang *et al.* (2020). A critical examination of compound stability predictions from machine-learned formation energies. *NPJ Computational Materials*, *6*(1), 97.

[51] L. Chanussot, A. Das, S. Goyal *et al.* (2021). Open catalyst 2020 (OC20) dataset and community challenges. *ACS Catalysis*, *11*(10), 6059–6072.

[52] C. Molnar, G. Casalicchio, and B. Bischl (2020). Interpretable machine learning — A brief history, state-of-the-art and challenges. In *Joint European Conference on Machine Learning and Knowledge Discovery in Databases*. Springer, pp. 417–431.

[53] T. Xie and J. C. Grossman (2018). Crystal graph convolutional neural networks for an accurate and interpretable prediction of material properties. *Physical Review Letters*, *120*(14), 145301.

[54] B. Sanchez-Lengeling and A. Aspuru-Guzik (2018). Inverse molecular design using machine learning: Generative models for matter engineering. *Science*, *361*(6400), 360–365.

[55] T. Xie, X. Fu, O.-E. Ganea *et al.* (2021). Crystal diffusion variational autoencoder for periodic material generation. *arxiv:2110.06197*.

[56] O. Kononova, T. He, H. Huo *et al.* (2021). Opportunities and challenges of text mining in materials research. *Iscience*, *24*(3), 102115.

[57] D. Chen, Y. Bai, S. Ament *et al.* (2021). Automating crystal-structure phase mapping by combining deep learning with constraint reasoning. *Nature Machine Intelligence*, *3*(9), 812–822.

© 2023 World Scientific Publishing Company
https://doi.org/10.1142/9789811265679_0024

Chapter 24

Artificial Intelligence for Accelerating Materials Discovery

Ankit Agrawal[*] and Alok Choudhary[†]

Department of Electrical and Computer Engineering,
Northwestern University, Evanston, USA
[*] ankit-agrawal@northwestern.edu
[†] a-choudhary@northwestern.edu

1. Introduction

The increasing availability of data from the first three paradigms of science (experiments, theory, and simulations), along with advances in artificial intelligence and machine learning (AI/ML), has offered unprecedented opportunities for data-driven science, which is the *4th paradigm of science* [1,2] (Figure 1). Within AI/ML, *deep learning* (DL) [3,4] has emerged as a transformative technology in the last few years, which is essentially a rediscovery of neural networks fueled by big data and big compute (Figure 2). Deep learning has rapidly become the AI/ML technique of choice due to its groundbreaking success in numerous real-world applications, such as natural language processing [5], computer vision [6], speech recognition [7], autonomous driving [8], and numerous others.

The field of materials science relies on experiments and simulation-based models to understand the "physics" of materials in order to better understand their characteristics, to subsequently discover and design new materials with improved properties. It is well-known that the key to almost everything in materials science depends on *processing-structure-property-performance* relationships (Figure 3), where the deductive *science* linkages of cause and effect go from left to right and the inductive *engineering* relationships of goals and means go from right to left. Furthermore, each science relationship is many-to-one, and consequently, the engineering ones are one-to-many, as depicted in the figure. Thus, multiple processing routes

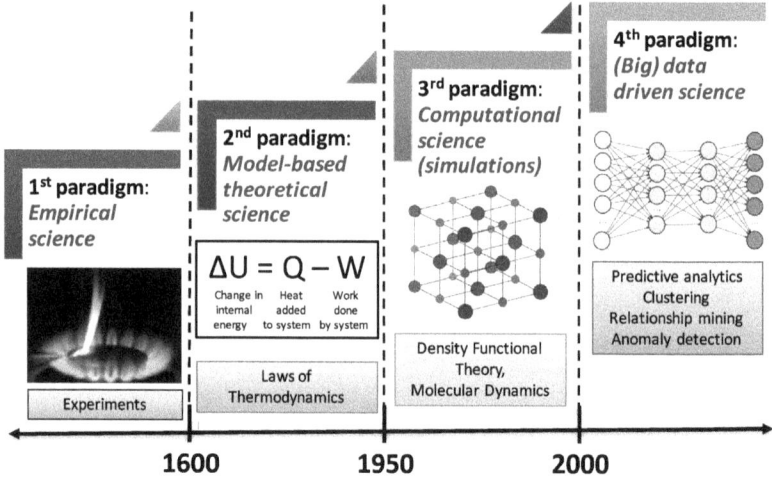

Fig. 1. The four paradigms of science: empirical, theoretical, computational, and data-driven (reproduced from [1]).

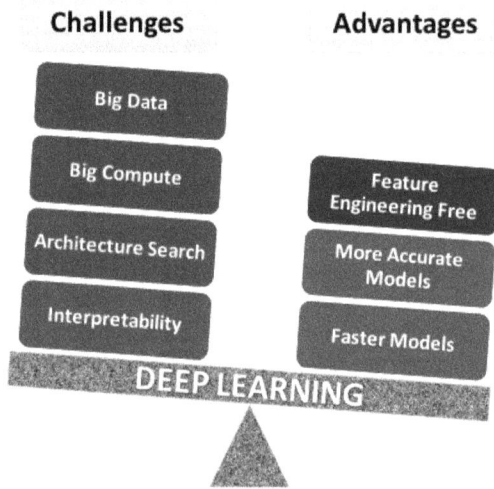

Fig. 2. The advantages of deep learning typically outweigh its challenges (reproduced from [3]).

can potentially result in the same structure of a material, and the same property could be potentially achieved by multiple materials.

In other words, for a given material, there is only one property, but for a given target property, there can be multiple materials, and it is

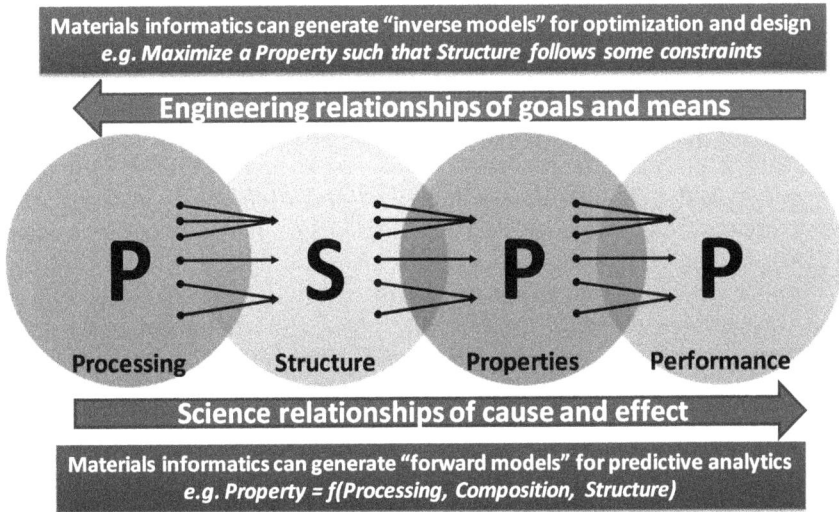

Fig. 3. The processing-structure-property-performance (PSPP) relationships of materials science and engineering. Materials informatics or the application of AI/ML techniques in materials science can help decipher invertible PSPP relationships via forward models of property prediction and inverse models of materials discovery and design (reproduced from [1]).

desirable to identify as many of them as possible, as some materials with a particular target property may not have other desired properties, or may be challenging to manufacture, and so on. This makes the inverse problem of learning the engineering of materials much more challenging as compared to the forward problem of learning the science of materials.

2. How Can AI Advance Materials Science and Engineering?

The AI/ML techniques can use data collected from experiments and simulations to build *forward models* that can predict the property of a given material represented by its composition, processing, and structure. The ML models have a prediction error associated with them, which can usually be reduced by exposing the model to more training data or incorporating known domain knowledge into the model. Since these are data-driven models, they are almost always orders of magnitude faster than the simulations and experiments and thereby can serve as useful proxies or surrogate models to get a reasonable estimate of the property of a given material without having to perform costly simulations and experiments.

Once the forward models are developed with satisfactory accuracy, they can in turn help realize the *inverse models* of materials discovery and design. Since inverse modeling is essentially an optimization problem over the design space of possible materials, the ability to query this space for a target property value using a low-cost AI/ML model can greatly help in identifying promising candidates, which can then be verified with more expensive and higher fidelity simulations and eventually validated with experiments. The AI models can thus intelligently reduce the search space of possible materials based on available historical data.

Furthermore, the forward and inverse models can be developed in an iterative fashion using *active learning*, where the recommendations from the first-generation inverse models, once verified/validated by simulations and experiments, are added back into the training dataset to build second-generation forward models followed by inverse models, which are usually more robust and accurate due to learning from a bigger training dataset. It is important to note that the results of all the additional simulations and experiments can and should be added to the training data, even if the predictions from the ML model turned out to be incorrect. In fact, such data can be invaluable for the ML model to learn to distinguish between materials with desirable and undesirable properties. This can significantly reduce the number of iterations to discover the optimal material, thereby accelerating materials discovery and design.

A *knowledge discovery workflow* for applying AI techniques to materials data is depicted in Figure 4, which can be used for different tasks by different users as shown. Depending on the specific use case of interest, a series of data-driven techniques can be used to integrate available information from heterogeneous materials databases, apply appropriate preprocessing and representation, develop and evaluate forward predictive models using a variety of modeling techniques, try to understand and interpret the models to make sure they are learning from the correct features, and use them to realize the inverse models to discover and design new materials.

Over the last decade, numerous AI works in materials science [9] have been undertaken for various use cases, such as steels [10], superconductors [11], thermoelectrics [12], metallic glasses [13], magnetoelastics [14], and high-entropy alloys [15], all of which can be understood to use some adaptation of the above-described workflow. The need to build upon the initial success of AI for materials science has been recognized by the 2021 Materials Genome Initiative (MGI) Strategic Plan [16].

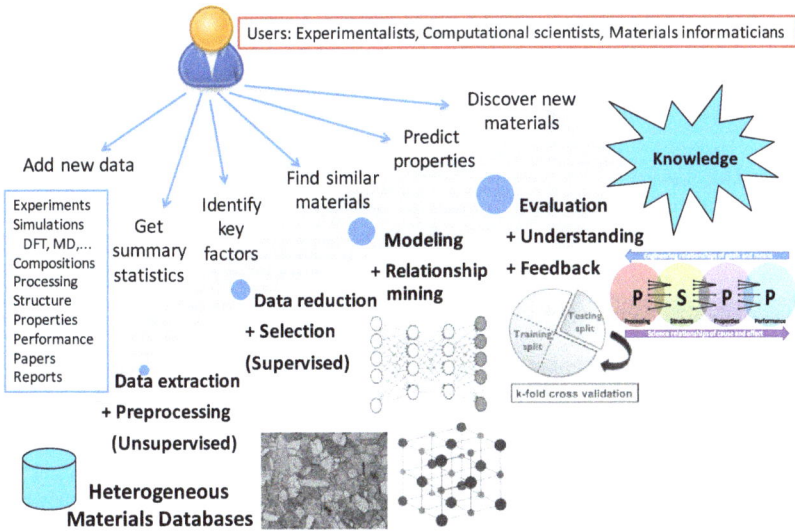

Fig. 4.   AI-driven knowledge discovery workflow for materials informatics. AI techniques, when carefully applied to heterogeneous materials databases can help extract invertible PSPP linkages to accelerate materials discovery and design (reproduced from [1]).

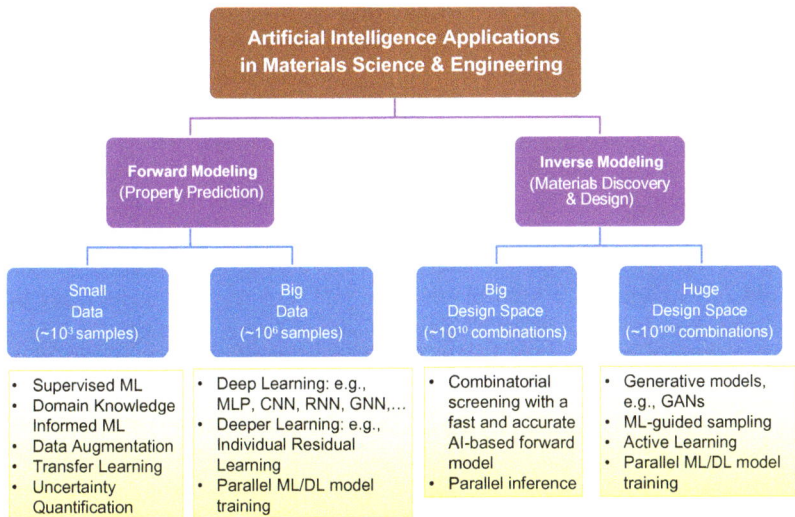

Fig. 5.   A framework for AI applications in materials science and engineering. The two major modeling tasks are in purple, their primary challenges are in blue, and the commonly used AI methodologies to address them are in yellow.

3. AI for Materials: Challenges and Opportunities

The availability of materials data is a prerequisite to perform any kind of AI/ML/DL modeling of materials. In this section, we discuss some unique data-related challenges in materials science and how AI can be used to tackle the same.

One of the biggest challenges for AI algorithms today is the *big data* challenge, i.e., how to extract actionable insights considering all available data, which can be exorbitantly large in many fields of science, such as cosmology and high-energy physics. Although there do exist several big datasets in materials science as well ($\sim 10^6$ samples), most of the materials datasets are relatively small ($\sim 10^3$ samples), thus posing the *small data* challenge. In other words, materials data, whether big or small, is both a resource as well as a challenge, that needs a careful design and application of AI methodologies to optimally utilize all available data.

In addition to data availability, the specific materials problem or use case often defines the design space, or the space of possible materials, a vast majority of which is usually unexplored by experiments or simulations. For example, if we only consider the number of possible ternaries, i.e., materials with three elements, there can be about a million combinations of elements from the periodic table, representing various materials systems. Considering all the possible stoichiometries, the set of possibilities could further expand by a few orders of magnitude. We call this *big design space* ($\sim 10^{10}$ combinations). Since we can never actually experimentally make or even simulate all these potential compounds, the availability of a fast and accurate AI/ML-based forward model is a big advantage for the inverse models in such cases, as we can potentially explore the entire design space using the forward model within a matter of hours and convert the big set of possibilities into a prioritized ranked list for further exploration by simulations and experiments.

However, when we go to microstructure-based representations, even a simple 2-D image of 20×20 pixels with just two possible values per pixel would lead to more than 10^{100} possibilities of the 2-D image. Actual 3-D microstructure images with multiple phases and orientations would simply explode the number of possibilities. We call this as *huge design space* ($\sim 10^{100}$ combinations). It is easy to see that with such an astronomical number of possibilities, even a fast and accurate forward model would be inadequate to explore the entire design space, thereby making inverse design in such cases an extremely challenging problem.

Considering the above-described challenges in materials science, almost all materials discovery problems for specific use cases can be characterized by their data availability (which can be *small* or *big*) and their design space (which can be *big* or *huge*). There exist several AI/ML techniques that have been developed and used by researchers to deal with these challenges in the context of materials science (Figure 5), but most of these are still very much open problems, highlighting the need for closer collaboration between materials scientists and computer scientists, to aid in the development of specialized AI/ML/DL methodologies to solve these problems efficiently.

4. AI for Materials: Illustrative Applications

4.1. *Enabling deeper learning for big materials data*

While the application of traditional ML techniques has become quite common in materials science, there have been limited applications of DL techniques, primarily because DL requires big data in general. Although materials datasets are typically not as big as in some other fields, they can still contain hundreds of thousands of samples at present, especially simulation-based datasets, and are regularly increasing in size. Given the demonstrated potential and advantages of DL and the increasing availability of big materials datasets, it is attractive to build deeper neural networks to try to enhance model accuracy. But quite contrary to what one might expect, arbitrarily making these networks deeper often leads to performance degradation instead of enhancement. This is primarily due to the so-called *vanishing gradient problem*, where the backpropagating gradients gradually become smaller and smaller as they go backwards layer by layer during the training due to being multiplied by small numbers at every layer. Thus, if the network is too deep, they become almost zero by the time they arrive at the beginning of the network, effectively halting the training.

Jha *et al.* [17] developed a DL framework based on individual residual learning (IRNet) to address the vanishing gradient problem in deep neural networks composed of fully connected layers, building upon the residual learning idea that was originally proposed for convolutional neural networks [18]. They introduced the so-called skip connections after every layer of the neural network in order to build very deep neural networks that can work with any vector-based materials representation as input to build accurate property prediction models. This work demonstrated how to enable deeper learning for cases where big materials data are available, by building deep neural networks with up to 48 layers.

IRNet models were recently tested [19] on a variety of materials datasets based on density functional theory (DFT) simulations, such as OQMD [20], AFLOW [21], Materials Project [22], and JARVIS [23], as well as experimental datasets [24], with sizes ranging from a few thousand to a few hundred thousand. The models were found to not only successfully alleviate the vanishing gradient problem and enable deeper learning but also build significantly (up to 47%) better predictive models for a variety of materials properties and input representations as compared to plain DL networks as well as traditional ML models, especially on datasets with more than 20,000 data points.

4.2. *Deep transfer learning for small materials data*

Although the size and availability of materials datasets are increasing, for most cases, it is still far from the big data sizes we see in other domains. This small data problem is especially prevalent for experimental data in materials science, which is often significantly more expensive and time-consuming than simulations. Since DL usually requires big data in order to build accurate models, most of the AI applications on small materials data are limited to using traditional ML algorithms. Thus, building accurate predictive models for small experimental datasets is a major and common challenge in materials science.

In order to take advantage of the high learning capacity of DL models for small materials data, Jha *et al.* [25] used the notion of transfer learning to first build a source DL model from scratch on a big source dataset, which could be from a simulation like DFT, and used the trained model as a starting point for training the target DL model on the small target dataset, which could be experimental. In other words, instead of randomly initial-izing the weights while training the target DL model, the learned weights of the source model were used. This is known as the fine-tuning method of transfer learning, as the network weights learned on the source dataset are fine-tuned using the target dataset. This simple yet powerful idea was found to result in up to 50% more accurate models compared to models trained from scratch. Interestingly, the accuracy of these transfer learning models w.r.t. experimentally observed values of formation energy was comparable and, in some cases, slightly better than even DFT's own accuracy, which is quite remarkable, as the AI models are much faster than DFT.

A key limitation of such transfer learning models is the need for the availability of a large source dataset of the *same* property as the target property, which is not an issue for some properties like formation energy, but there are numerous other materials properties such as exfoliation energy, for which large source datasets are not readily available to directly perform transfer learning. Gupta *et al.* [26] recently built upon earlier works on transfer learning to develop a cross-property transfer learning framework, wherein the source and target properties are allowed to be different. In addition to the fine-tuning method usually used for transfer learning, they also explored feature extraction-based transfer learning, which uses the source model to extract features or semantic vectors on the target dataset, which could then be used as alternate representations of the materials in the target dataset to build any ML/DL model on top of it. The cross-property transfer learning models were evaluated on 39 different target properties and were found to be more accurate than scratch models in 38/39 cases when both types of models used only raw elemental fractions as input. In a more stringent test for cross-property transfer learning models, only the scratch models were allowed to use more informative physical attributes as input, and the cross-property transfer learning models still performed better than scratch models in 27/39 cases, underscoring the wide applicability and usefulness of the framework to tackle the small data challenge in materials science.

4.3. *Deep adversarial learning for microstructure design*

As illustrated earlier, microstructure design is an extremely challenging inverse problem in materials science due to the huge design space of possible microstructure patterns. This is primarily due to the high dimensionality of the microstructure representations. Thus, one of the key challenges for the inverse design of microstructures is the identification of a low-dimensional microstructure representation that could be used for design.

Generative AI models based on deep adversarial learning — in particular, generative adversarial networks (GANs) — have been successfully used for microstructure design. A GAN model consists of two neural networks, called generator and discriminator, which are trained together while competing against each other. The goal of the generator is to produce a fake image, whereas the goal of the discriminator is to learn to distinguish between a real and a fake image. Thus, when trained properly, both the networks then become stronger and stronger until convergence, at which point, the generator is capable of producing realistic fake images.

Yang and Li *et al.* [27] used GANs to develop an end-to-end solution for learning a low-dimensional nonlinear embedding of microstructures for microstructural materials design. The architecture of the generator network took a latent variable matrix consisting of 16 variables arranged as a 4×4 image as input, which was progressively up sampled to generate a 128×128 image. Conversely, the discriminator network took a 128×128 image as input and progressively down sampled it into a probability distribution, in order to classify the input image as real or fake. The GAN model was trained on 5,000 synthetic microstructure images, which enabled it to rapidly generate new realistic microstructure images simply by randomly sampling the 4×4 latent design variable matrix. The GAN-generated images were found to be statistically similar (but not identical) to the training images, indicating successful training.

The developed GAN model was subsequently used with Bayesian optimization to find the optimal latent variables that would generate the microstructure image with the highest optical absorption performance as calculated by rigorous coupled wave analysis simulation. GAN-based optimization discovered microstructures with up to 17% better property values as compared to randomly sampled microstructures, thus confirming the efficacy of GAN-based microstructure design framework. Furthermore, the trained generator was found to be capable of generating higher-resolution microstructure images as well, without the need of retraining the GAN, simply by modifying the dimensions of the latent variable matrix. The authors also found that the discriminator network could be used as a pre-trained model for developing structure–property prediction models.

5. AI for Materials: Outlook and Broader Impact

The numerous applications of AI in materials science that have emerged over the last decade have amply demonstrated its potential to advance materials science. However, the success of this vision hinges on the availability of AI-ready data, for which it is necessary to incentivize and implement FAIR (Findable, Accessible, Interoperable, and Reusable) [28] data practices at a large scale, as also identified by the 2021 MGI Strategic Plan [16]. Furthermore, since materials science data can be quite heterogeneous and noisy, appropriate data quality assessment measures also need to be put in place to maximize the impact of AI techniques in materials science.

Materials are the foundational building blocks of our society. Our advancement thus critically depends on the development of new and improved materials. An informed application of AI in materials science has the potential to enable AI-driven materials research at scale, by integrating it with simulations and experiments, allowing us to efficiently navigate the practically infinite design space of materials in an autonomous manner (self-driving laboratories). In turn, these advances could translate to large-scale manufacturing and deployment, thereby significantly reducing costs and time to insertion of advanced materials.

6. Summary

Recent advances in AI have influenced practically all fields of science and engineering, and materials science is no exception. In this chapter, we discussed how AI can help in advancing materials science and engineering via forward and inverse models that constitute a knowledge discovery workflow, and the major challenges in gainfully implementing such a workflow from the viewpoint of data availability (small and big) and design space of materials (big and huge). A few illustrative examples of AI research works addressing these challenges and some broader impacts of AI in materials science were also discussed. The growing adoption of FAIR data principles in materials science, along with pioneering advances in AI/ML/DL, offers a lot of promise to accelerate the discovery and deployment of advanced materials, which is the vision of MGI.

Acknowledgments

This work is supported in part by: NIST award 70NANB19H005; DOE awards DE-SC0019358, DE-SC0021399; NSF award CMMI-2053929, and Center for Nanocombinatorics at Northwestern University.

References

[1] A. Agrawal and A. Choudhary (2016). Perspective: Materials informatics and big data: Realization of the "fourth paradigm" of science in materials science. *APL Materials*, *4*(053208), 1–10.

[2] T. Hey, S. Tansley, and K. Tolle (2009). *The Fourth Paradigm: Data-Intensive Scientific Discovery*. Redmond, Washington, USA: Microsoft Research.

[3] A. Agrawal and A. Choudhary (2019). Deep materials informatics: Applications of deep learning in materials science. *MRS Communications*, *9*(3), 779–792.

[4] Y. LeCun, Y. Bengio and G. Hinton (2015). Deep learning. *Nature*, *521*(7553), 436–444.

[5] R. Collobert and J. Weston (2008). A unified architecture for natural language processing: Deep neural networks with multitask learning. In *Proceedings of the 25th International Conference on Machine Learning*, pp. 160–167.

[6] A. Krizhevsky, I. Sutskever, and G. Hinton (2017). Imagenet classification with deep convolutional neural networks. *Communications of the ACM*, *60*(6), 84–90.

[7] G. Hinton, L. Deng, D. Yu *et al.* (2012). Deep neural networks for acoustic modeling in speech recognition: The shared views of four research groups. *IEEE Signal Processing Magazine*, *29*(6), 82–97.

[8] S. Grigorescu, B. Trasnea, T. Cocias *et al.* (2020). A survey of deep learning techniques for autonomous driving. *Journal of Field Robotics*, *37*(3), 362–386.

[9] K. Choudhary, B. DeCost, C. Chen *et al.*, (2022). Recent advances and applications of deep learning methods in materials science. *NPJ Computational Materials*, *8*(1), 1–26.

[10] A. Agrawal and A. Choudhary (2018). An online tool for predicting fatigue strength of steel alloys based on ensemble data mining. *International Journal of Fatigue*, *113*, 389–400.

[11] V. Stanev, C. Oses, A. G. Kusne *et al.* (2018). Machine learning modeling of superconducting critical temperature. *NPJ Computational Materials*, *4*(1), 1–14.

[12] A. Furmanchuk, J. Saal, J. Doak *et al.* (2018). Prediction of Seebeck coefficient for compounds without restriction to fixed stoichiometry: A machine learning approach. *Journal of Computational Chemistry*, *39*(4), 191–202.

[13] L. Ward, A. Agrawal, A. Choudhary *et al.* (2016). A general-purpose machine learning framework for predicting properties of inorganic materials. *NPJ Computational Materials*, *2*(1), 1–7.

[14] R. Liu, A. Kumar, Z. Chen *et al.* (2015). A predictive machine learning approach for microstructure optimization and materials design. *Scientific Reports*, *5*(1), 1–22.

[15] J. Rickman, G. Balasubramanian, C. J. Marvel *et al.* (2020). Machine learning strategies for high-entropy alloys. *Journal of Applied Physics*, *128*(22), 221101.

[16] Subcommittee on the Materials Genome Initiative (2021). Materials Genome Initiative Strategic Plan.

[17] D. Jha, L. Ward, Z. Yang *et al.* (2019). IRNet: A general purpose deep residual regression framework for materials discovery. In *Proceedings of the 25th ACM SIGKDD International Conference on Knowledge Discovery and Data Mining (KDD)*, pp. 2385–2393.

[18] K. He, X. Zhang, S. Ren *et al.* (2016). Deep residual learning for image recognition. In *Proceedings of the IEEE Conference on Computer Vision and Pattern Recognition*, pp. 770–778.

[19] D. Jha, V. Gupta, L. Ward *et al.* (2021). Enabling deeper learning on Big Data for materials informatics applications. *Scientific Reports*, *11*(1), 1–12.

[20] S. Kirklin, J. Saal, B. Meredig *et al.* (2015). The open quantum materials database (OQMD): Assessing the accuracy of DFT formation energies. *NPJ Computational Materials*, *1*(1), 1–15.

[21] S. Curtarolo, W. Setyawan, G. L. Hart *et al.* (2012). Aflow: An automatic framework for high-throughput materials discovery. *Computational Materials Science*, *58*, 218–226.

[22] A. Jain, S. P. Ong, G. Hautier *et al.* (2013). Commentary: The materials project: A materials genome approach to accelerating materials innovation. *APL Materials*, *1*(1), 011002.

[23] K. Choudhary, K. F. Garrity, A. C. Reid *et al.* (2020). The joint automated repository for various integrated simulations (JARVIS) for data-driven materials design. *NPJ Computational Materials*, *6*(1), 1–13.

[24] L. Ward, A. Dunn, A. Faghaninia *et al.* (2018). Matminer: An open source toolkit for materials data mining. *Computational Materials Science*, *152*, 60–69.

[25] D. Jha, K. Choudhary, F. Tavazza *et al.* (2019). Enhancing materials property prediction by leveraging computational and experimental data using deep transfer learning. *Nature Communications*, *10*(1), 1–12.

[26] V. Gupta, K. Choudhary, F. Tavazza *et al.* (2021). Cross-property deep transfer learning framework for enhanced predictive analytics on small materials data. *Nature Communications*, *12*(1), 1–10.

[27] Z. Yang, X. Li, C. Brinson *et al.* (2018). Microstructural materials design via deep adversarial learning methodology. *Journal of Mechanical Design*, *140*(11), 10.

[28] M. D. Wilkinson, M. Dumontier, I. J. Aalbersberg *et al.* (2016). The fair guiding principles for scientific data management and stewardship. *Scientific Data*, *3*(1), 1–9.

Particle Physics

© 2023 World Scientific Publishing Company
https://doi.org/10.1142/9789811265679_0025

Chapter 25

Experimental Particle Physics and Artificial Intelligence

David Rousseau

Université Paris-Saclay, CNRS/IN2P3, IJCLab, 91405 Orsay, France
david.rousseau@ijclab.in2p3.fr

1. Introduction

Experimental particle physics relies on two steps: (i) collect data from a particular interaction (e.g., high energy proton–proton collision) with an appropriately designed detector and (ii) infer from the data collected a measurement (a confidence level) on a nature parameter. The data collected comes in generally as a collection of "events", where an event is all the data collected about a particular event, e.g., a proton collision or a neutrino interaction.

In the old days of particle physics, the data were actual pictures obtained, e.g., from bubble chambers. The parameters (origin, direction, energy, and identity) of the visible particles were obtained by humans doing geometrical measurements (with rulers) on each picture, in what can be called **particle-level inference**. Since the breakthrough of the Multiwire Proportional Chamber invented by Georges Charpak in the seventies, raw particle measurements have been read out electronically, and their parameters are inferred algorithmically. The properties of the particles of a single event are then combined to infer what has happened in this particular event. The more interesting heavy particles being studied are very unstable and decay in a cascade of other particles in a cubic millimeter volume before reaching any detecting element. Only particles of a handful of different types are detected. Still, the signature of the original heavy unstable particles can be hinted at more or less clearly through feature engineering, in what can be called **event-level inference**. Finally, the study of all the recorded data (often billions of events), with the help of very accurate simulators, allows inferring fundamental laws of nature, more specifically a confidence interval on a specific parameter, in what can be called **experiment-level inference**.

The experimental particle physics field is used to deal with a large amount of data and was doing Data Science well before the term was coined, compared with, for example, genomics, where complete genomes have only become routine in the last decade. Hence, AI algorithms are evaluated with respect to already sophisticated benchmarks. There is no low-hanging fruit. The first documented attempt to use Artificial Intelligence in particle physics was by Bruce Denby in 1987 [1] using Neural Networks for calorimetry and tracking, which has become again a very active topic. He was quickly followed by [2] in the early nineties, who have notably developed JetNet [3], a generic NN software, which has had some success in the particle physics community in the nineties with over 300 citations. This was followed by an "AI winter" like in other fields.

In Computer Science, various flavors of Boosted Decision Trees [4] have taken the lead in the first decade of the century (and for a while, "Machine Learning" was used instead of "Artificial Intelligence"). They have started to be applied first at MINOS (neutrino) experiment in 2007 and at a much larger scale at the D0 ([5] and others) and CDF ([6] and others) experiments, until 2012. The expertise was carried over to the Large hadron Collider, and AI has significantly impacted Higgs boson Physics at LHC [7], where if a number has to be given, AI allowed a gain in sensitivity equivalent of order 50% more data. For a billion euros worth of infrastructure, it is quite significant.

Since then, the field of application of AI in the Experimental Particle Field has broadened considerably. The purpose of this chapter is a short review of the state of the art on a few selected topics; more details are available in books like [8], even more in the almost comprehensive bibliography in [9], as well as promising avenues. The first sections deal successively with particle-level inference, event-level inference, and experiment-level inference (particularly a subsection on "uncertainty aware training"). The fourth section deals with simulation before the conclusion.

2. Particle-level Inference

The success of deep learning has stemmed first from computer vision on benchmarks like MNIST and ImageNet. Time series and tabular data are also common formats. Particle physics's specificity is to deliver a large quantity of semi-structured data for which off-the-shelf tools are inadequate.

A few examples are displayed in Figures 1–4. Experiments on the Large Hadron Collider like ATLAS or CMS are designed to measure and identify

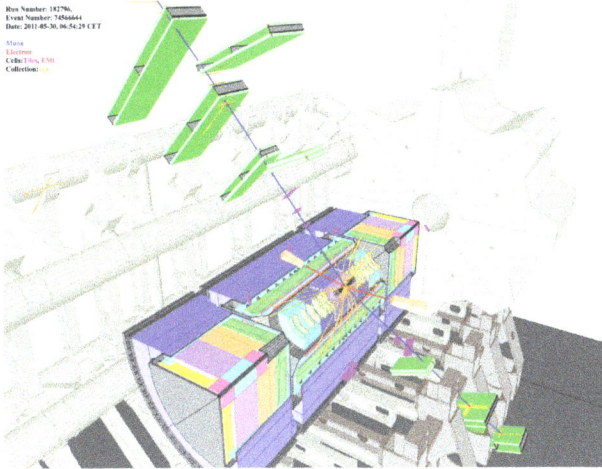

Fig. 1. A candidate for a Higgs boson decaying in two electrons and two muons in the ATLAS detector. The interaction takes place in the center of the detector cut out for visibility. The two muons exit the detector at the bottom right and top left, and the two electrons are stopped in the calorimeter at the right and the left (credit CERN).

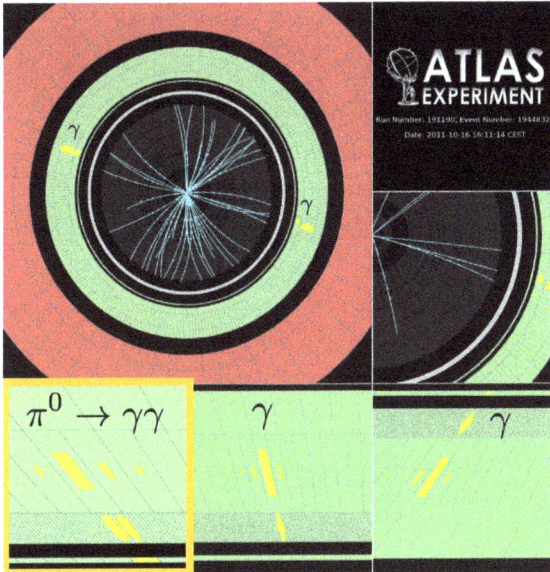

Fig. 2. A candidate for a Higgs boson decaying in two photons (labeled γ) in the ATLAS detector. The bottom left inset shows how a background particle π^0 would look in the calorimeter; the yellow areas are proportional to the energy measured in each cell (the green trapezes) (credit CERN).

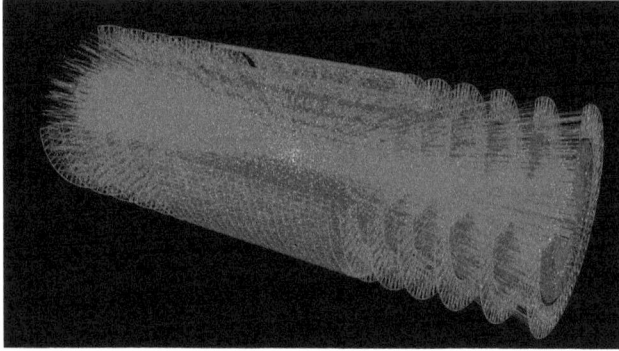

Fig. 3.   Tracks in a TrackML challenge in [11]. The white dots are the measurements to be associated into trajectories (the red lines).

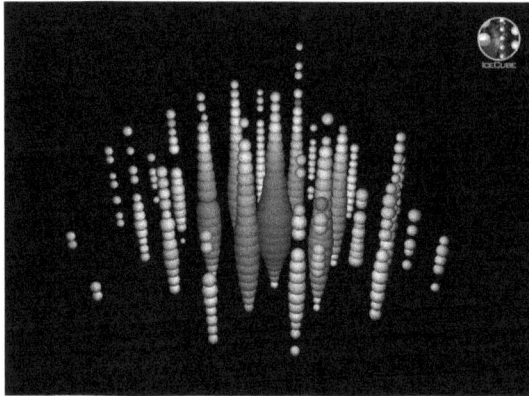

Fig. 4.   A very large energy neutrino candidate. The size of the spheres indicates the amount of light measured, and the color encodes the time of arrival (credit: IceCube collaboration).

as much as possible the firework of particles emerging from the interaction point. Inside out, charged tracks are first measured and then the calorimeter measures the energy and direction of all outgoing particles (charged or not), except for muons which sail through the calorimeter and are measured in the last layers of the experiment and except for neutrinos which are not detected at all.

Figure 1 is a representation of the data which allowed us to identify this event as a possible Higgs boson candidate decaying into two muons (top and bottom) and two electrons (the yellow trapezoids).

Figure 2 shows a 2D projection of the data, which allowed us to identify this event as a possible Higgs boson candidate decaying into two photons: a photon being identified as a compact energy deposit in the calorimeter without any particles pointing to it and with a dense shape (compared to a possible π^0 background). The zoom on the calorimeter shows (with textbook images) that shape analysis allows distinguishing photons from the background. Machine learning can be used to separate photons from the background. However, a classical convolutional neural network will not work on such irregular-shaped pixels, even more when one considers the third dimension does not appear in these images. ML is also used to regress the energy of the photon or electron, for now using Boosted Decision Tree [10] trained on expert-build features. Neural networks would be able to extract more information from the pattern. However, they would rely on accurate simulation to provide training data, which has delayed their adoption.

Figure 3 shows the complexity of reconstructing the trajectories of charged tracks, especially in the context of High-Luminosity LHC, the final upgrade of the LHC to start at the end of the decade. Typically, there are 10,000 charged tracks in one event, which intersection with 10 layers of silicon detectors leave precisely measured 3D points. The crux of the problem is to take the 100,000 points and associate them with tracks which are trajectories that are constrained to be an approximate arc of helices with a well-defined axis and originating from close to the center of symmetry. Moreover, the problem has to be solved quickly (subsecond) as it has to be done for billions of real and simulated events each year.

A two-step competition has been organized to find new algorithms for tracking, first without any speed incentive (on Kaggle [11]) and then with a substantial speed incentive (on Codalab [12]). ML algorithms were shown to be very accurate in the first phase. However, it was not the case when speed was considered. The conclusion was that significant progress would come from hybrid algorithms where ML techniques are combined with optimized combinatorial algorithms (another concrete case showing that there are no low-hanging fruits). In particular, it has shown that graph neural networks will play a more and more important role in such cases. Graph neural networks allow exploiting data that are semi-structured, in particular very unlike images [13].

Figure 4 is a representation of the data from an event in the IceCube experiment in a completely different context. Lines of photomultipliers buried in the ice in the Antarctic detect the Cherenkov light emitted by particles produced by high-energy neutrino, which have crossed the earth before interacting shortly before exiting. Again, despite the very different context, the flexibility of graph neural networks shows promising results [14].

3. Event-level Inference

At this point, now that particles have been identified with a variety of detector technologies, what is known about the event being examined is a list of particles of different types, with an estimation of their kinematic (direction and energy) and estimation of their point of origin, as well as an estimate of the accuracy of their identity and other measurements. The next question is to infer what happened during the collision, mainly what unstable particles have been created and immediately decayed.

It turns out that the unstable particles leave hints of their short existence among the visible particles. One classic example is the invariant mass: energy and momentum are conserved when a particle decays in n secondary particles. The sum of energy and the vectorial sum of the momentum of the secondary particles are one of the original particles. Then, by applying a fundamental law of special relativity (with appropriately chosen units) $E^2 = P^2 + M^2$, one gets $M = \sqrt{(\sum_n E_i^2 - |\sum_n \mathbf{P}_i|^2)}$, where M is the mass of the unstable particle. This is illustrated with the measurement of the Higgs boson decaying into four leptons, one of the channels used to report its discovery in 2012, and still to this day for further studies (a four-lepton event candidate is shown in Figure 1). Figure 5 shows the mass distribution of lepton quadruplets; the peak at 125 GeV is evidence of the existence of the Higgs boson existence, even though assessing this property is part of experiment-level inference (see Section 3). This is a textbook example of how an event-level feature is used for experiment-level inference. Things get more involved when (i) some of the final particles are poorly measured or identified, (ii) not measured at all (case of the neutrinos), or (iii) there are ambiguities in determining the list of particles to be combined. The traditional approach is to craft features based on expected distributions to maximize the sensitivity. The AI approach combines expert-built high-level features or particle kinematics with algorithms like boosted decision trees or more and more neural networks.

A challenge was organized on Kaggle in 2014, the Higgs Boson Machine Learning challenge (HiggsML in short)[15] to explore such cases. Given a simulated dataset of 250k events used for the evidence of the Higgs boson decaying in a tau lepton pair [16], how to maximize the sensitivity? The winner used an ensemble of (3-layer) deep neural networks. However, his/her final score was marginally better than the runner-up who's used random forest. XGBoost [17], a gradient boosting BDT algorithm, was developed and advertised for this challenge and has obtained a score close to the best with much simpler tuning. XGBoost has meanwhile become the *de facto* standard BDT algorithm in the whole Computer Science field. The NN approach was revisited recently [18] using modern NN software and techniques and has obtained marginally better results.

The first complete study using deep learning to identify a specific final state was performed in [19] and will be shortly summarized here. The final state being studied is $\ell\nu$bbjj, where ℓ is a lepton (electron or muon) accurately identified and measured, ν is a neutrino which is poorly measured, and only along two directions, jj are two jets which are somewhat well measured, and bb are two jets created by b quarks, which have been tagged by a special algorithm (making a particle-level inference). The b-tag is not certain, and the corresponding score is an additional feature of each jet. The training is done on 11 million simulated events, either a hypothetical supersymmetric Higgs boson as a signal or a well-known top quark pair as a background. Each particle is represented by a 3-coordinate vector (2 for the neutrino), and the four jets have an additional b-tag score. So, there are 21 low-level features which can be used directly in a classifier. High-level features like the invariant mass mentioned at the beginning of this section can also be used, even though they do not add any information to the low-level features. The paper shows that a shallow neural network (with a single hidden layer) has a classification power that is improved when high-level features are added as extra features, indicating that the shallow NN cannot extract the full information. However, a deep neural network (with three hidden layers, which is hardly deep by today's standard) has, in all cases, better classification power than the shallow one but, more importantly, does not need engineered features, which could be summarized by "the NN learns physics".

However, a similar study by the same authors on a different final state reached a different conclusion; the classifier was still improved when using high-level features [20].

The key message from these studies is that, yes, deep learning can reach higher sensitivity than a simpler BDT. However, it requires a much larger training dataset to reach this sensitivity. It explains the slow adoption of NN for event-level inference because accurately simulated events are very expensive, so a typical analysis will only afford order 100k (billions of events are simulated to analyze the data from a particular experiment, but (i) the simulation budget is split between many different analysis topics and (ii) a significant fraction of simulated events (especially for backgrounds) are lost at pre-selection level). The proof of concept papers uses cheap simulation, which is sufficient to demonstrate the potential of new techniques but cannot be used for inference on real data.

Several recent developments have attempted to facilitate the training of NN for such 4-momentum final states (and more complex ones) by complexifying the neural network structure, as overviewed in [21].

To be complete, there is a line of development called "end-to-end learning" to do event-level inference directly from the raw data by-passing particle-level inference [22].

4. Experiment-level Inference

The discovery of the positron (the antimatter positive electron) was claimed by Anderson from a few pictures obtained from a cloud chamber, where a naked-eye visible trajectory, thin like the one of an electron, appeared to be turning in the wrong direction in a magnetic field. Nowadays, a typical event at the Large Hadron Collider contains thousands of particles reconstructed by sophisticated algorithms. And the existence of the Higgs boson was claimed after an analysis of billions of events.

In some cases, like shown in Figure 5, the Higgs boson manifests itself as a clear peak on a feature. However, the evidence for the decay of the Higgs boson into a tau lepton pair was brought by training a Boosted Decision Tree (BDT) on a dozen variables. The BDT was trained to score Higgs-like events with values close to +1 and background-like events with values close to −1. The resulting analysis is shown in Figure 6, where evidence for the Higgs boson is the excess of data over predicted background contribution in the one or two right-most bins.

In recent years, the LHC experiments have moved from producing evidence of the Higgs boson to measuring in detail its properties and that of other particles. For example, there is today no known mechanism explaining why the universe is made of matter, while matter–antimatter asymmetry has been measured to be tiny. Hints on such a mechanism could be obtained by precisely measuring the angular distribution of Higgs boson decay particles (see, for example, [23]). Such measurement requires sophisticated statistical analysis.

It is usually done (see in particular G. Cowan Statistics review in [25]) by building a maximum likelihood from the binned one dimension event yield distribution (like the ones in Figures 5 and 6), the event yield in one bin following a Poisson distribution, which parameter depends on the estimated background and possible signal contribution. The background estimation is taken from Monte Carlo event simulations, which benefited from a lot of effort to carefully calibrate all its details on auxiliary distributions. In practice, multiple 1D distributions are often used simultaneously to maximize the sensitivity.

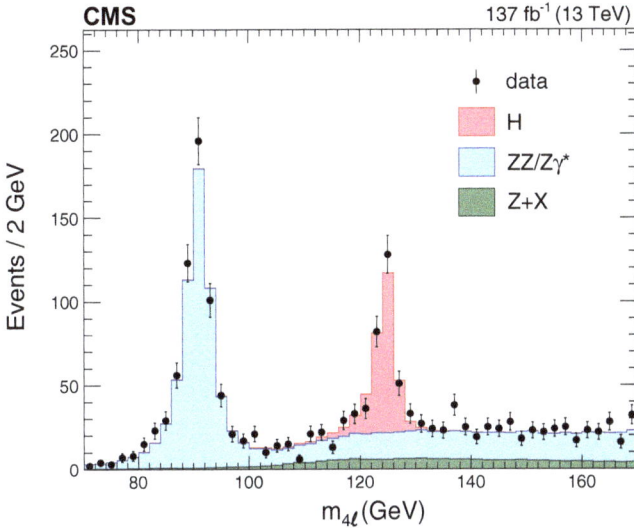

Fig. 5.   Invariant mass distribution of the 4-lepton final state measured by the CMS experiment. The peak at 91 GeV is a rare decay of the Z boson while the peak at 125 GeV is a clear evidence for the Higgs boson [24].

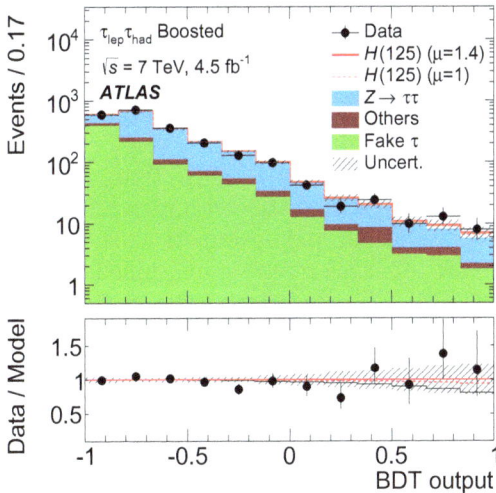

Fig. 6.   BDT discriminant distribution obtained by the ATLAS experiment searching for the Higgs boson decaying into a tau lepton pair. The dots show the data, while the colored histograms show the background prediction. The maybe less clear evidence for the Higgs boson comes from the excess of data over the predicted background in the two rightmost bins, in the distribution shown and five others [16].

A machine learning classifier, as in Figure 6, is effectively reducing the dimension of the feature space to 1 without losing sensitivity as long as it is just a matter of counting signal events. However, at the Large Hadron Collider, the goal is now to do precise measurements of the fundamental theory, which necessitates spotting minor deviations in the whole feature space dimension. The classical way to do it is to use Matrix Elements, which are first principles quantum field theory calculations of each event probability given the entire feature space. While this technique does bring sensitivity, it requires very detailed theoretical calculations, which are not necessarily done with a sufficient level of precision for all processes, and the experimental effects are difficult to take into account.

A machine learning set of techniques called Simulation-Based Inference (formerly called Likelihood-Free Inference) [26] promises to reach the maximal sensitivity with an unbinned multidimension maximum likelihood fit, where a neural network estimates the likelihood. A key ingredient for these techniques is a very accurately calibrated simulator; the field has developed such simulators for the more classical techniques. However, they would be challenged by these techniques at unprecedented levels.

4.1. *Uncertainty aware training*

The primary output of the field of experimental particle physics is publications with a measurement with a confidence interval. Assessing the confidence interval through the careful examination of the behavior of the negative log-likelihood around its minimum is part of the standard procedure (see also [25]). In the simple case of a well-behaved, parabolic, minimum, the confidence interval is $\pm\sigma = \pm(\sigma_{\text{stat}} \oplus \sigma_{\text{syst}})$, where $\oplus$ indicates a quadratic sum, σ_{stat} the statistical uncertainties, and σ_{stat} the systematical uncertainties. The statistical and systematical uncertainties (as they are called in physics) are often referred to in machine learning as aleatoric and epistemic uncertainties [27], respectively. The statistical uncertainty would vanish in the limit of infinite data, while the systematical uncertainty is unchanged (unless the model is adapted). Systematical uncertainties cover all the uncertainties due to the uncertainty on the auxiliary inputs to the measurement (often called Nuisance Parameters) and possible departure from the underlying hypothesis to the measurement.

The first issue is to continue to build trustable confidence intervals while machine learning is used more and more in the pipeline. For example, as related in [7] already mentioned, several first papers using machine learning in analyses at the Large Hadron Collider were quoting in addition to the primary measurement, a backup measurement using traditional cut-based (or rule-based) techniques which were both compatible and less precise. The backup measurement was used to convince, first, the other co-authors and, second, the whole community that ML techniques could be demonstrated to be trustable through a thorough study of their behavior in auxiliary feature space regions. More recent papers do not exhibit such backup measurements as the trust in ML techniques has improved. Needless to say, careful checks of ML techniques on auxiliary feature space regions continue to be done.

A second issue is to go further, to trust ML actually to reduce the overall uncertainty, including the systematical uncertainties. What is usually done is to optimize the ML technique to reduce the statistical uncertainty while maintaining the level of systematical uncertainties through common sense prescription, like avoiding using features that are not well described by the simulation. The next level is to consider the systematic uncertainty already at the training stage, hence "uncertainty-aware training".

Various techniques are being developed; see, for example, [28], some flavor is given in the following. The "pivot" technique [29] uses a neural network adversarial architecture to train a minimizer while reducing its sensitivity to a Nuisance Parameter. Figure 7 shows the significance (in standard deviations, the higher, the better) of a simplified benchmark analysis. The maximum of each curve shows the maximal significance of an analysis using a given classifier. The coupling λ allows tuning the adversarial piece of a NN from 0 (falling back to a classical NN) to large values minimizing the dependency on the Nuisance Parameter. Inevitably reducing σ_{syst} comes at the price of increasing σ_{stat}; hence a tuning is needed to minimize the overall σ, equivalent to maximize the significance, here for $\lambda = 10$.

A more involved technique called INFERNO [30] is built on the fact that a 1D histogram is often used to measure the parameter of interest while other 1D histograms are used to constrain the Nuisance Parameters. With INFERNO, the summary statistics (=the 1D histogram) are built automatically in an optimal way. Figure 8 shows that with this technique (on a simple benchmark), the profiled likelihood is narrower than in the standard case, indicating a reduction of the overall uncertainty. Other techniques have been developed, so far only on simple benchmarks. A danger of injecting a model of the systematic at the training stage is Goodhart's law [31], well known in economy and management: "When a measure becomes a target, it ceases to be a good measure". In other words, if the model is "informed" about the Nuisance Parameter, how to trust the evaluation of the systematics (the impact of the Nuisance Parameter) coming from that same model before it was evaluated separately?

Further progress will benefit significantly from shared datasets and benchmarks with sufficient complexity so that these advanced techniques

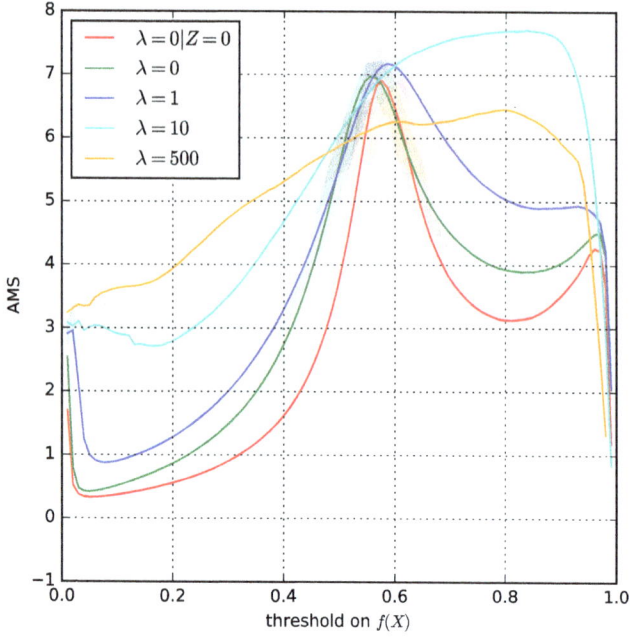

Fig. 7.   Significance of a benchmark analysis as a function of the threshold on the classifier score, for different values of the λ coupling parameter [29].

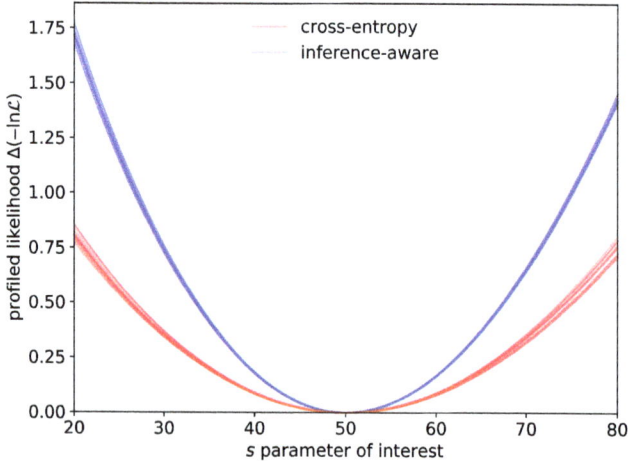

Fig. 8.   Profiled likelihood around the expectation value for the parameter of interest of 10 trained inference-aware models (built with the INFERNO technique) and 10 trained cross-entropy loss based models [30].

can be compared and well understood to build the trust of the entire community.

5. Simulation

Simulation plays a significant role in the design of future experiments but also in the analysis of the current ones, as detailed in the previous section. The primary interaction of particles like the collision of two protons at the Large Hadron Collider can be relatively accurately described by simulators like MadGraph [32] (see also [33] and [34] in this book). The set of particles obtained is then tracked with a simulation engine like Geant4 [35] through a virtual detector where they leave energy deposition and interact. Finally, the readout of these energy depositions is simulated to obtain data with the same format as the one coming from the real detector, associated with the ground truth. These simulators have been developed since the seventies [36, 37] and have become quite sophisticated. However, this comes with the price of being heavy in resources: one single event fully simulated with Geant4 in an LHC experiment requires about 1000 CPU seconds. Various fast parameterization techniques have been developed. However, they need careful hand-crafted tuning.

AI generator models are being developed in particular for the simulation of calorimeters [38] (as illustrated in Figure 9), which is tempting for several reasons:

- The calorimeter simulation is by far dominating the total simulation time.
- One particle impacting a calorimeter can lead to thousands of secondary particles (called the shower) to be tracked through the detector, while only the total energy deposit per sensitive element (a cell) is useful. So, it is tempting to bypass the intermediate complex state with secondary particles generation to go directly from the impacting particle parameter to the cell energy deposits.
- Calorimeters are designed to be linear (in the mathematical sense) to an excellent approximation, that is, the raw signal from an event with thousands of particles can be calculated as the sum of the raw signal from each particle.

So, if a generator model can be trained to reproduce individual showers from Geant4, it could be used within the simulation framework to speed it up considerably. Several proofs of concepts have been developed, using either Generative Adversarial Networks or Variational Auto Encoders. The beauty of the technique is that although the generators are trained to match the N individual cell energy distributions, they will learn about

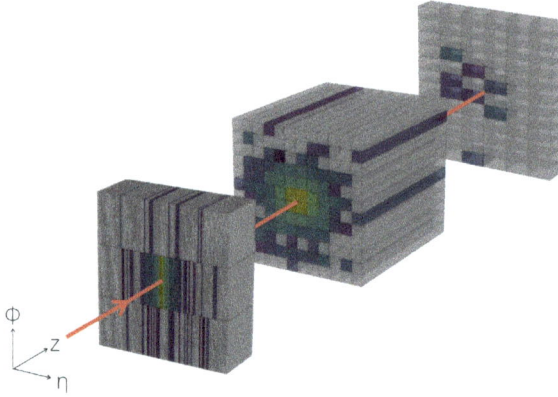

Fig. 9.   Electromagnetic shower in a simplified description of the ATLAS electromagnetic calorimeter. The three layers have been staggered for visibility. The complete calorimeter is a cylinder with two end-caps; only a small portion is represented here. The color encodes the amount of energy deposited in each cell [39].

all the correlations so that high-level observables like shower shapes (n-th moment, secondary minima) will also match without explicit constraint. The challenges still to be overcome are the following:

- Determining how accurate is accurate enough: a small systematic bias on individual showers can have a big impact on the total event simulation as it accumulates through the thousands of individual showers.
- Improve the description of the long tails of distribution: occasional fluctuations rarely appear in the training sample yet have to be included in the model as they are often amplified by the event selection process.
- Describing a detector in its full complexity: real-life calorimeters are complex 3D objects, where cells can be seen as voxels of irregular shape. Proof of concepts usually picks a region where translation symmetry holds. However, a production model should be able to deal with edges and changes in granularity.

6. Conclusion

Like in other scientific fields, artificial intelligence is used more and more in experimental high-energy physics to exploit the last bit of information produced from billions of euros in infrastructures. There has been progress in many areas, mainly through the design of neural network architecture adapted to the specificities of the data produced and the tasks. Relying primarily on supervised machine learning, accurate, fast simulators are needed. One challenge is to obtain the several orders of magnitude speed-up promised by generator models while maintaining the accuracy of the current heavy simulators. Another area (not covered in this short review) where the inference speed of trained NN models can be leveraged is the trigger [40], where fast particle-level and event-level inference, implemented in dedicated hardware like FPGA [41], is used to decide online whether an event should be retained for further analysis.

Parallel to the growing use of AI in society (like in medical diagnostic), there is a component of trust which has to be taken into account while AI is used more and more in physics papers. In a physics paper, the trust is quantified by the systematic uncertainty, but there is also an unquantifiable part: Is the reader convinced or not? Open datasets and challenges [42] participate in building the trust allowing different algorithms to be compared and studied on the same reference and trigger in-depth exchanges between experts of both AI and physics about the merit of different approaches. More is needed, particularly for experiment-level inference, where many innovative Proof-of-Concept papers have been published, but experimental papers using these techniques are rare.

And to conclude on a topic which could not be covered here, the LHC experiments (due to continuing to take data well into the thirties) were designed in the nineties when AI was not on the horizon. A new generation of experiments is being developed, with AI playing an essential role in data reduction. A fascinating avenue is to have AI play an essential role in designing the experiments themselves to maximize their sensitivity *a priori* (and not *a posteriori* once the data have been collected). A variety of techniques are being explored like Bayesian Optimization, Reinforcement Learning, Differential Programming, and Topological Optimization, see, for example, [43].

References

[1] B. H. Denby (1988). Neural networks and cellular automata in experimental high-energy physics. *Computer Physics Communications, 49*, 429–448.

[2] L. Lonnblad, C. Peterson, and T. Rognvaldsson (1990). Finding gluon jets with a neural trigger. *Physical Review Letters, 65*, 1321–1324.

[3] C. Peterson, T. Rognvaldsson, and L. Lonnblad (1994). JETNET 3.0: A versatile artificial neural network package. *Computer Physics Communications, 81*, 185–220.

[4] Y. Coadou (2022). Boosted decision trees. In *Artificial Intelligence for High Energy Physics*. World Scientific, pp. 9–58. https://doi.org/10.1142/9789811234033_0002.

[5] V. M. Abazov, B. Abbott, A. Abdesselam *et al.* (2001). A Quasi model independent search for new physics at large transverse momentum. *Physical Review, D64*, 012004.

[6] T. Aaltonen, A. Abulencia, J. Adelman *et al.* (2008). Model-independent and Quasi-model-independent search for new physics at CDF. *Physical Review, D78*, 012002.

[7] A. Radovic, M. Williams, D. Rousseau *et al.* (2018). Machine learning at the energy and intensity frontiers of particle physics. *Nature, 560*(7716), 41–48.

[8] P. Calafiura, D. Rousseau, and K. Terao (eds.) (2022). *Artificial Intelligence for High Energy Physics.*World Scientific.

[9] HEP ML Community (2022). A living review of machine learning for particle physics. https://iml-wg.github.io/HEPML-LivingReview/.

[10] M. Aaboud, G. Aad, B. Abbott *et al.* (2019). Electron and photon energy calibration with the ATLAS detector using 2015–2016 LHC proton-proton collision data. *Journal of Instrumentation, 14*(03), P03 017–P03 017. https://doi.org/10.1088/1748-0221/14/03/p03017.

[11] S. Amrouche, L. Basara, P. Calafiura *et al.* (2019). The tracking machine learning challenge: Accuracy phase. In *The NeurIPS 2018 Competition.* Springer International Publishing, pp. 231–264.

[12] S. Amrouche, L. Basara, P. Calafiura *et al.* (2022). The tracking machine learning challenge: Throughput phase. *Computing and Software for Big Science, 5*, to be published.

[13] J. Duarte and J.-R. Vlimant (2022). Graph neural networks for particle tracking and reconstruction. In *Artificial Intelligence for High Energy Physics.* World Scientific, pp. 387–436. https://www.worldscientific.com/doi/abs/10.1142/9789811234033_0012.

[14] R. Abbasi, M. Ackermann, J. Adams *et al.* (2021). Reconstruction of neutrino events in IceCube using graph neural networks. *PoS, ICRC2021*, 1044.

[15] C. Adam-Bourdarios, G. Cowan, C. Germain *et al.* (2015). The Higgs boson machine learning challenge. In C. Cowan, I. Germain, Guyon, B. Kégl, and D. Rousseau, (eds.), ser. *Proceedings of Machine Learning G. Research*, Vol. 42. Montreal, Canada: PMLR, pp. 19–55. http://proceedings.mlr.press/v42/cowa14.html.

[16] G. Aad, B. Abbott, J. Abdallah *et al.* (2015). Evidence for the Higgs-boson Yukawa coupling to tau leptons with the ATLAS detector. *JHEP, 4*, 117.

[17] T. Chen and C. Guestrin (2016). XGBoost: A scalable tree boosting system. In *Proceedings of the 22nd ACM SIGKDD International Conference on Knowledge Discovery and Data Mining*, ser. KDD '16. New York, NY, USA: ACM, pp. 785–794. http://doi.acm.org/10.1145/2939672.2939785.

[18] G. C. Strong (2020). On the impact of selected modern deep-learning techniques to the performance and celerity of classification models in an experimental high-energy physics use case. *Machine Learning: Science and Technology, 1*(4), 045006. http://dx.doi.org/10.1088/2632-2153/ab983a.

[19] P. Baldi, P. Sadowski, and D. Whiteson (2014). Searching for exotic particles in high-energy physics with deep learning. *Nature Communications, 5*(1). http://dx.doi.org/10.1038/ncomms5308.

[20] P. Baldi, P. Sadowski, and D. Whiteson (2015). Enhanced Higgs Boson to $\tau^+\tau^-$ search with deep learning. *Physical Review Letters, 114*(11), 111801.

[21] P. Baldi, P. Sadowski, and D. Whiteson (2022). Deep learning from four vectors. In *Artificial Intelligence for High Energy Physics*. World Scientific, pp. 59–83. https://doi.org/10.1142/9789811234033_0003.

[22] A. Aurisano and L. H. Whitehead (2022). End-to-end analyses using image classification. In *Artificial Intelligence for High Energy Physics*. World Scientific, February, pp. 313–353. https://doi.org/10.1142/9789811234033_0010.

[23] G. Aad, B. Abbott, B. Abbott *et al.* (2020). Test of CP invariance in vector-boson fusion production of the Higgs boson in the H to tau tau channel in proton-proton collisions at s=13TeV with the ATLAS detector. *Physics Letters B, 805*, 135426.

[24] A. Sirunyan, A. Tumasyan, W. Adam *et al.* (2021). Constraints on anomalous Higgs boson couplings to vector bosons and fermions in its production and decay using the four-lepton final state. *Physical Review D, 104*(5), 052004.

[25] P. A. Zyla, R. M. Barnett, J. Beringer *et al.* (2020). Review of particle physics. *Progress of Theoretical and Experimental Physics, 2020*(8), 083C01. https://doi.org/10.1093/ptep/ptaa104.

[26] J. Brehmer and K. Cranmer (2022). Simulation-based inference methods for particle physics. In *Artificial Intelligence for High Energy Physics*. World Scientific, February, pp. 579–611. https://doi.org/10.1142/9789811234033_0016.

[27] E. Hüllermeier and W. Waegeman (2021). Aleatoric and epistemic uncertainty in machine learning: An introduction to concepts and methods. *Machine Learning, 110*(3), 457–506. http://dx.doi.org/10.1007/s10994-021-05946-3.

[28] T. Dorigo and P. de Castro (2022). Dealing with nuisance parameters using Machine Learning in high energy physics: A review. In *Artificial Intelligence for High Energy Physics*. World Scientific, pp. 613–661. https://doi.org/10.1142/9789811234033_0017.

[29] G. Louppe, M. Kagan, and K. Cranmer (2017). Learning to pivot with adversarial networks. In I. Guyon, U. V. Luxburg, S. Bengio, H. Wallach, R. Fergus, S. Vishwanathan and R. Garnett (eds.), *Advances in Neural Information Processing Systems*, Vol. 30. Curran Associates, Inc. https://papers.nips.cc/paper/2017/hash/48ab2f9b45957ab574cf005eb8a76760-Abstract.html.

[30] P. De Castro and T. Dorigo (2019). INFERNO: Inference-aware neural optimisation. *Computer Physics Communication, 244*, 170–179.

[31] M. Strathern (1997). 'Improving ratings': Audit in the British university system. *European Review, 5*(3), 305–321. https://www.cambridge.org/core/journals/european-review/article/abs/improving-ratings-audit-in-the-british-university-system/FC2EE640C0C44E3DB87C29FB666E9AAB.

[32] J. Alwall, R. Frederix, S. Frixione *et al.* (2014). The automated computation of tree-level and next-to-leading order differential cross sections, and their matching to parton shower simulations. *JHEP, 7*, 079.

[33] A. Butter and T. Plehn (2022). Generative networks for LHC events. In *Artificial Intelligence for High Energy Physics*. World Scientific, pp. 191–240. https://doi.org/10.1142/9789811234033_0007.

[34] R. Gupta (2022). Particle physics theory and AI. In *Artificial Intelligence and Science*, to appear.

[35] S. Agostinelli, J. Allison, K. Amako *et al.* (2003). GEANT4: A simulation toolkit. *Nuclear Instruments and Methods A*, *506*, 250.

[36] R. Brun, R. Hagelberg, M. Hansroul *et al.* (1978). Geant: Simulation program for particle physics experiments. User guide and reference manual. 76 pages. CERN-DD-78-2, CERN-DD-78-2-REV.

[37] H.-U. Bengtsson and T. Sjostrand (1986). PYTHIA: The Lund Monte-Carlo for hadronic processes. *Conference Proceeding C*, Vol. 860623, p. 311.

[38] M. Paganini, L. de Oliveira, B. Nachman, D. Derkach, F. Ratnikov, A. Ustyuzhanin, and A. Ghosh (2022). Generative models for fast simulation. In *Artificial Intelligence for High Energy Physics*. World Scientific, February, pp. 153–189. https://doi.org/10.1142/9789811234033_0006.

[39] M. Paganini, L. de Oliveira, and B. Nachman (2018). CaloGAN : Simulating 3D high energy particle showers in multilayer electromagnetic calorimeters with generative adversarial networks. *Physical Review*, *D97*(1), 014021.

[40] P. Harris and N. Tran (2022). Machine learning for triggering and data acquisition. In *Artificial Intelligence for High Energy Physics*. World Scientific, February, pp. 265–309. https://doi.org/10.1142/9789811234033_0009.

[41] T. Aarrestad, V. Loncar, N. Ghielmetti *et al.* (2021). Fast convolutional neural networks on FPGAs with hls4ml. *Machine Learning: Science and Technology*, *2*(4), 045015.

[42] D. Rousseau and A. Ustyuzhanin (2022). Machine learning scientific competitions and datasets. In *Artificial Intelligence for High Energy Physics*. World Scientific, pp. 765–812. https://doi.org/10.1142/9789811234033_0020.

[43] T. Dorigo (2020). Geometry optimization of a muon-electron scattering detector. *Physics Open*, *4*, 100022. https://doi.org/10.1016/j.physo.2020.100022.

© 2023 World Scientific Publishing Company
https://doi.org/10.1142/9789811265679_0026

Chapter 26

AI and Theoretical Particle Physics

Rajan Gupta[*,‡], Tanmoy Bhattacharya[*,§], and Boram Yoon[†,¶]

[*]*Los Alamos National Laboratory, Theoretical Division T-2, Los Alamos, NM 87545, USA*

[†]*Los Alamos National Laboratory, Computer Computational and Statistical Sciences CCS-7, Los Alamos, NM 87545, USA*

[‡]*rajan@lanl.gov*
[§]*tanmoy@lanl.gov*
[¶]*boram@lanl.gov*

1. Introduction

Modern high-energy physics analyses make extensive use of large-scale computing, and many advances in computing were driven by the needs of this community. The needed computational resources are, however, fast outpacing the growth in hardware capability, therefore new techniques and algorithms are needed to reach the design goals of precision experiments and to make predictions of the Standard Model (SM) and theories beyond in order to compare them to experiments. Machine Learning (ML) provides a very important tool in this respect: it provides a general approach for devising algorithms to approximately solve a multitude of problems at far less cost — both for code development and for execution — than traditional methods.

One can view machine learning as a data-driven development of pattern matching, interpolation schemes, or surrogate models. Most of the powerful machine learning systems available today are black boxes, whose detailed analytical structure is difficult, if not impossible, to elucidate. This, however, is nothing new to computational high-energy physicists: numerical methods like lattice quantum chromodynamics (QCD) [1,2] have long supplanted analytical calculations even though the simulations are inscrutable (see Section 7). The only true requirement, as always, is not an analytic understanding but correctness guarantees assured by a principled estimation of bias and uncertainty in the predictions. In this chapter, we discuss the application of machine learning in speeding up predictions of the SM and beyond the standard model (BSM) theories, speeding up simulations of lattice QCD, in fitting data including global fits to obtain parton distribution functions (PDFs), and constraining the space of possible BSM and string theories. The scope of ongoing research is large and the pace is frantic. We aim to communicate some of the excitement in this review.

2. Surrogate Models: Looking for a Needle in a Haystack

Three very high impact and related uses of ML in high-energy physics (HEP) are to (i) connect individual detector outputs from billions of events (petabytes of experimental data) to an [un]characterized signal, (ii) provide signals that distinguish different BSM theories as a function of the free parameters that characterize these theories, and (iii) survey large regions of possible [string] theories that are not ruled out by known low-energy physics. Machine learning is very well suited for such pattern matching and searches to find a signal (well characterized or hidden) from a large body of data. It is typically a data-driven process without an underlying theory, but symmetries and constraints of the theory can/should be built in to make it more physics-aware. In the following, we give examples of how ML systems have transformed such analyses.

2.1. *Classifying an event*

A typical event in collider experiments consists of hits (energy or charge deposition) in thousands of detector units. These hits (called particle-level events) are caused by standard model particles that survive the evolution between the initial collision vertex and the final detection or are created in between as illustrated in Figure 1. What we are interested in are signatures of new physics. This requires reconstructing the vertex since novel particles are expected to survive for a very short time, i.e., in a millimeter or smaller-sized region about the vertex. This involves deciphering from a large volume of high-dimensional particle-level detected data the [virtual, exotic] particles produced right after the initial collision (labeled parton level) and their decay channels. The straightforward first use of ML to reduce dimensionality is to show it millions of such events and train it to classify patterns. While this is doable, it is inefficient. SM theory tells us that charged energetic SM particles produce jets (collimated beams of particles typically coming from a single progenitor) and building in this knowledge is essential for efficiency. For example, for strong interactions

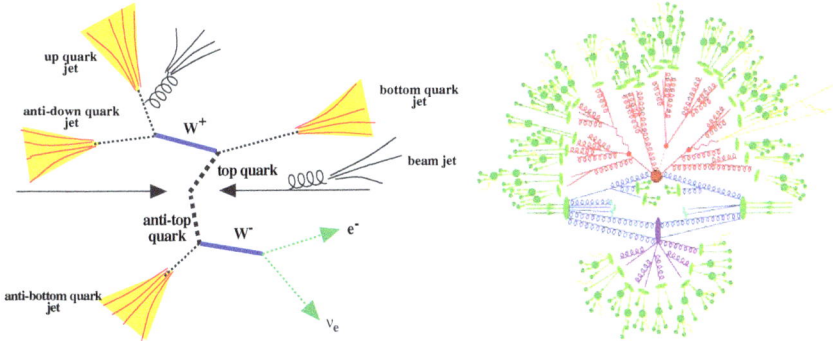

Fig. 1. *(Left)* An event initiated by electron–antielectron (or quark–antiquark) annihilation into a $t, \bar{t}$ quark pair production. The t and $\bar{t}$ are very short lived (5×10^{-25} sec) and decay into $W^- b \; W^+ \bar{b}$. The W boson and the b quarks also decay rapidly (3×10^{-25} and $\sim 10^{-12}$ secs, respectively) producing bottom, up, and antidown quark ($b, \bar{b}, u, \bar{d}$) jets. Also shown are two other jets: one from the radiation of an energetic photon from the initial electron and one from gluon emission from the up quark. In this event, the final state has six partons ($b, \bar{b}, u, \bar{d}, g$, and γ) that produce jets, and the neutrino (ν_e) and e^- from W^- decay that fly away. (Figure courtesy Pekka Sinervo). *(Right)* A pp event with hard collision between two constituent partons (red circle) that creates parton jets (red). Collisions between remnants of pp (purple) similarly produce away side partons. These partons also transform into jets of hadrons (green) that trigger the detectors. Soft gluons that neutralize color are not shown in either figure.

described by QCD, one could classify jets by whether they arose from a quark or a gluon progenitor. Thus, one could first train a ML system to recognize quark and gluon jets and how to distinguish between them and then classify each particle-level event (hits in thousands of detectors) in terms of jets and their progenitors. This reduction in dimension (data compression) from detector signals to jets to a collision (called particle-level to parton-level to event-level) is the sought for translation between signals in detectors and the language of physics [3–5].

ML systems are ideally suited for this task and are now ubiquitous and essential for such analyses (see David Rousseau, *ibid*). Examples of recent developments are given in [6] for extracting information on jet substructure and in [7] for SymmetryGAN used for inferring symmetries.

2.2. *Scattering amplitudes and cross-sections*

Theoretical predictions of expected outcomes in high-energy collider experiments are differential cross-sections. These require the calculation of quantum mechanical amplitudes for a certain well-specified initial state going into a given final state of partons (amplitude for parton-level description) as illustrated in Figure 1. These partons are then transformed into particles that reach the detectors using jet generators.

For higher precision and greater detail, theorists calculate differential cross-sections with increasingly more partons in the final state and with fewer phase space variables (4-momenta of various particles) integrated over. These corrections to the basic interaction are ordered in terms of details: leading order (LO), next-to-leading order (NLO), and so forth. Attaining each order of these theoretical calculations has required years of effort by the community. These amplitudes, say at next-to-next-to-leading order (NNLO), involve multidimensional integrals over the allowed phase space (momentum) of each virtual particle. The integrands are convolutions and complex; they can have large logarithms, singular regions, large cancellations, and highly peaked structures that require care during numerical integration. Physicists know how to deal with these and get finite physical answers, however, the evaluation is very computationally expensive (up to millions of core hours per event).

The output, on the other hand, is a well-behaved number (distribution). Furthermore, these results are governed by symmetries such as invariance under rotation about the initial collision axis that have to be implemented in the analysis. The goal is to replace these expensive calculations with ML regression models. A typical procedure for generating parton-level amplitudes is to (1) choose random samples of phase space points for a given initial state in a known theory (say the standard model) and evaluate the amplitudes or cross-sections using traditional approaches, (2) train an ML regression model to predict the same quantities for each phase space point, and (3) use the trained ML to predict amplitudes or cross-sections for new desired points, instead of the computationally expensive traditional calculations. In this procedure, the ML regression model learns about the correlation between the input and output variables and efficiently interpolates and extrapolates from the input parameters (or output) used for the training data for new evaluation points.

The reduction in the computation cost due to not having to do the complex integrals can be factors of $10^3 - 10^6$ or even more. These data can then be compared to experimental data (similarly compressed) to look for signals (agreements, disagreements, or anomalies) via pattern matching.

In [8], the authors trained a gradient boosting decision tree (GBDT) regression algorithm to make predictions of the amplitudes of the $gg \to ZZ$ process for a given phase space point. A similar approach approximating the multivariable scattering amplitudes of $e^+e^- \to$ 5-jets using a fully connected neural network has been explored in [9].

To constrain the parameters of a BSM theory, this process can be carried out for various values of couplings and masses and a further ML model can be used to interpolate over possible values. In [10], the authors trained a distributed Gaussian processes (DGP) regression algorithm to predict the Minimal Supersymmetric SM (MSSM) cross-sections at NLO.

A key issue in using such surrogate models, or any numerical calculation in general, is uncertainty estimation. This is important in many fields where the results of ML form the basis of action with serious consequences for incorrect decisions. But, in scientific disciplines as well, the same control over uncertainties is needed for the field to make progress. The purpose of theoretical calculations such as these is often to provide, as a gold standard, predictions of the theory against which other approximate techniques or experimental evidence can be evaluated. Not having a robust estimate of the uncertainty in the gold standard dilutes its use, except when they are known to be negligible compared to other uncertainties in the calculation.

The problem with black box ML methods that we focus on is that they are often not amenable to an analysis of systematic errors. To counter this, they are often used in situations where they form an inner component of a self-correcting calculation: conceptually, they generate hypotheses whose correctness affects the computational load but not the accuracy of the answers. An example of such use is in constructing proposals for an update of a gauge configuration in a Metropolis accept/reject step as discussed in Section 5. For a general method for bias correction for averages of a surrogate observable, see Section 8.

3. ML Models as Fitting Functions

In some analyses of physics data, the exact fitting functional form describing the underlying physics theory is not known. For such cases, ML regression models can be used to parameterize the physics data. The NNPDF collaboration (http://nnpdf.mi.infn.it/) proposed an approach for the global analyses of parton distribution functions (PDFs) using machine learning, called the NNPDF framework [11–13]. PDFs describe the probability density of quarks and gluons in a hadron as a function of the momentum fraction x carried by the parton. They cannot be computed directly but are extracted from data using a very systematic combined analysis of theoretical predictions and experimental results, initially from HERA (Hamburg, Germany) and now from the large hadron collider (LHC) at Geneva, Switzerland, etc. The output is a Monte Carlo representation of PDFs and their uncertainties: a probability distribution in a space of functions. These PDFs are essential inputs in the search for new physics in such experiments.

As an example of the analysis, a neural network is used to parameterize the PDFs $f_k(x, Q_0)$ as

$$x f_k(x, Q_0) = A_k x^{1-\alpha_k} (1-x)^{\beta_k} \mathrm{NN}_k(x), \tag{1}$$

where k is the index of the eight different PDF bases, which are linear combinations of the quarks, antiquarks, and gluons, Q_0 is the parametrization scale, and $\mathrm{NN}_k(x)$ is the neural network regression model. The NNPDF framework generates artificial Monte Carlo data replicas based on the experimental covariance matrix of each experiment and determines the free parameters A_k, α_k, β_k, and the neural network parameters. To avoid the issue of the scale of the momentum fraction x, the regression model takes two input variables of $(x, \ln x)$, and to minimize the over-fitting risk, they use a relatively small fully connected neural network of 2-25-20-8 neurons, where the first and last numbers indicate the number of input and output nodes and the two middle numbers indicate the size of the hidden layers. In the latest framework, NNPDF4.0, a single neural network with eight output nodes is successfully trained for all eight different PDF bases indexed by k.

Two more examples are from lattice QCD. First, to describe the potential between two heavy quarks, [14] used an artificial neural network as a general fitting function. They trained two artificial neural networks to represent the real and imaginary parts of the heavy quark potential using the lattice QCD data and obtained a good model-independent empirical description of the heavy quark potential. Second, in Ref. [15], ML was used to tune a relativistic heavy-quark action for charm quarks. The action, described by five parameters, was first tuned using the experimental charmonium ground-state masses with various quantum numbers and then validated by simulating it to reproduce the same spectrum.

4. Multidimensional Integration Using Machine Learning

Many physics calculations involve multidimensional integration whose analytic solution is not known. Numerical integration methods are used to evaluate the integrals and are often computationally expensive and bottlenecks in the overall analysis. When the dimension of the integration is large, as in lattice QCD (LQCD), Monte Carlo methods are the most efficient. Monte Carlo integration has two steps — efficient but random sampling of the space of independent variables and the evaluation of the integrand for each random sample; ML can speed up both steps.

In most Monte Carlo integration algorithms implementing importance sampling, the goal of the random sampling is to draw samples from a specific distribution, such as the absolute value of the integrand whose value is accessible only through numerical evaluation for a given sample point. Various approaches, such as the VEGAS [16–18] and hybrid Monte Carlo (HMC) [19] algorithms, have been developed, and recently, new algorithms based on generative ML models have been proposed [20–24].

Reference [20] provided a general numerical integration algorithm using ML and published an integration library: *i-flow*. They implemented the importance of sampling using normalizing flows [25,26], which is a family of generative models for efficient sampling and density evaluation of a specified probability distribution, and demonstrated its efficiency on various problems. For each sample, the integrand is calculated and the integral is estimated as its expected value.

For multidimensional integration, recognizing the efficient interpolation ability of ML models, [27] proposed training a regression model to emulate the integrand using the collected samples and obtain a better estimate of the integral. In this approach, the effect of the difference between the true integrand and the ML model is quantified using the bias correction method described in Section 8.

Lattice QCD calculations typically require integration over the gauge fields and the integration dimension in state-of-the-art calculations is $\mathcal{O}(10^{10})$. Markov Chain Monte Carlo (MCMC) methods are used to draw the samples but are computationally expensive and produce samples with large autocorrelations. New approaches using generative ML models are under active development [21–24,28]. A more detailed discussion of LQCD and the generation of lattices in LQCD is given in Sections 5 and 6.

5. Lattice QCD

Quantum chromodynamics (QCD) [29,30] is the fundamental theory of nature describing the strong interactions between quarks and gluons. Together with weak and electromagnetic interactions, it constitutes the standard model of elementary particles and their interactions [31]. The coupling constant of QCD, $\alpha_s(q^2)$, depends on the energy scale, q^2, of the interactions. For all natural phenomena characterized by $q^2 < 1 \text{ GeV}^2$, it is large, $O(1)$; consequently, standard methods based on perturbation theory (expansion in a small parameter) that are highly successful for weak and electromagnetic interactions are unreliable. In 1974, Wilson formulated QCD on a 4-D Euclidean lattice that provided a first principle method for solving the theory using numerical evaluations of its path-integral formulation [32–34]. Physical results are obtained by taking the infinite volume and continuum limits of data produced at many values of input parameters. Today, large-scale simulations of LQCD provide many high-precision results that test QCD, provide input needed in the analysis of experiments, and give a detailed description of hadrons, the bound states of quarks and gluons [35].

Classical numerical simulations of LQCD generate gauge configurations using Markov Chain Monte Carlo (MCMC) with importance sampling. The Boltzmann weight, e^{-S}, is highly peaked; consequently, analysis on 10^3–10^4 importance sampled configurations provides accurate estimates of many interesting quantities. These configurations are characterized by five input parameters, the QCD coupling constant and four (up, down, strange, and charm) quark masses.[1] On these configurations, correlation functions, O, are calculated as expectation values (ensemble averages):

$$\langle O \rangle = \frac{1}{Z} \int \mathcal{D}U \; e^{-S[U]} O[U] \approx \frac{1}{N} \sum_i O[U_i] \tag{2}$$

where $Z = \int \mathcal{D}U \; e^{-S[U]}$ is the partition function, S is the action of the theory that is a functional of the gauge configurations U_i, and N is the number of importance sampled configurations, i.e., configurations generated with the distribution $e^{-S[U]}$. For example, the properties of a proton are obtained by choosing O to be the 2-point function illustrated in Figure 2 (left). It represents the creation of a proton by putting in an external source consisting of quark fields with proton's quantum numbers, allowing it to evolve in time, and then annihilating it at a later time τ. Its interactions with say electromagnetism are obtained by inserting an additional probe with the quantum numbers of the vector current (marked by $\otimes$) at intermediate times t, i.e., the 3-point function shown in Figure 2 (right). As the number of such correlation functions and their complexity have grown to provide detailed predictions of QCD, their measurement has now exceeded the cost of generation of configurations.

The expectation value of each correlation function has statistical and systematic errors. The latter are due to discretization (putting QCD on a finite lattice of dimension $(L/a)^4$ and spacing a). The field theory is recovered in the limit $a \to 0$ with L held fixed in physical units. Real-world physics is obtained by tuning the coupling and quark masses to their physical values by matching predictions of five hadronic observables (for example, the masses of π^+, proton, kaon, Ω^-, and η_c hadrons) to their experimental values. Results in the continuum limit and with physical values of the quark masses are achieved by performing simulations at multiple values of the lattice volume and spacing and then extrapolating. This is a costly procedure. To provide context, these classical simulations

---

[1]The other two quark masses, bottom and top, are too heavy to significantly affect the gauge-field distribution.

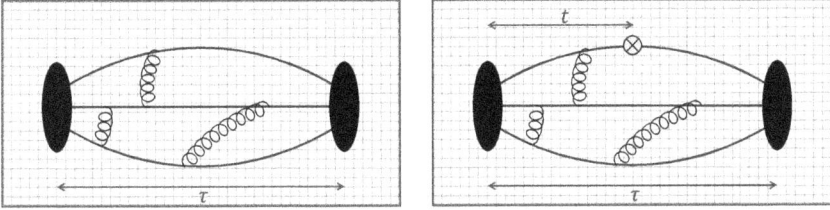

Fig. 2. Quark-line diagrams of the two (left) and three-point (right) functions of the proton. The black blobs denote nucleon source and sink, separated by Euclidean time τ. The insertion of the operator in the 3-point function (labeled by $\otimes$) is done at time slice t to calculate its matrix element within the nucleon state.

are analogous to those of spin models (Ising, XY, $O(N)$, etc.) except that both the generation of decorrelated configurations and measurements of correlation functions require about $10^9 - 10^{12}$ times more flops.

ML methods are being developed to speed up all three steps in such calculations [36]: (i) generation of gauge configurations (see Section 6), (ii) measurement of correlation functions [37–40] (see the following example), and (iii) their analysis to extract physics [41–46]. The first two steps in LQCD, and ML systems, are computational and are therefore labeled "black boxes". In Section 7, we give our thoughts on why they have this label and contrast their opacities.

Once expectation values have been calculated, they are characterized by five input parameters and can be expanded in terms of these. Thus, in principle, one expects correlations between them, but at what level — expectation values or correlation functions? A first such application of ML methods to predict correlation functions that are harder (more expensive) to calculate using the input of simpler ones was demonstrated in [41] using a GBDT regression algorithm available in scikit-learn Python ML library [47]. The gain in the computational cost of expectation values was modest, 9–38%. Using different ML models does not significantly improve the gain, presumably because the correlations are strong and essentially linear and the GBDT algorithm does a very good job of finding them. Nevertheless, this demonstration is non-trivial since the ML algorithm took as input a two-point correlation function and output a set of three-point functions configuration by configuration. The ML system provided no picture or understanding of the correlations between fluctuations on a given configuration, but it did find them! We discuss this point further in Section 7.

The second important contribution of [41], a general method for bias correction to remove the systematic errors from such ML-based predictions in expectation values, is reproduced in Section 8.

6. ML Methods for Efficient Generation of Gauge Configurations: Application to Lattice QCD

Generation of ensembles of configurations with importance sampling via Markov Chain Monte Carlo (MCMC) methods is an essential step in numerical simulations of the path integral of statistical mechanics systems and field theories. MCMC methods provide an efficient way to generate samples from the highly peaked probability density functional characterizing the theory by turning it into a stationary distribution. The limitation is that since Markov chains are stochastic processes, local [1,33] or small step-size global update schemes such as Hybrid Monte Carlo (HMC) — the algorithm of choice in today's simulations — suffer from long autocorrelation times (critical slowing down) near the quantum critical points defining the continuum limit.

In a HMC algorithm using microcanonical time evolution, changes are proposed by generating independent Gaussian distributed momentum variables conjugated to the position variables. This system is evolved using microcanonical dynamics (it keeps the total energy fixed) with a small step size (to reduce discretization errors) but for $O(1)$ unit of time. The proposed configuration is accepted using the probability $e^{-\Delta H}$, where ΔH is the change in the action (energy) [1,48]. This evolution is guaranteed to converge to the desired Boltzmann distribution $e^{-H} \equiv e^{-S}$. At each step of the microcanonical evolution, detailed balance (reversibility) is maintained, i.e., $P(A)P(B|A) = P(B)P(A|B)$ for the initial and final configurations A and B. (If not, one can correct by the ratio of probabilities of the proposed configuration and its inverse at the accept/reject step.) It also satisfies the ergodicity requirement. However, even though the momentum variables are refreshed at the start of each trajectory, keeping the system on a constant energy surface to enforce small ΔH (and, thus, a large acceptance), the configuration (position variables) changes by a small amount and the evolution suffers from critical slowing down as the correlation length in the continuum limit $a \to 0$ becomes infinite in lattice units. This limit is needed to recover the field theory. In practice, one pushes the calculations to small enough a (high enough energy scale) where various perturbative expansions become reliable and can be used to extrapolate to $a = 0$. With current algorithms, and for the precision required by experiments, the generation of lattice configurations is facing the problem of large autocorrelations before this desired matching is achieved.

It has been difficult to design efficient global update schemes that make large changes leading to fast decorrelations between configurations, as required for high statistics calculations. This is in spite of the few requirements for proposed changes as stated above: ergodicity (all configurations have equal weight, any configuration should be reachable), and detailed balance (reversibility) is maintained so that $P(A)P(B|A) = P(B)P(A|B)$ for any two configurations A and B. After thermalization, the configurations should satisfy the Gibbs distribution. What has revolutionized the calculations over the last decade is the development of the adaptive multigrid algorithm [49] for inverting the Dirac operator, the essential but extremely time-consuming part of the microcanonical evolution. The goal is to replace the proposed change based on microcanonical evolution with a ML algorithm, especially those that can be trained without generating a sufficiently large ensemble in the first place.

Here, we outline the promising method of normalizing flows [50] for the generation of gauge configurations that is being actively pursued. The goal is to combine ML with the MC method to generate configurations without autocorrelations.

Mathematically, there exist transformations that take a lattice configuration of uncorrelated variables (independent Gaussian distributed variables) to any desired Boltzmann ensemble. The practical question is as follows: Can machine learning be used to find approximations to such transformations that (i) preserve the symmetries (local gauge invariance, parity, etc.) and conservation laws (Gauss's law) of the theory, (ii) maintain ergodicity, and (iii) have a tractable Jacobian that is needed to calculate the probability of the proposals? Finding such a transformation allows one to propose large global changes (since the proposed new configuration is independent of the old one) in a Metropolis accept/reject scheme [1,48]. If the approximation is good enough to make the acceptance rate reasonable, using ML to transform Gaussian variables to the normalized distribution will generate an ensemble at a much lower cost and with essentially no autocorrelations. Correctness (generating configurations with the desired Boltzmann distribution) will be preserved provided the ML process is reversible and ergodic. For simple actions, the efficacy of the neural network-based normalizing flow, illustrated in Figure 3, has already

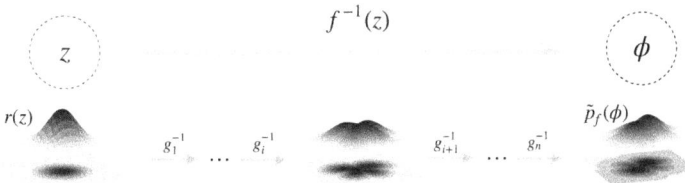

Fig. 3.   Normalizing flow transforming the samples z from a simple distribution $r(z)$ to the samples ϕ that follow the distribution $\tilde{p}_f(\phi)$, an approximation to $p_f(\phi) \propto e^{-H}$, through the mapping $\phi = f^{-1}(z)$ constructed by stacking the inverse layers g_i^{-1}. The figure is taken from [22].

been demonstrated, see [51] for a review. There is considerable activity in the community to extend the method to QCD, a non-abelian gauge theory in four dimensions [36].

7. Contrasting Two Black Boxes: Lattice QCD and ML

In this section, we present some thoughts on statements commonly made about both LQCD and ML — that they do not provide intuition or an understanding of the calculation and are essentially black boxes and therefore unappetizing.

LQCD involves two steps that are "black". The first is the generation of ensembles of gauge configurations. These configurations provide a statistical description of the ground (vacuum) state of QCD. One has no quantitative measure or understanding of what the fluctuations in any of the $SU(3)$ matrices attached to each link on the lattice mean, not only because of local gauge invariance but also because the examination of a single finite volume configuration does not specify the distribution from which it is drawn. The second is the construction of the quantum wavefunction of a state and its properties. For example, the mass of the proton, M, is obtained from a fit to the expectation value of the 2-point function, C_{2pt}, versus the separation τ between the source and the sink points in Euclidean time, $C_{2pt} \sim e^{-M\tau}$. The building block of C_{2pt} is the quark propagator, which is the inverse of the Dirac operator defined on a given configuration. It has no knowledge of a proton or any other hadron or any n-point correlation function. Information of the proton is built on averaging this 2-point function (an appropriate stitching together of three quark propagators to achieve proton quantum numbers) over thousands of configurations (doing the path integral) that picks out the relevant gauge interactions — it constructively adds fluctuations in gauge fields to create the wavefunction that correlates with the quantum numbers of the created state. It does this at each time τ and also builds into the wavefunction the knowledge that as τ increases, the excited states are exponentially damped. Said another way, it is the averaging that specifies the distribution.

Unfortunately, the simulation process gives us no idea of what the gauge fields or their fluctuations that exist within a proton state (i.e., its wavefunction) look like. The computer constructs the fully quantum wavefunction through the averaging process but does not provide any picture of it in terms of the spatial distribution of gauge fields. But once the wavefunction is created "within the computer", all gauge invariant quantities such as the distribution of the electric charge, spin, and momentum of quarks within the proton can be calculated. In summary, because the vacuum state and the wavefunction of any state created via appropriate external probes has no analytical or pictorial representation, simulations of QCD are regarded as a black box.

The calculated expectation values of correlation functions are well-behaved numbers that are rigorous outputs of QCD. They are trusted not only because of theoretical arguments but also because the hundreds of results one obtains from the same set of configurations by measuring different correlation functions exhibit all the subtle features of QCD. And all results obtained so far agree with experimental measurements where available [35]. Their variations with respect to the five tunable input parameters are also understood and quantifiable as power series[2] with approximately known coefficients, especially near the physical point where the artifacts are small and perturbative expansions in a, the pion mass M_π (surrogate for masses of the light, u and d quarks), and L work. Fits using these ansätze are then used to extrapolate data to physical values of the input parameters. Bias (systematic uncertainty) in results can arise from an incomplete sampling of the phase space of the path integral, usually checked by increasing the statistical sample by factors of 10–100, and those due to using truncated versions of the fit ansätze for the extrapolations by increasing the number of data points and simulating closer to the physical point in a controlled way.

ML has the potential to provide the ensemble of decorrelated lattices much more cheaply, to predict an expectation value with the input of another [41], and to interpolate and/or extrapolate results to other values of the input parameters [36]. It too is regarded as a black box for the following reasons.

For many applications, the ML model can be viewed as finding a "spline" to parameterize the data within a certain range of parameter values for an unknown function or a function that is very expensive to calculate. It is a black box because the "spline" is the very large number of weights on links in a network that have no physical or intuitive connection to the problem (see developments in Section 12). Furthermore, the number of these links is much larger than the degrees of freedom in the data. The process of getting a good ML model consists of (i) choosing the [neural] network architecture, (ii) the training schedule and the cost function, (iii) stopping criteria for the training, and (iv) the choice of data representation. There usually is little or no quantifiable determinism or logic for choosing between options for any of these four steps. The practice is to develop a model, train it and see if it works on a given dataset, and then tweak these steps. Even when a model works, the connectivity and the weights remain a black box.

---

[2]It is implicit that we first need to isolate non-analytic terms known from general arguments.

Bias in results, from ML systems where the desired distribution cannot be guaranteed, can come from any of the above four steps and if the dataset is not comprehensive, for example, if the data are limited or there was a bias in the collection or the training set is insufficient or different from the test set. Having a comprehensive data (and training) set is essential. Unfortunately, when one is looking for a tiny or uncharacterized signal, there is no, *a priori*, way to know if the training set is comprehensive other than a failure. One practical method for exposing failures, biases, and lack of robustness is continuous monitoring of results to look for the lack of robustness under variations in the four steps and adding more data at all levels, something unappetizing to purists.

Preserving the symmetries of QCD in LQCD formulations and calculations plays a very important role. In ML too, one can impose symmetries at the level of the model (a penalty for models that break it or build it into the tuning of weights) or data (data representation itself builds in the symmetry or perform data augmentation to realize the symmetry). Ongoing work suggests that incorporating an understanding of the science or the dynamics of the system into ML is likely to dramatically increase its power [23,37,38,52].

Overall, lattice QCD is a rigorous field theory but its simulations are a black box. To merge it with ML, one should simply continue to regard simulations of it as a computational challenge — start with input values of the five parameters and predict the correlation functions or even the expectation values directly. The guts of the process can be an efficient combination of simulations of lattice QCD and ML.

The intuitively apparent difference between ML and simulations of lattice QCD is that in LQCD the same set of gauge configurations provide the answers to all physics questions that can be formulated in terms of correlation functions, whereas in ML, one expects a different setup with respect to any of the four steps which may be more appropriate for each observable or application as even the underlying notions of the vacuum state and the wavefunction are lost. We re-emphasize this point: the fluctuations in LQCD configurations contain information on all correlation functions, even correlation functions that violate the symmetries of QCD, for example, parity, charge conjugation, or baryon number. All one needs in the latter case is to calculate the appropriate correlation functions and the reweighting factor to account for the difference in the Boltzmann weights. Naively, one has a hard time accepting that such richness could be built into a ML system trained on one set of correlation functions. Examples of progress in this direction are given in Section 9. Thus, there is a strong possibility that even this difference will blur with experience.

Our hunch is that the generation of decorrelated configurations in LQCD using methods such as normalizing flows [50] will be one of the first successes beyond the examples of predicting expensive to calculate correlation functions in terms of cheaper ones as discussed in [41]. Another exciting application of ML in the analysis of data is to estimate the real-time spectral function from lattice data for the Euclidean 2-point function [42,43,53,54], a notoriously difficult "inverse" problem since the latter is the Laplace transform of the former.

As these ML methods mature, a key issue will be the detection and correction of bias in ML predictions. The next section first describes a general method for bias correction followed by some additional comments.

8. A General Method for Bias Correction in ML Predictions of Averages

Consider M samples of independent measurements of a set of observables $\mathbf{X}_i = \{o_i^1, o_i^2, o_i^3, \ldots\}$, $i = 1, \ldots, M$, but the target observable O_i is available only on $N << M$ of these. These N are called the *labeled data* (LD) and the remaining $M - N$ are called the *unlabeled data* (UD). The goal is to build a ML model F that predicts the target observable $O_i \approx O_i^{\mathrm{P}} \equiv F(\mathbf{X}_i)$ by training a ML algorithm on a subset $N_t < N$ of the labeled data. The bias corrected estimate $\overline{O}$ of $\langle O \rangle$ is then obtained as

$$\overline{O} = \frac{1}{M - N} \sum_{i \in \{UD\}} O_i^{\mathrm{P}} + \frac{1}{N_b} \sum_{i \in \{BC\}} (O_i - O_i^{\mathrm{P}}), \tag{3}$$

where the second sum is over the $N_b \equiv N - N_t$ remaining labeled samples that corrects for possible bias. Here, O_i^{P} depends explicitly on $\mathbf{X}_i$ and implicitly on N_t and all training data $\{O_j, \mathbf{X}_j\}$. For fixed ML model F, the sampling variance of $\overline{O}$ is then given by

$$\sigma_{\overline{O}}^2 = \frac{\sigma_O^2}{N} \left\{ s^2 \frac{N}{M - N} + \frac{1}{f}[(1 - s)^2 + 2s(1 - r)] \right\}, \tag{4}$$

where σ_O^2 is the variance of O_i, $s \equiv \sigma_{O^P}/\sigma_O$ is the ratio of the standard deviations of the predictor variable O^P to the true observable O, r is the correlation coefficient between these two, and $f \equiv N_b/N$ is the fraction of observations held out for bias correction. Equation (4) shows that when $s \approx 1 \approx r$, this procedure increases the effective sample size from N, where O_i are available, to about $M - N$. For simplicity, in deriving Eq. (4), details such as the statistical independence of the data were ignored. One way to account for the full error, including the sampling variance of the training and the bias correction datasets, is by using a bootstrap procedure [26] that independently selects N labeled and $M - N$ unlabeled items for each bootstrap sample. While the bias correction removes the systematic shift in the prediction, it can increase the final error, i.e., the systematic error due to biased ML prediction is converted to a statistical error —— the advantage is, of course, that the standard statistical techniques like bootstrap can estimate the latter accurately. Nevertheless, since the bias is explicitly estimated in this procedure, in specific applications, one can evaluate whether to prefer a precise biased estimator to an unbiased, but imprecise, estimator.

9. Examples of Physics-aware Machine Learning Models

When applied to physics data, ML learns about the symmetries and constraints of the system inferred from the data and utilizes such information to make predictions. By explicitly implementing the physical rules in the ML procedure, however, one can obtain more precise ML predictions with a smaller number of training data. In [37], for example, the authors proposed a new structure of the convolutional neural network, named Lattice Gauge Equivariant Convolutional Neural Networks (L-CNNs), that preserves gauge equivariance. They introduced a set of network layers that preserve gauge symmetry exactly: convolutions, bilinear layers, activation functions, exponentiation layers, trace, plaquette layers, and Polyakov layers, which can be stacked arbitrarily to form gauge equivariant networks. An example of the L-CNN's construction is illustrated in Figure 4. Also studied is how to impose global translational invariance on convolutional neural network (CNN) architectures for the analysis of scalar field configurations on two-dimensional lattices [38]. For the study of the gauge generation, described in Section 6, a flow-based generative model satisfying the exact gauge invariance for lattice gauge theories has been proposed by defining gauge-invariant flows and coupling layers [23]. Also, in [52], the accuracy of the ML predictions of the matrix elements for $e^+e^- \to$ up to 5-jets, described in Section 2.2, has been significantly improved by exploiting the knowledge of the factorization properties of the matrix elements.

When constrained by an incorrect theory, however, the trained ML tends to generate biased predictions. In Eq. (1), for example, a prefactor $x^{1-\alpha_k}(1-x)^{\beta_k}$ multiplies the neural network parametrization of the PDFs to enforce the large-x behavior $f_k(x = 1) = 0$ required by the constituent counting rules [55] and the small-x behavior inspired by the Regge theory [56]. However, the prefactor provides more strict constraints than those allowed by the physics rules and may introduce bias in the predictions and uncertainty estimations [57]. To avoid such bias, [57] proposed to implement minimal constraints by removing the prefactor and replacing

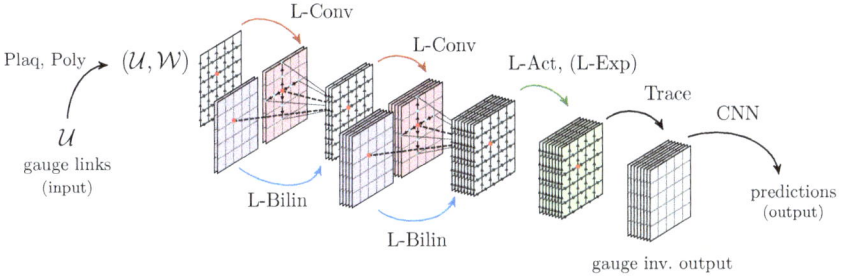

Fig. 4. An example of the gauge equivariant L-CNNs constructed from the lattice gauge equivariant convolutions (L-Conv), bilinear layers (L-Bilin), activation functions (L-Act), exponentiation layers (L-Exp), trace layers (Trace), and plaquette and Polyakov layers (Plaq and Poly). The input of lattice gauge fields, $\mathcal{U}$, and Wilson lines ending at the starting point, $\mathcal{W}$, is processed by the operations preserving the physical symmetry of the gauge equivariance to make accurate predictions. The figure is taken from [37].

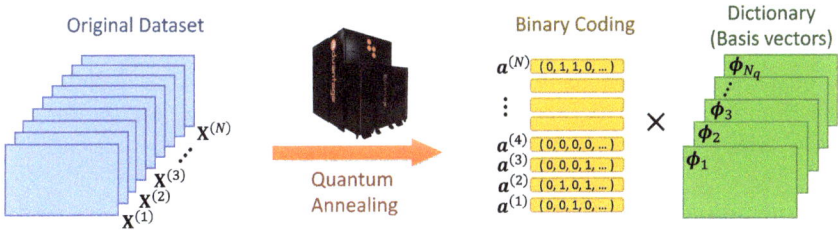

Fig. 5. An illustration of the ML-based compression algorithm proposed by [59]. Exploiting the correlation in physics data, the algorithm finds a lower-dimensional binary representation of the original floating-point data that can be stored in a small memory space but can precisely reconstruct the original data from a set of basis vectors. A quantum annealer was used to solve the NP-hard optimization problem of finding the optimal binary coding.

Eq. (1) by

$$x f_k(x, Q_0) = A_k \left[\mathrm{NN}_k(x) - \mathrm{NN}_k(1) \right]. \tag{5}$$

They find no loss in efficiency and good agreement with previous results.

10. Unsupervised ML Approaches

Modern physics experiments and simulations produce a deluge of data but many analysis models are not capable of dealing with and getting the most out of such large and complex data. However, the complicated physics data can be explained by a small number of features lying on a lower-dimensional manifold. For example, translational symmetry of a physics system could explain all the data symmetric under translations. Unsupervised ML is a class of algorithms drawing inferences from untagged data by building a compact internal representation of the data. By applying unsupervised ML algorithms to physics data, one can find a natural clustering and key features of the data, find anomalous events, and generate synthetic data.

Although experimental data are one of the best candidates for the unsupervised ML applications (for example, as discussed in Section 2.1 for classification of events, and see the chapter by David Rousseau, *ibid.*), many studies find useful applications in the analysis of data from theoretical particle physics. The generative models used for the Monte Carlo simulations explained in Section 4 are good examples of such applications. Reference [58] also applied generative adversarial networks to produce pseudo-samples of the Monte Carlo PDF data. With the dataset enhanced by the synthetic replicas, they were able to find a better subset accurately representing the underlying probability distribution of the original dataset than the standard method. Exploiting the correlation between physics data, [59] developed a lossy compression algorithm for statistical floating-point data through a representation learning with binary variables on quantum annealers, as illustrated in Figure 5. Based on the algorithm explained in Section 8, they further presented a bias correction method for the inexact reconstruction from lossy-compressed data.

11. Exploring the Space of Possible Theories

Even though the standard model of particle physics (SM) is an incredibly successful theory with no known deviation between its predictions and any known experiments, it, nevertheless, has major shortcomings. Three important ones are related to the large-scale structure of the observed universe: dark matter, dark energy, and an explanation for the matter–antimatter asymmetry. Possible mechanisms for the latter are baryogenesis or leptogenesis [60–63]. Thus, the SM needs to be extended to include the standard model of cosmology and possibly particles and interactions from beyond the standard model needed to explain these observations. At an even more fundamental level, the classical theory of general relativity that explains gravity and the large-scale evolution of the universe has not been successfully quantized. A fully unified theory needs to include quantum gravity. The number of possible theories are, however, huge. Given that the search for the fundamental or the "next" standard model is at the core of HEP research, it is not surprising that ML methods are already being used to help with this construction.

We discuss two examples. The first is to make predictions of a given BSM theory defined by specific values of the unknown parameters, particles, and interactions and generate synthetic data with a small number of output variables that characterize its predictions as described in Section 2.2. To determine if it is the theory of nature, one would again design a second ML system to compare predictions to experimental data. A flow chart of calculations to efficiently explore the space of input parameters (using the minimal supersymmetric model (MSSM) theory as an example) is as follows. Calculate the NLO cross-sections using conventional approaches for well-distributed values of the MSSM model parameters, such as gluino and squark masses, and interpolate these results using DGP to obtain the cross-sections for arbitrary values of model parameters. Again, symmetries, conservation laws, and other physics knowledge can be built into ML models or the output. The space of allowed couplings can be progressively constrained by matching these predictions to experimental data. Such ML systems can then be extended to search between BSM theories.

The second example is string theories. The reigning fundamental theory that incorporates both general relativity and quantum field theory is called the "M-theory" [64]. It is believed to be unique and various string theories appear as fluctuations around its many vacuua or false vacuua. The only freedom one has in developing a model for our universe is choosing between these vacuua. Unfortunately, these vacuua are parameterized by a set of integers, and by some estimates, there are more than 10^{10^5} of these [65]. A visualization is shown in Figure 6. This poses three grand challenge questions: How to choose which vacuua to analyze, do *any* of these have the standard model as a low energy effective theory, and what are the novel predictions of these theories [66,67]?

At their core, these questions can be framed as an algebraic problem [15, 70]. For example, the number of "particle species" that exist around any of these vacuua is an integer-valued function of the integer parameters that characterize the vacuum. This is a very difficult function to evaluate, and ML has been used to get surrogate functions for problems like this with over 90% match to the true function in some domains [71,72]. More interestingly, one can train a ML architecture to identify regions of parameter space within which polynomial approximations with theoretically expected structures work or where a certain structure believed to be important for the standard model or our universe exists [73,74].

This example illustrates the strength of combining human ingenuity in formulating string theory with ML tools to sift through the very large number of possible vacuua!

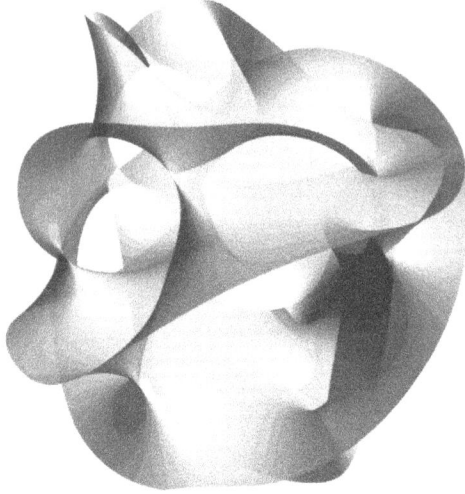

Fig. 6. A cross-section of the quintic Calabi–Yau manifold. In the F-theory approach to string theory, the various string vacuua arise from choosing a Calabi–Yau manifold structure and values of fluxes on it. Picture in public domain [68] where it was created using the methods described in [69].

12. Interpreting Extra Dimensions from Deep Neural Nets

Lastly, a particularly interesting connection of deep neural networks to modern theories of HEP is provided by the recently discovered latticed AdS-CFT correspondence [75,76]. In 1998, Maldecena made the profound discovery that conformal field theories (CFTs) appear as the description of the physics at the remote boundary of gravitational theories on an anti-de Sitter (AdS) background with a black hole horizon at its inner boundary, i.e., the AdS/CFT correspondence [77,78]. From the point of view of the CFT, the meaning of the extra dimension is completely opaque, but [75] and [76] provide an interpretation of the slices along the extra dimension as the layers of a neural network that computes the black hole horizon from the field theory data. Specifically, a neural net was designed such that its internal weights, interpreted as metric components on a discretized space-time, satisfy the gravitational equations of motion. Since the black hole boundary is fixed and known, one can now "train" this network to "learn" the black hole boundary condition when shown simple known field conformations as input at the remote boundary, and the weights in the trained network would then approximate the AdS geometry corresponding to the boundary theory.

13. Conclusions

Hard computational problems abound in theoretical high-energy physics. Dealing with the complexity of each event at the high-luminosity LHC and the rate of events, subpercent precision from lattice QCD, and finding the right vacuum of M-theory that describes our universe all require new tools. This chapter touched on how machine learning methods for optimization, pattern recognition (e.g., collider events), numerical integration, generative models, extrapolation, interpolation, regression, and surrogate models can transform many areas of research.

We have devoted considerable space to lattice QCD, not only because ML methods hold the promise to significantly reduce the large computational needs but also because LQCD illustrates how, by giving up analytical control (understanding, visualization) in the intermediate steps of calculations, the rich structure and predictions of strongly interacting quantum field theories can be obtained. Relying on large-scale simulations of LQCD and turning QCD into a numerical problem may not satisfy a purist but results from simulations have become palatable because of the rigorous foundation of the calculations in the Feynman path integral formulation. What these simulations highlight is that while the creation of the quantum ground state and the wavefunctions of hadrons in the computer is a "black box", this statistical description provides the means to calculate many observables of interest with increasing precision. In the future, methods such as normalizing flows are likely to supplant standard Markov Chain Monte Carlo methods for generating gauge configurations — all that is needed is a transformation, no matter how opaque, from a simple distribution to the desired distribution. The evolution in the thinking of a theorist needed is that it does not matter how one gets, say an ensemble of configurations for lattice QCD, as long we can validate they obey the Boltzmann distribution and guarantee that the results for correlation functions are bias-free.

We anticipate that, even as ML methods become more powerful and calculations using them become opaque, the need for understanding the physics will not decrease, and physics-aware development of ML will be more efficient. The trend towards collaborative teams of physicists, mathematicians, computer scientists, and statisticians is bound to enrich research, especially in areas requiring hard calculations that need to be repeated billions of times (event generators, lattice QCD) or to manage and process large complex datasets (experiments at the LHC).

Acknowledgments

We thank Phiala Shanahan for reading though the manuscript and providing feedback. T. Bhattacharya and R. Gupta were partly supported by the U.S. Department of Energy, Office of Science, Office of High Energy Physics under Contract No. 89233218CNA000001. T. Bhattacharya, R. Gupta, and B. Yoon were partly supported by the LANL LDRD program.

References

[1] M. Creutz (1985). *Quarks, Gluons and Lattices*, Cambridge Monographs on Mathematical Physics. Cambridge, UK: Cambridge University Press. ISBN 978-0-521-31535-7.

[2] C. Gattringer and C. B. Lang (2010). *Quantum Chromodynamics on the Lattice*, Vol. 788. Berlin: Springer. ISBN 978-3-642-01849-7, 978-3-642-01850-3. doi: 10.1007/978-3-642-01850-3.

[3] G. Kasieczka, T. Plehn, A. Butter *et al.* (2019). The Machine learning landscape of top taggers. *SciPost Physics, 7*, 14. doi: 10.21468/SciPostPhys.7.1.014, *arXiv:1902.09914 [hep-ph]*.

[4] T. Faucett, J. Thaler, and D. Whiteson (2021). Mapping Machine-Learned physics into a human-readable space. *Physical Review D, 103*(3), 036020. doi: 10.1103/PhysRevD.103.036020, *arXiv:2010.11998 [hep-ph]*.

[5] L. Bradshaw, S. Chang, and B. Ostdiek (2022). Creating simple, interpretable anomaly detectors for new physics in jet substructure. *arXiv:2203.01343 [hep-ph]*.

[6] P. T. Komiske, I. Moult, J. Thaler *et al.* (2022). Analyzing n-point energy correlators inside jets with CMS open data. *arXiv:2201.07800 [hep-ph]*.

[7] K. Desai, B. Nachman, and J. Thaler (2021). SymmetryGAN: Symmetry discovery with Deep Learning. *arXiv:2112.05722 [hep-ph]*.

[8] F. Bishara and M. Montull (2019). (Machine) Learning amplitudes for faster event generation. *arXiv:1912.11055 [hep-ph]*.

[9] S. Badger and J. Bullock (2020). Using neural networks for efficient evaluation of high multiplicity scattering amplitudes. *JHEP, 6*, 114. doi: 10.1007/JHEP06(2020)114, *arXiv:2002.07516 [hep-ph]*.

[10] A. Buckley, A. Kvellestad, A. Raklev *et al.* (2020). Xsec: The cross-section evaluation code. *European Physical Journal C, 80*(12), 1106. doi: 10.1140/epjc/s10052-020-08635-y, *arXiv:2006.16273 [hep-ph]*.

[11] S. Carrazza and J. Cruz-Martinez (2019). Towards a new generation of parton densities with deep learning models. *European Physical Journal C, 79*, 8, 676. doi: 10.1140/epjc/s10052-019-7197-2, *arXiv:1907.05075 [hep-ph]*.

[12] R. D. Bal, S. Carrazza, J. Cruz-Martinez *et al.* (2021a). *The Path to Proton Structure at One-Percent Accuracy. arXiv:2109.02653 [hep-ph]*.

[13] R. D. Ball, S. Carrazza, J. Cruz-Martinez *et al.* (2021b). An open-source machine learning framework for global analyses of parton distributions. *European Physical Journal C, 81*(10), 958. doi: 10.1140/epjc/s10052-021-09747-9, *arXiv:2109.02671 [hep-ph]*.

[14] S. Shi, K. Zhou, J. Zhao *et al.* (2022). Heavy quark potential in the quark-gluon plasma: Deep neural network meets lattice quantum chromodynamics. *Physical Review D, 105*(1), 014017. doi: 10.1103/PhysRevD.105.014017, *arXiv:2105.07862 [hep-ph]*.

[15] D. S. Berman, Y.-H. He, and E. Hirst *et al.* (2022). Machine learning Calabi-Yau hypersurfaces. *Physical Review D, 105*(6), 066002. doi: 10.1103/PhysRevD.105.066002, *arXiv:2112.06350 [hep-th]*.

[16] G. P. Lepage (1978). A new algorithm for adaptive multidimensional integration. *Journal of Computational Physics, 27*(2), 192–203. https://doi.org/10.1016/0021-9991(78)90004-9, http://www.sciencedirect.com/science/article/pii/0021999178900049.

[17] G. Lepage (1980). VEGAS — An adaptive multi-dimensional integration program. Tech. Rep. CLNS-447, Cornell Univ. Lab. Nucl. Stud., Ithaca, NY. http://cds.cern.ch/record/123074.

[18] G. Lepage (2021). Adaptive multidimensional integration: VEGAS enhanced. *Journal of Computational Physics, 439*, 110386. doi: 10.1016/j.jcp.2021.110386, *arXiv:2009.05112 [physics.comp-ph]*.

[19] S. Duane, A. D. Kennedy, B. J. Pendleton *et al.* (1987). Hybrid Monte Carlo. *Physical Letters B, 195*, 216–222. doi: 10.1016/0370-2693(87)91197-X.

[20] C. Gao, J. Isaacson, and C. Krause (2020). i-flow: High-dimensional integration and sampling with normalizing flows. *Machine Learning: Science and Technology, 1*(4), 045023. doi: 10.1088/2632-2153/abab62, *arXiv:2001.05486 [physics.comp-ph]*.

[21] J. M. Pawlowski and J. M. Urban (2020). Reducing autocorrelation times in lattice simulations with generative adversarial networks. *Machine Learning: Science and Technology, 1*, 045011. doi: 10.1088/2632-2153/abae73, *arXiv:1811.03533 [hep-lat]*.

[22] M. S. Albergo, G. Kanwar, and P. E. Shanahan (2019). Flow-based generative models for Markov chain Monte Carlo in lattice field theory. *Physical Review D, 100*(3), 034515. doi: 10.1103/PhysRevD.100.034515, *arXiv:1904.12072 [hep-lat]*.

[23] G. Kanwar, M. S. Albergo, D. Boyda *et al.* (2020). Equivariant flow-based sampling for lattice gauge theory. *Physical Review Letter, 125*(12), 121601. doi: 10.1103/PhysRevLett.125.121601, *arXiv:2003.06413 [hep-lat]*.

[24] D. C. Hackett, C.-C. Hsieh, M. S. Albergo *et al.* (2021). Flow-based sampling for multimodal distributions in lattice field theory. *arXiv:2107.00734 [hep-lat]*.

[25] D. J. Rezende and S. Mohamed (2016). Variational inference with normalizing flows. *arXiv:1505.05770 [stat.ML]*.

[26] B. Efron (1979). Bootstrap methods: Another look at the jackknife. *The Annals of Statistics, 7*(1), 1–26.

[27] B. Yoon (2021). A machine learning approach for efficient multi-dimensional integration. *Scientific Report, 11*(1), 18965. doi: 10.1038/s41598-021-98392-z, *arXiv:2009.06697 [physics.comp-ph]*.

[28] M. S. Albergo, D. Boyda, K. Cranmer *et al.* (2022). Flow-based sampling in the lattice Schwinger model at criticality. *arXiv:2202.11712 [hep-lat]*.

[29] J. Campbell, J. Huston, and F. Krauss (2017). *The Black Book of Quantum Chromodynamics: A Primer for the LHC Era*. Cambridge, UK: Cambridge University Press. ISBN 9780199652747. doi: 10.1093/oso/9780199652747. 001.0001.

[30] B. L. Ioffe, V. S. Fadin, and L. N. Lipatov (2010). *Quantum Chromodynamics: Perturbative and Nonperturbative Aspects*. Cambridge University Press. ISBN 978-1-107-42475-3, 978-0-521-63148-8, 978-0-511-71744-4. doi: 10.1017/CBO9780511711817.

[31] P. Langacker (2017). *The Standard Model and Beyond*. Taylor & Francis. ISBN 978-1-4987-6322-6, 978-1-4987-6321-9, 978-0-367-57344-7, 978-1-315-17062-6. doi: 10.1201/b22175.

[32] K. Wilson (1974). Confinement of quarks. *Physical Review D, 10*, 2445–2459. doi: 10.1103/PhysRevD.10.2445.

[33] K. Wilson (1975). Quarks and strings on a lattice. In *13th International School of Subnuclear Physics: New Phenomena in Subnuclear Physics*, p. 0069.

[34] K. Wilson (1980). Monte Carlo calculations for lattice Gauge theory. *NATO Science Series B, 59*, 363–402. doi: 10.1007/978-1-4684-7571-5_20.

[35] Y. Aoki, T. Blum, G. Colangelo *et al.* (2021). FLAG Review 2021. *arXiv:2111.09849 [hep-lat]*.

[36] D. Boyda, S. Calì, S. Foreman *et al.* (2022). *Applications of Machine Learning to Lattice Quantum Field Theory*. *arXiv:2202.05838 [hep-lat]*.

[37] M. Favoni, A. Ipp, D. I. Müller *et al.* (2022). Lattice Gauge equivariant convolutional neural networks. *Physical Review Letters, 128*(3), 032003. doi: 10.1103/PhysRevLett.128.032003, *arXiv:2012.12901 [hep-lat]*.

[38] S. Bulusu, M. Favoni, A. Ipp *et al.* (2021). Generalization capabilities of translationally equivariant neural networks. *Physical Review D, 104*(7), 074504. doi: 10.1103/PhysRevD.104.074504, *arXiv:2103.14686 [hep-lat]*.

[39] W. Detmold, G. Kanwar, H. Lamm *et al.* (2021). Path integral contour deformations for observables in $SU(N)$ gauge theory. *Physical Review D, 103*(9), 094517. doi: 10.1103/PhysRevD.103.094517, *arXiv:2101.12668 [hep-lat]*.

[40] R. Zhang, Z. Fan, R. Li *et al.* (2020). Machine-learning prediction for quasi-parton distribution function matrix elements. *Physical Review D, 101*(3), 034516. doi: 10.1103/PhysRevD.101.034516, *arXiv:1909.10990 [hep-lat]*.

[41] B. Yoon, T. Bhattacharya, and R. Gupta (2019). Machine Learning estimators for lattice QCD observables. *Physical Review D, 100*(1), 014504. doi: 10.1103/PhysRevD.100.014504, *arXiv:1807.05971 [hep-lat]*.

[42] L. Kades, J. M. Pawlowski, A. Rothkopf *et al.* (2020). Spectral reconstruction with deep neural networks. *Physical Review D, 102*(9), 096001. doi: 10.1103/PhysRevD.102.096001, *arXiv:1905.04305 [physics.comp-ph]*.

[43] S. Y. Chen, H. T. Ding, F. Y. Liu *et al.* (2021). Machine learning spectral functions in lattice QCD. *arXiv:2110.13521 [hep-lat]*.

[44] K. A. Nicoli, S. Nakajima, N. Strodthoff *et al.* (2020) Asymptotically unbiased estimation of physical observables with neural samplers. *Physical Review E, 101*(2), 023304. doi: 10.1103/PhysRevE.101.023304, *arXiv:1910.13496 [cond-mat.stat-mech]*.

[45] K. A. Nicoli, C. J. Anders, L. Funcke *et al.* (2021a). Estimation of thermodynamic observables in lattice field theories with deep generative models. *Physical Review Letters, 126*(3), (032001). doi: 10.1103/PhysRevLett.126. 032001, *arXiv:2007.07115 [hep-lat]*.

[46] K. A. Nicoli, C. J. Anders, L. Funcke *et al.* (2021b). Machine Learning of thermodynamic observables in the presence of mode collapse. In *38th International Symposium on Lattice Field Theory. arXiv:2111.11303 [hep-lat]*.

[47] F. Pedregosa, G. Varoquaux, A. Gramfort *et al.* (2011). Scikit-learn: Machine learning in Python. *Journal of Machine Learning Research, 12*, 2825–2830.

[48] N. Metropolis, A. W. Rosenbluth, M. N. Rosenbluth *et al.* (1953). Equation of state calculations by fast computing machines. *Journal of Chemical Physics, 21*, 1087–1092. doi: 10.1063/1.1699114.

[49] J. Brannick, R. C. Brower, M. A. Clark *et al.* (2008). Adaptive multigrid algorithm for lattice QCD. *Physical Review Letters, 100*, 041601. doi: 10. 1103/PhysRevLett.100.041601, *arXiv:0707.4018 [hep-lat]*.

[50] I. Kobyzev, S. J. Prince, and M. A. Brubaker (2021). Normalizing flows: An introduction and review of current methods. *IEEE Transactions on Pattern Analysis and Machine Intelligence, 43*(11), 3964–3979. http://dx.doi.org/ 10.1109/TPAMI.2020.2992934.

[51] M. S. Albergo, D. Boyda, D. C. Hackett *et al.* (2021). Introduction to normalizing flows for lattice field theory. *arXiv:2101.08176 [hep-lat]*.

[52] D. Maître and H. Truong (2021). A factorisation-aware Matrix element emulator. *JHEP, 11*, 066. doi: 10.1007/JHEP11(2021)066, *arXiv:2107.06625 [hep-ph]*.

[53] T. Spriggs, G. Aarts, C. Allton *et al.* (2022). A comparison of spectral reconstruction methods applied to non-zero temperature NRQCD meson correlation functions. *EPJ Web Conference, 258*, 05011. doi: 10.1051/ epjconf/202225805011, *arXiv:2112.04201 [hep-lat]*.

[54] J. Horak, J. M. Pawlowski, J. Rodríguez-Quintero *et al.* (2022). Reconstructing QCD spectral functions with Gaussian processes. *Physical Review D, 105*(3), 036014. doi: 10.1103/PhysRevD.105.036014, *arXiv:2107.13464 [hep-ph]*.

[55] S. J. Brodsky and G. R. Farrar (1973). Scaling laws at large transverse momentum. *Physical Review Letter, 31*, 1153–1156. https://link.aps.org/ doi/10.1103/PhysRevLett.31.1153.

[56] H. D. I. Abarbanel, M. L. Goldberger, and S. B. Treiman (1969). Asymptotic properties of electroproduction structure functions. *Physical Review Letters, 22*, 500–502. https://link.aps.org/doi/10.1103/PhysRevLett.22.500.

[57] S. Carrazza, J. M. Cruz-Martinez, and R. Stegeman (2021a). A data-based parametrization of parton distribution functions. *arXiv:2111.02954 [hep-ph]*.

[58] S. Carrazza, J. M. Cruz-Martinez, and T. R. Rabemananjara (2021b). Compressing PDF sets using generative adversarial networks. *European Physical Journal C, 81*(6), 530. doi: 10.1140/epjc/s10052-021-09338-8, *arXiv:2104.04535 [hep-ph]*.

[59] B. Yoon, N. T. T. Nguyen, C. C. Chang *et al.* (2022). Lossy compression of statistical data using quantum annealer. *Scientific Report, 12*, 3814. doi: 10.1038/s41598-022-07539-z, *arXiv:2110.02142 [quant-ph]*.

[60] A. Sakharov (1967). Violation of CP invariance, c Asymmetry, and Baryon asymmetry of the universe. *Pis'ma v Zhurnal Èksperimental'noi i Teoreticheskoi Fiziki, 5*, 32–35. doi: 10.1070/PU1991v034n05ABEH002497.

[61] J. D. Barrow and M. S. Turner (1981). Baryosynthesis and the origin of galaxies. *Nature, 291*, 469–472. doi: 10.1038/291469a0.

[62] M. Fukugita and T. Yanagida (1986). Baryogenesis without grand unification. *Physical Letter B, 174*, 45–47. doi: 10.1016/0370-2693(86)91126-3.

[63] S. Davidson, E. Nardi, and Y. Nir (2008). Leptogenesis. *Physics Reports, 466*, 105–177. doi: 10.1016/j.physrep.2008.06.002, *arXiv:0802.2962 [hep-ph]*.

[64] E. Witten (1995). String theory dynamics in various dimensions. *Nuclear Physics B, 443*, 85–126. doi: 10.1016/0550-3213(95)00158-O, *arXiv:hep-th/9503124*.

[65] W. Taylor and Y.-N. Wang (2015). The F-theory geometry with most flux vacua. *JHEP, 12*, 164. doi: 10.1007/JHEP12(2015)164, *arXiv:1511.03209 [hep-th]*.

[66] nLab wiki. Landscape of string theory vacua. (2022). https://ncatlab.org/nlab/show/landscape+of+string+theory+vacua.

[67] Y.-H. He (2017). Machine-learning the string landscape. *Physics Letters B, 774*, 564–568. https://doi.org/10.1016/j.physletb.2017.10.024, https://www.sciencedirect.com/science/article/pii/S0370269317308365.

[68] Wikimedia Commons (2015). https://commons.wikimedia.org/wiki/File:Calabi_yau_formatted.svg, derivative work: Polytope24 / Calabi yau.jpg: Jbourjai (using Mathematica output), "Calabi yau formatted", marked as public domain.

[69] A. Hanson (1994). A construction for computer visualization of certain complex curves. *Notices of the American Mathematical Society, 41*, 1156–1163.

[70] J. Bao, Y.-H. He, E. Heyes *et al.* (2022). Machine Learning Algebraic Geometry for Physics. *arXiv:2204.10334 [hep-th]*.

[71] F. Ruehle (2017). Evolving neural networks with genetic algorithms to study the String Landscape. *JHEP, 8*, 38. doi: 10.1007/JHEP08(2017)038, *arXiv:1706.07024 [hep-th]*.

[72] Y.-H. He (2017). Deep-Learning the Landscape. *arXiv:1706.02714 [hep-th]*.

[73] E. T. Parr (2020). *Machine learning in string theory*, Ph.D. thesis, Technische Universität München.

[74] R. Deen, Y.-H. He, S.-J. Lee *et al.* (2022). Machine learning string standard models. *Physical Review D, 105*(4), 046001. doi: 10.1103/PhysRevD.105.046001, *arXiv:2003.13339 [hep-th]*.

[75] K. Hashimoto, S. Sugishita, A. Tanaka *et al.* (2018). Deep learning and the AdS/CFT correspondence. *Physical Review D, 98*(4), 046019. doi: 10.1103/PhysRevD.98.046019, *arXiv:1802.08313 [hep-th]*.

[76] K. Hashimoto (2019). AdS/CFT correspondence as a deep Boltzmann machine. *Physical Review D, 99*(10), 106017. doi: 10.1103/PhysRevD.99. 106017, *arXiv:1903.04951 [hep-th]*.

[77] J. M. Maldacena (1998). The large N limit of superconformal field theories and supergravity. *Advances in Theoretical and Mathematical Physics, 2*, 231–252. doi: 10.1023/A:1026654312961, *arXiv:hep-th/9711200*.

[78] A. V. Ramallo (2015). Introduction to the AdS/CFT correspondence. *Springer Proceeding of Physics, 161*, 411–474. doi: 10.1007/978-3-319-12238-0_10, *arXiv:1310.4319 [hep-th]*.

Part D. The Ecosystem of AI for Science

ITER Tokomak fusion reactor under construction. Credit © ITER Organization, http://www.iter.org/.

© 2023 World Scientific Publishing Company
https://doi.org/10.1142/9789811265679_0027

Chapter 27

Schema.org for Scientific Data

Alasdair Gray*,†,¶, Leyla J. Castro*,‡,‖, Nick Juty*,§,**, and Carole
Goble*,§,††

*Bioschemas Steering Council
†Department of Computer Science, Heriot-Watt University, Edinburgh,
UK
‡ZBMED Information Centre for Life Sciences, Germany
§Department of Computer Science, The University of Manchester, UK
¶A.J.G.Gray@hw.ac.uk
‖ljgarcia@zbmed.de
**nick.juty@manchester.ac.uk
††carole.goble@manchester.ac.uk

1. Introduction

Data accessibility, data management, data quality, and data governance are
essential to the adoption of AI and machine learning. Models need data to
learn from and data on which they can work to build their predictions. The
results of AI are, themselves, data. The FAIR Data Principles [1] set out a
worldwide guide rail for making data Findable, Accessible, Interoperable,
and Reusable, putting at its heart the *machine actionability* of the metadata
associated with the data. With machine actionable metadata, we are
more readily able to build the Knowledge Graphs so often associated
with AI. Moreover, Machine Learning requires the formulation of the data
requirements for models, used to identify or generate the datasets needed
to develop the models by the data scientists. The FAIR principles present a
metadata framework for bridging between the data providers and the data
scientists. A common meme is that FAIR data is "FAIRly AI Ready" and
that AI is at the center of FAIR.

Leaving aside the challenges of making data suitably interoperable
and reusable to feed AI algorithms, we need to tackle the simpler issue

of enabling relevant data to be discovered at Web scale. Searching for data on the Web is problematic as they are often poorly described [2]. Web search is the obvious first step. However, the major search engines struggle to interpret what a Web page is actually about, i.e., the machine interpretability of its content, even with the extensive computational power and the advanced techniques available to them [3]. To improve Web search results, the embedding of machine-interpretable knowledge representation within Web pages has been developed over the last 10 years.

Schema.org [3] is a lightweight vocabulary of terms that has been developed by a collaboration of leading search engines — including Google, Microsoft, Yandex, and Yahoo! — to allow Web page authors to embed machine-interpretable data about the content of their site. This has led to improved search results and interfaces, e.g., "rich snippets" which provide a summary of the result page are generated for specific content types such as movies. These rich snippets give basic information about the movie, such as the actors, director, and release date, and aggregated viewer ratings. The embedded markup is also used to populate the knowledge graphs of the search engines, benefiting from the Interoperability gained by using a common vocabulary of terms, which are exploited to further improve results to user queries [4]. Furthermore, Interoperability and Reuse are improved as the added data are visible not only to search engines but also to all web users, making it easier for data aggregators to collect data across common but not necessarily interconnected data-based Web sites.

In this chapter, we discuss the use of knowledge representation to improve the Findability and Interoperability of data through the embedding of machine-interpretable markup within Web pages. The markup provides a high-level description of what the page is about, without providing all the (scientific) context and nuances required to fully interpret the data. The markup can be accessed by all, using standard Web protocols, i.e., HTTP GET requests are used to retrieve the page and its markup in the same way that it is for a Web browser, and the data are often available in the developer-friendly format of JSON-LD, i.e., common JSON libraries can be used. This enables users to access the structured data without needing to understand bespoke site-specific APIs. This high-level, machine-interpretable data can be exploited by a wide variety of services from generic Web search, through dedicated search portals, and by domain- and community-specific services and registries. Additionally, the entry barrier for the data provider is low — just hosting a Web page — meaning that it is accessible to the long-tail of scientific data and not just major data providers in a particular field. There is a challenge in making the site known to others but this can be achieved by registering your site with domain registry services that can then make the existence of the data known to others.

In this chapter, we will explore how to make data more Findable and Interoperable on the Web. We specifically address work in the life sciences data community to extend the generic Web search vocabulary (Schema.org) with domain-specific terms (Bioschemas.org) to enable markup of subject-specific data and resources, and harvesting or consumption by dedicated community registries and knowledge graphs. Finally, we show how these general approaches are being used to populate a general-purpose research knowledge graph containing data about papers, projects, and the data that they relate to. As Schema.org and Bioschemas are evolving, the examples given are representative of the time of writing (April 2022).

2. Enhanced Web Search with Schema.org

For many years, search engines have been scraping the Web and making a best guess with respect to interpreting the page content. However, even after natural language processing techniques are applied to a page, there are significant ambiguities about the content of a page. To overcome this, the search engines recommend embedding machine processable markup within the page source using a standard vocabulary of generic terms, the Schema.org vocabulary [3], to provide a high-level overview of the content of the page. For example, for a page about a movie, the markup would state that it was about a Movie type (https://schema.org/Movie) and provide some characteristics of the movie such as its name (https://schema.org/name) and average user rating (https://schema.org/aggregateRating). It would also link to data about the people declared with the Person type (https://schema.org/Person) involved with the movie using properties such as actor (https://schema.org/actor), director (https://schema.org/director), and author (https://schema.org/author). Figure 1 provides the JSON-LD markup[1] that could be embedded in a Web page for the movie "True Grit".

The search engine crawlers, upon processing Web page markup, have improved the understanding of the content of the page by the common understanding of these declared types and properties. The search engines can now process the content and connect it with other pages about the same content, e.g., pages about the same film, or related content, e.g., the actors in the film — in Figure 1 @id is a mechanism to link to other data. This identification of concepts and subsequent linking of concepts ("things") forms a knowledge graph [5], which several of the major search

---

[1]Markup can be provided in a number of different formats including Microdata, RDFa, and JSON-LD. In this chapter, we follow the recommendation of Google to use JSON-LD (https://developers.google.com/search/docs/advanced/structured-data/intro-structured-data).

```
<script type="application/ld+json">
{
      "@context": "https://schema.org",
      "@type": "Movie",
      "@id": "http://example.com/movie/true_grit_2010",
      "name": "True Grit",
      "aggregateRating": "4",
      "datePublished": "2011-02-11",
      "director": [
            {
                  "@type": "Person",
                  "@id": "http://example.com/person/ethan_coen",
                  "name": "Ethan Coen"
            },
            {
                  "@type": "Person",
                  "@id": "http://example.com/person/joel_coen",
                  "name": "Joel Coen"
            }
      ]
      ...
}
</script>
```

Fig. 1.   Snippet of JSON-LD markup for the movie True Grit.

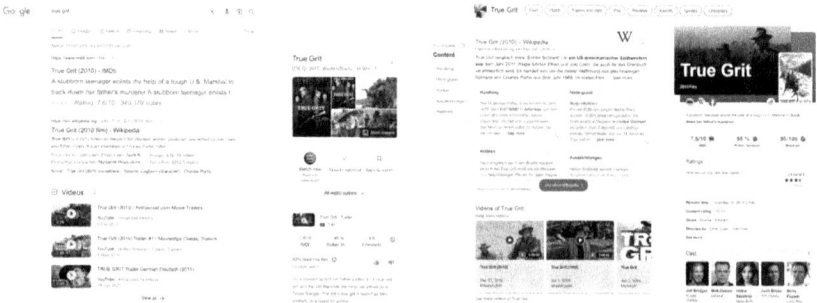

Fig. 2.   Search results provided by Google (left) and Bing (right) for the keyword search "True Grit". The main screenshot shows the rich snippets with aggregate ratings and facts about the film. These are generated based on markup embedded in Web pages. On the right of both results is the content displayed from the company's search Knowledge Graph which provides facts about the film True Grit, displayed in an "info box". Screenshots from April 2022.

engines now have [4,6,7]. Users see the effects of these knowledge graphs in their search results. Very often, rich snippets will be included with search results, giving some of the asserted facts about the page, together with a snippet of the page content (see Figure 2). Another feature of search results is an information box (info box) from the search engine's knowledge graph. This gives a detailed set of facts about the concept that was searched for. Figure 2 shows on the right the asserted facts from the knowledge graph about the movie that was searched for.

As of version 14[2], Schema.org contains 797 types — the "things" that can be described — and 1,453 properties — to specify the attributes of these "things". These are mostly targeted at the general Web with an emphasis on eCommerce. While the vocabulary is not a World Wide Web Consortium (W3C) Recommendation, the community group that oversees the development of the Schema.org vocabulary is hosted by the W3C and overseen by representatives from the major search companies.[3] This provides agility to the development of the vocabulary as well as consensus across the search engines. The semantics of the vocabulary are loosely defined, as is appropriate for a search scenario, giving enough common ground to allow for things to be found, but not enough to accurately capture all aspects, or properties, of the "thing" being described.

The Schema.org vocabulary is evolving with a wide range of communities providing contributions and suggestions, so it is not just defined by the search engines. The inclusion of new types and properties is driven by use cases for specific vocabulary terms that exploit markup found on Web pages. This has led to contributions for terms covering, e.g., automobiles, learning resources, and bibliographic resources.

3. Dataset Search: A Dedicated Search Portal

The main focus of Schema.org is to support Web search in general. However, specialized search portals that exploit a small number of types from the vocabulary have been developed. These benefit from a limited set of properties that can be used to provide rich search functionality. Google offers several dedicated search portals such as Google Scholar[4] for academic papers and patents, Google Careers[5] for job adverts, and Google Dataset Search[6] for collections of data.

The Dataset Search Portal is dedicated to searching for collections of data, where the user is given a standard keyword search interface, with autocomplete functionality for the names of datasets. Details of the dataset that is the top search result for the query are shown giving metadata about

---

[2] https://schema.org/docs/releases.html, accessed April 2022.
[3] https://www.w3.org/community/schemaorg/, accessed April 2022.
[4] https://scholar.google.com/, accessed April 2022.
[5] https://careers.google.com/, accessed April 2022.
[6] https://datasetsearch.research.google.com/, accessed April 2022.

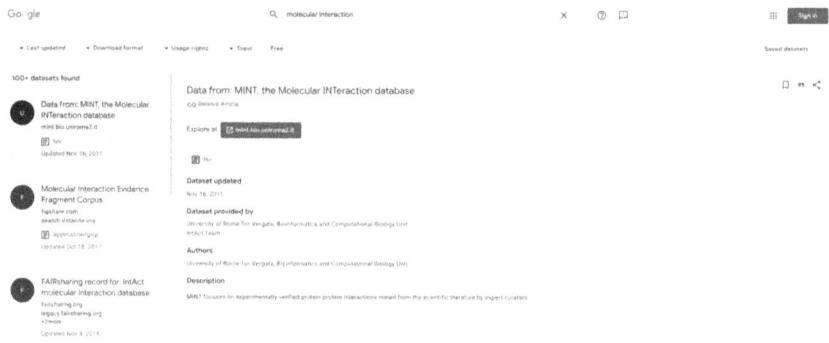

Fig. 3.   Search results from the Google Dataset Search portal searching for "molecular interaction" in April 2022.

the dataset, e.g., name, description, authors, and license, as well as links to related research articles on the dataset and the data download location (see Figure 3). The names and some key information of alternative search results are shown in a scrollable box on the left, which, if a result is clicked on, will then show the fuller metadata retrieved. There are some search facets across the top that allow the user to refine their results on parameters that are pertinent to datasets, viz. when they were last updated, the format of the data, associated license, and the high-level topic of the dataset. Recently, the outputs of the Dataset Search Portal have been incorporated into the results returned on the standard Google search portal.

The content underlying Google Dataset Search Portal is scraped from individual pages about datasets, where the Schema.org Dataset type has been embedded. The definition of what counts as a dataset is very permissive: "A body of structured information describing some topic(s) of interest" (https://schema.org/Dataset). This definition includes everything from a single CSV file, to a collection of files, to a database of curated content. At Web scale, it is difficult to rely on providers giving correct and detailed descriptions of their content. According to a study [8], after title and description — which must be provided to be included in Google's registry — provider and keywords are provided around 80% of the time, URL about 70%, and information about downloads, date modified, and license only 30–40%. Once a page is crawled, Google does a substantial amount of processing to curate the data and consolidate it into its internal knowledge graph [9].

Marking up a dataset resource is potentially a daunting task, particularly when taking into account that the properties for the Dataset type (https://schema.org/Dataset) number about 150. To support dataset providers in getting their data included in the search portal, Google has provided a usage guide identifying the key properties to include about a dataset,[7] together with a description of their purpose. These descriptions differ from those of the primary Schema.org description for the properties since they have been tailored for use with datasets. Additional usage notes and examples for each property focus on increasing data quality for searching for a dataset. There are 17 recommended properties not all of which are applicable to all datasets, e.g., a dataset about proteins is unlikely to have a geospatial coverage. Only two properties are actually required: name and description. These serve as the lowest common denominator for describing any sort of dataset on the Web.

The Google Dataset Search Portal is one of the biggest corpora aggregating datasets, growing from 500 thousand records to 28 million in a span of four years, from 2016 to 2020 [8]. The corpus contains datasets from a wide range of topics; with Social Sciences (about 26%) and Geosciences (about 19%) dominating; both were the focus of the portal's launch in September 2018. The portal is reliant on the markup provided by Web developers. An analysis published in 2021 found that only 61% of Web pages that included Dataset markup actually correspond to datasets, although there is work to alleviate deviant markup providers [10]. However, the portal does not support search into the content of the datasets; e.g., it is not possible to search for datasets on information about a specific protein, e.g., ACE2 which interacts with the virus COVID-19. To enable such a detailed search, markup of the content of datasets would be required, with extensions to the Schema.org vocabulary.

4. Bioschemas: Schema.org for the Life Sciences

Due to its conception by the major search engines, the Schema.org vocabulary has a focus on the most widely used parts of the Web, i.e., eCommerce (products); books, movies, and TV (creative works); people and organizations; and places. The vocabulary was extended to cover specialized types and properties, e.g., datasets to enable Google Dataset Search Portal. However, the content of these datasets cannot be described beyond high-level topical coverage using the Schema.org vocabulary and therefore are less meaningful when embedded within Web pages about the individual concepts, e.g., a page from a database of proteins about the human protein ACE2 (https://www.uniprot.org/uniprot/Q9BYF1). The other challenge

---

[7] https://developers.google.com/search/docs/advanced/structured-data/dataset, accessed April 2022.

for a domain adopting Schema.org is the number of available properties on many of the types. Markup providers, typically Web developers, need to be guided as to which of the properties are essential for allowing others to Find and Reuse their content. While Google has provided the *de facto* standard for describing datasets and a few other types that they use in their products, they do not provide these usage guidelines for all types. Additionally, these usage guidelines are developed for Google's internal use and may not meet the needs of the wider community.

Bioschemas (https://bioschemas.org) is a grassroots initiative that aims to tailor Schema.org to the life sciences community so that their resources become more Findable and Interoperable. It does this through two objectives:

1. Develop new types and properties to be included in the Schema.org vocabulary to allow the representation of life sciences concepts.
2. Define usage profiles to identify the essential properties for representing a life science resource.

Since its inception in 2015, Bioschemas has developed 23 types for describing life sciences concepts, of which six have now been included in Schema.org.[8] The community has also defined 37 profiles over these and existing Schema.org types with the goal of making them more accessible to life sciences resource providers. We are aware of over 80 sites with deployments of Bioschemas profiles.[9] To facilitate adoption and ease implementation of markup, Bioschemas provide tutorials giving step-by-step guides on developing markup for Web pages. The community has also developed software tools to support the development of markup, validation of deployed markup against the Bioschemas profiles, and a data harvester that can be used to extract the deployed markup site-wide.

4.1. *Schema.org types for the life sciences*

The Bioschemas community has been proposing new types and properties for the Schema.org vocabulary of relevance to the life sciences community. Many of these are specific to the life sciences, e.g., a Gene type (https://schema.org/Gene) for representing genes and a Protein type (https://schema.org/Protein) for representing proteins. Other types are relevant to the life sciences and closely related disciplines, e.g., the

---

[8]Schema.org releases note about the inclusion of Bioschemas types (https://schema.org/docs/releases.html#13.0, accessed April 2022).

[9]Bioschemas maintains a list of known deployments which can be accessed at https://bioschemas.org/developer/liveDeploys (accessed April 2022).

Taxon type (https://schema.org/Taxon) for taxonomies is relevant for the Biodiversity community and the BioSample type (https://bioschemas. org/BioSample) for biological samples has significance for Biomedical applications. The community has also been contributing to the evolution of existing types, e.g., suggesting and commenting on properties for the Course (https://schema.org/Course) and CourseInstance types (https://schema. org/CourseInstance) and developing new types that will be applicable in a wide number of fields, e.g., ComputationalWorkflow (https://bioschemas. org/ComputationalWorkflow) for describing computational workflows over Web services. The full list of types, together with their development status, i.e., whether they are recommended by the community (released) or still in draft, can be found on the Bioschemas website.[10]

The development of the Bioschemas types has followed the philosophy of the Schema.org vocabulary.[11] The type proposals do not seek to accurately capture the underlying biology; there are plenty of domain-specific ontologies that model the biology at differing degrees of granularity.[12] Instead, the developed types aim to capture the characteristics that are most widely used when searching for, or providing initial descriptions of, the concept. The types and their properties have been inspired by the leading ontologies in their domain with minor adaptations as required to fit within the Schema.org philosophy, e.g., the definitions for ChemicalSubstance (https://schema.org/ChemicalSubstance) and MolecularEntity (https:// schema.org/MolecularEntity) are taken from ChEBI [13], Protein (https:// schema.org/Protein) from UniProt [14], and Taxon (https://schema.org/ Taxon) from Darwin Core [15]. The Bioschemas proposals do not intend to replace any of the domain ontologies but to build on and link to them, to enable Schema.org to become relevant to the life sciences community.

4.2. *Bioschemas profiles*

The second contribution of the Bioschemas community is to provide usage guidelines, known as *profiles*, over the types. Figure 4 depicts the

---

[10]Bioschemas community type proposals (https://bioschemas.org/types/, accessed April 2022).

[11]The Schema.org README file describes the process for contributing to the development of the Schema.org vocabulary (https://github.com/schemaorg/schemaorg/# improving-schemas, accessed April 2022).

[12]See the content of BioPortal (http://bioportal.bioontology.org/, accessed April 2022) which currently contains 972 ontologies [11] or the EBI Ontology Lookup Service (https://www.ebi.ac.uk/ols, accessed April 2022) which currently contains 273 ontologies [12].

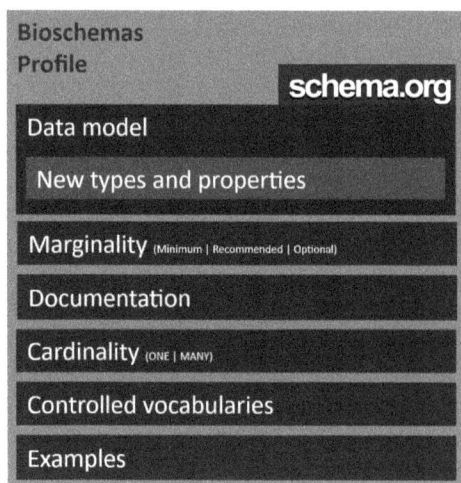

Fig. 4.   The components of a Bioschemas profile.

components of a Bioschemas profile, which consists of grouping properties
into marginality levels, refinements of expected types and descriptions to
ease understanding of the use of the property, declarations of the cardinality
of the property (i.e., should it only be used once or can it be used many
times), recommendations on the vocabulary terms to use as data values
of the property, and examples of the markup. There are three marginality
levels. The *Minimum* level identifies the properties of a type as those that
are required, i.e., all markup instances would always provide these data
items. Typically, these are the properties that are searched upon when
looking for an instance of the type. The *Recommended* level identifies the
properties that are commonly available for the concept. These properties are
helpful for discerning between search results. The *Optional* level identifies
other properties that are relevant for the type in a life sciences context but
generally do not help for the search use case.

   One of the key aspects of the profiles is to identify a core set of
properties, from the larger possible total set available for a particular type.
By limiting the number of properties, typically to about six at the Minimum
and Recommended levels respectively, the process of developing markup for
a site is simplified, allowing markup developers to focus on modeling their
own data to the identified properties for the type, rather than needing to go
through all the available properties for the type and decide which ones are
relevant or being overwhelmed by the number of available properties. This
recommendation of properties also ensures greater consistency in markup
deployment, since developers are guided to use the same properties, rather

than each resource deciding which are the most relevant and providing different subsets of properties to other sources. This consistency of markup allows consumers to rely on the presence of given properties. The full list of Bioschemas profiles, together with their development status, i.e., whether they are recommended by the community (released) or still in draft, can be found on the Bioschemas website.[13]

4.3. *Tools to support markup deployment and consumption*

To support the adoption and use of markup within the life sciences, the Bioschemas community has developed dedicated tooling and training materials. While the profiles are aimed to ease the process of mapping content to the Schema.org vocabulary by identifying the most pertinent properties, there is still a great deal of background knowledge that is required, e.g., adding JSON-LD blocks within a Web page. The Bioschemas community has developed a dedicated training portal for understanding the main terms and concepts and to support the deployment of markup within a Web site. Additionally, a markup generator tool[14] has been developed to enable preliminary markup to be generated by completing a simple Web form which is generated directly from the specification of the Bioschemas profile.

Testing of deployed markup is mainly achieved with the Schema.org Markup Validator.[15] This checks that the markup can be extracted from the Web page and uses terms from the Schema.org vocabulary. Markup containing the Bioschemas extensions to Schema.org is not recognized as valid, and hence the Schema.org tool reports errors in the deployed markup. Additionally, the Schema.org Markup Validator is unaware of the Bioschemas profiles so does not check that the most useful (Minimum) properties have been provided. The Bioschemas community is developing its own validators, which are just coming online, to test the markup against the declared profiles. For example, the "Inspect" feature of FAIR-Checker[16] [16] can be used to validate deployed markup against the Bioschemas profiles used in the markup.

To support the Reuse of markup in other applications, the community has developed the Bioschemas Markup Scraper and Extractor (BMUSE[17]) to harvest markup embedded in Web pages as either RDFa or JSON-LD.

---

[13] https://bioschemas.org/profiles/, accessed April 2022.
[14] http://www.macs.hw.ac.uk/SWeL/BioschemasGenerator/, accessed April 2022.
[15] https://validator.schema.org/, accessed April 2022.
[16] https://fair-checker.france-bioinformatique.fr/, accessed April 2022.
[17] https://github.com/HW-SWeL/BMUSE, accessed April 2022.

BMUSE extracts markup from a specified list of URLs or sitemaps.[18] The markup is extracted and provenance data added to track where and when the markup data were retrieved.

5. Applications Consuming Bioschemas

In this section, we provide details of three applications from the life sciences domain that are exploiting embedded markup from source sites. In each subsection, we highlight the benefits of consuming markup conforming with a widely agreed lightweight vocabulary and discuss the challenges resolved to enable the application.

5.1. *Training and event search*

The TeSS[19] Training Portal [18] provides a specialized search service for a particular context, in this case, life sciences training material and courses. There are a large number of institutions providing these specialist courses and online tutorials which are advertised through their own Web pages. The TeSS provides an aggregated view over this multitude of institutions so that life science researchers have a single location to discover training resources. Users can search for resources based on life sciences terminology or browse through by content type. For example, to search for training resources related to toxicology, the user can simply type "toxicology" in the search interface. As the context of the TeSS is training resources, all the search results are either online tutorials or courses that have some relationship to toxicology. Figure 5 shows the faceted browsing interface for finding and exploring available training materials. The user can refine the set of materials shown using a large set of facets: scientific topic, operation, tool (e.g., blast), database or policy, audience, keyword, expertise level (i.e., beginner, intermediate, and advanced), author, related resource, contributor, license, country, organization, and resource type (e.g., videos and slides). These facets are populated based on content in the TeSS registry.

There are several ways that content can be provided to TeSS. These include manually entering content, which is only advised if a provider has a small number of resources that do not change regularly; providing an RSS or calendar feed, which limits the available metadata that can be provided but content is updated as new items are available on the feed; or embedding

---

[18]A sitemap is a standard mechanism for listing all the pages in a Website and can additionally give expected change frequencies [17].

[19]https://tess.elixir-europe.org/, accessed April 2022.

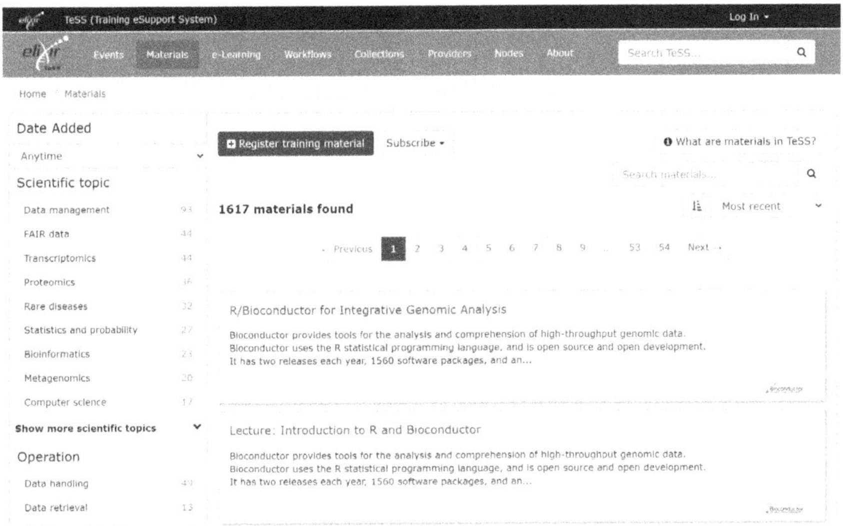

Fig. 5. Faceted browsing of life sciences training materials through TeSS. The screenshot shows the results for a search for toxicology made in November 2021.

Schema.org markup within the training material Web pages, which supports rich metadata and regular updates. TeSS consumes Course (http://schema.org/Course), CourseInstance (http://schema.org/CourseInstance), and LearningResource (http://schema.org/LearningResource) type markup conforming with their corresponding Bioschemas profile; note that the profile over LearningResource is named TrainingMaterial (https://bioschemas.org/profiles/TrainingMaterial). These provide usage guidelines reducing the 100s of possible properties to key 20–30 properties required to represent a training resource to allow it to be discovered and distinguished from other similar resources. Sites that provide markup within their pages can register a sitemap with the TeSS which lists all the pages containing markup and allows them to be visited to populate the TeSS registry. Sites are periodically reharvested to refresh the records.

By exploiting markup embedded in Web pages, TeSS is able to consume content from a large number of providers using a single common API and data model. The API is the Web standard HTTP, using the GET method. The data model is the community-agreed profiles over the three Schema.org types. Within TeSS, there is no need to merge content from different providers; each is seen as the canonical source for their content which may have links to content from other providers but won't be a duplication of the content and thus should be returned to users as separate entries.

5.2. Domain knowledge graph

Within scientific subdomains, there are large numbers of specialized data sources and individual Web sites with relevant experimental results, a.k.a. the long-tail of science. For a researcher to get a comprehensive overview of the domain, they need to gather and consolidate all of this knowledge. This is challenging both in terms of Finding all the data and also in Interoperability, due to sources using their own data models and APIs. Community-specific registries that aggregate data from sources are an increasingly adopted approach but currently need to be implemented on a "per community" basis due to the differing data models and APIs of the data providers. The long tail of small providers is often missed due to the need to implement bespoke wrappers to gather those data. Additionally, as these registries are based on community-specific approaches, they eliminate the possibility of wider exploitation of the data by other research communities. Instead, inserting markup within Web pages, using widely agreed profiles, enables gathering that data exposed through common representations, through the global API of the Web, HTTP GET requests. The data can be harvested comprehensively using sitemaps to discover all pages within a site.

One such example of this is the Intrinsically Disordered Protein Knowledge Graph (IDP-KG) [19] which harvests markup data embedded in the Web pages of specialist data providers and is being used as the basis for the IDP community registry IDPcentral.[20] The IDP-KG currently harvests data from three Intrinsically Disordered Protein data providers using the Protein (https://bioschemas.org/profiles/Protein), SequenceAnnotation (https://bioschemas.org/profiles/SequenceAnnotation), and SequenceRange (https://bioschemas.org/profiles/SequenceRange) profiles from Bioschemas. The data sources contain overlapping data about proteins that are intrinsically disordered but from different perspectives. The registry aims to support the discovery of relevant data, but not to centralize and replicate all the data. The IDP-KG thus provides sufficient richness to power the registry, using Schema.org extensions.

The harvested markup from the different sites cannot be directly used as a knowledge graph as each data provider uses its own identifiers to denote the proteins in its database. Rather than have multiple representations of the same protein, which must be consolidated into a common identifier space, the IDP-KG relies on identifier cross-references provided by the originating data source, allowing the merging of multiple representations of a protein into a single node in the knowledge graph. The IDP-KG allows

---

[20]https://idpcentral.org/, accessed April 2022.

multiple values for each property rather than distinguishing any one source as the provider of canonical information. The provenance for each data item is tracked and linked back to the original source.

The construction of the IDP-KG is an example of the development of a domain knowledge graph to support a community-specific registry. During its construction, there are no site or domain-specific APIs to learn. The multiple representations of a concept were combined using sameAs (https://schema.org/sameAs) links within the markup. As new sources provide markup conforming to the same community-agreed profiles, it is possible to increase the coverage of the knowledge graph without needing to implement per-site wrappers. The markup is also available for other communities to consume and reuse for novel applications.

5.3. *Research knowledge graph*

There is currently a lot of focus on generating knowledge graphs to capture the relationships between research outputs, authors, and funders. One such activity is the OpenAIRE Research Graph that aggregates data from a variety of sources to capture the links between research products [20]. The existing focus has been on linking research publications with their research authors and the projects and funding received. The research graph is populated by harvesting content from existing repositories provided by research institutions, data archives, and journals. The existing content about datasets is limited to metadata describing the dataset — as with the Google Dataset Search Portal (see Dataset Search Section) — rather than the data items in the data. By harvesting Schema.org/Bioschemas markup embedded within Web pages, the summary information about the concepts in the datasets can be linked to the publications and authors.

The OpenAIRE Research Graph uses the Datacite vocabulary for its internal representation of its data [21]. To reuse the markup, the harvested markup needs to be transformed from the Schema.org vocabulary into the Datacite model. This requires a mapping that identifies the properties of interest in the Schema.org model and connects these to their equivalent in the Datacite model. The life science-specific types do not exist in the Datacite model, so these are captured as extensions of the dataset concept. Not all aspects of the harvested markup will be included in the OpenAIRE Research Graph. The focus is on having a name and description with the identifier for the concept, together with links to the publications related to the concept. This then extends the coverage of the OpenAIRE Research Graph to cover the concepts within the datasets previously captured. This mapping approach to move between metadata standards, often mediated through Schema.org, is also evidenced for other domains, as demonstrated by the Research Metadata Schemas Working Group.[21] This group has also produced a crosswalk between various domains [22].[22]

6. Conclusions and Future Research Directions

The use of machine-processable embedded markup within Web pages has the potential to achieve the Web of Data envisioned by Tim Berners-Lee [23]. The widely used approach of annotating Web pages with terms from a loosely defined but widely agreed upon vocabulary of terms makes the content accessible for both human and machine consumption. While this is not the full vision of the Semantic Web [24] with intelligent agents acting on our behalf and using reasoning to infer meaning, a lot can still be achieved using these looser but widely agreed upon semantics. Web page embedded markup using the Schema.org vocabulary is already widely used by search engines to improve search results — improving **F**indability — and to populate their internal knowledge graphs — exploiting **I**nteroperability, providing benefits to billions of people on a daily basis. Benefits are also achievable for research disciplines using domain-focused registries that aggregate data from numerous sources, and cross-community knowledge graphs with the latest research interlinked and readily accessible linked to data, publications, researchers, and funders.

The **F**indability of datasets can be enhanced by embedding Dataset (https://schema.org/Dataset) markup within the homepage of the dataset. When this markup is crawled by Google, the dataset will be added to their internal knowledge graph and become discoverable through their dedicated search portal for datasets as well as their main search results. However, this is based on keyword summaries of the dataset; it allows you to find datasets about diseases but until you retrieve and inspect each one, you won't know if the specific disease you are interested in, e.g., COVID-19, is present within them. This is a time-consuming and costly process. Bioschemas has extended the Schema.org vocabulary with life sciences-specific types to enable a slightly deeper inspection of the contents of the resources while not delving to the detail of accurately modeling the data. In other words, it provides a lightweight representation of the key characteristics of the resource, enabling an initial level of **I**nteroperability, but to get the full set of features, you need to retrieve the data from its original source in the detailed representation format in which it is published. To simplify the process of

---

[21] https://www.rd-alliance.org/groups/research-metadata-schemas-wg, accessed April 2022.
[22] https://rd-alliance.github.io/Research-Metadata-Schemas-WG/, accessed December 2021.

implementing markup within sites, Bioschemas have developed community-agreed usage profiles over the Schema.org types. These profiles identify the core set of properties (typically about 10) to describe a resource of a specific type from the sometimes 100s of available properties on the type. Web page developers simply follow the profile rather than needing to pick and choose which properties to use. The profiles also increase the consistency of the markup available to consuming applications meaning that the data are more viable for **R**euse. The third pillar of Bioschemas is to support the deployment and consumption of markup by providing community training and tooling. We showcased three different applications where markup is exploited by consuming applications. The applications highlighted that there needs to be some way to identify all the pages within a site, typically through a sitemap. If the data sources being harvested and aggregated overlap, then there needs to be a mechanism to reconcile the multiple identities for a concept into a single identifier scheme; relying on sameAs declarations in the data is a simple first step here, but additional research into identifying equivalent resources is required. This is an area where machine learning is being adopted. Finally, depending on the application of the markup data, there may need to be a transformation of the data into the model of the application exploiting the markup.

Harvesting data at scale and ensuring its completeness is an open challenge that even the well-resourced Internet search engines have not solved. The Bioschemas community spent a month in late 2021 harvesting data from a number of sources known to have markup within their pages [25]. By the end of the month, 413,748 pages had been harvested from 25 sites. This represents only a small sample of the available content within the sites harvested — some of which contained millions of pages — and only a small sample of the sites known to have Bioschemas markup. While the markup can be harvested using standard HTTP GET requests, the way some sites are implemented — as single-page applications — requires the consuming client to render the page content prior to extracting the markup. This greatly increases the time and resources required to harvest markup. For small sites, in the region of a few thousand pages, this is not overly problematic as the markup can still be extracted in a few hours. However, for large sites, typical of pages representing the content of databases, this is a slow and inefficient way of accessing the data, requiring several weeks to retrieve all pages. Additionally, this data harvesting approach of visiting every page in a site is also a costly operation for the data provider in terms of both bandwidth and processing, as calls need to be made to the underlying database to retrieve the data. Overcoming this data exchange challenge is an active area of discussion both within the Bioschemas and the Schema.org communities with an initial proposal[23] for publishing the data for a site as a collection of data files rather than exclusively on a page-by-page basis. This would enable the markup for the whole site to be retrieved from a single standardized location on the site, akin to the location of robots.txt, ensuring completeness of the data gathering process.

The key benefit of the Schema.org vocabulary is that it is a globally agreed model for representing data. The definition of domain-specific minimal information models supports the detailed exchange of data within a specific community. However, typically only the key datasets in the domain can implement the model, and the long-tail of small datasets is missed. Additionally, the data are only available to that community. With the Schema.org approach, while important details for specific domains are glossed over, it makes the data usable beyond the immediate community of interest, and due to the low deployment effort, it is accessible to the long-tail of small datasets. Relying on the emerging metadata ecosystem, data marked up using Schema.org can be consumed both by community-specific registries and wider cross-domain registries, thus dramatically increasing the reach of the data. This is true not only for data but also for, e.g., software and machine learning models; while the first is already supported by Bioschemas, the latter are under construction with support for the Data, Optimization, Model, and Evaluation (DOME) recommendations (see Chapter 22) among the first specifications to be produced.

Acknowledgments

This work reports on the activities of the Bioschemas Community which has received funding from ELIXIR, the research infrastructure for life-science data; the European Union's Horizon 2020 research and innovation programme under grant agreement 676559 (ELIXIR-EXCELERATE), 82408 (EOSC-Life), 871075 (ELIXIR-CONVERGE), 730976 (IBISBA1.0), 871043 (DISSCo), 823830 (BioExcel-2); and the Innovative Medicines Initiative Joint Undertaking under grant agreement 802750 (FAIRplus).

We would like to acknowledge the inputs of all members of the community to the development of profiles, types, training materials, and supporting software. This was enabled through participation at the BioHackathon-Europe (https://biohackathon-europe.org) in 2018, 2019, 2020, and 2021 and other community-run events.

---

[23] https://schema.org/docs/feeds.html, published February 2022, accessed April 2022.

Schema.org logo by Loominade (automatically generated with wkhtml topdf) — Schema.org, CC BY-SA 4.0, https://commons.wikimedia.org/w/index.php?curid=51534848.

References

[1] M. D. Wilkinson, M. Dumontier, I. J. Aalbersberg *et al.* (2016). The FAIR guiding principles for scientific data management and stewardship. *Scientific Data*, *3*(1), Article no. 1. doi: 10.1038/sdata.2016.18.

[2] A. Chapman, E. Simperl, L. Koesten *et al.* (2020). Dataset search: A survey. *VLDB Journal*, *29*(1), 251–272. doi: 10.1007/s00778-019-00564-x.

[3] R. V. Guha, D. Brickley, and S. Macbeth (2016). Schema.org: Evolution of structured data on the web. *Communications of the ACM*, *59*(2), 44–51. doi: 10.1145/2844544.

[4] N. Noy, Y. Gao, A. Jain *et al.* (2019). Industry-scale knowledge graphs: Lessons and challenges: Five diverse technology companies show how it's done. *Queue*, *17*(2), 20:48–20:75. doi: 10.1145/3329781.3332266.

[5] A. Hogan, E. Blomqvist, M. Cochez *et al.* (2021). Knowledge graphs. *Synthesis Lectures on Data, Semantics, and Knowledge*, *12*(2), 1–257. doi: 10.2200/S01125ED1V01Y202109DSK022.

[6] Introducing the Knowledge Graph: Things, not strings. *Google*, May 16, 2012. https://blog.google/products/search/introducing-knowledge-graph-things-not/ (accessed 19 April 2020).

[7] More Intelligent Autocomplete: Academic and movie search. *Microsoft Bing Blogs*, 9 September 2016. https://blogs.bing.com/search-quality-insights/September-2016/more-intelligent-autocomplete/ (accessed 16 November, 2021).

[8] O. Benjelloun, S. Chen, and N. Noy (2020). Google Dataset search by the numbers. In *The Semantic Web — ISWC 2020*, Cham, 2020, pp. 667–682. doi: 10.1007/978-3-030-62466-8_41.

[9] D. Brickley, M. Burgess, and N. Noy (2019). Google Dataset search: Building a search engine for datasets in an open Web ecosystem. In *The World Wide Web Conference*, New York, NY, USA, pp. 1365–1375. doi: 10.1145/3308558.3313685.

[10] T. Alrashed, D. Paparas, O. Benjelloun *et al.* (2021). Dataset or not? A study on the veracity of semantic markup for dataset pages. In *The Semantic Web – ISWC 2021*, Cham, pp. 338–356. doi: 10.1007/978-3-030-88361-4_20.

[11] N. F. Noy, N. H. Shah, P. L. Whetzel *et al.* (2009). BioPortal: Ontologies and integrated data resources at the click of a mouse. *Nucleic Acids Research*, *37*, no. Web Server issue, W170–W173. doi: 10.1093/nar/gkp440.

[12] S. Jupp, T. Burdett, J. Malone *et al.* (2015). A new ontology lookup service at EMBL-EBI. In *8th International Conference on Semantic Web Applications and Tools for Life Sciences*, Cambridge, UK, 2015, Vol. 1546, pp. 118–119. http://ceur-ws.org/Vol-1546/paper_29.pdf.

[13] J. Hastings, G. Owen, A. Dekker *et al.* (2016). ChEBI in 2016: Improved services and an expanding collection of metabolites. *Nucleic Acids Research*, *44*(D1), D1214–D1219. doi: 10.1093/nar/gkv1031.

[14] The UniProt Consortium (2021). UniProt: The universal protein knowledgebase in 2021. *Nucleic Acids Research*, *49*(D1), D480–D489. doi: 10.1093/nar/gkaa1100.

[15] J. Wieczorek, D. Bloom, R. Guralnick *et al.* (2012). Darwin Core: An evolving community-developed biodiversity data standard. *PLOS ONE*, *7*(1), e29715. doi: 10.1371/journal.pone.0029715.

[16] T. Rosnet, V. Lefort, M.-D. Devignes *et al.* (2021). FAIR-Checker, a web tool to support the findability and reusability of digital life science resources, presented at the *Journées Ouvertes en Biologie, Informatique et Mathématiques (JOBIM 2021)*, Paris, France, July 2021. doi: 10.5281/ZENODO.5914307.

[17] sitemaps.org - Protocol v0.9, *Sitemap Protocol*, 21 November 2016. https://www.sitemaps.org/protocol.html (accessed 26 November 2021).

[18] N. Beard, F. Bacall, A. Nenadic *et al.* (2020). TeSS: A platform for discovering life-science training opportunities. *Bioinformatics*, *36*(10), 3290–3291. doi: 10.1093/bioinformatics/btaa047.

[19] A. J. G. Gray, P. Papadopoulos, I. Asif *et al.* (2022). *Creating and exploiting the intrinsically disordered protein knowledge graph (IDP-KG)*, Leiden, The Netherlands.

[20] M. Baglioni, A. Bardi, A. Kokogiannaki *et al.* (2019). The OpenAIRE Research Community Dashboard: On blending scientific workflows and scientific publishing. In A. Doucet, A. Isaac, K. Golub, T. Aalberg, and A. Jatowt (eds.), *Digital Libraries for Open Knowledge*, Vol. 11799. Cham: Springer International Publishing, pp. 56–69. doi: 10.1007/978-3-030-30760-8_5.

[21] P. Manghi, A. Bardi, C. Atzori *et al.* (2019). The OpenAIRE research graph data model. doi: 10.5281/zenodo.2643199.

[22] M. Ojsteršek, M. Eriksson, K. Kurowski *et al.* (2021). Crosswalk of most used metadata schemes and guidelines for metadata interoperability. Zenodo. doi: 10.5281/zenodo.4420116.

[23] T. Berners-Lee (2006). Linked data — Design issues. *w3.org*. https://www.w3.org/DesignIssues/LinkedData (accessed 20 August 2021).

[24] T. Berners-Lee, J. Hendler, and O. Lassila (2001). The semantic web. *Scientific American*, *284*(5), 34–43. doi: 10.1038/scientificamerican0501-34.

[25] A. J. G. Gray, P. Papadopoulos, A. Gaignard *et al.* (2022). Bioschemas data harvesting project report. *BioHackrXiv Preprints*. doi: 10.37044/osf.io/y6gbq.

© 2023 World Scientific Publishing Company
https://doi.org/10.1142/9789811265679_0028

Chapter 28

AI-coupled HPC Workflows

Shantenu Jha*,†,‡, Vincent Pascuzzi†,§, and Matteo Turilli*,†,¶

*Rutgers University, New Brunswick, NJ 08901, USA
†Brookhaven National Laboratory, Upton, NY 11973, USA
‡shantenu.jha@rutgers.edu
§vrpascuzzi@gmail.com
¶matteo.turilli@rutgers.edu

1. Introduction

Scientific discovery increasingly requires sophisticated and scalable workflows. Workflows have become the "new applications", wherein multi-scale computing campaigns comprise hundreds to thousands of heterogeneous executable tasks. Introducing AI/ML models into traditional high performance computing (HPC) workflows has been an enabler of highly accurate modeling, and has been demonstrated to be a promising approach for significant performance improvements.

Advances in statistical algorithms and runtime systems have enabled extreme scale ensemble-based applications [1] to overcome limitations of traditional monolithic simulations. However, in spite of several orders of magnitude improvement in efficiency from these ensemble algorithms, the complexity of phase space and dynamics for modest physical systems require additional orders of magnitude improvements and performance gains. Integration of traditional HPC workflows with AI/ML methods holds real promise for overcoming such barriers [2].

In many application domains, the integration of AI/ML into a computational workflow is a favorable way to obtain large performance gains, and presents an opportunity to jump a generation of simulation enhancements. For example, one can view the use of learned surrogates as a performance boost that can lead to substantial speedups, as calculation of a prediction from a trained network can be many orders of magnitude faster than full execution of the simulation [3,4]. In addition to the use of learning for advanced sampling as mentioned above, other simple examples include the use of a surrogate to represent a chemistry potential [5], or a larger grain size to solve the diffusion equation underlying cellular and tissue level simulations [6].

There are various modes (couplings) of integrating traditional HPC methods and simulations, with AI/ML methodologies, resulting in diverse types of AI/ML "enhanced" HPC workflows. This chapter provides an overview the various couplings and how they can result in the adaptive execution of workflow applications comprising heterogeneous tasks. We identify the core characteristics of such workflow applications, as well as discuss state-of-art tools and workflow applications.

2. Learning Everywhere Paradigm

There are two classes of interplay between HPC and ML. In the first, ML directly enhances and impacts applications; in the second class, ML enhances the HPC environment on which those applications operate. This chapter exclusively focuses on the former.

Central to the first class, as well as the re-examination and overcoming the performance barrier, is the need to integrate ML methodologies and HPC. In this approach–learning enhanced simulations and campaigns–we include the use of neural surrogates, with a neural network directly predicting either the full results of simulations, or components thereof. This also includes using learning methods to control and steer simulations, for example, efficient campaigns that steer ensembles smartly through phase space[7–10]. We have identified three high-level modes of integrating ML with HPC [3,11,12]: **ML-in-HPC**, **ML-out-HPC**, and **ML-about-HPC**.

ML-in-HPC represents the scenario when an ML model is introduced in lieu of a component of the HPC simulations, or possibly, in lieu of the total simulation itself, i.e., ML model serves as a "total surrogate". **ML-out-HPC** captures situations wherein a ML model resides "outside" of the traditional HPC simulation loop, but dynamically controls the progression of the HPC workflow. For example, Active Learning and Reinforcement Learning control of computational campaigns. Finally, **ML-about-HPC** represents the situation where ML models are concurrent and coupled to the main HPC tasks. Figure 1 illustrates these primary modes coupling AI/ML to HPC workflows. These three modes are not mutually exclusive, and will increasingly be used collectively.

The *learning everywhere* paradigm [3,11,12] contends that increasingly, scientific applications will achieve performance gains and methodological advances by using all three modes of combining learning approaches with

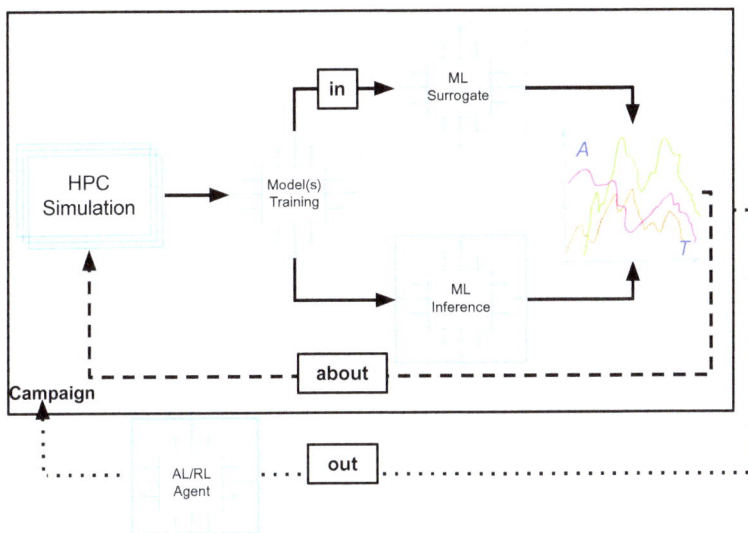

Fig. 1. Illustrating the three modes of ML-x-HPC: (1) ML-in-HPC: AI/ML surrogate models are used to replace part or entire simulations. (2) ML-about-HPC: AI/ML complements traditional computational tasks and possibly steers the tasks, improving their scientific results or efficiency. (3) ML-out-HPC: A high-level AI/ML based algorithm, such as active learning or reinforcement learning is used to dynamically control the campaign, or steer the workflow as a whole (as opposed to just the tasks). Typically, ML-in and ML-about are directly responsible for producing output for further analysis, while ML-out drives this production.

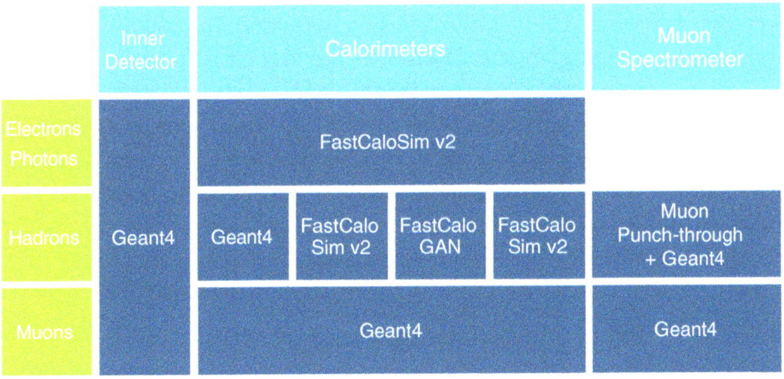

Fig. 2. Illustration of ML-in-HPC, showing a configuration of different surrogate modules replacing Geant4 in the ATLAS detector. Different ML-based components can be employed, depending on the type of process being modeled, specific subdetectors, particle types and energies. Image from [14].

HPC simulation-based techniques. In the next section, we will discuss multilevel drug selection as a canonical example of learning-everywhere paradigm, but additional prominent examples include materials design and earth-systems modeling [4].

There are many open challenges that implementing and translating the paradigm to practice poses. For example, how and where can ML effectively enhance or accelerate HPC simulations? How to make ML methods that work in tandem with HPC simulations scalable, robust, and reliable? For a given computational campaign what is the optimal mix and execution plan of ML-in, out and about HPC? Furthermore, there are system and software challenges and opportunities in combining ML and HPC systems software, hardware, and overall infrastructure. What are the correct programming models and abstractions to manage the diverse "computational tasks" viz., ML training & inference along with traditional HPC workloads? What runtime systems are needed to manage the heterogeneous workload effectively? What are the general motifs of interaction between ML and HPC, and their influence on design of runtime systems?

A leitmotif of the learning everywhere paradigm is **effective performance**, i.e., the performance improvement obtained by substituting a traditional HPC method with an integrated HPC and learning method. Effective performance measures the improvement in application performance metric (e.g., computational cost, improved time-to-solution, or the achievement of scientific objective) when using ML methods in conjunction with HPC, as compared to using HPC methods stand-alone. For example, effective performance can be measured as the time-to-solution ratio of the traditional approach vs. the learning-enhanced approach. If a traditional parameter study ran 1000 simulations to determine an optimal engineering design, while a model-based optimizer produced the same optimum in 100 simulations, the effective performance of the learning enhanced application is 10. If, additionally, the ML-based approximations in the simulation accelerated computation by a factor of 10, the effective performance would be 100. These orders-of-magnitude increase in effective performance as learning-enhanced high-performance computing takes root [13] are at the heart of the motivation for this new paradigm of computation.

3. Learning Everywhere Examples

This section provides an overview of various use cases and exemplar applications, across scientific domains which couple HPC and ML/AI. Table 1 groups use cases and exemplar applications using the three modes described in Section 2. Use cases and applications were selected to provide a representative overview of the ML techniques currently employed to couple

Table 1.   Examples of ML-x-HPC modes across scientific domains.

Mode	Domain	Application	Coupling mechanism
ML-in-HPC	High Energy physics	Atlfast3	Surrogate methods
	Molecular Dynamics	DeePMD-kit	Surrogate methods
ML-about-HPC	Atomistic simulations	Proxima	Runtime surrogate tuning
	Material engineering	Colmena	Runtime model (re)training/ configuration
	RAS protein/ Cancer	MuMMI	Runtime ML-based selection
ML-out-HPC	Cancer research	DeepHyper	Automated machine learning
	Cyberinfrastructure	SIOX	Offline ML
	Materials Science	EXARL	ML-guided simulations

ML with HPC, and to cover diverse scientific domains in which this coupling is bringing innovation and unprecedented performance improvement.

3.1. *ML-in-HPC*

Workflows in high energy physics are multi-scale, comprising quantum field theoretic calculations, detector simulations, and classical reconstruction of physical objects. Each scale has considerable computational requirements and, using only traditional methods, it is impossible to produce sufficient numbers of Monte Carlo events to maintain statistical adequacy with recorded data. As such, ML techniques, including generative adversarial networks, are becoming an increasingly attractive alternative to standard frameworks implementing step-by-step model predictions.

For example, Figure 2 shows an illustration of the ATLAS Collaboration's "fast" simulation framework, Atlfast3 [14], where ML-based techniques are used in place of intensive Geant4 [15] simulations. In this configuration, surrogates are employed in lieu of full Geant4 simulations for specific particle types, energies and subdetectors to reduce overall simulation times up to several orders of magnitude. At the same time, those surrogates allow to maintain accurate detector modeling for new physics searches, statistically-limited analyses, background processes, and detector upgrades.

Another significant example of ML-in-HPC can be found in the traditional *ab initio* MD (AIMD) methods for modeling atomistic phenomena. Due to demanding computational requirements (cubic scaling in the number of electronic degrees of freedom), most AIMD applications are limited to $O(1000)$ atoms. However, AIMD plays a major role in addressing many issues related to, e.g., drug discovery, complex chemical processes and nanotechnology. As such, tremendous efforts have been afforded to more efficient methods, including ML.

Jia *et al.* [5] offer a powerful example of ML-in-HPC applied to AIMD. Jia's approach employs an ML-based simulation protocol which uses surrogates (Deep Potential MD) in conjunction with a highly-optimized code (a GPU-accelerated DeePMD-kit [16]) to simulate $O(10^8)$ nanosecond-long trajectories in 24 hours. This record-setting accomplishment efficiently scaled to the whole 4,560 nodes of the Summit supercomputer, reaching double/mixed-single/mixed-half precision performance of 91/162/275 PFLOPS. Compared to other state-of-the-art, Jia *et al.* showed more than $O(10^{-3})$ reduction in time-to-solution (TTS) [s/step/atom].

Reference [5] is a prime example of how ML-in-HPC, which is on the cusp of a paradigmatic change as learning approaches influence the way both ODE and PDEs are being solved. For example, Karniadakis *et al.* [17] are investigating how to solve and discover new PDEs via deep learning. For partial differential equations (PDEs), neural operators directly learn the mapping from any functional parametric dependence to the solution. Thus, they learn an entire family of PDEs, in contrast to classical methods which solve one instance of the equation [18].

3.2. *ML-about-HPC*

Replacing computationally intensive computations with surrogate approximators aims to reduce TTS often by sacrificing accuracy with respect to more complete models. Optimally balancing TTS and accuracy is a non-trivial task, and the former is often neglected in order to reach the desired accuracy. Proxima [19], provides real-time feedback from executing simulations and it has been utilized to develop systematic and automated methods for dynamically tuning surrogate configurations. An iterative simulation workflow, representative of the ML-about-HPC mode, evaluates uncertainties associated with the use of surrogates, concurrently updating configurations based on a distance metric to learn features and an accuracy metric to evaluate prediction. Between iterations, surrogates evolve and replace less optimized ones, providing the coupling between concurrent surrogate tuning and the main HPC campaign.

The Proxima framework has been demonstrated in a Mone Carlo sampling application, where the first-principles Hartree-Fock [20] prediction target is replaced with a Proxima-managed surrogate. Mean absolute error (MAE) and TTS comparisons are made between Proxima and a surrogate strategy with a fixed distance threshold (based on scientific trial-and-error). In certain scenarios, the fixed strategy outperforms Proxima in terms of TTS. However, the utility of user-defined error bounds ensures more robust results with Proxima. By determining values for surrogate configurations automatically during workflow execution, Proxima is able to satisfy error bounds while achieving as much as 5.5x speedup in TTS.

Estimating properties of large collections of molecules is often necessary to find candidates for medical therapeutics, next-generation batteries, etc. However, the number of possible candidates for a single application, and therefore the number of different experimental configurations required to test them all, is often intractable. Large-scale workflows have thus come to adopt methodologies to provide an ML model training and retraining runtime to decide which computations to perform based on previous outputs.

The Colmena framework [21] facilitates a user-defined steering for workflow execution. Using an example application involving an ML-guided search of 10^5 molecules with high resistance to oxidation electrolyte design, the Colmena workflow provides components to actively train and learn as simulations are executed. Colmena performs a concurrent execution mode, having ML and traditional simulations running side-by-side throughout the workflow. Candidacy of molecules is evaluated using ML models which are scored based on selection criteria and then are ordered based on their score. Molecules appearing at the top of the ordered list reflect most suitable candidates, and subsequently additional simulations are executed. Colmena is reported to find candidate molecules at rates 100 times that of traditional computational solutions, and scaling up to 1024 nodes (65,636 cores) on Theta supercomputer.

A naturally more complicated scenario is the development of therapeutics. This type of R&D can take years or decades to come to fruition due to the complicated computational modeling involved in searches for candidate drugs and strict FDA approval procedure. In the context of cancer treatments, for example, it is suggested that Ras proteins are involved in nearly a third of all human cancers in the US [22]; however, many physiochemical properties of Ras-Raf-membrane dynamics are not fully understood. The inherent multi-scale nature of such processes makes computational modeling challenging, and each scale is traditionally simulated separately.

The massively parallel Multiscale Machine-Learned Modeling Infrastructure (MuMMI) [23,24] couples three resolution scales with ML-based selection, effectively promoting important configurations from coarse-grained to all atomistic (highest resolution). The autonomy and full power of MuMMI is realized through dynamic co-scheduling of tasks which is achieved by tying together application and coordination layers of the workflow. MuMMI achieves a 98% GPU occupancy for more than 83% of 600,000 node hours, coordinating 24,000 jobs and managing several terabytes of data daily. Furthermore, the split architecture, separating the workflow application from coordination, permits generalizability, making the infrastructure attractive beyond drug design.

3.3. *ML-out-HPC*

Increasing computational power helps to produce more rapidly predictive models, larger volumes of collected data enables higher fidelity predictions. However, improving models typically implies introducing additional complexity such as substantially increasing trainable parameters. As such, building ML models for complex diseases — such as cancer — involves a significant amount of trial-and-error, and intervention from both epidemiologists and ML experts, making diagnosis, detection, prognosis and prediction extremely time-consuming tasks.

Work from Balaprakash *et al.* [25] introduces a reinforcement, learning-based neural architecture search for autonomous deep learning development. By targeting specific class of cancer data, the automated approach finds neural architectures requiring fewer trainable parameters — thus reducing training time — which produce equivalent or better accuracy to manually finely-tuned architectures. Scalability is demonstrated using 1024 nodes of the Theta supercomputer, with the best neural architecture outperforming the manually designed network in terms of scientific results, and having 11.5× fewer trainable parameters and 2.5× faster training time. These results suggest ML-driven neural architecture search has the potential to accelerate cancer research, allowing researchers in the field to automate neural architecture discovery using HPC.

To accommodate needs of scientists and non-ML experts, a recent effort providing flexible user tools for distributed and scalable reinforcement learning (RL) is the EXARL [26] from the Co-Design Center for Exascale Machine Learning Technologies (ExaLearn). EXARL enables interfacing with existing exascale applications — *e.g.*, LAMMPS [27] and NWChem [28] — which domain scientists can guide using RL algorithms and associated neural network architectures. In addition to the miniGAN proxy application [29], the ExaLearn team has demonstrated its usefulness and exercise its scalable RL to a block copolymer application [30]. This is generally a complicated problem as materials may evolve toward generic states or become trapped in a metastable state, and thus requiring hundreds of experimental trials to reach a target state. By mapping this problem to RL, wherein a NN is trained to update annealing temperatures for subsequent block copolymer simulations, EXARL was able to show learning convergence for guiding the annealing process to both equilibrium and non-equilibrium states. Ongoing and future work includes expanding to new scientific domain use-cases, and enablement of further scaling and execution of multi-process applications.

While HPC drives much of scientific research and discovery, the platforms themselves require continuous performance analysis and optimizations to reach their full potential. This is particularly difficult for I/O systems which are commonly bottlenecks in computing systems, trailing in performance with respect to computational capabilities by several orders of magnitude. This is due to complexity of I/O systems, requiring intimate knowledge of the underlying components and potentially thousands of parameters need to mutual optimization.

The SIOX Project [31] monitors, diagnoses and optimizes I/O system parameters of HPC platforms. The modular design of SIOX provides plug-and-play capability, allowing to use diverse monitoring tools for data production. Plugins use offline ML to predict the performance gains or losses for different optimization actions and online ML to perform anomaly detection. SIOX implements actuator tasks to apply the selected optimizations and evaluator tasks to measure achieved performance.

3.4. *Learning EveryWhere: A canonical example*

The three modes of coupling ML with HPC are not mutually exclusive. In fact, the most ambitious multi-scale or multi-stage campaigns involve all three modes. For example, considering the universe of about 10^{68} possible drug compounds, efficient and high throughput frameworks for early stage drug discovery [32] are needed. *In silico* methodologies need to be improved to better select lead compounds that can proceed to later stages of the drug discovery protocol accelerating the entire process [33–35]. Innovations that integrate AI and simulation at multiple levels are demonstrating promise in overcoming fundamental limitations.

We discuss IMPECCABLE as a representative campaign that is comprised of ML-in-, ML-out-, and ML-about-HPC workflows, supplanting traditional HPC with learning everywhere. Although, IMPECCABLE

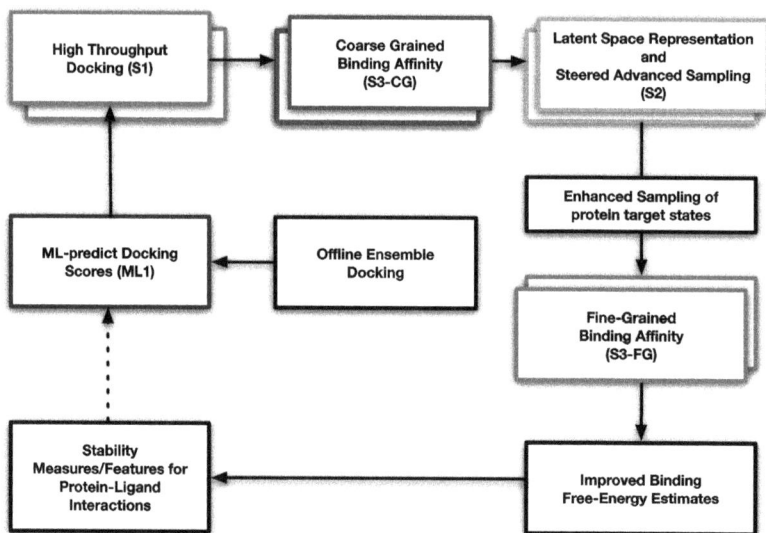

Fig. 3. IMPECCABLE is a virtual drug discovery pipeline, from hit to lead through to lead optimization. The constituent components are deep-learning based surrogate model for docking (ML1), Autodock-GPU (S1), coarse and fine-grained binding free energies (S3-CG and S3-FG) and ML-enhanced MD simulations.

was developed for COVID-19 therapeutics, the multi-stage and AI-HPC integrated campaign is representative of a range of campaigns in material and molecule design, climate science, inter alia.

The campaign consists of an iterative loop initiated with ML predictions (ML1), followed by data processing stages S1, S2, S3. ML/AI techniques (ML1 and S2) interfaced with physics-based methods estimate docking poses of compounds that are promising leads for a given protein target (S1) and binding free-energy computations (S3). Put together, the campaign glues together learning methods with innovative physics-based methods, with iterative algorithms allowing both upstream and downstream feedback to overcome fundamental limitations of classical *in silico* drug design [8]. It includes high-throughput structure-based protein-ligand docking simulations, followed by iterative refinements to these virtual screening results to filter out compounds that "show promise" in biochemical or whole-cell assays, safety and toxicology tests.

ML techniques overcome the limitations of S1 and S3 by predicting the likelihood of binding between small molecules and a protein target (ML1), and accelerating the sampling of conformational landscapes to bound the binding free-energy values for a given protein-ligand complex (S2).

Interfacing ML approaches with physics-based models (docking and MD simulations), we achieve at least three orders of magnitude improvement in the size of compound libraries that can be screened with traditional approaches, while simultaneously providing access to binding free-energy calculations that can impose better confidence intervals in the ligands selected for further (experimental or computational) optimization.

S1 is an example of ML-in-HPC mode(i.e., training and using a surrogate in lieu of computations), while S2 [36] represents a common instance of the ML-about-HPC mode. Although ML-out-HPC was not implemented on HPC platforms at the time of publication, prototypes were used to determine optimal allocation of computational resources across S1-S3 [37].

The impact of the algorithmic, methodological and infrastructural innovations resulted by measuring both raw throughput — defined as ligands per unit time, scientific performance — defined as effective ligands sampled per unit time, as well as the quality of ligands selected [8,9,38,39]. Thus, the IMPECCABLE [9,38] drug discovery pipeline is the quintessential example of the learning everywhere paradigm.

4. Machine Learning and Scientific Workflow Applications

The coupling of AI/ML methods to HPC simulations, poses unprecedented challenges to the development of middleware systems to support the execution of scientific workflow applications on increasingly heterogeneous computing platforms. We outline three main challenges, and discuss how the six use cases introduced in §3 address those challenges.

4.1. *Challenges*

Traditionally, scientific workflows were defined as either High Throughput Computing (HTC) or High Performance Computing (HPC). The former came to define the distributed workflows of the grid era; the later epitomized by complex and large DAGs of processing. The increasing importance and popularity of ensembles of HPC simulations, resulted in a convergence of these two primary modes — high-throughput of high-performance computing (HT-HPC). And ultimately workflows involving dependencies between large number of (parallel) tasks, and represented by DAG taskgraph. The current workflow middleware reflects these dominant paradigms and trends. Moving forward, they will be supplanted by middleware systems which support ML coupling to HT-HPC workflows at multiple levels of the application.

Integrating ML methods with HPC simulations, results in three primary classes of workflows: (1) Hybrid HPC-HTC workflows; (2) ML-coupled workflows, discussed in §3; and (3) Edge-to-center workflows, which typically involve integrating distributed ML with HPC workflows (e.g., with ML on the edge). This is rapidly becoming an increasingly important type of workflow with distributed data production and ML execution, and their need to couple to large data-centers.

Unsurprisingly, coupling ML to HPC simulations also introduces many challenges — at application, middleware and resource levels. In this chapter we focus on three main middleware development challenges related to resource and task execution management to realize the full potential of ML for scientific workflow applications: (1) task heterogeneity; (2) adaptive execution; and (3) application performance.

ML introduces multiple levels of task heterogeneity. Alongside traditional CPU, GPU and, possibly, multi-node MPI tasks, ML usually requires the execution of high-throughput function calls, often implemented in an interpreted language as Python, and that may depend on datasets distributed across repositories managed by diverse organization and platforms. As a consequence, the middleware that manages the execution of the workflow application, has to be able to concurrently schedule, place and execute MPI executables alongside Python functions with wildly varying execution lifetimes — the former for hours, the latter for as little as fractions of seconds.

One of the main scientific reasons to use ML in workflow applications is to improve the analysis that can be done on the data produced by part of the tasks of the workflow application. While some tasks progress, ML models can be used to learn relevant features and better drive the progress of the workflow at runtime. In order to leverage the potential of ML-based analysis, the workflow application has to become adaptive, i.e., being able to integrate the results of ML inferences and alter the workflow graph accordingly, and define the amount of learning to perform at runtime, especially when that amount cannot be known in advance, before execution [36]: simulations must be paused and restarted with new starting points, and/or a diverse number, type or size of simulations must be started to account for changed requirements, based on ML inferences. Further, ML training can vary at runtime, both in amount per model and across multiple models, when used. That has consequences for the capabilities of the workflow execution middleware. Alongside the capability of traversing an acyclic direct graph (DAG) to produce a concrete execution plan, workflow middleware has to update that DAG, pausing/restarting the execution of some of its nodes, adding/removing some nodes, and/or dynamically changing the amount of resources allocated to those nodes.

Finally, for ML to be useful it must enable improvements in both scientific and execution performance. On one side, the use of ML modeling and inference needs to improve the scientific computation that it drives, e.g., the accuracy and/or physically simulated duration. On the other side, ML has to effectively and efficiently use available resources when integrated within a workflow application. Resource efficiency depends on both the amount of time those resources are used in order to achieve the planned goal of the workflow application, and the percentage of available resources utilized to achieve that goal. This means that the workflow execution middleware has to manage the concurrent execution of heterogeneous tasks in a way that maximizes resource utilization while minimizing the workflow application total time to completion.

4.2. *Framework and middleware solutions*

The ML-enabled workflow frameworks described earlier address some or all the challenges of task heterogeneity, adaptive execution and framework's performance (as opposed to scientific performance), at different levels of the middleware software stack.

Proxima [40] is implemented as a Python library used to wrap a Python function. Based on its inputs, Proxima calculates when to infer via a surrogate model or running the wrapped function. Inferring via a surrogate model is often faster than executing the wrapped function, resulting in an overall speedup. Proxima continually monitors the function execution, dynamically adapting the surrogate configuration parameters and determining when to retrain the surrogate model at runtime. While Proxima executes different types of functions (inference, monitoring, evaluation, configuration and retraining), it is not optimized for HPC and does not concurrently execute those different functions at scale. Proxima implements adaptivity, by retraining at runtime and parametrizing the model. Finally, Proxima performance as Python library is evaluated in terms of Proxima logic, model (re)training, surrogate usage, and inference.

Colmena [21] a general-purpose Python library for steering ensembles of experiments on HPC computing systems. Colmena is designed to execute different types of tasks, including: simulation, inference (via surrogate models) model training, and candidate generation. Different from Proxima, Colmena is designed to scale on HPC platforms, addressing the heterogeneity challenge by coordinating the (possibly concurrent) execution of different types of tasks. Similar to Proxima, Colmena enables adaptivity via surrogate parameterization and (re)training. Colmena uses Parsl as its runtime, avoiding a reimplementation of a ML-specific and general-purpose runtime capabilities. Colmena's performance is measured in terms of communication overheads (e.g., requests or result object, and data input or output), and scaling performance with different task duration, result size, and number of workers.

EXARL [29] is a Python framework build on OpenAI Gym to enable the implementation of arbitrary reinforcement learning (RL) algorithms and their execution at scale. EXARL implements agents, each based on a learner/actors architecture in which each agent concurrently uses a scalable number of learners. Learners can be implemented as multi-process or MPI executables; multiple agents can be executed concurrently. EXARL does not offer specific capabilities for mapping and launching its agents, relying on third party tools like, for example, batch system and an MPI infrastructure. As such, EXARL does not support task heterogeneity and implementing adaptivity requires coding capabilities on top of its agents. Performance is currently under evaluation, in terms of scalability of the size of each learners, and number of concurrent learners and agents.

MUMMI [23,24] is a Python workflow manager that coordinated the execution of massively parallel multiscale simulations. MUMMI allows to coordinate the concurrent execution of macro- and micro-scale simulation tasks, coupling them via ML methods to decide what space of the macro-scale simulations should be explored by the micro-scale ones. MUMMI uses the Flux job scheduler to coordinate the scheduling and execution of heterogeneous tasks on both CPUs and GPUs, and the Maestro workflow plugin to interface its workflow manager component to Flux. MUMMI enables adaptivity, allowing (re)training of ML models at runtime and using them for steering the simulations. MUMMI's performance is evaluated in terms of resource utilization and number of concurrent simulations executed.

IMPECCABLE [8,9] is a drug discovery pipeline that executes heterogeneous tasks (i.e., MD simulations, ML training and inference) on both CPUs and GPUs at scale. Implemented using RADICAL-Cybertools as workflow middleware and runtime systems, it also uses DeepDriveMD. IMPECCABLE enables adaptivity by clustering MD trajectories to steer the ensemble of MD simulations. This may include either starting new simulations (i.e., expanding the pool of initial MD simulations), or killing unproductive MD simulations (i.e., simulations stuck in meta-stable states). IMPECCABLE also supports runtime evaluation of training of docking surrogate(s). IMPECCABLE's performance is evaluated in terms of resource utilization, framework's overheads, and total time to completion of the pipeline and each of its stages.

Importantly, the capabilities offered by DeepDriveMD and RADICAL-Cybertools are portable across use cases and computational campaigns.

DeepDriveMD and RADICAL-Cybertools capabilities which are utilized for IMPECCABLE, also allowed for coordinating the diverse simulations coupled to ML models, and automate their execution at scale for the #COVIDIsAirborne [41] campaign. Work is underway to use RADICAL-Cybertools to support workflow orchestration, heterogeneous task execution and adaptivity at scale.

5. Discussion

The success of ML-enabled HPC workflows brings to the forth several challenges and opportunities: (1) Engineering middleware and frameworks to support for ML-enabled HPC workflows; (2) ML-HPC Benchmarks to measure both execution and effective performance; (3) Online ML model engineering, to name just a few.

Consistent with the current workflow application landscape, many ML methods are being implemented as single-point software solutions, supporting specific user-facing interfaces, use cases and HPC platforms. Nonetheless, as seen in §4.2, some solutions are built over existing middleware, seeking benefits of well-engineered and general-purpose systems. Thus, one of the main requirements in middleware engineering for ML and HPC will be to progressively separate the applications, framework, middleware and platform concerns, enabling ML support across the stack, without having to code a plethora of independent solutions that all implement similar capabilities.

Another of the main items of the ML-enabled HPC workflow applications roadmap, is to promote the integration among existing middleware solutions to support the development of domain-specific ML frameworks. While the middleware layer should be domain-agnostic, offering general-purpose resource and runtime management capabilities, often domain scientists require frameworks tailored to their programming models and abstractions. For example, some scientists may prefer a configuration-based interface to set their applications' parameters, while others require an API to manage parallelism at loops level. The goal will be to develop frameworks tailored to ML-enabled workflow applications, that leverage runtime capabilities already available, and expose dedicated abstractions to the users while hiding low-level details.

Currently, filesystem performance and implementation of in-memory data sharing are among the main limitations faced by ML-driven workflow applications on HPC platforms. Often, filesystems become bottlenecks for the I/O intensive operations required by ML, especially when performed on data continuously generated at runtime. In-memory approach to data exchange among diverse types of workflow tasks still requires using task-level capabilities [42]. That creates friction between using middleware capabilities to implement coordination protocols and the need to implement those protocols within the tasks themselves because of in-memory communication requirements. That impedes a clean separation of concerns between middleware and tasks, hindering the development of general-purpose, production-grade solutions.

Finally, with the growing number of datasets stored on cloud platforms and the need to leverage diverse programming and computation paradigms, integrating cloud and HPC resources has become a priority. Developing robust and reliable solutions for such integrations is a sociotechnical challenge. Socially, cloud and HPC resources leverage different economic models, making difficult to reconcile two different resource allocation processes. Technically, the HPC multitenant batch systems with their non-elastic resource allocations, heavily biased towards large and long single MPI jobs, does not match the platform, container and function as a service models implemented by cloud providers. It will be important to develop resource brokering systems, designed to seamlessly execute large-scale, ML-enabled workflow applications on diverse and heterogeneous resources.

Performance will be critical for the future development of ML-enabled workflow applications. Steady-state performance and resource utilization for large-scale workflows is a known challenge. For example, workflows that helped advance research and response to COVID-19 and underpinned the Gordon Bell 2020 Special Prize for COVID-19 finalists had impressive peak performance, but modest steady-state performance. With increasing heterogeneity and temporal variation in the duration of tasks and services — as can be expected with ML-coupled HPC workflows, improving steady-state performance and resource utilization becomes challenging.

Effective performance, and its measure of scientific improvement over other methods, will have to be complemented by runtime performance to assure effective and efficient utilization of available computing resources. In that context, Benchmarks will play a fundamental role to drive both software and platform development. Benchmarks will have to be accessible and recognized by relevant scientific communities, enabling to compare performance among algorithmic methods and application execution. Without those benchmarks, it will not be possible to converge towards effective algorithmic solutions and, importantly, asses how efficiently future platform architectures will support ML-enabled workflows.

The learning everywhere examples show how ML methods will have to be integrated at multiple levels within workflow applications and the middleware that enable their executions. Whereas the real impact will arise from computational campaigns that integrate ML with HPC, ML methods will also play a fundamental role for the middleware, improving online monitoring, tracing and profiling. ML methods will also enable improved scheduling algorithms, essential for the effective placement of tasks at the upcoming exascale, and preemptive data staging and caching.

Acknowledgments

The authors would like to thank Jack Well and Tom Gibbs (NVIDIA), and Addi Malviya Thakur (ORNL) for valuable suggestions on early drafts. SJ acknowledges Geoffrey Fox for many useful discussions. SJ acknowledges funding from DOE (ECP CANDLE and ExaWorks, and DE-SC0021352), as well as NSF-1931512 (RADICAL-Cybertools).

References

[1] P. M. Kasson and S. Jha (2018). Adaptive ensemble simulations of biomolecules. *Current Opinion in Structural Biology*, *52*, 87–94. Cryo electron microscopy: The impact of the cryo-EM revolution in biology Biophysical methods.

[2] E. Hruska, V. Balasubramanian, S. Jha *et al.* (2020). Extensible and scalable adaptive sampling on supercomputers. *Journal of Chemical Theory and Computation (accepted)*. https://arxiv.org/abs/1907.06954.

[3] G. Fox, J. Glazier, J. C. S. Kadupitiya *et al.* (2019). Learning everywhere: Pervasive machine learning for effective high-performance computation. In *IEEE International Parallel and Distributed Processing Symposium Workshops*, pp. 422–429. IEEE. https://arxiv.org/abs/1902.10810.

[4] M. F. Kasim, D. Watson-Parris, L. Deaconu *et al.* (2021). Building high accuracy emulators for scientific simulations with deep neural architecture search. *Machine Learning: Science and Technology*, *3*, 015013.

[5] W. Jia, H. Wang, M. Chen *et al.* (2020). Pushing the limit of molecular dynamics with ab initio accuracy to 100 million atoms with machine learning. In *SC20: International Conference for High Performance Computing, Networking, Storage and Analysis*, pp. 1–14.

[6] J. L. Peterson, R. Anirudh, K. Athey *et al.* (2019). Merlin: Enabling machine learning-ready HPC ensembles. *arXiv preprint arXiv:1912.02892*.

[7] H. Lee, M. Turilli, S. Jha *et al.* (2019). Deepdrivemd: Deep-learning driven adaptive molecular simulations for protein folding. In *2019 IEEE/ACM Third Workshop on Deep Learning on Supercomputers (DLS)*, pp. 12–19. IEEE.

[8] H. Lee, A. Merzky, L. Tan *et al.* (2021). Scalable HPC and AI infrastructure for COVID-19 therapeutics. In *Platform for Advanced Scientific Computing Conference (PASC '21)*, July 5–9, 2021, Geneva, Switzerland. ACM, New York, NY, USA.

[9] A. Al Saadi, D. Alfe, Y. Babuji *et al.* (2021). Impeccable: Integrated modeling pipeline for covid cure by assessing better leads. In *50th International Conference on Parallel Processing (ICPP '21)*, 9–12 August 2021, Lemont, IL, USA. ACM, New York, NY, USA, p. 12.

[10] L. Casalino, A. C. Dommer, Z. Gaieb *et al.* (2021). AI-driven multiscale simulations illuminate mechanisms of sars-cov-2 spike dynamics. *International Journal of High-Performance Computing Applications (IJHPCA)*. https://journals.sagepub.com/doi/10.1177/10943420211006452.

[11] S. Jha and G. Fox (2019). Understanding ML driven HPC: Applications and infrastructure. In *2019 15th International Conference on eScience (eScience)*, pp. 421–427. IEEE. https://arxiv.org/abs/1909.02363.

[12] G. Fox and S. Jha (2019). Learning everywhere: A taxonomy for the integration of machine learning and simulations. In *2019 15th International Conference on eScience (eScience)*, pp. 439–448. IEEE. https://arxiv.org/abs/1909.13340.

[13] A. Karpatne, G. Atluri, J. H. Faghmous *et al.* (2017). Theory-guided data science: A new paradigm for scientific discovery from data. *IEEE Transactions on Knowledge and Data Engineering*, *29*(10), 2318–2331, October.

[14] G. Aad, B. Abbott, D. C. Abbott *et al.* (2022). Aad. Atlfast3: The next generation of fast simulation in ATLAS. *Computing and Software for Big Science*, *6*(1), 7.

[15] S. Agostinelli, J. Allison, K. Amako *et al.* (2003). Geant4 — A simulation toolkit. *Nuclear Instruments and Methods in Physics Research Section A: Accelerators, Spectrometers, Detectors and Associated Equipment*, *506*(3), 250–303.

[16] H. Wang, L. Zhang, J. Han *et al.* Deepmd-kit (2018). A deep learning package for many-body potential energy representation and molecular dynamics. *Computer Physics Communications*, *228*, 178–184.

[17] M. Raissi, P. Perdikaris, and G. E. Karniadakis (2019). Physics-informed neural networks: A deep learning framework for solving forward and inverse problems involving nonlinear partial differential equations. *Journal of Computational Physics*, *378*, 686–707.

[18] Z. Li, N. Kovachki, K. Azizzadenesheli *et al.* (2020). Fourier neural operator for parametric partial differential equations. *arXiv preprint arXiv:2010.08895*.

[19] P. Balaprakash, R. Egele, M. Salim *et al.* (2021). Proxima: Accelerating the integration of machine learning in atomistic simulations. In *Proceedings of the International Conference on Supercomputing*, pp. 242–253. ACM.

[20] C. F. Fischer (1977). Hartree–fock method for atoms. A numerical approach. 1.

[21] L. Ward, G. Sivaraman, J. G. Pauloski *et al.* (2021). Colmena: Scalable machine-learning-based steering of ensemble simulations for high performance computing. In *2021 IEEE/ACM Workshop on Machine Learning in High Performance Computing Environments (MLHPC)*, pp. 9–20. IEEE.

[22] D. K. Simanshu, D. V. Nissley, and F. McCormick (2017). Ras proteins and their regulators in human disease. *Cell*, *170*(1), 17–33.

[23] F. Di Natale, H. Bhatia, T. S. Carpenter *et al.* (2019). A massively parallel infrastructure for adaptive multiscale simulations: Modeling RAS initiation pathway for cancer. In *Proceedings of the International Conference for High Performance Computing, Networking, Storage, and Analysis*, pp. 1–16. ACM/IEEE.

[24] H. Bhatia, F. Di Natale, J. Y. Moon *et al.* (2021). Generalizable coordination of large multiscale workflows: Challenges and learnings at scale. In *Proceedings of the International Conference for High Performance Computing, Networking, Storage, and Analysis*, pp. 1–16. ACM/IEEE.

[25] P. Balaprakash, R. Egele, M. Salim *et al.* (2019). Scalable reinforcement-learning-based neural architecture search for cancer deep learning research. In *Proceedings of the International Conference for High Performance Computing, Networking, Storage and Analysis*, pp. 1–33.

[26] V. Ramakrishnaiah, M. Schram, J. Suetterlein *et al.* (2020). Easily extendable architecture for reinforcement learning (EXARL). https://github.com/exalearn/EXARL.

[27] A. P. Thompson, H. M. Aktulga, R. Berger *et al.* (2022). LAMMPS — A flexible simulation tool for particle-based materials modeling at the atomic, meso, and continuum scales. *Computer Physics Communications*, *271*, 108171.

[28] E. Aprà, E. J. Bylaska, W. A. de Jong *et al.* (2020). Nwchem: Past, present, and future. *The Journal of Chemical Physics*, *152*(18), 184102.

[29] J. Ang, C. Sweeney, M. Wolf *et al.* (2020). ECP report: Update on proxy applications and vendor interactions, pp. 1–3.

[30] F. J. Alexander, J. Ang, J. A. Bilbrey *et al.* (2021). Co-design center for exascale machine learning technologies (exalearn). *The International Journal of High Performance Computing Applications*, *35*(6), 598–616.

[31] J. M. Kunkel, M. Zimmer, N. Hübbe *et al.* (2014). The SIOX architecture–coupling automatic monitoring and optimization of parallel i/o. In *International Supercomputing Conference*. Springer, pp. 245–260.

[32] R. S. Bohacek, C. McMartin, and W. C. Guida (1996). The art and practice of structure-based drug design: A molecular modeling perspective. *Medicinal Research Reviews*, *16*(1), 3–50.

[33] D. A. Antunes, D. Devaurs, and L. E. Kavraki (2015). Understanding the challenges of protein flexibility in drug design. *Expert Opinion on Drug Discovery*, *10*(12), 1301–1313.

[34] Y. Zhou, F. Wang, J. Tang *et al.* (2020). Artificial intelligence in COVID-19 drug repurposing. *The Lancet Digital Health*, *2*(12), E667–E676.

[35] J. S. Smith, A. E. Roitberg, and O. Isayev (2018). Transforming computational drug discovery with machine learning and AI, *9*(11), 1065–1069.

[36] A. Brace, I. Yakushin, H. Ma, *et al.* (2022). Coupling streaming ai and hpc ensembles to achieve 100–1000× faster biomolecular simulations. In

2022 IEEE International Parallel and Distributed Processing Symposium (IPDPS), pp. 806–816. IEEE.

[37] H.-M. Woo, X. Qian, L. Tan, *et al.* (2021). Optimal decision making in high-throughput virtual screening pipelines. *arXiv preprint arXiv:2109.11683*.

[38] A. Clyde, S. Galanie, D. W. Kneller *et al.* (2021). High-throughput virtual screening and validation of a sars-cov-2 main protease noncovalent inhibitor. *Journal of Chemical Information and Modeling, 62*(1), 116–128.

[39] Y. Babuji, B. Blaiszik, T. Brettin *et al.* (2020). Targeting SARS-CoV-2 with AI-and HPC-enabled lead generation: A first data release. *arXiv preprint arXiv:2006.02431*.

[40] Y. Zamora, L. Ward, G. Sivaraman *et al.* (2021). Proxima: Accelerating the integration of machine learning in atomistic simulations. In *Proceedings of the ACM International Conference on Supercomputing*, pp. 242–253.

[41] A. Dommer, L. Casalino, F. Kearns *et al.* (2021). #covidisairborne: AI-enabled multiscale computational microscopy of delta SARS-CoV-2 in a respiratory aerosol (preprint).

[42] J. Y. Choi, J. Logan, K. Mehta *et al.* (2019). A co-design study of fusion whole device modeling using code coupling. In *2019 IEEE/ACM 5th International Workshop on Data Analysis and Reduction for Big Scientific Data (DRBSD-5)*. IEEE, pp. 35–41.

© 2023 World Scientific Publishing Company
https://doi.org/10.1142/9789811265679_0029

Chapter 29

AI for Scientific Visualization

Chris R. Johnson[*,‡] and Han-Wei Shen[†,§]

*Scientific Computing and Imaging Institute, University of Utah,
Salt Lake City, UT, US
†Department of Computer Science and Engineering, The Ohio State
University, Columbus, OH, US
‡crj@sci.utah.edu
§Shen.94@osu.edu

1. Introduction

Numerical simulations are routinely used to model complex scientific phenomena. Scientific visualization plays a key role in the verification, presentation, and exploration of these complex phenomena. Specifically, analysis and visualization pipelines involve the processing of large amounts of multidimensional data representing the complex phenomena. Among the primary objectives of scientific visualization and analysis are the extraction of features and identification of patterns that provide insight and can lead to scientific advancement. With rapid advances in computing, machine learning techniques which are well suited for modeling and data analysis are expected to play an increasingly important role in processing data produced by numerical simulations.

As supercomputers become more powerful, scientists can now simulate their problems at very fine spatial and temporal scales that were not previously possible. Because of the constraints in storage space and I/O speed, not all simulation output can be stored and analyzed. What is now a common practice is to store the simulation data at reduced spatial and temporal resolutions, even at the risk of throwing away crucial scientific features. Methods to retain the quality of data produced by simulations while keeping the computational cost under control are becoming a central focus of research and development in scientific data management, analysis, and visualization. To date, many data reduction and summarization methods have been proposed. One straightforward solution is to apply data compression. However, since most scientific data are high precision, compression of scientific data does not have as much success as compressing texts or images. Also, data compression does not consider preserving important domain-specific features that do not have concrete mathematical definitions. Because of these reasons, data compression alone is not sufficient. Another strategy is to extract features from the data and only output information that is related to the features. Examples of features are flowlines, vortices, isosurfaces, and volume-rendered images. While the size of features is often much smaller than the raw data, these types of methods do not allow users to perform exploratory analysis queries that require raw data.

In the following sections, we briefly discuss the specific challenges encountered in the scientific analysis visualization pipeline, followed by a classification of several impactful and relevant machine learning studies in this research area, and conclude with a closer look at two specific use cases of applying AI to tackle scientific analysis and visualization exploration challenges.

2. Specific Challenges

In this section, we provide specific challenges one might encounter when analyzing and visualizing data generated by numerical simulations. In particular, we focus on the significant challenge of performing analysis and visualization of data from an ensemble of large-scale simulations which require careful consideration of both input and output spaces.

Scientists from multiple disciplines routinely simulate complex real-world phenomena with advanced computational models. These models are controlled by a multitude of input parameters which in turn will determine the outcome of the simulation. Due to the lack of ground truth, the output can be approximated by running an ensemble of simulations, where various techniques such as using different computational models, sampling the input parameter space, stochastically changing the initial condition, etc., can be employed. An example of an ensemble simulation is weather forecasting using the WRF model [1]. The model takes the current weather condition of the region of interest as input and simulates/predicts the future weather conditions under the control of multiple convective parameters such as the coefficient related to downdraft mass flux rate and the maximum turbulent kinetic energy. To understand the impact of different initial conditions and parameter settings on the simulation output or model accuracy, scientists execute multiple runs of the simulation model with varying initial conditions and parameter settings. The output, which is a collection of spatiotemporal results from multiple runs of a simulation model, is called an ensemble. To fully take advantage of an ensemble simulation, robust analysis of the computational model is required to determine the most likely scenarios as well as low probability but potentially hazardous events. This will require a thorough understanding of the simulation inputs and outputs, both qualitatively and quantitatively. However, as some of the ensemble models contain parameters that have no immediate connection to the physical phenomena and are subject to various degrees of uncertainties, it is not always clear how parameter tuning and calibration should be done to improve the quality and the variety of the simulation output.

To analyze and visualize data generated by large-scale scientific ensemble simulations, there exist major challenges in the volume, variety, and velocity of the data as explained in the following:

- **Volume:** A single time-varying simulation run can generate data in the range of several hundred gigabytes to tens of terabytes. To produce a collection of possible outcomes, an ensemble simulation can consist of tens or even hundreds of such individual simulations. As a result, the total size of data can far exceed the available capacity of I/O devices, and the amount of data movement required to perform effective data analysis will be overwhelming.
- **Variety:** Most ensemble simulations model transient phenomena, with hundreds or thousands of timesteps. In each of the timesteps, many variables in the form of scalars, vectors, and/or tensors will be produced, which collectively describe the physical phenomena that are being simulated. To produce a wide range of possible outcomes and improve the prediction confidence, a large number of samples in the high-dimensional input parameter space are needed. Finally, to maximize the accuracy and minimize the simulation cost, scientists often need to run the simulations in a multiresolution setting. Understanding the relationships among all these dimensions is a challenging task.
- **Velocity:** As an ensemble scientific simulation can produce data at a very high rate, it is often impossible to store the multidimensional output on disk. A recent trend is to perform data analysis and visualization while the simulation is running, i.e., *in situ*. Since the simulation continues to produce data at a very high rate, there is only a small time slice made available to the data analysis and visualization code. The high velocity of data greatly limits the complexity of the analytics algorithms that can be used in practice.

Besides the challenges of investigating complex large-scale multidimensional data, the application of machine learning techniques is not always straightforward. Although machine learning has been utilized extensively in fields such as computer vision and image processing, we are still in the early stages of exploring the full potential of such techniques for scientific data analysis and visualization. Understanding whether the application of a machine learning technique is appropriate and choosing the right approach are critical for success. Furthermore, generalization of models across scientific datasets, generation of appropriate training data, and scaling training processes for large three-dimensional spatial data remain challenging.

3. Scientific Visualization and AI

Visualization researchers have been experimenting with using AI methods for quite some time. In scientific visualization, Ma and his colleagues [2,3] use traditional neural networks (nowadays deemed to be "shallow" neural networks as opposed to modern DNNs) for classifying multivariate volume data for 3D visualization, and neural networks were recognized as a promising direction for visualization research [4]. With the explosive growth of modern deep learning techniques, the community recently has focused on applying the capabilities of DNN to address various scientific visualization problems, for example, in volume visualization [5–11] and flow visualization [12–20]. In the following, we select a sample of papers published in top visualization venues that have a focus on using AI techniques for scientific visualization. Following a general order of visualization processing pipeline, we divide recent work in scientific data analysis and visualization that utilizes AI into the following categories: (1) data prediction, (2) feature extraction, (3) data reduction, (4) rendering, (5) super resolution, (6) simulation surrogates, (7) similarity and comparison, and (8) interaction.

3.1. *Data prediction*

Considering the spatiotemporal nature of scientific simulations, the applications that make use of neural networks to generate or predict simulation results fall into two categories: global and local methods. Global methods regard one timestep output of the simulation as an entity and apply neural networks (CNNs) to encode it into a latent representation. After that, a recurrent network (RNN or LSTM) is applied to the latent vectors to predict the next timestep. There are three studies [21–23] that fall into this category. This latent space can be divided into independent components so that external control of different simulation parameters like time and density is possible [22,23]. Wang *et al.* [24] also adopted a global method for data generation. However, instead of predicting flow fields, they predicted 3D organ models from single-view 2D medical images.

Similarly, CNN is applied to extract features from 2D images to guide 3D data generation. Local methods rely on the local neighborhood to perform temporal prediction. Tkachev *et al.* [25] used a local prediction model for spatiotemporal datasets and used the prediction error to assist volume visualization. Jakob *et al.* [26] released a 2D ensemble vector field dataset on which they tested neural flow map local interpolation. Their dataset can work as the benchmark for future neural network studies on vector field prediction. Because of the locality-based nature of these methods, they can scale to even larger datasets. Relating to the benchmark dataset for neural network studies on scientific simulations, Eckert *et al.* [16] captured a real-world large-scale volumetric dataset which can be used in machine learning studies.

3.2. *Feature extraction*

The term feature in scientific applications has different definitions in various scientific domains. In general, feature extraction is identifying specific patterns of interest in the dataset. Neural network-based methods for feature extraction basically fall into two categories: supervised and unsupervised. Unsupervised feature detection makes use of autoencoders. Autoencoders transform the original data representation into a latent representation which usually has lower dimensionality but is still capable of retaining important information. Han *et al.* [27] applied convolutional neural network (CNN) autoencoders to convert streamlines and stream surfaces into latent vectors and extract flow features by clustering the streamlines in the latent space. Supervised feature detection injects human knowledge into neural networks by providing labels of detected features in the training data. Supervised feature extraction can achieve higher accuracy although there is a cost associated with generating labels. Supervised feature extraction is employed in many scientific domains. Cheng *et al.* [7] first trained a CNN to segment a volumetric medical image into different complex structures and then use the activation map in the CNN as a feature vector to design transfer functions. In another work, Xu *et al.* [28] trained a predictive neural network on diffusion tensor images to study the effects of neurodegenerative diseases on neural pathways. Wang *et al.* [29] combined the supervision in 2D and 3D to obtain a higher accuracy in micro vessel structure segmentation. In the field of geographic information systems, Borkiewicz *et al.* [30] applied U-Net, a special architecture of CNN, to identify and remove artifacts. Finally, for the analysis of flow fields, Kim and Günther [14] extracted steady reference frames from unsteady 2D vector fields using CNN. Berenjkoub and Chen [31] identified vortex boundaries using CNN. To solve the load-balanced problem for parallel particle tracing, Xu *et al.* [32] treated the workload distribution across the processors as a feature and detected this feature using reinforcement learning.

3.3. *Data reduction*

For large-scale simulations, due to the storage and bandwidth limitations, scientists cannot save all the simulation output. Instead, only a fraction of or a compact representation of the data can be saved. For spatial data reduction, there are mainly two directions: generating compact statistical data representations or using neural network-based data representations. Among them, GMMs, CNNs, autoencoders, and implicit neural networks are commonly used. For example, in [33], the authors proposed a statistical down-sampling technique where each block is summarized by a Gaussian Mixture Model (GMM). The high-resolution volumes are reconstructed with GMM sampling, and the locations of the re-sampled data are assigned by the spatial information retrieved from a dictionary computed from learned simulation data. In [34], the authors represented a scalar field as an implicit function using implicit neural networks which maps a position in the domain to a scalar value. They limited the network capacity (the number of weights) and further performed network weight quantization to obtain highly compact representations of scalar fields. [23] used an autoencoder to reduce the spatial data size. Temporal data reduction is highly related to key timestep selection and temporal prediction. In this case, CNNs, LSTMs, autoencoders, and some prediction models are usually used. For example, [35] proposed representative timestep selection based on autoencoders. They first extracted feature descriptors of each timestep using the autoencoder and then performed representative timestep selection in the reduced space. [36] presented an error-controlled data reduction method based on autoencoders. During the simulation, they performed *in situ* key timestep sampling. For *post hoc* reconstruction, instead of a single decoder, they utilized multibranch deep decoders to reconstruct the discarded timesteps from previously sampled timesteps with quality control. And [23] proposed an end-to-end trained neural network to predict the complex physical dynamics of fluid flows. In their framework, an autoencoder is used for spatial compression and a LSTM is used for temporal prediction. Their network can achieve significant speedups compared to traditional solvers. Another direction of data reduction is to replace original data with a compact representation such that the similarity comparison or distance computation is fast and scalable. For example, [37] converted persistence diagrams into concise binary code representations using a GAN model. The topological similarity of original diagrams is maintained when comparing these binary codes with Hamming distance.

3.4. *Rendering*

In visualization, rendering is the process of converting features to visual forms. Machine learning in rendering work can be divided into two parts: higher-quality rendering and helping visual analysis by rendering. Higher-quality rendering is always an important topic in visualization. People perform volume rendering given a viewpoint, a transfer function, and other rendering parameters, where machine learning can help us to predict the rendering result. Shi and Tao [10] developed a CNNs-based viewpoint estimation pipeline to improve viewpoint selection. Related to transfer function, Quan *et al.* [38] used hierarchical 3D convolutional sparse coding to help transfer function design, and Hong *et al.* [9] applied GAN to replace the need for transfer function design with training images and synthesize new views with the same transfer function setting. Ambient occlusion is another important rendering effect, and Engel and Ropinski [39] came up with a deep volumetric network to predict ambient occlusion interactively during the process of direct volume rendering. Machine learning also helps other types of rendering. For example, deep scattering [40] is designed for rendering atmospheric clouds by combining Monte Carlo integration with deep radiance-predicting neural networks. ML-enhanced rendering methods are also developed to help them better analyze data. For example, Berger *et al.* [8] developed GAN-VR and used it to analyze transfer function sensitivity and explore the opacity of TF latent space. Weiss and Westermann [41] made volume rendering fully differentiable, which can be used for automatic viewpoint selection, transfer function optimization, and per-voxel densities' optimization.

3.5. *Super resolution*

Super resolution for scientific visualization is typically used *post hoc* as a method to increase the spatial and/or temporal resolution of some simulation output or the spatial resolution of images of scientific data. The methods are typically applied to scalar fields, or vector field data with specialized approaches being made for the vector field data, such as using the magnitude and the angle loss [42]. As a benefit of using SR, users may recover lost data that was downsampled or thrown away (a storage-reduction approach) or they may run simulations at lower resolutions and upscale them *post hoc* (a computation-reduction approach). Spatial super resolution (SSR) methods [42] typically use convolutional neural networks

(CNNs) to train on upscaling regular grid simulation data by a constant factor such as 4x. A 4x SSR network would increase a 128^3 volume to 512^3. Other methods learn a continuous representation for upscaling which allows users to query the network for any spatial point within the volume, normalized between [–1, 1][]. Temporal super resolution (TSR) methods use a combination of recurrent neural networks (RNNs) such as long short-term memory (LSTM) networks in combination with CNNs to create a convolutional LSTM [43]. These approaches learn deep spatial features through convolutions and then learn how these features are blended to generate a frame between t_0 and t_1. Other approaches for TSR use a continuous representation through a fully connected network and allow querying time at any point, normalized between 0 (the first timestep) and 1 (the last timestep) []. Lastly, spatiotemporal super resolution (STSR) approaches create a single neural network which increases both the spatial resolution and temporal resolution [44]. These approaches also use a combination of recurrent and convolutional methods in their network architecture to extract both deep spatial and temporal features before upscaling. Many of the above networks also employ generative adversarial network (GAN) training [45,46], which adds a discriminator network to distinguish between the output of the network and ground truth data. The generator (upscaling) network attempts to trick the discriminator into thinking the output is ground truth data. The result is the upscaled data that "look" more similar to the ground truth training data, and typically higher frequency features are added.

3.6. *Simulation surrogates*

Scientific visualization helps scientists analyze simulation results given different input parameters, thus useful for parameter exploration. However, exploring the simulation parameter space requires exhaustive search of the complicated parameter space by running a batch of computationally expensive simulations. To reduce the computational cost, researchers develop surrogate models to mimic the original expensive simulation model. Because of machine learning models' high fitting ability, they are well suited as surrogate models. Visualization of surrogate models can be divided into two categories: image-based and data-based. Image-based surrogate models such as InSituNet [47] rendered the generated simulation data directly after the simulation and used the images as supervision. Data-based surrogate models [48,49] predicted raw data.

3.7. *Similarity and comparison*

Measuring the similarity between two objects or distributions in feature space that encodes some high-level data semantics can be helpful in comparative visualization, feature extraction, and tracking. DNN as an end-to-end feature learning process can transform data into a favorable feature space specific to the downstream task, such that the similarity of features can be measured for comparative analysis. Virtually, all components of DNN can be leveraged, including input, activation, prediction, and loss value, according to the analysis goal. Features extracted from image and volumetric data by CNN, for example, are often used as a foundation of comparative analysis attributing to its capacity to encode low- to high-level semantics of the data resulting from various-sized receptive fields during convolution. V2V [50] used Conv and DeConv-based U-Net features and KL Divergence to calculate distribution similarity. Huang *et al.* [51] extracted feature maps and prediction score vectors from ResNet to analyze X-ray scattering images. He *et al.* [52] utilized the loss values and prediction scores of a binary classification CNN to measure the dissimilarity of two ensembles and analyze common members between them. DNN can also be used for distance-preserving hashing. Qin *et al.* [37] utilized a CNN to transform a persistent diagram to a 64-bit binary code such that the Wasserstein distance between training diagrams is approximated by the Hamming distance between their corresponding codes. Siamese neural network is a feature learning framework such that similar inputs will conform to similar output features. Similar ideas in the ML community are proposed from many emerging topics such as contrastive learning. Tkachev *et al.* [53] proposed a self-supervised siamese neural network to identify similar spatiotemporal regions given a query region. Positive samples during training are determined by spatiotemporal locality, and distant regions will be treated as negative samples. After training completes, the activation prior to the prediction can be used as the basis of similarity calculation and region matching.

3.8. *Interaction*

Interactive visualization is important for data exploration and understanding. Intelligent data selection is desired for such systems, but it is difficult to achieve because of the occlusion from 3D volume projected to 2D image, lack of label, etc. For 3D point cloud or particle lasso selection, traditional heuristics-based algorithms are based on data property, which is not applicable to many datasets. Supervised DNN, once trained on a labeled dataset, can produce accurate 3D data with selection on the 2D visualization and generalize to similar datasets. Permutation-invariant neural networks like PointNet [54], which is composed of point-wise MLP with global pooling, are usually adopted for point cloud data.

4. DNN Use Case: Visualization Surrogates

In this section, via a specific use case, we discuss how researchers use deep neural networks (DNNs) to assist ensemble parameter exploration by developing visualization surrogates, where the goal is to use DNNs to predict simulation results for unseen simulation parameters.

4.1. *Neural network assisted visual analysis for scientific simulations*

Complex computational models are often designed to simulate real-world physical phenomena in many scientific disciplines ranging from biology to cosmology. To model phenomena with a high degree of accuracy, simulations require high spatiotemporal resolutions and are often computationally very expensive and involve many simulation input parameters. These simulation parameters need to be thoroughly analyzed and properly calibrated before the models can be applied for real scientific studies. This requires performing exploratory analysis tasks, which involve repeated execution of the expensive simulations on new and unseen parameter configurations. For compute-intensive simulation models with high-dimensional input and output spaces, this can become a computationally prohibitive and non-trivial analysis task.

In the field of simulation sciences, a popular and effective strategy to address this issue has been to create a simpler statistical/mathematical surrogate model, mimicking the original expensive simulation model [55–59]. The surrogate is then utilized to perform detailed analysis tasks instead of the expensive simulation model. A well-trained surrogate model can greatly facilitate the analysis workflow of complex simulation models. To this end, it is possible to use neural network-based surrogate models to facilitate the design of interactive exploratory visual-analytic frameworks for the simulation/computational scientists.

Compared to popular surrogate model options like polynomial fitting or Gaussian processes, neural networks are particularly well suited for designing interactive visual analysis systems. This is primarily because, besides accurately predicting the output of high-dimensional nonlinear functions, they can also be utilized to extract and analyze interesting properties about the original simulation by opening the black box of the trained neural networks. Recent advances in the field of interpretability and explainability of neural network-based models [60] have resulted in many useful *post hoc* analysis techniques, making them more transparent in the process. This has led to a surge in their usage as proper analysis tools in many scientific domains [61–64].

Besides predicting the simulation output for new parameter configurations, a trained neural network-based surrogate model can support a multitude of useful analysis activities. We can facilitate in-depth parameter sensitivity analysis by utilizing the intrinsic differentiability of the different layers of neural networks to calculate partial derivatives. A recent work [65] showed that we can achieve uncertainty quantification in traditional neural networks (non-Bayesian models) by activating the dropout layers in the prediction/testing phase. We can support parameter optimization in our analysis system by utilizing the Activation Maximization framework [66] for trained neural networks to recommend optimal parameter configurations that can maximize/minimize the simulation outputs at specific user-selected regions of interest. We can also support extensive model diagnosis/validation by visualizing the network metadata such as the weight matrices and/or feature maps. The ability to extract and validate the knowledge learned by the surrogate model during its training process can pave ways into discovering new insights about the data with the help of such neural network assisted visual analysis systems.

In Ref. [67], researchers collaborated with computational biologists to design an interactive visual analysis framework, backed by a neural network-based surrogate model, which can assist them in analyzing and visualizing a complex yeast cell polarization simulation model [68]. The model simulates the concentration of important protein molecules along the membrane of a yeast cell (single-cell microorganism) during its mating process. The simulation model comprises 35 uncalibrated input parameters and generates a 400-dimensional output. Figure 1 offers a high-level overview of the proposed visual analysis framework. The system visually guides the users to discover new parameter configurations, which can be later used to execute the original simulation model and discover multiple new parameter configurations, which can trigger high cell polarization results in the original simulation model as well as identify interesting insights about the high-dimensional parameter space. The visual analysis framework can be extended to incorporate more complex analysis tasks like the set of recently proposed testing with concept activation vectors (TCAVs) [69]. This will allow the scientists to validate high-level domain-specific scientific concepts in the surrogate model. Moreover, the proposed visual analysis framework is independent of the architecture of the surrogate network. Therefore,

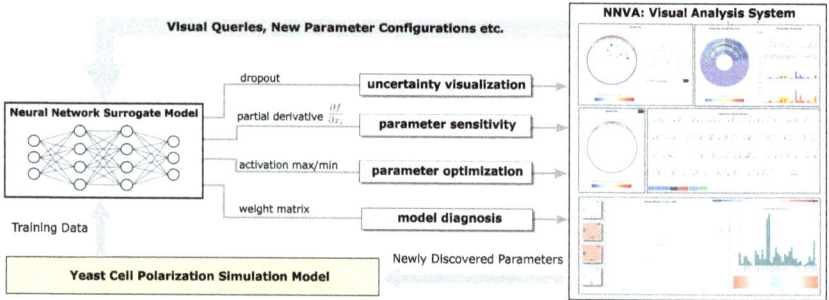

Fig. 1. A trained neural network-based surrogate model acts as the back-end analysis framework, driving our interactive visual analysis system for analyzing a computationally expensive yeast simulation model.

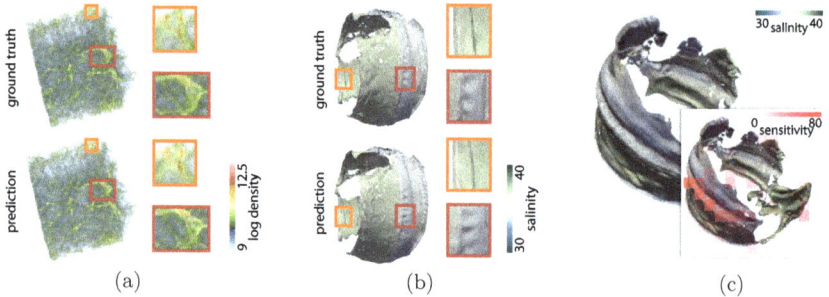

Fig. 2. (a) and (b) Comparing the predicted images with the ground truth. (c) Sensitivity of subregions of an image computed with backpropagation.

depending on the complexity of the simulation, different neural network-based models (generative models, autoencoders, reinforcement learning models, etc.) can be constructed while still utilizing the overall proposed analysis workflow.

4.2. *Image space parameter space exploration of ensemble simulations*

Parameter space exploration of ensemble simulations aims at investigating the influence of different simulation parameters on the simulation outputs. With parameter space exploration, scientists often expect to infer simulation outputs for new parameter settings and understand the sensitivity of different parameters. However, simulation parameter space exploration is not trivial, because the relationship between the simulation parameters and outputs is often highly complex. Moreover, the extreme scale of simulations makes data exploration even more challenging, because the raw simulation data cannot be all stored. To this end, one solution is to use a deep regression model to find the mapping between simulation parameters and outputs using only the visualization images produced at simulation time, i.e., an image database generated using *in situ* processing.

To develop an image space simulation surrogate, He *et al.* [70] use a deep regression model called regressor based on the training data collected *in situ*, which include simulation parameters Psim, *in situ* visualization parameters Pvis such as viewpoints and transfer functions, and the corresponding visualization images I. The regressor then learns a function F that takes the parameters as inputs and outputs the corresponding visualization result, which can be defined as $F(P_{sim}, P_{vis}) \rightarrow I$.

To this end, the regressor adjusts the weights iteratively with respect to the difference between the prediction and the ground truth. To improve the accuracy and fidelity of the prediction, the authors use the adversarial theory of GANs [71]. Specifically, we train another network called discriminator along with the regressor to differentiate the prediction and the ground truth and use the discriminator to stimulate the regressor to generate better results to fool the discriminator. With the trained model, scientists are able to infer the visualization results for arbitrary parameters within the parameter space through forward propagations and investigate the sensitivity of different parameters through backward propagations.

Figure 2 demonstrates the results of their experiments. In (a) and (b), the images predicted by the trained regression models are compared with the ground truth images for the Nyx [72] and MPAS-Ocean [73] simulations, respectively. We can see that high-quality images similar to the ground truth can be generated with trained regression models. In (c), it demonstrates that the trained model can be used to calculate the sensitivity of subregions of an image with respect to the simulation parameters. The deep regression model can be extended to *in situ* visualization and analysis approaches besides image-based techniques. For example, features such as isosurfaces and flow lines can be extracted *in situ*, and the regression model can be used to predict features for new simulation parameters and different feature extraction parameters such as isovalues.

References

[1] W. C. Skamarock, J. B. Klemp, J. Dudhia *et al.* (2019). A description of the advanced research WRF model version 4. In *National Center for Atmospheric Research*, Boulder: CO, USA, Vol. 145, p. 145.

[2] F.-Y. Tzeng, E. B. Lum, and K.-L. Ma (2003). A novel interface for higher-dimensional classification of volume data. In *Proceeding IEEE Visualization '03*, pp. 505–512.

[3] F. Tzeng, E. B. Lum, and K. Ma (2005). An intelligent system approach to higher-dimensional classification of volume data. *IEEE Transactions on Visualization and Computer Graphics, 11*(3), 273–284.

[4] K.-L. Ma (2007). Machine learning to boost the next generation of visualization technology. *IEEE Computer Graphics and Applications, 27*(5), 6–9.

[5] Z. Zhou, Y. Hou, Q. Wang *et al.* (2017). Volume upscaling with convolutional neural networks. In *Proceedings of Computer Graphics International*, pp. 38:1–38:6.

[6] M. Raji, A. Hota, R. Sisneros *et al.* (2017). Photo-guided exploration of volume data features. In *Proceedings of Eurographics Symposium on Parallel Graphics and Visualization*, pp. 31–39.

[7] H.-C. Cheng, A. Cardone, S. Jain *et al.* (2019). Deep-learning-assisted volume visualization. *IEEE Transactions on Visualization and Computer Graphics, 25*(2), 1378–1391.

[8] M. Berger, J. Li, and J. A. Levine (2019). A generative model for volume rendering. *IEEE Transactions on Visualization and Computer Graphics, 25*(4), 1636–1650.

[9] F. Hong, C. Liu, and X. Yuan (2019). Dnn-volvis: Interactive volume visualization supported by deep neural network. In *2019 IEEE Pacific Visualization Symposium (PacificVis)*. IEEE, pp. 282–291.

[10] N. Shi and Y. Tao (2019). CNNs based viewpoint estimation for volume visualization. *ACM Transactions on Intelligent Systems and Technology, 10*(3), 27:1–27:22.

[11] S. Weiss, M. Chu, N. Thuerey *et al.* (2019). Volumetric isosurface rendering with deep learning-based super-resolution. *arXiv preprint arXiv:1906.06520*.

[12] F. Hong, J. Zhang, and X. Yuan (2018). Access pattern learning with long short-term memory for parallel particle tracing. In *Proceedings of IEEE Pacific Visualization Symposium*, pp. 76–85.

[13] S. Wiewel, M. Becher, and N. Thuerey (2019). Latent-space physics: Towards learning the temporal evolution of fluid flow. *Computer Graphics Forum, 38*(2), 71–82.

[14] B. Kim and T. Günther (2019). Robust reference frame extraction from unsteady 2d vector fields with convolutional neural networks. In *Computer Graphics Forum*, Vol. 38, no. 3. Online Library, 2019, pp. 285–295.

[15] Y. Xie, E. Franz, M. Chu *et al.* (2018). tempoGAN: A temporally coherent, volumetric GAN for super-resolution fluid flow. *ACM Transactions on Graphics, 37*(4), 95:1–95:15.

[16] M.-L. Eckert, K. Um, and N. Thuerey *et al.* (2019). ScalarFlow: A large-scale volumetric data set of real-world scalar transport flows for computer animation and machine learning. *ACM Transactions on Graphics, 38*(6), 239:1–239:16.

[17] M. Werhahn, Y. Xie, M. Chu *et al.* (2019). A multi-pass GAN for fluid flow super-resolution. *arXiv preprint arXiv:1906.01689*.

[18] L. Prantl, B. Bonev, and N. Thuerey (2019). Generating liquid simulations with deformation-aware neural networks. In *Proceedings of International Conference for Learning Representations.*

[19] B. Kim, V. C. Azevedo, N. Thuerey *et al.* (2019). Deep fluids: A generative network for parameterized fluid simulations. *Computer Graphics Forum*, *38*(2), 59–70.

[20] M. Han, S. Sane, and C. Johnson (2022). Exploratory Lagrangian-based particle tracing using deep learning. *Journal of Flow Visualization and Image Processing.* doi: 10.1615/JFlowVisImageProc.2022041197.

[21] S. Wiewel, M. Becher, and N. Thuerey (2019). Latent space physics: Towards learning the temporal evolution of fluid flow. In *Computer Graphics Forum*, Vol. 38, no. 2. Wiley Online Library, pp. 71–82.

[22] B. Kim, V. C. Azevedo, N. Thuerey *et al.* (2019). Deep fluids: A generative network for parameterized fluid simulations. In *Computer Graphics Forum*, Vol. 38, no. 2. Wiley Online Library, pp. 59–70.

[23] S. Wiewel, B. Kim, V. C. Azevedo *et al.* (2020). Latent space subdivision: stable and controllable time predictions for fluid flow. In *Computer Graphics Forum*, Vol. 39, no. 8. Wiley Online Library, pp. 15–25.

[24] Y. Wang, Z. Zhong, and J. Hua (2019). Deeporgannet: On-the-fly reconstruction and visualization of 3d/4d lung models from single-view projections by deep deformation network. *IEEE Transactions on Visualization and Computer Graphics*, *26*(1), 960–970.

[25] G. Tkachev, S. Frey, and T. Ertl (2019). Local prediction models for spatiotemporal volume visualization. *IEEE Transactions on Visualization and Computer Graphics*, *27*(7), 3091–3108.

[26] J. Jakob, M. Gross, and T. Günther (2020). A fluid flow data set for machine learning and its application to neural flow map interpolation. *IEEE Transactions on Visualization and Computer Graphics*, *27*(2), 1279–1289.

[27] J. Han, J. Tao, and C. Wang (2019). FlowNet: A deep learning framework for clustering and selection of streamlines and stream surfaces. *IEEE Transactions on Visualization and Computer Graphics*, accepted.

[28] C. Xu, T. Neuroth, T. Fujiwara *et al.* (2020). A predictive visual analytics system for studying neurodegenerative disease based on dti fiber tracts. *arXiv preprint arXiv:2010.07047.*

[29] Y. Wang, G. Yan, H. Zhu *et al.* (2020). Vc-net: Deep volume-composition networks for segmentation and visualization of highly sparse and noisy image data. *IEEE Transactions on Visualization and Computer Graphics*, *27*(2), 1301–1311.

[30] K. Borkiewicz, V. Shah, J. Naiman *et al.* (2021). Cloudfindr: A deep learning cloud artifact masker for satellite dem data. In *2021 IEEE Visualization Conference (VIS)*. IEEE, pp. 1–5.

[31] M. Berenjkoub, G. Chen, and T. Günther (2020). Vortex boundary identification using convolutional neural network. In *2020 IEEE Visualization Conference (VIS)*. IEEE, pp. 261–265.

[32] J. Xu, H. Guo, H.-W. Shen *et al.* (2021). Reinforcement learning for load-balanced parallel particle tracing. *arXiv preprint arXiv:2109.05679.*

[33] K.-C. Wang, J. Xu, J. Woodring *et al.* (2019). Statistical super resolution for data analysis and visualization of large scale cosmological simulations. In *2019 IEEE Pacific Visualization Symposium (PacificVis)*. IEEE, pp. 303–312.

[34] Y. Lu, K. Jiang, J. A. Levine *et al.* (2021). Compressive neural representations of volumetric scalar fields. In *Computer Graphics Forum*, vol. 40, no. 3. Wiley Online Library, pp. 135–146.

[35] W. P. Porter, Y. Xing, B. R. von Ohlen *et al.* (2019). A deep learning approach to selecting representative time steps for time-varying multivariate data. In *2019 IEEE Visualization Conference (VIS)*. IEEE, pp. 1–5.

[36] Y. Zhang, H. Guo, L. Shang *et al.* (2022). A multi-branch decoder network approach to adaptive temporal data selection and reconstruction for big scientific simulation data. In *IEEE Transactions on Big Data*, 8(6), 1637–1649. DOI: 10.1109/TBDATA.2021.3092174.

[37] Y. Qin, B. T. Fasy, C. Wenk *et al.* (2021). A domain-oblivious approach for learning concise representations of filtered topological spaces. *arXiv e-prints*, *arXiv–2105*.

[38] T. M. Quan, J. Choi, H. Jeong *et al.* (2017). An intelligent system approach for probabilistic volume rendering using hierarchical 3d convolutional sparse coding. *IEEE Transactions on Visualization and Computer Graphics*, 24(1), 964–973.

[39] D. Engel and T. Ropinski (2020). Deep volumetric ambient occlusion. *IEEE Transactions on Visualization and Computer Graphics*, 27(2), 1268–1278.

[40] S. Kallweit, T. Müller, B. Mcwilliams *et al.* (2017). Deep scattering: Rendering atmospheric clouds with radiance-predicting neural networks. *ACM Transactions on Graphics (TOG)*, 36(6), 1–11.

[41] S. Weiss and R. Westermann (2021). Differentiable direct volume rendering. *IEEE Transactions on Visualization and Computer Graphics*, 28(1), 562–572.

[42] L. Guo, S. Ye, J. Han *et al.* (2020). Ssr-vfd: Spatial super-resolution for vector field data analysis and visualization. In *Proceedings of IEEE Pacific Visualization Symposium*.

[43] J. Han and C. Wang (2020). TSR-TVD: Temporal super-resolution for time-varying data analysis and visualization. In *IEEE Transactions on Visualization and Computer Graphics*, 26(1), 205–215. doi: 10.1109/TVCG.2019.2934255.

[44] Y. An, H.-W. Shen, G. Shan *et al.* (2021). Stsrnet: Deep joint space–time super-resolution for vector field visualization. *IEEE Computer Graphics and Applications*, 41(6), 122–132.

[45] J. Han and C. Wang (2022). SSR-TVD: Spatial super-resolution for time-varying data analysis and visualization. In *IEEE Transactions on Visualization and Computer Graphics*, 28(6), 2445–2456. doi: 10.1109/TVCG.2020.3032123.

[46] J. Han, H. Zheng, D. Z. Chen *et al.* (2021). Stnet: An end-to-end generative framework for synthesizing spatiotemporal super-resolution volumes. *IEEE Transactions on Visualization and Computer Graphics*, 28(1), 270–280.

[47] W. He, J. Wang, H. Guo *et al.* (2020). InSituNet: Deep image synthesis for parameter space exploration of ensemble simulations. *IEEE Transactions on Visualization and Computer Graphics*, *26*(1).

[48] N. Umetani and B. Bickel (2018). Learning three-dimensional flow for interactive aerodynamic design. *ACM Transactions on Graphics (TOG)*, *37*(4), 1–10.

[49] S. Hazarika, H. Li, K.-C. Wang *et al.* (2020). NNVA: Neural network assisted visual analysis of yeast cell polarization simulation. *IEEE Transactions on Visualization and Computer Graphics*, *26*(1).

[50] J. Han, H. Zheng, Y. Xing *et al.* (2020). V2v: A deep learning approach to variable-to-variable selection and translation for multivariate time-varying data. *IEEE Transactions on Visualization and Computer Graphics*, *27*(2), 1290–1300.

[51] X. Huang, S. Jamonnak, Y. Zhao *et al.* (2020). Interactive visual study of multiple attributes learning model of X-ray scattering images. *IEEE Transactions on Visualization and Computer Graphics*, *27*(2), 1312–1321.

[52] W. He, J. Wang, H. Guo *et al.* (2020). Cecav-dnn: Collective ensemble comparison and visualization using deep neural networks. *Visual Informatics*, *4*(2), 109–121.

[53] G. Tkachev, S. Frey, and T. Ertl (2021). S4: Self-supervised learning of spatiotemporal similarity. *IEEE Transactions on Visualization and Computer Graphics*.

[54] C. R. Qi, H. Su, K. Mo (2017). Pointnet: Deep learning on point sets for 3d classification and segmentation. In *Proceedings of the IEEE Conference on Computer Vision and Pattern Recognition*, pp. 652–660.

[55] N. V. Queipo, R. T. Haftka, W. Shyy (2005). Surrogate-based analysis and optimization. *Progress in Aerospace Sciences*, *41*(1), 1–28. http://www.sciencedirect.com/science/article/pii/S0376042105000102.

[56] A. Sobester, A. Forrester, and A. Keane (2008). *Engineering Design via Surrogate Modelling — A Practical Guide*. John Wiley & Sons, West Sussex: UK.

[57] D. Gorissen, I. Couckuyt, P. Demeester *et al.* (2010). A surrogate modeling and adaptive sampling toolbox for computer based design. *Journal of Machine Learning Research*, *11*, 2051–2055. http://dl.acm.org/citation.cfm?id=1756006.1859919.

[58] S. Razavi, B. A. Tolson, and D. H. Burn (2012). Review of surrogate modeling in water resources. *Water Resources Research*, *48*(7). https://agupubs.onlinelibrary.wiley.com/doi/abs/10.1029/2011WR011527.

[59] Y. Jin (2011). Surrogate-assisted evolutionary computation: Recent advances and future challenges. *Swarm and Evolutionary Computation*, *1*(2), 61–70. http://www.sciencedirect.com/science/article/pii/S2210650211000198.

[60] G. Montavon, W. Samek, and K.-R. Müller (2018). Methods for interpreting and understanding deep neural networks. *Digital Signal Processing*, *73*, 1–15. http://www.sciencedirect.com/science/article/pii/S1051200417302385.

[61] B. Alipanahi, A. Delong, M. T. Weirauch *et al.* (2015). Predicting the sequence specificities of dna- and rna-binding proteins by deep learning. *Nature Biotechnology, 33,* 831–838.

[62] J. Khan, J. S. Wei, M. Ringner *et al.* (2001). Classification and diagnostic prediction of cancers using gene expression profiling and artificial neural networks. *Nature Medicine, 7*(6), 673–679, June. http://dx.doi.org/10.1038/89044.

[63] I. Sturm, S. Lapuschkin, W. Samek *et al.* (2016). Interpretable deep neural networks for single-trial EEG classification. *Journal of Neuroscience Methods, 274,* 141–145. http://www.sciencedirect.com/science/article/pii/S0165027016302333.

[64] K. T. Schütt, F. Arbabzadah, S. Chmiela *et al.* (2017). Quantum-chemical insights from deep tensor neural networks. *Nature Communications, 8*(1), 1–8.

[65] Y. Gal and Z. Ghahramani (2016). Dropout as a Bayesian approximation: Representing model uncertainty in deep learning. In *Proceedings of the 33rd International Conference on International Conference on Machine Learning – Volume 48,* ser. ICML'16. JMLR.org, pp. 1050–1059. http://dl.acm.org/citation.cfm?id=3045390.3045502.

[66] A. Nguyen, A. Dosovitskiy, J. Yosinski *et al.* (2016). Synthesizing the preferred inputs for neurons in neural networks via deep generator networks. In *Advances in Neural Information Processing Systems,* pp. 3387–3395.

[67] S. Hazarika, H. Li, K.-C. Wang *et al.* (2020). Nnva: Neural network assisted visual analysis of yeast cell polarization simulation. *IEEE Transactions on Visualization and Computer Graphics, 26*(1), 34–44. https://doi.org/10.1109/TVCG.2019.2934591.

[68] M. Renardy, T.-M. Yi, D. Xiu *et al.* (2018). Parameter uncertainty quantification using surrogate models applied to a spatial model of yeast mating polarization. *PLOS Computational Biology, 14*(5), 1–26. https://doi.org/10.1371/journal.pcbi.1006181.

[69] B. Kim, M. Wattenberg, J. Gilmer *et al.* (2018). Interpretability beyond feature attribution: Quantitative testing with concept activation vectors (TCAV). *ICML.*

[70] W. He, J. Wang, H. Guo *et al.* (2020). Insitunet: Deep image synthesis for parameter space exploration of ensemble simulations. *IEEE Transactions on Visualization and Computer Graphics, 26*(1), 23–33. https://doi.org/10.1109/TVCG.2019.2934312.

[71] I. J. Goodfellow, J. Pouget-Abadie, M. Mirza *et al.* (2020). Generative adversarial networks. *Communication of the ACM, 63*(11), 139–144. https://doi.org/10.1145/3422622.

[72] A. S. Almgren, J. B. Bell, M. J. Lijewski *et al.* (2013). Nyx: A massively parallel AMR code for computational cosmology. *The Astrophysical Journal, 765*(1), 39.

[73] T. Ringler, M. Petersen, R. L. Higdon *et al.* (2013). A multi-resolution approach to global ocean modeling. *Ocean Modelling, 69,* 211–232.

© 2023 World Scientific Publishing Company
https://doi.org/10.1142/9789811265679_0030

Chapter 30

Uncertainty Quantification in AI for Science

Tanmoy Bhattacharya[*,§], Cristina Garcia Cardona[†,§], and Jamaludin Mohd-Yusof[‡,‖]

*T-2, Los Alamos National Laboratory, Los Alamos,
New Mexico, USA
†CCS-3, Los Alamos National Laboratory, Los Alamos,
New Mexico, USA
‡CCS-7, Los Alamos National Laboratory, Los Alamos,
New Mexico, USA
§tanmoy@lanl.gov
¶cgarciac@lanl.gov
‖jamal@lanl.gov

1. Introduction

Machine learning (ML), especially using deep neural networks (DNNs), has become an indispensable part of the modern arsenal of tools we bring to bear upon complex problems. Because of its immense representational power [1], it can exploit the correlations with a myriad of input features to make predictions in complex systems even when analytical understanding is lacking. Standard statistical techniques like careful cross-validated [2] regularization are then needed to tune the model complexity and avoid overfitting on limited data and to provide global measures of performance.

In many fields, however, such predictions are not actionable without a more careful understanding of the uncertainty in predictions [3]. In particular, the use of ML in science is severely restricted without uncertainty quantification (UQ) — they can then be used only in those places where the inaccuracies in ML predictions are either corrected by independent mechanisms [4, and references therein] or where they provide a negligible contribution to the total uncertainty. The difficulty in this task lies mainly in the implicit nature of the model space: as opposed to spline fits or

Experiment Design

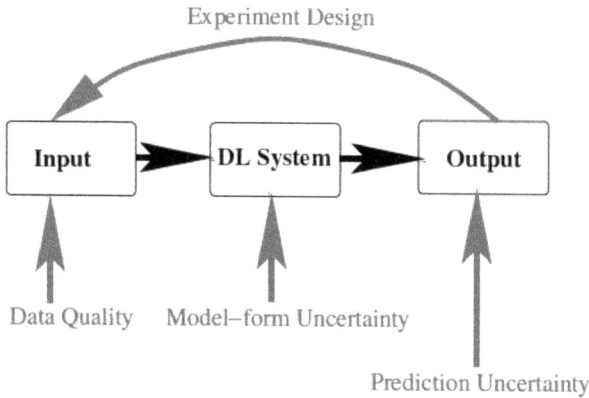

Fig. 1.　Uncertainty quantification forms a part of an improvable AI system.

other data-driven techniques for interpolation and extrapolation, where the assumptions are explicit, the function space modeled by a deep learning (DL) model is implicitly specified only by the regularization criteria and are often inscrutable. Any underlying theoretical knowledge of imperfectly known causal models is used mainly to tailor data representation or DL net architecture or to penalize unlikely models, rather than to restrict the model space explicitly. Furthermore, the power of these ML approaches arises from their being able to exploit high-order correlations among many input features, but model uncertainty resulting from the sparseness of data in high-dimensional spaces cannot be ascertained as easily. In fact, it is fair to say that in such high dimensions, almost all data lie near the boundary of the occupied region and the resulting uncertainty depends mainly on whether the boundary is, or should be, *relevant* to the prediction. As a result, the sensitivity of the models to statistical differences between training data and the data on which the predictions are desired is difficult to gauge: it is well known, for example, that one can always design input data on which even a well-trained model fails spectacularly [5].

To fully exploit the promise of these novel methods, therefore, needs us to make simultaneous advances in techniques for increasing the power and generalizability of the learned models and for providing local uncertainty estimates. A principled approach to ascertaining uncertainty can be exploited to form a systematically improvable AI system that assesses the effect of data quality and model-form uncertainty and designs data acquisition tailored to reducing prediction uncertainty (see Figure 1). In this chapter, we discuss some strategies to provide uncertainty estimates in DL.

2. Review of UQ in DL

As discussed in the introduction, DL models have been very successful in multiple applications mainly due to their ability to find high-order correlations in data. This results in highly accurate predictions and their efficient deployment, which can accelerate inference by orders of magnitude. On the flip side, they often require large amounts of data to learn the desired input–output mapping and result in large uncertainty in data-poor regions of the input space. Recent efforts have turned the attention to a systematic assessment of the error associated with their individual predictions. This type of analysis increases trustworthiness and reliability in DL models, improving decision-making, but is challenging due to the black box, high-dimensional, data-driven nature of the models.

2.1. *Preliminaries: Definitions and notation*

Prediction uncertainty can be broadly decomposed into (i) statistical (aleatoric) uncertainty, which is an inherent property of the data distribution and is generally irreducible, and (ii) systematic (epistemic) uncertainty, which arises from the imperfect assumptions encoded in the model and is often the result of approximations made. Data-driven methods with a model space ultimately capable of representing any data dependence blur the distinction between these two, since the epistemic uncertainty is now encoded by the ordering of models to be favored and is implicitly determined by network architectures, data-representation choices, training methods, and regularization procedures. This implicit specification makes it almost impossible to analyze these except in a data-driven fashion.

The basic DL model we will discuss in this chapter is the multilayer feedforward neural network (NN), though much of the conceptual framework generalizes beyond them. In this simple NN architecture, the information propagates layer-wise. A broad-enough neural net with at least three layers and a non-polynomial activation function provides a system capable of approximating an arbitrary continuous function [6]. Similar results also exist for deep-enough networks with bounded width [7]. In principle, a DL network implies a large number of layers comprising the NN, which in turn requires a huge number of parameters. We will, however, relax notation and use NN and DL interchangeably.

The overall mapping computed by the NN can be denoted as $f^{\omega}(\mathbf{x})$, or $\mathbf{f}^{\omega}(\mathbf{x})$ for a model with multiple outputs, where ω denotes the set of all the network parameters (i.e., the collection of all weight vectors and biases for all the neurons in all the layers). Training a DL model requires using training data to adjust the parameters ω with the goal of optimizing a performance metric. In a supervised setup, a matched collection of observed data $\mathcal{D} = (\mathbf{X}, \mathbf{Y}) = \{(\mathbf{x_i}, \mathbf{y_i})\}_{i=1}^{N}$ of N samples is known, where $\mathbf{x_i} \in \mathbb{R}^d$ represents the i-th input pattern, $\mathbf{y_i} \in \mathbb{R}^{d_{out}}$ the corresponding i-th expected output tuple (for one output: $y_i \in \mathbb{R}$), and $(\mathbf{X}, \mathbf{Y})$ the complete matched dataset. The performance of the network can be quantified by a loss function that measures the difference between the expected output $\mathbf{y_i}$ and the output computed by the model $\mathbf{f}^\omega(\mathbf{x_i})$. By minimizing the loss function, an optimal set of parameters $\omega^\star$ can be estimated.

For regression problems, where the outputs are continuous values, a commonly used loss function is the mean squared error (MSE),

$$\text{MSE}\left(\mathbf{f}^\omega; \mathcal{D}\right) = \frac{1}{N} \sum_{i=1}^{N} \|\mathbf{y}_i - \mathbf{f}^\omega(\mathbf{x}_i)\|^2 , \tag{1}$$

whereas for classification problems, where the outputs of the model $\mathbf{f}_{\mathfrak{C}}^\omega$ are scores denoting class membership in one of the C classes, a commonly used loss function is the cross-entropy, or softmax (SM), loss,

$$\text{SM}\left(\mathbf{f}_{\mathfrak{C}}^\omega; \mathcal{D}\right) = -\frac{1}{N} \sum_{i=1}^{N} \log\left(\hat{p}_{i,c_i}\right), \quad \hat{p}_{i,c_i} = \frac{\exp(\mathbf{f}_{c_i}^\omega(\mathbf{x}_i))}{\left(\sum_{c=1}^{C} \exp(\mathbf{f}_c^\omega(\mathbf{x}_i))\right)}. \tag{2}$$

Note, however, that these metrics do not provide information about the confidence in the predictions made, since even in the classification task, the softmax correlates with uncertainty only asymptotically. As a result, a large number of data-driven approaches have been developed to quantify uncertainty in black box models like DL (see Figure 2 for a hierarchy of methods we review in some detail in the following).

2.2. UQ models for DL

DL models can account for aleatoric uncertainty by specifying a noise distribution which translates into a likelihood function [8]. Two formulations are frequently used: *homoscedastic* and *heteroscedastic*. Both of these formulations model the noise as a normal random variable, but while the homoscedastic assumes constant parameters through the input domain, the heteroscedastic assumes that the parameters change and are dependent on the input. The learning task, then, involves the simultaneous prediction of the mean and the variance for the normal random model, but since the estimation of higher cumulants are generally more data intensive, the regularization demanded by the two simultaneous tasks may be vastly different. Alternative models use less restrictive assumptions, such as assuming the uncertainty to be given by a *mixture* of normal

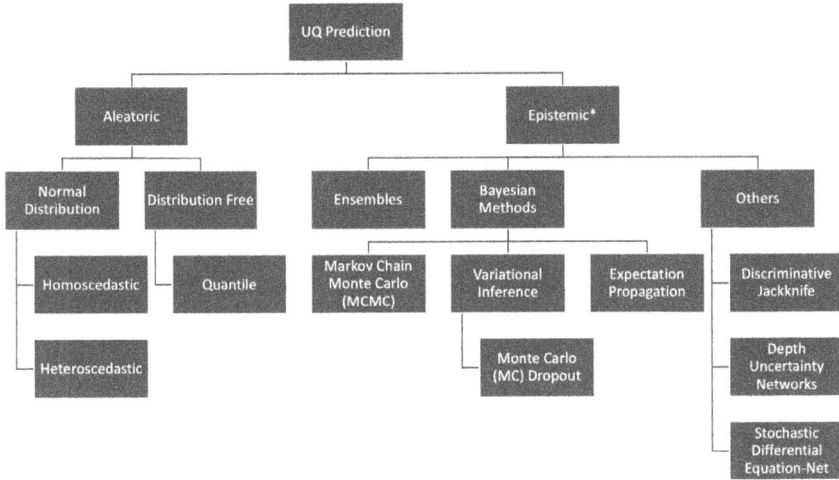

Fig. 2.   Schematic of UQ models for DL — the asterisk in "Epistemic*" denotes the fact that in data-driven UQ models, it is usually difficult to disentangle epistemic uncertainty from aleatoric uncertainty, so the separation is somewhat conventional.

distributions, or use the *quantile* formulation, which aims to partition the distribution into regions with a specified density mass (see Figure 3).

For example, the heteroscedastic loss for regression problems is based on the negative log-likelihood (NLL) of an univariate normal distribution and can be formulated as

$$\mathcal{L}_{\text{HET}}\left(f^{\boldsymbol{\omega}}, \sigma^{\boldsymbol{\omega}}; \mathcal{D}\right) = \frac{1}{N} \sum_{i=1}^{N} \frac{1}{2\sigma^{\boldsymbol{\omega}}(\mathbf{x_i})^2} \left\|y_i - f^{\boldsymbol{\omega}}(\mathbf{x_i})\right\|^2 + \frac{1}{2} \log \sigma^{\boldsymbol{\omega}}(\mathbf{x_i})^2, \qquad (3)$$

where $f^{\boldsymbol{\omega}}(\mathbf{x_i})$ represents the mean and $\sigma^{\boldsymbol{\omega}}(\mathbf{x_i})^2$ represents the variance. In contrast, the quantile loss is composed by the sum over the individual quantile losses of the entire dataset

$$\mathcal{L}_{\text{QTL}}\left(\{f^{\boldsymbol{\omega}}\}^{\alpha}; \mathcal{D}\right) = \sum_{\alpha} \frac{1}{N} \sum_{i=1}^{N} \mathcal{L}_{\alpha}\left(y_i - f^{\alpha}(\mathbf{x}_i)\right), \qquad (4)$$

with f^{α} corresponding to the predicted α-quantile (omitting the $\boldsymbol{\omega}$ dependence for simplicity) while the quantile loss L_{α} is computed as

$$\mathcal{L}_{\alpha}(\xi_i) = \begin{cases} \alpha\, \xi_i & \text{if } \xi_i \geq 0 \\ (\alpha - 1)\, \xi_i & \text{if } \xi_i < 0 \end{cases}, \qquad (5)$$

where $\xi_i = y_i - f^{\alpha}(\mathbf{x}_i)$. In this notation, the median corresponds to $\alpha = 0.5$.

Epistemic uncertainty, on the other hand, can be quantified in terms of the uncertainty in the architecture of the model and uncertainty in the

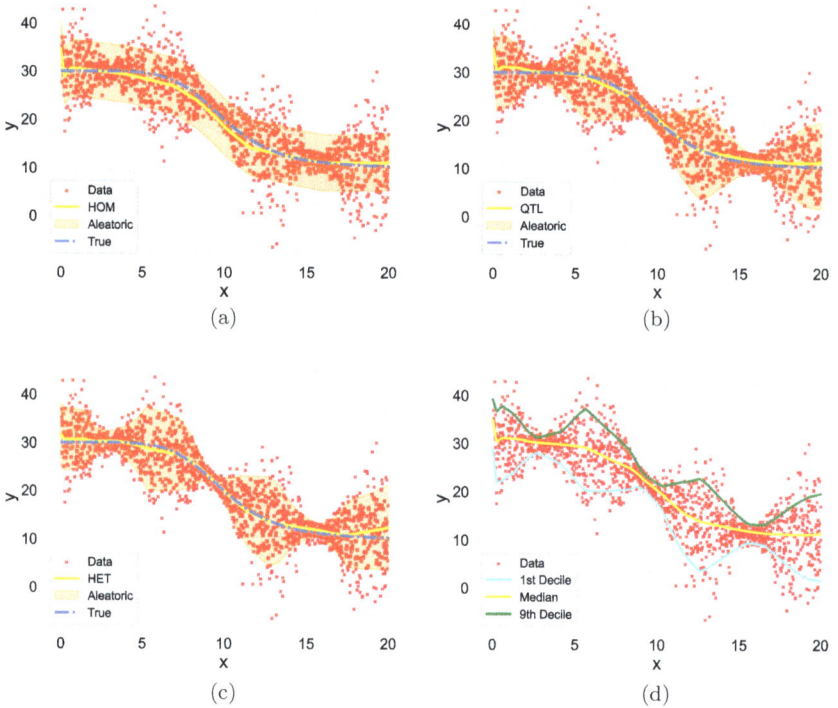

Fig. 3. Illustration of aleatoric uncertainty estimation for regression. In each panel, we show the prediction as a solid line along with a band designed to capture the middle 80% of the data. (a) Homoscedastic formulation: the prediction is given by the mean and the band shows 1.28 times the estimated standard deviation. Note that though correct on average, it significantly overestimates the uncertainty at some places and underestimates at others. (b) Heteroscedastic formulation: the prediction is again given by the mean and the band is 1.28 times the standard deviation, estimated as a function of the input. The band now captures the fluctuations in uncertainty better. (c) Quantile formulation: the prediction is given by the median and the band is the inter-decile range. (d) Quantile formulation — detail of median and 1st and 9th deciles used for aleatoric prediction, showing that it quantitatively captures the fluctuations in the data.

parameters of the model. As discussed by [9], it is less common for DL models to capture epistemic uncertainty explicitly. Instead, one usually studies sensitivity to introduced structural perturbations to increase the (epistemic) uncertainty awareness of DL models.

2.2.1. *Ensemble methods*

Ensemble methods train a collection of base models under different data sampling conditions, and epistemic uncertainty is quantified by the

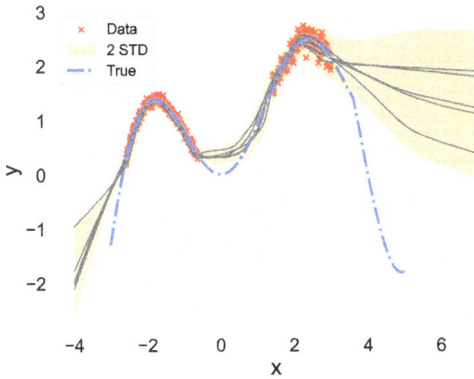

Fig. 4.   Illustration of uncertainty estimation based on ensemble method for regression. Gray lines correspond to individual realizations, and the bands are calculated from their variation. As can be seen, the uncertainty is large when data are sparse.

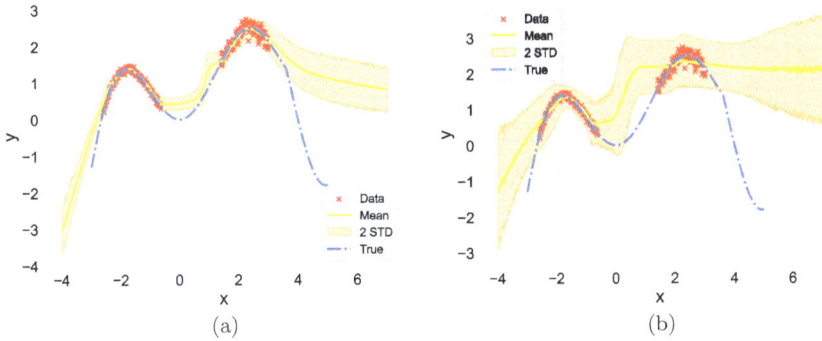

Fig. 5.   Illustration of MC dropout for regression. The dropout works like a prior on our uncertainty estimate: the larger the dropout, the more data are needed to constrain the prediction. Shown is a comparison between dropout rates of (a) 0.05 and (b) 0.5.

dispersion of predictions produced when evaluating the trained models in the inference stage (see Figure 4). Since this technique does not set a prior distribution over models, it can be regarded as a *frequentist* approach [9].

Ensemble methods can be classified in two general types [10]: *randomization*-based approaches, where the base learners do not interact (e.g., random forest), and *boosting*-based approaches that fit the models sequentially. The latter is useful to improve accuracy when the base learners are cheap to compute but is less practical for large-scale DL. There are also approaches that introduce the randomness using adversarial corruption.

2.2.2. *Bayesian methods*

Bayesian analysis allows one to express the probability of an outcome based on prior information and to update such probability after observations are made. Parametric models that use a Bayesian framework write the model parameters as random variables generated from a prior distribution $p(\boldsymbol{\omega})$. Given a matched collection of observed data $\mathcal{D} = (\mathbf{X}, \mathbf{Y})$, a model likelihood $p(\mathbf{Y}|\mathbf{X}, \boldsymbol{\omega})$ expresses the degree to which the model parameters and the inputs explain the outputs. The application of Bayes' theorem enables the estimation of a posterior distribution,

$$p(\boldsymbol{\omega}|\mathcal{D}) = \frac{p(\mathbf{Y}|\mathbf{X}, \boldsymbol{\omega})\, p(\boldsymbol{\omega})}{\int p(\mathbf{Y}|\mathbf{X}, \boldsymbol{\omega})\, p(\boldsymbol{\omega})\, d\boldsymbol{\omega}}, \tag{6}$$

which denotes the updated belief in the model parameters. The prediction for a new given input $\mathbf{x}^*$ is estimated by

$$p(\mathbf{y}^*|\mathbf{x}^*, \mathcal{D}) = \int p(\mathbf{y}^*|\mathbf{x}^*, \boldsymbol{\omega})\, p(\boldsymbol{\omega}|\mathcal{D})\, d\boldsymbol{\omega}. \tag{7}$$

Loosely speaking, NN models that incorporate any form of prior over their parameters, and thus allow for posterior inference, can be called Bayesian Neural Networks (BNNs). The resulting estimate encodes both epistemic uncertainty (given by the distribution of predictions from different parameter sets) and aleatoric uncertainty (given by the conditional over the data) [9]. The price to pay for comprehensive uncertainty representation is complexity. In most cases, the posterior and the predictive distribution cannot be computed analytically. Therefore, approximations are made, allowing for different trade-offs between tractability and quality, giving rise to different methods. Crucially, the quality of the predictive uncertainty obtained depends not only on the characteristics of the approximation but also on the selection of the prior distribution [10]. This is true of any Bayesian program, but the choice of priors is often less transparent in this domain.

Markov Chain Monte Carlo (MCMC) Methods MCMC methods are simulation methods employed to generate samples from a target distribution. MCMC enables Bayesian analysis by sampling from posterior and predictive distributions or from convenient approximations or reformulations, without making assumptions about the form of the distributions. However, MCMC-based methods can be slow, requiring a large number of iterations to converge. Hamiltonian Monte Carlo [11] and Laplace approximation [12] are some of the methodologies developed to accelerate computations. To mitigate its downsides, alternatives such as stochastic gradient MCMC [13] have been proposed. These improve data scalability but can add noise into the model and hurt the uncertainty predictions [8].

Variational Bayesian Methods In variational inference (VI) [14], a parametric function $q_{\boldsymbol{\theta}}(\boldsymbol{\omega})$ is used to approximate the posterior distribution, whose quality can be measured by the Kullback–Leibler (KL) divergence

$$\mathrm{KL}\left(q_{\boldsymbol{\theta}}(\boldsymbol{\omega})\|p(\boldsymbol{\omega}|\mathcal{D})\right) = \int q_{\boldsymbol{\theta}}(\boldsymbol{\omega})\log\left(\frac{q_{\boldsymbol{\theta}}(\boldsymbol{\omega})}{p(\boldsymbol{\omega}|\mathcal{D})}\right)\,d\boldsymbol{\omega}. \tag{8}$$

In order to deal with the intractability of the posterior distribution $p(\boldsymbol{\omega}|\mathcal{D})$, expression (6) is replaced in expression (8), yielding

$$\min_{\boldsymbol{\theta}}\left[\mathrm{KL}\left(q_{\boldsymbol{\theta}}(\boldsymbol{\omega})\|p(\boldsymbol{\omega}|\mathcal{D})\right) \equiv -\mathcal{L}_{\mathrm{VI}}\left(\mathbf{f}^{\boldsymbol{\omega}}, q_{\boldsymbol{\theta}}; \mathcal{D}\right)\right]$$

$$= \max_{\boldsymbol{\theta}} \sum_{i=1}^{N} \int q_{\boldsymbol{\theta}}(\boldsymbol{\omega})\log\left(p(\mathbf{y}_i|\mathbf{f}^{\boldsymbol{\omega}}(\mathbf{x}_i))\right)\,d\boldsymbol{\omega} - \mathrm{KL}\left(q_{\boldsymbol{\theta}}(\boldsymbol{\omega})\|p(\boldsymbol{\omega})\right). \tag{9}$$

This has a nice interpretation: the first term encodes data fidelity, while the second measures deviation from the prior and can be regarded as a regularization.

Nevertheless, there are some design choices and challenges associated with the VI loss (9). Some of the main design choices include (i) prior distributions over the weights of the model $p(\boldsymbol{\omega})$, (ii) structure of approximating parametric function $q_{\boldsymbol{\theta}}(\boldsymbol{\omega})$, and (iii) architecture of learning model $\mathbf{f}^{\boldsymbol{\omega}}$. Though reasonably efficient, the method also faces formidable challenges: (i) scalability for large datasets, (ii) computing the (frequently intractable) expected log-likelihood, and (iii) training the DL model. All the design choices come with associated trade-offs that can improve representation capacity (e.g., by modeling weight correlations, using deeper learning models, or avoiding over-fitting) but affect data scalability and overall model tractability (e.g., by increasing the number of parameters and the computation complexity). The plethora of approaches arising is a reflection of the diverse set of possible compromises.

Monte Carlo (MC) Dropout An insightful connection was made when it was demonstrated that dropout can be regarded as VI with MC estimation of the expected log-likelihood [15]. In other words, training DL models with dropout layers is equivalent to doing inference with a particular BNN architecture, and consequently, these models can be effectively deployed for predictive uncertainty (see Figure 5). More generally, selecting a stochastic regularization technique when training a DL model is equivalent (under certain conditions[1]) to setting a specific form for the approximating distribution $q_{\boldsymbol{\theta}}(\boldsymbol{\omega})$ and a specific prior distribution $p(\boldsymbol{\omega})$

---

[1] Associated with the KL condition for the selected $p(\boldsymbol{\omega})$ and $q_{\boldsymbol{\theta}}(\boldsymbol{\omega})$ distributions [15].

for a VI-based BNN. Two examples of this are as follows: (i) dropout-based variational inference [16], which corresponds to a BNN with a Bernoulli-based factorization of the approximating distribution $q_\theta(\omega)$ and independent normally distributed weights for the prior $p(\omega)$, and (ii) the variational dropout [17], which corresponds to a BNN with a normal-based factorization of $q_\theta(\omega)$ and improper log-uniform weights for $p(\omega)$.

To perform predictive uncertainty with a dropout-based DL model, the mean prediction can be estimated via MC integration. When using dropout, this is equivalent to computing a number T of stochastic forward passes through the network, i.e., with dropout enabled in testing too, and averaging the results. Other quantities, such as the test log-likelihood, a measure of the quality of the model fit to the data, can also be estimated by MC integration [15]. These estimations require minimal modifications to the normal DL model, but the evaluation timescales by T, a relatively small concern when using parallel computation frameworks. One difficulty is that it requires tuning the model variance σ^2 based on training data, as well as other parameters (prior over weights, which can be related to other factors such as dropout rate or regularization level), but it is not easy to verify that these hyperparameters have been set optimally. Reference [10] argues that dropout may also be interpreted as an ensemble of NNs with parameter sharing and that this is a more realistic scenario specially when the dropout rate is not tuned.

Expectation Propagation   Expectation propagation (EP) [18] is a different approach for dealing with the posterior distribution. The approximating distribution is constructed by an iterative process, based on analytical expressions that update expectations, namely mean and variance, enabled by choosing a convenient factorization of the approximating posterior (e.g., exponential family). Improved scalability and accuracy are obtained by probabilistic backpropagation (PBP) [19], which mimics the two-stage process of backpropagation but over a probabilistic network (random weights) and also produces calibrated estimates of the posterior uncertainty.

2.2.3. *Other approaches*

While the previous sections have described a subset of well-known landmark works in the field, a much more exhaustive collection of references, including plenty of real-world applications, can be found [8,9, and references therein]. Here, we conclude this overview of UQ models for DL by highlighting a few novel interesting threads.

The work of [20] moves away from both Bayesian and non-Bayesian UQ prediction methods, arguing that those methods do not guarantee coverage. As an alternative, they introduce *discriminative jackknife*, a procedure for estimating pointwise frequentist confidence intervals based on the jackknife, i.e., leave-one-out (LOO), resampling technique and on influence functions. These confidence intervals jointly capture epistemic and aleatoric uncertainties and have theoretical guarantees of coverage but applicability is limited due to their computational complexity.

The work of [21] introduces Depth Uncertainty Networks (DUNs), where the depth of a NN is treated as a random variable, modeled via a categorical distribution, while the network weights are treated as learnable hyperparameters. The marginalization process is equivalent to combining the predictions from a set of deep models (progressively deeper NNs) enabling quantification of model uncertainty while requiring only one forward pass over the network. This approach produces well-calibrated uncertainty estimates with good scalability for large datasets.

Finally, the work of [22] develops a neural stochastic differential equation model (SDE-Net) that uses two separate neural nets to represent drift and diffusion terms in a stochastic differential equation, capturing aleatoric and epistemic uncertainty, respectively. The work shows promising results in classification and regression setups for problems such as out-of-distribution detection, misclassification detection, and active learning.

3. Separating the Wheat from the Chaff

As discussed above, many methods have been developed for uncertainty quantification in deep learning. Here, we discuss a novel development in addressing a particular application problem highlighting a common situation that arises when the input instances are highly heterogeneous in their complexity. In such situations, one can develop a system where the ML approach can automatically sort out the less complex cases, leaving the more complex cases for separate, possibly manual, evaluation (see Figure 6).

3.1. *Background*

The National Cancer Institutes' Surveillance, Epidemiology and End Results (NCI SEER) program is responsible for curating large numbers of cancer reports, collected from various cancer registries. Each of these registries is responsible for annotating various aspects of these reports, including primary site, histology type, grade, laterality, and behavior of the tumor, typically through a combination of manual and automated workflows.

Through collaboration with NCI, the Department of Energy (DOE) is deploying machine learning to unify and automate these workflows, with the aim of improving the consistency and throughput of the annotation task. Various approaches have been attempted [23–28], but the overall

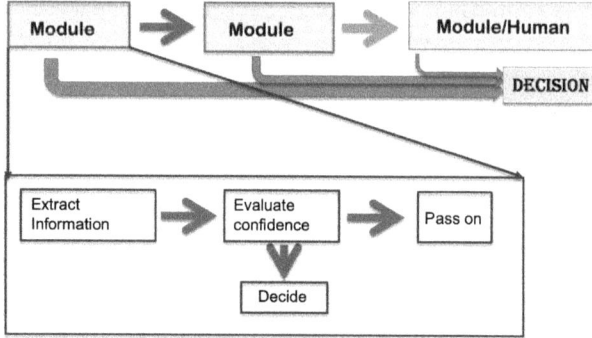

Fig. 6. A calibrated measure of uncertainty can be used to design modules that can be chained together. A less expensive, but more error-prone, classifier can be used to classify the simple cases, leaving the more difficult cases for a more expensive module or a human.

observation is that baseline accuracies are generally lower than that provided by human annotation, sometimes by a significant margin. Some form of triage is therefore needed to automate the classification of those high-confidence samples while deferring more ambiguous samples for human annotation.

Attempts to filter the output of an existing trained network have met with mixed success. In particular, the calibration of the output values for a neural network is not assured, and data-driven calibration was difficult at these extremely high accuracies needed. Therefore, we introduced the concept of an abstaining classifier to allow low-confidence samples to remain unclassified and be deferred for later annotation.

3.2. *Abstaining classifier in a multitask setting*

A deep abstaining classifier (DAC) [29] is a regular DNN classifier but with an extra (abstention) class and a custom loss function that permits abstention during training. This allows the DNN to abstain from (i.e., decline to classify) confusing samples while continuing to learn and improve performance on the non-abstained samples. The custom loss function, discussed in the following, behaves like a regular cross-entropy loss on the original classes and adds an additional tuning parameter α that controls the propensity of abstention. Since the balance between these terms depends on the data and the characteristics of the noise, the optimal value of α must be tuned during the training process. This tuning can be chosen to satisfy various criteria, as dictated by the problem at hand. The DAC can learn unlabeled features in the data which may be correlated only with label noise rather than with any particular output label [29].

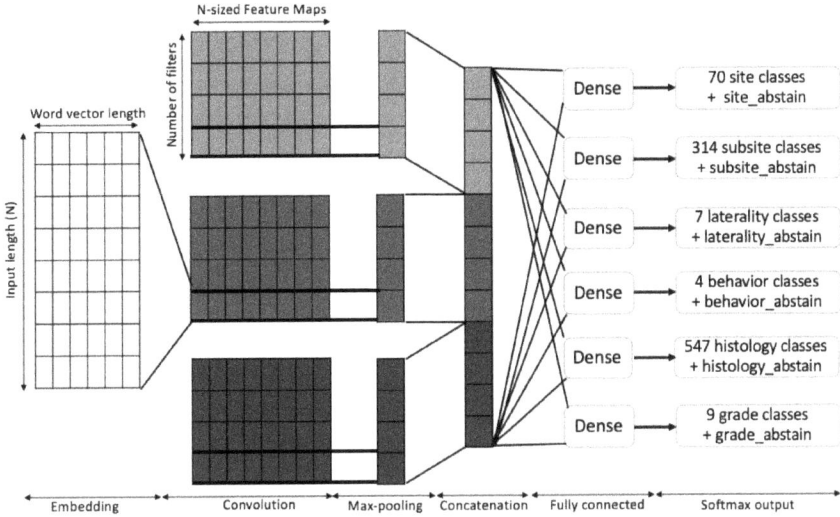

Fig. 7. Architecture of our model; the model is largely similar to [30] other than an extra task and the additional abstain classes for each of the tasks. It has an embedding layer [31,32], which feeds to three independent convolutional layers followed by one-dimensional max pooling layers. The outputs of these max pooling layers are then concatenated and fed to six independent fully connected layers with softmax output (one for each task) which return the predictions for each individual task.

We modified the multitask convolutional neural network (MTCNN) model [30] to include abstention for each task. Their model uses a word-level CNN in a multitask learning setting for automatic extraction of cancer information from unstructured text pathology reports to make predictions on five tasks: primary site (65 classes), laterality (4 classes), behavior (3 classes), histological type (63 classes), and histological grade (5 classes). Our model is an extension of theirs, where we trained a model of similar architecture for six tasks (subsite, in addition to the five previously listed) and a higher number of classes per task. The diagram of the model with the extra "abstain" classes is shown in Figure 7.

3.3. Loss function analysis: Learning the true class

Loss on a training sample x is given by

$$\mathcal{L}(x) = (1 - p_{k+1}) \left(-\sum_{i=1}^{k} t_i \log \frac{p_i}{1 - p_{k+1}} \right)$$

$$- \alpha \log(1 - p_{k+1}) - \kappa \mathcal{H}^{1\ldots k} \tag{10}$$

Table 1. Accuracy of baseline classifier with no abstention and abstention rate and accuracy of abstaining classifier on retained samples for individual tasks on data from four registries. The results show that the method abstains from samples difficult to classify but obtains a higher accuracy on the retained set. The last two columns show that the trained model continues to perform on out-of-sample data.

Task	Louisiana - Kentucky			Utah - New Jersey	
	Base acc (no abs)	Abs rate	Accuracy (retained)	Abs rate	Accuracy (retained)
Behavior	97.91%	0.00%	97.85%	0.00%	96.63%
Grade	76.71%	24.09%	83.35%	29.70%	78.20%
Histology	77.57%	38.75%	90.27%	47.36%	87.88%
Laterality	91.34%	43.94%	98.45%	48.19%	97.36%
Site	91.98%	24.46%	98.80%	28.90%	98.05%
Subsite	65.11%	20.41%	73.72%	21.72%	71.40%

where $\mathcal{H}^{1 \dots k}$ is the entropy over the real classes, i.e.,

$$\mathcal{H}^{1 \dots k} = \left(-\sum_{i=1}^{k} \frac{p_i}{1 - p_{k+1}} \log \frac{p_i}{1 - p_{k+1}} \right) \tag{11}$$

Note that $p'_i \equiv p_i/(1 - p_{k+1})$ is precisely the softmax output in the absence of the extra class. So, p'_j increases as we descend along the gradient, checked only by the entropic regulator in the usual fashion.

In Table 1, we show an example from [33] demonstrating the ability of the DAC to vastly improve the accuracy of a multitask CNN, albeit at the cost of significant abstention. In this case, the model was trained on data from Louisiana and Kentucky cancer registries. Application of the model to a dataset from Utah and New Jersey registries shows that although the model generalizes well, there is a small reduction in accuracy and increase in abstention when tested on such out-of-sample data.

3.4. *Other training-based calibration methods*

The DAC approach uses the notion of abstaining on a subset of the samples which exhibit traits correlated with low confidence. The approach differs from the *a posteriori* calibration methods insofar as it modifies the training of the network to learn features correlated with noise. In that sense, it is related to some leave-one-out (LOO) approaches which attempt to isolate samples that anomalously affect training [34].

4. Closing Remarks

Needless to say, the field of UQ in DL, and AI in general, is a developing field. Space did not allow us to discuss the extremely interesting subject of uncertainty quantification in predictions of or from time series data, in situations involving data fusion, and problems arising from biased coverage of the input space. The last is an example of a general problem — that of an undetected failure of the implicit assumptions of statistical identity of the training and calibration data with the data the methods are applied on. Being data-driven, current methods do not bound the magnitude of these errors. It should be possible to constrain these and separate the aleatoric and epistemic components better, with knowledge of the appropriate subject matter, but this is a direction that needs further research.

Furthermore, although various methods discussed here provide statistical bounds on the uncertainty of ML models, they ultimately remain as inscrutable to human interpretation as the predictions themselves. Especially in situations where the consequences for error are high, or when legal considerations require one to be able to explain one's actions, there may be a need to provide reassurance that the decisions are based on features that align with those used by a human expert and do not take into account complex correlates of features legally prohibited from consideration. The notion of interpretability or explainability of ML predictions is, therefore, closely linked to uncertainty quantification. In particular, methods such as Local Interpretable Model-agnostic Explanations (LIME) [35] and Counterfactuals [36] have proved to be useful in demonstrating that real-world applications of ML have, in fact, learned human-meaningful features in the data. The newly developed UQ methods such as DAC are specifically designed with easy coupling to these explainability frameworks. This argues for further research into extending the idea of abstention to problems beyond classification. Successful deployment of ML in real-world situation will require a combination of both UQ and interpretability to become a viable alternative to traditional methods.

References

[1] C. Zhang, S. Bengio, M. Hardt *et al.* (2016). Understanding deep learning requires rethinking generalization. *CoRR*, *abs*/1611.03530.

[2] G. C. Cawley and N. L. C. Talbot (2010). On over-fitting in model selection and subsequent selection bias in performance evaluation. *Journal of Machine Learning Research*, *11*(70), 2079–2107.

[3] E. Begoli, T. Bhattacharya, and D. Kusnezov (2019). The need for uncertainty quantification in machine-assisted medical decision making. *Nature Machine Intelligence*, *1*, 20–23.

[4] D. Boyda, S. Cali, S. Foreman *et al.* (2022). Applications of machine learning to lattice quantum field theory. In *Proceedings of Snowmass 2022*, Vol. 2.

[5] C. Szegedy, W. Zaremba, I. Sutskever *et al.* (2014). Intriguing properties of neural networks, *arXiv:1312.6199 [cs.CV]*.

[6] A. Pinkus (1999). Approximation theory of the MLP model in neural networks. *Acta Numerica*, *8*, 143–195.

[7] S. Park, C. Yun, J. Lee *et al.* (2020). Minimum width for universal approximation. *CoRR, abs/2006.08859*.

[8] M. Abdar, F. Pourpanah, S. Hussain *et al.* (2021). A review of uncertainty quantification in deep learning: Techniques, applications and challenges. *Information Fusion*, *76*, 243–297, December.

[9] U. Bhatt, J. Antorán, Y. Zhang *et al.* (2021). Uncertainty as a form of transparency: Measuring, communicating, and using uncertainty. In *AIES '21: Proceedings AAAI/ACM Conference on AI, Ethics, and Society*, July, pp. 401–413.

[10] B. Lakshminarayanan, A. Pritzel, and C. Blundell (2017). Simple and scalable predictive uncertainty estimation using deep ensembles. In *Advances in Neural Information Processing Systems*, Vol. 31. Curran Associates, Inc., pp. 6405–6416.

[11] R. M. Neal (1996). *Bayesian Learning for Neural Networks*, ser. Lecture Notes in Statistics, 118. New York: Springer-Verlag.

[12] D. J. C. MacKay (1992). A practical Bayesian framework for back-propagation networks. *Neural Computation*, *4*(3), 448–472.

[13] T. Chen, E. Fox, and C. Guestrin (2014). Stochastic gradient Hamiltonian Monte Carlo. In *Proceedings International Conference on Machine Learning*, ser. Proceedings of Machine Learning Research. Bejing, China: PMLR, 22–24 June, Vol. 32, pp. 1683–1691.

[14] A. Graves (2011). Practical variational inference for neural networks. In *Advances in Neural Information Processing Systems*, Vol. 24, pp. 2348–2356.

[15] Y. Gal (2016). Uncertainty in deep learning. Ph.D. dissertation, University of Cambridge, Cambridge, United Kingdom, September.

[16] Y. Gal and Z. Ghahramani (2016). Dropout as a Bayesian approximation: Representing model uncertainty in deep learning. In *Proceedings Machine Learning Research*. New York, USA: PMLR, 20–22 June, Vol. 48, pp. 1050–1059.

[17] D. P. Kingma, T. Salimans, and M. Welling (2015). Variational dropout and the local reparameterization trick. In *Advances in Neural Information Processing Systems*. Curran Associates, Inc., Vol. 28, pp. 2575–2583.

[18] T. Minka (2001). Expectation propagation for approximate Bayesian inference. In *Proceedings of the 17th Annual Conference on Uncertainty in Artificial Intelligence (UAI-01)*. Morgan Kaufmann, pp. 362–369.

[19] J. M. Hernández-Lobato and R. Adams (2015). Probabilistic backpropagation for scalable learning of Bayesian neural networks. In *Proceedings International Conference on Machine Learning ICML'15*. July, Vol. 37, pp. 1861–1869.

[20] A. M. Alaa and M. van der Schaar (2020). Discriminative jackknife: Quantifying uncertainty in deep learning via higher-order influence functions. In *Proceedings International Conference on Machine Learning*, Vienna, Austria, pp. PMLR 119:165–174.

[21] J. Antorán, J. Allingham, and J. M. Hernández-Lobato (2020). Depth uncertainty in neural networks. In *Advances in Neural Information Processing Systems*. Curran Associates, Inc., Vol. 33, pp. 10620–10634.

[22] L. Kong, J. Sun, and C. Zhang (2020). SDE-Net: Equipping deep neural networks with uncertainty estimates. In *Proceedings International Conference on Machine Learning*, Vienna, Austria, pp. PMLR 119:5405–5415.

[23] J. X. Qiu, H.-J. Yoon, P. A. Fearn *et al.* (2017). Deep learning for automated extraction of primary sites from cancer pathology reports. *IEEE Journal of Biomedical and Health Informatics*, *22*(1), 244–251.

[24] A. Jagannatha and H. Yu (2016). Structured prediction models for RNN based sequence labeling in clinical text. In *Proceedings Conference on Empirical Methods in Natural Language Processing*. Austin, Texas: Association for Computational Linguistics, November, pp. 856–865.

[25] S. Gao, M. T. Young, J. X. Qiu *et al.* (2018). Hierarchical attention networks for information extraction from cancer pathology reports. *Journal of the American Medical Informatics Association*, *25*(3), 321–330.

[26] S. Gao, J. X. Qiu, M. Alawad *et al.* (2019). Classifying cancer pathology reports with hierarchical self-attention networks. *Artificial Intelligence in Medicine*, *101*, 101726.

[27] H.-J. Yoon, A. Ramanathan, and G. Tourassi (2016). Multi-task deep neural networks for automated extraction of primary site and laterality information from cancer pathology reports. In *INNS Conference on Big Data*. Springer, pp. 195–204.

[28] M. Alawad, S. Gao, J. X. Qiu *et al.* (2020). Automatic extraction of cancer registry reportable information from free-text pathology reports using multitask convolutional neural networks. *Journal of the American Medical Informatics Association*, *27*(1), 89–98.

[29] S. Thulasidasan, T. Bhattacharya, J. Bilmes *et al.* (2019). Combating label noise in deep learning using abstention. In *Proceedings International Conference on Machine Learning*.

[30] M. Alawad, S. Gao, J. X. Qiu *et al.* (2020). Automatic extraction of cancer registry reportable information from free-text pathology reports using multitask convolutional neural networks. *Journal of the American Medical Informatics Association*, *27*, 89–98.

[31] T. Mikolov, I. Sutskever, K. Chen *et al.* (2013). Distributed representations of words and phrases and their compositionality. *Advances in Neural Information Processing Systems (NIPS)*.

[32] T. Mikolov, K. Chen, G. Corrado *et al.* (2013). Efficient estimation of word representations in vector space. In *International Conference of Learning Representations (ICLR) Workshop*.

[33] S. Dhaubhadel, J. Mohd-Yusof, K. Ganguly *et al.* (2020). Why I'm not answering: Understanding determinants of classification of an abstaining classifier for cancer pathology reports.

[34] D. Krstajic (2021). The costs and potential benefits of introducing the "I don't know" answer in binary classification settings. Preprints.

[35] M. T. Ribeiro, S. Singh, and C. Guestrin (2016). "Why should i trust you?": Explaining the predictions of any classifier.

[36] J. Klaise, A. V. Looveren, G. Vacanti *et al.* (2021). Alibi explain: Algorithms for explaining machine learning models. *Journal of Machine Learning Research*, *22*(181), 1–7.

© 2023 World Scientific Publishing Company
https://doi.org/10.1142/9789811265679_0031

Chapter 31

AI for Next-Generation Global Network-Integrated Systems and Testbeds

Mariam Kiran* and Harvey B. Newman[†]

*Energy Sciences Network (ESnet), Lawrence Berkeley National
Laboratory,
Berkeley, CA, USA
[†]Physics, Mathematics and Astronomy Division, Caltech,
Pasadena, CA, USA

1. Introduction

The continued cycles of innovation and discovery in many fields of data intensive science, from high energy physics and astrophysics to climate science, genomics, seismology, and biomedical research, depend on extracting the wealth of knowledge, whether subtle patterns, small perturbations, or rare events, buried in massive datasets. Each of these fields demands reliable and predictable data flows across multidomain local, regional, continental, and transoceanic networks, coordinated with the use of resource-intensive computation and storage.

The scale and complexity of the workflows that support the largest science collaborations, including the Large Hadron Collider (LHC) [15], the International Gravitational Wave Observatory Network (IGWN), IceCube, the Vera Rubin Observatory, the multiscale Brain Initiative (Börner, Silva, and Milojević, 2021; Borner, Silva, and Milojevic), and others in earth observation, genomics, have continued to grow (super-)exponentially over time. This has led to unprecedented challenges: in global data distribution, processing, access, and analysis that rely on the coordinated use of massive but still limited computing, storage, and network resources, and in the operation and collaboration within global science programs each encompassing hundreds to thousands of scientists located throughout the world.

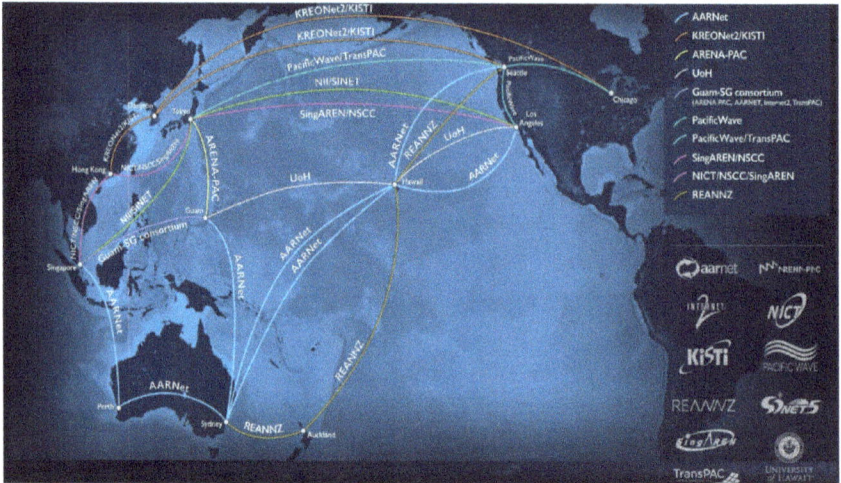

Fig. 1.   Asia-Pacific Science Network as it grows for more science.

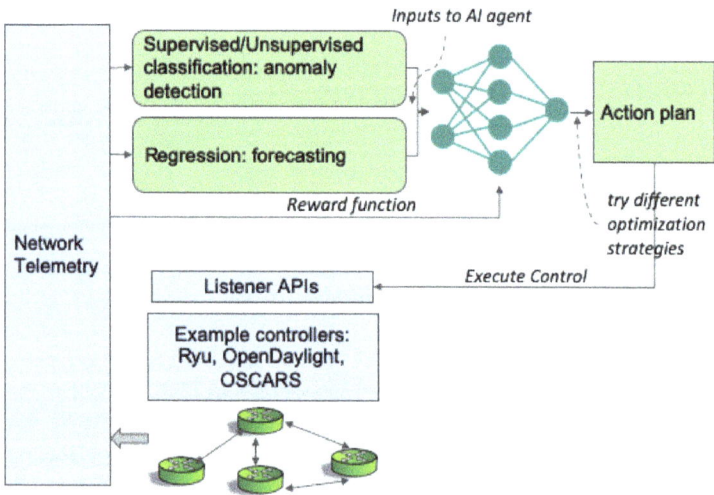

Fig. 2.   Summary of adapting AI to networking.

Maximizing the discovery reach of global-scale collaborative science programs such as these relies in turn on continuous cycles of innovation: developing and exploiting machine learning or artificial intelligence (ML/AI) and other state-of-the-art approaches to aid in the execution, coordination, and management of large distributed science workflows. Figure 1 shows an example of globally connected science communities and their supporting networks.

In networking, advances, such as software-defined networks (SDNs [32]) that have enabled programmable switches and end devices to dynamically control the provisioning and mapping of flows onto network paths, have until now been hindered by diverse device management and control planes and slow progress in developing optimized software–network interactions. Emerging agile and scalable services architectures that can adapt to dynamic network conditions, coupled to novel solutions based on deep learning and advances in pattern recognition and AI, have demonstrated the ability to help meet the diverse transfer demands and optimize the overall throughput while respecting policy constraints and data delivery deadlines across complex network topologies.

In this chapter, we tackle and describe how AI can aid in meeting the networking challenges, along with the key issues and current progress in the design, development, and prototyping of a next-generation dynamic network system that combines the use of AI, deep learning, overlay networks of virtual circuits with bandwidth guarantees, flow monitoring and steering, network and site resource management, and orchestration services to advance scientific discovery.

The field of **intelligent or self-driving networks** is evolving rapidly, and the science community has considered many ideas for improving and implementing hardware and developing new mathematical frameworks and algorithms to improve network capabilities. This chapter makes a number of significant contributions by

- addressing the current progress in AI, network software, and hardware to help realize self-driving networks for science,
- discussing open research challenges with a focus on specific target areas in networks where AI can help,
- discussing two use cases where networks are using prediction and self-learning to learn how to improve traffic engineering and overcome the challenges.

2. Innovations Brought on by AI

Industry efforts have recognized the importance of advanced intelligent decision-making or machine learning (ML) to help improve network application performance and management [33] and the IRTF forum (https://irtf.org/nmrg). Machine learning algorithms can be used to predict network behavior such as "which path selection, capacity, or QoS change will cause what result or event X with what probability P". Detecting anomalies will cut down costs and the time spent finding impaired segments or misbehaving devices in complex network infrastructures. Also, actively forecasting traffic demands can allow engineers to anticipate congestion and proactively perform better capacity planning for continued reliable connectivity and throughput for critical experimental programs. Network performance depends heavily on the topology configured across devices, the paths provisioned, application–network behavior, and meeting QoS requirements and underlying traffic restrictions. Making these decisions in near real time requires sufficient data processing power to rapidly digest all the relevant traffic datasets as time series, recognize the multiple factors that affect the application performance and application–network interaction, and build algorithms that use these factors to improve upon and eventually optimize the behavior.

Other application areas where deep learning algorithms which have had a major impact on network research include security [18], detecting malware, DOS attacks [1], as well as user–network interaction [44]. A DOE report [6] recognized that ML and deep learning methods can have huge potential in solving exascale computing demands, both within supercomputing sites and across their metro and wide area networks, by managing workloads to meet diverse application demands. The ML/AI methods that can be leveraged in network research include the following:

- Supervised and unsupervised classification: Supervised learning encompasses ML approaches that use labeled datasets to train or "supervise" algorithms that can help classify data into specific classes. Unsupervised ML, on the other hand, works with unlabeled datasets to learn underlying patterns, perform dimensional reduction, or learn via association to detect, express, and utilize latent relationships among the datasets. In networking datasets, it is often difficult to find labeled datasets, as performance logs are rarely labeled except in major event scenarios. Unsupervised classification is mainly used, for example, to recognize good flow performance or label security anomalies [18].
- Regression and Prediction: while classification helps predict a data label for a given sample, regression works by predicting a continuous quantity of the data sample, given historical datasets. Many examples such as linear, Bayesian methods, or least square regression are some examples where given a sample, the algorithms predict what the future values will be. More commonly used in time series data, this becomes extremely useful for network logs, where nearly all the data are time based. Predicting the future traffic or bandwidth consumption by learning daily

or weekend/weekday behavioral patterns, or predicting conditions that cause a variable to deviate from a pre-set threshold or control band, can help respond to, or preemptively deal with anomalies when or before they occur, and better plan future network resource usage.

• Reinforcement learning: Reinforcement Learning (RL) is a type of machine learning that allows an agent to interact in an environment by trial and error and use feedback on its actions and experiences to learn optimal behavior. Mostly used in games until now, such as AlphaGo or Chess, a reinforcement learning approach requires a simulation environment that captures the key characteristics and responses of the target environment so that an AI agent (or a set of agents) can try multiple strategies and learn optimal behaviors. RL does not need previous data to start. In networks, recent examples of RL have been used to learn optima in resource management, such as provisioning virtual machines, diverting flows to alternative paths, or learning behaviors leading to basic improvements in traffic engineering concepts. However, as RL needs a sufficiently realistic platform, simulations should be complemented by field trials that allow agents to learn while operating in a real environment.

  As allowing agents to learn under real conditions and trigger changes in a real set of networks is tricky, and the usual lack of such a platform has also limited the potential of how this AI technique can help improve networks. The recent emergence of multiregional collaborations among research and education networks and data-intensive science teams, such as the Global Network Advancement Group (GNA-G) http://www.gna-g.net/, has however opened the way towards a more comprehensive development of next-generation networks, including the use of RL and other ML-based techniques for traffic prediction and optimization.

There are multiple ways in which AI algorithms can be used for networking research and development. In this chapter, we will discuss some examples of how AI can be used (1) to recognize traffic patterns across complex networks, (2) to predict future traffic patterns and anticipate network path performance, and (3) to help learn and develop corrective actions to prevent failures and avoid or mitigate application workflow bottlenecks.

Some ML/AI techniques can be very costly due to the computational power and time required to train an algorithm. In complex systems such as the multidomain networks shared by major science programs, the ensemble of policies and constraints is often difficult to capture and express, and so the construction of an effective multiobjective set of metrics to be optimized is itself part of the longer-term learning process. Thus, this kind of research needs to leverage interdisciplinary skills combining distributed software engineering and data management, machine learning, and network architecture and engineering, and associated resources, to allow networks to autonomously react to, or interact and negotiate with applications as needed in an exascale era. This is an area vital for applications which are mission-critical to breakthroughs in a wide range of data and computationally intensive disciplines, from high energy physics and astrophysics to weather and climate forecasting to genomics.

Figure 2 presents a summary of various AI techniques that can be adopted in network operations. All kinds of network data collections, such as security logs, NetFlow records, TCP statistics, and more, can be used as input to various AI modules that perform classification, regression, and/or reinforcement learning to train a neural network architecture to learn optimum control strategies. Once trained, the AI agent needs to communicate these decisions back to the network, which is shown in the figure as a Listener API that communicates to multiple controllers (e.g., OpenDaylight, Ryu, and OSCARS) to allow network reconfiguration. The reward function depends on the optimization criteria and is discussed in Section 6.2.

3. Open Research Challenges

Using AI to control and optimize networking infrastructures has had major impacts on a broad range of science and commercial applications. One example of this is the LHC experiments, which require high-speed transfers of petabytes of already-filtered data per day to multiple research sites and storage facilities. On the other hand, genomics applications request dedicated flows, with reserved bandwidth and quality of service (QoS), to ensure high-speed connections among multiple research labs located around the world. Additionally, climate forecasting and advanced light source (ALS) experiments [6] have rising network demands on memory management for near real-time data processing, visualization, and high-volume bulk transfers. With these increasingly complex and diverse large-scale applications, the connecting network paths need to become intelligent to efficiently manage and respond to these multiple requirements. Developing AI to automate the decision-making process is a way to advance the effectiveness of the infrastructure and reduce the operational manpower burden while reducing and in some cases eliminating the cost of upgrading all the middleware and the capacity of many communication links. Some examples of open research challenges where automation is required are as follows.

3.1. *Network-integrated workflows and automation*

Some major challenges in networks are presented by data and network-intensive programs, where one has to manage computational and storage facilities at more than 170 institutions providing resources (e.g., the Worldwide LHC Computing Grid). The LHC, for example, has experienced network traffic growth of 40–60% annually over the last 5–10 years and has reached an annualized data volume transferred of 2.1 exabytes in the fourth quarter of 2021. The upgrades for the High Luminosity LHC (HL-LHC) [7] are projected to lead to a further 30x growth in the annual primary data volume, along with an order of magnitude growth in the computing and network capacity requirements by 2028. Additionally, one of the two largest experiments at the LHC is expected to yield 364 PB of RAW data in 100 days, spread across many national facilities in 100 days (along with the yield from the ATLAS experiment which has similar science goals and similar projections), accompanied by tens of petabytes of further-processed data distributed among the sites in several formats suited for subsequent analysis. At the same time, RAW data are produced at a rate of 400 Gbits/sec (400G) during data-taking periods, in addition to the simulated data volumes produced continuously by the ensemble of the experiment's facilities. The new data are transferred from CERN to globally distributed disk pools and tape archives, while the previous year's RAW data are transferred out of the archives to processing centers. Overall, this results in a projected need for terabit/sec links to the major national (Tier-1) centers and 400G at smaller laboratories and campuses hosting Tier-2 centers by 2028. Overall, we expect the aggregate of these transfers to grow over the next few years from a few hundred Gigabit/sec to Terabit/sec bursts lasting hours to days, accompanied by similar bursts across the Atlantic and Pacific and within Europe and Asia as well as selected sites in Latin America and Australia.

Network providers have until now largely avoided the need for network bandwidth management by deploying excess capacity. The combination of continued exponential historical growth with the advent of the x30 step function increase foreseen at the beginning of the HL-LHC era and the large increase foreseen in the number and diversity of big data communities renders such an approach financially challenging if not impossible. Equally importantly, the large science data transactions must coexist, in a compatible and flexible way, with the "river" of data flows from individuals and small groups throughout the community working to process and analyze their data, and/or conduct a wide range of other everyday tasks. This "peaceful coexistence" requirement adds another dimension to the optimization problem.

3.2. Wide Area Network (WAN) traffic prediction

Network traffic forecasting in research WANs is a formidable task because of the lack of regular patterns in how users and software agents acting on their behalf access and perform data transfers across the networks. Compared to general-purpose Internet WANs, which tend to have periodic patterns and relatively small flows, research WANs have larger flows (or groups of flows) and random traffic spikes that are difficult to understand and anticipate. The traffic patterns depend on which experiments and devices are running and which groups are involved, characterized by high-variability data transfers lasting minutes, hours, and in some cases days. Network monitoring tools such as Simple Network Management Protocol (SNMP), sFlow, and NetFlow allow the collection of traffic information on network nodes and flow transfers as time-stamped data, resulting in gigabytes (GB) of recording log files. Most monitoring tools collect data at sufficiently frequent intervals (30 seconds is currently typical) to give a fine-grained view that includes other key features such as the protocols used (e.g., TCP and UDP), interfaces, source and destination IP addresses, and flow rates in some cases. These datasets can be leveraged to develop data-driven forecasting methods.

3.3. Self-driving (or learning) for traffic engineering

The application of machine learning to network routing is not new. Broadly speaking, there are two main approaches used here to optimize routing configurations: (1) by predicting future traffic conditions depending on past traffic patterns or (2) based on a number of feasible traffic scenarios which aim to improve a set of performance parameters. Software-defined networking (SDN) and reinforcement learning have been leveraged to explore path computation, formulated as a resource allocation problem, and they are also being used together with other ML techniques to develop and provide viable solutions for dynamic flow management.

While SDN's centralized control offers great promise, these calculations cause overhead for high-performance networks and need global management to work, which is difficult in a large multidomain network. Recent successes of machine learning in complex decision-making problems such as Alpha-Go, cooling data centers, and self-driving cars suggest feasible pathways to solutions that are applicable to our problem space. In particular, reinforcement learning (RL), which is actively being applied in robotics, allows agents to learn how to make better decisions by interacting directly with the environment. Using concepts of rewards and penalties, the agents can learn through experience to optimize a given objective function (or reward).

3.4. *Federated infrastructures for Networking, Compute, and Storage*

As the various compute and network facilities have become increasingly large and complicated to manage, there is a need to perform real-time analysis for machine control, fault prediction, automation, and optimization of these resources. User facilities [39] have argued for the use of ML/AI solutions to aid in the design and control of their facilities, enable real-time capabilities to analyze large data volumes, automatically steer data collection for in-the-loop experiments, and allow experimentalists to harness the power of distributed DOE facilities. Additionally, an autonomous network can rectify or mitigate, and potentially foresee and avoid some of the effects of impairments or failures as they occur.

In order to achieve end-to-end workflow performance, one needs to perform real-time analysis across all the involved facilities and workflow managers. However, research in the areas of workflow and resource management is limited due to the lack of both standardized and benchmark facility operational data, and behavioral data characterizing the interaction of workflows with diverse facilities. These federated services infrastructures are complex because of their inherent characteristics: resource heterogeneity and limits, deployment of complex and heterogeneous system software stacks, and policies that constrain use, enforce diverse fair-sharing concepts, and/or specify a complex set of profiles and priorities for classes of work.

There are relatively few examples where one can predict the performance of complex science workflows executing on distributed computational and data infrastructure, detect and diagnose infrastructure and workflow anomalies, and even recommend workflow and infrastructure adaptations that optimize performance. The study of such systems and interactions also has been hindered by the lack of simulation frameworks and testbeds. This makes it difficult to assess and train AI algorithms to deliver optimal workflow configurations.

4. Statistics from Real Networks: Case Study from US Network (ESnet)

A major research and education (R&E) network, the U.S. Department of Energy (DOE) Energy Sciences Network (ESnet), provides international high-speed connectivity to over 55 research laboratories, universities, and other facilities in a global collaborative context. Similar to many other

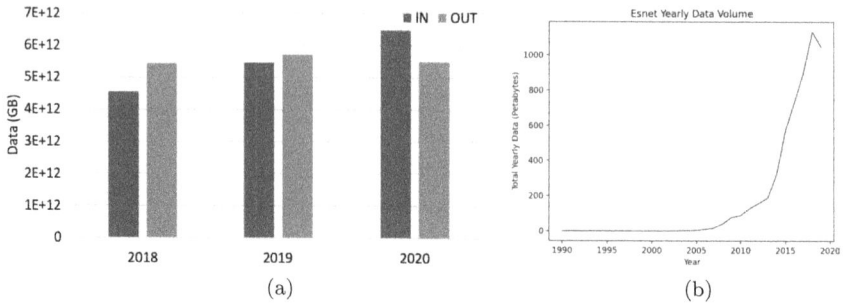

Fig. 3.   Rise in network transfers over the years [23]: (a) total traffic in and of DOE Facilities in 2018, 2019, and 2020; (b) yearly traffic totals since January, 1990.

wide area networks (WAN), ESnet employs multiple connections to other organizations which provide performance access to commodity resources, experiments, and other major R&E networks such as Internet2, GEANT, JANET, SURFnet, RNP, and many others. ESnet is responsible for carrying regular user traffic as well as science data generated from experimental facilities at DOE National Labs, the LHC, and universities and collaborators worldwide. To ensure reliability and availability, the network capacity and services are provisioned to account for unexpected traffic surges which allows experiments to grow, while keeping costs down [40]. Figure 3(a) shows the total yearly traffic volumes from 2018 to 2020 among the high-performance computing facilities. Multiple applications such as data processing and analysis in physics and near real-time calculations in nuclear science have large bandwidth requirements. Additionally, the total network traffic, among all the network equipment at the various sites, is projected to increase exponentially (Figure 3(b)). Application traffic therefore needs to be optimized to minimize packet loss, to maintain high transfer speed for large flows, and to be monitored and tracked in order to understand the throughput and contributing factors such as the distance (number of hops and round trip time) traveled by the data. Availability needs to maintain an ideal 99.99% level, with reduced disruptions and reduced expense associated with the capacity upgrades needed to respond to increased demands.

5.   Background: Current and Emerging Networking Technologies

A number of current approaches and techniques already developed to better control the network can leverage AI to provide a more effective end-to-end solution. Examples range from generally applicable open source to bespoke multidomain network solutions. Examples include virtual circuit-based multidomain network designs and operational software frameworks, state-of-the-art data transfer node (DTN) end-system designs coupled to high throughput applications and controls, multiresource model (MRML [47])-based site and network orchestration, SDN controllers, dynamic circuit and infrastructure development and software-defined exchanges (SDX [17]), and high throughput Named Data Networking caching and access methods. Additional developments in Software Defined Infrastructure (SDI) can be interfaced to the target program data management frameworks (such as Rucio [4], Pegasus [13], and more). Since data-intensive science requires large volumes of data being ingested, stored, distributed, and processed in a timely and economic fashion, an SDI-based solution can respond well to such requirements by leveraging these existing technologies.

As of this writing, many of the approaches and techniques are being pursued in the framework of the Global Network Advancement Group (GNA-G) and its working groups, with a view towards the development of the next-generation network paradigm described above.

5.1. *SENSE orchestrators and controllers*

Communicating the results of the AI algorithms to a network to help reconfigure it requires one to build tools that can take AI inputs. Connecting an SDN to end-to-end networking science, as in the SENSE controller for WANs [37], utilizes the use of orchestrators (SENSE-O) and resource managers (SENSE-RM). The RMs are administrative or technology domain-specific that can be responsible for committing and managing resources, based on a resource model exchange and manipulation paradigm. The resource model provided by each RM includes a description of its domain resources and a definition for their interconnects to external resources. For example, the SENSE-O receives resource descriptions from the SENSE-RMs and constructs a semantic model-based graph of the end-to-end SDN topology. This end-to-end model-based graph provides the basis for the SENSE-O to respond to user requests and construct workflows for service provisioning interactions with the proper RMs.

The SENSE notion of end-to-end orchestrated SDN includes the multidomain wide area, regional, and end-site networks, the site topologies and relationships among the components, as well as the network stack inside the end systems. The inclusion of the end-system networking stack enables deterministic and automated service provisioning, monitoring, and troubleshooting. The practical application of this approach is to manage the networking stack all the way to the network socket of the host operating system, virtual machine, or container where the application process interacts with the network. This is designed to provide a foundation for science workflow management systems to coordinate the use of network along with computational and storage resources. The end systems included in the SENSE end-to-end orchestration are often Data Transfer Nodes (DTNs) or clusters of DTNs inside Science DMZs [12]. However, the SENSE model ontology and Resource Manager functions are sufficiently extensible to be adapted to any networked system that may be associated with instruments, compute, and/or storage systems.

The associated data plane capabilities of the SENSE system include (i) Layer 2 point-to-point with QoS, (ii) Layer 2 multipoint with QoS, and (ii) Layer 3 flow QoS and routing customization. The SENSE system's model-based architecture and services implementation enables automated end-to-end network service instantiation across administrative domains. An intent-based interface allows applications to express their high-level service requirements, and an intelligent orchestrator and resource control systems allow for custom tailoring of scalability and real-time responsiveness, based on individual application and infrastructure operator requirements. This allows science applications to use the network as a first-class schedulable resource, as is currently the case with instruments, compute, and storage systems.

5.2. *SONiC: An open-source network operating system*

SONiC [9] is an example of an open-source network operating system that can run on switches and smart interfaces from multiple vendors. The software decouples network software from the underlying hardware and is built on the Switch Abstraction Interface (SAI) programming API. Supported network features include the Border Gateway Protocol (BGP), remote direct memory access (RDMA), QoS, and various other Ethernet/IP technologies. SONiC offers a full-suite of network functionality that has been production-hardened in the data centers of some of the largest cloud-service providers. It offers teams the flexibility to create the needed network solutions while leveraging the strength of a large ecosystem and a growing user/developer community.

5.3. *Intent-based networking*

Intent-based networks are designed to allow user "intent" to be communicated to the network, mostly done via a language that networking devices understand. These semantic models are formal descriptions using the Resource Definition Framework (RDF) and Web Ontology Language (OWL) to help model what network languages would configure [24].

Semantic models of spatio-temporal flows are dynamic graphs where resources are represented by interconnected vertices and properties and relationships are represented by edges. Examples include MRML or markup languages that can be integrated into end-to-end model graphs.

5.4. *P4 programmability*

P4 Open-Source Programming Language

Programming Protocol-independent Packet Processors (P4.org) is a domain-specific language for network devices, specifying how data plane devices (switches, network interface cards, routers, filters, etc.) process packets [8]. The P4 language and software ecosystem enables application developers and network engineers to implement specific behaviors in the network. This enables changes that can be made in minutes, instead of months to years as in the older network model based on vendor-specific silicon-associated hardware functions.

Additionally, the P4 Integrated Network Stack (PINS (https://opennetworking.org/pins/) is an industry collaboration bringing SDN capabilities and P4 programmability to traditional routing devices that rely on embedded control protocols (such as BGP). Specifically, PINS uses P4 to model the software-based SAI pipeline, adds externally programmable extensions to the pipeline, and introduces P4Runtime as a new control plane interface for controlling the pipeline. PINS, which enables P4-capable switches to control network paths that include non-P4 fixed-function switches, leverages the evolving capabilities of the SONiC operating system.

PINS uses real-time deep packet inspection enabled by the use of P4-programmable switches, edge systems with FPGA- and data processing unit (DPU)-based smart network interfaces [21], combined with the emerging generation of open-source network monitoring tools, and associated software and firmware acceleration technologies, to enable user/developers to build applications that are capable of interacting with the network, discover expected performance metrics, negotiate performance parameters, and receive real-time status/troubleshooting information.

5.5. *RARE: Router for Academia, Research, and Education*

The Router for Academia, Research, and Education (RARE) project aims to create a full-featured router running on open, commodity networking hardware. RARE, which is being developed under the auspices of the GÉANT [34] pan-European network, focuses on research and education (R&E) institutions as well as national research and education networks

(NRENs), which often require features that are not supported by commercial vendors. Another target audience is institutions that want to customize their networks to support new protocols. Building on an earlier effort that produced freeRouter, an open-source router, the RARE project uses P4 to program the data plane, resulting in a platform that combines an open-source IP router with a rich set of additional protocols and a wide range of advanced features.

5.5.1. *Source routing*

An effort collaborating with the RARE project that uses P4 to provide a novel form of source-based routing is PolKA [14]: Polynomial Key-based Architecture for Source Routing. PolKA is a means to efficiently select paths and load balance among them to adapt to variable workloads. In PolKA, the ability for a source to specify all segments of a network path (source-based routing) without packet rewrites along the path and without router tables is achieved through the use of arithmetic operations that use a Residue Number System (RNS) based on the Chinese Remainder Theorem (CRT). This avoids the limitations of traditional source-based routing schemes and makes it possible to handle complex use cases. Additionally, a new demonstration on HECATE [22] attempts to show multiobjective optimization among network utilization, loss and latency by investigating current application needs and traffic patterns, running bespoke data-driven deep reinforcement learning that learn optimal controls to improve traffic engineering, and rendering HECATE decisions to SDN and path computation engine (PCE) technologies to bring AI to real networks. The technique attempts to use source routing to help specify and construct the new paths.

5.6. *NDN: Named Data Networking*

Along with the developments summarized above, we are also exploring and developing the use of Named Data Networking (NDN), a data-centric future Internet architecture where data objects or collections are referred to by name rather than location. The NDN for Data Intensive Experiments (N-DISE [38], for example, focuses on developing a highly efficient and field-tested petascale data distribution, caching, access, and analysis system, built on recently developed high-throughput NDN caching and forwarding methods and containerization techniques. N-DISE leverages the integration of NDN and SDN systems' concepts and algorithms with the mainstream data distribution, processing, and management systems, as well as the integration with FPGA acceleration subsystems, to deliver

LHC and genomic data over wide area networks at throughputs approaching 100 Gbps.

5.7. *Metrics of success: from simple to complex*

Since multiple disciplines and programs share a common network infrastructure within or among nations, a set of common technical success metrics and levels of performance, stability, and reliability must be met so the scientists can meet their data processing, analysis, and ultimately, science goals. A set of metrics of success for an automated network could include the following characteristics and/or capabilities: (1) packet-loss free operation, (2) detection and identification of anomalies or impairments, (3) avoidance of saturation of any network segment, (4) localization and repair of impaired segments, (5) dynamic re-allocation to route or switch around the affected segments, (6) queuing and/or scheduling of transfers to meet deadlines, taking policy and priority into account when dealing with competing requests, (7) adjustments to allocated resources when transfer rates fall short of expectations and the allocated capacity is underused for an extended period, when deadlines are approached for selected tasks, or when higher priority requests are received, (8) inclusion of attributes that permit partial responses to requests and/or negotiation to allow efficient use of the available capacity, and (9) development of multiobjective metrics and the corresponding expressions composed of the above elements that express how well the ensemble of transfers meet the deadlines, priorities, policies, and turnaround time and resource-usage targets of the science programs.

5.8. *Monitoring data*

ML-based optimization of workflow progress and coordinated use of resources can benefit from the use of monitoring data and analytics from a host of in-network and edge and site sources. These include the following: data management and transfer tools; routing and caching services; path construction, selection, and load balancing services; and network and site resource allocation and queuing services. The optimization of networks with built-in intelligence also can benefit from edge-focused extreme telemetry data from programmable switches and end hosts with smart NICs or DPUs.

The above technologies, taken in combination according to the use case and optimized according to both program-specific and some of the general success metrics mentioned, can provide a common software-defined network fabric and analytics base with the range of capabilities needed to serve the science programs in many disciplines and world regions while respecting the capacity limits of the national and global ensemble of networks on which the programs rely.

6. A WAN Traffic Prediction Case Study

Classical statistical time series forecasting methods such as ARIMA and Holt-Winters have been investigated for network traffic forecasting but have been less effective for research WANs, as regular and seasonal patterns are difficult to deduce [26]. Forecasting methods based on classical ML methods such as random forest and SVM have been developed to provide per-site forecasts, but these fail to take the whole network and its spatial patterns into account, making them less robust with respect to dynamic traffic. New opportunities presented by deep learning (DL) methods for forecasting, such as convolutional neural networks (CNNs) and long short-term memory (LSTM) methods, have shown to provide better accuracy than classical statistical techniques.

Seminal works of Wolski *et al.* [46] highlighted the importance of network forecasting to improve TCP performance for scheduling computations. Azzouni *et al.* [3] trained LSTMs on the GEANT network to predict the traffic during 15-minute intervals. LSTMs and stacked autoencoders [45] were used to predict traffic in 15-, 30-, and 60-minute intervals by adding more hidden layers. Recently, innovations in graph-based models have been shown to remarkably improve the prediction accuracy relative to previous forecasting approaches [48] by including spatio-temporal data. The new approaches have been used to successfully predict Los Angeles road traffic [27] as well as WAN traffic, as a result of their being able to capture the key features of both the nonlinear temporal dynamics and the associated spatial properties in the data. Compared to simple CNNs, where one assumes that one is working with a grid-based Euclidean space, Graph neural networks (GNNs) are able to capture network topologies and distances as properties in the model, allowing them to capture the dependencies among the network links [29].

Using SNMP Monitoring Data. Network operators monitor link capacity and data movement across routers using SNMP [16], NetFlow, sFlow, and other monitoring tools. Table 1 shows a snapshot of an SNMP data sample during a two-way transfer between Sunnyvale, California and Sacramento, California. The traffic is collected in moving gigabytes (GBs) across router interfaces at 30-sec intervals. In our case study, we aggregated the data in 1-hour intervals in order to smooth over very short term bursts and treated these as discrete observations in our model. This helped reduce the model complexity and led to faster training and more rapid predictions [11].

Table 1.   A sample timestamped traffic trace collected from one router, including traffic in both directions between Sacramento and Sunnyvale.

Timestamp	SACR_SUNN_in (GB)	SACR_SUNN_out (GB)
1514822400	14110930202	1025131246
1514826000	13453619303	9191557943
1514829600	12168879944	7793842045
1514833200	11231198033	7097237528
1514836800	10780847622	8048293939

For example, the data shown in Figure 4 show traces from 1 January 2018 to 31 December 2018, with two-way traffic. Here sometimes we miss recording traffic movements at specific intervals, such as missing values in the Washington–Chicago link during a 1-week interval in November. To address this issue, one can calculate average data values for the missing points from the surrounding values to fill in the gaps.

6.1. *Using graph neural networks to model the WAN*

We denote L as the number of network links in a WAN network. For each link $l \in L$, traffic is measured as a time series $y_{(l,t)}$, where $t \in T$ is the time in hours and y is the aggregated traffic data (normalized) moving in one direction on the link l in time t. The training set contains the time-step data $[t_1, \ldots, t_m]$, the validation set is $[t_{m+1}, \ldots, t_{m+Y}]$, and the test data that are used as the ground truth are $[t_{m+Y+1}, t_{m+Y+2}, \ldots]$, where Y denotes the time interval we are predicting in the future.

Here, we also construct a correlation analysis to measure the linear and nonlinear relationships among the site nodes and traffic traces, such as when traffic moves across the links. This is modeled as a graph $G = (V, E, A)$, where V is a set of N nodes that represents the sites, E is a set of directed edges representing the connections among the nodes, and $A \in R^{N \times N}$ is the weighted adjacency matrix representing the strength of connectivity between nodes.

Given the historical traffic observations at each node in the graph, the goal is to learn a function f(.) that takes traffic observations t timesteps as input to forecast the traffic for the next $t + Y$ timesteps,

$$X(t-1), X(t); G \xrightarrow{\text{f}(.)} X(t+1), \ldots, X(t+Y)$$

The Pearson correlation r [5] can be used to measure the strength and direction of a linear relationship between links, calculated by dividing the covariance of two variables by the product of their standard deviations. This helps rank the relationships among each pair of links.

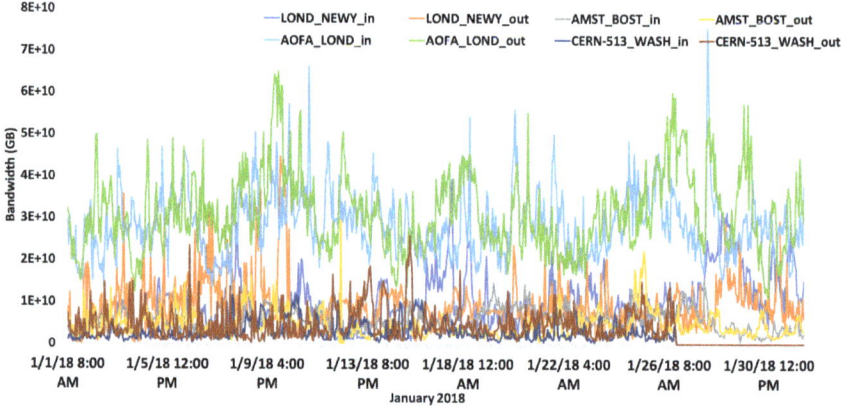

Fig. 4.   Traffic patterns in January 2018 on all transatlantic links in ESnet, including London, New York, Amsterdam, Boston, 32 Avenue of the Americas (AOFA), CERN, and Washington, D.C.

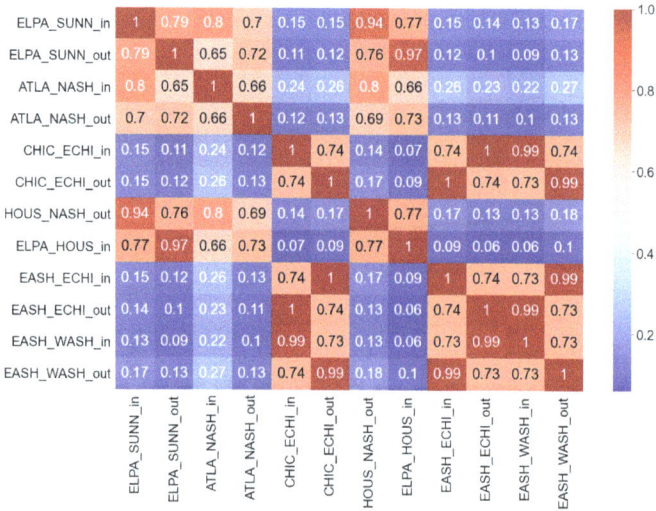

Fig. 5.   Correlation matrix of only 12 sites.

Equation (1) shows the Spearman coefficient, where $(\sigma_{rk_A}, \sigma_{rk_B})$ are the standard deviations of the rank variables, $cov(rk_A, rk_B)$ are the covariances of the rank variables, and ρ is the Pearson correlation coefficient applied to the rank variables. r_s ranges between -1 and 1, and we use 0.5 and above to indicate a positive correlation among two traffic traces and -0.5

and below to indicate a negative correlation. Figure 5 shows the correlation among 12 sites in 2018, represented as a heatmap.

$$r_s = \rho_{rk_A, rk_B} = \frac{cov(rk_A, rk_B)}{\sigma_{rk_A}, \sigma_{rk_B}} \tag{1}$$

Figure 6 shows the neural network architecture for the graph neural network. As WAN networks are highly dynamic, we update the graph neural network to take dynamic inputs represented by the correlation matrices shown in Figure 5. This model architecture is based on the diffusion convolutional neural network (DCRNN) [27], which was used to model and predict LA road traffic statistics in the past.

There are two inputs to the DCRNN model: 1) an adjacency matrix representing the traffic correlation among the sites of the WAN (Figure 5) and 2) the time series data or traffic at each node of the graph. The encoder of the DCRNN network encodes the input into a fixed-length vector and passes it to the decoder. The decoder forecasts future traffic conditions and loops through to find the best prediction function. During this training phase, the data from t timesteps on N nodes are fed in as input; the correlation matrix is computed on the time series data and given as the weighted adjacency matrix for diffusion convolution. The DCRNN is trained using a minibatch stochastic gradient and a mean absolute error (MAE) loss function.

Measuring Prediction Accuracy. There are multiple ways to measure the prediction accuracy of the model. Commonly used measures include the mean squared error (MSE) or its square root (RMSE), or the Mean Absolute Error (MAE) between the actual and predicted variables. In machine learning, most researchers use all three of these to show the model accuracy in assessing the model performance. A fourth measure, the coefficient of determination R^2, calculated as 1 - (the sum of squares of residuals)/(the total sum of squares), gives the proportion of the variance that can be explained by the predictor variables in a regression model. The higher the R^2 value, the better a model fits the data. R^2 often ranges between 0 and 1 but can be negative if the data were not used in deriving the regression model, including in cases such as ours where future data values are predicted.

Figure 7 presents the results of the DCRNN model and shows that it outperforms several other models. Linear regression models such as ARIMA, random forest, gradient boosting, and simple neural network variants, which have previously been used for traffic forecasting, all tend to show lower and often negative R^2 scores, while the DCRNN tends to have a higher, positive score.

Achieving higher prediction accuracy presents several advantages for self-driving networks, such as performing informed routing decisions for new

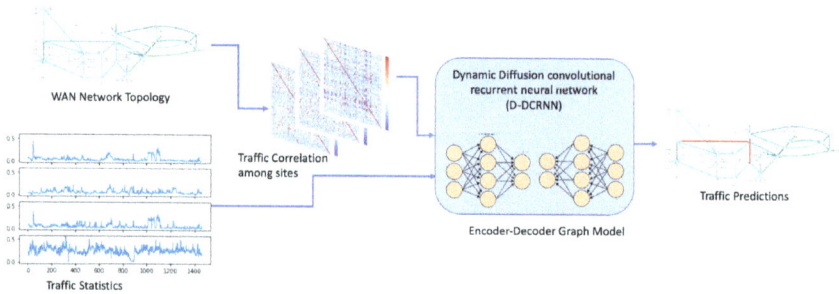

Fig. 6. DCRNN model architecture. The encoder–decoder deep neural network is used to forecast the network traffic for multiple timesteps.

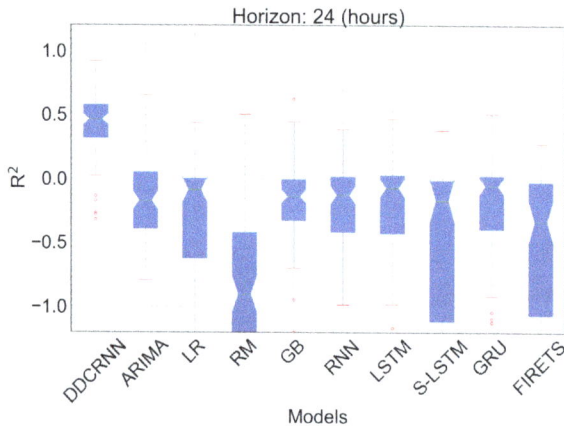

Fig. 7. Traffic prediction results in R^2 for several models, showing that the DCRNN outperforms all the other models tested.

flows on a currently congested network or finding least used paths that can be modified for better use of network resources. This prediction approach exposes many potentials to allow informed flow and routing allocations for network operations, such as scheduling long-running flow on alternative routes to prevent congestion points for other smaller flows. Eventually, these can be coupled with a controller to test how congestion-free routing will impact the average utilization of a network in practice. Additionally, there is further work on WAN traffic prediction in other continental-scale networks such as Internet2 [43], GEANT [25], and CANARIE [31] which is worthy of study.

6.2. *A self-driving (learning) traffic steering case study*

Traffic congestion can directly cause performance deterioration, such as when links are oversubscribed causing bottlenecks [10]. Many services rely on having high-throughput transfers and need high-capacity links such as 100 Gbps. However, even for the busiest link, the current average utilization is only between 40 and 60%, to account for unanticipated peaks [19]. Traffic engineering and path computation techniques such as Multiprotocol Label Switching Traffic Engineering (MPLS-TE) [2], Google's B4 [20], and Microsoft's Software Driven WAN (SWAN) [19] have proposed ways in which routers can greedily select routing patterns for arriving flows, both locally and globally, to increase path utilization. However, these techniques require meticulously designed heuristics to calculate optimal routes and also do not distinguish among the characteristics of arriving flows.

One can view the traffic steering problem as a "path computation" challenge, where using AI (or reinforcement learning (RL)) can help find optimal paths (or routes) based on past experience. Here, the system would first learn optimal paths by selecting random paths between source and destination, given the current network conditions. The AI will compute a reward function based on its selections and store these values in memory. Over time, the AI could become so aware that given a similar network condition or pattern, it will know how to steer the traffic in real time. This is known as Q-learning: a value-based gradient reinforcement learning method [49] in simplest form, but there are more complex RL algorithms that can be tried.

6.3. *Using deep reinforcement learning for the learning controller*

A reinforcement learning (RL) problem is formulated with an agent, situated in a partially observable environment, learning from past inter-action data to make current decisions. The agent receives data in the form of environment snapshots, processed in some manner, with specific relevant features. After receiving information and computing the value for future actions given the current state, an agent then acts to change its environment, subsequently receiving feedback on its action in the form of rewards, until a terminal state is reached. The objective is to maximize the cumulative reward over all actions at the time the agent is active. Almost all the deep RL problems can be framed as Markov Decision Processes (MDPs), which consist of four key elements $\langle \mathcal{S}, \mathcal{A}, P, R \rangle$. More specifically, at each decision epoch t, the intelligent agent can stay in state s_t that belongs to the state space $\mathcal{S}$ of the environment or choose to take an action

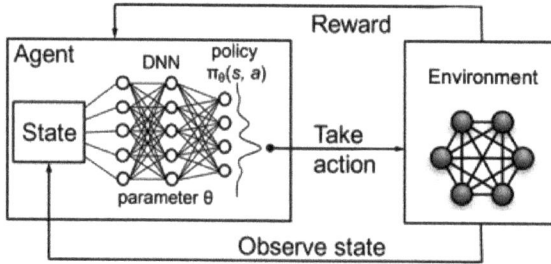

Fig. 8.   A RL agent learning network states.

a_t that belongs to the action space $\mathcal{A}$ to switch from one state to another. The probability that the process moves into its new state s_{t+1} is given by the state transition function $P(s_{t+1}|s_t, a_t)$. Once an action is taken, the environment delivers a reward r as feedback. Figure 8 shows the general process of reinforcement learning.

Reinforcement learning research has investigated multiple techniques such as multiarmed bandit problems, resource allocation, or finding routes through a maze [35]. Deep reinforcement learning builds upon classical models, replacing learning with a neural network to approximate policy and value functions. Here, the function approximates the environment state space with actions and rewards. Particularly when the state space is too large to store, this approach has proved feasible in learning approximate conditions.

Learning Formulation. A Q-value represents a state-action combination. Better Q-values show better chances of getting higher rewards which are earned at the end of a complete episode. The Q-value is calculated using a function that approximates the Q-value at each step by using the prior Q-values, a short-term and a discounted future reward. This way, optimal control policies are found across all environment states. Q-learning is an off-policy reinforcement learning algorithm [36] that uses a table to store all Q-values with possible state/action pairs. This table is updated using the Bellman equation [36], allowing the action to be chosen using a greedy policy, where γ is the discounting factor,

$$Q(s, a) = R(s, a) + \gamma \max_{a'} Q(s', a')). \tag{2}$$

Other RL Approaches. Other RL approaches such as value-based RL algorithms [41] attempt to learn the tabular value or an approximation of the state-action value $Q_\pi(s, a)$ and select the action based on the maximal function value among all available actions for a given state. Policy-based RL training algorithms work to learn the policy $\pi_\theta(a_t|s_t)$, which depends on a vector of parameters θ, that maximizes the expected cumulative reward function. Policy-based algorithms can learn stochastic policies. It is worthwhile to note that stochastic means stochastic in some action-state pairs where it makes sense. Usually, value-based algorithms, which choose the actions with the maximal reward values, can only follow deterministic policies or stochastic policies with predetermined distributions. That is not quite the same as learning the real optimal stochastic policy. Since the current communication networks are highly dynamic and stochastic, we can expect the policy-based RL algorithms to perform better than the value-based RL algorithms in certain scenarios, where the optimal policy is stochastic.

Furthermore, RL algorithms can be subcategorized into different groups: on-policy vs off-policy [42] and model-based vs model-free algorithms. Off-policy algorithms, as compared to on-policy, have a greedy learning approach. In on-policy learning, the RL performs an action that is immediately recommended by the neural network, while in off-policy learning, the RL iterates through all available action strategies to select the action with the highest perceived award. Given this look-ahead training nature, off-policy learning is "less risky" because the RL does not need to interact with the environment, while for on-policy learning, the RL has to interact with the environment for learning, risking to create undesirable operations of the system when the controller is not well-trained. In model-based learning, the controller learns the system dynamics first and then uses the learned system dynamics for planning, while model-free algorithms learn the optimal control without learning the system dynamics. The model-based algorithms are usually more computationally expensive because the algorithm is required to first learn an accurate environment model, which is usually a difficult task in real applications, then to an optimal policy based on the model. Thus, model-free algorithms are more popular as they are usually less computationally expensive. Figure 9 shows how a model-based and model-free approach differ. A model-based approach could learn the traffic patterns, peaks, and user request patterns over time and use this information to make decisions. However, in a model-free approach, the AI agent will use current state information, such as current path utilization, loss, and other data, to determine what action to take next.

Several papers used a neural network to approximate the action-value functions [36,41]. In 2015, Mnih *et al.* [35] introduced the Deep Q-Network (DQN), which was the first successful usage of a combination of deep neural networks and Q-learning algorithms. This work is responsible for the rapid growth of the field of deep reinforcement learning (DRL). In addition to using neural networks, the DQN approach includes the use of a replay buffer and two neural networks to approximate the action-value function and to

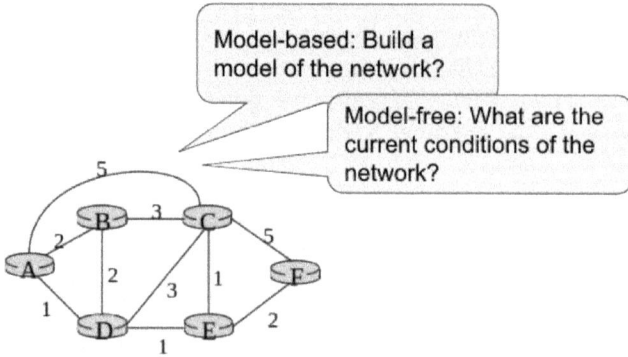

Fig. 9. Model-based versus model-free learning.

overcome the instability issues of previous approaches. The replay buffer is used to store a relatively large number of observations of transitions (s_t, a_t, r_t, s_{t+1}). Mini-batches of these transitions are sampled randomly (using a uniform distribution), which allows the algorithm to update the neural network from a set of uncorrelated transitions at each iteration. To reduce the correlation between the action values $(Q_\pi(s_t, a_t))$ and $r(s_t, a_t) + \gamma max_{a'} Q_\pi(s_{t+1}, a')$, DQN uses two neural networks. The weights of the first one are updated at each iteration, and this network is directly interacting with the environment. The weights of the second neural network, called the target network, are updated after a fixed number of iterations by simply copying the weights of the first network.

While the DQN approach can handle environments with high-dimensional state spaces, it can only be used with discrete and low-dimensional action spaces. In fact, DQN relies on finding the action that maximizes the action-value function, which requires an iterative optimization at every step, if used with an environment that has continuous actions. In theory, one can discretize the action space, however, this solution is likely to be intractable for problems that require fine control of actions (i.e., finer-grained discretization). The high number of discrete action spaces are difficult to explore efficiently. Moreover, a naive discretization strategy of the action spaces can exclude important information about the action domain, which can be essential for finding optimal control policy in several problems. To overcome this issue of discrete action spaces, Lillicrap *et al.* [28] introduced the Deep Deterministic Policy Gradient (DDPG) algorithm, which is a model-free, off-policy algorithm that can learn control policies in high-dimensional, continuous action spaces. Deep

Table 2.   Various RL algorithms.

Technique	Model	Policy	Observation space	Action space	Reward
Q-learning	Free	Off-policy	Discrete	Discrete	Q-value
DQN	Free	Off-policy	Discrete	Continuous	Q-value
DDPG	Free	Off-policy	Continuous	Continuous	Q-value
TRPO	Free	Off-policy	Continuous	Continuous	Advantage
A3C	Free	Off-policy	Continuous	Continuous	Advantage

Q-learning is based on value-based algorithms, whereas DDPG, which uses an actor-critic approach, leverages both value and policy-based learning to reach a better robust trained agent. Additionally, other examples of algorithms such as trust region policy optimization (TRPO) [42] or proximal policy optimization (PPO) [28] are designed to allow the agent to learn optimal policies quicker, again reducing the training time. In deep RL literature, most of these algorithms have been developed to tackle discrete versus continuous state and action spaces or improve the training of the agent without compromising the robustness of the solution produced [41]. Selecting the right algorithms, either value-based or policy-based, can have a significant impact on the results produced [41]. Table 2 shows a summary of these approaches.

Recent experiments by Tedeschi *et al.* [50] showed how RL can be used to perform Smart Caching for the CMS experiment at the LHC. Their goal was to optimize caching efficiency by using fewer storage resources. They were able to improve the throughput and network cost considerably, as compared to other caching methods. Given the initial success of their study, the remaining challenge is the real-world translation of RL approaches to help control the networks, optimally build paths, and allocate the available network resources and coordinate those allocations with site resources. Recent implementations such as HECATE and the use of prediction models, adapting some of the directions summarized above, are aiming to achieve this goal for real-world problems.

6.3.1. *Modeling traffic engineering*

Within the context of traffic steering, network providers may have different requirements such as minimizing congestion, utilizing maximum bandwidth, load balancing, and/or maximizing the success rate of meeting data delivery deadlines. Wide area networks allow a number of pathways to exist between pairs of end hosts. These paths can have equal or different cost distributions such as settings for bandwidth, latency, throughput, uptime, and more.

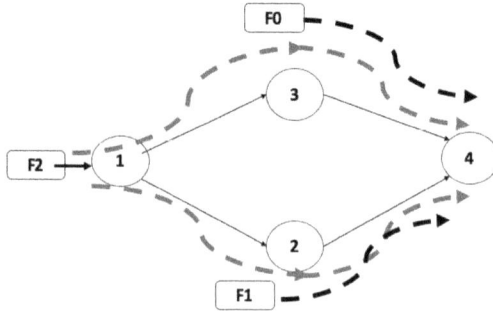

Fig. 10.   Example of routing a new flow F1 from 1→4. There are two possible paths to take through Node-3 or Node-2.

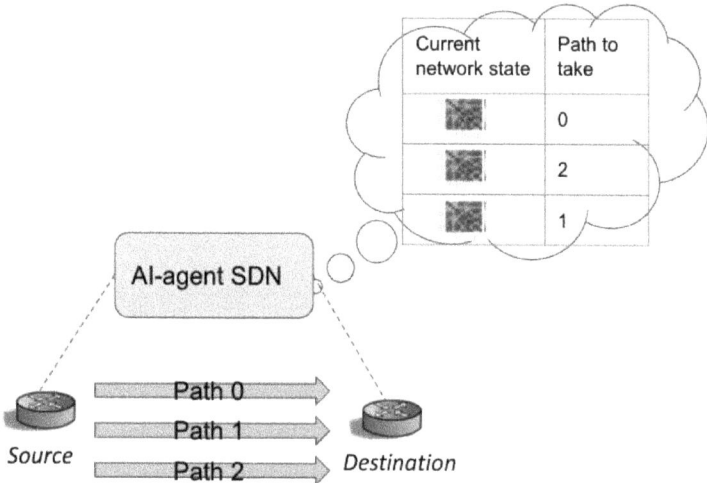

Fig. 11.   An AI-agent coupled with an SDN controller, working to optimize a state-dependent flow pattern.

These settings can determine how quickly and how reliably the arriving flow will reach its destination and can be allocated using different egress ports to choose the path to take. Equal-cost multi-path (ECMP) routing is an example of this, where packet forwarding to a single destination can occur over multiple best paths with equal routing priority, where this method can lead to unbalanced distribution among paths with different costs. One can design an AI agent using RL algorithms with customized reward functions in order to define an optimal network condition that overcomes these limitations.

Figure 10 shows a new flow F2 being allocated to one of the paths. There might be other previously allocated flows F0 and F1, already allocated on part of the paths. This means that while the link costs can be set in advance, the available bandwidth on the links is continuously changing and difficult to anticipate when selecting paths. The RL algorithm can be optimized to take this into consideration when allocating new paths to incoming flows.

Network monitoring data as State. Assuming the network is using an SDN controller to divert flows across multiple paths, if the controller is equipped with an AI agent, it can use current and recent network monitoring data to characterize the network state and divert flows accordingly. These data can include packet loss, link utilization, and other information available to the network operators. Additionally, the current topology can also help the AI agent make better decisions. This is shown in Figure 11. The AI-SDN agent can choose one of the paths depending on what the network monitoring data look like (represented as a 2D chart). Each path can have different bandwidth and latency definitions, state variables, and constraints, which allows the agent to generate variable flow topologies as it works towards its optimum.

The agent selects a path and receives a reward after a flow has been completed. This results in a delayed reward, where the delay is greater for flows that take longer to finish. The sequence of rewards acts as signals to adjust the forwarding-link priorities, which enhances or diminishes the probability a specific next-hop is selected for the flow. The agent learns to adjust the path selection policies based on experience, through the continual selections and modifications of the rewards. The goal of the model is to move all arriving flows from source to destination as quickly as possible.

6.3.2. *AI-agent design*

In this example, the objective of the AI agent is to get as many flows completed as it can, as soon as possible. When a flow of duration r_i finishes, it computes its completion time c_i by adding its duration with path latency. This is then inverted to give the flow's slowness rate by $l_i = c_i/r_i$. Similar to [22], we normalize this, to prevent skewing results for longer flows.

State Space. The state of the environment is what the AI (RL) agent learns against. In this example, we define this as (1) the currently available bandwidth across all paths, (2) the size of the flow being allocated, and (3) the currently allocated flows. For example, after an allocation on path0, the bandwidth availability is (actual-flow size), which can form part of the state information.

Action Space. There are three paths so three possible actions. Once some 100 flows are allocated, we assume the AI agent assesses its performance and records a reward. The simulation is run for a number of iterations containing many episodes. The total reward is calculated per episode when all 100 flows have been allocated.

Reward Calculation. At the end of each episode, the AI agent calculates if any flows have finished and the total completion time is recorded.

The AI agent is trained for multiple iterations, with each iteration generating a new set of flows and learning by allocating these flows onto the paths. Figure 12 shows the reward function, measured in the flow slowness time with the RL versus the shortest possible route algorithm (being used as a baseline). The graph shows that over time, the RL algorithm, because it uses more information from the network to make the allocations, is able to produce a better flow allocation over the network traffic than the default shortest possible algorithm (SPA), since the SPA does not learn over time.

The improved RL performance is recorded again when measuring network load and packet loss in the simulated case (Figure 13). As the network load increases, the RL agent is able to achieve lower packet delivery times for a longer time than the SPA. Additionally, we see that the packet loss is significantly reduced as the RL agent is able to learn optimal paths to deliver the traffic.

While the above example illustrates how an RL approach can be very effective in optimizing throughput across a network topology, further work and developments are ongoing in order to apply these techniques to the real multiuser, multiorganization case involving global research and education networks. In dealing with realistic demands from multiple individuals and teams, the objective function to be maximized will also take other variables into account expressing one or more of the following aspects (as well as others): network state, policy, relative priority, short- and long-term resource usage by each user or group, deadlines, coordination with job queues and site computational and storage resources, and the rates of workflow progress in different classes of work. Deriving objective functions and methods which are judged to be optimal in terms of satisfying the needs and operational constraints and missions of the major science programs, the at-large academic and research community, and the research and education network community is itself an important goal and ongoing focus of the communities mentioned, working in frameworks such as the Global Network Advancement Group.

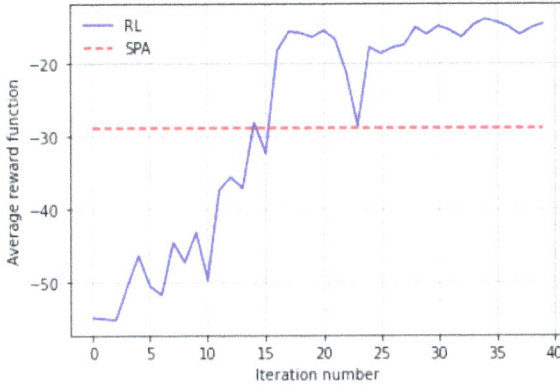

Fig. 12.   Measuring the performance of the AI agent compared to shortest possible route.

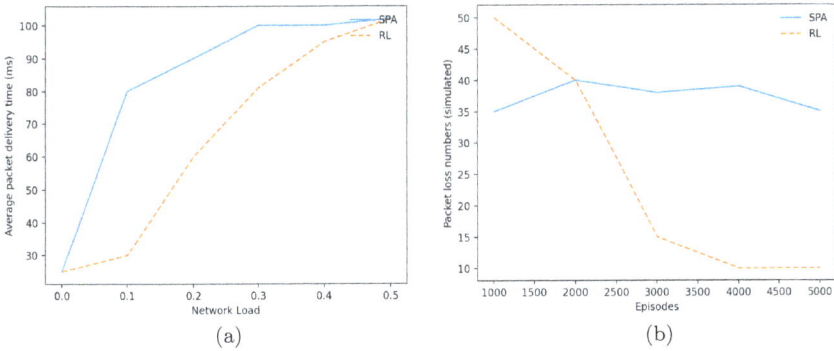

Fig. 13.   Comparing the results obtained with the shortest possible route algorithm and with the RL agent-based approach: (a) Comparing network load; (b) Comparing packet loss.

7. Towards Building Self-driving Networks

Autonomic describes self-management. This is not *autonomous* or *automatic*, where devices behave on their own or follow a predefined script. **Autonomic devices follow human-directed goals but interpret them locally and adapt, depending on their own capability and environment.** Human administrators have little direct influence and the devices can self-regulate by use of high-level policies.

IBM introduced the autonomic computing initiative [23] which argued for the use of autonomy principles focused on developing concepts that allow systems to self-correct and operate independently. These systems are built to follow adaptive behavior, perceive changes from the environment, reason, and correct themselves automatically.

"Autonomic computing is the ability of an IT infrastructure to adapt to change in accordance with business policies and objectives. Quite simply, it is about freeing IT professionals to focus on higher value tasks by making technology work smarter, with business rules guiding systems to be self-configuring, self-healing, self-optimizing, and self-protecting."

Autonomic networking follows the same concepts of autonomic computing that can handle increasing complexity by self-regulating its components and resulting behaviors using high-level policies. Also described in terms of the *Self-x* properties, it focuses on the following:

- Self-configuration: Automatic configuration of components.
- Self-healing: Automatic discovery of anomalies and fault correction.
- Self-optimization: Automatic monitoring and resource optimization to ensure optimal functions of resources, given high-level requirements are met.
- Self-protection: Proactive identification and protection from attacks.

The Internet Research Task Force (IRTF) describes autonomic networks as being composed of many autonomic agents that can communicate through an autonomic control plane, functioning on an abstract, high-level policy, or intent provided by a central authority. Figure 15 describes the reference model for an autonomic network node and how this translates into a WAN-controller scenario. Telemetry allows multiple monitoring data sources to be analyzed to make inferences about the current network state. This can include logs, packet statistics, topology information, and device data. As shown in Figure 15, each autonomic network node (or element) has its own self-network knowledge, such as service discovery, and can communicate with other autonomic service agents to make decisions. The autonomic control plane communicates high-level intents to the agents for their expected goals.

However, this architecture follows centralized control. The IRTF extends the concept by the use of individual control loops with every autonomic agent in a distributed network to allow immediate feedback and decentralized control. In practice, autonomic Self-x properties are essential for a smart network but are challenging to support in a large network ecosystem, because of the complex and distributed nature of both the hardware and software and operational rules involved. Enhancing individual network devices, such as routers for intelligent packet routing,

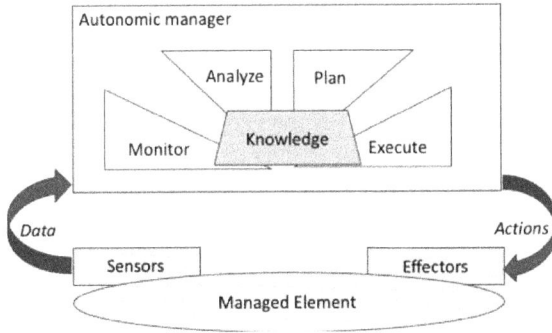

Fig. 14.   IBM's concept of a deliberative cycle of autonomic elements [23].

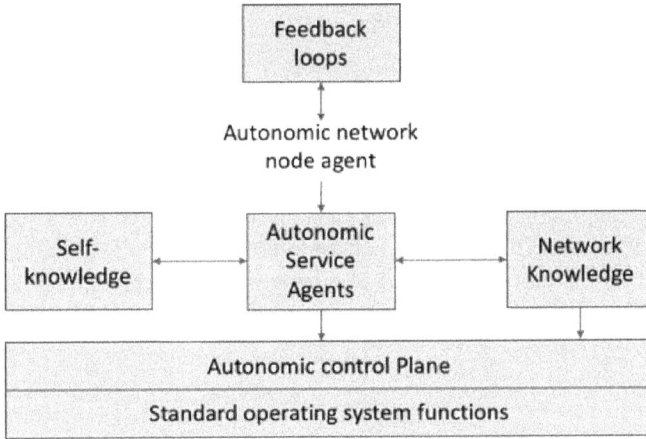

Fig. 15.   Autonomic network architecture showing a set of service agents each using self-knowledge and network knowledge to interact with a network node agent, receive high-level intents, and communicate with other service agents via an autonomic control plane.

dynamic policy adaptation, continual adjustment of resource utilization, or automatic initiation against malicious attacks, and early warnings to reduce latency are some strategies for an autonomic element. Additionally, individual elements can collectively help achieve various levels of autonomic intelligence, improving network capacity, reliability, and security. Multiple AI techniques can aid in achieving these four Self-x properties.

7.1. *Node-level and system-level intelligence*

One goal of this paper is to motivate researchers to treat network design with (at least) two levels of intelligence: node level and system level. At *node level*, each networking element (or device) is designed with feedback loops and allowed to interact with the others, in order to gain local intelligence at individual node level. At *system level*, interactions with controllers and feedback loops allow individual elements to interact with central elements for system-wide intelligence. Each element exhibits autonomic behavior thereby adapting to its own changing environment and minimizing human or central management. In complex or multiregional networks, this concept can be extended to include additional intermediate levels, distinguished by their geographic extent, or other organizational or technical factors.

Figure 16 shows a controller using information to optimize how paths are utilized for system-level packet routing. Similar decisions can optimize throughput or minimize loss, depending on the goal of the autonomic controller in this scenario.

While current AI implementations can optimize the network at various levels, there are some general research topics that should be addressed in order to lay the foundation for potential AI-enabled autonomic or self-driving network solutions.

In complex multiregional cases such as those referred to throughout this chapter, the individual agents will be embedded in a multiagent services infrastructure organized around the programs, nations, and regional and transoceanic consortia involved.

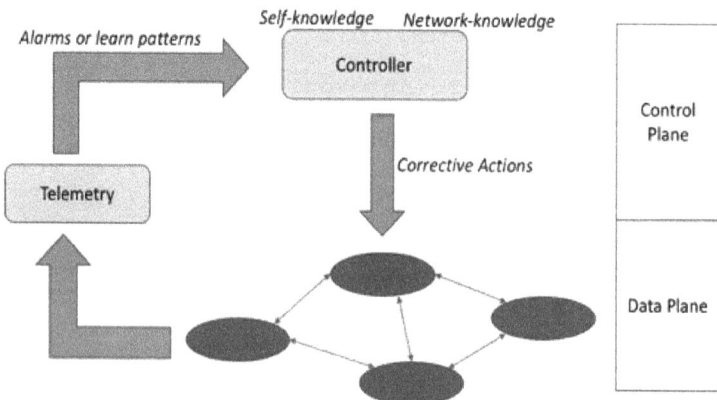

Fig. 16.   The (node-level) controller is an autonomic agent that uses knowledge and environment data to learn current state to perform corrective actions.

8. Outlook and Next Steps

As we have demonstrated in this chapter, deep learning approaches including the Deep Q-Learning Network concept (DQN), graph neural networks, and diffusion convolution recurrent neural network (DCRNN) architectures offer promising development directions for both network traffic prediction and decision support for traffic engineering in global research and education networks, to meet the challenges posed by frontier programs in data-intensive sciences. Beyond the imminent and decadal big data challenges of the Large Hadron Collider program in high energy physics, future astrophysics programs such as the Square Kilometer Array (SKA) and the genomics challenges of the future [18], the DCRNN, and its variants have been shown to be effective in predicting multiscale time series in several other important fields including vehicle road traffic [25] such as neuroimaging: causal inference in brain networks [26] and air quality forecasting [27]. Recent work on Graph networks can prove useful in combining multiple approaches to optimize networks [30]. Using Graph networks to model a computer network can help improve predictions, anomaly detection, and learning details flow patterns. These can then be combined with reinforcement learning to allow the AI module to learn more details and strategies to optimize the network. Moving forward, the agent-based architecture envisaged for global network traffic prediction and engineering shares analogous elements and aspects, in the structure and roles, of the mapping, real-time demand and control services, and platform optimization subsystems foreseen in the Smart Transportation Brain described by Yan Liu at ICML 2019 [45]. This indicates both that the study of smart transportation systems which deal with multiscale dynamic time series with complex traffic patterns may provide further insights for our future work and that conversely, our developments with many partners on research and education network traffic prediction and control, in the context of the new paradigm described in this chapter, may have broad impact on smart transportation and beyond.

9. Conclusion

Beyond machine learning optimization aspects which are a central theme of this chapter, the collaborative work among the network and data-intensive science communities on a global scale, in a joint multiyear shared mission in frameworks such as the Global Network Advancement Group, itself holds the promise of long-term transformational impact. Part of this promise is a deeper understanding of how to operate and manage multiregional systems driven by persistent (scientific and technical) goals; systems and solutions that likely could not exist were it not for the decade-long nature of the scientific missions themselves. The greatest value arising from this global effort, apart from its societal impact and value in promoting mutual understanding among nations through open cooperation, is perhaps in the prospect of greater scientific productivity, especially of a new round of discoveries that will transform our understanding of the world around us and the nature of our universe at its most fundamental level.

References

[1] J. Ashraf and S. Latif (2014). Handling intrusion and ddos attacks in software defined networks using machine learning techniques. In *2014 National Software Engineering Conference*, pp. 55–60. doi: 10.1109/NSEC.2014.6998241.

[2] D. Awduche, J. Malcolm, J. Agogbua *et al.* (1999). Requirements for traffic engineering over MPLS. RFC Editor. doi: 10.17487/RFC2702.

[3] A. Azzouni and G. Pujolle (2018). Neutm: A neural network-based framework for traffic matrix prediction in SDN. *NOMS*.

[4] M. Barisits, T. Beermann, F. Berghaus *et al.* (2019). Rucio: Scientific data management. *Computing and Software for Big Science*, *3*(1), 11. https://doi.org/10.1007/s41781-019-0026-3.

[5] J. Benesty, J. Chen, Y. Huang *et al.* (2009). Pearson correlation coefficient. In *Noise Reduction in Speech Processing*, Springer, pp. 1–4.

[6] M. Berry, T. E. Potok, P. Balaprakash *et al.* (2015). Machine learning and understanding for intelligent extreme scale scientific computing and discovery. DOE Workshop Report:15-CS-1768.

[7] K. Börner, F. N. Silva, and S. Milojević (2021). Visualizing big science projects. *Nature Reviews Physics*, *3*(11), 753–761. https://doi.org/10.1038/s42254-021-00374-7.

[8] P. Bosshart, D. Daly, G. Gibb *et al.* (2014). P4: Programming protocol-independent packet processors. *SIGCOMM Computer Communication Review*, *44*(3), 87–95. https://doi.org/10.1145/2656877.2656890.

[9] M. Branscombe (2019). Is sonic, the open source network OS, ready for mainstream? DataCenter Knowledge.

[10] D. Clark, S. Bauer, K. Claffy *et al.* (2014). Measurement and analysis of Internet interconnection and congestion. In *Telecommunication Policy Research Conference*.

[11] P. Cortez, M. Rio, M. Rocha *et al.* (2006). Internet traffic forecasting using neural networks. In *IEEE International Joint Conference Neural Network Proceedings*.

[12] E. Dart, L. Rotman, B. Tierney *et al.* (2013). The science dmz: A network design pattern for data-intensive science. In *SC '13: Proceedings of the International Conference on High Performance Computing, Networking, Storage and Analysis*, pp. 1–10. https://doi.org/10.1145/2503210.2503245.

[13] E. Deelman, K. Vahi, G. Juve *et al.* (2015). Pegasus, a workflow management system for science automation. *Future Generation Computer Systems*, *46*, 17–35. https://doi.org/10.1016/j.future.2014.10.008, https://www.sciencedirect.com/science/article/pii/S0167739X14002015.

[14] C. Dominicini, D. Mafioletti, A. C. Locateli *et al.* (2020). Polka: Polynomial key-based architecture for source routing in network fabrics. In *2020 6th IEEE Conference on Network Softwarization (NetSoft)*, pp. 326–334. https://doi.org/10.1109/NetSoft48620.2020.9165501.

[15] L. R. Evans (2009). *The Large Hadron Collider: A Marvel of Technology*. EPFL Press: Fundamental Sciences.

[16] S. M. Feit (1993). *SNMP: A Guide to Network Management*. McGraw-Hill McGraw-Hill Series on Computer Communications, McGraw-Hill.

[17] A. Gupta, L. Vanbever, M. Shahbaz *et al.* (2014). SDX: A software defined internet exchange. In *Proceedings of the 2014 ACM Conference on SIGCOMM*, SIGCOMM '14 (Association for Computing Machinery, New York, NY, USA), pp. 551–562. ISBN 9781450328364, https://doi.org/10.1145/2619239.2626300.

[18] S. Hao, A. Kantchelian, B. Miller *et al.* (2016). Predator: Proactive recognition and elimination of domain abuse at time-of-registration. In *Proceedings of the 2016 ACM SIGSAC Conference on Computer and Communications Security*, CCS '16 (Association for Computing Machinery, New York, NY, USA), pp. 1568–1579. ISBN 9781450341394, https://doi.org/10.1145/2976749.2978317.

[19] C.-Y. Hong, S. Kandula, R. Mahajan *et al.* (2013). Achieving high utilization with software-driven wan. *SIGCOMM Computer Communication Review*, *43*(4), 15–26. https://doi.org/10.1145/2534169.2486012.

[20] S. Jain, A. Kumar, S. Mandal *et al.* (2013). B4: Experience with a globally-deployed software defined wan. *SIGCOMM Computer Communication Review*, *43*(4), 3–14. http://doi.acm.org/10.1145/2534169.2486019.

[21] E. F. Kfoury, J. Crichigno, and E. Bou-Harb (2021). An exhaustive survey on p4 programmable data plane switches: Taxonomy, applications, challenges, and future trends. *IEEE Access*, *9*, 87094–87155. https://doi.org/10.1109/ACCESS.2021.3086704.

[22] M. Kiran, S. Campbell, and N. Buraglio (2022). Hecate: Ai-driven wan traffic engineering for science. In *2022 Innovating the Network for Data-Intensive Science Workshop (INDIS)*, Supercomputing '22.

[23] M. Kiran, S. Campbell, F. B. Wala *et al.* (2021). Machine learning-based analysis of COVID-19 pandemic impact on us research networks. *SIGCOMM Computer Communication Review*, *51*(4), 23–35. https://doi.org/10.1145/3503954.3503958.

[24] M. Kiran, E. Pouyoul, A. Mercian *et al.* (2018). Enabling intent to configure scientific networks for high performance demands. *Future Generation Computer Systems*, *79*, 205–214. https://doi.org/10.1016/j.future.2017.04.020, https://www.sciencedirect.com/science/article/pii/S0167739X1730626X.

[25] A. M. Koster and M. Kutschka (2011). Network design under demand uncertainties: A case study on the abilene and geant network data. In *Photonic Networks, 12. ITG Symposium* (VDE), pp. 1–8.

[26] N. Krishnaswamy, M. Kiran, K. Singh *et al.* (2020). Data-driven learning to predict wan network traffic. In *Proceedings of the 3rd International Workshop on Systems and Network Telemetry and Analytics*, SNTA '20 (Association for Computing Machinery, New York, NY, USA), ISBN 9781450379809, pp. 11–18. https://doi.org/10.1145/3391812.3396268.

[27] Y. Li, R. Yu, C. Shahabi *et al.* (2018). Diffusion convolutional recurrent neural network: Data-driven traffic forecasting. In *International Conference on Learning Representations.* https://openreview.net/forum?id=SJiHXGWAZ.

[28] T. P. Lillicrap, J. J. Hunt, A. Pritzel *et al.* (2015). Continuous control with deep reinforcement learning. *arXiv preprint arXiv:1509.02971.*

[29] X. Ma, Z. Dai, Z. He *et al.* (2017). Learning traffic as images: A deep convolutional neural network for large-scale transportation network speed prediction. *Sensors, 17*(4), 818.

[30] T. Mallick, P. Balaprakash, E. Rask *et al.* (2020). Graph-partitioning-based diffusion convolutional recurrent neural network for large-scale traffic forecasting. *Transportation Research Record, 2674*(9), 473–488. https://doi.org/10.1177/0361198120930010.

[31] S. Marcos (1992). The Canadian network for the advancement of research, industry, and education (canarie).

[32] N. McKeown, T. Anderson, H. Balakrishnan *et al.* (2008). Openflow: Enabling innovation in campus networks. *SIGCOMM Computer Communication Review, 38*(2), 69–74. https://doi.org/10.1145/1355734.1355746.

[33] D. Meyer (2016). Networking meets artificial intelligence: A glimpse into the (very) near future, CTO corner, 19 August 2016.

[34] K. Meyer (2020). The rare project, bringing back the network innovation within research and education community. GEANT Connect https://connect.geant.org/2020/01/17/rare-project-bringing-back-the-network-innovation-within-research-and-education-community.

[35] V. Mnih, K. Kavukcuoglu, D. Silver *et al.* (2015). Human-level control through deep reinforcement learning. *Nature, 518*(7540), 529–533. https://doi.org/10.1038/nature14236.

[36] E. Mocanu, D. C. Mocanu, P. H. Nguyen *et al.* (2019). On-line building energy optimization using deep reinforcement learning. *IEEE Transactions on Smart Grid, 10*(4), 3698–3708.

[37] I. Monga, C. Guok, J. MacAuley *et al.* (2018). SDN for end-to-end networked science at the exascale (sense). In *2018 IEEE/ACM Innovating the Network for Data-Intensive Science (INDIS)*, pp. 33–44. https://doi.org/10.1109/INDIS.2018.00007.

[38] NSF (2019). N-dise: NDN for data intensive experiments.

[39] D. Ratner and B. Sumpter (2019). Bes roundtable on producing and managing large scientific data with artificial intelligence and machine learning. DOE Roundtable Report:10.2172/1630823.

[40] H. Rodrigues, I. Monga, A. Sadasivarao *et al.* (2014). Traffic optimization in multi-layered wans using SDN. In *Proceedings of the 2014 IEEE 22nd Annual Symposium on High-Performance Interconnects*, HOTI '14 (IEEE Computer Society, Washington, D.C., USA), ISBN 978-1-4799-5860-3, pp. 71–78. http://dx.doi.org/10.1109/HOTI.2014.23.

[41] R. Sutton and A. G. Barto (2018). *Reinforcement Learning: An Introduction (2nd edition)*, Cambridge: MIT Press.

[42] R. S. Sutton, D. McAllester, S. Singh *et al.* (1999). Policy gradient methods for reinforcement learning with function approximation. In *Proceedings of the 12th International Conference on Neural Information Processing Systems*, NIPS'99, MIT Press, Cambridge, MA, USA, pp. 1057–1063.

[43] B. Teitelbaum, S. Hares, L. Dunn *et al.* (1999). Internet2 qbone: Building a testbed for differentiated services. *IEEE Network*, *13*(5), 8–16.

[44] A. Vieira (2016). Predicting online user behaviour using deep learning algorithms. *arXiv:1511.06247 [cs.LG]*.

[45] W. Wang, Y. Bai, C. Yu *et al.* (2018). A network traffic flow prediction with deep learning approach for large-scale metropolitan area network. In *NOMS 2018-2018 IEEE/IFIP Network Operations and Management Symposium*, pp. 1–9. IEEE.

[46] R. Wolski, N. T. Spring, and J. Hayes (1999). The network weather service: A distributed resource performance forecasting service for metacomputing. *Future Generation Computer Systems*, *15*(5-6), 757–768. http://dx.doi.org/10.1016/S0167-739X(99)00025-4.

[47] X. Yang, T. Lehman, R. Kettimuthu *et al.* (2018). A model driven intelligent orchestration approach to service automation in large distributed infrastructures. In *Proceedings of the 1st International Workshop on Autonomous Infrastructure for Science*, AI-Science'18 (Association for Computing Machinery, New York, NY, USA), ISBN 9781450358620. https://doi.org/10.1145/3217197.3217207.

[48] W. Yoo and A. Sim (2016). Time-series forecast modeling on high-bandwidth network measurements. *Journal of Grid Computing*, *14*(3), 463–476. http://dx.doi.org/10.1007/s10723-016-9368-9.

[49] C. Zhu, H. Leung, S. Hu *et al.* (2019). A Q-values sharing framework for multiple independent Q-learners. In *International Conference on Autonomous Agents and MultiAgent Systems*, pp. 2324–2326. ISBN 978-1-4503-6309-9. http://dl.acm.org/citation.cfm?id=3306127.3332099.

[50] T. Tedeschi, M. Tracolli, D. Ciangottini *et al.* (2021). Reinforcement Learning for Smart Caching at the CMS experiment, International Symposium on Grids & Clouds 2021 (ISGC2021) — Data Management & Big Data, 378.

© 2023 World Scientific Publishing Company
https://doi.org/10.1142/9789811265679_0032

Chapter 32

AI for Optimal Experimental Design
and Decision-Making

Francis J. Alexander*,§, Kristofer-Roy Reyes†,¶, Lav R. Varshney*,‖, and
Byung-Jun Yoon‡,**

*Brookhaven National Laboratory, Upton, NY 11973, USA
†University at Buffalo, Buffalo, NY 14260, USA
‡Texas A&M University, College Station, TX 77843, USA
§falexander@bnl.gov
¶kreyes@buffalo.edu
‖lvarshney@bnl.gov
**bjyoon@tamu.edu

1. Introduction

High-performance (near exascale) computing, natural language processing (NLP), artificial intelligence/machine learning (AI/ML) methods, experiments with exquisite accuracy, and collaborative tools have afforded substantial mechanisms for the continued advancement of modern science and engineering, often at an unprecedented pace.

Yet, despite these notable technological advances and the speeds at which they have been derived, modern science and engineering are now facing serious challenges in their ability to innovate at the momentum needed to provide tangible impacts. One of these challenges stems from the need to tackle problems that increasingly are larger scale and more complex than ever. Although there are exponentially growing amounts of data (e.g., in absolute terms of bytes), the quantity of *relevant* data often remains sparse relative to the problems at hand. Climate, urban systems, cancer, and other biological and health-related areas are among the many examples where problem complexity often exceeds the amount of *relevant* data available. Also, model development for complex systems — perhaps, more importantly, model validation — faces serious hurdles. Just as scientists are trying to comprehend more subtle and challenging scientific knowledge, claims are becoming less trusted, further complicating matters. Alarms of a "crisis in science" have been raised, necessitating reliable methods for reproducibility, explainability, and even trust in resources. It seems paradoxical that even with exquisite experiments, computational resources, large data, and advanced analysis tools available, science is experiencing a complicated convergence of obstacles that are impeding the continued effective rate of progress.

The hypothetico-deductive approach to scientific research (i.e., experimental hypothesis-testing process) that has accounted for the spectacular advances in science and led to multiple technological marvels largely has taken shape over the last five centuries [1]. By all accounts, this approach has proven a resounding success embodied by trust in peer-reviewed science and formal institutions, such as learned societies [2]. This "institutional trust" has enabled the scaling of the scientific enterprise beyond small groups of scientists [3] to large international collaborations. Still, this traditional framework may prove insufficient when faced with a variety of modern challenges.

An additional challenge is that of reduced "effective" productivity — a measure that factors in all of the aforementioned advances in experimental capacity, computational capability, etc. The number of disruptive papers [4] and novel concepts produced per unit cost [5] has tapered off. The scientific community's response to the COVID-19 pandemic has brought these issues to the fore. Under pressure, scientists and institutions are bypassing their prevailing practices [6]. The needed structural changes in the scientific foundation have not been made.

Nevertheless, we foresee these challenges as surmountable. Novel cognitive and communication tools have the ability to accelerate scientific progress. Breakthroughs in communication have changed scientists' cognitive and collaborative processes. Modern statistical and computational tools have enabled discovery within large datasets, and AI technologies are poised to suggest novel hypotheses [7]. We propose the application of a Bayesian approach — a **Bayesian Update** — coupled with these new tools to ameliorate the limitations of the hypothetico-deductive approach, making it more responsive for 21st-century problems and applications.

Science and engineering efforts commonly encounter sparse, noisy, and heterogeneous data, information, and/or knowledge sources. To deal with this, we first must integrate these data in an uncertainty-aware way, i.e., the *Bayesian Update* part: some posterior distribution obtained on conditioning whatever data/knowledge we can find and encode. Second, we acknowledge that the objective is not building AI models. Instead, it is to **do science or engineering**. As such, we have to take actions and/or make decisions using these posteriors with specific objectives in mind while being aware of the uncertainties contained therein.

Scientific knowledge is not immutable and continually evolves as new investigations are conducted. The same empirical results may be interpreted by different scientists variously if they have differing priors. Here, we argue that crowdsourcing and semi-automated annotation of metadata with findings could allow for the Bayesian Update of facts from throughout the scientific literature. In fact, meta-analyses may be automated from raw data directly or by using AI techniques to read papers and perform such analyses. This type of constant assessment and incorporation of new results can accelerate science.

In what follows, we will offer a vision of how the *Bayesian Update* approach to scientific modeling, coupled with advances in AI/ML and NLP, can address the aforementioned challenges to continued useful innovation. This work describes how to convert scientific knowledge into an optimal prior. As complex systems (climate, health, and networked systems) generically are highly uncertain, we provide a brief description of decision-making under uncertainty (DMU), as well as the concept of optimal experimental design (OED) under uncertainty. These processes are crucial to drive and propel the scientific cycle. We further detail a path to incorporate computational creativity algorithms into the scientific process through automated hypothesis generation, in a way not just updating probabilities but expanding possibilities.

2. Bayesian Approach

When thinking about how we can effectively apply AI/ML to science, perhaps it is best to distill the key processes underpinning the scientific endeavor. When studying some system or phenomenon, we use prior knowledge and preliminary data to form a scientific hypothesis and then design experiments to test such a hypothesis. Key to the progress of science is the acknowledgment that such hypotheses are just that — uncertain guesses of the ground truth based on limited and incomplete prior knowledge. Science advances when outcomes of experiments lead us to either (1) confirm the hypothesis (that is, decrease our uncertainty in our guesses) or (2) change our hypotheses and our interpretation of prior knowledge to incorporate the new data obtained from experiments.

This procedure — where prior knowledge begets hypotheses we test via experiments, the outcomes of which impact our understanding of the system of interest — fits naturally within a Bayesian perspective. In this perspective, we model imperfect knowledge and uncertainties about the system under study through probability distributions. These distributions capture Bayesian beliefs about the validity of scientific knowledge. They measure (in a strict sense) confidence about hypotheses of this ground truth. For any hypothesis and experimental observations, we can also model the observations' likelihood for the given hypothesis. Together, we can rigorously combine prior beliefs about the ground truth along with this likelihood to refine our beliefs. This Bayesian Update of our beliefs in light of new data emerges from Bayes' law, the central equation of the Bayesian method:

$$p(H|\mathcal{O}) = \frac{p(\mathcal{O}|H)}{p(\mathcal{O})}p(H).$$

Here, H represents a specific hypothesis and $\mathcal{O}$ is the experimental observation. The probability $p(H)$ is the prior probability of the hypothesis H before making observations $\mathcal{O}$, while $p(H|\mathcal{O})$ is the updated or posterior probability that integrates the prior with the data. The likelihood $p(\mathcal{O}|H)$ represents the probability of observing the given observations under the assumption that the hypothesis H is true. The probability $p(\mathcal{O})$, often called the evidence, is the total probability of observing the data under any hypothesis.

In addition to a Bayesian perspective in modeling and updating beliefs about the ground truth, a critical step in the scientific method is proposing experiments to confirm or reject hypotheses. Within the Bayesian perspective, this process is one of decision-making or experimental design under uncertainty, where we capture uncertainties in Bayesian beliefs. Methods to select experiments to run in the presence of uncertainties must, at a minimum, balance the expected utility of running specific experiments with resolving uncertainties inherent in any such utility measure given our imperfect knowledge of the ground truth.

Thus, within this Bayesian perspective, when considering the necessary tasks in which mathematical modeling, statistics, and AI can help, we may enumerate them as follows:

(1) encoding or parameterizing what a hypothesis is and describing a probability measure around the space of such hypotheses,
(2) developing a likelihood model to measure observations (however they are represented) against specific hypotheses,
(3) calculating, approximating, sampling, or otherwise characterizing the posterior distribution (which can be a computationally expensive task),
(4) encoding or parameterizing the space of feasible experimental actions we may take to obtain further observations,
(5) making optimal decisions of such actions under the uncertainty encoded by our Bayesian beliefs.

The act of encoding hypotheses is typically tantamount to identifying what quantities are unknown about the system under study. We model probability measures on such quantities in the Bayesian perspective, so a proper and efficient representation of hypotheses is essential. Here, we use "quantities" in a broad sense and state that they can include the following: from a finite collection of unknown physical parameters, experimental response function viewed as a black box, the "right-hand side" of a system's governing equations, to even encoding unidentified semantic connections between posited phenomena and processes which could potentially explain observable responses.

Similarly, encoding experimental actions requires proper and efficient representation. Sometimes, actions and hypotheses are modeled jointly, as is the case of representing an observable response as a function of such actions. In this case, dimensionality reduction and latent-space methods are proving fruitful. With such methods, latent, machine-learned vector-space representations serve as the requisite encoding of actions, while black box statistical models such as Gaussian processes model beliefs on response functions over such latent representations.

Another place we can bring AI/ML methods to bear within this Bayesian perspective is by developing surrogate forward models. Such models map actions and hypotheses to digital twins of observable responses. We can leverage ML regression/classification models to build such digital twins here. We can then use these twins in likelihood calculation, sampling from posterior distributions, and decision-making, where we often perform forward simulations to select experiments that yield high utility on average.

Above, we have given a brief glimpse of the interface between AI/ML and a Bayesian-oriented approach to science. In the following, we will expand on a few points along this interface, including how prior knowledge is captured and encoded and how Bayesian decision-making algorithms select experimental actions to gather additional, information-rich data.

3. Prior Construction

Given a specific representation of the unknown quantities of the system under study, i.e., a representation of hypotheses on some unknown ground truth, we may consider how to incorporate and fuse a heterogeneous set of known or assumed properties of the system. This prior knowledge can come from various sources, including existing data from related systems or tasks, assumptions about the relationships underpinning the complex system under study, or from domain expert opinion. A crucial task is encoding this prior knowledge for subsequent use in Bayesian models and decision-making. This process of prior construction is synonymous with how we do science in general: no scientist forms hypotheses in absolute ignorance but instead makes an educated guess based on their experience and implicit assumptions about the system under study. Similarly, we must rigorously encode prior knowledge and assumptions through the Bayesian prior distribution $p(H)$ for our Bayesian models.

There are several prior construction methods available. Indeed, reasonable priors are the crux of effective Bayesian methods. Consequently, priors are often the target of scrutiny when examining the predictions made by Bayesian models or decisions made by algorithms that use such models. There has been a strong focus on Bayesian prior construction, and the focus has generally split between two competing dogmas. First is objective Bayesianism, which (in broad strokes) attempts to limit what assumptions the prior encodes. To an objective Bayesian, priors exist to be as broad as possible. In this camp, people often speak of non-informative priors which satisfy the maximum entropy principle.

On the other end of the spectrum is subjective Bayesianism. With subjective Bayesian statistics, priors exist to encode what is known or assumed about the systems we study. This knowledge or these assumptions are often subjective, often explicitly coded into the models by the statistician or domain scientist. With subjective Bayesian priors, we have other tools available to capture and encode such knowledge and assumptions. Bayesian transfer learning can help build priors from data for related systems or tasks. Statistical elicitation methods can model domain expert knowledge. Other methods (such as the MKDIP method described in the following) allow us to encode more complex assumptions of our system (such as semantic information). The use of such external sources of information is especially essential in scientific applications where direct experimental data are limited. As such, we are strong advocates for the subjective Bayesian school and illustrate two example methods in the following.

3.1. *Expert elicitation*

One source for prior information is the human, in our case, a domain expert scientist. In general, the act of modeling and transforming what a human knows — including knowledge representation, unstructured information, cognitive models, and accounting for human fallacy — is a daunting task. The aim of statistical elicitation is to pose well-defined, structured questions to a domain expert, obtain similarly well-defined answers, and (for our purposes) use the answers to form a Bayesian prior. Discussions involved during statistical elicitation can be as broad as specifying problem definition, identifying quantities of interest, quantifying expert biases, or extracting a probability distribution from the expert [8,9].

For example, one generic elicitation procedure attempts to build a multivariate probability distribution on a finite number of quantities $\theta_1, \theta_2, \ldots, \theta_n$ [10]. Such quantities could represent, e.g., unknown parameters to a physical model or experimental responses at a fixed and finite set of "inputs". Questions posed to the domain experts ask the experts to estimate specific marginal distributions:

$$\mathbb{P}\left(\theta_1 \in [a_1, b_1], \ldots \theta_n \in [a_n, b_n]\right) = A.$$

Answers to such questions represent a domain expert's opinion that the quantities lie within a hyperinterval $[a_1, b_1] \times \cdots \times [a_n, b_n]$. We may then aggregate answers to several such questions, each with a different hyperinterval, to characterize a distribution on the θ_i values. While a closed-form formula does not exist, we can obtain a regression estimate of this distribution's probability density function, sufficient to describe the distribution.

The compilation of this distribution from the data is itself a Bayesian procedure. A non-informative prior for this distribution is combined with expert answers to form a posterior distribution, the average of which is the regression estimate of the PDF. The posterior of the elicitation procedure serves as an informative prior distribution for use in subsequent modeling or decision-making. Indeed, under this perspective, the act of acquiring information from the domain expert is not particularly distinguished from acquiring information from physical experiments — both are viewed as information-generating processes that we can incorporate within our Bayesian perspective.

This perspective allows us to envision incorporating such elicitation procedures with Bayesian decision-making. We can, for example, use methods in optimal experimental design to design informationally optimal questions to pose to the domain expert. Alternatively, we can view elicitation within a broader experimental campaign, one of several information sources a decision-making algorithm selects from to obtain data.

3.2. *Knowledge-based prior construction*

While it may be practically impossible to learn a model that accurately represents a complex system under scientific investigation solely from data, there may be prior scientific knowledge relevant to the system that may be used to tighten the uncertainty of the model. Although such knowledge may be partial and incomplete, it may nevertheless effectively complement the available data for learning or constraining the model. For example, suppose one wants to infer the gene regulatory network from gene expression data. Even for well-studied and relatively simple model organisms such as *Escherichia coli* (gut bacteria) and *Saccharomyces cerevisiae* (baker's yeast), inferring the regulatory relations among thousands of genes from gene expression data (typically obtained from microarrays or RNA sequencing) is very challenging. Partial regulatory relations among subsets of genes, typically captured by the so-called pathway diagrams, may be used to guide or constrain the network inference process thereby improving the quality of the learned network.

Although it is not uncommon that such prior knowledge is used in a heuristic manner to enhance model inference, it is also possible to take advantage of the available scientific knowledge to construct a prior distribution that represents the model uncertainty in a Bayesian paradigm. One notable example is the maximal knowledge-driven information prior (MKDIP) proposed by Boluki *et al.* [11,12]. In this work, the authors proposed a general method for constructing the prior for the feature-label distribution that governs the condition-dependent gene expression. For this purpose, gene regulatory relations in a genetic pathway are used to define a set of constraints in the form of conditional probability statements, which are then used to construct the optimal prior based on a specific criterion (e.g., Maximum-Entropy, Maximum Data Information, and Expected Mean Log-Likelihood) that obeys the constraints at hand. The efficacy of MKDIP was demonstrated by constructing priors using genetic pathway knowledge (e.g., mammalian cell-cycle pathway and p53 pathway) and utilizing the constructed priors for optimal Bayesian classification (OBC). Results showed that MKDIP clearly outperforms other existing prior construction methods when such prior knowledge is available.

While MKDIP mainly considered relational knowledge in the form of genetic pathways for prior construction and applied the resulting prior to classification, the theory is fairly general going beyond the examples considered in the original work [11]. We envision that a similar knowledge-based prior construction method may be used to translate various types of prior knowledge available in diverse science domains into effective Bayesian priors that can enhance learning and decision-making based on complex uncertain systems.

4. Decision-Making under Uncertainty

The Bayesian perspective allows us to encode what we know and what we do not through uncertainty quantification. Through Bayesian priors, we can measure the plausibility over a family of scientific hypotheses, though how the priors measure this plausibility depends strongly on the representation of such hypotheses. We must engage in experiments and specifically decide which experimental actions to perform to test such hypotheses. Our Bayesian perspective can assist us in this task. Coupled with a forward model (physics-based or a ML model) that maps actions and hypotheses to predicted observable outcomes, Bayesian beliefs on hypotheses induce beliefs on outcomes for any given action. That is, uncertainties in hypotheses yield uncertainties in experimental outcomes.

By characterizing the utility of any particular outcome, we can encode the objectives of a campaign. The induced distribution of outcomes further induces a distribution on utility on such outcomes. That is, a given tentative action and a distribution on hypotheses yield a distribution on outcomes, which in turn yields a distribution on the utility of that experiment. A reasonable decision-making strategy is to select the actions that maximize this utility on average. Of course, computing this average utility per action and maximizing this over the space of actions could be computationally intensive. Here, ML/AI can offer its assistance through ML surrogates of the forward model, utility function, or the decision policy function (here viewed as a function that maps beliefs to a selected optimal action).

The utility assigned to an experimental outcome captures the objectives of performing experiments. For example, suppose the goal of an experiment is to decrease uncertainties about hypotheses globally. In that case, we may imagine prescribing a utility based on how much a potential experiment can change our beliefs overall. If x is an experimental action and $\mathcal{O}_x$ is the outcome of the experiment, we can form the Bayesian posterior $f(H|\mathcal{O}_x)$ via Bayes' law. We can then compare some measure of the difference between this posterior and prior, such as the Kullback–Leibler divergence, to measure the utility of performing experiment x and observing outcome $\mathcal{O}_x$:

$$Q(x, \mathcal{O}(x)) = D_{\mathrm{KL}}\left[f(H|\mathcal{O}_x), f(H)\right].$$

Then, the average utility for any given experimental action x is just the weighted average of this utility over outcomes $\mathcal{O}_x$:

$$\bar{Q}(x) = \mathbb{E}\left[Q(x, \mathcal{O}_x)\right].$$

Here, the expectation is the weighted average over outcomes, where the outcomes are obtained from the distribution of outcomes induced by the prior beliefs on hypotheses. A decision-making policy would then select the experiment that maximizes this expected utility: $x^\star = \max_{x \in X} \bar{Q}(x)$.

Often, refining beliefs and globally reducing uncertainties is not the true objective of an experimental campaign. For example, we may wish to identify a set of experiments that maximize some response, say in an engineering application. We may instead want to learn some low-dimensional features about a response function. A mismatch between the true campaign objectives with those encoded in the utility could lead to inefficient decision-making. Therefore, it is essential to correctly model objectives within a utility function. In Section 5, we outline a method that selects experiments that resolve uncertainties in this objective-driven manner.

Up to now, we have been abstract in how we view experimental actions. Yet, the choice of parameterization or representation of actions is crucial for developing forward models and effective decision-making policies. In the simplest case, actions can encode the settings of tunable knobs to a fixed, well-defined experimental protocol, such as temperatures, pressures, and concentrations. However, actions can model broader definitions of an "experiment" through proper parameterization. For example, we may encode a choice between running a physical experiment, performing a simulation, searching the literature, or querying a domain expert — viewing such examples as information-generating processes. In addition, the actions can model a choice of experimental technique, such as choosing a characterization or analysis method to characterize a material. We hope to convey the flexibility of this Bayesian-driven decision-making through this broader perspective.

5. Optimal Experimental Design

5.1. *Objective-based uncertainty quantification*

Scientific problems often involve complex systems whose complexity may be far "bigger" than any "big" data that may be available for investigating the system. For such systems, it will be practically impossible to construct accurate models — from data, and possibly using relevant prior system knowledge that may exist in the domain — that faithfully represent the given systems in all aspects. Uncertainty in the learned model is inevitable, requiring effective strategies for quantifying, handling, and reducing uncertainty. The concept of objective-based uncertainty quantification (objective UQ) via mean objective cost of uncertainty (MOCU) [13,14] provides effective means for coping with uncertainty in complex systems by focusing on understanding the nature and impact of the model uncertainty on the scientific or engineering objectives it serves. For example, one may aim to design a novel material with a desired property using an uncertain model that describes the structure—property—function relationships. Or one may be interested in modeling the gene regulatory network with the goal of designing robust intervention strategies based on the model to beneficially alter the dynamics and future trajectories of the genetic network. A relevant real-world example would be designing a robust and effective Dynamic

Treatment Regimes that could enhance patient outcomes for a complex disease such as cancer. When there is model uncertainty, we may want to design a robust operator (e.g., predictor, controller, and classifier) that is expected to maintain reasonably good performance despite the uncertainty rather than designing an operator that may be optimal for a specific model but whose performance may significantly degrade in case of model mismatch. Consequently, model uncertainty leads to an increase in the operational cost due to having to use the optimal robust operator (with the best expected performance across all possible models) rather than the optimal operator for the true model (which is unknown). MOCU calculates this additional cost induced by model uncertainty, thereby quantifying the impact of model uncertainty on the operational objective at hand.

5.2. *Design of optimal experiments for effective reduction of model uncertainty*

From a practical point of view, the main significance of a metric for objective-based quantification of uncertainty lies in its utility for devising effective data or knowledge acquisition strategies for model improvement. Consider the problem of active learning, where one can actively select new data points to be labeled. Or consider the case when a domain scientist can pick the next experiment among a set of possible experiments to improve the model. How can one design the best data or knowledge acquisition scheme that can enhance the present model in the most cost-effective manner? An effective strategy that would lead to the best model improvement on average would be to evaluate the available options based on their expected efficacy in reducing the model uncertainty that "matters" and select the option with the highest predicted efficacy. For example, we may evaluate the efficacy of a given experiment by computing the MOCU that is expected to remain after performing the experiment and incorporating its outcomes. Among all possible experiments, we should select the one with the smallest expected remaining MOCU, as it is expected to maximally reduce the objective model uncertainty. In fact, MOCU has been shown to be very effective for optimal experimental design [15–19] and active learning [20–22], clearly demonstrating the power of "objective-based" UQ in making robust decisions regarding data/knowledge acquisition that enables effective learning.

Figure 1 illustrates a general optimal experimental design (OED) loop. The prior distribution that governs the model uncertainty may be constructed via expert elicitation (described in Section 3.1) or MKDIP (elaborated in Section 3.2). The constructed prior can be subsequently used for robust decision-making in the presence of uncertainty. Furthermore,

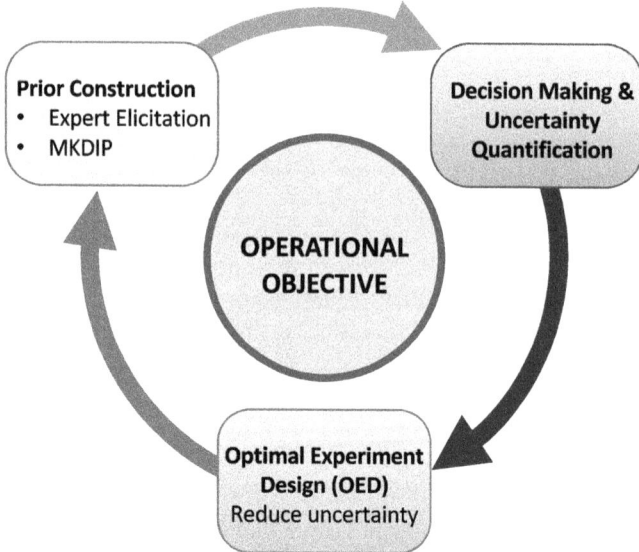

Fig. 1.   Illustration of a general optimal experimental design (OED) cycle.

we may quantify the impact of this model uncertainty on the operational objective via MOCU [13,14]. Note that MOCU estimation also involves the design of the optimal operator that is robust to the uncertainty at hand. Experiments in the design space can be prioritized based on the expected efficacy of each experiment for reducing the model uncertainty and enhancing the performance of the optimal robust operator (or decision-making). The knowledge (or data) acquired by performing the predicted optimal experiment can be used to update the prior (or obtain the posterior), and the OED loop may be iterated as desired within the given time/resource constraints, if any.

5.3. *An example: Optimal experimental design for gene regulatory networks*

Consider a gene regulatory network (GRN), where some of the regulatory relations are uncertain. If our operational objective is to perform network intervention to minimize the steady-state probability mass at phenotypically undesirable states, which uncertain relations should we aim to experimentally uncover first? Previous studies [15,16] investigated this problem based on the MOCU-based OED scheme elaborated in Section 5.2.

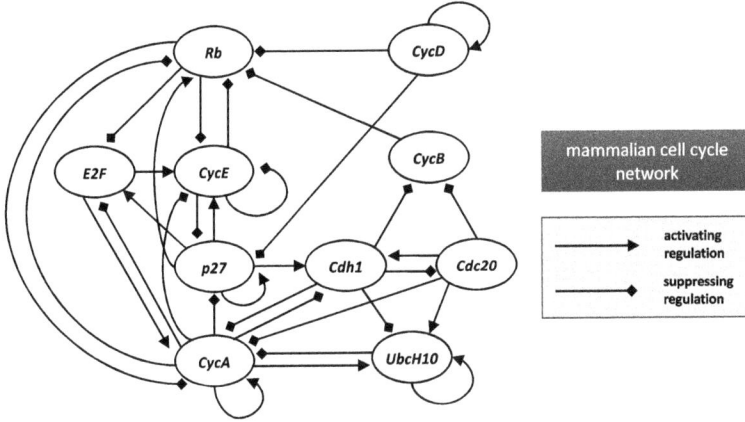

Fig. 2. A gene regulatory network (GRN) model representing the mammalian cell cycle. The nodes represent genes and the arrows indicate gene regulations. (Image adapted from [14]).

Suppose we would like to perform the optimal network intervention in the mammalian cell cycle network [23] shown in Figure 2 in the presence of model uncertainty. The network consists of 10 genes (i.e., CycD, Rb, p27, E2F, CycE, CycA, Cdc20, Cdh1, UbcH10, and CycB) represented as nodes in Figure 2, where the edges connecting the nodes depict regulatory relations between the genes. Pointed arrows represent activating gene regulations and blunt arrows represent suppressing regulations. The dynamics of this network can be modeled using a Boolean network with perturbation (BNp) [16]. States with down-regulated CycD, Rb, and p27 ($X_1 = X_2 = X_3 = 0$) may be considered as undesirable states, representing cancerous phenotypes, as they lead to continuous cell cycles even in the absence of extra-cellular stimuli.

Now, if the type of regulation (activation vs. suppression) is uncertain for a number of edges in the GRN shown in Figure 2 and if one can perform a series of experiments, each of which can unveil the type of a given gene regulation, how should one prioritize the experiments? In [16], MOCU-based OED strategy was used to prioritize the experiments based on their expected impact on enhancing the network intervention performance. The study showed that for the simplest case of $k = 2$ uncertain regulations (hence only two possible experiments to choose from), the OED scheme was capable of finding an experiment that was as effective as or outperformed the other (unselected) experiment 76% of the times. As the model uncertainty increased, the experiment selected by the OED scheme outperformed the other alternatives with a higher probability. For example, for $k = 5$ uncertain regulations, the optimal experiment predicted to be most effective outperformed (was at least as effective as) the experiment predicted to be least effective 68% of the times (90% of the times) on average.

6. Conclusion: From Refining Probabilities to Expanding Possibilities

Thus far we have discussed settings where the pieces of scientific inquiry are already on the game board, and we aim to conduct experiments to reduce uncertainty/gain information about them. But what about unseen elements? Scientific exploration is concerned not just with experiments to refine beliefs but also with the discovery of new mammalian species, chemical elements, and exoplanets [24,25]. Much creative work in engineering and also in science is concerned with generating new elements that are (Bayesian) surprising [26–28] and have never been imagined before, now often with cognitive support from computational creativity and generative artificial intelligence algorithms [29–31].

As in [32,33], imagine preparing for a journey of discovery where one may estimate the probabilities of encountering different mammalian species: perhaps initially assigning probability 1/2 to elephants, 1/6 to zebras, and 1/3 to lions. But what about some new category or species of mammal that has never been seen: perhaps to be called a nyala. How would a Bayesian approach be developed here [34]?

To address this unseen elements problem, Laplace proposed adding 1 to the count of each species, including to the collection of unseen ones [35], thereby assigning probability $(3 + 1)/10 = 0.4$ to elephants, $(1 + 1)/10 = 0.2$ to zebras, $(2 + 1)/10 = 0.3$ to lions, and $(0 + 1)/10 = 0.1$ to unseen species. The Laplace and other add-constant estimators [36] correspond to the expected value of the posterior distribution, using a symmetric Dirichlet distribution with parameter as the add-constant as a prior distribution from a Bayesian point of view.

Such add-constant estimators, however, are not effective in settings with a very large possible space of discovery; instead, it is common to use techniques like the Good-Turing (GT) estimator [32,33]. The GT framework assigns unseen elements a probability proportional to the number of events with a single appearance in the sample. Bayesian non-parametric estimation of the discovery probabilities corresponds to GT estimation under priors of a superpopulation with two-parameter Poisson–Dirichlet distribution [37].

Going forward, it will be of interest to connect the unseen elements estimation framework to MOCU, in characterizing how to balance pursuing new possibilities with refining uncertain probabilities for efficient but serendipitous scientific discovery. This will allow the overall process to be effectively guided by the main objective(s) of the scientific investigation at hand.

Acknowledgments

We would like to thank Edward R. Dougherty, Charity Plata, and Xiaoning Qian for extremely helpful discussions and helping us clarify the ideas presented here. The work of F. J. Alexander and B. J. Yoon was supported by the U.S. Department of Energy, Office of Science, Office of Advanced Scientific Computing Research, Mathematical Multifaceted Integrated Capability Centers program under Award DE-SC0019303.

References

[1] S. Shapin and S. Schaffer (1986). *Leviathan and the Air-Pump: Hobbes, Boyle, and the Experimental Life*. Princeton University Press, Princeton, NJ, USA.

[2] J. McClellan (2003). Scientific institutions and the organization of science. In R. Porter, (ed.), *The Cambridge History of Science*. Cambridge: Cambridge University Press, Vol. 4, pp. 87–106.

[3] R. Netz (1999). *The Shaping of Deduction in Greek Mathematics: A Study in Cognitive History*. Cambridge: Cambridge University Press.

[4] L. Wu, D. Wang, and J. A. Evans (2019). Large teams develop and small teams disrupt science and technology. *Nature, 566*(7744), 378–382.

[5] S. Fortunato, C. T. Bergstrom, K. Börner *et al.* (2018). Science of science. *Science, 359*(6379), eaao0185.

[6] M. Apuzzo and D. D. Kirkpatrick (2020). Racing for cure, scientists unite in global effort. *New York Times, 58*(651), A1–A10.

[7] T. Lookman, S. Eidenbenz, F. Alexander *et al.* (2018). *Materials Discovery and Design: By Means of Data Science and Optimal Learning*. Springer, Cham, Switzerland.

[8] T. O'Hagan (2005). Elicitation. *Significance, 2*(2), 84–86.

[9] A. O'Hagan (2019). Expert knowledge elicitation: Subjective but scientific. *The American Statistician, 73*(sup 1), 69–81.

[10] F. A. Moala and A. O'Hagan (2010). Elicitation of multivariate prior distributions: A nonparametric bayesian approach. *Journal of Statistical Planning and Inference, 140*(7), 1635–1655.

[11] S. Boluki, M. S. Esfahani, X. Qian, *et al.* (2017a). Incorporating biological prior knowledge for bayesian learning via maximal knowledge-driven information priors. *BMC Bioinformatics, 18*(14), 61–80.

[12] S. Boluki, M. S. Esfahani, X. Qian, *et al.* (2017b). Constructing pathway-based priors within a gaussian mixture model for Bayesian regression and classification. *IEEE/ACM Transactions on Computational Biology and Bioinformatics, 16*(2), 524–537.

[13] B. J. Yoon, X. Qian, and E. R. Dougherty (2013). Quantifying the objective cost of uncertainty in complex dynamical systems. *IEEE Transactions on Signal Processing, 61*(9), 2256–2266.

[14] B. J. Yoon, X. Qian, and E. R. Dougherty (2021). Quantifying the multi-objective cost of uncertainty. *IEEE Access, 9*, 80351–80359.

[15] R. Dehghannasiri, B. J. Yoon, and E. R. Dougherty (2015a). Efficient experimental design for uncertainty reduction in gene regulatory networks. *BMC Bioinformatics, 16*(13), S2.

[16] B. J. Yoon, X. Qian, and E. R. Dougherty (2015b). Optimal experimental design for gene regulatory networks in the presence of uncertainty. *IEEE/ACM Transactions on Computational Biology and Bioinformatics (TCBB), 12*(4), 938–950.

[17] G. Zhao, X. Qian, B. J. Yoon *et al.* (2020). Model-based robust filtering and experimental design for stochastic differential equation systems. *IEEE Transactions on Signal Processing, 68*, 3849–3859.

[18] Y. Hong, B. Kwon, and B. J. Yoon (2021). Optimal experimental design for uncertain systems based on coupled differential equations. *IEEE Access, 9*, 53804–53810.

[19] H. M. Woo, Y. Hong, B. Kwon *et al.* (2021). Accelerating optimal experimental design for robust synchronization of uncertain kuramoto oscillator model using machine learning. *IEEE Transactions on Signal Processing, 69*, 6473–6487.

[20] G. Zhao, E. R. Dougherty, B. J. Yoon *et al.* (2021a). Uncertainty-aware active learning for optimal Bayesian classifier. In *9th International Conference on Learning Representations (ICLR)*.

[21] G. Zhao, E. R. Dougherty, B. J. Yoon *et al.* (2021b). Bayesian active learning by soft mean objective cost of uncertainty. In *24th International Conference on Artificial Intelligence and Statistics (AISTATS)*.

[22] G. Zhao, E. R. Dougherty, B. J. Yoon *et al.* (2021c). Efficient active learning for gaussian process classification by error reduction. In *35th Conference on Neural Information Processing Systems*.

[23] A. Fauré, A. Naldi, C. Chaouiya *et al.* (2006). Dynamical analysis of a generic boolean model for the control of the mammalian cell cycle. *Bioinformatics, 22*(14), e124–e131.

[24] S. Arbesman and N. A. Christakis (2011). Eurekometrics: Analyzing the nature of discovery. *PLoS Computational Biology, 7*(6), e1002072.

[25] A. Vempaty, L. R. Varshney, and P. K. Varshney (2017). A coupon-collector model of machine-aided discovery. In *KDD Workshop on Data-Driven Discovery*, Halifax, Canada.

[26] L. Itti and P. Baldi (2009). Bayesian surprise attracts human attention. *Vision Research, 49*(10), 1295–1306.

[27] L. R. Varshney (2013). To surprise and inform. In *Proceedings of the 2013 IEEE International Symposium on Information Theory (ISIT)*, July, pp. 3145–3149.

[28] J. G. Foster, F. Shi, and J. Evans (2021). Surprise! Measuring novelty as expectation violation. SocArXiv 10.31235/osf.io/2t46f.

[29] L. R. Varshney, F. Pinel, K. R. Varshney *et al.* (2019). A big data approach to computational creativity: The curious case of Chef Watson. *IBM Journal of Research and Development, 63*(1), 7:1–7:18.

[30] L. R. Varshney (2019). Mathematical limit theorems for computational creativity. *IBM Journal of Research and Development, 63*(1), 2:1–2:12.

[31] P. Das and L. R. Varshney (2022). Explaining AI generation and creativity. *IEEE Signal Processing Magazine*, to appear.

[32] I. J. Good (1953). The population frequencies of species and the estimation of population parameters. *Biometrika, 40*(3-4), 237–264.

[33] A. Orlitsky, N. P. Santhanam, and J. Zhang (2003). Always Good Turing: Asymptotically optimal probability estimation. *Science, 302*(5644), 427–431.

[34] D. J. Navarro and C. Kemp (2017). None of the above: A Bayesian account of the detection of novel categories. *Psychological Review, 124*(5), 643–677.

[35] M. De Laplace (1995). *A Philosophical Essay on Probabilities.* New York, NY, USA: Springer-Verlag, a. I. Dale, translated from ed. 5, 1825.

[36] R. E. Krichevsky and V. K. Trofimov (1981). The performance of universal encoding. *IEEE Transactions on Information Theory, IT-27*(2), 199–207, March.

[37] A. Cerquetti (2019). Exact Good-Turing characterization of the two-parameter Poisson-Dirichlet superpopulation model. *arXiv:1901.09665 [math.ST]*.

© 2023 World Scientific Publishing Company
https://doi.org/10.1142/9789811265679_0033

Chapter 33

FAIR: Making Data AI-Ready

Susanna-Assunta Sansone*,§, Philippe Rocca-Serra*,¶, Mark Wilkinson†,‖,
and Lee Harland‡,**

*Data Readiness Group, Oxford e-Research Centre, Department of
Engineering Science, University of Oxford, UK
†Departamento de Biotecnología-Biología Vegetal, Escuela Técnica
Superior de Ingeniería Agronómica, Alimentaria y de Biosistemas, Centro
de Biotecnología y Genómica de Plantas. Universidad Politécnica de
Madrid (UPM) – Instituto Nacional de Investigación y Tecnología Agraria
y Alimentaria-CSIC (INIA-CSIC). Campus Montegancedo 28223 Pozuelo
de Alarcón (Madrid), Spain
‡SciBite Limited, Cambridge, UK
§susanna-assunta.sansone@oerc.ox.ac.uk
¶philippe.rocca-serra@oerc.ox.ac.uk
‖mark.wilkinson@upm.es
**lee@scibite.com

1. The FAIR Principles: A Prerequisite for Data Science

Effective and trustworthy data-driven science requires the use of data at
scale and a transition from the current closed and silo-based approaches to
research towards more networked scholarship. However, the vast majority
of public domain data, which include datasets, code, algorithms, workflows,
models, and software, is still not reusable, for a number of reasons. This
is mainly because the data are poorly described for third-party use. Data
still require a substantial amount of preparation before the researchers can
even begin to use them and answer sophisticated research questions. In
2016, a group of internationally recognized leaders in data management co-
authored the FAIR Principles — a set of guiding principles to ensure that
contemporary data resources and scholarly output are Findable, Accessible,
Interoperable, and Reusable (FAIR) [1]. The FAIR Principles, simplified in

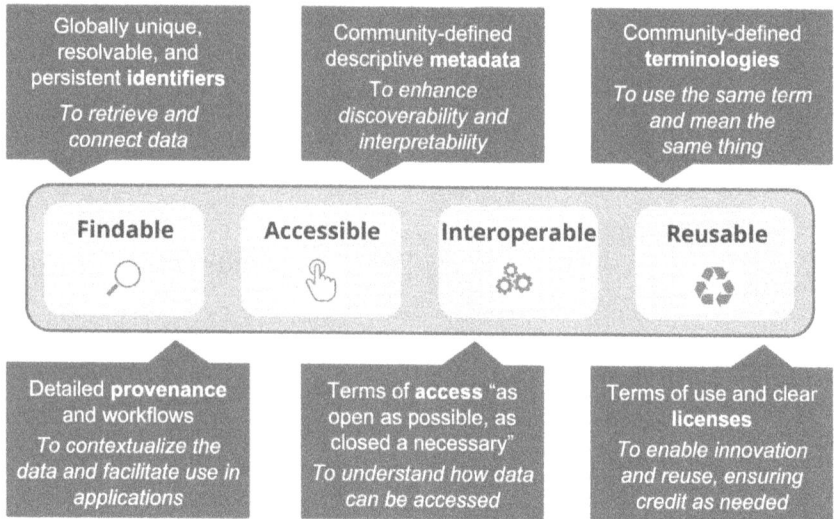

Fig. 1.   The FAIR principles in a nutshell.

Figure 1, put specific emphasis on enhancing the ability of machines to automatically find and use the data, in addition to supporting its reuse by individuals.

As we begin to invest heavily in extracting value from data, FAIR is no longer optional. FAIR data are essential to enable powerful new AI analytics to access data for Machine Learning (ML) and prediction. Machine-readable and actionable FAIR data natively understand semantic context and provide provenance of the information. FAIR data are essential to the future of human–machine collaboration and autonomous machine-to-machine communication. FAIR data are pivotal in all areas where decisions are made with minimal human intervention and where readiness for use (by machines) is prerequisite for success.

1.1. *The FAIR journey*

Today, FAIR has *de facto* become a global norm for good data stewardship, a prerequisite for reproducibility, and has guided data policies actions and professional practices in the public and private sectors. In their commitment to encouraging FAIR research data, meetings of international policymakers, such as the G20 and the G7, and the OECD Committee for Scientific and Technological Policy have publicly endorsed FAIR data; funding bodies are consolidating FAIR into their funding agreements; publishers, libraries, and unions have united behind FAIR as a way to promote and remain at the forefront of open research; and in the private sector, FAIR is adopted and enshrined in policy in major biopharmas, in particular. FAIR data, however, is not just a technical necessity; it is also economically advantageous. A report by the European Commission [2] has estimated the cost of not having FAIR data at €10.2M per year, and the impact of FAIR on innovation alone could add another €16M. The actual cost is likely to be much higher due to unquantifiable elements, such as the value of improved research quality and other indirect positive spill over effects of FAIR research data.

FAIR is not a standard, or a "one size fits all"; not a protocol or specification nor a specific architecture, technology, or platform; they are not synonymous with open or anything to do with quality. The FAIR Principles are aspirational. They do not strictly define "how" to achieve a state of FAIRness but rather describe a continuum of features, attributes, and behaviors that will move a digital resource closer to that goal. Although the principles have accelerated global discussion about better data stewardship across all disciplines, they still need to be turned into practice. Turning FAIR into reality requires new technological and social infrastructure, as well as cultural and policy changes, supported by educational and training elements that target not just researchers but all stakeholders involved in the data life cycle: from developers, service providers, librarians, journal publishers, funders, societies in the academic as well as in the commercial and governmental setting.

The FAIR journey has just begun, and there are many roads. The number of ongoing activities and initiatives, tackling one or more aspects of the FAIR ecosystem, is vast; we are not attempting to capture it all. In this article, we focus on two distinct perspectives related to the use of data at scale — one technical and one practical. The former involves a discussion of metadata, semantics, and the FAIR evaluation environment, while the latter focuses on a critical use-case — the need for FAIR-backed ML and Artificial Intelligence (AI) within the pharmaceutical sector.

2. Machine-Readable Metadata Matters

Along with globally unique, persistent identifiers, and the accessibility level of the data, metadata (i.e., descriptive data about the data) is a pillar of the FAIR Principles. Metadata provides the contextual information essential to interpret and reuse the data. Identifiers and metadata are the interoperability standards that enable the operational processes underlying exchange and sharing of information between different systems and need to be implemented by an array of registries, catalogs, tools, databases, and services that are needed to find, store, manage (e.g., mint, track provenance, and version), and aggregate (e.g., interlink and map) digital objects. Extant community-defined identifier schemas and metadata standards are described in FAIRsharing [3] (https://fairsharing.org), a globally recognized informative and educational resource on FAIR-enabling standards. Metadata standards encompass: reporting guidelines (or minimum information checklists), terminology artifacts (or semantics) ranging from dictionaries to ontologies, models, and formats. In the following sections, we highlight converging practices on metadata at the data resource-level to ensure that data published on the Web are discoverable, and then at data level, to enable their exploration by AI-based agents.

2.1. The data resource level

By and large, the major "general-purpose" data publishers, such as Zenodo, Dataverse, and Dryad, already fulfill the majority of the metadata requirements of the FAIR Principles. In particular, they provide globally unique identifiers, often Digital Object Identifiers (https://doi.org/10.25504/FAIRsharing.hFLKCn), which can be resolved to a metadata record and/or a landing page containing both human and machine-readable metadata. The metadata records may also fulfill other FAIR requirements such as containing references to ontological concepts describing the data, as well as outward cross-referencing links. In this way, data authors who utilize these services will get a large portion of FAIR "for free". Nevertheless, FAIR takes a broad view of what comprises "data", and this includes a variety of other digital resources that do not easily fit into the data repository model, such as software, workflows, web-accessible domain-specific registries, and "boutique" databases. Moreover, none of these general-purpose data publishers currently provides a reliable or discoverable way for the data creator to add their own domain-specific metadata to their data record — the detailed description of the data content, context, and its provenance, that makes data truly and reliably reusable. A variety of standards, tools, and emergent technologies are becoming widely recognized as being effective ways to fill these remaining FAIR publishing gaps.

Generic metadata is applicable across multiple general-purpose and domain-specific data resources, such as repositories, registries, data catalogs, and databases, and two standards merit special mention: schema.org (https://doi.org/10.25504/FAIRsharing.hzdzq8) and DCAT (https://doi.org/10.25504/FAIRsharing.h4j3qm). Developed by a collaboration between Google, Yahoo, Microsoft Bing, and Yandex, schema.org is a collection of structured data schemas designed to facilitate discoverability and indexing by internet search engines. The schema.org markup is designed to be embedded in web pages and site maps, where it can be harvested by machines to be indexed and aggregated. Therefore, this is a simple and powerful mechanism for metadata acquisition that does not require APIs. However, schema.org provides a core, generic vocabulary and expects domains of practice to extend this core to meet their own community needs, as demonstrated by the initiatives in the life sciences (Bioschemas, https://bioschemas.org, https://doi.org/10.25504/FAIRsharing.20sbr9) and in the earth and environmental sciences [4]. The Data Catalogue (DCAT, and its newer version DCAT2, https://www.w3.org/TR/vocab-dcat-2, and the newest version DCAT3, https://www.w3.org/TR/vocab-dcat-3) is an RDF vocabulary that provides a mechanism for capturing information about Web resources such as catalogs, data warehouses, datasets, and data files, facilitating interoperability. Moreover, the DCAT model is hierarchical, offering a reliable path for an AI agent to "drill down" from catalog-level metadata, into dataset repository metadata, to dataset metadata, and finally to a downloadable representation of the data itself. Each layer has appropriate metadata to allow an agent to decide which path is most likely to achieve its goals and to a limited extent, to determine if the data is usable by providing a predictable place to automatically locate the data license. While the licenses themselves are not machine-interpretable, there is some harmonization around the Creative Commons (CC) license suite (https://creativecommons.org), where both globally unique and resolvable identifiers are provided for each license, as well as a (trivially) machine-readable RDF representation of each. This would allow AI agents to reliably determine their authorization to use the data, at least in the case of the cc licenses. The recent DCAT2 specification also enables descriptors of other kinds of digital resources such as interfaces and APIs, which up to recently have had no predictable approach to authoring metadata descriptors of the data behind the API. While there are longstanding approaches to making the APIs themselves more machine-readable (e.g., OWL-S, https://www.w3.org/Submission/OWL-S; WSMO, https://www.w3.org/Submission/WSMO; openAPI, https://www.smart-api.info), the description of these interfaces — both for the purpose of FAIR discovery and for the purpose of automated decision-making regarding the utility of the interface for the agent's problem — had not been standardized. Both schema.org and DCAT have a broad uptake globally, and their impact is likely to become significant with respect to describing Web interfaces in the near future. The RDA Research Schemas Working Group (https://www.rd-alliance.org/groups/research-metadata-schemas-wg) brings together communities using, or working to extend, these standards to identify and bridge gaps in existing schemas and define common patterns for publishing metadata landing pages with structured data markups.

2.1.1. FAIR deployments: exemplars

To simplify the publication of DCAT records, software has been developed that both assists in record authoring, as well as provides a simplified way to publish this on the Web. The FAIR Data Point (FDP, https://www.fairdatapoint.org) is a metadata registry that follows two agent-accessible standards — DCAT(2) and the Linked Data Platform (LDP, https://www.w3.org/TR/ldp). LDP not only provides a standardized approach to adding FAIR content into the Web (i.e., making the Web writable, not only readable) but also provides an alternative, standardized approach to guiding an agent through a complex, hierarchical repository. Thus, the combination of DCAT and LDP greatly facilitates AI agents in their intelligent exploration of (and even enrichment of!) complex data spaces. In addition, the FDP client provides a DCAT record authoring interface, such that users can manually build correctly formatted DCAT descriptors of their digital resources. Deployment of an FDP has been simplified to a self-bootstrapping docker image, leading to the description of this process as "FAIR-in-a-box", and was widely deployed during the COVID-19 epidemic in Africa, as part of the VODAN initiative (https://www.vodan-totafrica.info).

While the VODAN deployment of FAIR focused on discoverable metadata, other "FAIR-in-a-box" initiatives are exploring approaches to dynamic transformations of the data itself into more AI-actionable, FAIR formats, such that data providers can become more FAIR without needing to have specific FAIR, modeling, or even coding expertise. An example of this is the "CDE-in-a-box" initiative from the European Joint Programme on Rare Disease (EJPRD), where Rare Disease Common Data Elements have been ontologically modeled for use by AI agents, and these models have been templatized such that CSV-formatted source data can be automatically used to create ontological instance data [5]. Models, and the transformation engine, are published as docker images, thus creating the "box" that only requires correctly formatted CSV to complete the FAIR transformation.

2.2. Bridging to the data level

Finally, and perhaps most critically, there is an emergent standard for publishing domain-specific, data-level descriptors that is compatible with existing general-purpose data publishers. The Research Object Crate (RO-Crate, https://doi.org/10.25504/FAIRsharing.wUoZKE) [6] provides a straightforward way to package research data, and their rich metadata, such that individual data files, and their contents, can be annotated to enable their exploration by AI-based agents. RO-Crates utilizes schema.org annotations for its highest level metadata elements, but, as one gets nearer to the data itself, the RO Crate model allows for more experiment-specific metadata, for example, in ISA format (https://doi.org/10.25504/FAIRsharing.53gp75) [7] and domain-specific structured representations with other models [8]. In addition, through being URI-based, it has the capacity to "virtually aggregate" data held in multiple locations. Finally, RO-Crates provides a predictable entry point for exploration of this metadata, such that an agent that has drilled down to an individual data deposition in, for example, Zenodo, may easily identify the gateway into the remaining metadata layers that allows them to examine the nature, purpose, and provenance of each of the deposited files.

3. FAIR Evaluation: Where Are We?

With intent, the FAIR Principles do not specify or promote any approach, technology, framework, or vocabulary that should be used to achieve the FAIR goals. This was to ensure that the Principles did not pick "winners and losers", but perhaps more importantly, to recognize that there are many ways to meet the goals of machine-supported data reuse and that these approaches, technologies, and standards would invariably evolve over time. Thus, while there seems to be a coalescence around a small set of particularly useful standards for FAIR data resources (described in the previous sections), there are still a wide range of scholarly domains and resources that take alternative approaches. Are these other approaches FAIR? Given that FAIR is defined largely in terms of the behaviors expected of a digital resource rather than any specific means of achieving those behaviors, is it possible to judge the FAIRness of a resource at all?

Starting in ~2019, a cottage industry emerged for FAIR testing and evaluation. As many as 13 different sets of FAIRness metrics (https://fairassist.org), supported by a variety of manual and automated metric testing tools, have been published based on these efforts. The majority of these are questionnaire-based, where each question addresses a distinct facet of FAIRness (e.g., Does the digital resource have a globally unique identifier? Does the digital resource link to a license?), while other approaches are fully or partially automated. This "explosion" of FAIR testing frameworks is, in some ways, positive, in that it speaks to the genuine desire of the data publishing community to *be* FAIR and to ensure that they are "doing it correctly". On the other hand, these frameworks are largely defined independently of one another, use different metrics, and measure those metrics in different ways. Thus, the results of any one testing framework cannot be compared to the output from any other, and unfortunately, they may produce dramatically different results. For example, in one case where two fully automated evaluation systems were compared using the same metadata record, the result was that 2/24 passed tests from one system and 20/22 passed tests for the other! This leads to the obvious question: Which result is correct?

3.1. Challenges: Reliability, repeatability, and governance

To evaluate the evaluators, it is first necessary to consider what it is that should be evaluated, for whom, and by whom. Beginning with the latter of these — who should undertake the evaluation? — we immediately encounter a problematic scenario. Data publishers tend to be domain experts in areas distinct from information science. One cannot realistically ask a clinical expert about globally unique identifiers or the metadata persistence policy of their preferred data repository. Similarly, one cannot ask the repository curators to evaluate if a given data deposit is following the best practices and standards of their specialist domain. This problem was borne out in an early attempt at questionnaire-based FAIR evaluation, where it was noted that different respondents interpreted a given question differently, depending on their own expertise [9]. This, on its own, suggests that human-questionnaire-based FAIR evaluation approaches will be unreliable and not comparable.

Moving to the issue of the evaluation consumer, there are many stakeholders in the FAIR ecosystem — from funding agencies to journal publishers to repository curators and data reusers. Each of these communities may place a greater or lesser weight on the various facets of FAIR or the individual subprinciples. Particularly in the area of reusability, the scholar who is attempting to correctly interpret the data they wish to reuse may have very little interest in the access protocol that was used to obtain it. Thus, it is worth reflecting on the utility of a "FAIR score" in general, versus a "FAIR-for-purpose" score, tuned to different stakeholder needs. This, then, speaks more to a modular FAIR testing approach, versus a broad, singular questionnaire. The "for whom" and "by whom" issues, therefore, provide support for a fully automated approach to FAIR evaluation, where the battery of tests applied to a given resource is defined by the relevant stakeholder community that needs the information. Moreover, a computational agent-based approach to FAIR evaluation addresses the primary goal of the FAIR Principles — that being, the ability of an intelligent agent to automatically find, access, integrate, and appropriately reuse data it encounters on the Web. This is something that cannot reliably be tested by humans and therefore absolutely requires a fully mechanized approach.

The final issues related to FAIR evaluation are the questions of what and how. As evidenced by the highly disparate scores that emerge from two of the existing fully automated and objective evaluation systems [10,11], there is clearly no agreement between the workers in the "cottage industry" about what the various principles intend or mean and how a resource's compliance with that intent should be measured. An RDA working group recently completed what is, to date, the most comprehensive survey and authoring exercise in the domain of FAIR Metric authoring [12], nevertheless a large proportion of those metrics are included in both of the fully automated evaluation systems described earlier, thus the disparities would appear to arise primarily from the implementation. As stated in the RDA WG's output document: "The maturity model is not meant as a 'how to', but instead as a way to normalize assessment". Who, then, will govern what should be tested, and more importantly, how? To date, there is no clear answer to this.

4. FAIR Data Strategy in Industry

While FAIR has its origins within the public research system, it has also taken hold within private commercial research organizations in the information and biopharma sectors. While the data within these companies are unlikely to be accessible beyond the company firewall, FAIR principles are still incredibly valuable. Indeed, it is estimated that commercial researchers spend too much of their time searching and integrating historical data, leading to considerable opportunities for efficiency savings [13]. Furthermore, in life sciences and other fields, knowledge workers benefit by combining internal data with that in the public domain. By applying consistent standards, across both types of data, researchers can ensure that powerful new AI analytics access more comprehensive datasets for ML and prediction. These sentiments have been expressed very clearly by members of the pre-competitive Pistoia Alliance (https://www.pistoiaalliance.org) who identified lack of findable, re-usable, high-quality data as the number one barrier to machine learning projects within the pharmaceutical industry [14]. Major companies such as Pfizer have declared ambitions to make "all of our data to FAIR data" (https://www.bio-itworld.com/news/2021/07/20/pfizer-s-digital-strategy-and-transformation) within the next few years. Many biopharma companies, which are highly complex, large, multinational enterprises, have already initiated strategic and operational projects internally, to demonstrate the practical impact, and business value of FAIR data [15].

Collaborative resources by "FAIR professionals" for "FAIR-doers" have also emerged from pre-competitive initiatives, such as the Pistoia

Alliance FAIR Toolkit (https://fairtoolkit.pistoiaalliance.org), and private-public-partnerships, such as the FAIR Cookbook (https://faircookbook. elixir-europe.org) created by major pharmas and ELIXIR members. These resources are helping to drive convergence in the way we turn FAIR into reality across companies. FAIR is truly seen as a major part of industry's "march to prosecution" of its data resources with AI/ML, and best practices have started to emerge to ensure their use in pharmaceutical and biotechnology research is underpinned by quality data that is fundamentally FAIR [16]. FAIR is a fundamental enabler for digital transformation [17], and although existing examples are in the life-science areas, similar assertions can be made across other knowledge-intensive industries.

4.1. *It is a matter of semantics*

Industry researchers cannot generate new insights from data if they cannot find it or if when found, the data are described too poorly to understand its origins. FAIR within industry specifically looks to address these critical issues. However, the variation of data within the life sciences poses a particular challenge. Roughly, we can group data into structured (e.g., quantitative values stored in a relational database), semi-structured (field-value-based mixed data, such as ClinicalTrials.Gov, https://clinicaltrials. gov), and unstructured text (patents, journal articles, and internal documents). All three types can benefit significantly through the application of standards to enable FAIR.

For structured data, the schema provides valuable metadata but can still frustrate researchers if columns are named using *ad hoc* convention. Fortunately, ontologies provide the backbone for standardization of these data, and several key resources such as OBI [18] and others under the OBO Foundry umbrella [19] provide unequivocal definitions to employ consistency. Quantitative data in structured and semi-structured data can also benefit through normalization with ontologies such as QUDT (https:// doi.org/10.25504/FAIRsharing.d3pqw7) which facilitates automated comparison and integration of similar data measured at different scales. Finally, we are left with the most difficult data of all, unstructured free text. Indeed, unstructured data have been estimated to be as much as 80% [20] of the entire data within an organization. The volume and heterogeneity of unstructured text can be overwhelming, from patents to journal articles and a huge variety of internal documents, and finding important information can be incredibly challenging. Textual data in particular suffers from the consequences of a lack of agreement on what we humans name any particular "thing". For instance, the drug acetaminophen is also known as paracetamol, Tylenol, Panadol, and many other names. Searching many information systems with one of these names usually will not return data associated with its other synonyms, even if they can be considered essentially the same physical thing for many purposes.

Fortunately, the last few years have seen the development of "semantic" search systems to alleviate this issue. Rather than searching to extract a string of characters entered by the user into a search box, these systems understand what the user *means* by the words and search for all synonyms which mean the same thing. Semantic search systems can vastly improve the findability of historical information within an organization. This is particularly important for ML use cases when searching experimental metadata for relevant datasets. Without semantic search, data scientists run the risk of missing large sets of data simply by using the wrong keyword. Systems such as PubTator (https://www.ncbi.nlm.nih.gov/research/pubtator/) and Europe PMC (https://europepmc.org/) integrate semantic concepts within standard literature search, providing this enhanced capability to all researchers. Semantic search systems achieve their success by using high-throughput Natural Language Processing (NLP, itself driven by AI algorithms) to annotate text with "cornerstone" ontologies, e.g., DO for disease (https://doi.org/10.25504/FAIRsharing.8b6wfq) [21], HGNC for genes (https://doi.org/10.25504/FAIRsharing.amcv1e), BAO for assays (https://doi.org/10.25504/FAIRsharing.mye76w), and many others. ML and semantics form a virtuous circle, whereby semantics helps prepare accurate high-quality data for ML methods, and those ML methods themselves can identify new concepts to add to the ontology [22].

4.2. *Open ontologies: The common good*

For industry, ontologies are the lynchpin of FAIR data, providing a consistent descriptor for the same "things" no matter how they may be named differently within different systems. Wherever possible, industry prefers to use open, public domain ontologies for this purpose. At first, this may seem counterintuitive as public ontologies are not as "controlled" as those which may be built internally. However, a standard is only a standard if it can be used without restriction across multiple parties. A good case study for this was described by the Genentech company (https://www.gene.com) highlighting a common industry model where different experiments are outsourced to different Contract Research Organisations (CROs) as part of a project. The role of the lead scientist is to bring all of these data together to form an overall picture of the system under study. The Genentech scientists describe the major inhibitor of this being the lack of standardization across different CROs [23], with different ways to represent even the most basic data such as sex, date, and treatment. Ontology-based

FAIR representation of these data is clearly a better way forward, but proprietary ontologies would prevent such wide adoption and hence not be a solution. Up until recently, however, industry has found working with public ontologies somewhat difficult [24]. While initial projects worked well, over time companies would want to add to the ontology, and these changes were not always communicated back to the original maintainer. Thus, the internal version of an ontology and the public domain version could very quickly diverge. Industry found it very difficult to subsequently "re-synchronize" and ultimately internal versions of ontologies became stale, becoming a major barrier to long-term stability of FAIR data. Fortunately, recent developments in ontology management have addressed this by developing new methodologies for routine ontology synchronization, thus allowing internal and public versions of the same ontology to remain in constant alignment (https://www.scibite.com/platform/centree).

5. Moving Forward

A data-centric approach is key to any digital transformation. The data management best practices underpinning the FAIR Principles are not new, but catalyzing stakeholder groups worldwide around a common set of data guidelines is unprecedented success. Let's be frank, the journey has just begun, and there are remaining gaps that would prevent the creation of AI agents capable of engaging in self-exploration of the global data space. Scalability is one. FAIRification to date has been mainly a retrospective activity, but we foresee more activities on prospective FAIRification in future to deliver data that are "born FAIR" by design.

FAIR is not just an essential precursor to data activities. FAIR practices will be part of the AI toolkit. Semantically enriched data have also been shown to directly improve the performance of many ML-focused solutions. One of the most celebrated AI success stories, the IBM Watson Jeopardy-playing system, was an example of the combination of AI and ontology-driven semantic data. FAIR data help with both the building of ML systems, addressing the "garbage-in/garbage-out" issue, and the interpretation of ML-generated results. There are numerous examples of these techniques working synergistically within the clinical domain, for instance, an AI-based tool to automatically scan skin images for signs of cancer, mimicking the actions of a dermatologist assessment [25]. In building the system, the authors noted that using a clinically driven taxonomy of dermatological diseases was crucial in generating training classes that performed best as ML classifiers as well as providing medically relevant results. Another example is the ground-breaking system created to diagnose conditions presented by juvenile patients entering the Emergency Room, even out-performing doctors in certain situations [26]. The construction of the platform followed a similar pattern, heavily relying on UMLS-style core FAIR standard for both the construction of training data and interpretation of the results of the AI by placing them in a clinically relevant context.

In an increasingly AI-driven world, FAIR data are more useful than ever. All signs point towards a future where FAIR data will become the norm, and FAIR competency a necessary skill set for efficient data science, knowledge discovery, and AI.

References

[1] M. D. Wilkinson, M. Dumontier, I. Jan Aalbersberg *et al.* (2016). The FAIR Guiding Principles for scientific data management and stewardship. *Scientific Data*, *3*, 160018.

[2] European Commission (2018). Cost-benefit analysis for FAIR research data: Cost benefit analysis for FAIR research data. http://doi.org/10.2777/02999.

[3] S. A. Sansone, P. McQuilton, P. Rocca-Serra *et al.* (2019). FAIRsharing as a community approach to standards, repositories and policies. *Nature Biotechnology*, *37*, 358–367.

[4] M. B. Jones, R. Richard, D. Vieglais *et al.* (2021). Science-on-Schema.org v1.2.0 (Version 1.2.0). *Zenodo*.

[5] R. Kaliyaperumal, M. D. Wilkinson, P. Alarcón Moreno *et al.* (2021). Semantic modelling of Common Data Elements for Rare Disease registries, and a prototype workflow for their deployment over registry data. *medRxiv* 2021.07.27.21261169.

[6] S. Soiland-Reyes, P. Sefton, M. Crosas *et al.* (2021). Packaging research artefacts with RO-Crate. *Data Science*, 1–42, 1 January 2021.

[7] S. A. Sansone, P. Rocca-Serra, D. Field *et al.* (2012). Toward interoperable bioscience data. *Nature Genetics*, *44*(2), 121–126.

[8] A. González-Beltrán, P. Li, J. Zhao *et al.* (2015). From peer-reviewed to peer-reproduced in scholarly publishing: The complementary roles of data models and workflows in bioinformatics. *PLOS ONE*, *10*(7), e0127612.

[9] M. D. Wilkinson, S. A. Sansone, E. Schultes *et al.* (2018). A design framework and exemplar metrics for FAIRness. *Scientific Data*, *5*, 180118.

[10] M. D. Wilkinson, M. Dumontier, S. A. Sansone *et al.* (2019). Evaluating FAIR maturity through a scalable, automated, community-governed framework. *Scientific Data*, *6*, 174.

[11] R. Huber and A. Devaraju, F-UJI: An automated tool for the assessment and improvement of the FAIRness of research data. In *Proceedings of the European Geosciences Union General Assembly Conference Abstracts*, EGU21, 15922 pp.

[12] RDA FAIR Data Maturity Model Working Group (2020). FAIR data maturity model: Specification and guidelines. *Research Data Alliance*. https://doi.org/10.15497/RDA00050.

[13] J. Wise, A. Moller, D. Christie *et al.* (2018). The positive impacts of real-world data on the challenges facing the evolution of biopharma. *Drug Discovery Today*, *23*, 788–801.

[14] M. R. Barnes *et al.* (2009). Lowering industry firewalls: Pre-competitive informatics initiatives in drug discovery. *Nature Reviews Drug Discovery*, *8*(9), 701–708.

[15] I. Harrow, L. Harland, S. M. Foord *et al.* (2022). Maximizing data value for biopharma through FAIR and quality implementation: FAIR plus Q. *Drug Discovery Today*, 20 January, S1359-6446(22)00024-1.

[16] V. A. Makarov, T. Stouch, B. Allgood *et al.* (2021). Best practices for artificial intelligence in life sciences research. *Drug Discovery Today*, *26*(5), 1107–1110.

[17] J. Wise, A. Grebe de Barron, A. Splendiani *et al.* (2019). Implementation and relevance of FAIR data principles in biopharmaceutical R&D. *Drug Discovery Today*, *24*(4), 933–938.

[18] A. Bandrowski, R. Brinkman, M. Brochhausen *et al.* (2016). The ontology for biomedical investigations. *PLOS ONE*, *11*(4), e0154556.

[19] B. Smith, M. Ashburner, C. Rosse *et al.* (2007). The OBO Foundry: Coordinated evolution of ontologies to support biomedical data integration. *Nature Biotechnology*, *25*(11), 1251–1255.

[20] C. C. Shilakes and J. Tylman, *Enterprise Information Portals*. Merrill Lynch. 1998. Archived from the original (PDF) on 24 July 2011.

[21] W. A. Kibbe, C. Arze, V. Felix *et al.* (2015). Disease Ontology 2015 update: An expanded and updated database of human diseases for linking biomedical knowledge through disease data. *Nucleic Acids Research*, *43*(D1), D1071–D1078.

[22] H. Liu, Y. Perl, J. Geller *et al.* (2020). Concept placement using BERT trained by transforming and summarizing biomedical ontology structure. *Journal of Biomedical Informatics*, *112*, 103607.

[23] M. D. Sorani, W. A. Ortmann, E. P. Bierwagen *et al.* (2010). Clinical and biological data integration for biomarker discovery. *Drug Discovery Today*, *15*(17–18), 741–748.

[24] L. Harland, C. Larminie, S. A. Sansone *et al.* (2011). Empowering industrial research with shared biomedical vocabularies. *Drug Discovery Today*, *16*(21–22), 940–947.

[25] A. Esteva, B. Kuprel, R. A. Novoa *et al.* (2017). Dermatologist-level classification of skin cancer with deep neural networks. *Nature*, *542*, 115–118.

[26] H. Liang, B. Y. Tsui, H. Ni *et al.* (2019). Evaluation and accurate diagnoses of pediatric diseases using artificial intelligence. *Nature Medicine*, *25*, 433–438.

Part E. Perspectives on AI for Science

Hybrid Solar-Wind Farm in the Californian Desert. Credit: narvikk at iStockphoto.

© 2023 World Scientific Publishing Company
https://doi.org/10.1142/9789811265679_0034

Chapter 34

Large Language Models for Science

Austin Clyde[*,§], Arvind Ramanathan[*,¶], and Rick Stevens[†,‡,‖]

*Data Science and Learning Division, Argonne National Laboratory,
Lemont, IL 60439 USA

†Department of Computer Science, University of Chicago, Lemont, IL
60439 USA

‡Computing, Environment, and Life Sciences Directorate, Argonne
National Laboratory, Lemont, IL 60439 USA

§aclyde@anl.gov

¶ramanathana@anl.gov

‖stevens@anl.gov

1. Introduction

Artificial intelligence is producing new ways of thinking about data [1,2], working with data [3,4], and reasoning about data products [5,6]. Data analysis and generative modeling are becoming the crux of science (along with humans and their creativity) [7]. How scientists read, interpret, and generalize data into a coherent theory is central to the scientific practice [8,9]. AI for science (AI4Science) is about fostering this deep connection between data, computing, and the scientific method to advance the next generation of discovery to deal with this generation of problems [10]. Foundational models for AI4Science are "any model that is trained on broad data at scale and can be adapted" [11]. In this chapter, we address the current generation of foundation models, large language models. Foundation models are meant.

Various campaigns fall under this umbrella, such as AI for chemistry or AI for material design [12,13], or even AI for COVID-19, where scientists use deep learning on novel data sources to rapidly identify infected individuals [14,15], or AI to simulate SARS-CoV-2 in droplets to understand the process of transmission and how it relates to the spike protein [16,17], or utilizing AI to understand the mechanism of drug candidates [18] and even screen vast libraries of compounds to locate drugs [19–22], or more broadly, AI for health where scientists are advancing the knowledge (and capability) for protein engineering and folding using the vast collections of simulation, structural data, and computing power amassed over the years [23,24]. AI for science has significant prospects for progress.

Nevertheless, AI for science's future potential can dwindle due to foreseeable challenges. An effort to identify those roadblocks and work towards them is essential for shaping the direction of scientific practice. A challenge we focus on in this article is dealing with natural language. As AI automatically performs much of the data analysis and moves towards notions of autonomous discovery [25], it is imperative for scientists to reflectively endorse the computational "science". This entails understanding the evidence and method by which an AI model concludes, balances evidence for or against hypotheses, proposes hypotheses, or even creates new concepts and theories. Furthermore, a more practical issue is that AI cannot operate over natural reasoning in the historical scientific literature or even analyze the unstructured data found in past literature or electronic health records. We call this challenge an interoperability challenge.

Interoperability is the ability for different systems to interact, share information, and understand each other. In software engineering, interoperability focuses on the ability of different systems to make sense and communicate with each other in a synergistic way [26]. For example, in the internet of things literature, it refers to the ability of different platforms to inter-exchange data [27]. When systems exchange data, they are both able to synergistically benefit from the exchange. Similarly, we can think about the general problem of explainable-AI (X-AI) in a similar vain where there is a fundamental interoperability problem between AI models and human social communication [28].

First, the lack of interoperability with human language prevents models from interacting with hundreds of years of scientific literature and discoveries. When scientists train models, the models are often trained on a dataset without any relationship to the body of knowledge and theory which they use to reason about the data. This can lead to inconsistencies between human literature and model predictions. There has been some progress in this area. For example, scientists may use a physics-based loss function to ensure that the model is constrained by the same laws the scientists view the world as constrained by [29]. The general ability to build on past literature relates to the ability to rely not just on data but on background scientific assumptions, which get tied into the language of scientific papers [30].

The second issue is that a lack of language understanding in computational models prevents models from explaining or even reasoning their predictions in an understandable human discourse. Because AI systems cannot support or disprove their claims with language, it is nearly impossible for humans to engage the models to understand the claims. This is an issue full of new research in human–computer interaction [31–33].

Lastly, if models cannot engage in human language, it limits the scope of what AI4Science can do. While research efforts in explainability pursue an ontologically aligned system (where AI systems can explain their predictions in terms of the data provided), this ambition ultimately limits the horizon of machine reasoning as ever being able to go beyond our prior understanding of the data [34]. The ability for AI systems to explain claims and even re-work an understanding of the data requires some use of language, and ideally, natural language.

This third point is visionary. It poses immense challenges for the philosophy of science, such as concept formation, analogical reasoning, and incorporating life-world experience into lifeless systems. Overcoming this language problem can create an opportunity to engineer new materials for climate change or discover new therapies. While interoperability is fundamental, spanning an extensive collection of issues regarding AI4Science, other equal challenges exist, such as developing opportunities for access to high-performance computing and fostering a more democratic scientific environment [35].

AI *foundation models* are "any model that is trained on broad data at scale and can be adapted" [11]. Current foundation models such as GPT-3 are trained on many different data sources [36]. This has meant impressive performance for applying foundation models to very distinct tasks ranging from text generation to code generation [37]. As models have become bigger, they are continually serving as the foundation of application-specific models such as ProtTrans, a model for predicting protein sequences [38]. Foundation models are a new paradigm of scientific modeling as they demonstrate increased homogenization and emergence. Increased homogenization means that more modeling tasks are starting to rely on the same foundation models, architectures, and learning algorithms (which also increases the overall risk of errors propagating to downstream tasks [39]). In turn, this means it is essential to invest in foundation models for creating next-generation capabilities, especially on the hardware and engineering fronts [11]. Increased emergence means that systems' behavior is increasingly "implicitly induced rather than explicitly constructed" (further increasing some fears of models becoming too powerful [40]) [11].

In this chapter, we make the case that large language models (LLMs) can advance AI4Science by directly integrating with scientific literature,

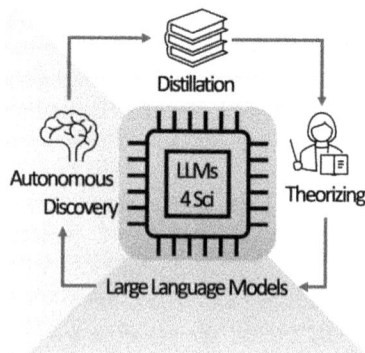

Fig. 1. **LLMs and AI for Science.** Large language models have shown equal state-of-the-art success on a variety of domain-specific and multimodal learning tasks. In transferring this success to science, it is imperative to develop an arsenal of techniques for applying LLMs to the discovery, distillation, and theorization components of science as a whole.

explainability, and concept formation, thus advancing the interoperability of AI and HPC with human scientific practice (Figure 1). LLMs are the current foundation models for AI4Science, although the future of foundation models need not be LLMs. LLMs have achieved impressive performance on generative text production and different reasoning tasks such as structuring data and forming knowledge bases, producing entailment between claims, and generating new text. The second section provides a high-level overview of LLM advances for natural language processing. The third section outlines how the current work can be applied to the scientific domain while outlining specific challenges that differentiate natural language processing from scientific reasoning. Finally, in the fourth section, we outline a series of challenges that look forward to designing interoperable systems for automated scientific reasoning.

NLP is a foundational subject in computer science [41]. NLP originates from government-funded machine translation campaigns driven by the various conflicts in the 20th century [42]. During the 1950s, there was considerable interest in automating translation between English and Russian. As imaginations grew with the advances in computing power, new opportunities in database retrieval and structured data fostered these imaginaries of computers reasoning about the soundness of arguments and scientific conclusions, for example, [43]. The idea of "computer reasoning" or "automated reasoning" eventually became the pinnacle topic curtailing on the formal semantic research programs such as Rudolf Carnap's [44]. While formal reasoning programs slowed down during the AI winter, modern LLM processing is far from the grounded techniques previously utilized [45]. Formal logic techniques required codified ground facts put into logical relations with each other. These sets of techniques eventually become part of a separate but closely related project of mathematical theorem proving [46]. The formal techniques for machine reasoning are largely distinct from the theorization of language used in modern large language modeling.

The next section will briefly overview the theoretical framework most common to large modeling design and discuss the state-of-the-art benchmarks.

1.1. *NLP preliminaries*

A challenge of modern NLP is encoding words into vectors obtained from the first few steps of NLP: vocabulary identification, tokenization, and embedding (see Figure 2). Many different techniques are available, and we only outline the preliminaries necessary for the current state-of-the-art LLMs. A *vocabulary* is a collection of valid tokens which are generally constructed from an initial text *corpus*. A vocabulary will have defined vector embedding to make the translation between natural language and vectors possible.

A simple tokenization method takes all words split by spaces from the corpus and assigns a unique number to it. Each word is then encoded as a one-hot vector of size $| V |$. The problem with this technique, especially for scientific domains, is that if a word is not encountered in the initial text corpus, then it must be assigned an unknown token. The unknown token, [UNK], either has to be applied to a variety of important words or the model must be retrained with the rare words added to the corpus.

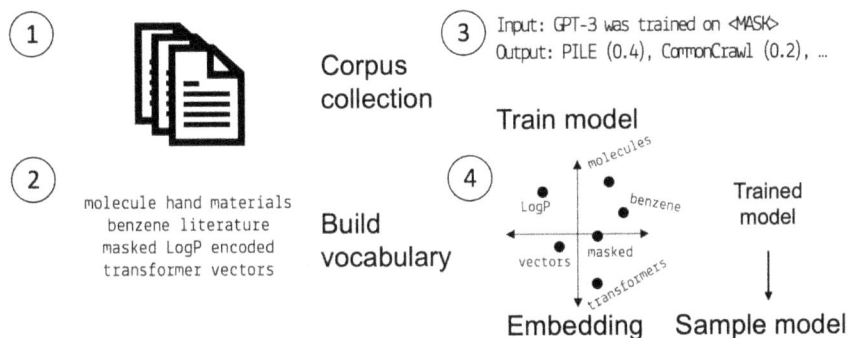

Fig. 2. **Overview of NLP**. There are four main components which include curating a collection of documents (1), building a vocabulary (2), training a model (3), and utilizing the model or its word embedding for downstream tasks.

Given the sheer number and frequency of rare words encountered in various scientific disciplines, having to retrain models or be unable to handle unseen words is not a desirable characteristic.

Hence, all modern LLMs such as Bidirectional Encoder Representations from Transformers (BERT), Generative Pretrained Transformer (GPT)-2, and GPT-3 utilize byte pair encoding (BPE). BPE combines word-level and character-level encoding by breaking up reoccurring character patterns into variable-length n-gram chunks [47]. Vocabulary sizes are fixed for GPT-2 and GPT-3 at 50257, but this is a hyperparameter [48]. Because the map between the embedding space and tokens is isomorphic, when we refer to a word as w may be referring to $w \in V$ — the token w in our vocabulary — or $w \in \mathbb{R}^{50257}$, the vector embedding of the word.

Modern large language models have two common paradigms. The first is *masked language modeling* which utilizes a special [MASK] token in the vocabulary, which can appear anywhere in a sentence. For example, the input sequence might look like "My dog went [MASK] to get his toy" where the model ought to predict the correct word where the [MASK] occurs. Models predict probabilities over all words in the vocabulary, so the most likely words might include "inside" or "outside" and likely would not include "car" or "bed" since the prepositions would not be correct. The model can use information from tokens before or after the mask, and thus the model represents probabilities of words in contexts. This scheme is used in BERT models [49].

Causal language models (CLM), on the other hand, do not explicitly use a [MASK] token but only predict the next word with dependencies traveling from left to right [50]. In the previous example, if one wanted to query what words might go into the masked position, the input would look like "My dog went" as causal models predict the next word. Causal models treat language autoregressively as each word depends on the previous words. A CLM, which provides the next token probabilities over the vocabulary given a list of words, can model the likelihood of a sentence as

$$P_{\Phi}(w_1, \ldots, w_n) = \prod_{i=1}^{n} P_{\Phi}(w_i \mid w_1, \ldots, w_{i-1}) \qquad (1)$$

given model parameters Φ. This allows direct sampling of sentences in a generative fashion which is not possible for MLMs like BERT as there appears to be no way to model sentence probabilities, though one could imagine pseudo-measures such as

$$P_{\Phi}^{(\text{psuedo})}(W) = \prod_{i=1}^{n} P_{\Phi}(w_i \mid w_1, \ldots, W_{\backslash t}), \qquad (2)$$

where $W = (w_1, \ldots, w_n)$ and $W_{\backslash t}$ is shorthand for the vector $(w_1, \ldots, w_{t-1}, [\text{MASK}], w_{t+1}, \ldots, w_n)$ [51].

1.2. *Architectures*

State-of-the-art LLMs such as BERT and GPT-3 are based on a transformer block architecture [52]. Transformer models follow an encoder–decoder structure where a set of tokens $(w_1, \ldots, w_n)$ are encoded to a latent representation vector $(z_1, \ldots, z_n)$ and subsequently decoded to the output space where decoding can be done within a causal or masked setup as described in the previous section.

The quintessential layer type for transformer-based models is called an *attention layer*. The intuition of an attention layer follows from the colloquial usage of the word attention in everyday life. For example, while considering the meaning of the word "it", it might be helpful to recall or "attend" to the previously mentioned subject.

Attention has a few different flavors [53–55], the most common being *scaled dot-product attention* which consists of a set of vectors called queries, Q, keys, K, and values, V, so computed as

$$\text{Attention}(Q, K, V) = \text{softmax}\left(\frac{QK^T}{\sqrt{d_k}}\right) V \qquad (3)$$

where d_k is the number of dimensions for vector k. Given an input vector $X \in \mathbb{R}^{s \times d_x}$ of tokens embedded into a space of dimension d_x with a sequence length of x, linear weights, W, can be used to produce vectors

$$Q = XW^Q \quad K = XW^K \quad V = XW^V. \qquad (4)$$

It should be clear given the dimensions of W^Q and W^K, both in $\mathbb{R}^{d_k \times s}$, that QK^T is a square matrix of dimension s by s which has softmax applied after normalizing. Intuitively, for each row representing a token, i, a column representing another token, j, is assigned a value close to 1 or 0. So, when V is multiplied on the right by this square matrix, it attends to which other token's information j is relevant when "thinking" about token i.

This can be thought of as an information retrieval mechanism like a dictionary look-up where the softmax term computes were exactly to perform the look-up. The values are where the information is retrieved from. Consider the sentence "I heard my cat meow". When thinking about what word might come after cat, we might want to attend to the word "heard" as it indicates a noise should follow. Therefore, the query and key matrix should result in values close to one for the j positions corresponding to those context words in the last row where the word meow should appear.

Three types of attention can occur in an encoder–decoder model: self-attention in the encoder, decoder, or encoder–decoder attention. In the case of encoder–decoder attention, the output sequence is used to attend to certain information from the input sequence,

$$Q = X_{\text{output}}W^Q \quad K = X_{\text{input}}W^K \quad V = X_{\text{input}}W^V. \tag{5}$$

Attention can also be masked or unmasked. For causal language models, attention is masked so that information from later parts of the sequence does not influence the current token. In contrast, unmasked attention uses all information and positions such as BERT.

Attention builds on the idea of recurrence in neural networks such as recurrent neural networks (RNNs), bidirectional RNNs, and convolutional neural networks (CNNs). These recurrent neural networks suffer from the degradation of long-range signals [56,57]. Attention is an attempt to reduce the information bottleneck associated with typical recurrent layers [54]. Continuing with the simple example of finding the referent of an "it" in a sentence, locating the subject which occurred in many word positions requires maintaining a vector either in a memory channel, in the case of long short-term memory (LSTM) networks or in the representation itself of the entire context [58]. In attention networks, because each token gets to specifically index and refers to another token through an attention query, the context does not need to be embedded into a single representation that flows through the sentence but instead can be retrieved. Recently, non-attention-based techniques for modeling these long-range decencies have been developed, such as LambdaNetworks [59].

Current LLMs utilize blocks of attention layers where attention layers have multiple heads. These multihead attention layers effectively perform h many loop-ups and concatenate the results together [36,48,52]. Blocks can be type encoder, decoder, or encoder–decoder, referring to the type of attention used, masked or unmasked. Blocks may combine a linear feed-forward network and possibly a normalization layer or a residual connection. GPT-2 and GPT-3 models utilize decoder-only blocks, and because they are autoregressive, the attention is masked self-attention.

1.3. *Training and fine-tuning*

LLMs require specialized training hardware both because (1) auto-regressive language modeling scales with sequence length and (2) the number of trainable parameters exceeds over 100 billion for a few of the largest models [36]. Training a LLM is not to be taken lightly. It is not a trivial computational task given the vast number of trainable weights and required data, often requiring the usage of a computing cluster and many days of training time. Some have even implicated environmental harms to the training of large language models [39].

LLMs over a few billion weights are expensive to train, requiring clusters of thousands of state-of-the-art GPUs to train over a few days to months.

Given the immense cost of initially training these models, the paradigm for LLMs is typically a single large upfront investment in training a model on a large overlapping corpus of a language, say from all web-scrabble material. From this initial "pre-trained" model, the model can be fine-tuned on downstream tasks using specialized datasets. This reduces the cost of specializing a model across multiple tasks and allows smaller amounts of data to generalize on the model, assuming that the general understanding and structure of language in the pre-training make it easier for the model to learn.

GPT-3 was trained on a subset of the CommonCrawl, which consisted of over 570GB of plain text which is over 400 billion BPE encoded tokens [36]. The CommonCrawl is a collection of raw web data extracted from public-facing websites. The Pile is an 800GB curated collection with an open-source generation script from a handful of high-quality sources [60]. The team showed that training GPT-3 on the Pile, instead of the CommonCrawl, resulted in better performance in some areas. GPT-NeoX is the largest publicly available LLM with over 20B weights which has been pre-trained on the Pile [61]. There are different publicly available training infrastructure managers such as Megatron and DeepSpeed [62,63].

1.4. *Language embedding*

The starting point of most of these models is from one-hot encoded tokens; however, as a result of the training process, tokens can be projected into an embedding space. Unlike one-hot encoded vectors where only a single axis will have a non-zero value, the embedding will have moved words around from their defined axis. While one-hot encoding is rapidly interpretable and easy to implement, they do not codify any initial information about a language, such as the fact that "king" and "queen" represent similar ideas and are much different than the words "plant" or "car", all while having connotations of "monarchy" or "royalty". Word embeddings, as opposed to one-hot encodings, attempt to learn this natural sense of connotations and similarity through the distance between words in a vector space. Naturally, this can result in inductive bias based on the data samples, such as identifying words with wrongful and biased linkages such as certain professions and gender [64,65].

Word embeddings do not necessarily need to come from LLMs, as discussed in previous sections. Two models such as continuous bag-of-words (CBOW) attempt to project surrounding words, $w_{t-2}, w_{t-1}, w_{t+1}, w_{t+2}$, to a latent space to predict the output word w_t [66]. The Skip-gram model is the reverse, projecting the word w_t to a latent space and predicting the four contextual words. Global Vectors for Word Representation (GloVe) improves on these methods, utilizing smaller vector sizes and performing better on smaller vocabulary sizes [67].

1.5. *Few-shot learning*

Few-shot learning consists of using only a handful of data examples to learn a task [68]. Pre-trained GPT-3 and other LLMs have been shown to be capable few-shot learners [36]. Furthermore, Brown *et al.* show that the more the weights, the more the models use in-context information (the few shots). The basic idea is that by providing an input sentence that begins with two or three examples of the kind of response desired, the model will learn from those initial few examples and structure its response based on generalizing the structure, style, and content. The limit to the amount of context or in-sequences examples is limited by the context window of the model, which for GPT-3 is 2048 tokens. One-shot learning is the same as few-shot, except only one example is shown.

Few-shot learning is the basis of GPT-3 multitude of tasks. The process of using GPT-3 as a few-shot learner is called "prompting" [69]. There is a spectrum of specialization for a specific task given a pre-trained LLM, from zero-shot learning to fine-tuning. Fine-tuning entails changing the weights of the pre-trained model to specialize a model to perform a task, which is still considered to produce the best results. Few-shot to zero-shot learning does not alter the model's weights but changes the amount of contextual information provided.

1.6. *Information retrieval*

Information retrieval applies to a variety of tasks such as search, question-answering, or even basic fact-checking [70]. Information retrieval is a challenging computational problem because, among other things, it is somewhat ill-posed. Given a particular context and a question, it's often not obvious what the best information is in real-world scenarios. There are factual or analytic questions for which there is a clear range of good answers (for example, "for an elementary school student, what is a planet?"). Some questions lack obvious answers or have answers that depend on the context ("what is a good cancer drug for a 50-year-old male with lung cancer?"). Information retrieval treats information as a ground truth where the problem is posed as a look-up. This distinction will play a prominent role when thinking about scientific literature and reasoning.

Given a set of documents (or, for example, webpages in the case of search), neural information retrieval encoded documents into a latent space. It used cosine similarity to retrieve documents from a query [71,72].

However, this method only links documents through a non-contextual global embedding. They do not result in the retrieval of specific information based on the query details. Cross-encoding solves this issue where a LLM uses the query to embed the documents [73]. Typically, a classical retrieval technique is used to limit a small set of documents for which the model then chooses the most relevant passages from [74]. LLMs for information retrieval are employed at scale for web search [69].

Thorne *et al.* (2018) utilize chunks of Wikipedia as ground-truth claims [70]. Given a claim, they annotate passages from Wikipedia if they support or refute claims. The pipeline they propose ingests a claim, utilizes an information retrieval system to locate n relevant documents, and finally uses a model to evaluate if any of the documents entail the input claim, thereby checking if the claim has supporting evidence or can be "verified".

Similarly, Guu *et al.* (2020) utilize a fully differentiable retrieve-then-predict model [75]. Given a masked query such as "The [MASK] is the powerhouse of the cell", the goal is to locate the correct term. To create a fully differentiable model that can be trained end-to-end, they utilize a differential document retrieval system, such as the LLM-based systems, to contextual input information from the retrieved document and the query to a model. One benefit to their system is that it works for supervised tasks, not just masked terms, like a question-answering system. Izacard (2020) utilizes a student–teacher paradigm to iteratively train a model on attention scores of a LLM on base QA tasks producing better performance than non-iteratively trained models [76].

Nevertheless, some disciplinary datasets have been aggregated through a collection of over 15k test questions [77]. There are multiple-choice questions based on textual passages spanning various disciplines from social studies to science in this collection. They report that non-structured autoregressive LLMs lack the reasoning required for complex analytical tasks such as law datasets or logical reasoning, failing to achieve better than random performance, while performing better on marketing and management test questions with over 60% accuracy (and a question-answer fine-tuned LLM, such as UnifiedQA [78], performed with 80% accuracy on these two tasks).

2. From Natural to Scientific Language

We will now discuss various approaches to translating LLMs from the scope of everyday language usage towards scientific reasoning. First, we will outline technical challenges for the direct application of language modeling techniques and then move towards how these models can work in a scientific practice through a review of some recent translational research.

2.1. *Scientific language versus natural language*

Scientific reasoning, assumptions, and culture are embedded in the texts scientists produce; however, the content and context of a scientific text are much different than that of, say, utterances from Reddit or even StackExchange found in the PILE or CommonCrawl. Scientific writing is generally structured into (1) observations, which are statements regarding things that have truly occurred, (2) analysis, which involves interpreting these observations in the context of background scientific assumptions and explicit models and theories, and (3) discussion, which may raise complicating issues such as data errors, inconsistencies with prior work, and new ideas to study. While non-exhaustive, these three different modes in scientific writing are essential to parse as distinctive constitutive components of a scientific claim. These components separate scientific writing from other sources found in NLP.

Science aims to track the truth, and important to this is some notion of what is "true". Whether it be a heuristic notion such as the one exercised by scientists in practice of basing the truth on some reasonable analysis of prior scientific literature in conjugation with their education or even grounding their observations in some application of logic to observed experimental evidence, scientists keep track of speculation versus scientific fact. Thus, an essential difference between scientific reasoning and natural language is how statements are justified in light of tracking this scientific truth. Statements in science come with justification that at some point need to be tracked down or have reasons made to defend their cogency.

There's a caveat even to this notion of scientific fact that also bears on thinking about the problem long-term: scientific facts do change. An ideal scientific reasoner can hold certain beliefs that are true and update those beliefs gradually or suddenly, depending on how the evidence presents itself. These changes can be just a reworking of facts such as "BRCA1 is not involved in cancer" rather than the current belief "BRCA1 is involved in cancer". But changes can also extend to more conceptual and ontological considerations that alter how entities such as "BRCA1" possess a status in scientific reasoning. New concepts can be created altogether.

2.1.1. *Bootstrapping understanding*

While philosophers of science hardly agree on how to systematize scientific understanding in general, there has been progress in codifying scientific theories into large-scale datasets. First, the scientific literature is strongly networked, which is well studied in the area of citation network analysis [79–81]. This means the bulk of scientific literature can be considered in a network based on citations, providing a primary mode of parsing out generalized claims from their support (one experiment could examine the entailment of a claim from its citations to evaluate the strength of support).

Second, largely accepted formal scientific theories are already structured and codified (to a certain extent) in online web portals and databases. Take, for instance, KEGG pathway data which codifies various gene, protein, and chemical interaction pathways into graphical diagrams with well-structured sets of relations, entities, and even citation information supporting the records [82–84]. These large structured graphs provide a basis for thinking about scientific theories and provide an impetus for progress. In the next section, we turn to some example questions and experiments one can begin on.

2.1.2. *Vocabularies*

A challenge in the history of scientific literature parsing has been the complexity of its vocabulary [85]. Various approaches have taken hold for dealing with this. First, utilizing the BPE scheme prevents complex and rarely seen scientific words from being removed from possible model inputs as often scientific terms break down into common prefixes which carry a component of the terms meaning [86]. Second, medical ontologies and categorization efforts have already created substantial nested lists of specific terminology and entities [87]. Third, NLP models can themselves be used to categorize words that are used in a similar context and within a specific range of uncertainty [88].

A further issue is linking entities together which have different names [89]. For example, genes have many other names which are often used interchangeably. A naive program tracing just the literal vocabulary might recognize they are similar but fail to collapse both terms into a single entity for reasoning. NLP models such as BERT have been used to extract and link together these named entities [90,91].

2.2. *Facticity*

Facticity refers to the qualities or aspects of being a fact. In general, NLP has a slightly different tone than science. In NLP, the idea of verifying facts is usually presented in the context of dealing with misinformation where there is a reduction in the quality of the verification from the scientific setting (i.e., simply checking that the information appears in a reputable source such as Wikipedia or a national news agency is sufficient), the complexity of the facts being verified (i.e., what year was X born), and the robustness of the reasoning required. Nevertheless, the advances in NLP can lay some foundational ideas for building a system with the more stringent requirements for a scientific LLM. One can view this problem from two angles: ensuring the output of LLMs is factually grounded and/or ensuring the model is constrained to factual or grounded claims. These two angles correspond to verifying and filtering output or imposing some structural and architectural design on the LLM such that the output is likely verifiable truthful or grounded. For this discussion, we will adopt the more lenient standard of verification, which is that the information can be found in a similar stated form from a reputable source.

One angle on the first issue of simply linking the output of an NLP model to some other source can be framed as an information retrieval problem as discussed in Section 1.6. For example, if a claim is detected in the output of a LLM, the claim can be searched in a database such as Wikipedia. If the claim appears and is in an equivalent form, the output of the LLM can be reported as verified. If the claim does not arise, the claim is unverified. If the claim appears but is presented in an incompatible form, it can be presented as counter-substantiated. This basic form of reference checking can be extended to output regarding scientific claims, such as locating sentences in the scientific literature that would follow, entail, and support this claim. One downside of this approach is that there may exist claims which are not entailed by current claims directly (i.e., it does not occur in a propositional form already). Still, in conjunction with applying different scientific reasoning techniques, it would follow. We deal with this in the following section.

Another unique training strategy used entity detection to replace similar entities in "factual" claims from Wikipedia, producing a more extensive set of claims based on the assumption that entities of a standard type should share a generalizable set of claims among them [92]. This approach relies on altering the training set of the model so that factual information is reinforced over less trustworthy data. In light of research that argues that the number of times a LLM is trained on a particular sentence is strongly correlated with the likelihood that the sentence is reproduced in model output, careful engineering of the training data for the scientific usage of models will likely improve the performance of the verifiability of the claims it produces [93].

2.3. *Reasoning*

Scientific reasoning allows a model's verified claims to be confirmed but to see if they can reasonably follow from other claims. Scientific reasoning leads to models which may produce information that is new to scientists but is grounded in material that is already found in current literature. We present two approaches to reasoning: One based on building up an internal representation of the state-of-the-art knowledge through a knowledge graph, and another based on contextual reason, which never maintains a complete state of the literature or ground truths.

One issue as the scientific literature grows is reference checking and updating. Over time, specific claims in papers may be disproven, generalized, or further qualified — this is the nature of science, not a deficit. Nevertheless, the current scientific practice of citing full research articles to support propositional claims leads to the inscrutability of evidence. Peer review aims to get around this, but it would be an unreasonable burden to place on reviewers to check every claim from a cited reference, where those claims often have cited references, and so on. This problem has been well studied in mathematics, where claims can be formalized to comprehend the exact genealogy and ground terms of a claim [94]. The use of natural language in science makes such an approach intractable without further research.

A knowledge graph is a heuristic for reasoning about the linkages between entities. A basic formulation consists of a set of entities E and a set of relations R which form a graph $G = (E, R)$. Given there can exist different relationships, one can imagine a set of triples of the form (p, e_1, e_2), where p is a propositional relationship in a set of relations $p \in \mathcal{R}$ and $e_1, e_2 \in E$. This set of material can be mined using few-shot learning and claim-extraction techniques from the NLP literature [95–98]. This technique is known more broadly as knowledge distillation [99–101]. The problem can be posed as a machine translation problem. Given a sentence as a sequence of NLP tokens, the aim is to translate it to triplet space such that some meaning of the sentence is maintained.

A different approach builds up local knowledge graph constructions from sentences and then compares them in knowledge-graph space to known databases such as Wikipedia [102]. This is another form of fact claim checking except that in this case the verification happens in graph space instead of natural language space as in the previous section. Greedy Neural Theorem Prover is one such example [103].

Under another approach, the idea is to enforce facticity in the model by altering the training data; however, this is difficult given the training objective only relates to co-occurrence and probability rather than facts. However, there is reason to believe that given a LLM, one can embed a subtask in the model through a formalized syntax [37,104]. For example, in Clyde *et al.* (2021b), a knowledge graph between chemicals is embedded into a transformer model. First, a graph $G = (M, E)$ is generated where M consists of molecular scaffolds and E is the super-graph relationship. Molecule m in M is represented by a text SMILES string which is a listing of a breadth-first search on the graph structure of the compound. These SMILES strings have no relationship to natural text besides consisting of a sequence of letters. The model is trained to translate m to m_{sup} where $m_{\text{sup}} \in E(m)$. Interestingly, the model is trained on a subset of $E(m)$ since it is not fully known what larger molecules contain this molecular scaffold as a subgraph. However, the model can correctly infer the full graph from the set of training examples. This example highlights the possibility of taking a knowledge graph, embedding it into a model, and examining if it can correctly learn some structure from the graph to extrapolate to a new connection. Given this task was on molecular structure and the model had no scientific literature pre-training, the question is still open if pre-training on a task-specific dataset might create synergies or if context based on some information retrieval objective is provided what kind of synergies might be possible.

3. Opportunities and Open Problems

This section outlines three areas of opportunity for applying LLMs to scientific practice.

3.1. *Structured retrievals*

A predictive model can be used for an inverse design for engineering and optimization problems, like drug discovery or material design. For example, a drug hunter may want to find a compound that maximizes inhibition's likelihood and satisfies various property constraints such as molecular weight.

Property predictive models with deep learning are highly successful at this task; however, they require structured data in tabular form. While many datasets are available for simple properties already in tabular form, the scientific literature is full of experimental properties for compounds that are not aggregated into any tabular format. Retrieving a structured table based on a pre-determined ontology would unlock predictive modeling on the historical, scientific literature.

Furthermore, in unstructured electronic health records (EHRs), the full application of predictive modeling has been slowed by, among other things, the inability to rapidly transform text, image, and handwritten data into a tabular form based on a common ontology. While this problem has had some recent growth due to the proliferation of more common standards through software, the practice is far from standardized. It still prevents looking back at the vast collections of historical even print medical records.

These examples would benefit significantly from a mechanism for taking an ontology (the tabular fields desired), applying it to a corpus of documents, and constructing a data table for downstream learning projects.

LLMs, as outlined in Section 1.5, have already been shown to be able to parse unstructured data from structured data. Adaption for the aforementioned problem would require new directions using multimodal documents, that is dealing with tables and figures in scientific papers and EHRs, with LLMs, designing a metric for the quality of transformations from unstructured text to structured text, addressing the normalization among different papers in the case of quantities, and preventing bias from only retrieving structured data from a certain class of unstructured documents.

For example, consider the pipeline representative of current EHR analysis projects: "(1) extracting clinical notes for the target population and preprocessing the data, (2) defining the annotation schema with a hierarchical structure, (3) performing document-level hierarchical annotation using the annotation schema, and (4) indexing annotations for a search engine system" [105]. LLMs can be used with nearly every level with some intervention at stage 2 to filter the annotation scheme to be precisely what would be useful for the clinicians [106].

3.2. *Future work*

3.2.1. *Autonomous discovery*

Autonomous discovery has two main components [107,108]. The first is the automation of the laboratory through the use of robotics and AI [109]. The second is goal setting, analysis, and hypothesis generation [110]. We believe that LLMs can be used to accelerate the research and incorporation of data into existing theories and knowledge graphs. First, LLMs can be used to extract claims from scientific data and embed them into a pre-existing knowledge graph. This can be used to detect inconsistencies, supporting evidence, or even interesting connections. By updating the knowledge graph based on experimental evidence, sampling and predictive techniques can be used to predict new experiments or questions which arise [111–114]. King *et al.* used a graph method to automatically choose and plan experiments [115].

Second, LLMs can be used to generate novel hypotheses not just at the scale of a knowledge graph but also at the scale of the literature considered as a whole [116]. It is obvious that science can be cleanly structured into computational facts even within a particular scientific moment or paradigm. Nevertheless, for creative new ideas and theories that reach beyond current understanding, it is clear that the previous structure will not work or require reworking at best — the kind of ontological shift that is computationally difficult to articulate [117]. Therefore there might be some benefit to using LLMs to articulate creativity in natural

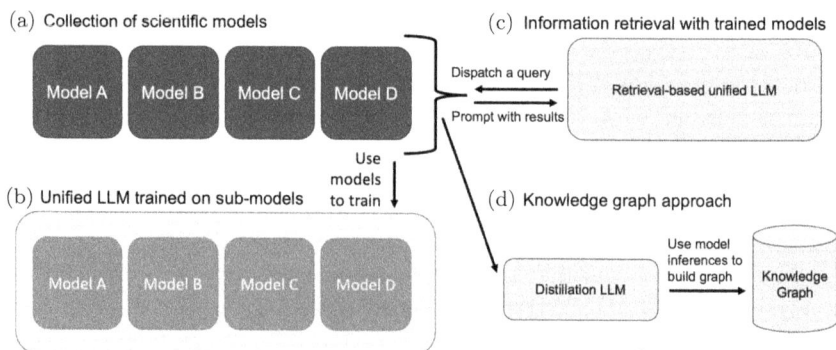

Fig. 3.   **Unifying scientific models with LLMs.** (a) A collection of specific-trained scientific models. (b) Inferences from (a) can be used to train a LLM to capture those task-specific tasks into a single model. (c) A model can be trained to utilize the collection of models like an information retrieval task. There are two parts. First is selecting which model to query and what to query, and second is utilizing the resulting inference to produce a result. (d) A distillation model can be used to attempt to distill the inferences from the collection of models to store in a knowledge graph for answering queries.

language through various kinds of summarizations which use analogical reasoning [118,119].

3.2.2. *Model unification*

In practice, many scientific laboratories create their own sets of specialized learning models based on shared data or experimental data. This leads to many unversioned scientific models that can be slightly different across different lab groups and lack organization. Furthermore, one model does not know about the existence of other models, while scientific thinking generally respects the background information of other scientific thinking. Therefore, there is reason to desire a unified model that can ingest other models, retain their accuracy and information, and locate synergies. Given that LLMs have been the only model type that has been trained with weights in the hundreds of billions, there is reason to believe the architecture might allow embedding and unifying other models within them.

Consider the following setup (illustrated in Figure 3(c)): Let (D_x, D_y) consist of supervised data and L be a loss function on D_y. Let C be some textual context regarding the data and let S be a specific task syntax. We say that $T = (D_x, D_y, L, C, S)$ is a task. For example, a molecular weight task might consist of smiles strings in D_x and their corresponding weights in D_y, $L(x,y) = \sum(\hat{y} - y)^2$, and the context is "a dataset consisting of molecules represented by SMILES strings and their corresponding molecular weights", and the syntax is MolWgt($\cdot$). Let $\mathcal{T} = \{T_0, T_1, \dots\}$ be a family of tasks.

The aim is to train a model M such that for every task $T \in \mathcal{T}$,

$$\underset{(x,y)\sim(D_x^T, D_y^T)}{\mathbb{E}}\left[L^T\left(M\left(S^T(x)\right), y\right)\right] \leq \underset{(x,y)\sim(D_x^T, D_y^T)}{\mathbb{E}}\left[L^T\left(M^T(x), y\right)\right] \quad (6)$$

where M^T is the best task-specific model. In other words, the aim is to create a single model M such that it performs at least as good as any task-specific model M^T.

In this formulation, there are many open questions. For example, the no free lunch theorem states that there exists no M such that it performs better than every M^T for all T [120]. Is it the case that naturally occurring scientific data are a subset of all possible tasks such that Equation (6) can hold? Does pre-training the model on a certain literature set improve its ability to subsume another model? How do numerical inputs D_x specific to a language prompt via S affect the learning? How does the model capacity of L affect the ability to learn a certain number of tasks? What is the effect of forgetting? Does using the context C as with prompting outlined in Section 1.5 improve performance?

4. Conclusion

LLMs are deep neural networks that aim to mimic language. Language is modeled autoregressively by using previous words to predict the next. This simple concept leads to the ability to retrieve information, demarcate information relations via attention, and generate new text. Information retrieval, information linkage, and generation are fundamental tasks that can be used for scientific progress, such as verifying scientific claims, building knowledge bases, and generating novel hypotheses. We outlined a few major research areas in transferring LLMs from NLP space to scientific language, focusing on the problem of scientific fact tracking. We presented a few projects LLMs can be immediately applied to, such as performing in-depth literature reviews, structuring electronic health records, and creating on-the-fly knowledge graphs for a specific experimental setup. These projects can be seen as part of a more significant future of AI4Science where LLMs are used to generate novel hypotheses and even unify other data-driven modeling techniques into a single source.

References

[1] S. Stall, L. Yarmey, J. Cutcher-Gershenfeld *et al.* (2019). Make scientific data FAIR. *Nature, 570*, 27–29, doi: https://doi.org/10.1038/d41586-019-01720-7, http://www.nature.com/articles/d41586-019-01720-7.

[2] A. J. Hey, S. Tansley, K. M. Tolle *et al.* (2009). *The Fourth Paradigm: Data-intensive Scientific Discovery*, Vol. 1. Microsoft Research Redmond, WA.

[3] N. Artrith, K. T. Butler, F.-X. Coudert *et al.* (2021). Best practices in machine learning for chemistry. *Nature Chemistry, 13*(6), 505–508.

[4] S. Leonelli (2016). *Data-centric Biology*. University of Chicago Press, Chicago.

[5] V. Dhar (2013). Data science and prediction. *Communications of the ACM, 56*(12), 64–73.

[6] J. Sadowski (2019). When data is capital: Datafication, accumulation, and extraction. *Big Data & Society, 6*(1), 2053951718820549.

[7] C. Anderson (2008). The end of theory: The data deluge makes the scientific method obsolete. *Wired Magazine, 16*(7), 16–107.

[8] V. Mayer-Schönberger and K. Cukier (2013). *Big Data: A Revolution that will Transform How We Live, Work, and Think*. Houghton Mifflin Harcourt.

[9] L. Floridi (2014). *The Fourth Revolution: How the Infosphere is Reshaping Human Reality*. OUP Oxford.

[10] R. Stevens, V. Taylor, J. Nichols *et al.* (2020). AI for Science: Report on the Department of Energy (DOE) Town Halls on Artificial Intelligence (AI) for Science. United States. https://doi.org/10.2172/1604756.

[11] R. Bommasani, D. A. Hudson, E. Adeli *et al.* (2021). On the opportunities and risks of foundation models. *arXiv preprint arXiv:2108.07258*.

[12] M. H. S. Segler, M. Preuss, and M. P. Waller (2018). Planning chemical syntheses with deep neural networks and symbolic AI. *Nature, 555*, 604–610.

[13] Q. Vanhaelen, Y.-C. Lin, and A. Zhavoronkov (2020). The advent of generative chemistry. *ACS Medicinal Chemistry Letters, 118*, 1496–1505.

[14] A. S. Imran, I. Posokhova, H. N. Qureshi *et al.* (2020). AI4COVID-19: AI enabled preliminary diagnosis for COVID-19 from cough samples via an app. *Informatics in Medicine Unlocked, 20*, 100378.

[15] X. Mei, H.-C. Lee, K. Diao *et al.* (2020). Artificial intelligence-enabled rapid diagnosis of patients with COVID-19, *26*(8), 1224–1228, https://doi.org/10.1038/s41591-020-0931-3, http://www.nature.com/articles/s41591-020-0931-3.

[16] L. Casalino, A. C. Dommer, Z. Gaieb *et al.* (2021). AI-driven multiscale simulations illuminate mechanisms of sars-cov-2 spike dynamics. *The International Journal of High Performance Computing Applications, 35*(5), 432–451.

[17] A. Dommer, L. Casalino, F. Kearns *et al.* (2021). # covidisairborne: AI-enabled multiscale computational microscopy of delta sars-cov-2 in a respiratory aerosol. *International Journal of High Performance Computing Applications 37*(1), 28–44, January.

[18] A. Clyde, S. Galanie, D. W. Kneller *et al.* (2021). High-throughput virtual screening and validation of a sars-cov-2 main protease noncovalent inhibitor. *Journal of Chemical Information and Modeling, 62*(1), 116–128.

[19] A. Clyde, S. Galanie, D. W. Kneller (2022). Ultrahigh throughput protein–ligand docking with deep learning. In *Artificial Intelligence in Drug Design*. Springer, pp. 301–319.

[20] H. Achdout, A. Aimon, E. Bar-David *et al.* (2020). Covid moonshot: Open science discovery of sars-cov-2 main protease inhibitors by combining crowdsourcing, high-throughput experiments, computational simulations, and machine learning. *COVID-19 Research*. The COVID Moonshot Consortium. https://doi.org/10.1101/2020.10.29.339317.

[21] A. A. Saadi, D. Alfe, Y. Babuji *et al.* (2021). Impeccable: integrated modeling pipeline for covid cure by assessing better leads. In *50th International Conference on Parallel Processing*, pp. 1–12.

[22] A. P. Bhati, S. Wan, D. Alfè *et al.* (2021). Pandemic drugs at pandemic speed: Infrastructure for accelerating COVID-19 drug discovery with hybrid machine learning-and physics-based simulations on high-performance computers. *Interface Focus, 11*(6), 20210018.

[23] K. K. Yang, Z. Wu, and F. H. Arnold (2019). Machine-learning-guided directed evolution for protein engineering. *Nature Methods, 16*(8), 687–694.

[24] J. Jumper, R. Evans, A. Pritzel *et al.* (2021). Highly accurate protein structure prediction with alphafold. *Nature, 596*(7873), 583–589.

[25] C. W. Coley, N. S. Eyke, and K. F. Jensen (2020). Autonomous discovery in the chemical sciences part I: Progress. *Angewandte Chemie International Edition, 59*(51), 22858–22893.

[26] Y. Naudet, T. Latour, W. Guedria *et al.* (2010). Towards a systemic formalisation of interoperability. *Computers in Industry, 61*(2), 176–185.

[27] M. Noura, M. Atiquzzaman, and M. Gaedke (2019). Interoperability in internet of things: Taxonomies and open challenges. *Mobile Networks and Applications, 24*, 796–809.

[28] T. Nickles (2020). Alien reasoning: Is a major change in scientific research underway? *Topoi, 39*(4), 901–914.

[29] J. Willard, X. Jia, S. Xu *et al.* (2020). Integrating physics-based modeling with machine learning: A survey. *arXiv preprint arXiv:2003.04919, 1*(1), 1–34.

[30] E. Rocca and F. Andersen (2017). How biological background assumptions influence scientific risk evaluation of stacked genetically modified plants: An analysis of research hypotheses and argumentations. *Life Sciences, Society and Policy, 13*(1), 1–20.

[31] D. Wang, J. D. Weisz, M. Muller *et al.* (2019). Human-AI collaboration in data science: Exploring data scientists' perceptions of automated AI. *Proceedings of the ACM on Human-Computer Interaction, 3*(CSCW), 1–24.

[32] D. Dellermann, A. Calma, N. Lipusch *et al.* (2021). The future of human-AI collaboration: A taxonomy of design knowledge for hybrid intelligence systems. *arXiv preprint arXiv:2105.03354.*

[33] P. Khadpe, R. Krishna, L. Fei-Fei *et al.* (2020). Conceptual metaphors impact perceptions of human-AI collaboration. *Proceedings of the ACM on Human-Computer Interaction, 4*(CSCW2), 1–26.

[34] R. M. Byrne (2019). Counterfactuals in explainable artificial intelligence (XAI): Evidence from human reasoning. In *IJCAI*, pp. 6276–6282.

[35] A. Clyde (2022). AI for science and global citizens. *Patterns, 3*(2), 100446.

[36] T. Brown, B. Mann, N. Ryder *et al.* (2020). Language models are few-shot learners. *Advances in Neural Information Processing Systems, 33*, 1877–1901.

[37] M. Chen, J. Tworek, H. Jun *et al.* (2021). Evaluating large language models trained on code. *arXiv preprint arXiv:2107.03374.*

[38] A. Elnaggar, M. Heinzinger, C. Dallago *et al.* (2020). Prottrans: Towards cracking the language of life's code through self-supervised deep learning and high performance computing. *arXiv preprint arXiv:2007.06225.*

[39] E. M. Bender (2021). On the dangers of stochastic parrots: Can language models be too big? In *Proceedings of the 2021 ACM Conference on Fairness, Accountability, and Transparency*, pp. 610–623.

[40] S. A. Wright (2020). AI in the law: Towards assessing ethical risks. In *2020 IEEE International Conference on Big Data (Big Data)*. IEEE, pp. 2160–2169.

[41] K. R. Chowdhary (2020). *Natural Language Processing.* Springer India, ISBN 978-81-322-3970-3 978-81-322-3972-7, pp. 603–649, ISBN 978-81-322-3970-3 978-81-322-3972-7, https://doi.org/10.1007/978-81-322-3972-7_19, http://link.springer.com/10.1007/978-81-322-3972-7_19.

[42] K. S. Jones (1994). Natural language processing: A historical review. *Current Issues in Computational Linguistics: In Honour of Don Walker*, pp. 3–16.

[43] W. A. Woods (1973). Progress in natural language understanding: An application to lunar geology. In *Proceedings of the June 4–8, 1973, National Computer Conference and Exposition*, pp. 441–450.

[44] W. A. Woods (1978). Semantics and quantification in natural language question answering. In *Advances in Computers*. Elsevier, Vol. 17, pp. 1–87.

[45] J. Hendler (2008). Avoiding another AI winter. *IEEE Intelligent Systems, 23*(2), 2–4.

[46] M. Davis, G. Logemann, and D. Loveland *et al.* (1962). A machine program for theorem-proving. *Communications of the ACM, 5*(7), 394–397.

[47] R. Sennrich, B. Haddow, and A. Birch (2016). Neural machine translation of rare words with subword units. In *Proceedings of the 54th Annual Meeting of the Association for Computational Linguistics (Volume 1: Long Papers)*. Association for Computational Linguistics, Berlin,

Germany, pp. 1715–1725. https://doi.org/10.18653/v1/P16-1162; https://aclanthology.org/P16-1162.

[48] A. Radford, J. Wu, R. Child *et al.* (2019). Language models are unsupervised multitask learners. *OpenAI blog*, *1*(8), 9.

[49] J. Devlin, M.-W. Chang, K. Lee *et al.* (2018). Bert: Pre-training of deep bidirectional transformers for language understanding. *arXiv preprint arXiv:1810.04805*.

[50] Y. Bengio, R. Ducharme, and P. Vincent (2000). A neural probabilistic language model. In T. Leen, T. Dietterich and V. Tresp (eds.), *Advances in Neural Information Processing Systems*, Vol. 13. MIT Press, https://proceedings.neurips.cc/paper/2000/file/728f206c2a01bf572b5940d7d9a8fa4c-Paper.pdf.

[51] J. Salazar, D. Liang, T. Q. Nguyen *et al.* (2019). Masked language model scoring. *arXiv preprint arXiv:1910.14659*.

[52] A. Vaswani, N. Shazeer, N. Parmar *et al.* (2017). Attention is all you need. In I. Guyon, U. V. Luxburg, S. Bengio, H. Wallach, R. Fergus, S. Vishwanathan and R. Garnett (eds.), *Advances in Neural Information Processing Systems*, Vol. 30. Curran Associates, Inc., https://proceedings.neurips.cc/paper/2017/file/3f5ee243547dee91fbd053c1c4a845aa-Paper.pdf.

[53] D. Britz, A. Goldie, M.-T. Luong *et al.* (2017). Massive exploration of neural machine translation architectures. *arXiv preprint arXiv:1703.03906*.

[54] D. Bahdanau, K. Cho, and Y. Bengio (2014). Neural machine translation by jointly learning to align and translate. *arXiv preprint arXiv:1409.0473*.

[55] Y. Kim, C. Denton, L. Hoang *et al.* (2017). Structured attention networks. *arXiv preprint arXiv:1702.00887*.

[56] S. S. Talathi and A. Vartak (2015). Improving performance of recurrent neural network with relu nonlinearity. *arXiv preprint arXiv:1511.03771*.

[57] Z. C. Lipton, J. Berkowitz, and C. Elkan (2015). A critical review of recurrent neural networks for sequence learning. *arXiv preprint arXiv:1506.00019*.

[58] S. Hochreiter and J. Schmidhuber (1997). Long short-term memory. *Neural Computation*, *9*(8), 1735–1780.

[59] I. Bello (2021). Lambdanetworks: Modeling long-range interactions without attention. *arXiv preprint arXiv:2102.08602*.

[60] L. Gao, S. Biderman, S. Black *et al.* (2020). The pile: An 800gb dataset of diverse text for language modeling. *arXiv preprint arXiv:2101.00027*.

[61] S. Black, S. Biderman, E. Hallahan *et al.* (2022). Gpt-neox-20b: An open-source autoregressive language model, *arXiv preprint arXiv:2204.06745*.

[62] D. Narayanan, M. Shoeybi, J. Casper *et al.* (2021). Efficient large-scale language model training on GPU clusters using megatron-lm. In *Proceedings of the International Conference for High Performance Computing, Networking, Storage and Analysis*, pp. 1–15.

[63] J. Rasley, S. Rajbhandari, O. Ruwase *et al.* (2020). Deepspeed: System optimizations enable training deep learning models with over 100 billion parameters. In *Proceedings of the 26th ACM SIGKDD International Conference on Knowledge Discovery & Data Mining*, pp. 3505–3506.

[64] T. Bolukbasi, K.-W. Chang, J. Y. Zou *et al.* (2016). Man is to computer programmer as woman is to homemaker? Debiasing word embeddings. In *Advances in Neural Information Processing Systems, 29*.

[65] J. Zhao, Y. Zhou, Z. Li *et al.* (2018). Learning gender-neutral word embeddings. In *Conference on Empirical Methods in Natural Language Processing. arXiv preprint arXiv:1809.01496*.

[66] T. Mikolov, K. Chen, G. Corrado *et al.* (2013). Efficient estimation of word representations in vector space. *arXiv preprint arXiv:1301.3781*.

[67] J. Pennington, R. Socher, and C. D. Manning (2014). Glove: Global vectors for word representation. In *Proceedings of the 2014 Conference on Empirical Methods in Natural Language Processing (EMNLP)*, pp. 1532–1543.

[68] Y. Wang, Q. Yao, J. T. Kwok *et al.* (2020). Generalizing from a few examples: A survey on few-shot learning. *ACM Computing Surveys (CSUR), 53*(3), 1–34.

[69] P. Liu, W. Yuan, J. Fu *et al.* (2021). Pre-train, prompt, and predict: A systematic survey of prompting methods in natural language processing. *arXiv preprint arXiv:2107.13586*.

[70] J. Thorne, A. Vlachos, C. Christodoulopoulos *et al.* (2018). Fever: A large-scale dataset for fact extraction and verification. *arXiv preprint arXiv:1803.05355*.

[71] P.-S. Huang, X. He, J. Gao *et al.* (2013). Learning deep structured semantic models for web search using clickthrough data. In *Proceedings of the 22nd ACM International Conference on Information & Knowledge Management*, pp. 2333–2338.

[72] H. Palangi, L. Deng, Y. Shen *et al.* (2016). Deep sentence embedding using long short-term memory networks: Analysis and application to information retrieval. *IEEE/ACM Transactions on Audio, Speech, and Language Processing, 24*(4), 694–707.

[73] R. Nogueira and K. Cho (2019). Passage re-ranking with bert. *arXiv preprint arXiv:1901.04085*.

[74] W. Yang, Y. Xie, A. Lin *et al.* (2019). End-to-end open-domain question answering with bertserini. *arXiv preprint arXiv:1902.01718*.

[75] K. Guu, K. Lee, Z. Tung *et al.* (2020). Realm: Retrieval-augmented language model pre-training. *arXiv preprint arXiv:2002.08909*.

[76] G. Izacard and E. Grave (2021). Distilling knowledge from reader to retriever for question answering. *ArXiv, abs/2012.04584*.

[77] D. Hendrycks, C. Burns, S. Basart *et al.* (2020). Measuring massive multitask language understanding. *arXiv preprint arXiv:2009.03300*.

[78] D. Khashabi, S. Min, T. Khot *et al.* (2020). Unifiedqa: Crossing format boundaries with a single QA system. *arXiv preprint arXiv:2005.00700*.

[79] K. Asatani, J. Mori, M. Ochi *et al.* (2018). Detecting trends in academic research from a citation network using network representation learning. *PloS one, 13*(5), e0197260.

[80] C. C. Loving and W. W. Cobern (2000). Invoking Thomas Kuhn: What citation analysis reveals about science education. *Science & Education, 9*(1), 187–206.

[81] S. Fortunato, C. T. Bergstrom, K. Börner *et al.* (2018). Science of science. *Science, 359*(6379), eaao0185.

[82] M. Kanehisa and S. Goto (2000). Kegg: Kyoto encyclopedia of genes and genomes. *Nucleic Acids Research, 28*(1), 27–30.

[83] M. Kanehisa (2019). Toward understanding the origin and evolution of cellular organisms. *Protein Science, 28*(11), 1947–1951.

[84] M. Kanehisa, M. Furumichi, Y. Sato *et al.* (2021). Kegg: Integrating viruses and cellular organisms. *Nucleic Acids Research,* 49(D1), D545–D551.

[85] S. Meystre and P. J. Haug (2006). Natural language processing to extract medical problems from electronic clinical documents: Performance evaluation. *Journal of Biomedical Informatics, 39*(6), 589–599.

[86] M. Pinnis, R. Krišlauks, D. Deksne *et al.* (2017). Neural machine translation for morphologically rich languages with improved sub-word units and synthetic data. In *International Conference on Text, Speech, and Dialogue.* Springer, pp. 237–245.

[87] Y. Zhang, Q. Chen, Z. Yang *et al.* (2019). Biowordvec, improving biomedical word embeddings with subword information and mesh. *Scientific Data,* 6(1), 1–9.

[88] K. Denecke (2014). Extracting medical concepts from medical social media with clinical NLP tools: A qualitative study. In *Proceedings of the Fourth Workshop on Building and Evaluation Resources for Health and Biomedical Text Processing.* Citeseer, pp. 54–60.

[89] A. B. Abacha and P. Zweigenbaum (2011). Medical entity recognition: A comparison of semantic and statistical methods. In *Proceedings of BioNLP 2011 Workshop,* pp. 56–64.

[90] U. Naseem, M. Khushi, V. B. Reddy *et al.* (2020). Bioalbert: A simple and effective pre-trained language model for biomedical named entity recognition. *arXiv, abs/2009.09223.*

[91] A. Liu, J. Du and V. Stoyanov (2019). Knowledge-augmented language model and its application to unsupervised named-entity recognition. *arXiv, abs/1904.04458.*

[92] W. Xiong, J. Du, W. Y. Wang (2020). Pretrained encyclopedia: Weakly supervised knowledge-pretrained language model. *arXiv, abs/1912. 09637.*

[93] S. Biderman and E. Raff (2022). Neural language models are effective plagiarists. *arXiv preprint arXiv:2201.07406.*

[94] J. Harrison, J. Urban and F. Wiedijk (2014). History of interactive theorem proving. *Computational Logic, 9,* 135–214.

[95] P. West, C. Bhagavatula, J. Hessel (2021). Symbolic knowledge distillation: From general language models to commonsense models. *arXiv preprint arXiv:2110.07178.*

[96] H. Lu Open-ended generative commonsense question answering with knowledge graph-enhanced language models.

[97] Y. Sun, S. Wang, S. Feng *et al.* (2021). Ernie 3.0: Large-scale knowledge enhanced pre-training for language understanding and generation. *arXiv preprint arXiv:2107.02137.*

[98]   T. Kim, Y. Yun and N. Kim *et al.* (2021). Deep learning-based knowledge graph generation for COVID-19. *Sustainability*, *13*(4), 2276.

[99]   J. Gou, B. Yu, S. J. Maybank *et al.* (2021). Knowledge distillation: A survey. *International Journal of Computer Vision*, *129*(6), 1789–1819.

[100]   S. Lee and B. C. Song (2019). Graph-based knowledge distillation by multi-head attention network. *arXiv preprint arXiv:1907.02226*.

[101]   C. Lassance, M. Bontonou, G. B. Hacene *et al.* (2020). Deep geometric knowledge distillation with graphs. In *ICASSP 2020-2020 IEEE International Conference on Acoustics, Speech and Signal Processing (ICASSP)*. IEEE, pp. 8484–8488.

[102]   I. V. Logan, L. Robert, N. F. Liu *et al.* (2019). "Barack's wife hillary: Using knowledge-graphs for fact-aware language modeling." arXiv preprint arXiv:1906.07241.

[103]   P. Minervini, M. Bošnjak, T. Rocktäschel *et al.* (2020). Differentiable reasoning on large knowledge bases and natural language. In *Proceedings of the AAAI Conference on Artificial Intelligence*, Vol. 34, pp. 5182–5190.

[104]   A. Clyde, A. Ramanathan, and R. Stevens (2021). Scaffold embeddings: Learning the structure spanned by chemical fragments, scaffolds and compounds. *arXiv preprint arXiv:2103.06867*.

[105]   J. Park, S. C. You, E. Jeong *et al.* (2021). A framework (socratex) for hierarchical annotation of unstructured electronic health records and integration into a standardized medical database: Development and usability study. *JMIR Medical Informatics*, *9*(3), e23983.

[106]   I. Li, J. Pan, J. Goldwasser *et al.* (2021). Neural natural language processing for unstructured data in electronic health records: A review. *arXiv preprint arXiv:2107.02975*.

[107]   T. Dimitrov, C. Kreisbeck, J. S. Becker *et al.* 2019. Autonomous molecular design: Then and now. *ACS Applied Materials & Interfaces*, *11*(28), 24825–24836.

[108]   E. Mjolsness and D. DeCoste (2001). Machine learning for science: State of the art and future prospects. *Science*, *293*(5537), 2051–2055.

[109]   P. S. Gromski, J. M. Granda and L. Cronin *et al.* (2020). Universal chemical synthesis and discovery with 'the chemputer'. *Trends in Chemistry*, *2*(1), 4–12.

[110]   J. H. Montoya, M. Aykol, A. Anapolsky *et al.* (2022). Toward autonomous materials research: Recent progress and future challenges. *Applied Physics Reviews*, *9*(1), 011405.

[111]   H. Xiao, M. Huang, and X. Zhu (2015). From one point to a manifold: Knowledge graph embedding for precise link prediction. *arXiv preprint arXiv:1512.04792*.

[112]   A. Rossi, D. Barbosa, D. Firmani *et al.* (2021). Knowledge graph embedding for link prediction: A comparative analysis. *ACM Transactions on Knowledge Discovery from Data (TKDD)*, *15*(2), 1–49.

[113]   R. Patel and Y. Guo (2021). Graph based link prediction between human phenotypes and genes. *arXiv preprint arXiv:2105.11989*.

[114] P. Rosso, D. Yang, and P. Cudré-Mauroux (2020). Beyond triplets: Hyper-relational knowledge graph embedding for link prediction. In *Proceedings of the Web Conference 2020*, pp. 1885–1896.

[115] R. D. King, K. E. Whelan, F. M. Jones *et al.* (2004). Functional genomic hypothesis generation and experimentation by a robot scientist. *Nature*, *427*(6971), 247–252.

[116] S. Spangler, A. D. Wilkins, B. J. Bachman *et al.* (2014). Automated hypothesis generation based on mining scientific literature. In *Proceedings of the 20th ACM SIGKDD International Conference on Knowledge Discovery and Data Mining*, pp. 1877–1886.

[117] T. S. Kuhn (1970). *The Structure of Scientific Revolutions*, Vol. 111. Chicago University of Chicago Press, Chicago.

[118] S. M. Glynn, B. K. Britton, M. Semrud-Clikeman *et al.* (1989). Analogical reasoning and problem solving in science textbooks. In *Handbook of Creativity*. Springer, pp. 383–398.

[119] P. Abrantes (1999). Analogical reasoning and modeling in the sciences. *Foundations of Science*, *4*(3), 237–270.

[120] S. P. Adam, S.-A. N. Alexandropoulos, P. M. Pardalos *et al.* (2019). No free lunch theorem: A review. In I. C. Demetriou and P. M. Pardalos (eds.), *Approximation and Optimization*. Springer International Publishing, Cham: Springer, Vol. 145, pp. 57–82. ISBN 978-3-030-12766-4 978-3-030-12767-1, https://doi.org/10.1007/978-3-030-12767-1_5, http://link.springer.com/10.1007/978-3-030-12767-1_5.

© 2023 World Scientific Publishing Company
https://doi.org/10.1142/9789811265679_0035

Chapter 35

AI for Autonomous Vehicles

Tom St. John[*,‡] and Vijay Janapa Reddi[†,§]

Cruise, San Francisco, CA, USA

†*John J. Paulson School of Engineering and Applied Sciences,
Harvard University, Cambridge, MA, USA*

‡*tom.stjohn@getcruise.com*

§*vj@eecs.harvard.edu*

1. Introduction

In a recent technical report by the National Highway Traffic Safety Administration (NHTSA), it was reported that 94% of accidents are caused by human error [17]. With an annual reported fatality rate of nearly 43,000 Americans in 2021 [13], technologies which would reduce or eliminate traffic fatalities due to human error have become a research area of utmost importance.

The autonomous vehicle market is projected to reach over $2 trillion USD by 2030 [1]. This revolution has been enabled by advances in artificial intelligence which have made the myriad engineering challenges encountered in this domain tractable. However, in order to achieve the level of safety guarantees necessary for mainstream deployment, further advances in the state of the art are still necessary.

We intend to provide an overview of the current state of the field for autonomous vehicles, as well as describe future directions for this industry.

2. Sensors

While the variety and number of sensors deployed in autonomous vehicles vary between companies, they typically fall into three categories:

- lidar,
- cameras,
- radar.

In Figure 1, we see Waymo's 5th-generation Waymo Driver [3] platform. As you would expect, they are using multiple sensors of each type, both to compensate for whatever shortcomings an individual sensor modality may have and also to provide redundancy.

2.1. *Lidar*

Lidar (Light Detection and Ranging) works by spinning continuously and firing lasers, measuring how long it takes these beams to return to the sensor. These data can then be represented as a 3D point cloud. In Figure 2, we see such a point cloud being generated by a Velodyne lidar [19].

Lidar is able to capture detailed 3D information about surroundings out to 200–300 m. Due to the fixed frequency of the sensor, data become more sparse as it travels further from the source, necessitating alternative sensor modalities for distances beyond the effective range of lidar. The accuracy of the data collected can also be negatively impacted by poor weather conditions (rain, snow, etc.)

2.2. *Cameras*

Cameras are frequently used in autonomous vehicles due to their low cost, high resolution, and ability to detect color information. However, cameras also face difficulty obtaining depth information and are susceptible to negative illumination conditions.

2.3. *Radar*

Radar is quite useful when compensating for the weaknesses of other sensor types. It operates well during bad weather and it provides range information. However, it frequently has difficulty detecting small objects at long range, so it needs to be supplemented by other sensors to compensate for this.

3. AV System Architecture

The AV system architecture can be thought of as a pipeline accepting input data and then proceeding through several computation phases in order to determine which actions the vehicle should take.

Fig. 1.   Suite of sensors used in Waymo's 5th-generation Waymo Driver.

Fig. 2.   A lidar point cloud created by Velodyne lidar.

The major phases are as follows:

- Perception
  - In this phase, input data coming in from sensors are processed to identify the state of the environment around the vehicle.

- Prediction
  - In this phase, data generated during the perception phase are used to determine how the state of the environment is expected to change (pedestrian movement, etc.).
- Planning
  - In this phase, the results from the prediction phase are used to determine the appropriate course of action for the vehicle to take.

4. Perception

Since perception is where AI has seen the most widespread adoption in the domain of autonomous vehicles, this is where we will focus the remainder of the chapter. In Figure 3 [2], we observe objection detection being carried out by a self-driving vehicle.

4.1. *3D object detection*

One of the modules of the autonomous driving pipeline which makes heavy use of deep learning techniques is 3D object detection.

Although work has been done to perform 3D object detection using only camera images [6,15,21], the lack of depth information makes this challenging, so network architectures leveraging lidar-based point clouds [4, 9,12,14,22,23] are far more prevalent.

4.1.1. *PointPillars*

We will consider the PointPillars architecture as an example of a lidar-based 3D object detection model.

The main components of the PointPillars network are a pillar feature network, 2D convolutional backbone, and SSD [10] detection head. The pillar feature network converts the point cloud into a sparse pseudo-image, the convolutional backbone processes the pseudo-image into a high-level representation, and the detection head detects 3D boxes.

Some newer models take advantage of multiple input modalities to improve the accuracy of 3D object detection. These models include MV3D [7], AVOD [8], and PointPainting [20], among others [11,16,24].

4.1.2. *PointPainting*

We will look at the approach used in the PointPainting architecture.

The PointPainting network takes point clouds and images as inputs and detects 3D boxes. The first step is to perform semantic segmentation on

Fig. 3.   An example of object detection.

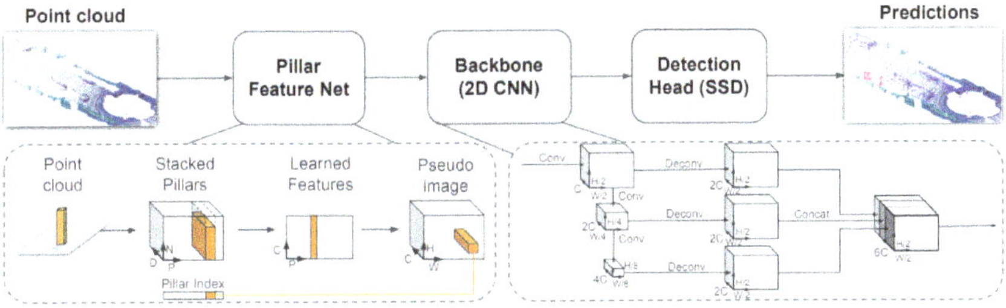

Fig. 4.   Network overview of PointPillars network.

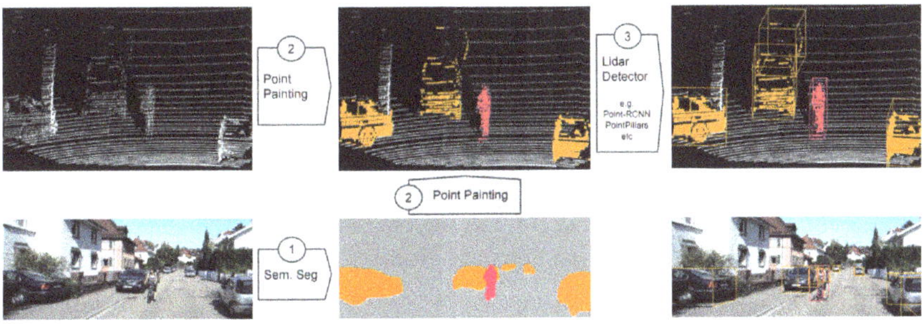

Fig. 5.   Overview of PointPainting architecture.

the input images, providing pixel-wise segmentation scores. Next, the lidar points are painted (fused) with the semantic segmentation scores computed in the previous step. Finally, a lidar-based 3D object detection network detects the 3D boxes.

PointPainting was initially developed to use DeepLabv3+ [5] as its image segmentation model, but newer models can be swapped in as the state of the art advances, allowing the PointPainting architecture to take advantage of improvements to individual components. Several lidar-based 3D detection models leveraged in PointPainting include PointPillars [9], VoxelNet [23], and PointRCNN [14]. However, as was also the case with the image segmentation models, newer 3D object detection models, such as Range Sparse Net [18], could be used as a replacement.

5. Conclusion

In conclusion, we have summarized some of the applications of artificial intelligence in the autonomous vehicle domain. Being able to detect and identify objects is critical for self-driving, and deep learning techniques have significantly boosted recognition accuracy compared to more traditional detection techniques.

We described the advantages and disadvantages of different sensor modalities and how they can be used to complement each other.

As deep learning continues to be applied to the remaining components of the AV system architecture (tracking, planning, etc.), this will create even more exciting opportunities for innovation.

References

[1] https://www.alliedmarketresearch.com/press-release/autonomous-vehicle-market.html.

[2] https://blogs.nvidia.com/blog/2018/08/10/autonomous-vehicles-perception-layer/.

[3] https://blog.waymo.com/2020/03/introducing-5th-generation-waymo-driver.html.

[4] R. Q. Charles, H. Su, M. Kaichun *et al.* (2017). PointNet: Deep learning on point sets for 3D classification and segmentation. In *2017 IEEE Conference on Computer Vision and Pattern Recognition (CVPR)*, pp. 77–85. doi: 10.1109/CVPR.2017.16.

[5] L. C. Chen, Y. Zhu, G. Papandreou *et al.* (2018). Encoder-decoder with atrous separable convolution for semantic image segmentation. In V. Ferrari, M. Hebert, C. Sminchisescu, and Y. Weiss (eds.), *Computer Vision — ECCV 2018*. Lecture Notes in Computer Science, Vol. 11211. Springer, Cham. https://doi.org/10.1007/978-3-030-01234-2_49.

[6] X. Chen, K. Kundu, Z. Zhang *et al.* (2016). Monocular 3D object detection for autonomous driving. In *2016 IEEE Conference on Computer Vision and Pattern Recognition (CVPR)*, pp. 2147–2156. doi: 10.1109/CVPR.2016.236.

[7] X. Chen, H. Ma, J. Wan *et al.* (2017). Multi-view 3D object detection network for autonomous driving. In *2017 IEEE Conference on Computer Vision and Pattern Recognition (CVPR)*, pp. 6526–6534. doi: 10.1109/CVPR.2017.691.

[8] J. Ku, M. Mozifian, J. Lee *et al.* (2018). Joint 3D proposal generation and object detection from view aggregation. In *2018 IEEE/RSJ International Conference on Intelligent Robots and Systems (IROS)*, pp. 1–8. doi: 10.1109/IROS.2018.8594049.

[9] A. H. Lang, S. Vora, H. Caesar *et al.* (2019). PointPillars: Fast encoders for object detection from point clouds. In *2019 IEEE/CVF Conference on Computer Vision and Pattern Recognition (CVPR)*, pp. 12689–12697. doi: 10.1109/CVPR.2019.01298.

[10] W. Liu, D. Anguelov, D. Erhan *et al.* (2016). SSD: Single shot multibox detector. In B. Leibe, J. Matas, N. Sebe, M. Welling, (eds.), *Computer Vision — ECCV 2016. Lecture Notes in Computer Science*, Vol. 9905, pp. 27–37, Cham: Springer. doi: 10.1007/978-3-319-46448-0_2.

[11] G. P. Meyer, J. Charland, D. Hegde *et al.* (2019). Sensor fusion for joint 3D object detection and semantic segmentation. In *2019 IEEE/CVF Conference on Computer Vision and Pattern Recognition Workshops (CVPRW)*, pp. 1230–1237. doi: 10.1109/CVPRW.2019.00162.

[12] G. P. Meyer, A. Laddha, E. Kee *et al.* (2019). LaserNet: An efficient probabilistic 3D object detector for autonomous driving. In *2019 IEEE/CVF Conference on Computer Vision and Pattern Recognition (CVPR)*, pp. 12669–12678. doi: 10.1109/CVPR.2019.01296.

[13] National Center for Statistics and Analysis (2022). Early estimates of motor vehicle traffic fatalities and fatality rate by sub-categories in 2021. *Tech. Rep.*

[14] S. Shi, X. Wang, and H. Li (2019). *PointRCNN: 3D object proposal generation and detection from point cloud*, pp. 770–779. doi: 10.1109/CVPR.2019.00086.

[15] X. Shi, Q. Ye, X. Chen *et al.* (2021). Geometry-based distance decomposition for monocular 3D object detection. In *2021 IEEE/CVF International Conference on Computer Vision (ICCV)*, pp. 15172–15181.

[16] V. A. Sindagi, Y. Zhou, and O. Tuzel (2019). MVX-Net: Multimodal Voxel-Net for 3D object detection. In *2019 International Conference on Robotics and Automation (ICRA)*, pp. 7276–7282. doi: 10.1109/ICRA.2019.8794195.

[17] S. Singh (2018). Critical reasons for crashes investigated in the national motor vehicle crash causation survey. *Tech. Rep.*, 2018.

[18] P. Sun, W. Wang, Y. Chai *et al.* (2021). RSN: Range Sparse Net for efficient, accurate LiDAR 3D object detection. In *2021 IEEE/CVF Conference on Computer Vision and Pattern Recognition (CVPR)*, pp. 5721–5730. doi: 10.1109/CVPR46437.2021.00567.

[19] https://velodynelidar.com/blog/guide-to-lidar-wavelengths/.

[20] S. Vora, A. H. Lang, B. Helou *et al.* (2020). PointPainting: Sequential fusion for 3D object detection. In *2020 IEEE/CVF Conference on Computer Vision and Pattern Recognition (CVPR)*, pp. 4603–4611. doi: 10.1109/CVPR42600.2020.00466.

[21] Y. Wang, W.-L. Chao, D. Garg *et al.* (2019). Pseudo-LiDAR from visual depth estimation: Bridging the gap in 3D object detection for autonomous driving. In *2019 IEEE/CVF Conference on Computer Vision and Pattern Recognition (CVPR)*, pp. 8437–8445. doi: 10.1109/CVPR.2019.00864.

[22] B. Yang, W. Luo, and R. Urtasun (2018). PIXOR: Real-time 3D object detection from point clouds. In *2018 IEEE/CVF Conference on Computer Vision and Pattern Recognition*, pp. 7652–7660. doi: 10.1109/CVPR.2018.00798.

[23] Y. Zhou and O. Tuzel (2018). VoxelNet: End-to-end learning for point cloud based 3D object detection. In *2018 IEEE/CVF Conference on Computer Vision and Pattern Recognition*, pp. 4490–4499. doi: 10.1109/CVPR.2018.00472.

[24] M. Zhu, C. Ma, P. Ji *et al.* (2021). Cross-modality 3D object detection. In *2021 IEEE Winter Conference on Applications of Computer Vision (WACV)*, pp. 3771–3780. doi: 10.1109/WACV48630.2021.00382.

© 2023 World Scientific Publishing Company
https://doi.org/10.1142/9789811265679_0036

Chapter 36

The Automated AI-driven Future of Scientific Discovery

Hector Zenil[*,†,§,¶] and Ross D. King[*,‡,§,‖]

*Department of Chemical Engineering and Biotechnology,
University of Cambridge, UK
†Kellogg College, University of Oxford, UK
‡Department of Computer Science and Engineering,
Chalmers University, Sweden
§The Alan Turing Institute, UK
¶hector.zenil@cs.ox.ac.uk
‖rk663@cam.ac.uk

1. Introduction

Computing and machine learning are now ubiquitous, pervading our social, cultural, and intellectual lives. Academic fields have been affected, many to such an extent that future progress has become almost unthinkable without the integration of a machine learning component.

Most modern machine learning methods produce very large models (in terms of the number of parameters and the complexity of their interactions) of phenomena, and it is left to the human scientist to ask "What has been learned?" The burgeoning field of model explanation (e.g., LIME [19]) attempts to help humans achieve a succinct understanding of what these large models are doing. But this approach is merely an attempt to fix a problem of our own creation.

AI for scientific discovery has to focus its efforts on breaking current barriers preventing scientific progress. Some of these are related to a lack of understanding of first principles, such as the origin of life, while others are more pragmatic in nature, having to do with how best to conduct massive experiments, as in systems biology and drug discovery.

Other obvious challenges are connected to climate change, energy and
environment, and waste management and disposal, where, for example,
materials science can play a key role. Another area is that of population
growth stagnation, which will also impact science and its practice since
fewer professionals may be available and automation will become more
necessary if the scientific enterprise is to remain efficient. When shortages
of personnel in certain areas such as medicine and engineering become even
more difficult to compensate for than they are now, new pathways will
be required, creating a demand for more efficient ways to serve an aging
population using fewer human resources [23].

More immediate problems are housing, migration (e.g., as a result of
current climate change patterns), and problems related to spending more
time indoors, like chemicals, waste, recycling, resource management (e.g.,
cooling and energy distribution) [6,12].

A larger and fundamental problem of great urgency is disease, both
chronic and infections, the former affecting high-income countries and the
latter affecting both high- and low-income countries. Included here is the
serious problem of antibiotic resistance, with drug discovery being key to
addressing this challenge [12,17].

When exploring challenges where AI-led automation for scientific discovery can contribute, one has to wonder whether certain challenges appear
insoluble by experimental means only because of a lack of imagination.
Consider, for instance, questions related to black holes and, e.g., the
information paradox and no-hair theorems, that is, that black holes,
like elementary particles, have no other features except mass, electric
charge, and angular momentum [16]. One would be somewhat incredulous
if told that experimental automation could test the validity of such a
theoretical statement, but in point of fact, AI-led automation can help
design experiments based on the generation of hypotheses compatible
with either the experimental validation or rejection of the consequences
of non-hair theorems, thereby controlling telescopes that scan the sky
or pointing them at specific objects [4]. The exercise of creativity and
vision is called for, the vision to find out how to experimentally validate
even heavily theoretical hypotheses, which indeed is something scientists
are not unfamiliar with, though the task is often not an easy one, as
witnessed in the Higgs boson, which took decades and billions of euros to
validate following its theoretical postulation, or the experiments validating
Einstein's general relativity, which though only a handful, took brilliant
minds to devise and then verify them. The following challenges have thus
to be read in this context, where areas of physics in particular may seem at
first glance difficult to translate into scientific experiments led or assisted
by AI. But the expectation of science is that all questions will eventually be

settled experimentally. Therefore, AI-led experiments are not only possible but are consistent with scientific methodology, even if deploying them in the early stages of scientific discovery is as yet untenable.

2. AI-led Automation in Science

AI applications to science are multiple but limited and not always systematic or standardized. One instance of the successful application of AI was the discovery of climate dipoles through machine learning [15] from climate data. Another application of AI in science is in creating self-driving robots, not just for exploring planetary surfaces such as that of Mars but also for use on the seabed, in prioritization work and in deciding on optimal routes for cabling, in prospecting for oil or exploring the surface of this and other planets [2,22]. AI has also had an impact on robot automation, having been incorporated into commercial and academic labs to different degrees, but it is companies that currently lead applications for lab automation.

Automation in science involves machine embodiment, simulating the performance of a human scientist, instrument-driven approaches where robotics are capable of making progress in physical experimentation. If not embodied, the scientific experiment may collapse into a problem of data analysis and inference, which is only a small part of the scientific discovery cycle. Only exploration of certain delimited regions of the possible scientific discovery space will be possible. Neural networks can help physical machines to embed themselves in a physical world for representation purposes, as neural networks have proven useful in representing all manner of content, such as images in numerical matrices or language as vectors. But to accommodate the full range and depth of scientific experiments, innovation will be required in the areas of robotics and mechatronics, in particular with respect to accuracy and precision — which should not present a problem — but also in relation to the current, very human problem of reproducibility [3]. Such innovations may be expected to have a significant positive impact on the reproducibility of science, as automating science requires semantic precision.

A fundamental goal of automation in science is the development and operation of highly autonomous AI/Robotics experimental laboratories in selected key research centers. These would enable the separate development of the hardware and software for AI scientists, and researchers working on new AI software would not confront the difficulties associated with running physical laboratories. Infrastructure that would need to be developed includes open and standard configurations, software and cloud platforms, APIs, and protocol sharing approaches to enable scalable and shareable AI scientist prototype components, initially targeting basic scientific research on microbials, mammalian cellular systems, and synthetic biology.

An initial core center may be established in one or more of the coordinating centers and later expanded to other sites as the proof-of-concept is validated. These laboratories would be remotely accessible. All this should be in place within the first five years [10]. But what should one choose to prioritize when contemplating automation in science? We have found consensus on a set of relevant criteria, which we present in the form of a dynamic AI-driven leaderboard incorporating answers to this question for each of the fields proposed:

1. feasibility and probability of success, e.g., based on the momentum of prior success,
2. expected cost of research/development,
3. complexity,
4. data availability,
5. size of parameter space,
6. interdisciplinarity (room to compete),
7. interdisciplinarity (number of different kinds of approaches),
8. scientific/conceptual breakthrough,
9. AI breakthrough,
10. number of lives (e.g., DALYs — disability-adjusted life years) affected,
11. ability to address global inequality.

3. Key Milestones

Lab automation is traditionally the use of instrumentation to perform laboratory processes with minimal or no human input [7]. Automation can be used anywhere, in a single step of an experimental process or throughout the entire workflow. While lab automation can be split into stages, and automated processes can be integrated across the board, application to all parts of the experimental process, automation of the entire experimental cycle in a fully closed loop from hypothesis generation to feature selection, model generation, and hypothesis testing has so far been rare.

The purpose of AI-led science must ultimately be to learn compact, modular, hierarchical theories to mirror current human scientific discovery. Our AI systems will need to suggest new concepts and specify their properties; build or use existing self-consistent mathematical objects to simplify a theory; compare the consistency of alternative theories even though they may work with different concepts. This learning process can and should draw on the many years of search, optimization, and knowledge representation work that lie behind us, but it is a distinct research direction.

Prioritizing data collection based on the available scientific knowledge. The trend in science is for more and more of the physical execution of experiments to be done using robotics. This will increase the productivity of science, as robots work cheaper, faster, more accurately, and for longer than humans.

One key task is to create AI systems for scientific discovery able to conduct experimentation and hypothesis testing independent of human instruction or with little to no human instruction. This is because what is desired to take scientific discovery to the next level is not the programming of algorithms able to conduct experiments but open-ended algorithms able to set their own goals and devise experiments using previous experiments as guides (their own or drawn from the human literature).

Two successful instances of lab automation in scientific discovery may be cited that close the discovery loop from hypothesis generation to validation, going through the entire experimental cycle.

An open question for current investigation by our group has to do with how to scale up these successes. A key finding from the Adam robot scientist project (Figure 1) is that reusing experimental results can be critical [20]. Semantically labeled results were recycled from a previous

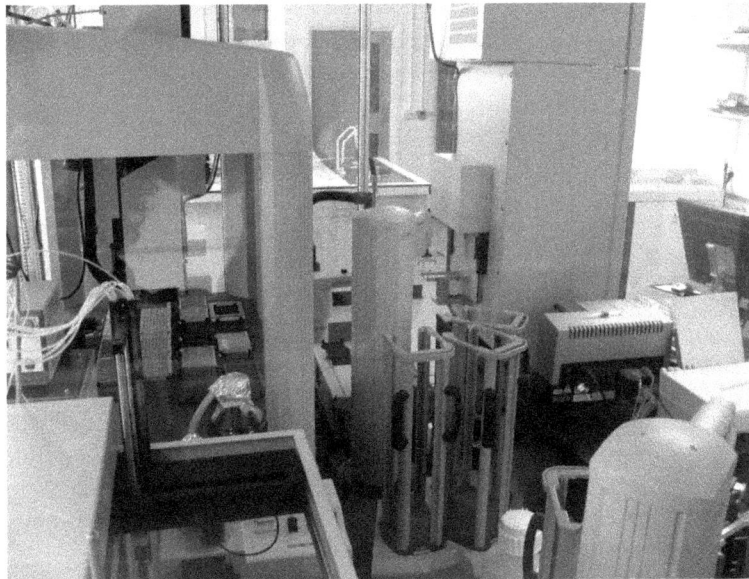

Fig. 1. Adam Robot Scientist. Adam is a computer system that fully automates the scientific process. Within limits, he can come up with new hypotheses, design, and carry out experiments to test them.

Fig. 2.   Eve robot scientist had as a first mission to identify and test drugs.

research purpose and used to make a new biological discovery. Adam was able to autonomously investigate gene function in yeast, even finding contradictions in current models of yeast growth, which is the type of discovery that gets into textbook accounts of the fundamentals of the scientific method. Adam discovered the genes responsible for "orphaned" yeast enzymes, the origins of which were previously unknown, in another example of a fully closed AI-led automated cycle in scientific discovery.

Eve, an artificially intelligent "robot scientist", made drug discovery faster and much cheaper by reducing the costs, uncertainty, and time involved in drug screening, an achievement with the potential to improve the lives of millions of people worldwide [25]. Eve (Figure 2) discovered that a compound called triclosan, used as an antiseptic, effectively targets an enzyme that is key to the growth of *Plasmodium vivax*, one of the parasites that causes malaria [6], a result that drug companies would struggle to achieve, given that their business model is designed to maximize profits from developed countries and not to serve developing ones. Even with computer-assisted tools, drug discovery is slow and based on trial and error.

Among several novel ideas being developed in our group at the Alan Turing Institute is an attempt to institutionalize this notion of recycling and reuse, with both Adam and Eve affording proof of concept. This entails the establishment of domain-specific labs bridging domain knowledge, lab automation, and AI, with the right proportion of scientific minds in each of these areas deeply interacting with each other, united by a single scientific purpose. Another suggestion is to find the metrics to properly evaluate the contribution of AI in a specific field or subject, progress on which we report in the next section. Yet another suggestion is to create and adopt a public library of automation protocols to accelerate adoption and translation of automation protocols across domains. But consideration has to be given to the open and stable nature of both the libraries and APIs, which should go beyond private ownership and private control.

4. The Future of AI-led Discovery in Science

Extensions of the Adam and Eve robot scientists are currently in development, for example, related to a central challenge in modern science, the development of systems biology models of eukaryotic cells. These models are central to the future of medicine (humans are eukaryotes), to agriculture (plants are eukaryotes), and to biotechnology (antibodies, food, etc.). Systems biology presents an extreme challenge to the traditional human based scientific method, as the existing models (thousands of causally interacting components) are so complex that they are beyond human intuitive understanding. The legendary complexity of biological systems also implies that the only way forward to build comprehensive system models will be to increase by orders of magnitude the number of hypothesis-led experiments. The Genesis hardware, developed at Vanderbilt, is designed to meet this challenge. It will consist of ten thousand individually programmable microchemostats connected to state-of-the-art mass-spectrometry and RNA sequencing. This will enable Genesis-AI to design and execute in parallel ten thousand closed-loop cycles of experiments per day. Each closed-loop cycle will consist of hypothesis formation, experiment planning, laboratory execution, and results interpretation. Each experiment will be designed to improve the complex systems biology model. This number of parallel cycles is a thousand times more than that of any previous AI closed-loop system and represents a step-change in AI methods for automating science.

In drug discovery, AI systems will be deciding what to make and screen, simply because they are faster and better at some tasks than humans. Automation can be the fifth paradigm of science in all areas, after empiricism (or experimentation, the first paradigm), theory (the second), computation (the third), and data (the fourth). The empirical approach is often inductive, in the sense that one tries to find common patterns, rules, or laws in observed data. Data-intensive statistical investigation (the fourth paradigm) could be viewed as a computer-led acceleration of the first paradigm, hence inductive as well. On the other hand, the second paradigm, theory, is deductive, in the sense that one makes a prediction based on a proposition that is a candidate hypothesis to be tested, something current approaches to statistical machine learning are ill-equipped to do. Computer simulation (the third approach) can be viewed as a computer acceleration of this theoretical deduction approach, based on rules, sometimes physics-related and following physical laws (e.g., weather prediction). In the fifth, ultimate AI paradigm, the whole cycle, including inductive and deductive processes, is expected to be combined and automated. AI possesses this capability and has not yet been developed and consistently or systematically applied, even in cases where impressive results have been obtained, such as with AlphaFold 2 in the challenge of protein folding [13,24].

One of the pieces still missing, in addition to highly automated discovery, is the synthesizing power of science, the piece that is added to textbooks. Currently, the discoveries of AlphaFold 2 will require scientists' interpretation beyond the crude classification of results. What is currently missing, and what current approaches such as deep learning have fallen short of, and which goes beyond robotized experimentation, is the means to automate execution of abductive inference that converts results from the inductive processing of data (e.g., classification) into hypotheses and models that are necessary to conduct deductive inference (or simulation), i.e., science, properly speaking, in its full cycle.

In areas such as planetary exploration, it is most likely that discovery will entirely be led by automated AI systems that will be able to categorize all sorts of planetary objects with great precision on the basis of well-defined signatures indexing some or most of the objects' properties, such as atmospheric conditions and even bio-markers. AI for scientific discovery will no doubt help process the many orders of magnitude that humans will keep generating.

In biology, research is most likely to become even faster and unrecognizable vis-a-vis today's state of the art. Challenges will probably involve predicting the kinds of changes that genetic perturbations will lead to, all the way from the coding to the behavioral layer, and the brain will be mapped with even greater detail, to the point where we may have full pathways from epigenetics to brain processes. Cancer most likely will be beaten in 30 years with the help of AI and even faster with AI systems for scientific discovery. Perhaps, other diseases will emerge due to novel challenges faced by human society (such as pandemics or climate change), but science has proven to be a fundamental tool for humans to use in confronting such challenges.

AI in the environmental sciences will most likely help find ways to clean up the world and make us more efficient at managing waste than we have been in the last century. It may help rid the seas of plastics and find new enzymes to fight microplastic generation. New materials will be used to replace plastic, and AI will contribute to making every aspect of our technology more efficient.

Mathematics will also most likely be transformed, and it is perhaps where human–machine collaboration will turn out to be most in evidence [9, 21], as it is human curiosity that will lead the AI, while the AI, through semi-supervised or unsupervised automatic theorem proving systems, will do most of the heavy work. Mathematicians will be freed to seek more analogies across mathematical fields and possibly more applications, as they produce theories already in computable form ready to be used in other areas.

5. The Evaluation of AI in Science

Today, there is no easy solution to the problem of how science is rewarded or how themes are chosen or research proposals are evaluated, but reproducibility, better quantification of impact, and a clearer display of purpose rather than method may represent an opportunity. AI may be able to optimize the choice of themes with the highest impact, which will give rise to new debates around these choices and how humans can relate to them, even if they are explained by the AI and even if they are based on purely quantitative performance indicators.

While human IQ tests are a measure of intelligence, they are probably not a sound measure of the skills that conduce to scientific discovery. We already know machines are better at most of the skills tested on an IQ test, such as logic, arithmetic, and calculus, which human IQ tests are heavily biased toward. Less impressive are the machine's capabilities to understand questions out of context and in a multiplicity of ways in which the same question can be asked possibly making them fail some IQ test questions. Most of the challenges are thus related to representation both internal and at the ingestion point, which neural networks have helped advance, but machines fail at producing hypotheses, selecting problems, synthesising models from data and noise, abstracting salient features, unstructured reasoning, reinterpretation of results, and the full closing of the discovery cycle (restarting it from the previous point) [11,14,18].

A hierarchy similar to that of SAE's (BS ISO/SAE 21434:2021) levels of autonomy of self-driving cars, in combination with the above, can be adopted to evaluate the degree of AI automation in science. But unlike driverless cars, where companies compete around which of their cars has logged more miles — in millions — AI in science should take the opposite direction and rely less on data and more on generating models able to make more and better predictions with less and less data.

The following is a hierarchy inspired by SAEs but in relation to quantifying the degree of AI-led automation in the process of scientific discovery:

Level 0 No Automation: Traditional, past human experimentation with no machine intervention, manual calculation, data processing, classification.

Level 1 Machine Assistance: Data science, statistical machine learning. Solve a problem within a closed set of rules (e.g., theorem provers). Search problem in a closed world.

Level 2 Partial Automation: An important aspect of the discovery cycle is fully automated, e.g., simulation or knowledge extraction. Test a proposition in open world (propose experiments necessary to test the proposition) -¿ search problem in open world.

Level 3 Model selection and generation, the equivalent of a knowledgeable peer possessing some agency. Given a set of hypotheses, the system is able to follow their consequences, test them, and arrive at a rejection or validation, i.e., a conclusion.

Level 4 Generates a hypothesis (a proposition that is a candidate for novel knowledge) in the way that testing it maximizes information gain defined by criteria specified by humans. The system possesses level 3 capabilities but can also generate and explore the hypothesis space on its own. There is at least one aspect of or one module in the discovery cycle that is not yet fully automated.

Level 5 Full Automation: Capable of level 4. No human intervention is required at any step. Is able to define the information gain criteria in level 3 autonomously, within the system itself. The system is able to deal with existing literature, from which the AI extracts all relevant elements to generate hypotheses, with open access to the full hypothesis space (or the equivalent for its human counterpart) and is able to reverse the scientific process from result back to hypothesis (abduction) when the result is of scientific interest (computational serendipity). Solves inverse problems as human do, equivalent (or superior) to a human scientist.

Areas of science will be so much more sophisticated than they are today that new challenges and directions are likely to emerge, unrelated to today's ones. For example, in physics, a replacement of the standard model may appear in the future (as a result of AI or not), and it is not clear whether this replacement will be simpler or more complicated — even if proves to be more encompassing — if the promise of areas such as quantum gravity and related unifying efforts are realized. So, the tools for evaluating the contributions of AI to scientific discovery are of the greatest importance in guiding and assessing the process.

6. Conclusion

When it comes to scientific discovery, purpose will become increasingly important and more salient, less hidden behind the complications of present-day AI black boxes. Scientific purpose will have to be specified and evaluated in a clear fashion.

In the next 25 years, technologies such as biological 3D bioprinting [1] will open up a far wider spectrum of possibilities for AI in scientific discovery, creating materials and objects. This is already possible at the cellular level and will most likely soon be possible even at the molecular level, with proteins and nucleic chains, say, and capable of creating or manipulating life from the smallest scale to the anatomical level.

This will also produce better and more malleable robotic systems which will introduce even greater changes and levels of sophistication, both in everyday life and scientific expertise, leading to snowballing scientific research, so that soon we may be even more overwhelmed by data, information, and knowledge than we are today. And again, AI will not only help us regain our bearings but most likely we will not be able to do so at all without AI.

A consensus is that we should explore all possible approaches: empowering human scientists with advanced AI tools; pure AI-based solutions with thousands of hypotheses tested in parallel and deep, flawless iterative reasoning; and hybrid approaches, that is, human–robot scientists.

Humans and human scientists will have to come together to define scientific purpose, that is, what is worth pursuing scientifically and toward what ends. Fields may flourish the sole purpose of which is to let scientists explore how far human and machine understanding can go, whether in abstract areas such as mathematics or in areas of immediate impact such as medicine and healthcare. Mechanisms to devise what is worth pursuing or promoting by national councils will be needed, as indeed they are today. It may be as difficult to decide as it is today what topics scientific councils should promote and fund, but AI for scientific discovery could also offer a chance to find mechanisms to decide these questions in a better, more systematic, and less biased manner, perhaps, paradoxically, making the process more humane.

References

[1] A. Tong, Q. L. Pham, P. Abatemarco *et al.* (2021). Review of low-cost 3D bioprinters: State of the market and observed future trends. *SLAS TECHNOLOGY: Translating Life Sciences Innovation, 26*(4), 333–366.

[2] M. Bajracharya, M. W. Maimone, and D. Helmick (2008). Autonomy for mars rovers: Past, present, and future. *Computer (Long Beach, CA), 41*(12), 44–50.

[3] M. Baker (2016). 1,500 scientists lift the lid on reproducibility. *Nature, 533*(7604), 452–454. doi: 10.1038/533452a.

[4] S. Bhagwat, X. J. Forteza, P. Pani, and V. Ferrari (2020). Ringdown overtones, black hole spectroscopy, and no-hair theorem tests. *Physical Review D, 101*(4), 044033.

[5] E. Bilsland, L. van Vliet, K. Williams *et al.* (2018). Plasmodium dihydro-folate reductase is a second enzyme target for the antimalarial action of triclosan. *Scientific Reports, 1038*, 8.

[6] B. K. Bose (2017). Artificial intelligence techniques in smart grid and renewable energy systems — Some example applications. *Proceeding IEEE Institute of Electrical and Electronics Engineering, 105*(11), 2262–2273.

[7] T. Chapman (2003). Lab automation and robotics: Automation on the move. *Nature, 421*(6923), 661, 663, 665–666.

[8] A. Cherkasov, K. Hilpert, H. Jenssen *et al.* (2009). Use of artificial intelligence in the design of small peptide antibiotics effective against a broad spectrum of highly antibiotic-resistant superbugs. *ACS Chemical Biology, 4*(1), 65–74.

[9] K. Hartnett (2021). Proof assistant makes jump to big-league math. https://www.quantamagazine.org/lean-computer-program-confirms-peter-scholze-proof-20210728/#.

[10] D. J. Hicks and R. Simmons (2019). The national robotics initiative: A five-year retrospective. *IEEE Robotics & Automation Magazine, 26*(3), 70–77.

[11] A. Holzinger, M. Kickmeier-Rust, and H. Müller *et al.* (2019). KANDINSKY patterns as IQ-test for machine learning. In *Lecture Notes in Computer Science*, Springer International Publishing, Cham, pp. 1–14.

[12] S. K. Jha, J. Bilalovic, A. Jha *et al.* (2017). Renewable energy: Present research and future scope of artificial intelligence. *Renewable and Sustainable Energy Reviews, 77*, 297–317.

[13] J. Jumper, R. Evans, A. Pritzel *et al.* (2021). Highly accurate protein structure prediction with AlphaFold. *Nature, 596*(7873), 583–589.

[14] F. Liu, Y. Shi, and Y. Liu (2017). Intelligence quotient and intelligence grade of artificial intelligence. *Annals of Data Science, 4*(2), 179–191.

[15] J. Liu, Y. Tang, Y. Wu *et al.* (2021). Forecasting the Indian ocean dipole with deep learning techniques. *Geophysical Research Letters, 48*, 20.

[16] S. D. Mathur (2009). The information paradox: A pedagogical introduction. *Classical and Quantum Gravity, 26*(22), 224001.

[17] M. C. R. Melo, J. R. M. A. Maasch, and C. de la Fuente-Nunez (2021). Accelerating antibiotic discovery through artificial intelligence. *Communications Biology, 4*(1), 1050.

[18] S. Ohlsson, R. H. Sloan, G. Turán, and A. Urasky (2016). Measuring an artificial intelligence system's performance on a verbal IQ test for young children. *Journal of Experimental & Theoretical Artificial Intelligence, 29*(4), 679–693.

[19] M. T. Ribeiro, S. Singh, and C. Guestrin (2016). "Why should I trust you?" Explaining the predictions of any classifier. In *Proceedings of the ACM SIGKDD International Conference on Knowledge Discovery and Data Mining*, Vol. 13, 17 August. https://doi.org/10.1145/2939672.2939778.

[20] R. D. King, M. Liakata, C. Lu *et al.* (2011). On the formalization and reuse of scientific research. *Journal of the Royal Society Interface, 63*, 8.

[21] P. Scholze (2021). Liquid tensor experiment — Xena. https://xenaproject.wordpress.com/2020/12/05/liquid-tensor-experiment/.

[22] A. Shukla and H. Karki (2016). Application of robotics in offshore oil and gas industry — A review part II. *Robotics and Autonomous Systems, 75*, 508–524.

[23] P. Skobelev (2018). Towards autonomous AI systems for resource management: Applications in industry and lessons learned. In *Advances in Practical Applications of Agents, Multi-Agent Systems, and Complexity: The PAAMS Collection*, Lecture notes in Computer Science, Springer International Publishing, Cham, pp. 12–25.

[24] J. Skolnick, M. Gao, H. Zhou *et al.* (2021). AlphaFold 2: Why it works and its implications for understanding the relationships of protein sequence, structure, and function. *Journal of Chemical Information and Modeling, 61*(10), 4827–4831.

[25] K. A. Williams, E. Bilsland, A. Sparkes *et al.* (2015). Cheaper faster drug development validated by the repositioning of drugs against neglected tropical diseases. *Journal of the Royal Society Interface, 104*, 12.

© 2023 World Scientific Publishing Company
https://doi.org/10.1142/9789811265679_0037

Chapter 37

Towards Reflection Competencies in Intelligent Systems for Science

Yolanda Gil

*Information Sciences Institute and Department of Computer Science,
University of Southern California, California, USA
gil@isi.edu*

1. Introduction: Eighty Years of AI for Science

Scientific discovery has long been of interest to AI researchers. Herbert Simon (Nobel Laureate and Turing award winner) worked on cognitive modeling of scientific discovery as early as the 1940s [1]. Edward Feigenbaum (also a Turing award winner) worked with Joshua Lederberg (himself a Nobel Laureate) and other colleagues at Stanford in the 1960s on using AI to automate the identification of organic molecules from their mass spectra [2]. Many more AI systems have been developed over the years to address major activities in scientific discovery such as problem formulation, experimentation and data collection, data analysis, machine learning, and model revision [3]. Indeed, a recent cover of *Science* states "artificial intelligence transforms science" [4].

Today, a major focus of AI for science is on machine learning. In the last few decades, advances in machine learning as well as data-intensive computing have pushed the envelope in the nature and scale of the scientific phenomena that can be addressed. Powerful learning paradigms and distributed computation work in unison to process data at scale, leading to spectacular discoveries in diverse areas such as high-energy physics, biomedicine, and geosciences. More recently, new deep learning approaches for machine learning and new intelligent techniques for data mining have given rise to modern data science, combining these powerful data-driven discovery capabilities with scalable computing and data systems that have completely changed how we look at data.

In addition to machine learning, many other areas of AI are making significant contributions to science. Examples include natural language processing to extract knowledge from publications [5], constraint reasoning to search for optimal solutions [6], experiment design and execution [7], and semantic data repositories to facilitate information integration [8].

Future AI systems can contribute much more to science. AI systems for scientific discovery today have very limited scope in the scientific research process, as they are given the learning goals, they are given the data, and they are given optimization metrics. The role of AI systems is limited to solving a well-defined task where the data and techniques are specified by a scientist. Confining intelligent machines to this narrow realm is severely limiting our ability to truly harness the potential of AI to tackle complex science questions. The limited incorporation of intelligent systems in science is also thwarting the pursuit of fundamentally new discoveries particularly at the fringe of current science practice. The increased complexity of the scientific questions that we face is challenging the abilities of human scientists. Imagine a new generation of AI systems that can formulate the learning problems needed to address a given science question, that can find or generate necessary data of appropriate quality, and that can incorporate background knowledge such as theories and scientific principles in order to discern what metrics would be appropriate to assess any new findings. Many scholars have shed light on the diverse and rich cognitive processes involved in scientific reasoning that AI still does not address, from discovering laws [1], to understanding causal mechanisms [9,10], to collaboration [11], to prioritizing problems [12–15], to producing paradigm shifts [16].

In this chapter, we argue that a much more expanded role for AI in scientific discovery will be necessary to tackle many of the challenges of our time. Scientists will need to partner with intelligent systems that are AI scientists capable of doing independent inquiry, proactive learning, and deliberative reasoning. A new generation of AI systems will enable a true partnership between scientists and machines. This partnership will be essential to tackle a new generation of science questions. And expanding the role of intelligent machines in the scientific discovery process will in turn enable significant advances in knowledge representation, reasoning, planning, meta-reasoning, and architectures for intelligence.

2. The Imperative of AI for Science

As scientific questions become more complex and multidisciplinary, the capabilities of scientists to do research will need to be augmented with intelligent machines. Compare the challenges of finding a cure for polio and finding a cure for cancer. Polio, a scourge that has affected humanity for millennia, was cured with a vaccine that was discovered by one scientist. Glioblastoma, a brain cancer that takes very few months to go to advanced stages and is very hard to detect and treat, is being studied by scores of scientists in multiple specialties. Different research groups have complementary information about the disease, with disparate data on genomics, proteomics, transcriptomics, MRIs, treatments, etc. It is a challenge to combine their independent partial findings and synthesize major discoveries. Similarly, compare the challenges of early river hydrology and physics modeling with the challenges of understanding the interacting hydro-bio-agro-human processes in our environment and ecosystems. Scientists with expertise in each of these areas develop complementary models that are very hard to integrate to study the intricate interactions that cut across them. Today's science processes require work that goes beyond what human scientists can do in the face of the complexity and multidisciplinarity of the research questions pursued. There are several key aspects in this matter.

First, keeping up with research innovation is challenging and costly for any scientist. Each discipline advances very quickly, with new sophisticated methods coming out continuously. It is challenging for any given research group to keep up with all the latest methods, so only a few are likely adopted. There is a high cost to understanding what new methods are becoming important and are crucial, learning their nuanced assumptions, and training younger researchers to use sophisticated methods properly. Scientists today do not have intelligent assistance to facilitate fast learning and adoption of new methods.

Second, collaborative research requires very significant effort. It is becoming harder for an individual researcher to tackle the more advanced science questions. Integrating all the information needed is very challenging, particularly across disciplines, and requires partnerships and collaborations. It can take a year of work by a dozen of scientists to integrate climate, hydrology, and agriculture models to understand and forecast food shortages. It takes two years of work by hundreds of scientists to assemble and analyze data to do a global climate study to see trends across the last few decades. It has taken thousands of scientists working for several years to discover the Higgs boson. These efforts require so much coordination (to secure funding, to organize the work, to coordinate responsibilities, to monitor progress, to assemble results, etc.) that they are far from being the norm and in some cases can be described as heroic. Scientists today do not have intelligent assistance to support these kinds of collaborative research tasks.

Third, accounting for new data requires continuous updates of prior findings that the science enterprise is not well equipped to do. When cancer data for a new cohort of patients become available, previously published studies for similar cohorts should be reconsidered and their findings updated to incorporate the new data. When new environmental data are continuously captured through sensors, or with improved quality with a new type of sensor, previous findings should be reconsidered and extended to account for the new data. When a new and more powerful analysis method comes to light, it should be applied to existing data that were previously analyzed. Each paper in the published literature provides a static snapshot of how scientists would answer a question, but researchers seldom have the resources to revisit published results. Scientists today do not have intelligent tools that automatically reproduce the methods and update the results.

Fourth, significant innovation could result from reimagining research methodologies and processes. There are many aspects of scientific research that could be automated, improved, or redesigned to incorporate capable intelligent systems. This could open the door to advance the frontiers of science in fundamentally new directions by tackling new kinds of questions and creating unconventional approaches. Scientists today do not have intelligent tools that complement and augment their abilities to create innovative changes in research.

In summary, in order to pursue increasingly complex science questions effectively and efficiently, we need the following:

1. AI systems that help scientists adopt new methods quickly so they can keep up with continuous advances in their field,
2. intelligent aids that reduce the effort to integrate knowledge across disciplines so scientists can tackle complex multifaceted phenomena with reduced effort and therefore more frequently,
3. automated AI systems that can incorporate newly available data into previously published studies in order to continuously update findings so scientists can keep up with all the new data that are being continuously collected,
4. AI approaches that can synthesize and innovate scientific research methodologies and processes so scientists have new avenues to address fundamentally new kinds of questions.

In turn, these avenues of AI research will lead to a new generation of intelligent systems capable of understanding the scientific research process, knowing the different ways to carry out the steps involved, and being able to learn the skills required to keep up with new methods and even create their own. These capabilities will be generally applicable beyond scientific domains, as they will become important tools for humanity to tackle complex problems.

What new avenues of AI research do we need to pursue in order to address these science needs?

3. General Intelligent Capabilities of AI Systems for Science: Thoughtful AI

Intelligent systems with some basic AI capabilities for science will soon become necessary for all scientists. At first, they will be used simply as tools that have no initiative or autonomy. AI systems will soon become assistants to scientists, carrying out tasks that a lab assistant or a research assistant would do. Intelligent systems will at some point become more independent, perhaps making contributions that deserve co-authorship and in some instances writing scientific papers on their own [17]. Eventually, they will become more than assistants and will act as partners to scientists. Some envision AI systems capable of making major scientific discoveries and even winning the Nobel prize [18].

In order to be assistants and partners for scientists, intelligent systems will need to be more collaborative, more resourceful and independent, and more responsible. These kinds of skills can be considered under the umbrella term of *thoughtful AI systems* which will act as is expected of human assistants and partners. Key design principles for such thoughtful AI systems are summarized in Table 1 and discussed in detail in [19].

Future AI research in these principles will enable successful approaches for developing intelligent systems that can be partners for scientists.

Table 1. Principles for designing *Thoughtful Artificial Intelligence Systems* (from [19]).

	Principle	Description
1	Rationality	Behavior is governed by knowledge
2	Context	Seek to understand the purpose and significance of tasks
3	Initiative	Proactively learn new knowledge relevant to their task
4	Networking	Access external sources of knowledge and capabilities
5	Articulation	Respond with persuasive justifications and arguments
6	Systems	Facilitate integration and collaboration with other systems
7	Ethics	Behavior that conveys scope and limitations

4. Specific Capabilities of AI Systems for Science: Core Competencies

What kinds of tasks and activities would intelligent systems carry out in pursuing scientific research? Defining core competencies required for scientific research that are shared across scientific disciplines is not an easy endeavor given the diversity and complexity of scientific work. As a starting point, we posit six core competencies needed in intelligent systems for science:

1. *Reflection.* This competency is focused on reasoning about scientific knowledge to formulate questions, identify strategies to pursue them, and situate new findings in the context of what is known. It will push the frontiers in AI in areas such as reasoning, meta-reasoning, and problem solving.
2. *Observation.* This competency focuses on data gathering through laboratory experiments, sensor management, remotely controlled robots and drones, and other science tasks focused on interactions with the physical world or the system under study. It will advance AI research in robotics and cyberphysical systems.
3. *Modeling.* This competency is about the analysis of complex scientific data to uncover patterns and create explanatory and predictive models. It will result in AI innovations in all aspects of machine learning, causality, and uncertainty reasoning.
4. *Probing.* This competency is focused on design and exploration of solutions through efficient search strategies. This competency is important in many science domains that are not so focused on modeling the world but in synthesizing new artifacts, such as drug design and materials discovery. This competency will emphasize AI search, constraint reasoning, and optimization.
5. *Extraction.* This competency is focused on pulling out and integrating information from the literature, online data repositories, and other Web sources. It will result in AI advances in natural language, vision, and information integration.
6. *Creation.* This competency is focused on generating new theories, designing new approaches, constructing new instruments, and other inventions that lead to significant inventions and paradigm changes that open fundamentally new directions in science. It will result in AI advances in creativity, design, and representation shift.

The six core competencies are summarized in Figure 1. Each will advance complementary areas of AI research and will need to be integrated

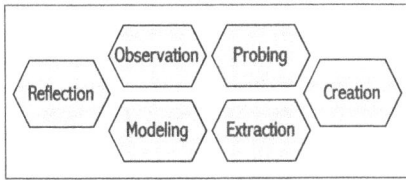

Competency	Description	AI Research Areas
Reflection	Formulate questions, identify strategies, understand findings	Reasoning and problem solving
Observation	Gather data through laboratory experiments or sensors	Robotics, cyberphysical systems
Modeling	Analyze data to uncover patterns and create predictive models	Machine learning, causality, uncertainty reasoning
Probing	Design and explore solutions through efficient search & optimization	Search, constraint reasoning, optimization
Extraction	Pull out and integrate information from diverse online resources	Natural language, vision, information integration
Creation	Significant inventions and paradigm changes	Creativity, design, representation shift

Fig. 1.   Six core competencies of AI scientists.

together to create powerful machines for science. Each competency can be explored separately, which will enable the AI community to make significant progress. Most of the work to date on AI for science has focused on the Observation Competency, Modeling Competency, Probing Competency, and Extraction Competency. The Reflection Competency and Creation Competency have not received as much attention. We discuss next some of our prior work on the Reflection Competency.

5. Reflection Competency in Intelligent Systems for Science

Intelligent systems for science will need reflection capabilities in order to formulate scientific questions, devise general strategies to answer them, execute methods that implement those strategies, and place new findings in the context of the original questions. These reflection capabilities are crucial to automatically generating new scientific findings, no matter the question or the domain.

Key research challenges for the Reflection Competency include the following:

- representing scientific knowledge to capture questions, hypotheses, and methods and relating those to one another,

- reasoning about hypotheses, the methods to test them, and the results obtained,
- implementing the scientific processes and steps involved in answering different types of questions, and that can be similar or differ significantly across science domains,
- integrating new findings into current theories and models, detecting inconsistencies, and resolving them with theory revisions or further questions,
- explaining findings and the supporting evidence appropriately, answering follow- up questions about the findings in the context of what is already known.

The development of a reflection competency will result in significant advances in many areas of AI, including cognitive architectures, knowledge representation, reasoning, planning, meta-reasoning, explanation, question answering, theory revision, and argumentation.

Figure 2 illustrates a proposed conceptual framework for reflection based on six major steps of the scientific research process, based on [3,20,21]. Scientific research often starts with an inquiry, which can be a hypothesis that can be tested or simply a question to explore. Next, a scientist will decide what approach to take to pursue the question, in terms of what kinds of data would be needed and how the data would be analyzed. Then, there would be a step for gathering data, which may mean carrying out experiments or retrieving data from an existing data repository. Once the data are available, different analyses are carried out for different subsets of the data or with different assumptions. The results of these analyses are consolidated in relation to the original question or hypothesis. Finally, a scientist would reflect on the nature and significance of the findings and revise existing theories or models in their domain.

This reflection framework focuses on inquiry-driven research, where a question or hypothesis prompts a scientist to gather evidence necessary to answer the questions posed. This is by no means a universal account of all scientific research processes, which may be more exploratory (starting with some data rather than driven by questions), analytical (driven by representation change and redesign of some body of knowledge), instrument-focused (design of a new instrument), synthesis (e.g., of new methods or algorithms), etc. This is a high-level process that captures commonalities in many scientific endeavors. This general reflection framework can be fleshed out based on the approaches and processes that are used in different science domains.

Figure 3 illustrates the use of this conceptual framework for reflection with real examples from multiomics (from [22]), neuroscience (from [23]),

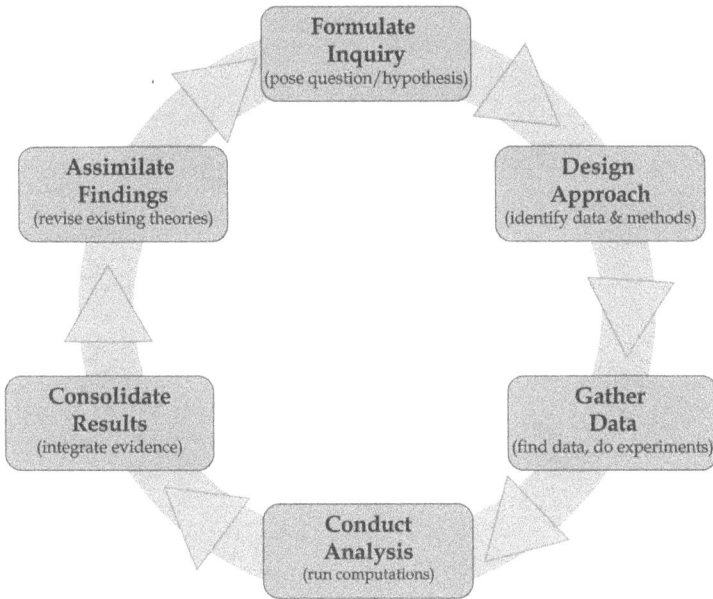

Fig. 2. An initial conceptual framework for reflection in the scientific research.

and flood prediction (from [21]). This highlights the generality of this framework and its flexibility to adapt to different kinds of inquiries, data types, and analyses. In multiomics, there are readily available data in shared repositories from many prior studies, and many specialized software tools that can be used for the analysis of proteomic and genomic data. Combining the results from these different modalities is an open area of research. In neuroscience, there are data available but specific features of interest have to be extracted from brain image data. Meta-analysis is needed to combine results from different studies. For example, in flood prediction, the analysis consists of running many simulations and the meta-analysis combines them to generate prediction ranges and assess uncertainty.

The reflection framework illustrates how this core competency can drive the development of other competencies:

- The Experimentation Competency would be prompted by the needs of the Gather Data step. The reflection process can provide context for the Experimentation Competency in terms of the kinds of data needed, the requirements for data collection, and the quality metrics that should drive experimentation.
- The Modeling Competency would be invoked by the needs of the Conduct Analysis step. The reflection process will determine what kind

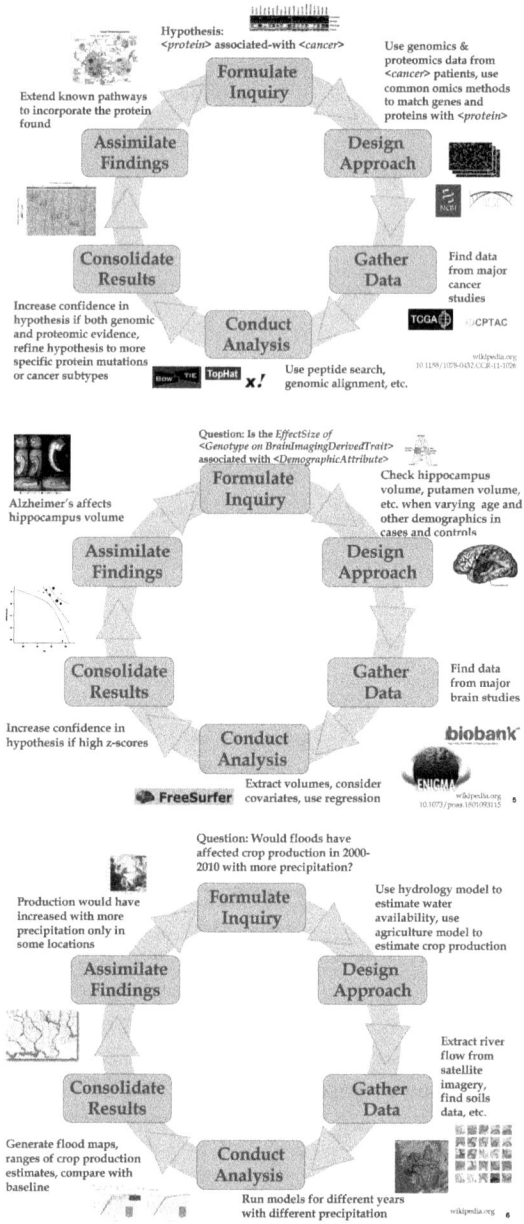

Fig. 3.   Illustrations of the reflection framework with real examples in three diverse areas of science: cancer omics (top), neuroscience (middle), and flood prediction (bottom).

of modeling needs to be done, the data available, the performance criteria for the resulting model, and other important information for modeling tasks.

- The Probing Competency would be driven by the needs of the Conduct Analysis step. The reflection process can determine the search objectives, optimization criteria, and the domain knowledge and data that can make the search more efficient.
- The Extraction Competency would be triggered by the needs of all the six steps, as it can extract theories to be used in the Formulate Inquiries step, domain knowledge to guide the Gather Data and Conduct Analysis steps, and fusion and integration methods to synthesize Consolidate Results and Assimilate Findings.
- The Creation Competency would be needed when the Design Analysis step cannot generate appropriate strategies to find data or methods to answer key questions, or when no findings result after several iterations of the cycle, or when findings remain inconsistent despite the iterations.

6. Conclusion

Future AI systems for science will be capable of pursuing independently substantial aspects of the research and therefore make their own discoveries. They will be capable of taking on significant problems by formulating their own research goals, proposing and testing hypotheses, designing theories, debating alternative options, and synthesizing new knowledge. They will also be able to explain their reasoning, compare their lines of inference to other possible ones, and situate their findings. They will communicate with scientists who have different levels of expertise and understanding in any given research topic.

The required capabilities will only be possible through substantial research advances in a diversity of areas of AI, including cognitive systems, machine learning, knowledge representation, constraint reasoning, problem solving and planning, meta-reasoning, reasoning under uncertainty, multiagent systems, natural language processing, collaboration, and robotics. AI research for science will also emphasize intelligent capabilities that have received less attention in the past, such as representational change and creativity.

Acknowledgments

We would like to thank our collaborators over the years, particularly Daniel Garijo, Deborah Khider, Maximiliano Osorio, Varun Ratnakar, Hernan Vargas, Suzanne Pierce, Emmanuel Johnson, Parag Malik, Ravali

Adusumilli, Neda Jahanshad, Alice Yang, Scott Peckham, Armen Kemanian, and Kelly Cobourn. We gratefully acknowledge support from the US Office of Naval Research through award N00014-21-1-2437, the National Institutes of Health through award 1R01AG059874-01, and the Defense Advanced Research Projects Agency through award W911NF-18-1-0027.

References

[1] H. A. Simon (1997). *Models of Discovery and Other Topics in the Methods of Science.* Springer. ISBN 978-94-010-9521-1. https://link.springer.com/book/10.1007/978-94-010-9521-1.

[2] R. K. Lindsay, B. G. Buchanan, E. A. Feigenbaum *et al.* (1980). *Applications of Artificial Intelligence for Organic Chemistry: The Dendral Project.* McGraw-Hill. ISBN 978-0070378957. https://profiles.nlm.nih.gov/spotlight/bb/catalog/nlm:nlmuid-101584906X7379-doc.

[3] Y. Gil, D. Garijo, V. Ratnakar *et al.* (2017). Towards continuous scientific data analysis and hypothesis evolution. In *Proceedings of the Thirty-First AAAI Conference on Artificial Intelligence (AAAI-17)*, San Francisco, CA.

[4] AI transforming science. *Science* Special Issue, *357*(6346), 7 July 2017. https://science.sciencemag.org/content/357/6346.

[5] A. Callahan, M. Dumontier, and N. H. Shah (2011). HyQue: Evaluating hypotheses using Semantic Web technologies. *Journal of Biomedical Semantics, 2*, S3.

[6] C. Gomes, T. Dietterich, C. Barrett *et al.* (2019). Computational sustainability: Computing for a better world and a sustainable future. *Communications of the ACM, 62*(9). https://doi.org/10.1145/3339399.

[7] P. Groth and J. Cox (2017). Indicators for the use of robotic labs in basic biomedical research: A literature analysis. *PeerJ, 5*, e3997. https://doi.org/10.7717/peerj.3997.

[8] V. Tshitoyan, J. Dagdelen, L. Weston *et al.* (2019). Unsupervised word embeddings capture latent knowledge from materials science literature. *Nature, 571*, 95–98. https://doi.org/10.1038/s41586-019-1335-8.

[9] C. F. Craver and L. Darden (2013). *In Search of Mechanisms: Discoveries across the Life Sciences.* University of Chicago Press.

[10] J. Pearl (2018). *The Book of Why: The New Science of Cause and Effect.* Basic Books Publishers.

[11] S. B. Trickett, C. D. Schunn, and J. G. Trafton (2005). Puzzles and peculiarities: How scientists attend to and process anomalies during data analysis. In M. E. Gorman, R. D. Tweney, D. Gooding, and A. Kincannon (eds.), *Scientific and Technological Thinking*. Mahwah, NJ: LEA, pp. 97–118.

[12] P. Thagard (2012). *The Cognitive Science of Science: Explanation, Discovery and Conceptual Change.* Cambridge, MA: MIT Press.

[13] R. Samuels and Wilkenfeld (eds.) (2019). *Advances in Experimental Philosophy of Science.* London, UK: Bloomsbury.

[14] M. Addis, P. D. Sozou, P. C. Lane *et al.* (2016). Computational scientific discovery and cognitive science theories. In V. C. Müller (ed.), *Computing and Philosophy*. Synthese Library, Vol. 375. Cham: Springer. https://doi.org/10.1007/978-3-319-23291-1_6.

[15] S. Chandrasekharan and N. J. Nersessian (2015). Building cognition: The construction of computational representations for scientific discovery. *Cognitive Science*, *39*, 1727–1763.

[16] T. S. Kuhn (1962). *The Structure of Scientific Revolutions*. University of Chicago Press.

[17] Y. Gil (2021). Will AI write the scientific papers of the future? *AI Magazine*, *42*(4). https://doi.org/10.1609/aimag.v42i4.18149.

[18] H. Kitano (2016). Artificial intelligence to win the Nobel Prize and beyond: Creating the engine for scientific discovery. *AI Magazine*, *37*(1). https://doi.org/10.1609/aimag.v37i1.2642.

[19] Y. Gil (2017). Thoughtful artificial intelligence: Forging a new partnership for data science and scientific discovery. *Data Science*, *1*, 119–129.

[20] Y. Gil, D. Khider, M. Osorio *et al.* (2022). Towards capturing scientific reasoning to automate data analysis. *Proceedings of the Annual Conference of the Cognitive Science Society*, 44. Retrieved from https://escholarship.org/uc/item/85d2d1xf.

[21] Y. Gil, D. Garijo, D. Khider *et al.* (2021). Artificial intelligence for modeling complex systems: Taming the complexity of expert models to improve decision making. *ACM Transactions on Interactive Intelligent Systems*, *11*(2), 1–49.

[22] A. Srivastava, R. Adusumilli, H. Boyce *et al.* (2019). Semantic workflows for benchmark challenges: Enhancing comparability, reusability and reproducibility. *Proceedings of the Pacific Symposium on Biocomputing (PSB)*, *24*, 208–219.

[23] Y. Gil, J. Honaker, S. Gupta *et al.* (2019). Towards human-guided machine learning. *Proceedings of the 24th ACM International Conference on Intelligent User Interfaces (IUI)*. New York, NY, USA: Association for Computing Machinery, pp. 614–624. https://doi.org/10.1145/3301275.3302324.

© 2023 World Scientific Publishing Company
https://doi.org/10.1142/9789811265679_0038

Chapter 38

The Interface of Machine Learning and Causal Inference

Mohammad Taha Bahadori* and David E. Heckerman[†]

Amazon
bahadorm@amazon.com
[†]*heckerma@amazon.com*

1. Introduction

A central tool of science is the ability to discover and quantify causal relationships and mechanisms. In particular, knowing cause and effect allows us to make predictions under interventions, a key goal of science. Discovering only correlations rather than causality does not enable prediction under intervention — it is merely a stepping stone to causal discovery.

Machine Learning (ML) has focused on identifying and quantifying correlations from data. The focus on correlation has achieved huge success in prediction tasks such as image recognition, machine translation, and speech recognition. However, in none of these tasks, do we discover any causal relationships. An important distinction in causal inference is whether the data are the result of interventions or are strictly observational. Inferring cause and effect with data resulting from interventions, especially random ones, is relatively straightforward. In contrast, inferring cause and effect with purely observational data is much more difficult. Observational causal inference has had a relatively slow start over the last century but is seeing accelerated progress [1–6]. Even more recently, the two fields of causal inference and ML are beginning to share insights that leverage one another, yielding advances in both fields.

Here, we examine progress in these two fields and how they are beginning to help one another. First, we address a common issue in ML — the inability to explain a deep neural net model. We show how an insight from the causal inference field enables better explanations. Second, we show how insights from optimization and end-to-end learning in ML can be used to infer causal relationships in difficult case where such relationships are continuous and nonlinear.

2. Explaining the Predictions of Deep Neural Networks

Modern deep neural networks are composed of multiple layers with nonlinear functions. Understanding the reasons behind predictions of neural networks is a difficult task [7,8]. For example, the well-known ResNet152 neural network [9] has about 60 million parameters, making its decisions effectively impossible to understand by inspecting the weights. Furthermore, a key requirement for interpreting neural networks is that the explanation should be understandable to human subject matter experts.

Here, we examine one approach for improving explanations of neural network predictions that makes use of high-level concepts provided by the model builder [10–13]. This approach leverages domain knowledge and has been used for applications including medical imaging [14], breast cancer histopathology [15], cardiac MRIs [16], and meteorology [17].

The example we consider here comes from the CUB-200-2011 dataset [18]. The dataset includes 11788 pictures of 200 different types of birds, annotated both for the bird type and 312 different concepts about each picture. Example concepts include "has throat color black", "has head pattern plain", and "has forehead color black". The goal is to label the bird type in each image and explain that label by listing a subset of all concepts that favor the predicted label.

In this original version of this approach, we fit a Concept Bottleneck Model (CBM) in which the discriminative information flows from the feature vectors $\mathbf{x}$ through the concept vectors $\mathbf{c}$ and reaches the labels $\mathbf{y}$. We assume that during the training phase, we are given triplets $(\boldsymbol{x}_i, \boldsymbol{c}_i, \boldsymbol{y}_i)$ for $i = 1, \ldots, n$ data points. In addition to the regular features $\boldsymbol{x}$ and labels $\boldsymbol{y}$, we are given a human interpretable concepts vector $\boldsymbol{c}$ for each data point. Each element of the concept vector measures the degree of existence of the corresponding concept in the features. To predict the labels, we learn two models: one that estimates $\mathbf{c}$ given the features (denoted $\widehat{\mathbf{c}}(\mathbf{x})$) and one that estimates $\mathbf{y}$ given the estimates of $\mathbf{c}$ (denoted $\widehat{\mathbf{y}}(\widehat{\mathbf{c}}(\mathbf{x}))$). To explain the prediction, we list the concepts with large values for $\widehat{\mathbf{c}}(\mathbf{x})$.

A key issue with this approach is that there can be hidden common causes (i.e., hidden confounders) of the feature and concept vectors. Our goal is to account for these confounders so that $\widehat{\mathbf{c}}$ explains the predictions more accurately.

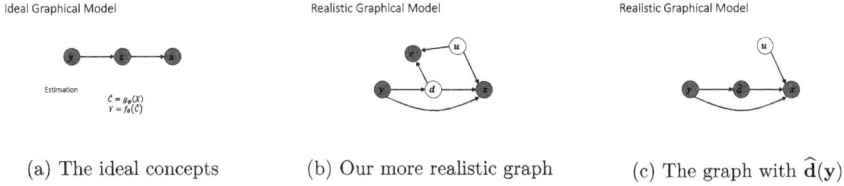

Ideal Graphical Model	Realistic Graphical Model	Realistic Graphical Model

(a) The ideal concepts (b) Our more realistic graph (c) The graph with $\widehat{\mathbf{d}}(\mathbf{y})$

Fig. 1. (a) The ideal view of the causal relationships between the features $\mathbf{x}$, concepts $\mathbf{c}$, and labels $\mathbf{y}$. (b) In a more realistic setting, the unobserved confounding variable $\mathbf{u}$ impacts both $\mathbf{x}$ and $\mathbf{c}$. The shared information between $\mathbf{x}$ and $\mathbf{y}$ goes through the discriminative part of the concepts $\mathbf{d}$. (c) When we use $\widehat{\mathbf{d}}(\mathbf{y}) = E[\mathbf{c}|\mathbf{y}]$ in place of $\mathbf{d}$, we eliminate the confounding link $\mathbf{u} \to \mathbf{c}$. Shaded and unshaded nodes are observed and unobserved, respectively.

2.1. *A new causal graphical model for CBMs*

To this end, let us consider several causal models for our task. A causal model is a directed acyclic graph in which nodes represent variables and each arc points from a cause to an effect. Associated with each node is a probability distribution of that node given its parents. Besides being a specification of cause and effect, each causal model provides a recipe for how to generate data from it: (1) start at a root node and generate data from the distribution at that node and (2) when all data for the parents of a node have been generated, generate data for that node given the data associated with its parents.

The causal model in Figure 1(a) shows the ideal situation in the CBM approach, where labels cause concepts and those concepts cause the features. The generative model corresponding to Figure 1(a) states that for generating each feature $\boldsymbol{x}_i$, we first randomly draw the label $\boldsymbol{y}_i$. Given the label, we draw the concepts $\boldsymbol{c}_i$. Given the concepts, we generate the features. The data generation flow in this graph is from nodes with less detailed information (labels) to more detailed ones (concepts and then features).

To model the confounding between concepts and features, we propose a new causal model in Figure 1b. Our model corresponds to a generative process in which to generate an observed triplet $(\boldsymbol{x}_i, \boldsymbol{c}_i, \boldsymbol{y}_i)$, we first draw a label $\boldsymbol{y}_i$ and a confounder $\boldsymbol{u}_i$ vector independently. Then, we draw the discriminative concepts $\boldsymbol{d}_i$ based on the label and generate the features $\boldsymbol{x}_i$ jointly based on the concepts and the confounder. Finally, we draw the observed concept vector $\boldsymbol{c}_i$ based on the drawn concept and confounder vectors.

Estimation of the model in Figure 1(b) is challenging because there are two distinct paths for the information from the labels $\mathbf{y}$ to reach the features $\mathbf{x}$. Our approach is to use a trick from the instrumental variables

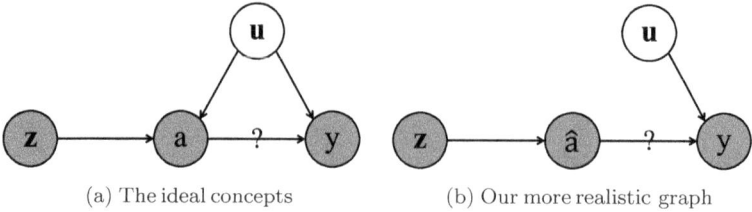

(a) The ideal concepts   (b) Our more realistic graph

Fig. 2.   (a) The classical instrumental variable setting for estimating the causal effect of cause a on outcome y. **z** is the instrumental variable, which is assumed (1) to directly influence a, (2) to be independent of confounders **u**, and (3) to not directly influence the outcome y. (b) The independence of **z** and **u** implies the independence of $E(a|\mathbf{z})$ and **u** so that the estimation of the causal effect of a on y is not confounded.

literature to remove the confounding factors impacting features and concept vectors. Use of an instrumental variable can simplify the process of learning cause and effect [4,19,20]. A typical setup is shown in Figure 2(a). Here, one or more instrumental variables **z** influence the treatment a and are independent of the confounders **u**. Variables **z** also do not directly influence the outcome y. In this context, a trick to estimate the effect of the treatment on the outcome is to first determine $E(a|\mathbf{z})$ (e.g., by regressing a on **z**) and then use this expectation in place of the treatment to predict the outcome, as shown in Figure 2(b). The independence of **z** and **u** implies the independence of this expectation and **u** so that the estimation of the causal effect of a on y is not confounded.

In our approach, we determine the expectation in the data of **c** as a function of **y**, by learning **c** as a function of **y** (e.g., with a neural network) and using these expectations as pseudo-observations of **d**. In notation form, we set $\widehat{\mathbf{d}}$ to $E[\mathbf{c}|\mathbf{y}]$. The graphical model corresponding to this procedure is shown in Figure 1(b), where **c** is no longer relevant and is ignored. Then, in the spirit of the instrumental variable trick, we have $\widehat{\mathbf{d}} \perp\!\!\!\perp \mathbf{u}$, so we can learn $\widehat{\mathbf{y}}(\widehat{\mathbf{d}}(\mathbf{x}))$ with the standard CBM procedure in a manner that is not confounded. For more details about the debiasing procedure, please refer to [21].

2.2. *CUB-200-2011 experiments*

Let us apply this approach to the CUB-200-2011 dataset.

Dataset and preprocessing. The 11788 pictures in the dataset include 11788 pictures that are portioned into 5994 and 5794 train and test partitions, respectively. The concept annotations are binary, whether the concept exists or not. However, for each statement, a four-level certainty score has been also assigned: 1: not visible, 2: guessing, 3: probably, and 4: definitely. We combine the binary annotation and the certainty score

Table 1. Mapping the concept annotations to real values.

Annotation	Certainty	Ordinal score	Numeric map
Doesn't exist	Definitely	0	0
Doesn't exist	Probably	1	1/6
Doesn't exist	Guessing	2	2/6
Doesn't exist	Not visible	3	3/6
Exists	Not visible	3	3/6
Exists	Guessing	4	4/6
Exists	Probably	5	5/6
Exists	Definitely	6	1

to create a 7-level ordinal variable as the annotation for each image as summarized in Table 1. For simplicity, we map the 7-level ordinal values to uniformly spaced values in the $[0, 1]$ interval. We randomly hold out 15% of the training set as the validation set.

Quantitative Results. Comparing to the baseline algorithm, our debiasing technique increases the average Spearman correlation between $\widehat{\mathbf{c}}(\mathbf{x})$ and $\widehat{\mathbf{c}}(\mathbf{y})$ from 0.406 to 0.508. For the above 10 concepts, our algorithm increases the average Spearman correlation from 0.283 to 0.389. Our debiasing algorithm also improves the generalization in the prediction of the image labels. The debiasing also improves the top-5 accuracy of predicting the labels from 39.5% to 49.3%.

To show that our proposed debiasing accurately ranks the concepts in terms of their explanation of the predictions, we use the RemOve And Retrain (ROAR) framework [22]. In the ROAR framework, we sort the concept using the scores $E[\widehat{\mathbf{d}}|\boldsymbol{x}_i] - \frac{1}{n}\sum_{i=1}^{n} E[\widehat{\mathbf{d}}|\boldsymbol{x}_i]$ in the ascending order. Then, we mask (set to zero) the least explanatory $x\%$ of the concepts using the scores and retrain the model that predicts labels from concepts. We perform the procedure for $x \in \{0, 10, 20, \ldots, 80, 90, 95\}$ and record the testing top-5 accuracy of predicting the labels $\boldsymbol{y}$. We repeat the ROAR experiments three times and report the average accuracy as we vary the masking percentage.

Figure 3 shows the ROAR evaluation of the regular and debiased algorithms. Because the debiased algorithm is more accurate, for easier comparison, we normalize both curves by dividing them by their accuracy at masking percentage $x = 0\%$. An immediate observation is that the plot for debiased algorithm stays above the regular one, which is a clear indication of its superior performance in ranking the explanatory concepts from important to unimportant. The results show several additional interesting insights. First, the prediction of the bird species largely relies on a sparse set of concepts as we can mask 95% of the concepts and still have a decent accuracy. Second, masking a small percentage of irrelevant concepts reduces

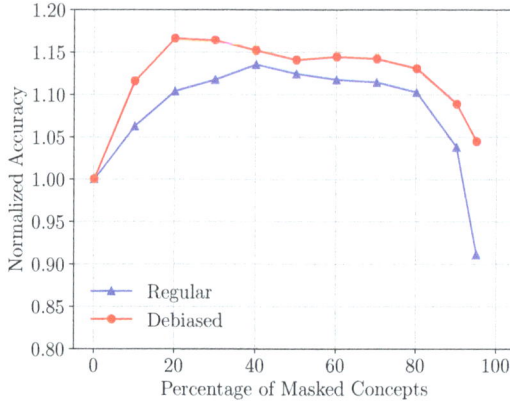

Fig. 3. The ROAR evaluation: We mask $x\%$ of the concepts that are identified by the methods as less explanatory of the labels and retrain the model of labels given predicted concepts. We measure the change in the accuracy of predicting the labels $\mathbf{y}$ as we increase the masking percentage. For better comparison of the trends, we have normalized them by their first data point ($x = 0\%$).

Fig. 4. Twelve example images where the debiasing helps. A common pattern is that the image context has either prevented or misled the annotator from accurate annotation of the concepts. From left to right, the birds are "Brandt Cormorant", "Pelagic Cormorant", "Fish Crow", "Fish Crow", "Fish Crow", "Ivory Gull", "Ivory Gull", "Green Violetear", "Green Violetear", "Cape Glossy Starling", "Northern Waterthrush", and "Northern Waterthrush".

the noise in the features and improves the generalization performance of both algorithms. Our debiased algorithm is more successful by being better at finding the noisy features before $x = 20\%$ masking. Finally, the debiased accuracy curve is less steep after $x = 80\%$, which again indicates its success in finding the most explanatory concepts.

Qualitative analysis of the results. In Figure 4, we show 12 images for which the $\widehat{\mathbf{d}}$ and the true value of $\mathbf{c}$ are significantly different. A common pattern among the examples is that the context of the image does not allow accurate annotations by the annotators. In images 3, 4, 5, 6, 7, 11, and 12 in Figure 4, the 10 color-related concepts listed at the beginning are all set to 0.5, indicating that the annotators have failed in annotation. However, our algorithm correctly identifies that, for example, Ivory Gulls do not have green-colored backs by predicting $\widehat{c} = 0.08$ which is closer to $\widehat{c}(\mathbf{y}) = 0.06$ than the true $c = 0.5$.

Another pattern is the impact of the color of the environment on the accuracy of the annotations. For example, the second image from the left is an image of Pelagic cormorant, whose back and upper tail colors are unlikely to be green with the per-class average of 0.12 and 0.07, respectively. However, because of the color of the image and the reflections, the annotator has assigned 1.0 to both of "has back color::green" and "has upper tail color::green" concepts. Our algorithm predicts 0.11 and 0.16 for these two features, respectively, which are closer to the per-class average. In Table 2, we list six examples to show the superior accuracy of the debiased CBM in ranking the concepts in terms of their explanation power.

3. Inferring a Nonlinear Causal Relationship with a Continuous Treatment

In this section, we focus on the problem of inferring cause and effect from observational data. In this setting, methods for inferring a causal relationship can be relatively straightforward when (1) relevant confounders are known and observed and (2) the putative causal relationship is linear or when the treatment is discrete and of low dimension (e.g., "take the pill" or "don't take the pill"). When the treatment is continuous and the relationship is nonlinear however, inferring the causal relationship has been extremely difficult [23,24, Chapter 1.2.6] even when relevant confounders are known and observed. Fortunately, advances in ML have made this task feasible in certain situations.

One example is quantifying the impact of the dose of a drug in treating a medical condition. In this example, we could find the minimum drug dose that is effective in increasing the survival of the patients. Here, we consider the example of estimating the impact of the level of air pollutant $PM_{2.5}$ on the cardiovascular mortality rate. The study by [25] shows that improvements in air quality have been *associated* with reduced cardiovascular mortality rates. Our goal is to perform a causal analysis and identify levels of air pollutants that are safe from a cardiovascular mortality point of view.

Describing the problem mathematically, suppose we have the triplet of $(\mathbf{x}, \mathrm{a}, \mathrm{y})$, where $\mathbf{x}$, a, and y denote the confounders, treatments, and response variables, respectively, from an observational causal study. In our continuous treatment setting, we denote potential outcomes as $\mathrm{y}^{(a)}$, which means the value of y after intervention in the treatment a and setting its value to a. Given an i.i.d. sample of size n, $\{(\boldsymbol{x}_i, a_i, y_i)\}_{i=1}^n$, our objective is to eliminate the impact of the confounders and identify the average

Table 2. Examples of differences between regular and debiased algorithms in ranking the concepts.

Image	Top 15 Concepts

Red winged Blackbird

Debiased: has throat color::black, has head pattern::plain, has forehead color::black, has breast color::black, has underparts color::black, has nape color::black, has crown color::black, has primary color::black, has bill color::black, has belly color::black, has wing color::orange, has breast pattern::solid, has upperparts color::orange, has wing pattern::multicolored, has bill length::about the same as head

Regular: has primary color::black, has wing color::black, has throat color::black, has upperparts color::black, has breast color::black, has primary color::blue, has underparts color::black, has belly color::black, has back color::black, has nape color::black, has upperparts color::blue, has tail pattern::solid, has crown color::blue, has under tail color::black, has forehead color::blue

Purple Finch

Debiased: has primary color::red, has crown color::red, has forehead color::red, has throat color::red, has nape color::red, has breast color::red, has underparts color::red, has belly color::red, has forehead color::rufous, has upperparts color::red, has crown color::rufous, has nape color::rufous, has wing pattern::multicolored, has primary color::rufous, has throat color::rufous

Regular: has underparts color::gray, has breast color::gray, has belly color::gray, has belly pattern::multicolored, has breast pattern::multicolored, has nape color::gray, has bill length::shorter than head, has breast color::red, has throat color::gray, has upperparts color::red, has back pattern::multicolored, has underparts color::red, has primary color::gray, has belly color::red, has throat color::red

Northern Flicker

Debiased: has bill length::about the same as head, has belly pattern::spotted, has underparts color::black, has bill shape::dagger, has breast color::black, has belly color::black, has breast pattern::spotted, has back pattern::spotted, has wing pattern::spotted, has nape color::red, has back color::black, has tail pattern::spotted, has under tail color::black, has upper tail color::black, has primary color::buff

Regular: has primary color::brown, has wing color::brown, has upperparts color::brown, has crown color::brown, has back color::brown, has forehead color::brown, has nape color::brown, has throat color::white, has breast pattern::spotted, has under tail color::brown, has breast color::white, has belly color::white, has underparts color::white, has upper tail color::brown, has breast color::brown

Table 2.   (*Continued*)

Image	Top 15 Concepts

Gadwall

Debiased: has shape::duck-like, has bill shape::spatulate, has size::medium (9–16 in), has bill length::about the same as head, has throat color::buff, has underparts color::brown, has breast color::brown, has belly pattern::spotted, has crown color::brown, has primary color::brown, has belly color::brown, has nape color::brown, has forehead color::brown, has upperparts color::brown, has belly color::purple

Regular: has belly color::gray, has underparts color::gray, has breast color::gray, has belly color::pink, has belly color::rufous, has underparts color::purple, has belly color::purple, has underparts color::pink, has throat color::gray, has primary color::gray, has belly color::green, has underparts color::rufous, has underparts color::green, has belly color::iridescent, has forehead color::gray

Rose breasted Grosbeak

Debiased: has throat color::black, has forehead color::black, has crown color::black, has primary color::black, has nape color::black, has breast color::red, has belly color::white, has underparts color::white, has underparts color::red, has back color::black, has primary color::white, has bill shape::cone, has breast pattern::multicolored, has primary color::red, has upperparts color::black

Regular: has nape color::black, has primary color::black, has nape color::rufous, has primary color::red, has wing color::orange, has nape color::red, has breast color::red, has crown color::black, has upperparts color::orange, has crown color::red, has underparts color::white, has upperparts color::rufous, has forehead color::black, has throat color::red, has back color::purple

White breasted Kingfisher

Debiased: has wing color::blue, has upperparts color::blue, has crown color::rufous, has primary color::blue, has bill color::rufous, has back color::blue, has under tail color::blue, has bill color::red, has upper tail color::blue, has wing pattern::multicolored, has nape color::rufous, has crown color::brown, has belly color::brown, has nape color::brown, has underparts color::brown

Regular: has primary color::red, has throat color::red, has underparts color::red, has breast color::red, has forehead color::red, has crown color::rufous, has crown color::red, has nape color::red, has belly color::red, has primary color::rufous, has throat color::rufous, has forehead color::rufous, has wing color::red, has nape color::rufous, has underparts color::rufous

treatment effect function $\mu(a) = \mathbb{E}[y^{(a)}]$, which is also called the response function.

Propensity score weighting [26,27] and stand-alone or combined with regression-based models to achieve double robustness [28,29] are one set of approaches that have been used. In this approach, each observational instance is weighted so as to make the confounders and treatments independent of expectation. This approach, however, faces two challenges: (1) the weights only balance the confounders in expectation, not necessarily in the given data [30], and (2) the weights can be very large for some subjects, leading to unstable estimation and uncertain inference.

As a possible remedy, entropy balancing [31] estimates the weights such that they (1) enforce zero correlations between confounders and treatments and (2) minimize a measure of dispersion on the weights to prevent extreme weights. Regarding the enforcement of zero correlations, we select a set of functions on the confounders $\phi_k(\cdot) : \mathbb{X} \mapsto \mathbb{R}$, for $k = 1, \ldots, K$, that are dense and complete in L^2 space. Given the ϕ functions, we approximate the independence relationship by $\widehat{\mathbb{E}}_n[a\phi_k(\mathbf{x})] = 0$, for $k = 1, \ldots, K$, where the empirical expectation $\widehat{\mathbb{E}}_n$ is performed on the pseudo population. Hereafter, we will denote the mapped data points as $\boldsymbol{\phi}(x_i) = [\phi_1(x_i), \ldots, \phi_K(x_i)]$. The $\phi_k(\cdot)$ functions can be chosen based on prior knowledge or learned [32]. Following [33,34], in the case of continuous treatments, we first demean the confounders $\boldsymbol{\phi}(x_i)$ and treatments a_i such that without loss of generality they are taken to have mean zero. The balancing objective is to learn a set of weights $w_i, i = 1, \ldots, n$, that satisfy $\sum_{i=1}^{n} w_i \boldsymbol{\phi}(x_i) = 0$, $\sum_{i=1}^{n} w_i a_i = 0$, and $\sum_{i=1}^{n} w_i a_i \boldsymbol{\phi}(x_i) = 0$. We can write these three constraints in a compact form by defining a $(2K+1)$-dimensional vector $\boldsymbol{g}_i = [\boldsymbol{\phi}(x_i), a_i, a_i \boldsymbol{\phi}(x_i)]$. The constraints become $\sum_{i=1}^{n} w_i \boldsymbol{g}_i = \mathbf{0}$. We stack the $\boldsymbol{g}$ vectors in a $(2K+1) \times n$-dimensional matrix $\boldsymbol{G}$ for compact notation. Note that it is also possible to generalize the constraint to higher order moments [23,35,36].

Regarding the prevention of extreme weights, a variety of dispersion metrics including entropy or variance of the weights have been proposed as objective functions for minimization [37]. [31] originally proposed minimizing the KL divergence between the weights and a set of base weights $q_i, i = 1, \ldots, n$. Details on the choice of base weights are discussed in the following, however, we note that $q_i = $ const. leads to minimization of the entropy of weights. Using this dispersion function and the balancing constraints, entropy balancing optimization is as follows:

$$\widehat{\boldsymbol{w}} = \underset{\boldsymbol{w}}{\operatorname{argmin}} \sum_{i=1}^{n} w_i \log\left(\frac{w_i}{q_i}\right), \qquad (1)$$

s.t.   (i) $\boldsymbol{G}\boldsymbol{w} = \mathbf{0}$,   (ii) $\mathbf{1}^\top \boldsymbol{w} = 1$,   (iii) $w_i \geq 0$ for $i = 1, \ldots, n$.

The above optimization problem can be solved efficiently using its Lagrangian dual:

$$\widehat{\boldsymbol{\lambda}} = \operatorname*{argmin}_{\boldsymbol{\lambda}} \, \log\left(\mathbf{1}^{\top} \exp\left(-\boldsymbol{\lambda}^{\top}\boldsymbol{G} + \boldsymbol{\ell}\right)\right), \tag{2}$$

where $\ell_i = \log q_i$ are the *log-base-weights*. Given the solution $\widehat{\boldsymbol{\lambda}}$, the balancing weights can be computed as $\boldsymbol{w} = \operatorname{softmax}(-\widehat{\boldsymbol{\lambda}}^{\top}\boldsymbol{G} + \boldsymbol{\ell})$, where $\operatorname{softmax}(\boldsymbol{v}) = \frac{\exp \boldsymbol{v}}{(\mathbf{1}^{\top}\exp \boldsymbol{v})}$ for any vector $\boldsymbol{v}$. We can also add an L_1 penalty term to the dual objective in Eq. (2), which corresponds to *approximate balancing* [37].

[31] suggests two approaches for choosing base weights: (1) use weights obtained from a conventional propensity score model and (2) use knowledge about the sampling design. [38] shows that with any arbitrary base weights, causal estimation using the weights $\widehat{\boldsymbol{w}}$ learned in Eq. (2) will be consistent. Thus, there is the potential to improve the quality of causal estimation by careful learning of these weights.

Now, let us bring in ML to address this task. End-to-end learning is the cornerstone of modern deep neural networks. It emphasizes the use of gradient descent to directly optimize the error in estimating the desired quantity without using intermediate steps such as feature engineering [39]. Here, we describe an application of end-to-end learning [38] that learns the weights in entropy balancing to improve the quality of causal estimation.

In this approach, we define the log-base-weights $\boldsymbol{\ell}$ as a parametric function (e.g., a neural network) of the treatment variable, i.e., $\ell_{\boldsymbol{\theta}}(\cdot)$. We learn the base weights with the goal of improving the accuracy of the subsequent weighted regression. This task is challenging because simply optimizing the weighted regression loss (e.g., weighted MSE) leads to degenerate results. That is, learning $\boldsymbol{\ell}$ to minimize the regression loss will lead to exclusion of the difficult-to-predict data points from the regression, which is undesirable. Thus, we need to find another loss function to optimize, ideally a loss function that directly minimizes the error in the estimation of the response function $\mu(a)$. To do so, we generate multiple pseudo-responses $\overline{y}$ with randomly generated (see the following) response functions $\overline{\mu}(a)$. Now that we know the true response function $\overline{\mu}(a)$ in the randomly generated data, we can perform causal inference and obtain the estimation of the known response curve $\widehat{\mu}(a)$ using the optimized weights. More concretely, first, we estimate the distribution of noise using the residuals of regressing mry on $(a, \mathbf{x})$, capturing the possible heteroskedasticity in the noise. Then, in each iteration, we draw a batch of possible datasets. To generate each dataset, we randomly choose a response function $\overline{\mu}(a)$ and use it to generate the entire dataset. For the collection of such datasets, we use ℓ_θ to compute the log-base-weights and subsequently learn the weights w. Then, we use a weighted regression algorithm to find our estimation $\widehat{\mu}(a)$ of the randomly generated $\overline{\mu}(a)$. Finally, we update θ to minimize the loss function (the mean squared error between $\widehat{\mu}(a)$ and $\overline{\mu}(a)$) and iterate. Further details, theoretical analysis, and empirical evaluations of this algorithm, called *End-to-End Balancing* (E2B), can be found in [38].

To choose the class of random response functions $\overline{\mu}(a)$, ideally, we should rely on domain experts to choose a function set that includes the true response function. Alternatively, we can choose broad function classes such as random piecewise smooth functions or polynomial functions with random coefficients. We can also use generative adversarial networks to generate data that are more similar to our sample [40].

3.1. *Application*

Returning to our application, we study the impact of $PM_{2.5}$ particle level on the cardiovascular mortality rate (CMR) in 2132 counties in the US using the data provided by the National Studies on Air Pollution and Health [41]. The data are publicly available under U.S. Public Domain license. The $PM_{2.5}$ particle level and the mortality rate are measured by $\mu g/m^3$ and the number of annual deaths due to cardiovascular conditions per 100,000 people, respectively. We use only the data for 2010 to simplify the experimental setup, using 75%–25% random train test split. Other than the treatment and response variables, the data include 10 variables such as poverty rate, population, and household income, which we use as confounders.

To train E2B, we create the random dataset using Hermite polynomials of max degree 3, $\mu_y = \left| h_{\gamma_{xy}} (\boldsymbol{\beta}_{xy}^\top \mathbf{x} / \|\boldsymbol{\beta}_{xy}^\top \mathbf{x}\|_2) + h_{\gamma_{ay}}(\mathbf{a}) \right|$. We use absolute value to capture the positivity of our response variable. The data also show heteroskedasticity, so we model our noise as a zero mean Gaussian variable with variance $\sigma^2(\widehat{y}) = 6.00\widehat{y}$. For regression, we use the non-parametric local kernel regression algorithm. We measure the uncertainty in the curves using the deep ensembles technique [42] with 100 random ensembles. That means, in each experiment, we initialize the neural network with different random values. To further improve the uncertainty estimation, in each training, we resample the dataset too.

Figure 5 shows the average treatment effect for the impact of CMR as a function of $PM_{2.5}$ concentration. We show the one standard deviation interval using the shaded areas. Starting around $PM_{2.5} = 5.3\mu g/m^3$, the curve increases with a steep slope; confirming the previous studies that increased $PM_{2.5}$ levels increase the probability of cardiovascular mortality. We can see that after $PM_{2.5} = 6.4\mu g/m^3$ the curve plateaus and the mortality rate stays at elevated levels. Looking at the histogram of the treatments in Figure 6, we observe that most counties have $PM_{2.5}$ between

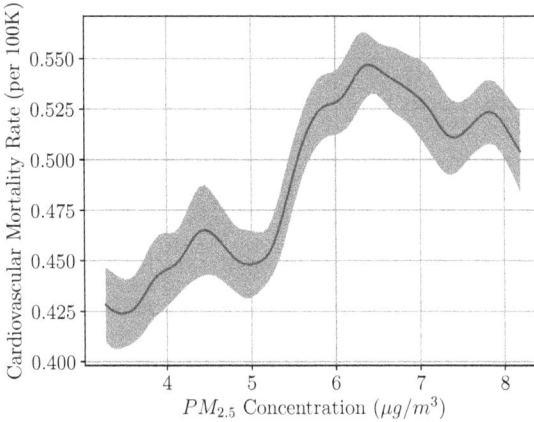

Fig. 5. The average treatment effect curve for measuring the impact of $PM_{2.5}$ concentration on the cardiovascular mortality rate. We perform the experiment 100 times and report the mean and ±std range.

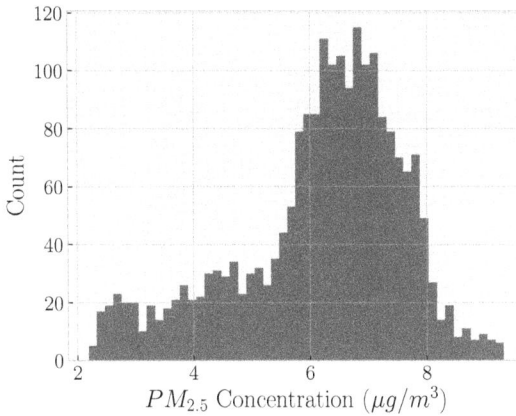

Fig. 6. Histogram of $PM_{2.5}$

6 and 8. This might justify the fluctuations that we see in this interval and suggests potential unmeasured confounders.

4. Conclusion

Enormous strides have been made in the recent decade in both machine learning and causal inference. Furthermore, a fortuitous overlap between the two endeavors has led to accelerated sharing of ideas and consequential progress. We believe that such advances are just the beginning.

References

[1] D. B. Rubin (2005). Causal inference using potential outcomes: Design, modeling, decisions. *Journal of the American Statistical Association, 100*(469), 322–331.

[2] J. M. Robins and A. Rotnitzky (1995). Semiparametric efficiency in multivariate regression models with missing data. *Journal of the American Statistical Association, 90*(429), 122–129.

[3] P. Spirtes, C. N. Glymour, R. Scheines *et al.* (2000). *Causation, Prediction, and Search.* Cambridge, MA: MIT Press.

[4] J. Pearl (2009). *Causality.* Cambridge, United Kingdom: Cambridge University Press.

[5] G. W. Imbens and D. B. Rubin (2015). *Causal Inference in Statistics, Social, and Biomedical Sciences.* New York, NY: Cambridge University Press.

[6] J. Peters, D. Janzing, and B. Schölkopf (2017). *Elements of Causal Inference: Foundations and Learning Algorithms.* The MIT Press.

[7] Z. C. Lipton (2018). The mythos of model interpretability: In machine learning, the concept of interpretability is both important and slippery. *Queue, 16*(3), 31–57.

[8] C. Molnar (2020). *Interpretable Machine Learning.* Lulu. com.

[9] K. He, X. Zhang, S. Ren *et al.* (2016). Identity mappings in deep residual networks. In *European Conference on Computer Vision.* Springer, pp. 630–645.

[10] B. Kim, M. Wattenberg, J. Gilmer *et al.* (2018). Interpretability beyond feature attribution: Quantitative Testing with Concept Activation Vectors (TCAV). In *ICML*, pp. 2668–2677.

[11] A. Ghorbani, J. Wexler, J. Y. Zou *et al.* (2019). Towards automatic concept-based explanations. In *NeurIPS*, pp. 9273–9282.

[12] L. Brocki and N. C. Chung (2019, December). Concept saliency maps to visualize relevant features in deep generative models. In *2019 18th IEEE International Conference on Machine Learning and Applications (ICMLA)* pp. 1771–1778. IEEE.

[13] M. Hamidi-Haines, Z. Qi, A. Fern *et al.* (2018). Interactive naming for explaining deep neural networks: A formative study. *arXiv:1812.07150.*

[14] C. J. Cai, E. Reif, N. Hegde *et al.* (2019). Human-centered tools for coping with imperfect algorithms during medical decision-making. In *Proceedings of the 2019 chi Conference on Human Factors in Computing Systems*, pp. 1–14. 2019.

[15] M. Graziani, V. Andrearczyk, and H. Müller (2018). Regression concept vectors for bidirectional explanations in histopathology. In *Understanding and Interpreting Machine Learning in Medical Image Computing Applications.* Springer, pp. 124–132.

[16] J. R. Clough, I. Oksuz, E. Puyol-Antón *et al.* (2019). Global and local interpretability for cardiac MRI classification. In *Medical Image Computing and Computer Assisted Intervention-MICCAI 2019: 22nd International Conference*, Shenzhen, China, 13–17 October, 2019, Proceedings, Part IV 22, pp. 656–664. Springer International Publishing.

[17] C. Sprague, E. B. Wendoloski, and I. Guch (2019). Interpretable AI for deep learning- based meteorological applications. In *American Meteorological Society Annual Meeting*. AMS.

[18] C. Wah, S. Branson, P. Welinder *et al.* (2011). *The Caltech-UCSD Birds-200-2011 Dataset*. California Institute of Technology, Tech. Rep. CNS-TR-2011-001.

[19] R. Blundell and J. L. Powell (2003). Endogeneity in nonparametric and semiparametric regression models. *Econometric Society Monographs*, *36*, 312–357.

[20] J. H. Stock (2015). Instrumental variables in statistics and econometrics. *International Encyclopedia of the Social & Behavioral Sciences*, *1*, 7577–7582.

[21] M. T. Bahadori and D. Heckerman (2021). Debiasing concept-based explanations with causal analysis. In *International Conference on Learning Representations*. https://www.amazon.science/publications/debiasing-concept-based-explanations-with-causal-analysis.

[22] S. Hooker, D. Erhan, P.-J. Kindermans *et al.* (2019). A benchmark for interpretability methods in deep neural networks. In *Advances in Neural Information Processing Systems 32*.

[23] D. Galagate (2016). *Causal Inference with a Continuous Treatment and Outcome: Alternative Estimators for Parametric Dose-Response Functions with Applications*. Ph.D. dissertation, University of Maryland.

[24] C. Ai, O. Linton, and Z. Zhang (2022). Estimation and inference for the counterfactual distribution and quantile functions in continuous treatment models. *Journal of Econometrics*, *228*(1), 39–61.

[25] L. H. Wyatt, G. C. Peterson, T. J. Wade *et al.* (2020). The contribution of improved air quality to reduced cardiovascular mortality: Declines in socioeconomic differences over time. *Environment International*, *136*, 105430.

[26] J. Robins, M. Hernán, and B. Brumback (2000). Marginal structural models and causal inference in epidemiology. *Epidemiology*, *11*(5), 550–560.

[27] K. Imai and D. A. Van Dyk (2004). Causal inference with general treatment regimes: Generalizing the propensity score. *Journal of the American Statistical Association*, *99*(467), 854–866.

[28] I. Díaz and M. J. van der Laan (2013). Targeted data adaptive estimation of the causal dose–response curve. *Journal of Causal Inference*, *1*(2), 171–192.

[29] E. H. Kennedy, Z. Ma, M. D. McHugh *et al.* (2017). Nonparametric methods for doubly robust estimation of continuous treatment effects. *Journal of the Royal Statistical Society. Series B, Statistical Methodology*, *79*(4), 1229.

[30] J. R. Zubizarreta, C. E. Reinke, R. R. Kelz *et al.* (2011). Matching for several sparse nominal variables in a case-control study of readmission following surgery. *The American Statistician*, *65*(4), 229–238.

[31] J. Hainmueller (2012). Entropy balancing for causal effects: A multivariate reweighting method to produce balanced samples in observational studies. *Political Analysis*, *20*(1), 25–46.

[32] S. Zeng, S. Assaad, C. Tao *et al.* (2020). Double robust representation learning for counterfactual prediction. *arXiv:2010.07866*.

[33] C. Fong, C. Hazlett, K. Imai *et al.* (2018). Covariate balancing propensity score for a continuous treatment: Application to the efficacy of political advertisements. *The Annals of Applied Statistics, 12*(1), 156–177.

[34] B. G. Vegetabile, B. A. Griffin, D. L. Coffman *et al.* (2021). Nonparametric estimation of population average dose-response curves using entropy balancing weights for continuous exposures. *Health Services and Outcomes Research Methodology, 21*(1), 69–110.

[35] R. K. Wong and K. C. G. Chan (2018). Kernel-based covariate functional balancing for observational studies. *Biometrika, 105*(1), 199–213.

[36] C. Hazlett (2020). Kernel balancing: A flexible non-parametric weighting procedure for estimating causal effects. *Statistica Sinica, 30*, 1155–1189.

[37] Y. Wang and J. R. Zubizarreta (2020). Minimal dispersion approximately balancing weights: Asymptotic properties and practical considerations. *Biometrika, 107*(1), 93–105.

[38] M. T. Bahadori, E. T. Tchetgen, and D. E. Heckerman (2022). End-to-end balancing for causal continuous treatment-effect estimation. In *International Conference on Machine Learning*, pp. 1313–1326. PMLR. https://proceedings.mlr.press/v162/bahadori22a.html.

[39] T. Glasmachers (2017). Limits of end-to-end learning. In *Asian Conference on Machine Learning*. PMLR, pp. 17–32.

[40] S. Athey, G. W. Imbens, J. Metzger *et al.* (2021). Using wasserstein generative adversarial networks for the design of monte carlo simulations. *Journal of Econometrics.*

[41] A. Rappold (2020). Annual pm2.5 and cardiovascular mortality rate data: Trends modified by county socioeconomic status in 2,132 US counties. https://doi.org/10.23719/1506014.

[42] B. Lakshminarayanan, A. Pritzel, and C. Blundell (2017). Simple and scalable predictive uncertainty estimation using deep ensembles. In *NeurIPS*, pp. 6405–6416.

Part F. Endpiece: AI Tools and Concepts

The Frontier Supercomputer at the US Department of Energy's Oak Ridge National Laboratory. Credit: Oak Ridge National Laboratory, U.S. Dept. of Energy.

© 2023 World Scientific Publishing Company
https://doi.org/10.1142/9789811265679_0039

Chapter 39

Overview of Deep Learning and Machine Learning

Alok Choudhary[*,§], Geoffrey Fox[†,¶], and Tony Hey[‡,‖]

*Electrical and Computer Engineering and Computer Science
Departments, Northwestern University, Evanston, IL, USA*
†*Biocomplexity Institute and Computer Science Department, University of
Virginia, Charlottesville, VA USA*
‡*Chief Data Scientist, Rutherford Appleton Laboratory, Science and
Technology Facilities Council/UKRI, Didcot, UK*
§*a-choudhary@northwestern.edu*
¶*vxj6mb@virginia.edu*
‖*tony.hey@stfc.ac.uk*

1. Introduction

The chapters in this book demonstrate that AI applications in science have recently focused on deep learning with some examples of older machine learning approaches still being used effectively. The summary of methods, tools, and solutions in Chapter 40 has lists of tools for both deep learning and classical machine learning. Deep learning exploits big data and can use this to build models parameterized by the weights of the associated neural network. The classical methods often required the user to supply the model, which is often hard to do. In the following section, we summarize three classical ML methods while Section 3 describes components used to build deep learning networks. Particular networks are illustrated in Section 4. These fields are all moving very fast and so references will inevitably be out of date. So, we are content with noting that Wikipedia covers all our topics while popular basic deep learning resources are Goodfellow and collaborators book [1] and Andrew Ng's online course [2]. Note that there are many examples in this book of two important types of AI.

Supervised learning is used when you are understanding new data in terms of a previously developed scheme so the training data samples are all labeled.

Unsupervised learning is used to discover previously unknown structures such as in clustering and autoencoders. It does not require labeled data.

Also, in this chapter, we do not distinguish between Deep Learning (DL) and Artificial Neural Networks (ANNs) viewing the former as the latter applied with large datasets. Sometimes, optimization problems are divided into regression and classification. The former involves continuous variables and is common in science while the latter, involving discrete categories, is more common in commercial applications.

2. Classical AI/Machine Learning

2.1. *Decision trees, LightBGM, XGBoost, and Random Forests*

A decision tree is a graph structure illustrated in Figure 1, where an internal node represents a "test", and each branch represents the result of the test, and each leaf node represents the decision corresponding to the test results along the path from the root to that leaf node. Random Forest is an important idea that uses an Ensemble of decision trees to represent the common situation that the tests do not have certain decisions and the final result can be an average over that of the constituent trees.

Boosting is a technique that builds Ensembles of "weak" (not so good) learners and combines them into "strong" learners. It is often used

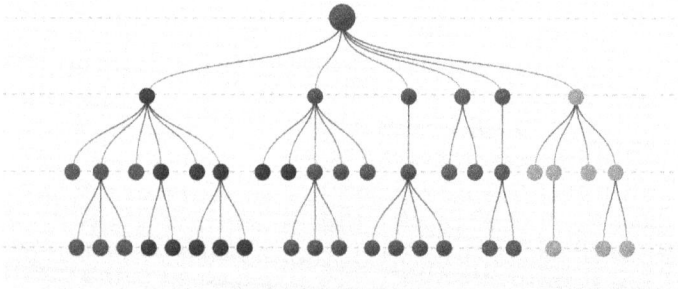

Fig. 1.   A decision tree.

as **Gradient boosting** when differentiable loss functions allow descent methods — move in the direction of the negative of the gradient (first derivative) of the loss function. Gradient boosting applied to decision trees typically outperforms Random Forests. **LightBGM** and **XGBoost** are two popular Gradient boosting implementations.

2.2. *Support vector machine (SVM)*

The SVM was historically one of the most successful machine learning algorithms which were used in classification problems. As shown in Figure 2, SVM finds the best hyperplane that cuts an arbitrary dimension space into two regions corresponding in the figure to a quantity with two possible states: red and blue. Of course, as in this example, the best solution may still misclassify some points. SVM has an important extension by using a kernel to map the input data into a feature space and find the hyperplane in this new space. Deep learning has often replaced SVM and here we see the clear advantage of a neural net being able to learn a model; the kernel is naturally learned.

2.3. *Clustering*

This is an unsupervised learning problem where data are as shown in Figure 3 divided into clumps. Points in each cluster are close to each other and in clean cases, far from points in other clusters. This algorithm depends critically on the existence of a distance metric in the space being clustered. One implicitly feeds in some measure of expected cluster size, often by the number of desired clusters. K-means which has many quite sophisticated variants is perhaps the best-known clustering method. There are important clustering problems where the clusters are not separated but rather the algorithm divides the dataset into regions of nearby points as, e.g., countries are divided into counties and states.

2.4. *Genetic algorithms (GA)*

Whereas neural networks are inspired by the mechanisms of the human brain, genetic algorithms (GA) are inspired by the slower process of evolution. One optimizes systems described by a sequence that is typically made up of discrete-valued variables and one minimizes a known loss function dependent on the sequence. One evolves an ensemble of solutions that are evolved by biologically inspired operators such as mutation, crossover, and selection. Decision trees and hyperparameter optimization are natural candidates for genetic algorithms.

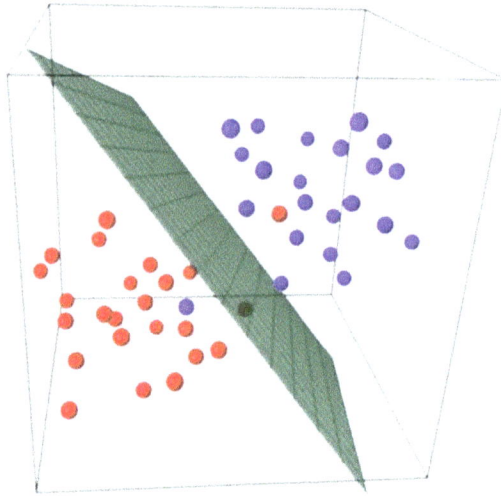

Fig. 2.   Illustration of an SVM hyperplane dividing the feature space into two categories.

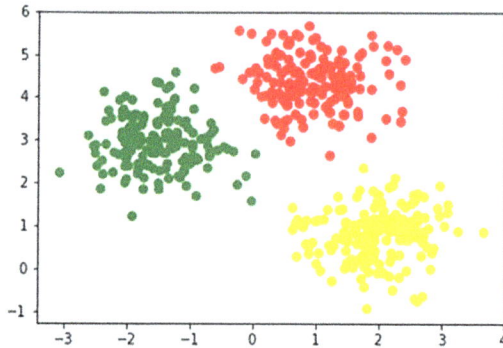

Fig. 3.   Point clustering illustrated with three clusters shown.

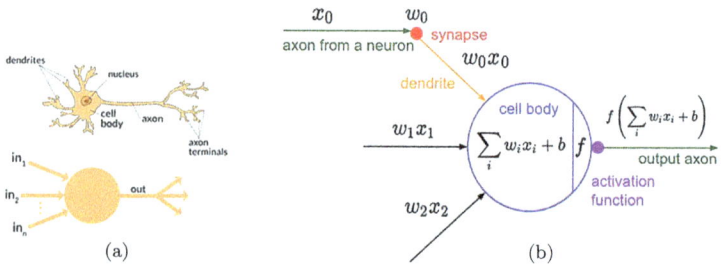

Fig. 4.   (a) A biological neuron contrasted with a mathematical node of a neural net. (b) The detailed structure of an activation layer.

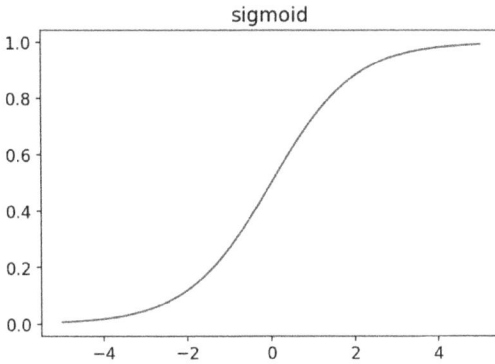

Fig. 5. A typical activation function — the Sigmoid.

3. Deep Learning Components

3.1. *Neurons. Weights and links*

Artificial neural nets, as shown in Figure 4(a), are built as graphs with nodes analogous to nucleus cells and inputs and outputs analogous to dendrites and axons. The ANN model is parameterized by weights associated with the links to the nodes. A signal is presented to the initial input layer and propagates through the network multiplying by the weights as shown in Figure 4(b).

3.2. *Activation (ReLU, Sigmoid, Tanh, SELU, Softmax)*

At a node, the inputs are summed and a possible bias is added. In the simplest case of an identity activation, this resultant signal is passed on to the output links for this node. In general, however, as shown in Figure 4(b), an activation function f is applied. This step introduces nonlinearity and is typified by the Sigmoid activation $\sigma(x) = 1/(1 + \exp(-x))$ and other activations such as Tanh and RELU similarly map the output into a bounded domain. Softmax is a special activation used in a layer of nodes to map node inputs to a probability that sums to 1 over all nodes.

3.3. *Layers*

Progress in deep learning has been accelerated by highly functional software models that allow one to build a model in a modular fashion as a set of linked (by weighted arcs) layers where layers are hierarchically constructed from collections of neurons called layers. This is illustrated in Figure 6 which exhibits seven layers: one input, one output, and five internal or hidden layers. Typically, one specifies some but not all the layers to be

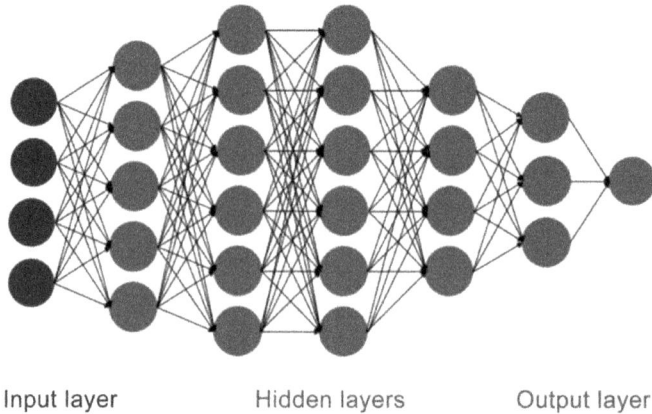

Fig. 6.   A fully connected network with hidden, input, and output layers.

associated with non-identity activation functions. The pipelined structure of that figure would be called the sequential architecture in Keras which was an early popular system in which general networks could be specified.

3.4. *Loss function, optimizer*

Optimization problems define a quantity — the loss function to be minimized. Example loss functions are the negative logarithm of the likelihood, mean square error and mean absolute error. Deep learning frameworks come with many built-in choices of the loss function and allow the user to specify their own. This loss function is minimized by an optimizer for which again there are many choices provided. For deep learning, direct use of the Newton–Raphson second-order method is impractical due to the large number of weights that need to be determined and so one uses variants of the first-order steepest descent method where steps are made in the negative direction of the first derivative gradient. At the simplest, this just needs a step size (called the learning rate) but there are many variations that try to speed up the convergence; some of these effectively estimate second-order effects. Well-known optimizers are AdaGrad, RMSProp, and Adam.

3.5. *Stochastic gradient descent SGD and batch size*

In classical algorithms, the analysis of a particular dataset would often have many iterations where the action at each iteration or epoch depended on calculations involving the full dataset. However, an important strategy used in deep learning is to divide the data into batches (perhaps as small as 64) and now an epoch consists of a set of steps, one for each batch. The resultant **stochastic gradient descent** algorithm is particularly suitable for first-order methods where updates are fast as there are no heavy Hessian-based computations. SGD has several advantages; if the dataset is large and the samples are correlated, one does not waste time summing over redundant samples. Second, the statistical fluctuations over the SGD steps may better avoid local minima than the one update per epoch approach.

3.6. *Backpropagation*

Given a loss function, and a choice of weights to be determined, one needs to calculate both the value of the loss and its first derivative with respect to the weights. If we have a cascade of layers f_i, then the loss takes the functional form $f_N(f_{N-1}(f_{N-2}, \ldots, f_1(f_0(\text{weights}))\ldots))$, where the input layer is f_0. To find the loss value, you iterate forward starting at f_0 but using the chain rule, calculating the first derivative starts at the other end with f_N. The derivative calculation is built into the deep learning packages and this is termed **backpropagation**.

3.7. *One-hot vector*

One-hot vectors are used in classification problems and refer to vectors of length N where the only allowed choices are vector components with $N - 1$ zeros and a single one. Then, if there is a quantity that consists of items each in one of N categories, then the ith item would have a one-hot representation with 1 in its $(i - 1)$th component and the other components zero.

3.8. *Vanishing gradient*

In large networks, one sometimes finds that derivates can be small and as these multiplied by the learning rate are the parameter change, this implies one can converge slowly. This small derivative is often caused by the nonlinear activation layers. One can alleviate this **vanishing gradient** problem by designing networks with "residual connections" or "skip connections" that provide long-distance links between layers that avoid the squashing effect of activation functions. One can also reduce the impact of the vanishing gradient by hierarchical training methods or the use of Rectified Linear units (ReLU) in the activations as these only saturate in one direction.

3.9. *Hyperparameters*

The key parameters in deep learning problems are the weight and biases, but in addition, one must also choose the metadata specifying the approach. These are exemplified by Batch Size, Number of Hidden layers, Number of LSTM layers, Size of hidden variables, Learning Rate, Number of Epochs, Optimization method, Number of Transformer heads, Regularization method, Number of branches in a decision tree, and Number of clusters in a clustering algorithm. These **hyperparameters** are typically investigated by a separate optimization either looping over a grid in these parameter values or using a Genetic algorithm. This can be computationally expensive and increase the training time by a factor of 100 or so. There is an extension of this that explores different network choices and is called **Neural Architecture Search**.

3.10. *Dropout*

Dropout is a surprisingly powerful method that both avoids overfitting (improves generalization), regularizes, and can be used to estimate uncertainty as explained in Chapter 30. One can specify layers to be dropouts and set a probability p (perhaps between 0.2 and 0.5). Then, in each batch optimization, one randomly drops independent nodes in a dropout layer with a probability p.

4. Deep Learning Networks

4.1. *Multilayer perceptron, feed-forward network, fully connected network*

This is the most straightforward but still important deep learning architecture illustrated by our original Figure 1 in Chapter 1 and Figure 6. Each layer has a set of nodes that are fully connected to the previous and following layers with each node being connected to all nodes in the adjacent layers and each connection having a weight attached to it. Some but typically not all the layers would have non-identity activations assigned.

4.2. *Convolutional neural networks*

Humans are very good at many tasks such as image and video recognition, pattern recognition, and natural language processing. Such data (e.g., images) have spatial relationships. Features (edges, colors, objects, etc.) are present at various levels. A CNN is inspired by how humans perform the task of object recognition, pattern recognition, etc. As shown in

Figure 7, the neural network combines those features to make predictions. Thus, unlike typical machine learning techniques which require feature engineering, a CNN architecture performs the task of feature extraction, feature hierarchy as well as learning from labeled data using a deep neural network. CNN layers include filters linking neighbors for input pixel data. This can produce the difference operators familiar from classical edge detection image processing algorithms. However, they are more general in that the width of interaction (at its simplest 1) is general and more interestingly the weights in difference operators are not fed in but learned from the data.

4.3. *Encoder–decoder network*

Many deep learning networks are built with two steps illustrated in Figure 8. The first step called the **Encoder** takes the input and builds a representation that includes features identified in this step. This is followed by a **Decoder** that converts the internal representation into the final form. Convolutional, Recurrent, Attention, and Fully connected layers can be present in either the Encoder or Decoder steps. Figure 12 illustrates an encoder–decoder architecture with very different architectures for the steps. However, sometimes it is natural to use similar architectures (the decoder is inverse to the encoder) as discussed in the next section.

4.4. *Autoencoder, variational autoencoder*

One important special case of encoder–decoder networks is an **autoencoder** which has the key feature that the output is identical to the input. This can be used to develop a clean representation (shown as the bottleneck in Figure 9) which can be applied to find low-dimension reductions of the original data. They can also be used to remove noise from the input. They can be used as sophisticated alternatives to dimension reduction methods of classical machine learning such as Principal Component Analysis (PCA) and Multidimensional Scaling (MDS). A **variational autoencoder** is a special autoencoder that generates probability distributions using a special loss function.

4.5. *Recurrent neural network (RNN)*

A variety of data in many practical applications is presented in a sequence or serial fashion. Any temporal or sequence dataset, such as natural language, stock market, weather data, and videos, has this characteristic. Therefore, for such datasets, the prediction depends not only on the current data but also on learned sequential patterns. There are two important problem

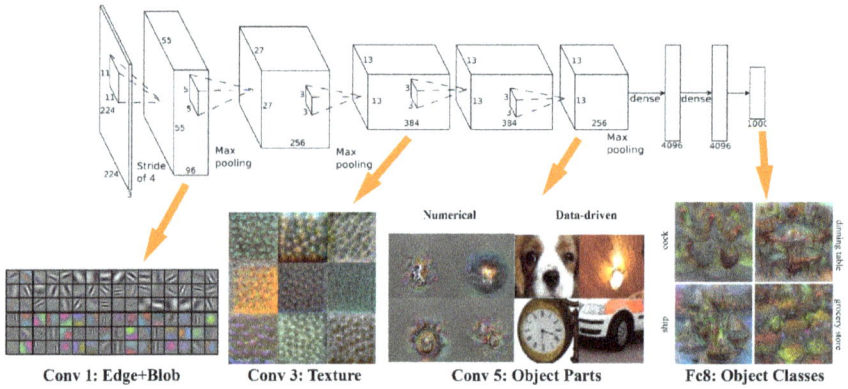

Conv 1: Edge+Blob   Conv 3: Texture   Conv 5: Object Parts   Fc8: Object Classes

Fig. 7.   The aspects of an image that are identified at different stages of a CNN network AlexNet.

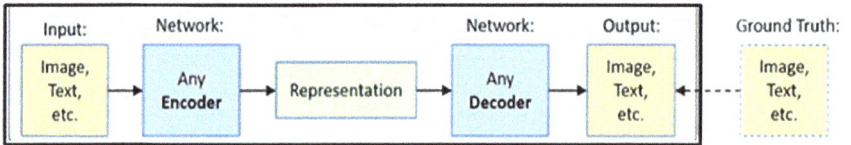

Fig. 8.   A generic encoder–decoder network architecture.

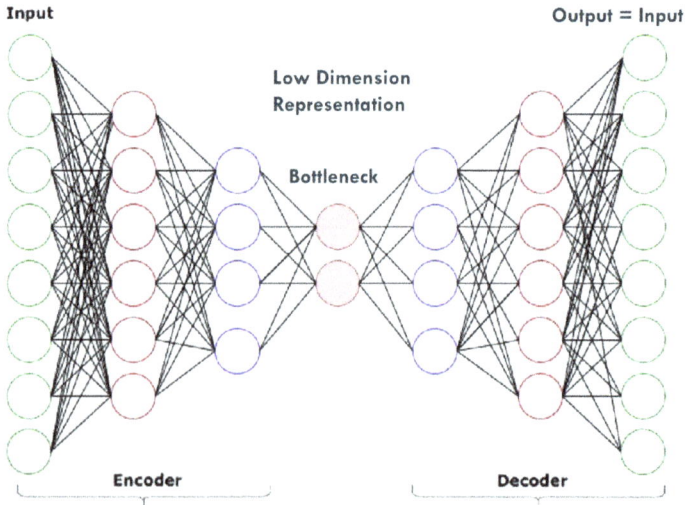

Fig. 9.   An autoencoder with identical input and output.

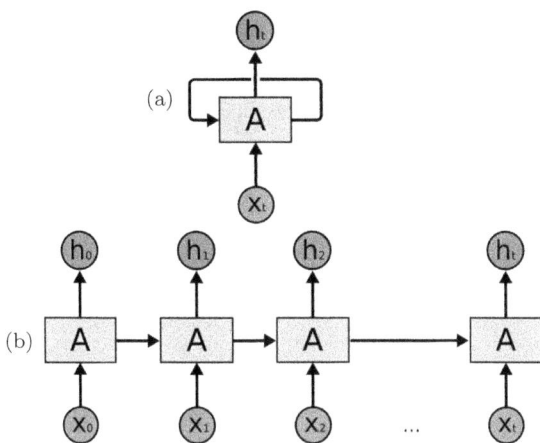

Fig. 10. A basic RNN showing in (a) a basic unit and (b) the unit replicated across a sequence.

classes called sequence to sequence (e.g., converting a stream of English into a different language) and sequence to forecast such as the word processor suggesting the next word to type.

Both of these problems can be addressed with recurrent neural networks (RNNs). These are illustrated in Figure 10 where there is a basic layer shown in Figure 10(a) which is replicated a number of times equal to the sequence length shown in Figure 10(b).

Therefore, training an RNN involves data from prior inputs and outputs (which are captured in memory or state), along with the current input and output of training data. However, the original base RNN suffers from what is called a "vanishing gradient" problem. Gradients typically carry information for parameter updates of a network. But when the gradients become so small for long sequences that parameter update practically stops, that is, the learning doesn't work. This led to the introduction of more complicated networks GRU and LSTM described in the following subsections and illustrated in Figure 11.

4.6. *Long short-term memory (LSTM) network*

To address the limitations of basic RNNs, particularly that of the "vanishing gradient", LSTM networks are used. Figure 11(b) shows a typical node of an LSTM. It addresses the long-term dependency problem with cell structure and various gates. The LSTM has three gates, namely, the forget gate, input gate, and output gate. These control the cell state. The first gate layer determines how much information to forget using a sigmoid function

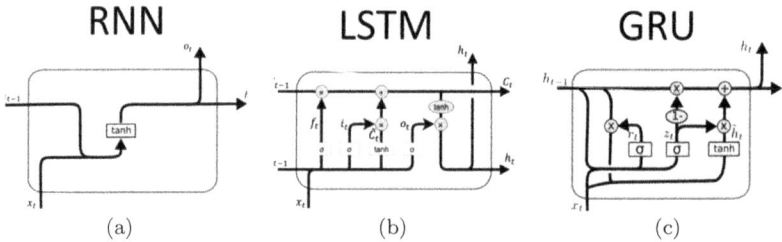

Fig. 11. Comparison of three recurrent neural networks: (a) Basic, (b) LSTM, and (c) GRU. https://deepai.org/machine-learning-glossary-and-terms/gated-recurrent-unit.

as a gating function. The second gate determines how much information to use from the current input (x_t). The cell states encode the long-term dependencies and relationships.

4.7. Gated recurrent unit (GRU)

Basic RNNs are rarely used today but a simplification of the LSTM termed the GRU Gated Recurrent Unit is still in active use and gives good results. LSTMs are typically preferred when the sequences are long and there is big data to be able to train the increased number of weights. Note that a GRU has two gates (reset and update gates), whereas an LSTM has three gates (namely input, output, and forget gates).

4.8. Transformer

Transformers have revolutionized deep learning, starting with the striking paper [3] "Attention is all you need" from a Google team that introduced the Transformer built around the earlier developed concept of Attention. Transformers have a sequence-to-sequence architecture that replaced recurrent networks by Attention heads. Appearing in the 2017 NeurIPS conference, this paper already has over 45,000 citations and has excellent online tutorials [4]. Attention looks over sequences and identifies common patterns and the most common form is the so-called "scaled dot product" formulation which introduces three vectors Q (query), K (key), and V (value) that are formed by passing embedded input through three separate dense layers. Labeling sequences $s(i)$, one determines the attention between two input items by comparing the query vector $Q(i)$ and finding the overlap with key $K(j)$ for every other item using the softmax activation layer to choose item j with the largest dot product. Then, $V(j)$

(a) **Encoder**   (b) **Decoder**

Nowcasted Future Earthquakes

Encoding 4x

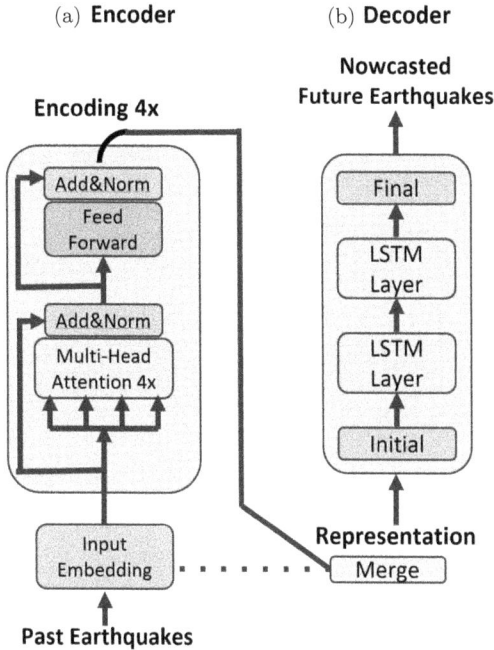

Past Earthquakes

Fig. 12.   A network aimed at earthquake nowcasting with a transformer-based encoder and an LSTM-based decoder.

is the resultant representation of the attention. Mathematically, attention $A(i) = \text{Softmax}(QK^T)V$ suitably normalized.

Attention is calculated in several layers, and in each layer, one calculates multiple attention candidates called heads. The original transformer paper had an encoder–decoder architecture with attention calculated in both encoder and decoder steps. However, attention can be used as a module (layer) in any network, and Figure 12 shows an Earthquake nowcasting application [5] with a similar encoder to the original Transformer paper but a decoder aimed at regression (numerical predictions).

4.9. *Generative adversarial network (GAN)*

GANs are typically used to generate new datasets from existing datasets, where new datasets are "similar" to the existing datasets. As Figure 13 shows (using images as a dataset example), there are two parts to a GAN, namely, a Generator and a Discriminator. The Generator generates a "fake image" and the Discriminator's goal is to predict whether the "fake

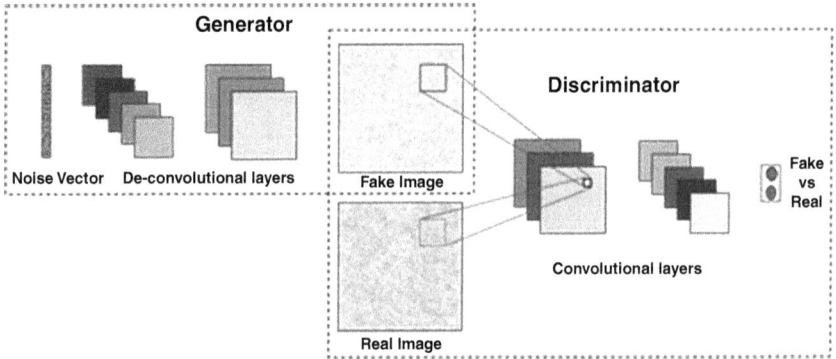

Fig. 13.   Architecture of a GAN.

image" is "fake" or "real". In other words, the Generator learns to generate new samples, whereas the Discriminator learns to distinguish between real examples and the ones that are generated. There are many practical applications of GANs, both good and bad. For example, GANs have been used to generate "deep fakes". GANs are also useful in many applications such as generating additional data when the number of observed datasets can be small due to many reasons. In order to improve learning, bigger datasets need to be generated that follow certain distributions and constraints. For example, in cybersecurity, models can be trained to learn "fake" patterns, thereby, then detecting "fakes" when presented to the network. Or, in healthcare, GANs can be used to understand the difference between images from cancerous tumors versus benign ones where it is impossible or very hard to create large datasets with features.

4.10. *Reinforcement learning*

The idea behind reinforcement learning is quite simple. An agent (learner) learns optimal behavior to achieve maximum rewards. For example, the way a dog learns how to detect explosives or drugs is based on the concept of reinforcement earning. The learner is presented with different scenarios (data points) and is rewarded when it makes the right decision and is not rewarded when it does not. It is different from supervised learning in the sense that the learner independently discovers actions and decisions that maximize rewards.

In supervised learning, the learner is presented with training data, where the outcome for each point is known. Reinforcement learning is, therefore, a very important technique to learn in an unseen environment. Important

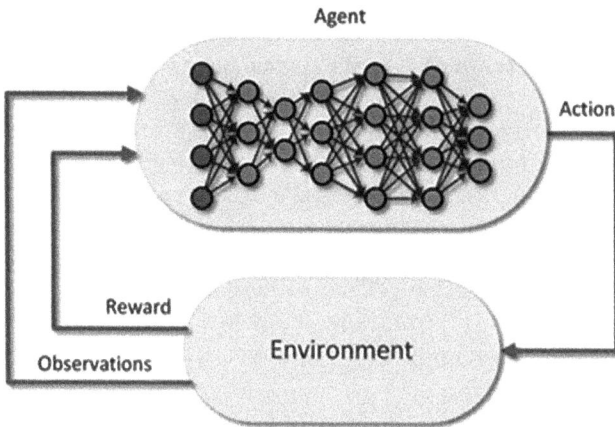

Fig. 14.   Reinforcement learning architecture.

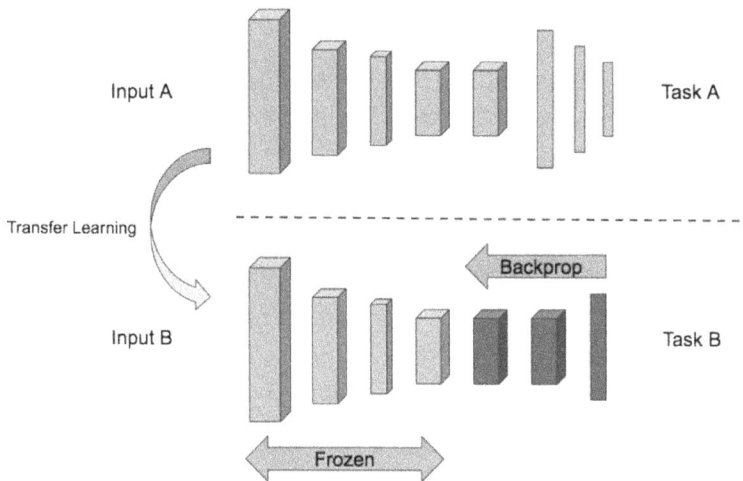

Fig. 15.   Transfer learning.

examples of the applications of reinforcement learning include AlphaGo, autonomous vehicles, robotics, etc. As shown in Figure 15, one typically builds the agent as a deep learning network that is learned in conjunction with state-action policy mapping. In the book, this approach is seen several times, especially in autonomous experiments and networks. It was famously successful in games such as AlphaGo [6].

4.11. *Transfer learning and pretraining*

Here, we use a **pretrained** model that has been trained on a large dataset that addresses a problem similar to the one that we want to solve. Then, as illustrated in Figure 14, we take the new dataset of interest and fine tune the pretrained network to represent the new problem. There are other useful forms of pretraining such as **Contrastive Learning** [7] which teaches a network as to which data points are similar or dissimilar.

We can see an example of transfer learning in remote sensing covered in Chapter 17 where there is often a paucity of labeled data. One can take networks such as those pretrained by ImageNet [8] and use transfer learning with modest data samples to find a remote sensing network [9].

4.12. *Foundation models*

Foundation models [10] are a bold extension of transfer learning and pretraining in the incredibly big data limit. They are illustrated by GPT-3 [11] from OpenAI with 175 billion learned parameters and explored in Chapter 34 of this book. These models are trained on large samples of multimodal data (say text and images) and are found to have emergent characteristics in successfully answering questions from datasets and fields not built into the original model. Chapter 34 stresses that the computational cost of the training of such models puts many research organizations at a disadvantage compared to private companies. One could imagine building Foundation models for surrogates of differential equation solvers or for geospatial time series. These models might need to be funded by governments in the same way as large scientific instruments.

4.13. *What are PyTorch, TensorFlow, JAX, and MXNET?*

Above we explained how deep neural networks were built modularly from linked layers and how they were trained using backpropagation invoking sophisticated optimizers. As an example, GPT-3 discussed in the previous section, contains 96 Transformer layers, while in image processing, ResNet-152 [12] has 152 layers. The resultant graph of layers (each of which could be many sublayers) is a nontrivial challenge and includes the need for automatic differentiation. This has led to several software packages supporting this model. Typically, these packages use popular scripting languages like Python but achieve high performance by invoking efficient (C + +) libraries. PyTorch [13] from Facebook, TensorFlow [14], JAX [15] from Google, and MXNET [16] from Apache are well-known frameworks of this type.

References

[1] I. Goodfellow, Y. Bengio, and A. Courville (2016). Deep learning. MIT Press. https://play.google.com/store/books/details?id=omivDQAAQBAJ.

[2] A. Ng, Y. B. Mourri, and K. Katanforoosh. Deep learning specialization online courses. https://www.deeplearning.ai/courses/deep-learning-speci alization/ (accessed 25 June 2022).

[3] A. Vaswani, N. Shazeer, N. Parmar *et al.* (2017). Attention is all you need. *Advances in Neural Information Processing Systems, 30*, 5998–6008. https://arxiv.org/abs/1706. 03762 https://proceedings.neurips.cc/paper/2017/file/3f5ee243547dee91fbd053c1c4a845aa-Paper.pdf.

[4] The TensorFlow Authors. Transformer model for language understanding: Google Colab Tutorial. https://colab.research.google.com/github/tensorflow/text/blob/master/docs/tutorials/transformer.ipynb (accessed 13 November 2020).

[5] G. Fox, J. B. Rundle, A. Donnellan *et al.* (2016). Nowcasting earthquakes. *Earth Space Science, 3*(11), 480–486. http://doi.wiley.com/10.1002/2016EA000185.

[6] AlphaZero is a computer program developed by artificial intelligence research company DeepMind to master the games of chess, shogi and go. https://en.wikipedia.org/wiki/AlphaZero (accessed 25 June 2022).

[7] T. Chen, S. Kornblith, M. Norouzi *et al.* (2020). A simple framework for contrastive learning of visual representations. In *Proceedings of the 37th International Conference on Machine Learning*, 13–18 July 2020, Vol. 119, pp. 1597–1607. https://proceedings.mlr.press/v119/chen20j.html.

[8] Stanford University. ImageNet image database organized according to the WordNet hierarchy. http://www.image-net.org/ (updated 11 March 2021)

[9] J. Lin, Z. Jiang, S. Sarkaria *et al.* (2019–2020). Special issue of Remote Sensing 'Deep Transfer Learning for Remote Sensing' MDPI. https://www.mdpi.com/journal/remotesensing/special_issues/DeepTransfer_Learning (accessed 25 June 2022).

[10] R. Bommasani, D. A. Hudson, E. Adeli *et al.* (2021). On the opportunities and risks of foundation models, *arXiv [cs.LG]*, 16 August 2021. http://arxiv.org/abs/2108.07258.

[11] OpenAI. GPT-3 Playground. https://gpt3demo.com/apps/openai-gpt-3-playground (updated 18 November 2021) (accessed 25 June 2022).

[12] K. He, X. Zhang, S. Ren *et al.* Deep residual learning for image recognition: ResNet-152 pre-trained model for PyTorch. https://www.kaggle.com/datasets/pytorch/resnet152, https://arxiv.org/abs/1512.03385 (accessed 25 June 2022).

[13] PyTorch Home page. An open source machine learning framework that accelerates the path from research prototyping to production deployment (Facebook). https://pytorch.org/ (accessed 14 March 2020).

[14] TensorFlow Home Page. An end-to-end open source machine learning platform (Google). https://www.tensorflow.org/ (accessed 14 March 2020).

[15] Google. JAX Quickstart. https://jax.readthedocs.io/en/latest/notebooks/ quickstart.html (accessed 25 June 2022).

[16] MXNET Home Page. A flexible and efficient truly open source library for deep learning (Apache Software Foundation). https://mxnet.apache.org/ (accessed 14 March 2020).

© 2023 World Scientific Publishing Company

https://doi.org/10.1142/9789811265679_0040

Chapter 40

Topics, Concepts, and AI Methods Discussed in Chapters

Alok Choudhary[*,§], Geoffrey Fox[†,¶], and Tony Hey[‡,‖]

Electrical and Computer Engineering and Computer Science Departments, Northwestern University, Evanston, IL, USA

†*Biocomplexity Institute and Computer Science Department, University of Virginia, Charlottesville, VA, USA*

‡*Chief Data Scientist, Rutherford Appleton Laboratory, Science and Technology Facilities Council/UKRI, Didcot, UK*

§*a-choudhary@northwestern.edu*

¶*vxj6mb@virginia.edu*

‖*tony.hey@stfc.ac.uk*

1. Overview

Here, we scanned chapters for key ideas and recorded them in tables. These list Nuggets of information, Goals, Concepts, Topics, and targets for AI applications. We identified Education discussions and Electronic Resources E such as datasets and Physical Resources R such as instruments. Very important is the list of Methods, and Tools (called solutions) in the AI and computing area. We also list Qualities such as explainability and FAIR principles.

Essentially, all chapters discuss deep learning and in more detail, common mentions are AlphaFold 14, Bayes 16, CNN 23, Deep 31, Explainable 9, FAIR 22, GAN 3, Generative 10, LSTM 9, RNN 9, SVM 2, Uncertainty 18, and XGBOOST 3.

Chapter 3. Data-Driven Science in the Era of AI: From Patterns to Practice

Alexander Szalay

Nuggets Mid-scale experiments averaging $10M–$100M

Topics What types of people are needed; Bioinformatics; Material Science; Disruptive assistance collaboration model

Concepts Big data is long-lived because too hard to replace; Cloud-based access replaces "disk at home"; Data from simulations and Observation; Fault Tolerance; Redundancy; Parallelism; Benchmarks

Solutions Federated Learning; computing locally, computing in the cloud, distributed computing

Computing Kubernetes; Databases

Qualities FAIR, Cost; Value; Sustainability

Resources Planet Labs; SkyServer and Sloan Digital Sky Survey SDSS; SciServer general science database access; Turbulence simulation Database; Ocean Circulation simulation Database; Indra cosmological simulations

Chapter 4. AI in the Broader Context of Data Science

Phil Bourne and Rafael C. Alvarado

Concepts AI within this 4+1 framework where the emphasis moves beyond algorithms into the realm of systems, human–computer interaction, ethics, policy, law, justice, psychology, and more; Comprehensive cross-disciplinary approach

Solutions AlphaFold

Computing DIKW (Data, Information, Knowledge, Wisdom) pipeline; GPU CUDA

Qualities Better Data; Understandable Explainable AI; FAIR

Education History of Data science; 4+1 model: systems, design, analytics, ethics + Domain

Chapter 5. AlphaFold — The End of the Protein Folding Problem or the Start of Something Bigger?

David T. Jones and Janet M. Thornton

Nuggets CASP competition every two years; evolved sophisticated metric GDT-TS and is limited in scope; Humans 20000 proteins; AF2 (AlphaFold2) will enable the field of structural biology to grow and contribute even more to our understanding of life at the molecular level

Topics Extensions include ligands and carbohydrate chains; Multiple sequence alignment in AF2, essential

Concepts Rotational and translational invariance enforced

Solutions Parts based on AlphaGo; Single fully differentiable neural net for end to end; Set of Transformers from amino acids to positions; Sequence to sequence map

Resources AF2 results at AlphaFold Protein Structure Database ftp://ftp.ebi.ac.uk/pub/database/alphafold; 1 million structures in the database, covering sequences from 49 organisms; The AlphaFold source code (https://github.com/deepmind/alphafold/) and Colab notebook (https://colab.research.google.com/github/deepmind/alphafold/blob/main/notebooks/AlphaFold.ipynb); https://medium.com/@salwasayeed236/alphafold-a-scientific-breakthrough-9cfe8364bb21

Chapter 6. Applications of AI in Astronomy

S. G. Djorgovski, A. A. Mahabal, M. J. Graham, K. Polsterer, and A. Krone-Martins

Nuggets multimessenger astronomy is observing multiple wavelengths including neutrinos

Topics AI for images of stars/galaxies and remove instrumental artifacts; sky surveys give billions of objects — AI flags interesting ones; Anomaly identification; Analyze publications; Identify gravitational lens; Photo-Z (multicolor) for redshifts

Concepts Supervised learning gives known objects; Unsupervised discovery of new phenomena; Time-dependent surveys need real time; Include domain knowledge with AI to give physics-based AI

Solutions Estimating errors with uncertainty quantification; Physics-based AI; Gaussian process regression (GPR) for missing data; surrogates for simulations; AIFeynman uses symbolic/memetic regression to learn equations; Supervised learning/classification (Artificial Neural Nets, Decision Trees, Deep Learning); Time Series Analysis (GPR and Recurrent Neural Networks); Dimensionality reduction (Deep Learning and XGBOOST); Regression analysis and prediction

Chapter 7. Machine Learning for Complex Instrument Design and Optimization

Barry C. Barish, Jonathan Richardson, Evangelos E. Papalexakis, and Rutuja Gurav

Nuggets Describes AI for designing instruments that gather data; not analysis of the data. Stresses richness of instrument data with over 10K channels or LIGO

Concepts Optimizing instrument design based on simulators — has similarities to hyperparameter searches; Domain knowledge needed to identify efficient datasets; Difficulties with GANs addressed by physics-guided AI and expert in loop; Replace simulators by GANs

Topic (Solution)s **Noise glitches in LIGO** (tensor factorization); **LIGO needs laser cavities to operate in resonant mode — failures are a control failure identified by anomalies.** (Use tree-based Outlier Detection algorithm called Isolation Forest); **nonlinear Noise removal** (unsupervised learning as can not be modeled); **Avoiding control failures by identifying (cf. fusion and earthquakes) precursors to failure** (Make binary classification Fail/Succeed using limited supervision)

Other Topics Anomaly Detection; Transient noise

Computing ML pipeline including explainability after analysis and use of expert in loop and limited supervision

Qualities Use explainable AI to identify precursor signals

Education Weak or limited supervision; Explainable models; Theory/physics-guided models; Human (expert)-in-the-loop real-time supervision and active learning; GAN

Resources LIGO (Gravitational waves); LHC (Hadrons); EIC (Electron-Ion); lists public datasets

Chapter 8. Artificial Intelligence (AI) and Machine Learning (ML) at Experimental Facilities

J. A. Sethian, J. J. Donatelli, A. Hexemer, M. M. Noack, D. M. Pelt, D. M. Ushizima, and P. H. Zwart,

Nuggets Guide scientific inquiry by designing/choosing experts

Education General discussion of AI avoiding hype on both sides pro and con

Concepts Self-driving laboratories for self-driving experiments; AI for Experimental Science — Price of being wrong is high

Topics Making Sense of Complex Data; Detecting Patterns across experiments; Tuning and Optimizing (self-driving) Experiments; Advancing theory and simulations by surrogates (computer is laboratory); AI/ML for Discovering and Understanding the broad Scientific Landscape built on common community approaches, standards, and resources

Topic (Solution) **(1) AI/ML and Optimized Self-Driving Experiments** (gpCAM system); **(2) Cryo-electron tomography images** (AI/ML for Limited Scientific Training Data, Mixed-Scale Dense Convolutional Neural Networks — new architecture needing less data); **(3) AI/ML for Automated High-Throughput Data Analysis for Xray scattering** (pyCBIR identify and classify images); **(4) Reconstructing 3D macromolecular structure from fluctuation X-ray scattering FXS experiments conducted at X-ray free-electron lasers: Reconstruct PBCV-1 virus** (Multi-Tiered Iterative Projections M-TIP for complex inversion problems); **(5) AI/ML for Designing Materials** (recommender systems)

High-level Solutions Bayesian Uncertainty Quantification UQ; Stochastic Processes; Random Fields; Gaussian Processes; ML-augmented Inversion; Constrained Function Optimization; Computational harmonic analysis; Optimization theory; Numerical linear algebra

Core Solutions: pyCIBR for Content-Based Image Retrieval; VGG-16; VGG-19; ResNet-50; Xception; Inception ResNet; Random Forest; Lightgbm; XGBoost; Extra Trees; Cat-boost

Chapter 9. The First Exascale Supercomputer: Accelerating AI-for-Science and Beyond

Satoshi Matsuoka, Mohamed Wahib, Aleksandr Drozd, and Kento Sato

Nuggets Fugaku supercomputer has A64FX Fujitsu Processor with CPU and GPU characteristics to cover not only the bandwidth-bound kernels but also the compute-bound kernels by wide vectorization; Design aimed at three main types of kernels: compute-bound, bandwidth-bound, and latency-bound applications. In practice, the majority of applications are bandwidth-bound as represented by the HPCG benchmark, and some are latency-bound as represented by the Graph500 benchmark; Discusses future architectures

Topics (Solutions) **Flood damage remote sensing** (Attention U-Net and LinkNet); **Clustering ensemble of simulations** (Generative Topographic Mapping GTM); **Tsunami Flooding** (Surrogates); **configurational sampling of multicomponent Solids** (Neural Network Potentials NNP); **DFT Density Functional Theory** (Surrogates); **Nonlinear modes of the three-dimensional flow field around a cylinder** (CNN); **Aerospace design** (Genetic Algorithm, MLP, Latin Hypercube Sampling, CNN, deep convolutional generative adversarial network; Supernova simulation (Surrogate); **Quantum Spin systems** (Boltzmann machines); **Compression** (PredNet); **Data representation in Quantum computer** (tensor network)

Qualities (solutions) **Explainable AI and causality for gene networks and cancer drug resistance** (Wide Learning plus DeepTensor and Tensor Reconstruction-based Interpretable Prediction, TRIP)

Resources Top500; MLCommons MLPerf HPC benchmarks CosmoFlow
and DeepCAM
Computing Deep Learning with PyTorch TensorFlow MXNET optimized;
CuDNN; OneDNN (Intel MKL); Model and data parallelism for ML;
BLAS and Horovod supported; ONNX exchange format

Chapter 10. Benchmarking for AI for Science

Jeyan Thiyagalingam, Mallikarjun Shankar, Geoffrey Fox, and Tony Hey

Education Discusses AI for science
Nuggets Discovery performance is different from Runtime performance
(which must be included) and can give the same (better systems) and
different (better science) goals
Topics Weather, Climate, Electron microscope
Concepts Develop taxonomy and organization; curation and distribution;
simulations (theory) to train models used to analyze observational data;
science model versus AI model
Solutions Deep Learning; Large Language Models; CNN; Generative models
for new data; surrogates
Computing System stack to support benchmarking
Resources References seven other benchmark resources; MLCommons

Chapter 11. Radio Astronomy and the Square Kilometer Array

Anna Scaife

Nuggets Science case for SKA and need for two telescopes in Australia and
South Africa; Description of SKA Apparatus
Concepts All processing done in software not custom signal processing
hardware; Network of regional data centers; Images formed from raw data;
Time Domain data so large that must be processed online; most important
scientific task of new astronomical observatories: discovery; deep-learning
approaches to object detection and morphological classification across a
range of astrophysical system types; Paucity of labeled data and need for
Augmented Datasets; Rotation, Reflection Symmetry preservation;
Unsupervised learning for discovering new structures
Topics (solutions) **denoising radio images** (convolutional autoencoders);
Fanaroff–Riley classification of radio galaxies (CNN, R-CNN);
Synthetic populations (structured variational inference with VAE and
Decoder); **Removal of RFI Radio Frequency Interference** (U-net);
Pulsar Classification (MLP, Gaussian Hellinger Very Fast Decision Tree
(GH-VFDT) online algorithm, single-qubit quantum neural network)

Solutions Capsule Networks; Transfer Learning; Transformers; Attention-gated CNN; Gaussian process modeling to augment training data; Bayesian deep-learning and cold posterior effect; semi-supervised learning (SSL) algorithms
Computing Data rates 300 PB per telescope per year; Apache Storm

---

Chapter 12. The Rise of the Machines

Andy Connolly

Nuggets Vera C. Rubin Observatory was known as the Large Synoptic Survey Telescope (LSST) and will carry out the Legacy Survey of Space and Time with 37 billion stars/galaxies each with 1000 observations finished in 2034; Netflix (which first offered a streaming option to its subscribers in 2007) streams more data every two hours than the total accumulated data expected from Rubin over its 2024–2034 LSST survey span; Nancy Grace Roman Space Telescope infra-red telescope launches soon after Rubin; PTF Palomar Transient Factory current surveys; Plots astronomy papers per time in three ML categories
Concepts Real-time online analysis and Batch processing of time series; SDSS has 400K citations; Integrate physics, e.g., redshifts into deep learning; Need for training and software engineers for research computing
Topics(solution) **PLASTICC challenge to classify astrophysically variable sources such as supernovae** (Gaussian Processes, LightGBM plus data augmentation improved by adding physics insight); **Remove noise with real-bogus classifiers** (Random Forest, Bloom)
Solutions CNN RNN LSTM on time series of images
Computing LSST Interdisciplinary Network for Collaboration and Computing (LINCC) to support the development of the required software frameworks; Serverless cloud computing; Apache Parquet; Apache Kafka; AXS Astronomy Extension to Spark; Ray; Dask

---

Chapter 13. AI for Net-Zero

Alberto Arribas, Karin Strauss, Sharon Gillett, Amy Luers, Trevor Dhu, Lucas Joppa, Roy Zimmermann, and Vanessa Miller

List of Tools in Tables 1 and 2
CV Computer Vision
NL Natural Language Processing
DF Data Fusion or Multi-sensor Data Fusion
TL Transfer Learning
UL Unsupervised Learning
RL Reinforcement Learning
GM Generative Models

Table 1. Summary and examples of previous uses of AI for net-zero.

Problem area and examples	Problem size	Data sources	CV	NL	DF	TL	UL	RL	GM	IN	CA	LC	CF	MD
Detection of emitting infrastructure/Tracking of emissions/Detection of GHG leaks/Monitoring of emissions from land use	**Accounting** ~50 Gt/year GHG emissions in 2021	Remote sensing *in situ* sensors census and reports data	X	X	X	X							X	
Electricity generation: Balancing variable generation/ Dynamic scheduling and pricing/Local-grid management and optimization	**Reducing** ~25% of GHG emissions	*in situ* sensors remote sensing	X				X	X	X					
Transport: Efficiency of transport system/Modal shift/Alternative fuels research	**Reducing** ~14% of GHG emissions	Vehicle sensors; mobile phones; remote sensing	X			X	X	X			X		X	
Manufacturing (and buildings): Real-time management of buildings/Carbon-free materials research	**Reducing** ~27% of GHG emissions	*in situ* sensors remote sensing mobile phones real-state data	X	X	X	X		X			X			
Land sector: Irrigation management/Crop yield prediction/Monitoring of emissions	**Reducing** ~24% of GHG emissions	*in situ* sensors remote sensing UAV	X			X		X			X			
Nature-Based Solutions: Monitoring of emissions	**Removing** ~5–10 Gt from 2050	Remote sensing *in situ* sensors UAV	X					X						
Technology: Materials research/Identification of storage locations	**Removing** ~5–10 Gt/year from 2050	*in situ* sensors	X		X		X							

First two columns from Rolnick *et al.* (2019) *Tackling climate change with machine learning*. For specific references, see text. Emission estimates from IPCC.

Table 2.　Key knowledge gaps and AI tools to address them.

Problem area and examples	Problem size	CV	NL	DF	TL	UL	RL	GM	IN	CA	LC	CF	MD
Accounting: Direct measuring of GHG for reliable accounting systems Direct measuring for reducing error bars from land sector and methane	∼50 Gt/year GHG emissions in 2021	X		X						X			
Electricity generation: Material science for energy storage	**Reducing** ∼25% of GHG emissions	X							X	X	X	X	X
Transport: Material science for sustainable fuels	**Reducing** ∼14% of GHG emissions	X							X	X	X	X	X
Manufacturing (and buildings): Material Science for carbon-free materials (e.g., cement, steel, and semiconductors)	**Reducing** ∼27% of GHG emissions	X							X	X	X	X	X
Land sector: Direct measuring of CO_2 and CH_4	**Reducing** ∼24% of GHG emissions	X		X						X			
Nature-Based Solutions: Direct measuring — verification and leakage	**Removing** ∼5–10 Gt from 2050	X		X						X			
Technology: Material Science for sorbent materials	**Removing** ∼5–10 Gt/year from 2050	X							X	X	X	X	X

IN Inference
CA Causality
LC Life Cycle Analysis
CF Computation Fluid Dynamics
MD Material Design

Chapter 14. AI for Climate Science

Philip Stier

Nuggets Simulations need wide ranges of scales with parameterizations of subscales; It seems inconceivable that anything else than hybrid models, combining numerical solutions of fundamental physical equations with faster and/or more accurate AI components will dominate the short- to medium-term future; The question remains primarily what fraction of the physical climate models will ultimately be replaced by AI

Topics Most AI applications in climate modeling have focused on the emulation of climate model parameterizations in existing climate modeling frameworks for better speed and accuracy; Global and regional climate models; Current climate model development and evaluation make use of only a small fraction of the information content from an unprecedented amount of Earth observations available — examples are classify clouds and ship tracks

Methods Perturbed Parameter Ensembles (PPE), varying climate model parameters within their uncertainty bounds; mechanism denial, perturbed parameter ensembles, or adjoint methods are widely used to identify and quantify causal relationships; fingerprinting methods have been developed for the detection of climate impacts and their attribution to specific anthropogenic forcers; Digital Twins; Objective functions; Regularization; Labeling of training datasets; Feature detection; Semantic segmentation; Graph-based structural causal models explained and causal inference; Approximate Bayesian Computation; Markov Chain Monte Carlo

Solutions Neural networks; Convolutional neural networks (CNNs); Relevance vector machines; Active learning; Gaussian Processes; Autoencoders; Explainable artificial intelligence (XAI); Random Forests; Causal forests; Long short-term memory (LSTM); Generative Adversarial Networks (GANs); Invertible neural networks; Residual neural networks; Gradient boosting decision trees (LGBM); k-means clustering; Principal Component Analysis; Ridge Regression; Supervised or semi-supervised machine learning; Super-resolution imaging compared to downscaling climate; Multisensor Fusion; U- Net, ResNet; Latin hypercubes; Zooniverse platform crowd-sourcing; fastai library; AI to detect changes and extreme events (anomalies)

Resources Coupled Model Intercomparison Experiment (CMIP6) 18PB output; A benchmarking framework based on CMIP6, ScenarioMIP, and DAMIP simulations performed by a full complexity climate model has been developed, combined with a set of machine learning-based models

---

Chapter 15. Accelerating Fusion Energy with AI

Steve Cowley, Dan Boyer, and Michael Churchill

Nuggets Tokomak Plasma exhibits turbulence and plasma instability; AI merge simulation and data to make operation efficient; simulations too slow so need DNN surrogates for observed and simulated results; Reactor control

Topics (solutions) **Full code for Trapped Gyro-Landau Fluid (TGLF) reduced quasilinear turbulence model run many times** (replace by an FCN surrogate million times faster); **Other codes** (replace kernels XGC of collision. Million samples give 5× speedup from encoder (CNN)–Decoder RNN)

Concepts Edge processing for real-time sensor analysis; Model-based Control; PDE operator learning

Solutions Loss involved physics constraints conserve particle, momentum, and energy; accelerate iterative solvers such as GMRES, by providing better initial guesses to the solver; ML to produce better preconditioners; differentiable simulations, and using neural networks in effect to learn subgrid models for kinetic simulations; end-to-end differentiable workflows to design future machines; Simulation Surrogates; Simulation-based inference (likelihood-free inference); Uncertainty Quantification essential if to use in control critical scenarios; Learning with physics-based constraints; Convolutional NNs; Transfer Learning; Active learning; Bayesian optimization; Time-series prediction; Reinforcement learning for operational control; Encoder–decoder neural networks; Normalizing flows (finding probability distributions)

Chapter 16. Artificial Intelligence for a Resilient and Flexible Power Grid

Olufemi A. Omitaomu, Jin Dong, and Teja Kuruganti

Nuggets Recent widespread and extreme natural disasters as well as the drive towards clean sustainable energy sources necessitate a transformational operational and technological approaches to improve power grid resilience; The goal of a smart grid is to transition the electric power grid from an electromechanically controlled system into an electronically controlled system, moving from a reactive system to a proactive system; Unlike the legacy power grid, the smart grid allows for customer participation in grid operations: consumers will not only consume electrons and generate data but can also respond to the dynamic processes in the system

Topics Physical layer, Sensor layer, analytics layer, Market layer; Distributed Energy Resources for Efficient Grid Services; Human–Machine Collaboration for Efficient Grid Operations

Concepts The two black boxes: humans and AI linked in a cooperative learning loop; computational burden of the data-driven approach is much smaller than the model-based approach so better for consumer at the edge; Problem of limited training data

Reinforcement learning for control and trading; off-the-shelf RL algorithm versus tailored RL or alternative AI algorithms; multiagent Q-learning at the edge as centralized solutions can't cope with size of action space

Solutions Multiobjective optimization; Knowledge Enhancement through Transfer Learning

Computing Cloud services; IOT; Real time; Edge computing; Data Preprocessing for AI using Fog Computing

Chapter 17. AI and Machine Learning in Observing Earth from Space

Jeff Dozier

Nuggets Article mainly future looking

Education Discusses AI v ML, explainable AI for Earth System Science

Topics EOS Earth Observing System; Snow properties; AI use in correcting current estimates from inverting the radiative transfer equations; Multitask Observation using Satellite Imagery and Kitchen Sinks (MOSAIKS) from Google Maps

Concepts Measurement of variables more important than recognizing objects; The choice of the training data matters more than the machine learning method

Solutions Gaussian process regression; Neural network fitting; Boosted and aggregated regression trees

Chapter 18. Artificial Intelligence in Plant and Agricultural Research

Sabina Leonelli and Hugh F. Williamson

Nuggets Many use cases described; Need to address the challenges of climate change, and food production; AI needs to deliver "precision" farming.

AI Role Elucidating and managing the complexity of biological data, organisms, and systems; Tackling changing environmental and climatic conditions to foster planetary health; Supporting conservation and the sustainable exploitation of biodiversity; AI to understand the impacts of our changing global climate and environments

Topics Big data from publicly shared genomic data; the development of platforms for high-throughput plant phenotyping in the laboratory, the greenhouse, and the field; and the proliferation of remote sensing devices on-farm; Integration of high throughput phenotyping data with other forms of research data, including genomic, field evaluation, and climatic data; predicting key traits of agronomic importance (including yield, protein content and flowering time), across several different plant species, based on vast quantities of data collected as part of the Australian National Variety Trial

Concepts diversity and variation central; Distributed computing for privacy; Need transdisciplinary collaborations

Solutions Broadly Computer Vision; Time Series; Deep supervised Convolutional Neural Networks (CNNs) are revolutionizing the scale and accuracy of field evaluation, agricultural monitoring, and the study of plant properties; ML in an image-based analysis of plants in the lab or the field (phenomics) offers many opportunities better to understand plant growth and environmental responses in detail and using non-destructive means; ML can also be used to augment longstanding statistical methods of in silico crop modeling; ML for automatic identification of species and traits and so enhancing biodiversity; Smartphone-based apps that use computer vision to provide plant disease detection and diagnostic services to farmers in locations where access to agricultural advisory services may be lacking, such as such as PlantVillage Nuru.

Qualities Governance of data important as many stakeholders; FAIR and related good data practices in Table 1

Chapter 19. AI and Pathology: Steering Treatment and Predicting Outcomes

Rajarsi Gupta, Jakub Kaczmarzyk, Soma Kobayashi, Tahsin Kurc, and Joel Saltz

Nuggets Digital histopathology — aimed at quantitative characterization of disease state, patient outcome prediction, and treatment steering; Whole slide images (WSIs) can be more than $100,000 \times 100,000$ pixels in size. WSIs can be generated at different levels of resolution; a pixel will commonly represent a 0.25 to 1-micron tissue region; EU BIGPICTURE will collect millions of slides; Goal is detecting, segmenting, and classifying objects (e.g., nuclei and cells), structures (e.g., stroma), and regions (e.g., tumor regions) within a WSI; best predictions are likely to require integrated analysis of microscopic tissue images, Radiology images, and clinical and molecular information

Topics Detection, Segmentation, and Characterization of Microanatomic Structures; WSI-level or patient-level annotations; Prediction of Patient Outcome and Treatment Response

Concepts AI better than traditional methods; deep learning assistant; Need labeled data — maybe Crowd sourcing; In digital pathology, deep learning methods are being used to carry out nuanced computational multiresolution tissue analyses

Solutions FCNs, convolutional neural networks (CNNs), multi-instance learning (MIL), attention mechanisms, recurrent neural networks (RNNs), and transformer; multistep deep learning pipeline for segmentation; watershed algorithm; CNN architecture, called HoVer-Net, to both segment and classify nuclei in a single method; GAN + CNN U-Net for data augmentation; 2-layer attention, MIL and RNN/LSTM for image level classification; ResNet for image level classification; K-Means SVM for image level classification; Inception-V3 for image level classification; Graph Convolutional Network for image level classification; CNN K-Means for Patient outcome; fully connected neural networks and the boosting Cox negative likelihood method; graph convolutional neural network for patient outcome; Cox proportional loss function for survival analysis; attention mechanisms in a multimodal deep learning framework, called Multimodal Co-attention Transformer for image-genome integration; ResNet-50 CNN for image data and fully connected networks for the other modalities and the integrated feature representation for clinical, imaging, and omic; continuous learning and improvement of AI on real-time patient data; Foundation models trained on lots of data and then customize

Qualities Interpretable and explainable AI

Chapter 20. The Role of Artificial Intelligence in Epidemiological Modeling

Aniruddha Adiga, Amanda Wilson, Srinivasan Venkatramanan, Jiangzhuo Chen, Andrew Warren, Bryan Lewis, Parantapa Bhattacharya, Stefan Hoops, Brian Klahn, Joseph Outtten, Przemyslaw Porebski, Benjamin Hurt, Gursharn Kaur, Henning Mortveit, Dawen Xie, Justin Crow, Stephen Eubank, Christopher L. Barrett, and Madhav V. Marathe

Nuggets What is a pandemic, epidemic. Consequences of no controlled experiments; Generalize as complex socio-technical system; For longer-term projections and understanding the effects of different kinds of interventions and counter-factual analysis, mechanistic models are usually more helpful.; Short-term: Compartment (disease states) models versus long-term: agent-based models. PatchSim includes commuting between spatial regions; discrete-time Susceptible-Exposed-Infectious-Recovered (SEIR) compartmental model with modeled Vaccination; Agent-based using individual interaction; Experience with Virginia modeling strategies to combat

Topics (solution) **Contact Tracing** (via phones); **Decision Support Tools to inform policy makers** (Visualization, NLP user queries); **Social media misinformation**; AI for **contact tracing**; AI for **vaccination**; AI for **drug discovery**; AI for **new variants**; **model human behavior** (Reinforcement Learning)

Concepts C causality, reasoning, and inference in complex systems, and some of the new ideas in AI, including explainability, fairness, and biases in AI systems, digital twins, and deep learning; Real-time analysis, and operationally relevant AI; Spectrum of models (see Remarks); Data-driven machine learning models are helpful for forecasting and short-term projections

Solutions Agents; Auto-Regressive models like ARIMA; Filtering methods (Kalman); Feed-forward, LSTM, graph-based spatio-temporal; Hybrid deep learning and mechanistic; Ensemble models across different choices; weighted with Bayesian Model Averaging Ensemble; Graph Neural Nets; Hybrid GNN (CausalGNN); RNN GRU LSTM

Qualities Overfitting, Explainability

Resources More data for COVID: Curated data regarding confirmed cases, hospitalizations, human mobility, deaths, and various social interventions are now available for all of the United States (US) at a county-level resolution; Scenario Hub https://covid19scenariomodelinghub.org/viz.html https://viz.covid19forecasthub.org/

Chapter 21. Big AI: Blending Big Data with Big Theory to Build Virtual Humans

Peter Coveney and Roger Highfield

Concepts Deep learning learns models unlike other ML; Combine mechanistiuc models with AI; old saw that correlation does not mean causation; What's wrong with just AI overfitting; AI methods are simply "black boxes" that reveal little about their inherent limitations, inbuilt assumptions, and intrinsic biases; Simulations do some things well, AI others

Topics AI for COVID-19 diagnosis from images failed; other COVID-19 AI worked; Breast Cancer; Blood flow; Weather; Electrocardiogram simulations

Solutions Epilepsy surgery planning from virtual brain model; Hybrid example of AI for docking and simulation for scoring binding free energies in drug candidates; AlphaFold with comments on limitations; Surrogates for Docking; GAN for drug discovery; Ensemble methods to cope with chaos and extreme sensitivity to input data; Enhanced Sampling of Simulation Phase Space; Surrogates for components of simulations (the fine-grain compute-intensive parts); Nowcasting short term weather; Physics Informed PINN

Resources Virtual brain open-source software

Chapter 22. A Roadmap for Defining Machine Learning Standards in Life Sciences

Fotis Psomopoulos, Carole Goble, Leyla Jael Castro, Jennifer Harrow, and Silvio C. E. Tosatto

---

Nuggets DOME covers supervised machine learning applications: data, optimization, model, and evaluation; The recommendations have been implemented as an ML reporting checklist

Concepts Any ML method requires both data and software, so making these openly available important

Qualities Reproducible; Trustworthy and fair (unbiased); FAIRness in ML could pave the road to more open and reproducible methods, facilitating trust of the outcome by the involved stakeholders

People CLAIRE and Pistoia Collaborative Consortia

Computing European Open Science Cloud and the data services associated with the European Health Data Space, the NIH Data Commons, and the Australian BioCommons

Resources DOME life science recommendations from ELIXIR; Bioschemas; Best Practices Toolkit for Machine Learning Ops (MLOps) in life sciences

---

Chapter 23. Artificial Intelligence for Materials

Debra J. Audus, Kamal Choudhary, Brian L. DeCost, A. Gilad Kusne, Francesca Tavazza, and James A. Warren

---

Education Supervised, unsupervised, semi-supervised, transfer, representation learning

Concepts Lack of data; Scientific Machine Learning incorporates Physics into AI; Need datasets designed to support AI; CASP and Alphafold should be generalized

Topics (Solution): **DFT Density Functional Theory**; **Phase mapping** (unsupervised); Force-field (surrogates); **Automated materials discovery** (Deep generative models); **Design and control high-throughput experiments in materials and chemistry** (Active Learning); **Recommend Research** (Active Learning)

Solutions Uncertainty quantification; Alphafold; PINN; **classic ML:** Linear models (standard regression, logistic regression, etc.); Gaussian process; Support Vector Machine; Tree-based models; Nearest neighbor regression/classification; **discriminative deep learning:** Convolutional neural network; Graph neural network; Recurrent neural Network; **deep generative models:** Autoencoding neural networks; Generative adversarial networks; Active learning; Scientific Machine Learning

---

Computing Metadata and semantic tools
Resources MGI Materials Genome Initiative did not have AI; Material image datasets; Material simulation datasets; Text from articles datasets; Open Catalyst is an example of a modern AI-oriented approach

Chapter 24. Artificial Intelligence for Accelerating Materials Discovery

Ankit Agrawal and Alok Choudhary

Nuggets Processing-structure-property-performance science pipeline (forward model); engineering is reverse (inverse model); Focus on metallic, inorganic materials (hard condensed matter); describes sizes
Concepts Inverse problem is given a set of properties, find possible materials that can be verified experimentally
Topics (Solutions) **Iterate forward and inverse** (active learning); **Tackle small data** (Deep transfer learning); **Microstructure** (Deep adversarial learning)
Resources IRNet is Individual residual learning to allow deep regression networks (FCN) without vanishing derivatives

Chapter 25. Experimental Particle Physics and Artificial Intelligence

David Rousseau

Nuggets four levels of analysis (Particle, Event, experiment, cross-experiment); Shallow Neural Nets used to identify jets ∼1990; Event level can use earlier particle level or original raw data
Topics Design of Experiments; calorimeter simulations (GAN, VAE)
Concepts Using AI increases data by 1.5; Use same tools to analyze event simulations as well as observed data; Deep learning better but needs much larger training set; Nuisance parameters
Solutions Confidence Levels, Statistical (aleatoric) and Systematic (epistemic), Simulation-Based Inference (formerly called Likelihood Free Inference); Bayesian Optimisation, Reinforcement, Learning, Differential Programming, Topological Optimisation; Graph Neural Networks; Boosted Decision Trees; CNN
Computing FPGA used in Trigger to reduce recorded data volume
Resources Kaggle competitions HiggsML 2014 (3-level FCN, XGBoost)

Chapter 26. AI and Theoretical Particle Physics

Rajan Gupta, Tanmoy Bhattacharya, and Boram Yoon

Nuggets A general method for bias correction and discussion of errors

Concepts AI/Deep Learning is no more of a black box than computational QCD; The only true requirement, as always, is not an analytic understanding, but correctness guarantees assured by a principled estimation of bias and uncertainty in the predictions; Gauge invariant networks as examples of physics aware AI

Topics Deep learning for identifying and classifying Jets (see the previous chapter); Use NN to fit functions such as parton distributions; Surrogates for integrals over phase space as functions of theory parameters using GBDT or FCN and distributed Gaussian processes (DGP) regression; Data compression with Representation Learning using Binary Variables

High-Level Solutions Normalizing flows (generative) for efficient importance sampling giving larger steps and avoiding critical slowing down; Replace MCMC for more efficient integrals combined with surrogate

Core Solutions Artificial Neural Networks; Gaussian Processes Regression; Generative Adversarial Networks; Surrogate Models; Gradient Boosting Decision Tree GBDT Regression; Lattice Gauge Equivariant Convolutional Neural Network; Normalizing flows; Representation Learning with Binary Variables

---

Chapter 27. Schema.org for Scientific Data

Alasdair Gray, Leyla J. Castro, Nick Juty, and Carole Goble

Nuggets Improve the Findability and Interoperability of data through the embedding of machine- interpretable markup within Web pages; Schema.org is a lightweight vocabulary of terms that has been developed by a collaboration of leading search engines — including Google, Microsoft, Yandex, and Yahoo!; Commercial motivation enhanced Web Search with Schema.org; Movie metadata as an example

Education Courses and Training including TeSS Training Portal

Concepts FAIR is important; Results of AI are data

Types Schema.org v14 has 797 types and 1,453 properties mainly ecommerce; Bioschemas.org extends Schemas.org for life sciences with 23 types with six included in Schema.org: ChemicalSubstance, MolecularEntity, Gene, protein, taxon, biosample

Tools Usage guidelines, known as profiles, over the types; Tools such as validators; Datacite vocabulary mapped to schema.org; Knowledge Graph

Computing Microdata, RDFa, and JSON-LD are possible formats. Use JSON-LD as recommended by Google; Bioschemas.org has ComputationalWorkflow type for computational workflows

Resources Google Dataset Search Portal

Chapter 28. AI-Enabled HPC Workflows

Shantenu Jha, Vincent Pascuzzi, and Matteo Turilli

Nuggets Classes of workflows: (1) Hybrid HPC-HTC workflows; (2) ML-coupled workflows, and (3) Edge-to-center workflows, with distributed ML with HPC workflows (e.g., with ML on the edge); Workflows of multiscale ensembles with ML improving path through phase space

Concepts Surrogates for all or part of an application; ML-in-HPC, full or partial surrogate; ML-out-HPC, ML controls simulation; ML-about-HPC. ML coupled to simulation; Effective performance of AI enhancement from the increase in speed through phase space to surrogate/original performance

Topics and solutions Atlas particle physics surrogates for event simulations; Molecular Dynamics potential surrogate; Proxima to increase accuracy in Hartree Fock; Colmena mixes surrogates and traditional simulations molecular dynamics; MUMMI for drug therapeutics; RL to control Neural Architecture Search NAS; IMPECCABLE for COVID19 therapeutics has all 3 ML-x-HPC styles (Docking by AI as in Chapter 21); Proxima Python, Colmena Python and Parsl, EXARL Python on OpenAI Gym; MUMMI workflow using Flux scheduler; miniGAN use RL to anneal

Computing RADICAL-Cybertools and DeepDriveMD; Integrate clouds (platform, container, and function as a service model) and supercomputer HPC systems (large and long single MPI jobs); need to execute large-scale, ML-enabled workflow applications on diverse, adaptive, heterogeneous resources; Python plus traditional HPC; EXARL is useful Reinforcement Learning system

Chapter 29. AI for Scientific Visualization

Han-Wei Shen and Chris Johnson

Overall Goal Interpreting an ensemble of Science simulations is basic problem

Topics(1) Data Prediction (Forward in Time, Spatial, Benchmarks); (2) Feature extraction (Streamlines, vortices, GIS artifacts, Medical images); (3) Data reduction (Essential as too much data to save unless used in situ, i.e., analyze data as it is produced, GMMs, CNNs, autoencoders, GANs, and implicit neural networks); (4) Rendering (Surrogates to represent the rendering); (5) Super-resolution (recovers averaged away data, GAN, LSTM CNN); (6) Simulation surrogates (Visualization and data- based, Detailed examples use GAN); (7) Similarity and comparison (DL representation compared, Siamese NN); (8) Interaction (PointNet, 3D data selection)

Solutions Uncertainty Quantification; CNN; RNN; Autoencoders
unsupervised feature extraction and compression; Reinforcement learning
for load balancing; Gaussian Mixture Model (GMM); Implicit Neural
Networks mapping domains to scalar values; GAN; Convolutional LSTM;
Temporal super resolution (TSR); Siamese NN; Pointnet; Surrogate

Chapter 30. Uncertainty Quantification in AI for Science

Tanmoy Bhattacharya, Christina Garcia Cardona, and Jamal Mohd-Yusof

Scope UQ for DL and NN same as DL; focus on MLP network (multilayer
feed forward)

UQ statistical (**aleatoric**) uncertainty, which is an inherent property of the
data distribution and is generally irreducible; and (ii) systematic
(**epistemic**) uncertainty, which arises from the imperfect assumptions
encoded in the model

Education Deep Learning DL compared to Spline Fits

Topics Cross-validation; Loss Functions for regression and classification;
Regression (output continuous); homoscedastic and heteroscedastic are two
forms of normal errors. Can use mixtures; Heteroscedastic Aleatoric
Uncertainty; Negative Log-Likelihood, Quantile Losses; Quantile Aleatoric
Uncertainty

Concepts Deep Learning assumptions unclear; In high dimensions all points
near boundary

Solutions Deep Ensemble Methods (Randomization, Boosting); Bayesian
Neural Networks (BNN) (NN models that incorporate any form of prior
over their parameters, and thus allow for posterior inference); Markov
Chain Monte Carlo (MCMC) for BNN; Variational Bayes Methods; Monte
Carlo Dropout is a form of variational inference (dropout-based variational
inference, variational dropout); Expectation Propagation using
exponentials for posterior distribution (Probabilistic Back Propagation);
Discriminative Jackknife using leave-one-out (LOO) resampling; Depth
Uncertainty Networks where depth variable; Neural Stochastic Differential
Equation (SDE-Net)

Example NCI Cancer images (Deep Abstaining Classifier (DAC) with an
abstaining category class, multitask convolutional neural network
(MTCNN), CNN)

Qualities Explainable UQ (Local Interpretable Model-agnostic Explanations
(LIME), Counterfactuals)

Chapter 31. AI for Next-Generation Global Network-Integrated Systems and Testbeds

Mariam Kiran and Harvey Newman

Topics Review of Federated infrastructures for Networking, Compute, and Storage; Compared to Road Traffic (Graph link weights from traffic time-series correlation); Autonomic Networks; Architecture for AI and networking in Figure 2; Research in the areas of workflow and resource management is limited; Software Defined Infrastructure; Software Defined Network; SDN for end-to-end networked science at the exascale (SENSE); SONIC network O/S open-source; P4 network programming; RARE; Source routing PolKA; NDN; Monitoring (SNMP)

Concepts Stresses the role of networking to enable worldwide big science in many fields

Computing CERN LHC experiments use Rucio and Pegasus workflow

Solutions Classification and anomaly identification; Regression (time series prediction); ARIMA, Random Forest, SVM for forecasting (replaced by DL); Graph neural networks for distributed system operation and optimization; Deep reinforcement learning; Markov Decision Processes; Autoencoders; Encoder–Decoder; Diffusion Convolutional Neural Network; Long short-term memory (LSTM); GNN to forecast the future from time series on links; Reinforcement Learning RL for Routing decisions; RL for Smart caching; Compare the shortest possible route algorithm with the RL agent-based decision; Divide RL training into episodes of 100 decisions

---

Chapter 32. AI for Optimal Experimental Design and Decision-Making

Francis J. Alexander, Kristofer-Roy Reyes, Lav R. Varshney, and Byung-Jun Yoon

---

Concepts Discovery of New things; Reduced productivity in large teams; Add Bayesian Update to Experimental hypothesis-testing process; The Bayesian perspective allows us to encode what we know and what we do not through **uncertainty quantification**

Central Approach Bayesian Prior distribution has different interpretations: Objective Bayesian and Subjective Bayesian (used in this chapter)

Topics Optimal Experimental Design (OED); Objective-Based Uncertainty Quantification UQ (MOCU mean objective cost of uncertainty, Active Learning); Design of Optimal Experiments for Effective Reduction of Model Uncertainty; OED for gene regulatory network (GRN)

Solutions NLP; Digital Twins; Surrogates; Bayesian Transfer Learning; Statistical Elicitation; Expert Elicitation constructs prior by "interviewing" expert; Knowledge-Based Bayesian Prior Construction; MKDIP (maximal knowledge-driven information prior); Optimal Bayesian classification (OBC); Kullback Leibler divergence

---

Chapter 33. FAIR: Making Data AI-Ready

Susanna-Assunta Sansone, Philippe Rocca-Serra, Mark Wilkinson, and Lee Harland

---

Goal This article looks at the FAIR journey, status, and key next steps

Topics The need for FAIR-backed ML and AI within the pharmaceutical sector; Different evaluation methods with IT and/or domain emphasis; Cope with different names for the same item using ontology management to synchronize evolving ontologies

Concepts We need data that are Findable, Accessible, Interoperable, and Reusable (FAIR); Machine -readable and actionable FAIR data natively understand the semantic context and provide provenance of the information; FAIR data are essential to the future of human–machine collaboration and autonomous machine-to-machine communication; FAIR is a goal, not an implementation; Economic benefit; DOI part of FAIR; FAIR describes generalized data, including software; DCAT2 specification also enables descriptors of other kinds of digital resources such as interfaces and APIs

Solutions DOI; Schema.org; DCAT3 https://www.w3.org/TR/vocab-dcat-3 RDF Data Catalog; Creative Commons (CC) license suite; The Research Object Crate (RO-Crate, packaging data, and metadata https://doi.org/10.25504/FAIRsharing.wUoZKE); FAIRness metrics (https://fairassist.org), Test and evaluate; OBO and OBI Biomedical ontologies; Semantic search and NLP; SciBite Ontology management

Resources Publishers Zenodo, Dataverse, and Dryad; FAIR Data Point (FDP, https://www.fairdatapoint.org) is a metadata registry that follows two agent-accessible standards, DCAT(2), and the Linked Data Platform (LDP, https://www.w3.org/TR/ldp). FAIR in a box

---

Chapter 34. Large Language Models for Science

Austin Clyde, Arvind Ramanathan, and Rick Stevens

Nuggets AI for science (AI4Science) builds a deep connection between data, computing, and the scientific method to advance the next generation of discovery; How scientists read, interpret, and generalize data into a coherent theory is central to the scientific practice; interoperability challenge: AI cannot operate over natural reasoning in the historical scientific literature or even analyze the unstructured data found in past literature or electronic health records

Assertion large language models (LLMs) can advance AI4Science by directly integrating with scientific literature, explainability, and concept-formation, thus advancing the interoperability of AI and HPC with human scientific practice

---

Topics Information retrieval; Knowledge Graph; NLP Natural language processing; HCI human– computer interaction; mathematical theorem proving

Solutions Corpus; Vocabulary; Embedding; Masked-language modeling; Causal language models; attention layer; scaled dot-product attention; Self-attention in the encoder, decoder, or encoder– decoder attention; Training infrastructure managers such as Megatron and DeepSpeed; continuous bag-of-words (CBOW); Global Vectors for Word Representation (GloVe); One shot-learning, Few-shot learning, Prompting; Retrieve-then-predict model; Ontology; Reasoning; Greedy Neural Theorem Prover; Foundation models; UnifiedQA LLM; BERT GPT-2 GPT-3 GPT-NeoX; LLM Large Language Models; Transformers; LSTMs and RNNs bidirectional RNNs

Qualities XAI Explainable AI

Resources CommonCrawl; The Pile

Chapter 35. Autonomous Vehicles

Tom St. John and Vijay Janapa Reddi
This chapter gives an overview of the current state of the field for autonomous vehicles, as well as describes future directions for this industry

Nuggets 94% accidents due to human error

Topics Lidar Camera Radar; Perception, Prediction, planning; Waymo; NVIDIA; Velodyne (Lidar) PointPillars; 3D Point Clouds; Object Detection

Solutions Deep Learning; Pillar Feature Net; 2D CNN; SSD Single Shot Detection; PointPainting; DeepLabv3+ PointPillars VoxelNet PointRCNN, Range Sparse Net

Computing Autonomous Vehicle System Architecture

Chapter 36. The Automated AI-Driven Future of Scientific Discovery

Hector Zenil and Ross D. King

Nuggets General discussion of AI for Science and how AI-driven experiments can address by speeding up and improving experimentation

Concepts Models are large; Analogy to self-driving cars SAE0-5 with SAE as Society of Automobile Engineers; Gives 11 criteria to judge which autonomous AI/Robotics experimental laboratories to establish; Industry leads robot automation

Topics Cancer cured; Mathematics; Pandemics; Planetary exploration; Environmental Science; 3D bioprinting
Solutions Examples Adam and Eve in Turing Lab biology experiments; Genesis Vanderbilt; Alphafold2
Qualities Explainability LIME system; But this approach is merely an attempt to fix a problem of our own creation

Chapter 37. Towards Reflection Competencies in Intelligent Systems for Science

Yolanda Gil

Education History AI for Science; Review of AI for Science
Topics Examples of reflection (prior work of author) in cancer omics neuroscience flood prediction
Concepts Implications of Global Team Science; Need faster learning of new methods; Need automatic update with new data; New AI methods; AI Assistant now to AI collaborator
Qualities Six competencies: **reflection (focus)**, observation, modeling, probing, extraction, and creation

Chapter 38. The Interface of Machine Learning and Causal Inference

Taha Bahadori and David Heckerman

Concepts ML great at correlation; this is not causality; Observation naturally gives correlation; intervention gives causality
Topics Explain a deep neural-net model for CUB-200-2011 Bird dataset; insights from optimization and end-to-end learning in ML can be used to infer causal relationships in the difficult case where such relationships are continuous and non-linear; Apply to impact of the level of air pollutant PM2.5 on the cardiovascular mortality rate
Solutions Features → concepts → label; hidden common causes (i.e., hidden confounders); instrumental variables; confounders, treatments, and response variables; Propensity score weighting; Double robustness; entropy balancing; minimize a measure of dispersion on the weights; Resnet152; Concept Bottleneck Model (CBM); RemOve And Retrain (ROAR) framework; KL-divergence; End-to- End Balancing (E2B); GANs for generating auxiliary data

© 2023 World Scientific Publishing Company.
https://doi.org/10.1142/9789811265679_bmatter

Index

www.ingramcontent.com/pod-product-compliance
Ingram Content Group UK Ltd.
Pitfield, Milton Keynes, MK11 3LW, UK
UKHW020859151025
3245IPUK00017B/1

9 789811 265662